Lives and Legacies:
An Encyclopedia of People Who Changed the World

Government Leaders, Military Rulers, and Political Activists

Edited by David W. Del Testa

Writers

David W. Del Testa

Florence Lemoine

John Strickland

ORYX PRESS
2001

The rare Arabian Oryx is believed to have inspired the myth of the unicorn. This desert antelope became virtually extinct in the early 1960s. At that time several groups of international conservationists arranged to have 9 animals sent to the Phoenix Zoo to be the nucleus of a captive breeding herd. Today the Oryx population is over 1,000, and over 500 have been returned to the Middle East.

© 2001 by The Oryx Press
An imprint of Greenwood Publishing Group
88 Post Road West, Westport, Connecticut 06881

Produced by The Moschovitis Group, Inc.
339 Fifth Avenue, New York, New York 10016
www.mosgroup.com

Publisher: Valerie Tomaselli
Project Editor: Stephanie Schreiber
Design and Layout: Annemarie Redmond
Original Illustrations: TurnStyle Imaging
Editorial Coordinator: Sonja Matanovic
Copyediting: Carole Campbell
Fact Checking: Colleen Sullivan
Proofreading: Joseph Reilly
Editorial Assistants: Stewart Rudy, Colleen Sullivan
Index: AEIOU, Inc.

Published simultaneously in Canada
Printed and Bound in the United States of America

ISBN 1-57356-153-3

Library of Congress Cataloging-in Publication Data

Government leaders, military rulers, and political activists : an encyclopedia of people
who changed the world / edited by David W. Del Testa.
    p.   cm.—(Lives and legacies series)
    Includes bibliographical references and index.
    ISBN 1–57356–153–3 (alk. paper)
    1. Heads of state—Biography—Encyclopedias.   2.
Statesmen—Biography—Encyclopedias.   3. Kings and rulers—Biography—Encyclopedias.
4. Dictators—Biography—Encyclopedias.   5. Emperors—Biography—Encyclopedias.   6.
Politicians—Biography—Encyclopedias.   I. Del Testa, David W.   II. Lives and legacies.
D107.G646 2001
920.01—dc21   2001034031

⊗ The paper used in this publication meets the minimum requirements of American National Standard for Information Science—
Permanence of Paper for Printed Library Materials, ANSI Z39.48, 1984.

Table of Contents

Listing of Biographies

Introduction

Qualities of Leadership

Scholars have only just begun to appreciate how the world's peoples, cultures, and ideas have influenced one another since the dawn of organized human civilizations some thousands of years ago. However, leadership, particularly political, military, and social leadership, has received comparatively little attention within the study of global interconnectivity because its impact has been seemingly obvious. Likewise, the idea of who and what qualities make a good leader has remained similarly unchallenged. Some scholars have recently begun to question the construction of leadership and its importance at various times in the past. In part, this questioning has reaffirmed or even improved the assessment of the leadership of many famous leaders, including Napoléon I, leader of France from 1799 to 1814–15, and Franklin Delano Roosevelt, who served as president of the United States from 1933 to 1945.

This new examination has also illuminated the achievements of previously ignored historical figures who have had a powerful and enduring impact on human civilization and global interconnectivity. For example, 25 years ago, few scholars would have known about the accomplishments of the eighteenth-century French political writer Olympe de Gouges or the twentieth-century British human rights activist Peter Benenson; fewer still would have dared to compare them with the canonical "greats" of human history. This volume, which introduces 200 of the greatest leaders throughout history, makes a broader reexamination of leaders and leadership, enhancing the reputation of some and illuminating other men and women previously overlooked. This volume is also located at the crossroads of the debate on how the societies of different parts of the world influenced one another and what impact they had on world history.

Unlike more conservative and traditional efforts, we have striven to introduce the reader to the broader forces that influenced the personal development of the historical figures considered, and to show how their leadership has

had an enduring and global impact. Every biography begins with a description of the life of the individual, followed by an analysis of the individual's legacy. In each entry, the leader's legacy carries equal or more weight than the actual life events. The long-term influence of a particular figure's leadership on the progress and shape of world history and the impact of global forces on that figure formed the major criteria for inclusion in this volume; they were also the core issues examined in the biographies.

As a word and a concept, leadership has many meanings. It may indicate, sometimes simultaneously, the ability to lead, the ability to choose the individual who leads, or the validation by others of the right to lead. In this volume, the subjects of the 200 biographies must have at least embodied the first definition, although they may or may not have served as the sole leader of a group, organization, or movement and may not have even initially had the right to lead. Naturally, many of the figures possessed personalities and skills that their society considered to be important traits for a true leader. Equally important, however, is to remember that sometimes what their societies may have initially considered deficiencies made the various historical figures better leaders over time. These supposed deficiencies, or differences, often were excellent alternatives to what the preceding leaders had offered as leadership.

By considering individuals with unconventional leadership characteristics, we were able to include leaders who have had an important impact on history but who did not necessarily have favorable reputations during their lifetimes. For example, because she was a stage actress and served as the mistress to wealthy men during her life, many of the peers of Olympe de Gouges questioned her character. Yet her social vantage point, combined with her own progressive sensibilities and qualities as a writer, allowed de Gouges to write insightful political tracts and argue for women's rights in a way most men would not have dared to do at the time. Likewise, Booker Taliaferro Washington, an African-American activist of the late nineteenth century, had an approach to the social emancipation of African Americans that some people consider a brilliant effort at making the status quo work to the benefit of African Americans and others view as an unhealthy surrender to the existing hierarchical and racist social structures. Indeed, some controversy probably surrounds the individuals in each of the biographies presented here.

Examining the importance of leaders and leadership in relation to world history and the interconnectivity of peoples and cultures creates a troublesome paradox. The sensitive writer, aware of her or his own prejudices and cultural background and trying to avoid the worst aspects of a "presentist" (historically insensitive) point of view, will try to discover what qualities people of the distant and recent past considered to be representative of a good leader. The definition and purpose of leadership has changed radically over time, even though the formal definitions of the political systems that were adopted by particular leaders have remained the same. For example, even though they both supported democracy and led great republics, Pericles, a leader of ancient Athens, and Thomas Jefferson, the third president of the United States, had very different understandings of by what authority and for what purpose they governed and who a "democracy" should include. Frequently, that leadership originated with a person receiving and claiming for him- or herself some kind of mandate. They and/or their followers often believed that this mandate came from a divine source or, more rarely, from the populace. However, in the past, fulfilling this mandate did not necessarily require a leader to consider the needs of his or her people. Rather, it was often better to appear strong as a leader than to have others feel good about one's leadership: displaying magnificence, acting brutal, and demonstrating the force of one's power often provided a visible confirmation that the leader had the right to remain in charge. The reader should not forget that the leadership of modern bureaucratic republics through mass and popular consensus and cooperative leadership is, in the long span of human history, very recent.

On the other hand, the historians who contributed to this volume could not fail to recognize that the subjects of the biographies often shared, for better or for worse, certain qualities that transcended time, space, and culture. We found that, although the various styles of and purposes for leadership in the historical figures considered were by nature strongly "historicist" (that is, defined by their time and place in history), these figures nonetheless had certain qualities in common. For example, Alexander III's personal dedication to a vision of a world unified by Greek culture was so convincing to his multinational followers that he successfully led an army of many nations and conquered the southwestern quarter of ancient Asia within a decade. He used violence to impose what he considered a universal civilization—Greek culture—on others. Peter Benenson, the English founder of Amnesty International, was so dedicated to ensuring that every person was guaranteed human rights that he inspired an influential, independent, and worldwide movement of great and enduring power. He helped to organize a huge following that has used peaceful means to cajole abusive leaders into introducing what he considered the basis of universal civilization—human rights—to their peoples. Both Alexander and Benenson strove to bring about changes that would make the world, in their estimation, a better place.

The generally positive valorization of Alexander and Benenson's accomplishments has its corollary in the infamous but influential impact of other leaders, such as ancient China's Shih Huang-ti and the Soviet Union's Joseph Stalin, whose vision of a better world similarly inspired millions to follow them. Unfortunately for those who lived under their rule, these leaders were brutal and dictatorial—a style of leadership that complemented their vision of a totalitarian society. In every case, however, dedication, single-mindedness, vision, tirelessness, and the ability to convince others of the importance of their vision and make them act on that vision on their behalf have marked the leaders presented here.

Even though the individuals included in this volume possessed strong leadership qualities, not all were successful in fulfilling their political campaigns or reaching their goals. In a few instances, we have chosen leaders who seem to be historical failures. These figures often precipitated the collapse of their societies or failed to provide, in a conventional sense, sufficiently effective leadership in a time of crisis. However, the leadership of individuals such as pre-colonial Mexico's Montezuma II, ancient Cambodia's Suryavarman II, and a twentieth-century leader of China, Chiang Kai-shek occurred during "golden ages" of their societies; they have remained very powerful models for future leaders, even if their own reigns were not so golden. For example, by stalling for time in a moment of obvious crisis, Montezuma II lost the opportunity to destroy the Spanish conquistador

Hernán Cortés and his men. Nonetheless, the civilization of Montezuma's age has come to be seen as the height of ancient Mexican society, which for some scholars and politicians is symbolic of indigenous power and creativity. Suryavyarman II, although a successful conqueror, so weakened ancient Cambodia socially and militarily that his successors and Cambodia itself never again achieved equal stature. Yet, the grandeur and power of his reign became the symbolic goal for many future Cambodian leaders, including twentieth-century communist dictator Pol Pot. Finally, Chiang Kai-shek showed that modern democracy could function in China and with the Chinese people, even if the regime he created failed to live up to the promise of representative democracy for all Chinese.

The three categories of leaders treated by this text—government leaders, military rulers, and political activists—all have commonalities that originate in the idea of leadership and transcend, to some degree, categorization. As the reader shall see, each historical figure included almost always possesses characteristics of a government, military, or activist leader. Even Mohandas Gandhi led an army of sorts. However, we feel the various classifications help define important aspects of a given person's leadership and show how and why that individual is remembered by history.

Government Leaders

Choosing which government leaders to emphasize presented us with myriad and, on the surface, easy choices. In many ways, history and habit had already made the choice of which government leaders had had the greatest impact on the course of human history and should figure in this volume. However, if history has made some of our choices obvious and made the accomplishments of these obvious choices well known, the global impact of these historical figures has remained obscured by habit. Therefore, we have searched for government leaders whose choices, methods, and actions had a global impact that other scholars may not have thought to illuminate because the interpretation of these figures has not yet been challenged or reexamined.

Humans have organized themselves into governments for thousands of years. Indeed, government—the organized management of a greater or lesser number of human affairs by a selected or self-selecting body—is one of the distinguishing characteristics of human societies.

The reader has to be careful not to confuse government with leadership because government is usually an administrative unit of more than one individual, whereas leadership is typically a quality possessed by an individual. Governments, whether composed of one person or many, manage the affairs of many other humans, usually with the potential to do so more efficiently and with fewer resources than a single human could.

The first government leaders emerged when the need for the efficient management of resources, material and human, became imperative. This occurred some thousands of years ago through two rival processes. First, religious figures, who people believed had the power to transcend the material world and enter into or receive direct inspiration from the spiritual world, began to organize societies to serve religious needs. Alternatively, these religious figures displayed rare and specialized knowledge, such as the ability to forecast floods or eclipses, that people considered divine in origin. Second, other figures, sometimes religious, sometimes not, organized governments to manage water and land with the goal of producing sufficient food for increasing populations. In return for higher guidance and administrative control, people surrendered individual authority. Indeed, for the early civilizations discussed in this book, including those of ancient Mesopotamia, Egypt, India, China, and the Americas, most government leaders embodied a spiritual state unattainable to everyday humans. Usually, these figures, such as the Mesopotamian leader Hammurabi, the Egyptian leader Menes, and the Cambodian Suryavarman II, were considered, to a greater or lesser degree, as gods on Earth; they officiated over relatively rigid societies in which strict rules and limits on behavior governed everyday activities. However, occasionally the social rules of demigods were challenged; for instance, the Egyptian woman Hatshepsut, through ambition and ability, became and was accepted as a king in ancient Egypt when women typically did not serve in this role. Furthermore, some leaders, such as Huayna Capac, flaunted their divinity with excessive arrogance and, as a result, lost the respect of their subjects. However, for the most part, the right of ancient leaders to govern descended from their display of spiritual powers, and average people defied these rulers only at great risk.

Even though the inherent ability of a government leader to serve as some sort of spiritual medium endured beyond the ancient world, the ability of a leader to manage the earthly affairs of a country's people, land, or resources became increasingly important. Indeed, sometimes well after the spiritual was no longer a strict criterion for leadership, its appearance in someone such as the fourteenth-century French military commander Joan of Arc could inspire massive support for particular causes. Above all, even as it became increasingly important for a leader to manage the affairs of a bureaucratic state rather than a mere personal following, the leader had to command the respect of his followers sufficiently to inspire or compel them to do the things the leader wanted done. A leader's ability to motivate others has evolved from a well-developed sense of personal loyalty and obligation to more subtle forms of influence solidified by the implementation of laws. However, all government leaders throughout history needed to demonstrate the ability to influence others in order to accomplish the goals of their administration.

What distinguished many of the government leaders in this volume was their ability to transform their entire society or even the course of human history. This sort of leader, who often believed that he or she had to lead not only the state but a whole civilization in a new direction, often made social and cultural choices that had enormous consequences lasting to the present day. For example, leaders such as the ancient Indian ruler Aśoka or the Roman leader Constantine I made decisions about religion that have influenced religious conflicts ever since. Others such as Kemal Atatürk or Pol Pot engaged in transformative social exercises with a religious fervor, even though they themselves were trying to eliminate religion and traditionalism from their societies. A slightly lesser though equally significant change occurred when some leaders—the communists Vladimir Ilich Lenin, Mao Tse-tung, and Ho Chi Minh, for example—imposed radical, new political systems that had a transformative social effect in themselves. Still others, such as the radical leader of the French Revolution Maximilien Robespierre, pushed profound though understandable political transformations to extremes. Finally, a few leaders, Adolf Hitler and Ruhollah Khomeini among them, looked to the past for inspiration and found radical, religious, or religion-like zealotry among millions to support their retrograde vision of the future.

However, most of the leaders discussed in this volume did not challenge the status quo so radically. Indeed, some defended it with such zealotry as to forestall significant changes, while others made revolutionary changes within known boundaries and limits. Saladin prevented a re-

Christianization of the Holy Land, thereby ensuring the continuing dominance of Islam throughout North Africa, the Middle East, and Southeast Asia. The mid-nineteenth-century Italian liberal parliamentarian Giuseppe Mazzini worked almost his whole life to achieve freedom for the entire Italian nation, a freedom already enjoyed by many European states of the time. The early-twentieth-century French socialist Jean Jaurès called for France to reform its government in order to become less concerned with its collective pocketbook and its guns and more concerned with its people. The seventeenth-century Russian tsar Peter I used his autocratic power to thrust Russia forward from a past he considered a weight on its progress, especially when faced with aggressive, "modern" neighbors to the west. All of these efforts stretched, yet did not necessarily break, the boundaries of the permissible, understandable, or appropriate. In the case of Peter, his autocratic manipulation of his country's resources, in an attempt to make Russia stronger, may have reinforced or even confirmed his mandate to lead.

Scholars have often focused on individuals who made, or almost made, the transition from political activists to government leaders because these figures have had such an important impact on societies and influenced so many other leaders, great and small. By force of will, sense of mission, or exemplary dedication, they led others to transform and improve an intolerable situation. All of the early Colonial American political leaders—George Washington, Benjamin Franklin, Thomas Jefferson—opposed the tyranny of the British and created a new political society. The great modern African leaders—Jomo Kenyatta, Robert Mugabe, Nelson Mandela, Léopold Sédar Senghor—transformed anticolonial activism and created new states and leadership positions for their people. Many Latin American leaders, such as Simón Bolívar, Fidel Castro, and Eva Duarte de Péron, used their positions to transform oppressive states into freer worlds for their fellow citizens or to protect those whom they believed had been unjustly deprived of a voice in their own affairs.

Finally, some of the individuals possessed such greatness that they provided inspiration to their people even if others forcibly took away their mandate to act as leaders. For instance, Chief Joseph, an American Indian leader of the second half of the nineteenth century, sought to accommodate and cooperate with an encroaching settler population based on principles of sharing, equal access, and mutual respect. Emiliano Zapata, who readers might also equally consider a political activist as much as a government leader, paid with his life for his support of peasant rights in Mexico during the first quarter of the twentieth century. It is perhaps from these tragic figures that future leaders might seek their own inspiration rather than look to the violence and intolerance that marks so many of the biographies presented here.

Military Rulers

In a biographical encyclopedia such as this, with its emphasis on broad holistic achievement rather than relatively narrow accomplishments and effects, singling out great military rulers from either figures of political or, less often, activist accomplishment presents enormous difficulties. In short, many of the most important military rulers also had important nonmilitary careers that created as much of a historical impact as their accomplishments on the battlefield or as commanders. Although it is easy to play "What if" with military leaders and posit various outcomes if military rulers had won or lost certain battles or had turned over their commands to civilian rulers sooner rather than later, our major criterion for choosing military leaders centered on whether or not their military exploits had a significant impact on an immediate and global scale.

Remarkable military rulers as a group share certain characteristics. They all seem to apply the skills and methods that made them successful military commanders to their careers as leaders of civilian governments. Almost universally, the successful application of military methods to the governing of civilians involves a holistic approach to leadership, meaning that these military men look beyond strategy, tactics, and soldiering to find ways of effective governance. It does not mean, however, the regimentation, rigidification, or militarization of society. We have not been the only ones to notice the power of a comprehensive approach to leadership by military men. The two most important and enduringly influential works on military strategy, Sun T'zu's fourth-century B.C.E. *The Art of War* and Karl von Clausewitz's 1831 *On War*, insist that success will come to military leaders only when they successfully manipulate the prevalent political environment as well as their troops. The military leaders in this volume, whether or not they read Sun T'zu or Clausewitz's theories, understood their wisdom.

Many military leaders in this volume used armies to effect social change or benefited from the social rewards of military careers. Napoléon I, the leader of France between 1799 and 1814–15, provides the best example of such a military ruler. Napoléon was a poor Corsican who became an officer in the French army through scholarships based on ability, aptitude, and merit. During his reign, Napoléon imposed on France, and tried to impose on many other European countries, the institutional apparatuses—schools, laws, and administration—that had, in a much earlier and diffuse form, helped him escape relative poverty and social isolation. "Imposed" is the operative word. Although he favored appointment by merit, he left no doubt that he—a general, consul, and finally, emperor—was in charge.

However, the reasoning behind the selection of which military rulers to include was not always as clear-cut as that of Napoléon. For example, Scipio Africanus the Younger, a famous Roman general and statesman of the second century B.C.E. who is not featured in this volume, had an enormous impact on the history of the ancient Mediterranean region, and he remained a model of behavior in Rome for hundreds of years. Yet history remembers Julius Caesar better because he engaged in military exploits of an even greater magnitude than Scipio and his behavior and assassination prepared Rome for the transformation from a republic to an empire, an event that had a far greater impact than Scipio's conquest of Carthage and ancient Spain. More striking perhaps is the reason for not including American General Douglas MacArthur while including General, and later president, Dwight David Eisenhower. Although contemporaries of one another and of equal rank, power, and vision, Eisenhower and MacArthur differed in one very important personal characteristic that destined Eisenhower for greater leadership in his era. Eisenhower encouraged people to work together, an important characteristic given the divisions between the Allies in World War II, whereas MacArthur led alone. Eisenhower's leadership style emphasized consensus, caution, and analysis of everything related to the military because he realized the awesome power and dangers of inherently undemocratic militaries, whereas MacArthur's style promoted personal isolation and insubordination among his soldiers. While both Scipio and MacArthur were certainly great military leaders, they remained focused on the act of waging war. Caesar and Eisenhower, perhaps without their conscious intent, commanded whole societies as they organized their troops on the field, or, later, led governments.

Political Activists

"Activism" is a relatively new word. The third edition of the *Oxford English Dictionary* records its first use in 1920. At that time, the word reflected a sense of vigorous activity, whereas the current usage, which originated in the 1950s, refers to the support of a particular cause, often political or social. Vigorous and often organized activism in support of a cause is as old as recorded time. The rebel Roman slave Spartacus and the Jewish rebel Bar Kokhba are two of the earliest examples of political activists in this volume. Accordingly, the relatively recent origin of the word does not define the limits of its meaning and application. What distinguishes the activism of the figures selected for this volume is that they had, in our estimation, a world-historical impact. We chose figures who have operated essentially outside dominant power structures and paradigms represented by the previous two groupings, government leaders and military rulers: in every case, these activists have transcended their immediate cultural or political environment to fight or work for what they believed in.

When choosing what political activists to include, we had to make much more of a moral judgment than required elsewhere in the volume, because political activists often engaged in efforts they considered beneficial for the common good. We specifically chose not to write on political activists who had enduring legacies but whose political choices ran against the common good of all the world's people. For example, readers will not find an entry on the founder of the Ku Klux Klan.

The concept of a common good, however, is naturally subjective. To determine which activists to include, we used a variety of subjective variables and performed a kind of moral calculus. Given this subjective moral framework, the basis for including or excluding a particular individual ultimately rested on whether he or she served as a model for large numbers of people to engage in subsequent and beneficial activism, promoted a new model of behavior in the world, or convincingly supported a people or cause that strongly altered what would otherwise have been a negative historical outcome. Moreover, the figures here also championed their cause in a particularly selfless way.

With some of the figures, we believe that their contribution to the common good has been widely accepted by scholars and is irrefutable. It seems that no one can reasonably argue against Bartolomé de Las Casas's advocacy for the Americas' native peoples in the sixteenth century, Mohandas Gandhi's peaceful and non-sectarian campaign against British colonialism during the first half of the twentieth century, and the support of political prisoners organized by Peter Benenson in the 1960s.

On the other hand, we understand that some readers might raise effective criticism against our choices because of the methods they chose. The best example of this ambiguity is Nelson Mandela, who at times advocated violence to destroy apartheid (the legalized discrimination against one racial group by another). Apartheid is insupportable from any perspective, but the use of violence to achieve political ends remains a hotly debated issue. In addition, many activists selected for the volume, including Ernesto Guevara, Rosa Luxemburg, and Eva Duarte de Péron, wanted to serve as government leaders, but were unsuccessful, or only partly successful, in doing so. Their impact at the time and their inspiration to the future are their legacies.

Finally, limitations of space forced us to narrow our choices to those who had a strictly defined political impact. Consequently, we could not include the incredible sacrifices and outstanding results of activists such as Raoul Wallenberg, who gave his life to ensure that over 100,000 Jews escaped from Nazi Germany in the 1930s, or Albert Schweitzer, who devoted his life to helping Africans overcome disease.

Conclusion

The biographies presented in this volume touch on the possibilities and limits of leadership. We hope that readers will recognize that a cause is needed to create a leader, and that the leaders in this volume, even if they seem to have led effortlessly, had to devote considerable time and energy to develop their abilities and knowledge. Oftentimes, the figures in this volume faced great adversity and even death to achieve their goals. In many cases, the effort—simply the trying—transformed time and space just as much as the efforts of those leaders who achieved their goals.

David Del Testa,
November 2000

The
Biographies

Adams, John Quincy

Sixth President of the United States
1767–1848

Life and Work

John Quincy Adams used a distinguished career in government to strengthen the international presence of the early United States and to solidify the power of the federal government in managing the country's affairs.

Born on July 11, 1767, John Quincy was groomed by his father, John Adams, already an important leader of the American Revolution and later the second president of the United States, for service in public life and government. John Quincy received an excellent primary education from tutors in Boston and while accompanying his father on diplomatic missions. He attended Harvard College, from which he received a degree in 1787, after only two years of study. Thereafter, John Quincy was "apprenticed" to a prestigious Boston lawyer from whom he learned the legal profession, a common practice before the advent of law schools.

Between 1794 and 1801, under Presidents Washington and Adams, John Quincy served as the minister of the United States to various nations, including the Netherlands, Prussia, and Portugal. As a diplomat, Adams developed a keen political sensibility in observing the competition of European nations during the Napoleonic Wars.

In 1803, based on his own reputation as well as that of his esteemed family, John Quincy was appointed, as was the practice of the time, by the Massachusetts legislature as a United States senator. He remained in office until 1808, when involvement in an unpopular embargo against Britain caused him to resign. Thereafter, he temporarily devoted his full attention to teaching at Harvard as professor of rhetoric and oratory, a post he had held since 1806. In 1809, under President James Madison, John Quincy served as minister to Russia and then, in 1815, as ambassador to Great Britain. During this time, he negotiated the Treaty of Ghent, which was signed in 1814, ending the destructive War of 1812 with Britain. With the 1815 election of James Monroe to the presidency, Adams's political fortunes improved, and he served as secretary of state from 1817 to 1824. His most famous accomplishments as secretary were fixing the border with Canada as far west as the Rockies, and acquiring from Spain territory for the United States. He ran for president in 1824 and became the only person ever elected to the office from a field of candidates with a majority of votes by the House of Representatives. Scandal made him unpopular, and he lost to Andrew Jackson in 1828 after an undistinguished presidency. However, John Quincy returned to politics in 1830 as a representative from Massachusetts. During this time, he railed against slavery as well as the 1846–48 Mexican–American War because of the illegal means by which it came about. He died in office on February 23, 1848.

Legacy

John Quincy Adams gave the early United States a strong diplomatic presence abroad while simultaneously trying to use great moral authority to force Americans to address divisive issues, such as slavery, with intellect and reason rather than emotions and prejudice.

Sympathetic to the Federalist cause, which strove for a strong and centralized government, John Quincy throughout his career sought the expansion and protection of the United States. The morality of such a government, he reasoned, would overcome the weaknesses of the country, such as slavery. However, he stood against the tyrannical tendencies pursued in the late 1790s by such measures as the Alien and Sedition Acts, which made almost all criticism of the United States illegal. Morality and reason were the foundations on which John Quincy built his reputation and influence.

John Quincy's desire for national strength extended to his actions in diplomacy as well.

These tendencies descended partly from the patriotic heritage of his family and partly from his belief that Providence had intended people like him to make the United States a continental power. Although embodying all the qualities of a cultivated, learned English gentleman, he distrusted the Europeans and detested the conniving monarchies that ruled the Continent. He manifested this dislike by not supporting THOMAS JEFFERSON and JAMES MADISON's desire for a close alliance with Britain, and by convincing President Monroe in 1823 to make the Americas off limits to foreign powers or threats, although the United States lacked the military strength to defend such a declaration. John Quincy's brainchild, the Monroe Doctrine, which stated that the United States would not tolerate renewed European colonization or imperialism in the Americas, remains a central tenet of American foreign policy to this day, and has often encouraged a paternalistic and interventionist attitude by the United States that its Latin American neighbors have not always appreciated.

Del Testa

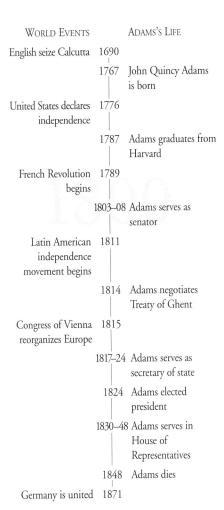

World Events		Adams's Life
English seize Calcutta	1690	
	1767	John Quincy Adams is born
United States declares independence	1776	
	1787	Adams graduates from Harvard
French Revolution begins	1789	
	1803–08	Adams serves as senator
Latin American independence movement begins	1811	
	1814	Adams negotiates Treaty of Ghent
Congress of Vienna reorganizes Europe	1815	
	1817–24	Adams serves as secretary of state
	1824	Adams elected president
	1830–48	Adams serves in House of Representatives
	1848	Adams dies
Germany is united	1871	

For Further Reading
Nagel, Paul. *John Quincy Adams: A Public Life, a Private Life.* Cambridge, Mass.: Harvard University Press, 1999.
Parsons, Lynn Hudson. *John Quincy Adams.* Madison, Wis.: Madison House Publishers, 1997.

Adenauer, Konrad

German Chancellor
1876–1967

Life and Work

During his long political career Konrad Adenauer guided West Germany into the post–World War II era, creating a stable, democratic West German republic and promoting European unity.

Adenauer was born on January 5, 1876, in Cologne, then in the German Empire, which had only become a unified nation-state in 1871. The son of a civil servant who insisted that his children receive a university education, Adenauer entered the University of Freiburg in 1894, studied law, received a degree in 1900, and joined a law firm in Cologne shortly thereafter. Adenauer, a Roman Catholic, joined the Center Party, a political party representing Catholics in a country dominated by the Protestant state of Prussia.

In 1906 Adenauer ran for and won a city council seat in Cologne; in 1909 he was appointed deputy mayor of that city. In 1917, during World War I, Adenauer was appointed mayor of Cologne by the city council, making him, at 41, the youngest mayor in the territories of the state of Prussia. Germany's defeat in World War I put an end to the empire; a republic (known as the Weimar Republic) was

proclaimed in 1919. In 1920 Adenauer, still serving as Cologne's mayor, became the chairman of the Prussian State Council and was considering a career in national politics.

However, in March 1933, the Nazis, who had just taken power under ADOLF HITLER, forced Adenauer out of office, in part because he had previously restrained Nazi violence in Cologne. Adenauer went into retirement but remained in Germany, neither supporting the Nazi government nor actively opposing it. In March 1945, as World War II drew to a close and with the defeat of the Nazis imminent, American forces asked Adenauer to resume his post as mayor of Cologne, which he did in May, just after Germany surrendered.

Later that year Adenauer joined the new Christian Democratic Union party (CDU), where he soon seized the leadership. In 1948 Adenauer was appointed chairman of the Parliamentary Council, convened by the occupying powers to draft a constitution for West Germany. Adenauer became the first chancellor of the Federal Republic of Germany (formerly West Germany) in 1949.

Adenauer cooperated with the Allies, and Germany joined NATO (the North Atlantic Treaty Organization, formed to counter the feared expansionist tendencies of the Soviet Union) in 1955. In 1963 he signed a "treaty of friendship" with France, a step toward cooperation with Germany's longtime enemy.

Adenauer retired in 1963 and died on April 19, 1967, in Rhöndorf, West Germany.

Legacy

Konrad Adenauer helped transform the defeated and demoralized population of West Germany into a prosperous and confident people committed to European unity.

After World War II, Adenauer demanded and received a measure of respect from the victorious Allies still occupying German lands, reduced the punitive measures taken by the Allies against Germany for starting the war, and won back (West) German sovereignty by 1955.

Adenauer pushed for German integration into the European Community that was forming in the late 1940s. West Germany received funds from the American Marshall Plan for European economic recovery (1947–48), joined the Organization for European Economic Cooperation (1949), the European

Coal and Steel Community (1951), and was a founding member of the European Economic Community (1957). By involving his country in efforts at European unity, Adenauer successfully made West Germany an equal partner in the postwar world order.

Adenauer's pragmatic and Western-oriented economic policies (boosted by the Marshall Plan) turned West Germany into a prosperous nation; in what became known as the "economic miracle," the country's productivity and standard of living grew by leaps and bounds in the 1950s and 1960s, ensuring stability.

Adenauer's center-right regime was sometimes criticized for its staunchly pro-Western orientation, willingness to appoint former Nazis to the cabinet, and mildly authoritarian tendencies. Adenauer nonetheless fostered a commitment among West Germans to a democratic political system. In response, the political rival of Adenauer's CDU, the Social Democratic Party (SPD), modified its revolutionary rhetoric and adopted a more moderate social-welfare platform. When the SPD won the elections of 1969, the CDU peacefully relinquished the power it had enjoyed for 20 years.

Although Adenauer's anticommunist policy facilitated the 40-year division of Germany into two states, it also made reunification with East Germany in 1990 possible on West German terms. Despite continued problems integrating the former East Germany into the West German social, political, and economic structure, the united Germany of today is a strong but stable leader among European states.

Lemoine

World Events		Adenauer's Life
Germany is united	1871	
	1876	Konrad Adenauer is born
Russo-Japanese War	1905	
World War I	1914–18	
Russian Revolution	1917	Adenauer appointed mayor of Cologne
Great Depression	1929–39	
	1933	Adenauer forced by Nazis to resign as mayor of Cologne
World War II	1939–45	
Communist China is established	1949	Adenauer becomes chancellor
	1963	Adenauer signs treaty with France; he retires
Israel defeats Arab nations in Six-Day War	1967	Adenauer dies

For Further Reading

Hiscocks, Richard. *The Adenauer Era*. Philadelphia: J. B. Lippincott, 1967.

Schwarz, Hans-Peter. *Konrad Adenauer: A German Politician and Statesman in a Period of War, Revolution and Reconstruction.* 2 vols. Oxford: Berghahn, 1995.

Akbar

Indian Mughal Emperor
1542–1605

Life and Work

A descendant of both Tamerlane and GENGHIS KHAN, Islamic Mughal Emperor Akbar (in full Abu-ul-Fath Jalal-ud-Din Muhammad Akbar) conquered much of northern, central, and Hindu India, yet fostered efficient government and tolerance in a religiously pluralistic Indian society.

The Mughal Empire (also called the Timurid Empire and the Mogul Empire) began in 1526 when Akbar's grandfather, Babur, Muslim ruler of Turkestan in Central Asia, invaded northern India and moved southward. Akbar was born in Umarkot, Sind (present-day Pakistan), on October 15, 1542, while his father, Humayun, was in exile, having been driven from his throne in 1539. Akbar experienced hardship during his early life and never learned to read or write. Humayan reconquered his empire in 1555. In 1556, at age 13, Akbar inherited the throne. His rule was immediately challenged, but Akbar, ably advised by his regent, Bayram Khan, defeated Hindu forces at Panipat to secure his rule. Bayram Khan acted as regent until his dismissal in 1560, when Akbar was 18 years old.

The early part of Akbar's reign was spent expanding his empire. Akbar applied his knowledge of military strategy to conquest; often personally leading his well-organized military, Akbar embarked on a remarkable series of conquests: the Punjab (1566); the Rajput (Hindu) kingdoms in northwestern India (1561–69); the Muslim states of Gujarat (1572–73) and Bengal (1576). In 1581 Akbar reconquered Kabul in Afghanistan. The conquest of Kashmir (1586–92) and Sind (1592) resulted in Mughal rule in most of northern and central India.

Akbar efficiently organized and administered these newly acquired territories, creating salaried administrators (*mansabdari*), recruiting Hindu (Rajput) officials, and marrying a Rajput princess. He introduced many administrative reforms, encouraged trade, and eliminated the poll tax imposed on non-Muslims. Although illiterate himself, he promoted artistic and literary life, and architectural improvements. Most important to the stability of the regime, Akbar promoted religious toleration. His efforts to integrate the practices of other religions into Muslim worship eventually so offended orthodox Sunnis, some of whom accused him of heresy.

The final years of his reign saw him preparing to conquer the Muslim sultanates on the Deccan plateau in south-central India. Akbar's death on October 17, 1605, was possibly caused by poisoning by his son, who succeeded him under the new name of Jahangir ("World Seizer").

Legacy

Akbar created a stable, rich, and powerful empire characterized by religious tolerance, enabling Mughal rule to last two centuries. Elements of his administrative framework endure in present-day India.

Although ruling according to Muslim law, Akbar established an administrative structure within conquered states and territories that was continued by his Mughal descendants as well as by British and post-colonial administrators. Akbar's *mansabdari* system dividing the administration into 33 ranks based on the theoretical number of cavalrymen that an official could bring to the battlefield, was a forerunner of the system of salaried government officials. Akbar also divided the land into provinces, which were subdivided into smaller units for efficient tax collection. The immediate impact of Akbar's stable, fair, and efficient rule was economic growth through increased domestic and international trade. Akbar's policy of opening his administration to talent regardless of faith was adopted, not always successfully, by the British. Elements of both forms of administration endure in independent India.

Akbar's descendants carried on his policies for a time. Akbar's focus on architecture continued under his son Jahangir and his grandson Shah Jahan, who built the famed Taj Mahal. His successors also continued to expand the empire, an effort that proved to be increasingly costly in lives and revenue. Akbar and his successors had difficulty maintaining control of the southern Indian territories, and their repeated invasions sparked fierce local resistance that plagued the Mughal Empire for generations.

Akbar's greatest achievement was his recognition of the pluralistic character of Indian society and religion. In a process of religious amalgamation, called *Mughlai*, the Mughals blended the religious and cultural traditions of Islam, Hinduism, Zoroastrianism, and even elements of Christianity to form a uniquely Indian Muslim rule.

Akbar attempted to create a national empire in which Muslims, Hindus and other ethno-religious groups worked together for the greater good of the empire. Indian nationalists adopted this policy in the late nineteenth century in a unified effort to resist and combat British imperial rule. Although eventually successful in driving out the British, Indians continued to face religious divisions and conflict throughout the twentieth century.

Lemoine

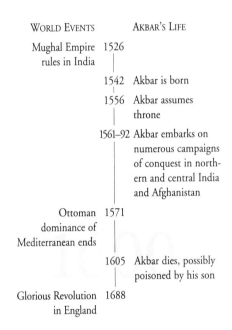

WORLD EVENTS		AKBAR'S LIFE
Mughal Empire rules in India	1526	
	1542	Akbar is born
	1556	Akbar assumes throne
	1561–92	Akbar embarks on numerous campaigns of conquest in northern and central India and Afghanistan
Ottoman dominance of Mediterranean ends	1571	
	1605	Akbar dies, possibly poisoned by his son
Glorious Revolution in England	1688	

For Further Reading

Burke, S. M. *Akbar: The Greatest Mogul*. New Delhi: Munshiram Manohalral, 1989.

Habib, Irfan. *Akbar & His India II*. New York: Oxford University Press, 1997.

Alexander II

Russian Tsar and Reformer
1818–1881

Life and Work

Alexander II ruled the Russian Empire in the face of grave political and military challenges. Committed to a series of courageous reforms, he met a tragic and ironic death at the hands of revolutionaries.

Alexander was born on April 29, 1818, in Moscow. In 1825 his father Tsar Nicholas I acceded to the throne amid an upheaval known as the Decembrist Revolt. In 1854, the weaknesses of his father's traditional order were revealed when England and France invaded Russia's Crimean peninsula. As an officer in the army, Alexander observed the resulting Crimean War (1854–56) closely and was shocked by the victories of Russia's more advanced enemies. In 1855 he succeeded Nicholas and in the following year obtained peace with the Treaty of Paris.

Alexander was impressed by the power industrialization and political reform had brought to his Western adversaries. Afraid that Russia was falling behind the West, he repudiated the conservative system of his father and launched what came to be known as the Great Reforms. On February 19, 1861 he issued the Emancipation Edict liberating Russia's serfs, who were attached to the property of a landlord. In 1864 he issued the Zemstvo Edict, creating provincial assemblies called *zemstvos*, as well as the Judicial Reform Edict overhauling the court system. A series of military reforms was brought to fulfillment in 1874 when the Military Reform Edict eliminated the exemption of the nobility from conscription and reduced the term of service. Other edicts created municipal councils and freed the press from censorship. In all, Alexander's Great Reforms were a bold effort by the tsar to improve and strengthen the Russian Empire.

These reforms, however, failed to create a stable alternative to the conservative order of Nicholas I. While millions of peasants now enjoyed personal freedom, continued economic hardships and confusion about the limits of the emancipation provoked uprisings in rural districts throughout the 1860s. The radical intelligentsia, freed to speak more openly, now issued a barrage of inflammatory statements. Most ominously, a revolutionary movement known as the *narodniki* ("populists") agitated for a peasant uprising during the 1870s. When this failed they resorted to terrorism and a group calling itself Narodnaya Volya ("People's Will") launched a series of assassinations after 1879. Alexander, who had nearly died from an assassin's bullet in 1866, was horrified by the disorders and took action to counter them, resorting in a limited way to the methods of his father, but also he authorized the creation of a liberal consultative assembly of nobles drawn from the *zemstvos*.

On March 1, 1881, the Narodnaya Volya ambushed Alexander's entourage in Saint Petersburg and were successful. Alexander died from his wounds later that day.

Legacy

Despite their failure, Alexander's Great Reforms had a lasting impact on the history of modern Russia.

With the assassination of Alexander in 1881, Russian statecraft entered a period that historians call the "era of counterreform." During this time rulers sought to reverse the Great Reforms. Upon his succession Alexander III (r. 1881–94) dismissed liberals from the government, reversed promises for a consultative assembly, restricted the powers of *zemstvos*, and reimposed censorship. Tsar NICHOLAS II (r. 1894–1917) maintained the policies of counterreform.

Although the Revolution of 1905 actually forced Nicholas to establish a much more liberal representative assembly known as the Duma, he continued to resist liberal reforms until 1917, when he and the entire tsarist system were completely overthrown.

Nevertheless, the Great Reforms left an enduring mark on the social structure and political attitudes of modern Russia. Alexander II was remembered as the "Tsar-Liberator" whose Emancipation Edict had freed 22 million peasants. Migrating to Russia's cities, many of these peasants became the first generation of industrial workers. Although workers would remain a small part of the population, it was this element to whom Marxist revolutionaries such as VLADIMIR ILICH LENIN looked to for justification of the Revolution of 1917.

The Emancipation Edict also affected political opinion. For conservatives it was a sign of the tsarist system's moral legitimacy; its peaceful implementation caused many to contrast Russia to the contemporary United States, where slavery was abolished only through the violence of the Civil War (1861–65). Even critics of the tsarist system were compelled to acknowledge the nobility of Alexander's act. Some actually feared it would ruin the revolutionary movement. When reflecting upon it from his London exile, for instance, Russia's leading socialist Alexander Herzen could not help repeating the despairing final words of the pagan Roman Emperor Julian the Apostate: "Thou hast conquered, O Galilean!"

Strickland

WORLD EVENTS		ALEXANDER II'S LIFE
Congress of Vienna reorganizes Europe	1815	
	1818	Alexander II is born
	1854–56	Alexander serves in Crimean War
	1855	Alexander accedes to throne
	1861–64	Alexander begins his "Great Reforms"
	1866	Alexander survives first assassination attempt
Germany is united	1871	
	1881	Alexander is assassinated by terrorists
Russo-Japanese War	1905	

For Further Reading

Lincoln, W. Bruce. *The Great Reforms: Autocracy, Bureaucracy, and the Politics of Change in Imperial Russia.* DeKalb, Ill.: Northern Illinois University Press, 1990.

Pereira, N. G. O. *Tsar-Liberator: Alexander II of Russia, 1818–1881.* Newtonville, Mass.: Oriental Research Partners, 1983.

Seton-Watson, Hugh. *The Russian Empire, 1801–1917.* Oxford: Oxford University Press, 1967.

Alexander III

Greco–Macedonian Conqueror
356–323 B.C.E.

Life and Work

Considered one of the great military geniuses in history, Alexander III (Alexander the Great), through his conquests, fostered the spread of Greek culture into Asia and Egypt.

Alexander was born in 356 B.C.E., son of King Philip II of Macedon, in the northern Balkan Peninsula. He was tutored by ARISTOTLE, absorbing Greek culture, and was groomed for military leadership. His mother, Olympias, fostered his interest in art and mysticism. At age 16 he was appointed regent while his father conducted almost continual military campaigns; he was also named a commander in his father's army. Despite the tension between Alexander and his father arising over Philip's many potential heirs, he assumed the throne as Alexander III (the Romans added "the Great" to his name many years later) after his father was assassinated in 336. Alexander built his empire on a Macedonian kingdom consolidated and strengthened by his father.

Alexander then launched a 10-year military campaign that transformed Macedonia into a vast empire. First, in 335, he suppressed rebellions against Macedonian rule arising among the northern tribes and the Greek city of Thebes. Beginning in 334 he invaded the traditional and ideological Greek enemy, the Persian Empire. The Battle of Granicus began Alexander's conquest of Asia Minor (modern-day Turkey). From there he moved into Syria, where his well-disciplined troops defeated the Persian army, led by Emperor Darius III himself, at the Battle of Issus in 333. Darius fled eastward, leaving Alexander in control of the western half of the Persian Empire.

In 332 Alexander turned south (into modern Lebanon and Israel–Palestine), destroying the ports at Tyre and Gaza that supported the Persian fleet, then marched into Egypt, founding the city of Alexandria. In 331, he returned eastward to defeat Darius again at the Battle of Gaugamela. Approximately one million people died during Alexander's wars of expansion.

Having utterly defeated the Persians, Alexander proclaimed himself "Lord of Asia," and continued eastward to India. Beginning in 327 he conquered Afghanistan, and in 326 defeated the northern Indian kingdom of Porus on the Hydaspes River. In 325 he was forced by his weary troops to retreat back to Persia where he died of fever, possibly induced by alcoholism, in Babylon, on June 13, 323.

Legacy

Alexander III's effort to create an empire of universal rule resulted in the spread of Greek culture throughout much of Egypt and western Asia. Alexander's example also inspired future military leaders with a similar vision.

In each land conquered, Alexander founded new cities (all called Alexandria) that transformed urban areas into provincial capitals serving the empire. City-states that were once independent political entities were absorbed into the empire and transformed into administrative, manufacturing, and commercial centers for each imperial province. The cities Alexander founded formed the central points of Hellenistic culture; the inhabitants adopted Greek patterns of government, institutions, and economic life. Educational, artistic, and intellectual activities flourished in these new Hellenistic cities; trade was expanded to include Arabia, India, and China.

Alexander's vast empire did not long survive his death, however, and was replaced by several successor states ruled by his generals, called the Diadochi. In Egypt, General Ptolemy founded a long-lasting dynasty, which came to an end with the death of Cleopatra in 30 B.C.E. In Asia, elite Persian families learned the Greek language and customs. A dialect of Greek, called Koines, became the lingua franca of the region.

The Roman conquests of the second century, and those of the Parthians to the east, diminished but did not destroy the influence of ancient Greek culture spread so widely by Alexander.

Alexander's vision of world domination was imitated by many ambitious rulers in the following centuries, beginning with AUGUSTUS Caesar, the first emperor of the Roman Empire.

Raised on Homer's warrior epics, the *Iliad* and the *Odyssey*, Alexander earned the support of the Greeks by undertaking the campaign against the Persians, traditional enemies of Greece. An accomplished orator, keenly aware of the heroic nature of his status as military leader, Alexander effectively cultivated a persona of the warrior-king, which inspired his troops to extraordinary feats of endurance. His successful and often ruthless conquests inspired the desire to establish universal rule under one law: his. NAPOLÉON I and ADOLF HITLER are two modern examples of rulers who sought world domination in much the same way as Alexander.

Lemoine

WORLD EVENTS	B.C.E.	ALEXANDER III's LIFE
China's "Warring States" Period begins	403	
	356	Alexander III is born
	340	Alexander is appointed regent
	336	Philip II is assassinated; Alexander succeeds him
	335	Alexander consolidates control of northern tribes and Greek city of Thebes
	334	Alexander begins campaign against Persian Empire
	333	Alexander defeats Persian army at Battle of Issus
	332	Alexander occupies Egypt, founds Alexandria
	331	Alexander defeats Persia
	327	Alexander conquers Afghanistan
	326	Alexander defeats Indian kingdom of Porus
Maurya Empire in India is founded	325	
Alexander the Great's empire at greatest size	323	Alexander dies of fever
Han Dynasty ends China's "Warring States" Period	206	

For Further Reading

Bosworth, A. B. *Conquest and Empire: The Reign of Alexander the Great.* Cambridge: Cambridge University Press, 1988.
Borza, Eugene N., ed. *The Impact of Alexander the Great.* Hinsdale, Ill.: Dryden Press, 1974.

Anthony, Susan Brownell

American Women's Rights Advocate
1820–1906

Life and Work

Susan Brownell Anthony campaigned for women's rights by bringing the abuse and second-class status of women to the world's attention.

Anthony was born on February 15, 1820, into a prosperous Quaker family in rural Massachusetts. In 1839 her family sent her to a Philadelphia Quaker girls' academy for additional education, a rarity at a time when women were often denied advanced educations. She had to leave the academy to help her family during an economic downturn. Anthony soon began a teaching career, which led to an appointment in 1846 as headmistress at the Canajoharie Academy in Rochester, New York.

Anthony began her political career in Rochester, joining the temperance (anti-alcohol) movement. She soon became involved in other political issues of the day—the abolition of slavery, workers' rights, and a woman's right to own property.

In 1851, Anthony met Elizabeth Cady Stanton, one of the organizers of the first women's rights convention (1848) in Seneca Falls, New York. They became friends and began to work as a team. Soon after their meeting, in 1852, Anthony attended her first women's rights convention, held in Syracuse, New York, and began to dedicate more and more of her time to women's rights. In 1860, she helped win the right of women to own property and to conduct legal business in New York state, her first big victory. She earned a reputation as a tireless and well-organized activist.

After the Civil War, Anthony and Stanton pushed for an amendment to the Constitution to enfranchise women, just as the Fifteenth Amendment had given the vote to all males (except Native Americans) over 21. In 1869, they formed the National Woman Suffrage Association, dedicated to gaining full voting rights at the national level; the opposing American Woman Suffrage Association, formed that same year, worked more for suffrage at the state level. (The two organizations would settle their differences and merge in 1890.) Anthony soon turned to more radical measures. She was arrested for voting in Rochester in November 1872 and even spoke out against immigration because she thought a flood of Roman Catholic men, deemed excessively patriarchal in a common contemporary stereotype, would forever tip the balance against the enfranchisement of women. At the forefront of the suffrage movement, she crisscrossed the country, campaigning vigorously. In 1883 Anthony and Stanton traveled to Europe to help form the International Council of Women, an international effort for women's rights.

By the mid-1890s, Anthony, in her seventies and declining health, began to stay closer to her home in Rochester. She made one last trip to Europe in 1904, where she could boast of much progress made for the rights of women. Indeed, throughout the 1880s and 1890s, women gradually gained property and certain political rights in the United States. She died on March 13, 1906. Fourteen more years would pass before Congress approved the Nineteenth Amendment, giving American women the vote in time for the 1920 presidential election.

Legacy

Susan B. Anthony gave the American women's rights movement form and momentum, and was pivotal in helping women gain the right to vote in the United States.

Although the call for women's rights had evolved out of the Enlightenment and was briefly popular in Europe during the French Revolution, the dominant religious and legal institutions in the early United States discouraged women from involvement in public life. Anthony challenged the prevailing political climate to awaken people to the just cause of women's rights. For example, she celebrated the idea of marriage, but said that women needed to have the right to manage their own property. Using the issue of "taxation without representation," Anthony struck a patriotic chord with many Americans when she insisted on the enfranchisement of women because they paid taxes as citizens. Later, she argued that the vote for women was a logical extension of the abolition movement.

It was this political astuteness that made her work so influential and helped to pave the way for the eventual ratification of the Nineteenth Amendment in 1920. She, along with Stanton, guided younger generations of women's rights activists. Stanton gave words to the suffrage movement through her eloquent speeches, while Anthony's exceptional organizational skills kept it moving forward. Women's rights activists today, indeed, still learn from their example.

Del Testa

World Events		Anthony's Life
Congress of Vienna reorganizes Europe	1815	
	1820	Susan Brownell Anthony is born
	1839	Anthony goes to Philadelphia to study
	1846	Anthony is appointed headmistress of school in Rochester, NY
	1851	Anthony meets Elizabeth Cady Stanton
	1860	Through Anthony's efforts, New York grants women right to own property
	1869	Anthony helps form National Woman Suffrage Association
Germany is united	1871	
	1872	Anthony is arrested for voting
	1883	Anthony visits Europe with Stanton
Russo-Japanese War	1905	
	1906	Anthony dies
World War I	1914–18	

For Further Reading

Barry, Kathleen. *Susan B. Anthony: A Biography of a Singular Feminist.* New York: New York University Press, 1988.

Sherr, Lynn. *Failure Is Impossible: Susan B. Anthony in Her Own Words.* New York: Times Books, 1995.

Weatherford, Doris. *A History of the American Suffragist Movement.* Denver, Colo.: ABC-CLIO, 1998.

Arafat, Yasir

Leader of the Palestinian
Liberation Organization
1929–

Life and Work

Palestinian leader Yasir Arafat forced international recognition of Palestinian nationalism and negotiated an agreement with Israel to establish a Palestinian state in Israeli occupied territories.

Arafat was born Mohammed Abed Ar'ouf, probably on August 4, 1929, in Cairo, Egypt (accounts differ), to a comfortable middle-class family, adopting the nickname Yasir ("easygoing"). Arafat became interested in politics as a student in Cairo. The defeat of the Arab states in the Arab–Israeli War of 1948–49, which created 750,000 Palestinian refugees when the state of Israel was proclaimed, provided Arafat with the cause of his life.

Arafat attended Fuad I University in Cairo (1952–1956) and studied electrical engineering, though he devoted his time to political activities. During his univerity years, he became the leader of the Palestinian Students' Union, adopting the headdress that became his trademark.

After graduation in 1956 he founded al-Fatah ("victory"), a Palestinian resistance group. When the Arab states formed the Palestinian Liberation Organization (PLO) in 1964, Fatah was poised to assume the leadership of the Palestinian umbrella organization.

After the crushing defeat of the Arab states by Israel in the Six-Day War of 1967, in which Arafat fought for Syria, he waged a guerrilla war in the territories now occupied by the Israelis, specifically the West Bank and the Gaza Strip. Arafat took control of the PLO away from the Arab states in 1969, and established its headquarters in Lebanon.

In the following decades, Arafat struggled to appear moderate to the international community and to appease the factions in the PLO that supported terrorism and guerrilla warfare against Israel. In 1974, after Arafat's speech to the U.N. General Assembly, the United Nations recognized the PLO as the sole representative of the Palestinian people. In 1982 Israel invaded Lebanon, forcing Arafat to move his headquarters to Tunisia.

By the 1980s Arafat and the Israelis were convinced of the need to negotiate. In 1987, Palestinian Arabs in the occupied territories began a resistance movement, the *intifada* ("shaking off"), making occupation of the West Bank and Gaza Strip more difficult for the Israelis. But Arafat could not completely control the *intifada.* In 1988, Arafat agreed to recognize the state of Israel and renounce terrorism, thus gaining official U.S. recognition for the PLO.

In 1993 and 1995, Israel and the PLO completed negotiations, known as the Oslo I and II accords, in which each formally recognized the sovereignty of the other. The agreements established Palestinian autonomy in the Gaza Strip and parts of the West Bank during a transition period, and put an end to the *intifada.* In 1996 Arafat was elected president of the nascent Palestinian state. He is currently negotiating with Israel on a variety of issues, including land transfers, the repatriation of refugees, and the status of Jerusalem, which is claimed by both sides as a capital.

Legacy

Yasir Arafat has transformed the PLO from a terrorist organization into a platform for Palestinian national sovereignty. In signing the Oslo accords, he has been instrumental in bringing a measure of peace and stability to the Middle East.

Arafat laid the groundwork—in both the Palestinian and international community— that would eventually give rise to Palestinian autonomy and the real possibility of a Palestinian state. He appealed to grass-roots public opinion in ways that bolstered his people's self-identify and sense of nationalism. He overcame manipulation by other Arab states and prepared the international community to recognize Palestinian national sovereignty.

Arafat's influence has been diminished by rival Palestinian groups, including radical Islamic fundamentalist groups, such as Hamas and Islamic Jihad, that opposed the Oslo peace accords. His influence has also been limited by Israel's slow schedule in implementing the Oslo accords and ongoing issues such as the status of Jerusalem, claimed by both the Israelis and the Palestinians as their political and religious capital.

The full extent of Arafat's legacy—of his work for Palestinian identity and statehood—will be seen in the outcome of current peace efforts and in the shape and structure of the future Palestinian state. Nevertheless, his influence in the region is remarkably extensive. His efforts have also sparked peace talks between Israel and other Arab states, Jordan and Syria among them.

Lemoine

WORLD EVENTS	ARAFAT'S LIFE
Great Depression 1929–39	
	1929 Yasir Arafat is born
World War II 1939–45	
Communist China 1949 is established	
	1952–56 Arafat attends Fuad I University in Cairo
	1956 Arafat founds al-Fatah
	1964 Arab states form Palestinian Liberation Organization (PLO)
Israel defeats 1967 Arab nations in Six-Day War	
	1974 Arafat addresses United Nations; UN recognizes PLO
Vietnam War ends 1975	
	1987 *Intifada* begins in Israeli-occupied territories
	1988 Arafat recognizes state of Israel and renounces violence
Dissolution of 1991 Soviet Union	
	1995 Oslo II accords signed, extending previous agreements

For Further Reading

Gowers, Andrew, and Tony Walker. *Arafat: The Biography.* London: Virgin, 1994.

Hart, Alan. *Arafat: A Political Biography.* London: Sidgwick & Jackson, 1994.

Smith, Charles D. *Palestine and the Arab-Israeli Conflict.* 3rd ed. New York: St. Martin's Press, 1996.

Arias Sánchez, Oscar

President of Costa Rica
1941–

Life and Work

By returning Costa Rica to a political course that emphasized democracy, independence, and civil society, Oscar Arias Sánchez kept his country from becoming embroiled in the destructive conflicts that rocked Central America throughout the 1980s.

Arias Sánchez was born on September 13, 1941, into wealth and privilege. His parents were affluent growers of coffee. He received an excellent education, graduating with a degree in economics from the University of Costa Rica and earning a doctorate in economics from the University of Essex in England. With public welfare an important personal concern and with Costa Rican politics increasingly empha-

World Events		Arias Sánchez's Life
World War II	1939–45	
	1941	Oscar Arias Sánchez is born
Communist China is established	1949	
Israel defeats Arab nations in Six-Day War	1967	
	1972–77	Arias Sánchez serves as minister of planning
Vietnam War ends	1975	
	1979	Arias Sánchez is elected secretary-general of Partido de Liberacion Nacional (PLN)
	1986	Arias Sánchez is elected president of Costa Rica
	1987	Arias Sánchez receives Nobel Prize for Peace
Dissolution of Soviet Union	1991	

sizing the growth of average income and political involvement, Arias Sánchez began to involve himself in the Partido de Liberacion Nacional (PLN) during the mid-1960s.

In 1972, in an atmosphere of growing social tensions, Costa Rican President José Figueres Ferrer appointed Arias Sánchez as minister of planning, a position he retained until 1977. Throughout his term, Arias Sánchez stressed the expansion of the market and conciliation with the economically weak elements of Costa Rican society in order to ease social tensions. In 1979, the membership of the PLN elected Arias Sánchez as the party's secretary-general, and in 1986 he won the presidential elections. He immediately began to address two of Costa Rica's thorniest problems—massive foreign debt and the spillover of the region's political strife into his country.

To ameliorate the crushing effects of indebtedness that had come with the rise of oil prices and the fall of commodity prices during the early 1980s, Arias Sánchez embarked on a program of fiscal austerity and promoted foreign investment and tourism. To deal with regional political strife, in which his predecessor, Luis Alberto Monge, had involved Costa Rica, Arias Sánchez first stood firm against the leftist Sandinista regime of his northern neighbor, Nicaragua, and then forbade the rightist insurgents, the Contras, to operate on Costa Rican soil. He then called upon the leaders of Honduras, Guatemala, Nicaragua, and El Salvador to sign a plan for peace for Central America; it was signed in August 1987. This plan set a timetable for cease-fires between rebels and governments, for the release of political prisoners, and for free and democratic elections. As a result, during the 1990s the countries of Central America have gradually evolved toward peace, although many of the region's social tensions have endured along with economic difficulties.

In October 1987, Arias Sánchez was awarded the Nobel Prize for Peace for his efforts in Central America. After his presidency ended in 1990, Arias Sánchez retired from politics.

Legacy

By standing his ground on Costa Rica's regional and international autonomy, Oscar Arias Sánchez stressed the positive qualities of Costa Rican political development—conciliation, accommodation, and inclusion—that

have made it Central America's most stable and prosperous country.

In the context of a Costa Rica heavily indebted to the United States after the economic crisis of the early 1980s and increasingly involved in bloody civil conflicts in El Salvador, Nicaragua, and Guatemala, Arias Sánchez returned the nation to an independent course that did not make it overly beholden to other interests. This reaffirmed a trend toward relative self-sufficiency and domestic cooperation temporarily interrupted by his predecessor, Alberto Monge, who had expanded the Civil Guard (Costa Rica has not had a military since the 1940s) and contracted large amounts of international debt. By refusing to allow the Contras to use Costa Rica as a base and by trying to improve Costa Rica's economy through government austerity rather than simply augmenting its debt through international borrowing, Arias Sánchez provided a model of how a Central American nation could become free and prosperous without resorting to extremism of the left or the right.

In addition, Arias Sánchez's Peace Plan, following his refusal to let the United States' base the Contra rebels along Costa Rica's border with Nicaragua, showed how regional leaders could cooperate successfully. The economic punishment meted out by the United States against Costa Rica in the late 1980s and early 1990s for not following its wishes highlighted to Arias Sánchez and his successors the wisdom of trying to work as much on their own as possible, and how peace was far better for Central America than war.

Del Testa

For Further Reading

Arias Sánchez, Oscar. *Horizons of Peace: The Costa Rican Contribution to the Peace Process in Central America.* Translated by Bernice G. Romero and Joaquín Tacsan. San José, Costa Rica: Arias Foundation for Peace and Human Progress, 1994.

Booth, John A., and Thomas W. Walker. *Understanding Central America.* 3rd ed. Boulder, Colo.: Westview, 1999.

Aśoka

Indian Emperor
c. 292–c. 233 B.C.E.

Life and Work

Building on the unification of India achieved by his grandfather, CANDRAGUPTA, Aśoka strengthened his empire's administration and commerce; he also converted to Buddhism, elevating it from a small sect to the status of a major world religion.

Aśoka was born about 292 B.C.E. to Bindusara, the emperor of the Mauryan Empire in India. He received the education reserved for young nobles, including eight to 10 years' study of mathematics, the Indian classics, economics, politics, and the military arts. As a young man, he applied these skills during "apprentice" governorships in the provinces surrounding the cities of Taxila, in northern India, and Ujjain, in central India. After these assignments, Aśoka was considered fit to succeed his father.

At the death of Bindusara in about 273, Aśoka immediately became involved in an unclear succession dispute, resolved only when he raised an army against, and possibly killed, his brother Sumana-Susima. The conflict divided the Mauryan Empire into factions, and Aśoka spent four years replacing untrustworthy administrators with candidates loyal to him. He took the throne in 269 or 268.

Aśoka quickly earned a reputation as an enthusiastic and diligent leader and under him the empire prospered. About 260, Aśoka invaded Kalinga, a rebellious semitribal area on India's eastern coast, with a large army. Although the invasion was successful, Aśoka was disgusted by the wholesale slaughter he witnessed. His horror coincided with philosophical discussions with Buddhist theologians and may have prompted his full conversion to Buddhism in 258.

After the conquest of Kalinga, Aśoka gradually imposed Buddhist laws on the Maurya Empire, including ending the practice of animal sacrifice. Aśoka heavily patronized Buddhist monasteries and arts, commissioning up to 80,000 *stupas* (domed Buddhist shrines) and many commemorative columns throughout India. He sought to make it safe and convenient for pilgrims to travel around his kingdom, which had the effect of improving internal trade. In every action, Aśoka sought to replace *danda* ("force") with *dharma* ("justice"). However, social conflict over the imposition of Buddhist law seethed across the empire. Aśoka died in 233 or 232.

Legacy

Aśoka cemented the idea of an Indian national identity but sowed the seeds of religious and cultural conflicts that endure today.

Aśoka ably managed his vast empire, strengthening internal government and further reinforcing the idea of a larger India in the entire Asian subcontinent. His adoption of Buddhism also showed to his people that many religions and cultures might peacefully exist side by side, a cultural tolerance with which India continues to struggle. Indeed, some Indian states have occasionally shown great religious and cultural tolerance.

However, Aśoka's imposition of Buddhist laws disrupted a centuries-old social order, with the Hindu Brahmanical (priestly) caste at its apex. With the growth of India's population in the centuries before Aśoka's reign, the priesthood had also expanded and the range of religious practices managed by Brahmanical specialists, most especially around specific types of animal sacrifice, had also grown. Aśoka's restrictions on animal sacrifice, based on his Buddhist beliefs, technically put much of India's elite out of work and out of power. This elite had vast influence over community governance and commercial development, even if it did not always engage directly in these activities. Aśoka's empire did not outlive him in any substantive way by more than a few decades because local officials refused to convert to Buddhism or its practices. Religious conflicts and cohabitation between Buddhists and Hindus, and, subsequently, Muslims, who arrived in the eighth century C.E., continues today.

Del Testa

World Events		Aśoka's Life
	B.C.E.	
Alexander the Great's empire at greatest size	323	
	c. 292	Aśoka is born
	273	Aśoka's father dies and he becomes involved in fight for throne
	269	Aśoka is coronated
	c. 260	Aśoka invades Kalinga
	258	Aśoka's converts to Buddhism
	c. 233	Aśoka dies
Han Dynasty ends China's "Warring States" Period	206	

For Further Reading

Ahir, D. C. *Asoka the Great*. Delhi: B. R. Publishing, 1995.
Nikan, N.A., and Richard McKeon. *The Edicts of Asoka*. Chicago, Ill.: University of Chicago Press, 1978.

Atatürk, Kemal

Founder of Modern Turkey
1881–1938

Life and Work

Kemal Atatürk, elected Turkey's first president, transformed the Ottoman Empire into a modern state.

Atatürk was born Mustafa in Salonika in Greece (then part of the Ottoman Empire) on March 12, 1881. His father, a minor civil servant, insisted he be educated at a secular school. There a teacher gave him the surname Kemal ("perfect"). He attended the War College in Istanbul, graduating in 1905. As punishment for participating in nationalist activity, Kemal was ordered to an army post in Syria, also Ottoman territory.

Kemal joined the nationalist Committee of Union and Progress (CUP) and the Young Turk movement. In 1908, Young Turks, led by army officers including Mustafa Kemal, forced the sultan of the Ottoman Empire to restore the constitution, promulgated in 1876 but immediately suspended. In 1909, when Kemal was serving in the army, the CUP (now a political party) deposed the sultan, replacing him with the more pliable Mehmed IV.

When the Ottoman Empire allied with Germany and Austria-Hungary in World War I, Kemal served on the Gallipoli Peninsula, where he became a national hero after repelling a British invasion in 1915. However, the

Ottoman Empire was defeated, along with the other Central Powers. The terms of the Treaty of Sèvres (1920) were harsh: the Ottoman Empire lost nearly all its European territory and control of the Bosphorus Straits. Kurdistan gained autonomy. What remained was an ethnic Turk enclave that today makes up Turkey.

Turkey, as it was now called, rebelled against the Treaty of Sèvres by declaring war on the Allied forces. Kemal led the nationalist movement. By 1922, the Turks were victorious. The Treaty of Lausanne (1923) confirmed their victory, dashing the Kurds' hopes for autonomy. The sultan, who had cooperated with the Allies, was deposed, the Ottoman Empire was abolished (1922) and the Turkish Republic was proclaimed (1923).

Kemal, as president and leader of the new Republican People's Party, continued the campaign, begun in the late-nineteenth century, to westernize Turkish institutions. A Western-style legal system was adopted (1926); the Latin alphabet was adopted (1928); women gained the vote (1934); mass education was introduced. In 1934, all Turks were required to adopt Western-style surnames; Kemal acquired the surname Atatürk, meaning "father of the Turks." The government also took control of key sectors of the economy and encouraged industrialization. Atatürk died of cirrhosis of the liver on November 10, 1938.

Legacy

Kemal Atatürk transformed his country from a multiethnic empire based on Islam into a secular nation-state, providing a model for newly independent countries facing similar challenges in the twentieth century.

Under Atatürk, Turkey recreated itself by adopting what Atatürk and other Turkish leaders believed to be the strengths of the West: secular political institutions and industrialization. Turkey's future leaders continued Atatürk's pro-Western policy, joining NATO in 1952, and becoming an associate member of the European Economic Community in 1964. When other regions of the world (such as India, Africa, and Southeast Asia) gained their independence, its leaders also had to decide which Western institutions to adopt or reject. Atatürk's transformation of Turkey provided a successful model for these emerging states.

Atatürk's task, turning Ottoman subjects into Turkish citizens, was not accomplished without

cost. The war Atatürk led against the Allied forces and the Treaty of Lausanne forced approximately 350,000 ethnic Turks to leave Greece and approximately one million ethnic Greeks to evacuate Turkey. Non-Turkish minorities who remained in Turkey were denied cultural and political rights. Atatürk's refusal to recognize the rights of ethnic minorities in Turkey led to civil unrest. Among the Kurds (whom Atatürk designated "Mountain Turks"), a nationalist movement was formed, factions of which resorted to terrorism. The Turkish government retaliated, sometimes brutally, to suppress the movement.

Atatürk's legacy resulted in both political instability and increased democracy, stemming from the conflict between his liberal-democratic ideals and authoritarian tendencies. In 1945, Atatürk's handpicked successor, Ismet Inönü, legalized other political parties, and in 1950 the conservative Democratic Party won national elections. However, three military coups occurred when the multiparty parliamentary system seemed unable to maintain stability. The constitution was rewritten twice, in 1961 and 1982, in an attempt to redress the problems of the previous constitutions.

Furthermore, despite the apparent success of Atatürk's secularizing reforms, not all Turks wanted to eliminate Islam from public life. An Islamic fundamentalist party, Refah (prosperity) gained power in 1996, challenging the secular rule created by Atatürk. Despite these problems, the Republic of Turkey has maintained the political institutions established by its first leader.

Lemoine

World Events		Atatürk's Life
Germany is united	1871	
	1881	Kemal Atatürk is born
Russo-Japanese War	1905	
	1909	Kemal participates in Young Turk coup
World War I	1914–18	
Russian Revolution	1917	
	1923	Republic of Turkey is established; Kemal becomes president
Great Depression	1929–39	
	1934	Kemal assumes name Kemal Atatürk
	1938	Atatürk dies
World War II	1939–45	

For Further Reading

Macfie, A. L. *Atatürk*. London: Longman, 1994.

Tachau, Frank. *Turkey: The Politics of Authority, Democracy, and Development*. New York: Greenwood Publishing, 1984.

Weiker, Walter F. *The Modernization of Turkey: From Atatürk to the Present Day*. New York: Holmes and Meier, 1981.

Attila

Hunnish King
c. 400–453

Life and Work

Attila ruled a powerful kingdom in central Europe that threatened both the Western and Eastern branches of the fifth-century Roman Empire.

Historians are uncertain about the exact date of Attila's birth. He was sure to have witnessed many military engagements while still a boy, for his uncle, a chieftain named Ruga, was responsible for leading the Huns in battles throughout eastern Europe. When Ruga died in 434, Attila and his brother, Bleda, became joint rulers of the kingdom. In the following year, Bleda arranged a favorable treaty with the eastern Roman Empire by which the Huns were to receive annual tribute from Constantinople. In 443 Attila had his brother murdered and was thereby able to proclaim himself sole ruler.

Attila's nine-year rule was a time of spectacular military expansion by the Huns, whose kingdom dominated central and eastern Europe. His first important act was to invade the Balkan peninsula. In 447 he led his armies on a sudden campaign that nearly reached the gates of Constantinople. Disease among his troops forced him to turn back, but not before Hunnish soldiers laid waste to numerous cities in their path.

In the meantime, Attila had received a furtive offer of marriage from Honoria, a princess of the Western empire. When she was compelled to rescind the offer, the enraged Attila invaded France. In 451 his armies began besieging and sacking one city after another. Their custom of massacring the inhabitants of fallen cities led contemporary Church leaders to call Attila "the scourge of God." He failed, however, to take Orleans, and by the end of the year his rampage had come to an end. At the Battle of Catalaunian Fields near the Marne River, his armies were defeated and he was forced to withdraw.

Never content in peace, Attila decided in 452 to cross the Alps and invade Italy. His goal was Rome itself, but an unexpected visit by Pope Leo I to the Hunnish camp caused Attila to change his mind and reverse course. Although not a Christian, religious portents often played a role in his campaigns, and the Pope's sudden appearance seems to have shaken his confidence.

In 453 Attila's life came to a sudden and ignoble end. After a drunken wedding feast, he collapsed in his tent with a severe nosebleed. Unconscious, he bled to death in the presence of his new bride.

Legacy

Attila's military campaigns in Europe had a great impact on contemporary and subsequent events. His use of mounted cavalry led to the development of new military tactics, while the destruction of Roman armies further weakened an already crumbling Western empire.

The Huns were one of the most successful military forces of their age. The flat Eurasian steppes from which they emerged enabled them to develop mounted armies with great effectiveness. It was just such an army that GENGHIS KHAN would lead in the thirteenth century. The Huns, when they arrived in eastern Europe at the end of the fourth century, encountered armies that relied mainly on foot soldiers. The Huns easily prevailed over their adversaries, in part with the use of terrifying weapons such as a special lanyardlike weapon with a hook at the end. Hurling this at an enemy solider, the Huns would entangle him with it and then finish him off with short hatchets and swords as he struggled to free himself. Attila deployed these irresistible tactics across the European continent and by doing so forced Roman generals to reconsider their traditional methods of warfare. For centuries afterward, the mounted solider would be integral to all European armies.

Attila's destructive campaigns also contributed to the collapse of the Western Roman Empire. Constantinople replaced Rome as the empire's capital during the fourth century. As a result, by the beginning of the fifth century, the western half of the empire was increasingly powerless to oppose the influx of barbarian tribes from central Europe. In 410, the Visigothic ruler Alaric even marched on Rome and sacked it. The Hunnish kingdom also participated in this barbarian onslaught. By consuming the military resources of the enfeebled Western empire, Attila thus hastened its final collapse, which came in 476.

Strickland

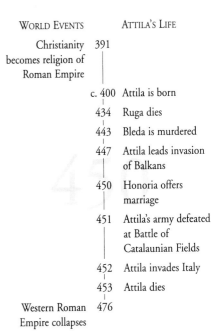

WORLD EVENTS		ATTILA'S LIFE
Christianity becomes religion of Roman Empire	391	
	c. 400	Attila is born
	434	Ruga dies
	443	Bleda is murdered
	447	Attila leads invasion of Balkans
	450	Honoria offers marriage
	451	Attila's army defeated at Battle of Catalaunian Fields
	452	Attila invades Italy
	453	Attila dies
Western Roman Empire collapses	476	

For Further Reading

Howarth, Patrick. *Attila, King of the Huns.* London: Constable, 1994.

Maenchen-Helfen, Otto J. *The World of the Huns: Studies in Their History and Culture.* Berkeley: University of California Press, 1973.

Thompson, E. A. *A History of Attila and the Huns.* Oxford: Blackwell Publishers, 1996.

Augustus

First Roman Emperor
63 B.C.–14 A.D.

Life and Work

Augustus consolidated the Roman Empire and ruled during its most brilliant period of growth.

Augustus was born Gaius Octavius in 63 B.C. His father died when he was only four years old, and he ultimately came under the protection of Rome's most powerful statesman, JULIUS CAESAR. He soon gained Caesar's paternal affection and assisted him in government and war. In 44 B.C., after campaigning with Caesar in Spain, Octavius was sent by his patron to Macedonia to study rhetoric. Only months after arriving, he received news that Caesar had been stabbed to death in Rome. He sped back to the capital, where upon his arrival he received even more remarkable news. Just before his death, Caesar had adopted the 18-year-old Octavius and named him his heir. Gaius Octavius adoptd the name Gaius Julius Caesar, but soon became known as Octavian.

The rule of Octavian was by no means assured. Although the conspirators were driven from Rome by a mob loyal to the memory of Caesar, their armies presented a grave challenge. The greatest threat came from Marc Antony, once Caesar's loyal lieutenant but now a commander who refused to accept the terms of the late dictator's will. After an initial clash between their forces, Octavian and Antony agreed upon a truce in 42 by which a triumvirate was formed with a third commander named Lepidus. This shaky alliance enabled Octavian to concentrate on the remaining armies of the conspirators, which were finally destroyed in the same year at the Battle of Philippi in Greece. Peace might have been secured, but Antony now sought the throne of Egypt by marrying Queen CLEOPATRA VII. This was a direct challenge to Octavian. Not only did Egypt represent a threat to Rome, but Antony was already married to Octavian's sister. As Antony sailed to Greece to rendezvous with Cleopatra, Octavian declared war and followed in pursuit. At the Battle of Actium in 31, the Roman navy smashed the forces of Antony and Cleopatra, who fled back to Egypt and committed suicide.

With no military rivals left, Octavian had finally recovered the authority of Julius Caesar. To emphasize his supreme status, he had the title *Augustus* ("venerable") bestowed upon him by the Senate in 27, and it was by this name that he was henceforth known. With the added title *Imperator* ("emperor"), as well as a host of others, he now controlled the Roman state like no previous ruler. Augustus was careful not to flaunt the changes in Roman statecraft that he had imposed. He always exercised power behind a facade of constitutional institutions such as the consulship.

In the meantime, decades of civil war had finally come to an end. With the exception of a crushing defeat inflicted by the Germans beyond the Rhine in 9 A.D., an era of peace and stability followed. Thus when he died in 14, he left a magnificent state behind him.

Legacy

The reign of Augustus laid the basis for nearly two centuries of Roman imperial rule.

By restoring the semblance of Rome's traditional republican constitution, Augustus was able to restore political stability after years of civil war. His exercise of absolute authority while doing so enabled him to make reforms that helped Rome enter a new stage of development. The imperial bureaucracy was strengthened, and the often unwieldy Roman army brought under greater control. Merchants were given the freedom to expand Italy's markets, and exports of textiles and ceramics boomed. In 28 B.C. Augustus ordered a census that gave the state more information about the expanding population it ruled. He also outlawed adultery, evidence of his interest in social morality and further population growth. According to the terms of this law, he even exiled his own daughter for profligacy.

The peace that followed the Battle of Actium also signaled the emergence of a new order. For nearly two centuries after his death, the empire maintained throughout the Mediterranean world what was known as the *Pax Romana* or Roman Peace. With the fall of Egypt, most of the Mediterranean coastline fell into the hands of Rome, creating a "Roman Lake." Peace in the region secured trade and communications, and the construction of roads and administrative outposts followed. Under these conditions, peoples who had formerly been isolated increasingly came into contact with one another. From Judea, for instance, which Augustus had annexed in 6 A.D., St. Paul was able to travel throughout the eastern Mediterranean on missionary journeys to spread the Christian faith.

Finally, Augustus's rule had a far-reaching impact upon the development of Latin literature. He was patron to some of the greatest poets of the age, and the atmosphere of civil order and prosperity that characterized the *Pax Romana* inspired some of their greatest works. As a result, the era came to be known as the Augustan Age. Perhaps the most remarkable poet was Virgil (70–19 B.C.), whose *Aeneid* is comparable in character to the epics of Homer. Other literary figures of the Augustan Age include Livy, Horace, and Ovid. The influence of Latin and the great works of these Augustan writers has lasted to the present.

Strickland

World Events		Augustus's Life
	B.C.	
Overland silk trade between Rome and China begins	c. 121	
	63	Gaius Octavius is born
Rome's conquest of Gaul completed	50	
	45	Spanish campaign with Julius Caesar
	44	Julius Caesar is assassinated in Rome
	42	Octavian forms ruling triumvirate with Antony and Lepidus
		Conspirators' armies defeated at Battle of Philippi
	31	Antony and Cleopatra VII defeated at Battle of Actium
	28	Octavian orders imperial census
	27	Title of Augustus is bestowed on Octavian by Senate
	A.D.	
	6	Rome annexes Judea
	9	Roman military defeat beyond Rhine
	14	Augustus dies
Jesus is crucified	c. 33	

For Further Reading

Carter, John M. *The Battle of Actium: The Rise and Triumph of Augustus Caesar.* New York: Weybright and Talley, 1970.

Rowell, Henry Thompson. *Rome in the Augustan Age.* Norman, Okla.: University of Oklahoma Press, 1962.

Southern, Pat. *Augustus.* London: Routledge, 1998.

Aung San Suu Kyi

Burmese Political Activist
1945–

Life and Work

Despite great adversity, Aung San Suu Kyi has used her status as the daughter of a famous Burmese independence activist and her own beliefs in freedom to challenge the corrupt military regime, the SLORC (State Law and Order Restoration Council), that rules Burma today. (Burma is also called Myanmar. See note below.)

Born in 1945, Aung San Suu Kyi came from a family already deeply involved in the creation and post-independence politics of modern Burma. Her father, General Aung San, was integral to fighting the colonial occupation of Burma by the British and was to serve as the first post-independence leader of Burma, but was assassinated in 1947. Her mother, Khin Kyi, became an important Burmese diplomat. As a child and teenager, Aung San Suu Kyi attended schools in Burma until 1960, when her mother was appointed as Burma's ambassador to India. In 1962, she was accepted to St. Hugh's College at Oxford University in England. There, she met her future husband, Michael Aris, whom she married in 1972.

In 1967, after graduating from Oxford, Aung San Suu Kyi went to work for the United Nations in New York. Later, during the 1970s and early 1980s, she accompanied her husband on advisory work in Bhutan and took up advanced study of English literature in Britain. After 1986, she embarked on an ambitious biography of her father.

In 1988, Aung San Suu Kyi traveled from England to Burma to take care of her dying mother. During that year, enormous protests erupted against the unpopular military dictator of Burma, Ne Win, who had ruled an impoverished Burma since 1962. Ne Win's government and military responded to the protests with a slaughter of demonstrators in the streets of Rangoon. Aung San Suu Kyi felt compelled to speak out against the government's violence, and in 1989 she helped found a political party, the National League for Democracy (NLD), which began a nonviolent campaign for human rights in Burma. As she campaigned around the country, she became increasingly popular, based partly on her father's heroic legacy and partly on her own convictions and personality. In an effort to stymie her growing popularity and snuff out a growing opposition, the government placed Aung San Suu Kyi under house arrest in 1989. In addition, the government restricted all contact between Aung San Suu Kyi and the outside world.

In 1990 the NLD sponsored candidates for nationwide elections, and these candidates won 80 percent of the vote. The military government, with its own new organization, the State Law and Order Restoration Council (SLORC), simply ignored the results and tightened its oppressive hold on the country.

Aung San Suu Kyi remained under house arrest for six years. But international protest was vociferous and she received greater recognition when she was awarded the Nobel Prize for Peace in 1991. In 1995, under intense foreign pressure, the SLORC allowed Aung San Suu Kyi freedom of movement within Burma, but maintained the right to restrict her contact with others. Despite this limitation, Aung San Suu Kyi has remained a vocal adversary of the regime.

Legacy

Aung San Suu Kyi has used her family's fame, her devotion to human rights, and her own determination to resist the abuses of the SLORC government.

Aung San Suu Kyi stands in opposition to a government controlled by a tyrant infatuated with mysticism, an economy supported by a broad traffic in narcotics, and a declining standard of living. Her failures, such the inability of the NLD candidates to take office in 1990 and the inability after 1995 to mount an effective political front, only illuminated more clearly the corrupt nature of the SLORC regime.

Aung San Suu Kyi's continuing struggle also reveals the two sides of international opinion in the politics of Burma. On one hand, grass-roots international protest, Aung San Suu Kyi's receipt of the Nobel Prize for Peace , declining aid from the West, and a virtual boycott of Burma by Western tourists in the mid-1990s showed how effectively international opinion might affect a dictatorship's actions. On the other, the demands of international business appear to outweigh international concern about Burma's human rights record, as foreign investment has increased since the mid-1990s and the Association of Southeast Asian Nations granted Burma membership in 1997. Aung San Suu Kyi's outspokenness ensures at least one widely heard voice calling for true democracy and human rights in Burma.

Note: In 1989, the government changed the country's name to Myanmar, Union of Burma. Because of the nation's political uncertainty—and, many feel, its illegitimacy—the new name has not taken hold universally.

Del Testa

World Events	Aung San Suu Kyi's Life
World War II 1939–45	
	1945 Aung San Suu Kyi is born
	1947 Aung San Suu Kyi's father is assassinated
Communist China 1949 is established	
Israel defeats Arab nations in Six-Day War	1967 Aung San Suu Kyi graduates from Oxford
Vietnam War ends 1975	
	1988 Aung San Suu Kyi returns to Burma
	1989–95 Aung San Suu Kyi is placed under house arrest
Dissolution of 1991 Soviet Union	
	1995 Aung San Suu Kyi is given limited freedom

For Further Reading

Ling, Bettina. *Aung San Suu Kyi: Standing up for Democracy in Burma.* New York: Feminist Press at the City University of New York, 1999

Victor, Barbara. *The Lady: Aung San Suu Kyi, Nobel Laureate and Burma's Prisoner.* Boston: Faber & Faber, 1998.

Aurangzeb

Indian Mughal Emperor
1618–1707

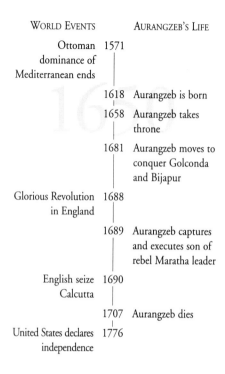

World Events		Aurangzeb's Life
Ottoman dominance of Mediterranean ends	1571	
	1618	Aurangzeb is born
	1658	Aurangzeb takes throne
	1681	Aurangzeb moves to conquer Golconda and Bijapur
Glorious Revolution in England	1688	
	1689	Aurangzeb captures and executes son of rebel Maratha leader
English seize Calcutta	1690	
	1707	Aurangzeb dies
United States declares independence	1776	

Life and Work

Under Aurangzeb, the Islamic Mughal Empire of India reached its greatest territorial extent, but his endless military campaigns against non-Muslims provoked revolts and weakened the empire, which collapsed soon after his death.

Aurangzeb was born on November 3, 1618, in Dohad, India, the third son of Mughal (or Mogul) Emperor Shah Jahan. Aurangzeb understood that because the Mughal dynasty, a Sunni Muslim ruling family, did not have a clear rule of succession, he and his brothers would have to fight for the throne. When his father was ill, he deposed and imprisoned him. After defeating and killing his three brothers, he took the throne in 1658.

Like his ancestor, Akbar, the greatest of the Mughal emperors, Aurangzeb possessed administrative talents and was single-minded in his determination to expand the Mughal Empire into southern India. Conflict with the Marathas (from western India near Bombay) began in the 1640s when Maratha leader Shivaji Bonsle seized Mughal fortresses in the south. This precipitated a war in which Aurangzeb was never completely successful. Furthermore, Shivaji had awakened a sense of Hindu nationalism that also threatened Aurangzeb's rule. In 1689 Aurangzeb captured and executed Shivaji's son, Sambhaji, hoping this would subjugate the Marathas permanently. Instead, a costly and difficult war dragged on, weakening the Mughals.

In 1681 Aurangzeb moved to conquer the Muslim south Indian states of Golconda and Bijapur. Although eventually successful, this prolonged conflict enabled the Sikhs of the Punjab, a religious group that combined a form of Hinduism and Islamic Sufism, and the Hindu Rajputs, to rebel. Aurangzeb ordered the execution of the Sikh guru and the destruction of Sikh temples.

The emperor's conquests extended to all of the Indian subcontinent, except for its southernmost tip. Yet they cost an estimated 100,000 lives a year, along with much of the imperial treasury. Increasing taxes on peasants resulted in revolts, which were brutally suppressed by the imperial army.

Aurangzeb, a pious Sunni Muslim, ended Akbar's policy of religious toleration and enforced a strict Muslim fundamentalism, alienating both Hindus and moderate Muslims. The Rajputs, Hindu subjects who had been welcomed in the Mughal court by previous emperors, rebelled after Aurangzeb ordered the destruction of Hindu temples in Benares (1669), and held the son of a Rajput general hostage at his court 10 years later. In 1680, Aurangzeb sent his own son, Akbar, to put down the revolt. Akbar, however, joined the Rajputs, but was defeated and fled into exile. Throughout his life Aurangzeb suspected his sons of plotting against him and periodically had them arrested and imprisoned.

Aurangzeb spent the rest of his life on military campaigns in the south, never to return to the capital. He died on March 3, 1707, in the southern city of Ahmadnagar.

Legacy

Through Aurangzeb's conquests the Mughal Empire reached its greatest extent, but his anti-Hindu policies promoted inner weaknesses that the British were later able to exploit for their own imperial purposes.

The costly wars and anti-Hindu religious policy drained Mughal resources and aroused too much opposition to permit the empire to remain strong after Aurangzeb's death. His sons conducted the traditional war of succession among themselves. Many provincial rulers lost confidence in the empire's central authority, and thus the autonomy of the provinces increased.

By the middle of the eighteenth century the Mughal empire was falling apart because of interregional religious wars, court incompetence and factionalism, and foreign invasion. The Maratha state, although formally acknowledging Mughal sovereignty, controlled more Indian territory than did the Mughals; Persia invaded the weakened empire in 1739, sacking and looting the capital, Delhi, and taking parts of Afghanistan.

Aurangzeb's wide-ranging wars initiated contact with the British at Madras, Surat, and Calcutta. Aurangzeb gave the British permission to trade in Bengal in 1690, the "wedge" Great Britain needed to eventually conquer all of India. The British did not depose the Mughal emperor, but kept him as a puppet ruler until the Indian Mutiny of 1857, in which rebels sought to restore the Mughal emperor to his former powers.

Lemoine

For Further Reading
Faruki, Zahiruddin. *Aurangzeb and His Times*. Delhi: Idarah-I Adabiyat-I Delli, 1972.
Lal, Muni. *Aurangzeb*. New Delhi, India: Vikas Publishing, 1988.

Bakunin, Mikhail

Russian Anarchist
1814–1876

Life and Work

Mikhail Bakunin's writings laid the foundations for anarchism in a time of rising unrest in Europe.

Mikhail Alexandrovich Bakunin was born on May 18, 1814, near Tver in Russia. His parents were members of the privileged nobility and, in Bakunin's words, raised their children "in a world filled with feeling and imagination." In this atmosphere Bakunin developed an early interest in idealistic philosophy. After an unsuccessful stint in the army, he left Russia in 1840 to study in Berlin. There he encountered a school know as the Left Hegelians (radical disciples of G. W. F. Hegel), whose atheistic claims about human freedom became an inspiration for both him and KARL MARX. In 1842, under this influence, Bakunin wrote an inflammatory article that ended with the claim that "the passion for destruction is also a creative passion." This statement became the leitmotif of his revolutionary anarchism.

Refusing to return to Russia to answer for his article, Bakunin traveled to Paris, where in February he witnessed the outbreak of the 1848 revolution. Convinced that a political cataclysm was at hand, he raced to central Europe to help accelerate it. In Prague, which had been taken over by revolutionaries

demanding secession from the Austrian Empire, he attended a Pan-Slavic conference and witnessed the bombing of the city by the authorities. He was in Dresden the following year fomenting another uprising with the help of the romantic composer Richard Wagner, but was arrested when it collapsed. Deported first to Austria, he was finally returned to Russia where he was incarcerated for six years. In 1857 he was exiled to Siberia, but a daring escape aboard an American ship ultimately returned him to Europe and the revolutionary movement he longed to lead.

In 1868 Bakunin joined the First International, a socialist organization influenced by Marx. Objecting to Marx's authoritarian tendencies, Bakunin soon fell into disagreement and was expelled in 1872. Seeking refuge in Italy, where his following had become strongest, Bakunin continued to work out his anarchistic revolutionary philosophy in hastily written and unsystematic books such as *The State and Anarchy* (1872). His last years were spent in Switzerland, where he collaborated with fellow Russian revolutionaries. One of these, Sergei Nechaev, provoked great controversy by murdering a young man in order to build loyalty to himself among a group of conspirators. This cold-blooded affair, which inspired Fyodor Dostoevsky's famous novel *Demons* (1872), discredited the aging Bakunin. In 1876 he died in Bern, Switzerland, virtually penniless.

Legacy

Mikhail Bakunin's contributions to the revolutionary movement inspired the rise of anarchism and hastened the downfall of Europe's political order.

Bakunin had grown up in what was probably the most repressive political order in Europe during the nineteenth century. His revolutionary philosophy, therefore, placed special emphasis upon the freedom of the individual from the state. Regarding the state as the source of all oppression, anarchism appealed to other frustrated revolutionaries during and after Bakunin's life. While some anarchists were nonviolent, Bakunin's record of spontaneous rebellion, coupled with his philosophical celebration of destruction, appealed to many who were impatient to realize the new order. The Italian Errico Malatesta, for instance, called

upon revolutionaries to lash out against any representatives of authority by committing "insurrectionary deeds" that would serve as propaganda by example.

Such statements supported the wave of political terrorism that swelled at the end of the century. In 1881 revolutionaries assassinated Tsar ALEXANDER II of Russia. In later years anarchists took the lives of political leaders in Italy, Spain, France, and, with the assassination of President McKinley in 1901, the United States. In 1914 Serbian Gavrilo Princip assassinated Archduke Franz Ferdinand of Austria, sparking World War I (1914–18), which would finally sweep away the monarchies of Germany, Austria, and, most destructively, Bakunin's native Russia.

Bakunin's anarchistic political philosophy was not his only contribution to the end of Europe's ancient monarchies. His participation in the unsuccessful revolutions of 1848 and 1849 also had a destabilizing effect. Both of the states, the Austrian Empire and Saxony, in which he helped lead revolutions survived his attacks but emerged from them greatly weakened. Austria, which was saved from a Hungarian revolt only by the intervention of Russia, was forced in 1848 to dismiss its chancellor KLEMENS VON METTERNICH and to institute political restructuring. The weakened government of Saxony was decisively overthrown in 1871 when Germany was united under OTTO VON BISMARCK. The tsarist system of Russia fell in 1917, creating, for a little while at least, what fellow revolutionary VLADIMIR ILICH LENIN would call the "freest country in the world."

Strickland

For Further Reading

Carr, Edward Hallet. *Michael Bakunin*. London: Macmillan, 1937.
Kelly, Aileen. *Mikhail Bakunin: A Study in the Psychology and Politics of Utopianism*. Oxford: Oxford University Press, 1982.
Mendel, Arthur. *Michael Bakunin: Roots of Apocalypse*. New York: Praeger, 1981.

WORLD EVENTS		BAKUNIN'S LIFE
Latin American independence movement begins	1811	
	1814	Mikhail Bakunin is born
Congress of Vienna reorganizes Europe	1815	
	1848	Bakunin witnesses revolution in Paris
	1849	Bakunin joins revolution in Saxony
	1857	Bakunin is exiled to Siberia
Germany is united	1871	
	1872	First International expels Bakunin
	1876	Bakunin dies
Russo-Japanese War	1905	

Balfour, Arthur

British Politician; Author of the
Balfour Declaration
1848–1930

World Events		Balfour's Life
Congress of Vienna reorganizes Europe	1815	
	1848	Arthur Balfour is born
Germany is united	1871	
	1874	Balfour is elected to House of Commons
	1891–1905	Balfour serves as prime minister
Russo-Japanese War	1905	
World War I	1914–18	
	1915	Balfour joins World War I coalition government
Russian Revolution	1917	Balfour issues Balfour Declaration
	1919	Balfour attends Paris Peace Conference
	1926	Balfour leads delegation to Imperial Conference
Great Depression	1929–39	
	1930	Balfour dies
World War II	1939–45	

Life and Work

A career British statesman, Arthur Balfour shaped Great Britain's relations with the United States and Europe and was the author of the Balfour Declaration, which encouraged the establishment of a Jewish state.

Arthur James Balfour was born on July 25, 1848, in Scotland, the oldest son in a wealthy merchant family. He was educated at Cambridge University, where he took an interest in philosophy. Under the patronage of his uncle, Member of Parliament Lord Salisbury, Balfour followed his father's footsteps and was elected to Parliament in 1874 as a Conservative. In 1887 he was appointed chief secretary for Ireland. In 1895 he took the leadership of the House of Commons and assisted Prime Minister Lord Salisbury.

Balfour became prime minister in 1891. He created the Committee of Imperial Defence (CID) to prepare for possible war with Germany; he also signed the so-called Entente Cordiale with France in 1904, which eventually became an alliance with both France and Russia. When his party was defeated in the elections of 1905, Balfour resigned as prime minister but retained his seat in the House of Commons.

In 1915, after the outbreak of World War I, Balfour joined the multiparty coalition government, serving as first lord of the admiralty, then as foreign secretary (1916–19). He led a mission to the United States to negotiate that country's entry into World War I. In November 1917, in order to gain worldwide Jewish support of the Allied war effort, Balfour drafted the Balfour Declaration, which stated "that the British government favored establishment in Palestine of national home for Jewish people, without prejudice to civil and religious rights of existing non-Jewish communities."

After the armistice ending World War I, Balfour attended the Paris Peace Conference (1919) as part of the British delegation. He supported the League of Nations and other efforts to promote world peace. He attended the Washington Conference (1921–22), which promoted a reduction in British, American, and Japanese navies in the Pacific; he also led a delegation to the Imperial Conference held in London in 1926, where his "Balfour Definition" delineated the relationship between Britain and its dominions.

Balfour served the government in various capacities until his retirement in 1929. He died on March 19, 1930, in Woking, England.

Legacy

A rthur Balfour's leadership in the early years of the twentieth century helped to prepare Great Britain for the harsh demands of waging World War I. His efforts during and after the war cemented an Anglo–American alliance for the future and encouraged Zionists to found the state of Israel in 1948.

Balfour's support for the League of Nations and world peace led to the establishment of the United Nations after World War II. Although the League of Nations failed to prevent the outbreak of another world war, Balfour's support of the League and his leadership at the Washington Conference cemented strong ties with the United States. In the post–World War II era the strong Anglo–American alliance he helped forge provided a crucial component to the direction of American Cold War policies.

The Balfour Definition paved the way for the future independence of British colonies by establishing a policy of equality among the dominions (Canada, Australia, New Zealand, South Africa, and the Irish Free State).

Many Israelis see the Balfour Declaration as the crucial turning point in the creation of the state of Israel. After World War I the League of Nations accorded Britain control over Palestine as a mandate (a form of trusteeship). Jewish immigration to Palestine increased in the years after World War I and swelled dramatically after World War II. In 1948 the British returned their mandate to the United Nations, after which Zionists (Jewish nationalists), led by DAVID BEN-GURION, founded the state of Israel. Balfour's policy, while helping to establish a Jewish homeland, displaced a significant percentage of Palestinians, thus setting the stage for continuing conflicts between Israelis and Arabs in the Middle East.

Lemoine

For Further Reading

Mackay, Ruddock F. *Balfour: Intellectual Statesman.* Oxford: Oxford University Press, 1985.

Tomes, Jason. *Balfour and Foreign Policy: The International Thought of a Conservative Statesman.* Cambridge: Cambridge University Press, 1997.

Begin, Menachem

Prime Minister of Israel

1913–1992

Life and Work

The leader of the ultranationalist Likud Party, Menachem Begin led Israel to its first peace treaty with the Arab state of Egypt.

Begin was born in Brest-Litovsk, Poland, on March 16, 1913, the son of a staunch Zionist (Zionists supported the establishment of a Jewish homeland in Palestine). Begin worked tirelessly for the Zionist youth group Betar, part of Vladimir Jabotinsky's Zionist Revisionists, becoming its Polish leader in 1938. Betar sought increased immigration to Palestine, declared illegal by the British authorities who administered Palestine for the League of Nations when the Ottoman Empire lost the territory after World War I.

At the outbreak of World War II in 1939, Begin fled Poland to Lithuania. Arrested by the Soviets as a spy in 1940, then released in 1941, he enlisted in the Free Polish Army and was sent to Palestine in 1942. Most of his family who remained died in the Holocaust.

Discharged in 1943, Begin became leader of the Irgun Zvai Leumi, the military wing of the Revisionists in Palestine, whose goal was to establish a Jewish state there. Irgun resorted to terrorist raids against British rule in Palestine, and against Palestinian Arabs, including, in 1946, bombing of British military headquarters at the King David Hotel, killing 91, and massacring Arab villagers in 1947.

In 1947, Britain withdrew from Palestine, handing its governance over to the United Nations. That same year, the United Nations partitioned Palestine into Arab and Jewish territories, which Jewish Labor Party leader DAVID BEN-GURION favored, but Begin opposed. Begin's desire for all of Palestine nearly resulted in a civil war. The need to unite in a war that had just begun against the Arab states forstalled any civil conflicts.

In 1948 Begin formed the right-wing Herut (Freedom) Party. He then spent two decades building it into a strong opposition party to Ben-Gurion's Labor Party. After merging with two other parties to form the Likud Party in 1973, Likud won the 1977 and 1981 elec-tions. Begin, appointed prime minister, pro-moted new controversial Israeli settlements in the West Bank (conquered in the 1967 Six-Day War), and adopted a hard-line policy toward Palestinian Arabs.

In 1978 Begin negotiated a peace treaty with Egyptian President ANWAR AS-SADAT, signing, at U.S. President Jimmy Carter's urg-ing, the Camp David accords in 1978, and the Egyptian–Israeli treaty in 1979, earning him and Sadat the Nobel Prize for Peace. In return-ing to Egypt the Sinai Peninsula (also con-quered in the Six-Day War) and ensuring a secure southern border, Begin believed he had strengthened Israel's hold on the West Bank.

In 1982 Begin ordered the invasion of Lebanon to destroy the Palestinian Liberation Organization (PLO). The operation bogged down and, in September 1982, Lebanese Christians massacred Palestinian refugees in Israeli-occupied Beirut. Blamed for the Lebanon debacle, Begin withdrew from poli-tics in 1983. Begin became a recluse, dying of heart failure on March 9, 1992.

Legacy

Menachem Begin's policy towards Israel's position in the Middle East continued well after his retirement.

Begin's expansionist and ultranationalist ide-ology, especially concerning the occupied terri-tories, formed the basis of much of his administration's policy. Coalition governments continued Begin's intransigence over the West Bank long after he had left public life. In response, Palestinian Arabs in the occupied terri-tories began a resistance movement, the *intifada* ("shaking off"). Mass demonstrations, boycotts, strikes, school closures, and other mostly non-violent protests posed a new and difficult task of maintaining order in a civilian revolt.

Some Israeli leaders saw the problems and limitations of Begin's policies. As a result, start-ing in 1991, Israel took a bold new direction in opening negotiations with Palestinians. These talks culminated in the Oslo accords of 1993 and 1995, which recognized the sover-eignty of the Palestinian Arabs under the lead-ership of YASIR ARAFAT and the Palestinian Liberation Organization (PLO). Palestinian autonomy was established in several towns in the West Bank, as well as in the Gaza Strip, another occupied territory.

However, both Islamic fundamentalists and right-wing Israelis opposed the Oslo accords, and both committed acts of terror against the other. Likud, which had lost the elections of 1992, continued to adhere to Begin's principles. Likud regained power in 1996, claiming it could ensure the security of Israeli citizens. Prime Minister Benjamin Netanyahu, following in Begin's footsteps, continued to promote the interests of the Israeli settlers in the West Bank and stalled the peace process with the PLO. Although Likud was defeated by the Labor Party in the 1999 elections, its policy, one Begin's ideas had helped to shape, ensured the continued presence of Israeli settlers in the West Bank.

Begin's other important initiative, the inva-sion of Lebanon, gave rise to fundamentalist Muslim terrorist groups, who committed ter-rorist acts in Israel, in Lebanon itself, and internationally. Unfortunately, his peace treaty with Egypt is overshadowed by the effects of this type of initiative, as well as his intransi-gence on the occupied territories.

Lemoine

For Further Reading

Schweitzer, Avraham. *Israel: The Changing National Agenda.* Dover, N.H.: Croom Helm, 1986.

Silver, Eric. *Begin: A Biography.* London: Weidenfeld and Nicolson, 1984.

Sofer, Sasson. *Begin: An Anatomy of Leadership.* New York: Basil Blackwell, 1988.

WORLD EVENTS		BEGIN'S LIFE
Russo-Japanese War	1905	
	1913	Menachem Begin is born
World War I	1914–18	
Russian Revolution	1917	
Great Depression	1929–39	
World War II	1939–45	
	1939	Begin escapes Poland
	1946	Begin orders bombing of British headquarters
Communist China is established	1949	
Israel defeats Arab nations in Six-Day War	1967	
Vietnam War ends	1975	
	1977	Begin appointed prime minister
	1978	Begin signs Camp David accords
	1982	Begin orders invasion of Lebanon
	1983	Begin retires
Dissolution of Soviet Union	1991	
	1992	Begin dies

Bell, Gertrude

British Diplomat
1868–1926

Life and Work

Using her extensive knowledge of and respect for Arab culture, Gertrude Bell helped to establish the states of the modern Middle East.

Born on July 14, 1868, to a family of wealthy English industrialists, Gertrude Margaret Lowthian Bell was tutored at home and later enjoyed a progessive education at Queen's College in London. In 1886 Bell entered Oxford University, a rarity for a woman at the time, and obtained high honors upon graduation in 1888.

Bell's independence and education did not exemplify the ideal of the late-Victorian–era woman. In 1892, Bell embarked on a second education, a 13-year rotation between Britain, the mountains of Switzerland, and the broad deserts of the Near and Middle East. During this time, she became expert in Arabic and Arab culture. She wrote a book, *Syria: The Desert and the Sown* (1907) that marked her as a professional Orientalist and earned her a great reputation. Bell befriended many Arab leaders, and, through the relationships she cul-

tivated, began to serve Britain's political interests in the Middle East. Because the Suez Canal, in the middle of the Arab world, linked the Mediterranean Sea and the Indian Ocean, Britain considered the Middle East vital to protecting its colonial, commercial, and strategic interests in East Africa and Asia. In addition, Britain had just begun the transition from coal to oil for its navy; thus, its need for oil, available in quantity only from the Middle East, had dramatically increased.

In September 1914, Bell filed her first report with the Foreign Office on the political relationships between the various Arab factions. Britain wanted to find allies in the Middle East to oppose the Ottoman Turks, allies of Germany in World War I. Her report was received with great eagerness. After a year of taking care of wounded British troops for the British Red Cross, Bell was summoned, along with THOMAS EDWARD LAWRENCE, to Port Saïd, Egypt, to help with Britain's Military Intelligence Bureau in the war against the Ottoman Empire. Bell spent much of the war in southern Iraq, helping calm the bitter rivalries of overlapping British bureaucracies, providing the British Army with maps, contacts, and advice, and arbitrating the conflicts between clans of Arabs and Bedouins.

Events toward the end of the war crowned Bell's involvement with the Middle East and British diplomacy. In 1917, she helped the British establish the state of Iraq. In 1919, she served as an advisor to the British delegation to the Paris Peace Conference. Throughout the early 1920s, Bell managed the collection of intelligence in Iraq for the British, and helped Faisal, son of local leader Sharif Hussein, to the throne. Although hopeful about and engaged with the progress of Iraq, Bell grew more and more morose as the years went on, frustrated by continuing conflicts in the Middle East and her own loneliness. She died in Baghdad on July 11, 1926, and was accorded a military burial at the British Military Cemetery in Iraq.

Legacy

As an Arab expert, Gertrude Bell was one of the main contributors to the creation of the modern states of the Middle East. As a woman, she was a model of activism, independence, and learning for women around the world.

As one of a handful of British experts on the Middle East on the eve of World War I, Bell facilitated the achievement of British aims and Arab nationalism in the Middle East. Bell's experience with the broad range of cultures and her understanding of the delicate harmony that kept the Middle East's peoples from destroying one another made her invaluable to the British Foreign Office and army. In part, the countries of Syria, Iraq, and Saudi Arabia exist as they do today because of Bell's advice to and guidance of the British government.

Bell also was an important symbol to women around the world. Although she detested publicity, she inspired many young women in Britain, the Middle East, and elsewhere to pursue their dreams and develop their abilities at a time when, although permitted education if they had sufficient money, women generally lacked opportunities to move beyond the traditional "women's work" professions such as teacher, nurse, or governess. Her independence, like that of many pioneering women, did not come without a cost. As a university-educated woman who traveled on her own, Bell was on the edge of British social norms; in the Middle East, she was outside of any cultural concept of normal female behavior. Although she moved in powerful circles, Bell found it hard to find permanent companionship and understanding. Despite espousing some distinctly Victorian values, such as her initial opposition to women's suffrage, Bell encouraged women to take charge of their lives and put their dreams into action.

Del Testa

WORLD EVENTS		BELL'S LIFE
Congress of Vienna reorganizes Europe	1815	
	1868	Gertrude Bell is born
Germany is united	1871	
	1886–88	Bell attends Oxford University
Russo-Japanese War	1905	
World War I	1914–18	
	1914	Bell active in Middle East as British agent
Russian Revolution	1917	Bell helps to establish state of Iraq
	1919	Bell attends Paris Peace Conference
	1926	Bell dies
Great Depression	1929–39	

For Further Reading

Bell, Gertrude. *Syria: The Desert and the Sown.* New York: E. P. Dutton, 1907.

Goodman, Susan. *Gertrude Bell.* Dover, N.H.: Berg, 1985.

Wallach, Janet. *Desert Queen: The Extraordinary Life of Gertrude Bell, Adventurer, Advisor to Kings, Ally of Lawrence of Arabia.* New York: Doubleday, 1996.

Ben-Gurion, David

First Prime Minister of Israel
1886–1973

Life and Work

As Israel's first prime minister, David Ben-Gurion ensured the fledgling state's survival and transformed Israel into an important ally of the United States.

Ben-Gurion was born David Gruen on October 16, 1886, in the Polish town of Plonsk, then ruled by Russia. Like his father, David Gruen was a Zionist (Zionists supported the establishment of a Jewish homeland in Palestine) before immigrating in 1906 to Palestine, then ruled by the Ottoman Empire. At first a farm laborer, he moved to Jerusalem in 1910 to edit the Workers' Zionist Party's newspaper, signing his articles with the name Ben-Gurion (a defender of Jerusalem against the Romans). An avid student, Ben-Gurion moved to Constantinople to study law, obtaining a degree in 1914, on the eve of World War I. The Ottoman Empire soon entered the war allied with Germany and Austria-Hungary.

In 1915, exiled for supporting the Allies, Ben-Gurion went to the United States, where he recruited Jews to immigrate to Palestine. When the British issued the Balfour Declaration in November 1917, which promised support for a Jewish homeland in Palestine, Ben-Gurion joined a British Army unit sent to fight in the Middle East. Discharged in Palestine in 1918, Ben-Gurion

returned to his pre-war activism and became Labor Party leader in 1930.

Meanwhile, the British, who ruled Palestine after World War I, restricted Jewish immigration to appease the Arab population, a policy they continued after World War II. Ben-Gurion organized illegal immigration, while extremists committed terrorist acts against British officials. The British withdrew in 1947, turning Palestine over to the United Nations. Ben-Gurion supported the U.N.-sponsored partition of Palestine into Israeli and Arab territories. On May 14, 1948, he declared Israel's independence, igniting a war with the Arab states. Ben-Gurion transformed scattered armed forces and terrorist groups into the Israeli army, defeating the Arabs.

Elected prime minister in 1949, Ben-Gurion launched an immigration program that doubled the population in four years. To pay for their resettlement and for development programs, and to maintain military superiority over the surrounding Arab states, Ben-Gurion sought international investment and accepted controversial reparations payments from West Germany.

Ben-Gurion resigned briefly in 1953, joining a kibbutz (a cooperative farming settlement), but returned after a scandal. As prime minister after the 1955 elections, Ben-Gurion cultivated alliances with France and Britain. In 1956, when Egyptian President GAMAL ABDEL NASSER nationalized the Suez Canal, France, Britain, and Israel invaded the Sinai Peninsula, Egyptian territory. Although the invasion was initially a diplomatic disaster, it brought Israel closer to the United States, which was concerned about Nasser's ties to the Soviet Union. Ben-Gurion consistently used the Cold War conflict to solidify international alliances.

Ben-Gurion resigned in 1963. Although he remained active in politics until 1970, his influence had diminished. He returned to his kibbutz and died on December 1, 1973.

Legacy

David Ben-Gurion guided Israel through its crucial early years, scoring both diplomatic and military successes that ensured Israel's survival as a thriving Middle East democracy.

Ben-Gurion laid solid military, demographic, and economic foundations for the new state of Israel upon which its future leaders could build a secure Jewish homeland. He defied the right-wing militants who opposed the Labor Party by developing the Israeli army on his own terms.

His political rivals later formed conservative, yet loyal, opposition parties, such as the Likud Party. Ben-Gurion encouraged Jewish immigration, especially from Europe, which created the demographic basis of the Labor Party's dominance until 1977.

Ben-Gurion's leadership of the military in the face of aggressive neighbors ensured the country's survival and enabled it to effectively defend itself in later conflicts. The military successes of the 1956 Sinai Campaign and the 1967 Six-Day War (when Israel defeated Arab forces and began its occupation of the West Bank and Gaza Strip) were attributable, in part, to his leadership. Ben-Gurion helped Israel to become a symbol to other nation-states established after World War II, for its determination to succeed in the face of constant hostility and economic underdevelopment.

Ben-Gurion's exploitation of the Cold War tensions between the United States and the Soviet Union bolstered Israel's prospects for security in a hostile region. After 1956 his military and diplomatic policies increased Israeli's security by establishing secret alliances with countries surrounding the Arab states, opening the way to securing an alliance with the United States against Soviet expansionism in the Middle East. In the decades following Ben-Gurion's death, Israel continued to be an important ally of the United States.

Lemoine

WORLD EVENTS		BEN-GURION'S LIFE
Germany is united	1871	
	1886	David Gruen is born
Russo-Japanese War	1905	
	1906	Gruen immigrates to Palestine
World War I	1914–18	
Russian Revolution	1917	Balfour Declaration
Great Depression	1929–39	
	1930	Ben-Gurion becomes Labor Party leader
World War II	1939–45	
	1948	Ben Gurion declares Israel independent
Communist China is established	1949	Ben-Gurion is elected prime minister
	1956	Ben-Gurion helps lead Sinai campaign against Egypt
Israel defeats Arab nations in Six-Day War	1967	
	1973	Ben-Gurion dies
Vietnam War ends	1975	

For Further Reading
Bar-Zohar, Michael. *Ben-Gurion: A Biography.* Translated by Peretz Kidron. New York: Delacorte Press, 1978.
Zweig, Ronald W., ed. *David Ben-Gurion: Politics and Leadership in Israel.* London: Frank Cass, 1991.

Benenson, Peter

Founder, Amnesty International
1921–

Life and Work

Peter Benenson built on years of human rights activism to create Amnesty International, an influential organization dedicated to liberating those people unjustly oppressed for their beliefs.

Born on July 31, 1921 in London, Benenson enjoyed a privileged upbringing. He attended Eton, one of Britain's most prestigious private

WORLD EVENTS		BENENSON'S LIFE
Russian Revolution	1917	
	1921	Peter Benenson is born
Great Depression	1929–39	
	1937	Benenson organizes Spanish Civil War relief committee
	1938	Benenson organizes group to rescue young German Jewish boys
World War II	1939–45	
	1947	Benenson begins career as lawyer and human rights activist
Communist China is established	1949	
	1961	Benenson and others hold original "Appeal for Amnesty"
	1962	Benenson founds Amnesty International
Israel defeats Arab nations in Six-Day War	1967	Benenson resigns from Amnesty International
Vietnam War ends	1975	
	1977	Amnesty International receives Nobel Prize for Peace
Dissolution of Soviet Union	1991	

schools, and went on to study history at Oxford University. Benenson committed himself to political causes early in life, forming a committee at Eton in 1937 to support children orphaned by the 1936–39 Spanish Civil War and another group in 1938 dedicated to rescuing young Jewish boys from Nazi Germany. During World War II, Benenson served in the intelligence branch of the Royal Navy. Between 1945 and 1947, while still in the military, he studied law. In 1947, in addition to taking conventional legal cases, Benenson began his career as a professional human rights activist by traveling to Spain to serve as the defense lawyer for oppressed labor leaders. Throughout the 1950s, Benenson actively defended human rights cases around the world.

In November 1960, Benenson read a newspaper report about two students who had been arrested by the military dictatorship in Portugal, and sentenced to eight years' imprisonment for publicly toasting the idea of freedom. In consultation with sympathetic, influential friends, Benenson decided that the best way to help such "prisoners of conscience" (people imprisoned for their beliefs) was by coordinating international pressure through letter-writing campaigns and media alerts.

In 1961 Benenson and his friends decided to hold an "Appeal for Amnesty" as a way to seek the release of prisoners of conscience and to improve their situation once released. Benenson organized a campaign to seek the release of six prisoners of conscience, each from a different country. On May 28, 1961, the London paper *The Observer* gave this campaign front-page coverage. Other papers around the world picked up the story, and soon information about thousands of prisoners of conscience flooded Benenson's law offices. In 1962, Benenson formed a new organization, Amnesty International, to build on the momentum of this initial campaign.

The tactics of Benenson's original Amnesty International were simple: a cell of three Amnesty International supporters coordinated by a national chapter would "adopt" three prisoners of conscience. They would then bombard the government, embassies, jailers, and newspapers of the given country with polite but firm letters in an attempt to concentrate media attention on the plight of the prisoner in question. Amnesty International maintained its nonpartisan nature was supported by a rule that no country's organization could

involve itself in the release of prisoners of conscience within its own country.

Amnesty International's first great success was the release in 1962 of Cardinal Josef Mindszenty of Hungary, imprisoned in 1948 by that country's Cold War–era communist government. In 1966, Amnesty International experienced its greatest crisis when allegations arose that a leader of the organization in London, Robert Swann, had, in collusion with the British government, suppressed an organization report attacking the torture and imprisonment used by officials in the British colony of Aden (on the Arabian Peninsula). Benenson almost resigned in protest. Then, in 1967, allegations arose that Benenson himself had made frivolous use of Amnesty International funds during missions to Nigeria and Rhodesia (now Zimbabwe). To stave off mounting criticism of the organization, Benenson resigned and an executive committee replaced him.

Benenson retired to his farm in the English countryside 1967, and has continued to work with Amnesty International, most recently working to bring the torturers of the former communist Eastern European nations to trial.

Legacy

Through Amnesty International, Peter Benenson raised awareness of human rights abuses and the suffering they caused. No group before had made personal, concerted, nonpartisan, and direct appeals the central method of securing rights for prisoners of conscience. By making the appeals simultaneously personal and political, Amnesty International shamed governments into treating prisoners of conscience better. Although Amnesty International cannot win every case, it has helped tens of thousands of people to find freedom.

Amnesty International has had an enormous impact on human rights throughout the world, and Benenson's priority of international over national appeals has remained essentially in place. However, the reasons for Benenson's departure have also been thoroughly reviewed since 1967, and Amnesty International has worked hard to improve its impartiality and independence from government sponsorship. This distance has ensured a continuing respect for the organization. Amnesty International received the Nobel Prize for Peace in 1977.

Del Testa

For Further Reading

Power, Jonathan. *Amnesty International: The Human Rights Story.* New York: McGraw-Hill, 1981.

Winner, David. *Peter Benenson: Taking a Stand Against Injustice.* Milwaukee, Wis.: Gareth Stevens, 1991.

Biko, Stephen

South African Civil Rights Activist
1946–1977

Life and Work

Stephen Biko became the leader of a new, more aggressive kind of opposition by blacks to white rule in South Africa, and in doing so he set in motion, at the cost of his own life, the destruction of apartheid.

Biko was born Bantu Stephen Biko on December 18, 1946, in eastern South Africa. Beginning in 1952, Biko attended a primary school near his home.

Since the time of European colonization in the early seventeenth century, South Africa had been a racially divided society. After 1948, one branch of the white-dominated power structure turned toward a policy of apartheid, or (racial) separateness. Racial discrimination became more highly legislated, and opportunities, support, and protection for blacks in South Africa declined precipitously. Anti-apartheid groups, such as the African National Congress (ANC) and the Pan-Africanist Congress (PAC), struck back, culminating in the bloody Sharpeville Riots of April 1960.

In this contentious environment, Biko entered high school in 1959. As a high school student, Biko began to protest against apartheid, resulting in his expulsion in 1963. Biko was able to continue his education at St. Francis College, a liberal boarding school in

eastern South Africa, and then entered the University of Natal Medical School in 1966.

In 1966, while at medical school, Biko joined the National Union of South African Students (NUSAS), a moderate, multiracial organization that supported equal rights for blacks. Finding NUSAS too passive and dominated by whites, in 1969 Biko co-founded the all-black South African Students' Organization (SASO). Influenced by black writers such as Frantz Fanon, who viewed white domination as a psychological condition, SASO had as its goal the improvement of black self-esteem.

Initially, the South African government tolerated SASO because it seemed to reinforce the government's own preference for separate racial communities. However, Biko and his fellow SASO supporters attacked not only the government but even supposed supporters, including white liberals and the leaders of black homelands (reservations). In February 1973, the government of South Africa issued orders limiting the rights of free movement and association of Biko and the other leaders of SASO. Biko continued his political activities covertly, shifting his attention to the creation of the Zimele Trust Fund, which began operation in 1975. The Trust supported families of imprisoned political activists.

South African Security forces arrested Biko four times between 1975 and 1977, often holding him for months without trial. On August 18, 1977, security forces seized Biko and some fellow activists in Port Elizabeth on charges of treason. Naked and manacled, Biko was beaten repeatedly by his jailers over the course of 24 hours, resulting in life-threatening brain lesions. Unconscious, Biko was transported 740 miles to Pretoria for hospitalization. He died there on September 12, 1977.

Legacy

Stephen Biko built the South African anti-apartheid movement into a powerful psychological reawakening for black South Africans.

After 1948, the white power structure of South Africa made a fateful decision to turn away from a slowly evolving cooperation between the races and to try instead to make blacks legally third-class citizens. Although opposition to white rule and racism had existed in South Africa since at least the founding of the African National Congress in 1912, it had used political and cultural rhetoric as the basis

for change. During the 1960s Biko argued that the remaking of the black mind was essential to the successful rejection of white rule. (In 1976 Biko said, "The basic tenet of black consciousness is that the black man must reject all value systems that seek to make him a foreigner in the country of his birth and reduce his basic human dignity.") Generating a positive self-image for blacks, the rejection of all whites, even liberal whites, and collaborating blacks, and violent noncooperation with any institution controlled by whites or blacks aligned with the government—these practices challenged white rule in South Africa to its very core and made white management of the state and its economy increasingly difficult. Whereas opposition to apartheid before Biko had centered around the actions of a few essential leaders, Biko transformed the movement into one of mass consciousness and mass action.

Biko became an international symbol of the injustice of South Africa's apartheid system. Biko's death, along with the 1976 Soweto Uprising, provoked international condemnation of and sanctions against South Africa during the 1980s. Internal revolt and international pressure became so severe that the South African government had to turn first, in 1986, to a four-year state of emergency and then, in 1990, to the abandonment of apartheid and the release of NELSON MANDELA to satisfy the demands that Biko had made so many years before.

Del Testa

WORLD EVENTS		BIKO'S LIFE
World War II 1939–45		
	1946	Stephen Biko is born
	1948	Legal apartheid is established in South Africa
Communist China is established	1949	
	1963	Biko is expelled from high school
	1966	Biko enters medical school
Israel defeats Arab nations in Six-Day War	1967	
	1969	Biko co-founds SASO
Vietnam War ends	1975	Frequent arrests of Biko begin
	1977	Biko is beaten to death while in police custody
Dissolution of Soviet Union	1991	

For Further Reading

Juckes, Tim J. *The Opposition in South Africa: The Leadership of Z. K. Matthews, Nelson Mandela, and Stephen Biko.* Westport, Conn.: Praeger, 1995.

Biko, Steve. *Black Consciousness in South Africa.* Edited by Millard Arnold. New York: Random House, 1978.

Bismarck, Otto von

German Statesman and Diplomat
1815–1898

Life and Work

Otto von Bismarck unified Germany under a conservative government and altered the balance of power in nineteenth-century Europe.

Otto Eduard Leopold von Bismarck was born to the Junker nobility of Prussia in 1815, the year peace was restored to Europe after the tumultuous Napoleonic Wars. In his youth he preferred drinking and duels to his law studies in Berlin and his later duties as a civil servant. Citing the inability "to tolerate my superiors," he returned to the comfort of his family estates and might have remained there had revolution not suddenly exploded in Germany in 1848, threatening to destroy the social and political order that he valued.

Germany at the time was divided into more than 30 separate states, with Prussia as the largest. Revolutionaries generally hoped to unify these states into a single national state, and to establish a liberal constitutional monarchy to govern it. Bismarck traveled to the Frankfurt Assembly to listen to their demands but left with the conviction that their form of liberal nationalism had no future in Germany. When the Prussian king arrested the Frankfurt Assembly in 1849, Bismarck expressed his approval. His support of the Prussian monarchy won him a post in the government, and in 1862 he was appointed chancellor.

World Events		Bismarck's Life
Latin American independence movement begins	1811	
Congress of Vienna reorganizes Europe	1815	Otto von Bismarck is born
	1862	Bismarck appointed chancellor of Prussia
Germany is united	1871	
	1878	Bismarck supports anti-socialist law
	1890	Bismarck is dismissed by William II
	1898	Bismarck dies
Russo-Japanese War	1905	

A political crisis awaited him, however, and his solution to it proved fateful for Germany and the rest of Europe. Within the Prussian Diet (legislature) liberal opponents of the king were claiming constitutional powers over army policy. Revealing a bold and politically astute mind, Bismarck told the deputies in a famous 1863 speech that the time had come to abandon liberalism, which he claimed was divisive, and focus solely upon the ideals of nationalism. Germany would be united, he told them, not by parliamentary debate but by "iron and blood." Within a decade he had led Germany toward unification through military action, thus undermining the liberals within the Diet. Victorious wars against Denmark (1864), Austria (1866), and France (1870–71) culminated in the creation of the German Empire under Kaiser William I in 1871.

Bismarck's first goal was to preserve as much of Prussia's absolute monarchy as he could, especially within the new Reichstag (parliament). Especially hostile to political parties who refused to conform to the authoritarian and secular character of German nationalism, he supported an 1878 law banning the Social Democratic Party; in a campaign known as the *Kulturkampf* ("struggle for civilization") he turned also against the Catholic Center Party, whose loyalty to a universal rather than a national church was considered unpatriotic. While these antisocialist and anti-Catholic policies were generally a failure, Bismarck achieved brilliant successes in diplomacy. After the Franco–Prussian War ended in 1871, the greatest threat to Germany came from the West, and he therefore sought alliances with the Great Powers of Austria and Russia in the East. In 1879 a Dual Alliance was forged with Austria, and in 1887 a Reinsurance Treaty brought Russia into Germany's orbit.

In 1888 Kaiser William I was succeeded by the capricious William II, who resented Bismarck's domination of government. Accordingly, William II dismissed Bismarck in 1890. Unable to defend himself against the absolute monarchy he had helped to preserve, Bismarck now watched helplessly as the new kaiser canceled the crucial Reinsurance Treaty, thereby driving Russia into a military alliance with vengeful France. In 1898 the frustrated "Iron Chancellor" died.

Legacy

By unifying Germany and establishing a conservative monarchy, Otto von Bismarck created a powerful and authoritarian force at the center of Europe.

The wars of German unification between 1864 and 1871 upset the balance of power that had been created by Klemens von Metternich at the Congress of Vienna in 1815. Europe's Great Powers were now confronted with an industrialized military power at the center of Europe. Bismarck's system of alliances with Austria and Russia, however effectively they isolated France, ultimately failed to make Germany secure and prevent another Continental war. With an increasingly pugnacious William II exercising control over German diplomacy after 1890, Russia was not the only Great Power to turn to France. William embarked on a *Weltpolitik* ("global policy") that further upset the diplomatic order. Now Great Britain, whose isolation from the Continent had reinforced Bismarck's system of alliance, was also driven into the arms of France with the Entente Cordiale of 1904. Thus in 1914, when World War I began, the diplomatic order established by Bismarck had evolved into two rival alliances: the Central Powers (Germany and Austria) and the Entente (Britain, France, and Russia). Germany was badly defeated in 1918 and thus fell victim to the Great Power status that Bismarck had forged.

The creation of a tense diplomatic order was not Bismarck's only negative legacy. Domestically, he helped empower a group of conservative elites within the bureaucracy and the military. With the suppression of liberalism in 1862 and the creation of a nationalistic monarchy in 1871, these elites continued to dominate the German government until its collapse in 1918. During this time respect for political compromise was diminished by efforts to subordinate all political interests to the power of the national state. Many groups were adversely affected by, including socialists, Catholics, Poles, and Jews. Although this aspect of the Bismarckian order was eliminated by the Weimar Republic in 1918, Adolf Hitler and the Nazis would revive some of its features with terrible consequences after 1933.

Strickland

For Further Reading

Eyck, Erich. *Bismarck and the German Empire.* 2nd ed. London: Allen and Unwin, 1958.

Taylor, A. J. P. *Bismarck: The Man and the Statesman.* New York: Vintage, 1955.

Waller, Bruce. *Bismarck.* 2nd ed. Oxford: Blackwell, 1997.

Wehler, Hans-Ulrich. *The German Empire, 1871–1918.* Translated by Kim Traynor. New York: Allen and Unwin, 1985.

Blanc, Louis

French Socialist and Historian
1811–1882

Life and Work

Louis Blanc's ideas shaped early-nineteenth-century socialist thought and anticipated the European democratic socialism of the twentieth century.

Louis Blanc was born on October 29, 1811, the son of a French official from a royalist family serving under NAPOLÉON I. He began his schooling at the College Royal in Rodez, France, in 1822. In July 1830, while France was undergoing the revolution that deposed the Bourbon King Charles X in favor of the more liberal King Louis-Philippe, Blanc moved to Paris. There Blanc faced unemployment and poverty, an experience that possibly radicalized his view of society. In desperation, Blanc took a position in 1832 as a tutor for the children of an industrialist in the provincial city of Arras.

Back in Paris in 1834, he became an increasingly influential republican journalist who wanted to overthrow the monarchy in favor of a republic. In 1839 Blanc founded the republican *Revue du Progrès,* which also advocated socialist reforms. Influenced by the democratic ideas of the Jacobins, the most radical faction of the French Revolution of 1789, Blanc advocated universal (male) suffrage and "co-operative socialism," where workers controlled industrial production, and consumption would be based on need, capacity, and work.

A number of publications established Blanc as a leader of the French socialist movement, which many, but not all, republicans supported. In 1840 he published *The Organization of Labor,* a work that argued that the state should provide cheap credit to form worker-controlled cooperative workshops. Another book, *The History of Ten Years, 1830–1840* (1841–43), attacked the constitutional monarchy of Louis-Philippe. Both works sold well and had a major impact on the public perception of the regime and the capitalist-industrial society then forming in France.

In February 1848, a revolution in France deposed Louis-Philippe; the provisional government soon proclaimed the Second Republic. Pushed into the provisional government by the revolutionary crowds of Paris, Blanc was distrusted by its conservative leaders. He was denied a post in the Ministry of Labor, presiding instead over the Luxembourg Commission, formed to study the problem of labor, but with no real power.

Conservatives in the government established national workshops that were nothing more than public relief projects rather than the cooperative enterprises envisioned by Blanc. Their ultimate failure, and the Parisian riots that followed their dissolution, was blamed on Blanc. He was forced into exile, his reputation ruined by the revolution that could have propelled him to real power.

While in exile in Great Britain, Blanc completed his work on the revolution of 1789, *The History of the French Revolution* (1862), which rehabilitated his reputation. Returning to France in 1870, he was elected to the Chamber of Deputies of the newly formed Third Republic, allying himself with the radical left. He died in southern France on December 6, 1882.

Legacy

With his faith in democracy and gradual, nonviolent social reform, Louis Blanc contributed to the destruction of the French constitutional monarchy and helped to keep the European socialist movement alive in the nineteenth century. His social and political policies anticipated peaceful social democratic movements in Europe and the world in the twentieth century.

Through his work as a journalist and historian, Blanc influenced and advanced the socialist movement before 1848. He opposed both capitalist competition and monarchy because they did not foster economic cooperation or true representative democracy. In an era of chronic underemployment, he proposed that all men had the "right to work," a concept future labor leaders in France and elsewhere later adopted. Furthermore, he asserted that the state was responsible for providing universal and free education to all its citizens. These proposals were popular initially among the working class, and would soon be embraced by most democratic societies. When the revolution of 1848 broke out, many workers looked to Blanc to lead the cause of social, as well as political, reform.

Blanc was the first socialist to take part in a French government—or in any government—in the nineteenth century. He was not an extremist; he argued that people must be prepared by ideas before taking action for social progress. He saw himself as a moderate, and, like other moderate socialists after him, was unwilling to undertake the brutal measures used to establish a socialist republic in France in 1848. The more conservative leaders of the Second Republic saw him as too radical to be allowed to have real power. Yet, by the end of the nineteenth century, socialists followed in his footsteps and began to take a legitimate role in many European governments.

Blanc was an advocate of the modern democratic socialism that gained legitimacy in the twentieth century, especially after World War II. Governments in Western Europe, gaining consensus across class lines rather than through class conflict, constructed mixed economies in which the state guided the economy to ensure social progress and worker protections, but left much of it in private hands. Although Blanc's vision of a network of worker-controlled enterprises has not come to fruition, his ideas resulted in the institution of progressive policies that have benefited the working class in France and other nations.

Lemoine

For Further Reading

Agulhon, Maurice. *The Republican Experiment, 1848–1852.* Translated by Janet Lloyd. Cambridge: Cambridge University Press, 1983.

Lubère, Leo. *Louis Blanc.* Evanston, Ill.: Northwestern University Press, 1961.

Sewell, William H., Jr. *Work and Revolution in France: The Language of Labor from the Old Regime to 1848.* Cambridge: Cambridge University Press, 1980.

WORLD EVENTS		BLANC'S LIFE
French Revolution begins	1789	
Latin American independence movement begins	1811	Louis Blanc is born
Congress of Vienna reorganizes Europe	1815	
	1839	Blanc founds *Revue du Progrès*
	1840	*The Organization of Labor* is published
	1841–43	*The History of Ten Years* is published
	1848	Blanc joins provisional government; Blanc is exiled
	1870	Blanc returns to France; is elected to Chamber of Deputies
Germany is united	1871	
	1882	Blanc dies
Russo-Japanese War	1905	

Bolívar, Simón

South American Independence Leader
1783–1830

Life and Work

Known as "El Liberator," Simón Bolívar led the battle against Spanish imperialism in South America, liberating five nations on that continent in the nineteenth century.

Born in Caracas, Venezuela, on July 24, 1783, Bolívar was a Creole (born in South America of Spanish descent) aristocrat. Orphaned at a young age, he nonetheless received a solid education in Europe, where he learned about the new ideologies of freedom, liberty, democracy, and republican (as opposed to monarchical) government, arising from the Enlightenment and the French Revolution. Bolívar returned home determined to free South America from Spain.

During this period, Creoles were largely denied the top positions in the colonial administration, which were given to men from Spain. In 1808 NAPOLÉON I invaded Spain and installed his brother on the throne. Many Creoles rejected the new king, declaring that the people of the Americas were sovereign and began forming provisional governments. Bolívar was one of the most ardent supporters of full independence.

In 1810 the colonial governor of Venezuela was deposed and a *junta* ("governing body") was formed. Bolívar was sent to London to seek an alliance with Britain. Although Britain refused to give the rebellion direct aid, Venezuela formally declared independence on July 5, 1811. Bolívar, at age 28, joined the Venezuelan army as

a colonel; however, royalist troops defeated the revolutionary army and Bolívar escaped to New Granada (present-day Colombia), where he made a famous speech in 1813 declaring a "war to the death" for liberation.

Promoted to general by the revolutionary government, Bolívar continued to fight, conducting a remarkable 90-day campaign and defeating five armies; he entered Caracas a hero in August 1813. He established a republic and appointed himself military dictator. In 1814, however, the royalists loyal to Spain inflicted another defeat and Bolívar was again forced to flee to New Granada. Bolívar mounted another revolutionary effort in Venezuela but was defeated; he fled to Jamaica in 1815.

Bolívar went to Haiti to refurbish his army, changing his strategy to attack the royalists within Venezuela from the interior. By 1822 both Venezuela and New Granada were liberated; Bolívar continued into Peru, which finalized the royalist defeat in 1825. Upper Peru was renamed Bolivia in honor of Bolívar, who became president of Colombia, Peru, and Bolivia. Bolívar sought to unite these countries into "Gran Colombia," but internal rebellions and other problems dissolved the union by 1829.

His failure to create "Gran Colombia," along with bitter infighting, exacerbated Bolívar's ill health. He died on December 17, 1830, in Colombia.

Legacy

Simón Bolívar was instrumental in the establishment of liberal democratic republics in South America.

Although Bolívar supported open and democratic governments, he recognized that a heterogeneous population consisting of a plurality of Indians, and minorities of blacks, *mestizos* (those of mixed Spanish–Indian blood), and whites, combined with a lack of political consensus and democratic traditions, made liberal constitutions unlikely in the immediate future. Bolívar agreed that there was a temporary need to postpone liberty in favor of order and security, and thus more authoritarian governments. However, his ideal of a strong government turned into government by strongmen ("*caudillos*"); the continent experienced much political and social instability that lasted into the twentieth century.

Bolívar was also a member of the Creole elite, which replaced the Spanish after liberation. After

independence, Creoles controlled political and economic institutions, while much of the remaining population lacked civil rights and languished in poverty. This, too, caused instability and led to coups and military takeovers.

Because the revolutionary period seriously disrupted the continent's economy, Bolívar welcomed British investment, which had long-term consequences for Latin American development. Governments focused on providing raw materials for export and imported finished goods from the industrialized countries, especially Britain. Britain was the predominant economic power of the nineteenth century, playing a large role in lending money to Latin American governments and in controlling export-import markets. This involvement made economic independence more difficult to achieve than political independence.

Although the Creole elites benefited from this arrangement, the rest of the population remained poor and isolated. Landowning elites collaborated with foreign export-import merchants to sell goods on the overseas market, and they received all the profits, with little "trickling down" to the working poor. The landowners would use the profits to import consumer goods from Europe or the United States. The export earnings, therefore, were not invested at home to diversify the economy, resulting in "growth without development." Because of a labor surplus, workers' wages remained low and groups outside the export sector received little benefit, resulting in unequal income distribution. This has been a fundamental problem for Latin America and it continues to limit Latin American national sovereignty.

Lemoine

World Events		Bolívar's Life
United States declares independence	1776	
	1783	Simón Bolívar is born
French Revolution begins	1789	
Latin American independence movement begins	1811	Bolívar joins Venezuelan army
	1813–15	Bolívar fails in two revolutions; flees to Jamaica
Congress of Vienna reorganizes Europe	1815	
	1822–25	Bolívar liberates five nations from Spain
	1830	Bolívar dies
Germany is united	1871	

For Further Reading

Brading, D. A. *Classical Republicanism and Creole Patriotism: Simon Bolívar (1783–1830) and the Spanish American Revolution.* Cambridge: Center of Latin American Studies, University of Cambridge, 1983.

Johnson, John J. *Simón Bolívar and Spanish American Independence: 1783–1830.* Princeton, N.J.: D. Van Nostrand, 1968.

Brezhnev, Leonid

Soviet Leader
1906–1982

Life and Work

Leonid Brezhnev served as leader of the Soviet Union for 18 years. His rule contributed both to the rise of the Soviet Union as a global military power and to the decline of communism.

Brezhnev was born on December 19, 1906, in the city of Dneprodzerzhinsk, then a part of the Russian empire. After joining the Communist Party in 1931, he enrolled in a metallurgical institute, graduating in 1935. Becoming a member of the party's Presidium (formerly the Politburo) in 1957, his moderate inclinations earned him the confidence of party conservatives at a time when NIKITA KHRUSHCHEV's support was eroding among them. When Khrushchev's erratic reforms finally provoked the Presidium to remove him from office in 1964, the leadership turned to Brezhnev as a reliable alternative.

Elevated to the post of party general secretary, Brezhnev secured the support of conservatives by canceling Khrushchev's plans to reorganize the party. Adopting a slogan called "stability of cadres," he sought to cooperate with the privileged elite known unofficially as the *nomenklatura* and was thereby able to steer a stable course for 18 years. During this time, he generally avoided changes and reforms to the economy and the state.

In the sphere of diplomacy, however, he led the Soviet Union to its pinnacle of influence. Issuing his Brezhnev Doctrine after the Soviet invasion of Czechoslovakia in 1968, he warned Eastern European states that any internal challenges to their communist systems would meet with a Soviet military response. He also sought to expand Soviet diplomatic influence throughout the non-European world, a policy that led to the 1979 invasion of Afghanistan. Finally, Brezhnev greatly strengthened the military. In 1965, for instance, an arsenal of intercontinental ballistic missiles (ICBMs) was introduced that finally brought nuclear parity with the United States. From this position of strength Brezhnev was able to promote a policy of détente. In 1972, he signed the Strategic Arms Limitation Treaty (SALT I), which placed limits upon the nuclear arsenals of the Soviet Union and the United States.

Despite his diplomatic achievements, Brezhnev's preoccupation with maintaining the power of party elites at home prevented him from experimenting with badly needed reforms in industry and agriculture. He died in 1982.

Legacy

Leonid Brezhnev ruled a communist superpower that was increasingly unable to meet the economic, intellectual, and spiritual needs of its population. In a sense, then, his leadership laid the groundwork for the crisis that followed his death.

In order to maintain power, Brezhnev was compelled to preserve the privileges and status of the *nomenklatura*. This meant that fundamental reforms to the totalitarian system created by JOSEPH STALIN, especially its command economy, were put off indefinitely in the hope that the system's weaknesses (which Khrushchev had begun to expose) would eventually correct themselves.

As the shortcomings of Brezhnev's leadership revealed themselves, intellectuals became bolder in their challenge to the system. Although usually restricted to unofficial publications and discussion groups, Soviet "dissidents" began to form a civil society that was both informed about the regime's shortcomings and committed to redressing them. Some were inspired by arms control agreements such as SALT I. Others formed human rights watch groups in the spirit of the Helsinki Accords of 1975. When the Soviet government, which signed these and other treaties, appeared to fall short of its ideals, it thus earned additional censure. After Brezhnev ordered the invasion of Afghanistan, for instance, ANDREY SAKHAROV protested so vehemently that he was forced into internal exile. Other leading dissidents such as Alexander Solzhenitsyn were deported for their views. The fact that they lived to direct their criticisms from abroad, however, revealed that communism no longer had the ruthless energy it had possessed in earlier times. Launching his own attack on what he called the Brezhnev "era of stagnation," Soviet leader MIKHAIL GORBACHEV would openly appeal to this element of civil society for political support after 1985.

Strickland

WORLD EVENTS		BREZHNEV'S LIFE
Russo-Japanese War	1905	
	1906	Leonid Brezhnev is born
World War I	1914–18	
Russian Revolution	1917	
Great Depression	1929–39	
	1931	Breshnev joins Communist Party
World War II	1939–45	
Communist China is established	1949	
	1957	Breshev becomes member of Politburo
	1964	Breshnev becomes General Secretary
Israel defeats Arab nations in Six-Day War	1967	
	1968	Brezhnev Doctrine is issued
	1972	SALT I treaty signed by Soviet Union
Vietnam War ends	1975	
	1979	Breshnev supports Soviet invasion of Afghanistan
	1982	Brezhnev dies
Dissolution of Soviet Union	1991	

For Further Reading

Breslauer, George W. *Khrushchev and Brezhnev as Leaders: Building Authority in Soviet Politics.* London: Allen and Unwin, 1981.

Edmonds, Robin. *Soviet Foreign Policy: The Brezhnev Years.* Oxford: Oxford University Press, 1983.

Keep, John L. H. *Last of the Empires: A History of the Soviet Union, 1945-1991.* Oxford: Oxford University Press, 1995.

Burke, Edmund

British Statesman
1729–1797

Life and Work

Edmund Burke, committed to reforming government, became an outspoken political conservative when confronted by the French Revolution.

Burke was born in Dublin, Ireland (then a part of Great Britain), on January 12, 1729. Although raised as an Anglican, he developed a tolerance for Roman Catholicism and became critical of laws that limited the rights of its adherents. In addition, he grew critical of other shortcomings in the political system, which he first expressed in *The Reformer*, a newspaper that he edited while a student at Trinity College in Dublin. As a young man, he dedicated himself

WORLD EVENTS		BURKE'S LIFE
English seize Calcutta	1690	
	1729	Edmund Burke is born
	1750	Burke moves to London
	1766	Burke wins seat in Parliament
United States declares independence	1776	
	1787	Burke prosecutes Warren Hastings
French Revolution begins	1789	
	1790	Burke publishes *Reflections on the Revolution in France*
	1797	Burke dies
Latin American independence movement begins	1811	

to public matters and won a seat in Parliament in 1766. For the remainder of his life he would be occupied almost exclusively with the burning political issues of the period.

Burke joined Parliament as a member of the liberal Whig Party. At a time when both Whigs and their Tory conservative adversaries tended to regard their seats merely as sources for personal gain, he used his position to address social and political abuses. He was a severe critic of King George III's fiscal policies in the American colonies, for instance, and when Warren Hastings, the governor of the East India Company, was accused of corruption in 1787, Burke prosecuted the case for impeachment. Burke supported William Wilberforce's efforts to abolish the African slave trade, and he urged Parliament to rescind legislation depriving Irish Catholics of civil liberties.

Burke's most memorable activity, however, occurred in response to the French Revolution. He had proven himself a sincere advocate of reform throughout his career, but in 1790, just a year after revolutionaries overthrew the monarchy of Louis XVI, he issued a highly conservative attack on their experiment in a book entitled *Reflections on the Revolution in France*.

Burke retired from Parliament in 1794. Having lived long enough to see some of his darkest prophecies fulfilled under the regime of Maximilien Robespierre, he died in 1797.

Legacy

Edmund Burke left a mixed legacy of reform and conservatism for later generations of political leaders in Britain and the world.

Educated during the eighteenth-century Enlightenment, Burke had taken an early interest in the efforts of contemporary philosophers to apply natural reason instead of religion to questions about human civilization. Many of his political writings expressed confidence in human reason to explain and justify government. Such an approach had sustained him in Parliament. His example would be followed by political reformers like William Ewart Gladstone in Britain during the nineteenth century.

Burke's attitude toward reform was complex, however. Historians credit him with introducing one of the earliest examples of the political philosophy known as conservatism. *Reflections on the Revolution in France*, the most elaborate exposition of his conservative philosophy, did

not attack reform as such. It criticized revolutionaries for tampering with customs hallowed by centuries of existence and for approaching the question of government from a purely secular perspective. The two principles behind these objections, prescription and moral pessimism, would provide a foundation for modern conservatism in later years.

Conservatives during the nineteenth century used the principle of prescription (the assignment of rights and titles according to historical custom) in an effort to prevent the erosion of traditional institutions such as the monarchy and the nobility. Klemens von Metternich of Austria, for instance, would apply this principle at the Congress of Vienna in 1815 in an effort to restore Europe's traditional political order after the upheavals of the French Revolution and the Napoleonic Wars. He oversaw the reestablishment of monarchy in France, and throughout eastern Europe sought to reimpose the power of social elites. In Russia, Tsar Nicholas II likewise sought to limit rights and titles according to historical precedent.

Finally, the moral pessimism of Burke's political philosophy, expressed in prescient claims that the French Revolution would ultimately degenerate into savagery and tyranny, impressed later conservatives who were disgusted by the spectacle of Robespierre's Reign of Terror. This principle, with its corollary that man's propensity for violence is best restrained by political institutions that have foundations in religious teaching, was elaborated vividly in the politically inspired novels of Fyodor Dostoevsky.

Strickland

For Further Reading

Lock, F. P. *Edmund Burke*. Oxford: Oxford University Press, 1998.

Macpherson, C. B. *Burke*. New York: Farrar, Straus & Giroux, 1980.

Russell, Kirk. *Edmund Burke: A Genius Reconsidered*. Wilmington, Del.: Intercollegiate Studies Institute, 1997.

Caesar, Julius

Roman Dictator
100–44 B.C.

Life and Work

Julius Caesar fought a series of successful wars to establish a dictatorship in ancient Rome.

Caesar (in full Gaius Julius Caesar) was born to a patrician (upper-class) family in Rome in 100 B.C. Because his parents were not wealthy, his future in the republic depended upon success in politics. To this end he received training in rhetoric and learned how to speak publicly with great effect. An initial opportunity to enter politics was lost, however, when his patron, Consul Marius, was overthrown by a powerful general named Sulla in c. 82–83 Caesar was forced to flee into exile.

Caesar was soon able to return to Rome, but instead of looking to the republican constitution to chart his course to power, he followed Sulla's example and turned to the army. As a patrician, he had the right to serve as an officer, and in 80 he was decorated for defeating the Greeks in Asia. A series of subsequent military campaigns brought him even greater distinction in Rome, where he was elected to the office of pontificate in 73. Aware that the Roman legions were the center of his power network, he distributed lavish bribes to his lieutenants. He also won the devotion of common soldiers by financing gladiatorial games. Thus in 59, when the Senate finally named him consul, he had become one of Rome's most powerful statesmen.

In the meantime he formed a ruling triumvirate with his two main rivals, Pompey and Crassus, and then left Rome to campaign in Gaul (modern-day France). His victories in the Gallic Wars, which included the invasion of Britain in 55, added enormous territories to a republican city-state that was poorly equipped to rule them. As Caesar's military leadership threatened the customary authority of the Senate in Rome, however, Pompey rallied traditional elites against the absent Caesar in 49. Hearing of this, Caesar made the decision to return across the Rubicon River that was the border between Gaul and Italy. The civil war that followed ended when Pompey's forces were defeated at the Battle of Pharsalus in 48.

Caesar was now the unrivaled military dictator of Rome. To consolidate his power, he decided to alter the republican constitution. He enlarged the Senate with men he believed would be loyal only to him, and he granted Roman citizenship to large numbers of people outside of Italy. Furthermore, believing he was descended from the gods, he began to mint coins bearing his image and to reorganize the calendar to include a month named July in his honor. His aspirations proved too great for a political system that had resisted monarchy for centuries, however, and on the Ides of March (March 15) in the year 44 a group of conspirators, including the formerly loyal Brutus, stabbed Caesar to death in the Senate chamber.

Legacy

Julius Caesar's rule was a watershed in the history of ancient Rome. His military expansion, dictatorial rule, and claims to divinity undermined the republic and laid the groundwork for an imperial system of government that lasted centuries.

When Caesar established himself as dictator, the republic was already in a state of crisis. For centuries its unwritten constitution had banned monarchy in favor of a consul elected by the patrician-controlled Senate. However, with Roman conquests in Italy and then the larger Mediterranean, the power of the army gradually came to displace that of the Senate. In one sense the civil wars that followed the collapse of the triumvirate and Caesar's subsequent dictatorship in 45 B.C. were the final outcome of the army's ascendance. By acquiring unprecedented power, however, to the point where he could even name his adopted son Octavius his successor, Caesar had established a new principle for rule.

Caesar's aggressive military expansion influenced both the development of Western Europe and the Roman state. Rome had already claimed much of Spain before Caesar's rise, but the Gallic Wars under his command brought even greater territorial gains in northern Europe. All of France and the southern half of Britain were brought under Roman authority; although these and other regions continued to resist Rome they were forever marked by its forms of civilization. Many great cities, including Paris, were founded or expanded under Caesar's successors, and vernacular languages became enriched through contact with Latin. In turn, control of these territories challenged the traditional military and administrative system of Rome and forced later emperors such as DIOCLETIAN to reorganize the state drastically.

Finally, Caesar's pretensions to divine lineage introduced a principle of emperor worship that would repeatedly alienate the empire's non-Roman population and, in the case of some rulers, invite gross abuses of power. While Caesar's immediate successor Octavius, who ultimately assumed the title AUGUSTUS ("venerable"), ruled on the whole with prudence and skill, the divine status claimed by him and other emperors created dissension within the empire's Jewish and Christian population. When the Jews were ordered to make public sacrifices to the emperor's image in 70 A.D. they revolted, provoking the Jewish War that brought the final destruction of the Temple in Jerusalem. Some emperors, such as Caligula (r. 37–41 A.D.) and Nero (r. 54–68 A.D.), were so outrageous in their claims to divinity (Caligula was said to have carried on conversations with a statue of Jupiter) that they felt free to tyrannize all who surrounded them. As a result both were overthrown at the cost of the empire's political stability.

Strickland

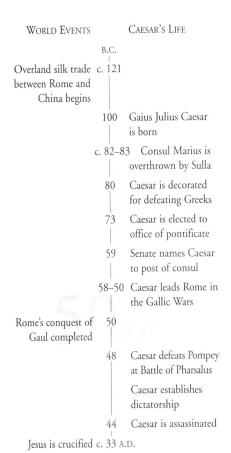

World Events	Caesar's Life
	B.C.
Overland silk trade between Rome and China begins	c. 121
	100 Gaius Julius Caesar is born
	c. 82–83 Consul Marius is overthrown by Sulla
	80 Caesar is decorated for defeating Greeks
	73 Caesar is elected to office of pontificate
	59 Senate names Caesar to post of consul
	58–50 Caesar leads Rome in the Gallic Wars
Rome's conquest of Gaul completed	50
	48 Caesar defeats Pompey at Battle of Pharsalus
	Caesar establishes dictatorship
	44 Caesar is assassinated
Jesus is crucified c. 33 A.D.	

For Further Reading

Bradford, E. D. S. *Julius Caesar: The Pursuit of Power*. London: Hamilton, 1984.

Caesar, Julius. *The Gallic War*. Translated by Carolyn Hammond. New York: Oxford University Press, 1996.

Meier, Christian. *Caesar*. Translated by David McLintock. New York: Harper Collins, 1995.

Weinstock, Stefan. *Julius Divus*. Oxford: Oxford University Press, 1971.

Candragupta

Emperor and Unifier of India
c. 348–c. 298 B.C.E.

WORLD EVENTS		CANDRAGUPTA'S LIFE
	B.C.E.	
China's "Warring States" Period begins	403	
	c. 348	Candragupta is born
	c. 330	Candragupta begins studies at Taxila
	327–24	Alexander invades and conquers western India
Maurya Empire in India is founded	325	
	324	Candragupta raises armies to oppose Alexander
Alexander the Great's empire at greatest size	323	
	322	Candragupta founds Maurya dynasty
	317	Candragupta retakes western India
	c. 298	Candragupta dies
Han Dynasty ends China's "Warring States" Period	206	

Life and Work

By unifying numerous Indian states into an empire and founding a dynasty to carry on that empire's governance, Candragupta made real the ideal of a united India.

Historians conjecture that Candragupta (also known as Candragupta Maurya) came from a relatively powerful family, but was orphaned at a young age and sold into a family of an unknown but unseemly profession or background. As a child, despite his poverty, Candragupta played games with his friends in which he took the role of king so well with his friends that Chanakya, a person of aristocratic or religious importance who by chance observed Candragupta, adopted him and raised him as a noble. About 330 B.C.E., at Taxila, in extreme northern India, Chanakya sent Candragupta to a military academy where he received a comprehensive education, including study of arts and letters, mathematics, and the military arts.

Candragupta's career as a statesman began immediately after he finished his studies at Taxila several years later. ALEXANDER III (Alexander the Great), who ravaged the whole of the Indus Valley between 327 and 324, had caused great consternation throughout India. Many feared he would conquer the whole subcontinent, despite the incredible force deployed against him. The main strategic fault of the Indians was, as observed by Candragupta, how they separated and thus dissipated their formidable resources. In 324 Candragupta traveled throughout northern India to raise troops to oppose Alexander. Although hated by the people of central India, in 322 Candragupta made himself emperor, founding the powerful Maurya dynasty. He retook most of Hellenized India by 317. Candragupta then moved against the Nanda family, overlords of central India who had earlier begun a process of unification.

Candragupta never forgot the Greek invasion, and moved to make Persia, rather than the Punjab, India's western frontier. In 305 he completed pushing India's boundaries westward toward Persia, probably in modern Afghanistan, to assure that a sufficient buffer existed between India and the West. Thereafter, Candragupta established friendly relations with the Persians and even the Romans. Candragupta rounded out his conquests with a bold move toward southern India, which gained him some land but also a bloody reputation. By 300, Candragupta ruled over an India that stretched from modern Afghanistan to Burma and from the Himalayas to nearly the southern tip of the subcontinent.

Fatigued of war and statecraft, Candragupta abdicated in favor of his son, Bindsutra, in 298, and lived the remainder of his days in spiritual isolation. He supposedly fasted to death, a great honor in the Jain religious tradition to which he is believed to have belonged.

Legacy

Candragupta created the idea of a greater India that endures to this day and pointed the way toward an effective method by which rulers might govern such a vast country.

By ending the Greek occupation of territory west of the Indus River and destroying Hellenic culture wherever he found it, Candragupta ensured an enduring presence of Indian culture throughout southern Asia that only the power of Islam was capable of challenging 1,500 years later. The essential part of administering such an empire was to have one culture throughout it. Although subsequent rulers adopted Buddhism or, much later, Islam, the core of Hindu legends and books, the Brahmin priesthood, and the caste system remained an important part of what Candragupta established as "India."

Candragupta realized that the strength of a state ultimately originated in its ability to extract resources from the territory and its people, and that military might was insufficient to ensure access to these resources. In order to extract resources from his kingdom and answer the needs of his people, he knew that he needed an effective administration and responsive government. Along with his prime minister and chief advisor, Kautalya, Candragupta put into place the beginnings of an effective bureaucracy based on salaried offices and inspectors. With an effective and theoretically incorruptible bureaucracy, Candragupta could extract the maximum of resources from his empire's farmers and artisans while understanding these producers' level of tolerance for taxation. Ever since, the linchpin of the effective governance of India has been the artful balance between might and an appreciation for how much the average person would contribute to the state without undue suffering or rebelling.

Del Testa

For Further Reading
Mookerji, Radhakumud. *Candragupta Maurya and His Times.* Delhi: Motilal Banarsidass, 1966.
Singh, Mahesh Vikram. *Society Under the Mauryas.* Delhi: Indological Book House, 1989.

Castro, Fidel

Cuban Revolutionary and Leader
1926–

Life and Work

Fidel Castro led the 1959 Cuban Revolution and has ruled the country since that time.

Castro was born Fidel Castro Ruz in 1926 and received a rigorous education at Jesuit schools. Castro enrolled at Havana University in 1945, joined the Law Faculty, an institution that groomed Cuba's elite, and earned his degree in 1950. In a university violently divided into political factions, Castro entered the Accion Radical Ortodoxo faction, which promoted revolution in Cuba's society and politics.

On March 10, 1952, Fulgencio Batista staged a coup and installed himself as dictator. Batista allied with Cuba's landowners and industrialists and initiated a political crackdown. Castro, knowing that reform within Batista's regime would be impossible, planned a countercoup in 1953, which failed miserably. After nearly two years in prison, Castro was granted amnesty in 1955 and planned another revolt. Launched in November 1956, the second rebellion was an even worse disaster than the first, forcing Castro and his followers to flee into Cuba's mountains.

Undeterred, Castro and his allies executed a brilliant military takeover in January 1959. As Cuba's new leader, Castro initiated a series of reforms, including the secularization of education and extensive land reform. In an atmos-phere suspicious of the previous regime and foreign influence, Castro suspended normal parliamentary procedure and ended the privileged economic relationship Cuba had enjoyed with the United States. The negative reaction of the United States, culminating in the disastrous May 1961 Bay of Pigs invasion, pushed Castro, who had originally hoped to have friendly relations with the United States, toward the Soviet Union.

Resulting from the stationing of Soviet nuclear missiles in Cuba, the Cuban Missile Crisis erupted in 1962. Castro was dissatisfied with the Soviet Union because it backed down in response to pressure from the United States. Always exercising Cuban independence, Castro engaged in development that was often at odds with mainstream socialism by its emphasis on the peasantry and local control. In a world in which the Soviet government believed it controlled the use of force between socialist nations, Cuba's independence peaked between 1975 and 1980 when, in defying the Soviet Union, Cuba dispatched soldiers to Angola to support its new socialist regime.

To maintain effective political control, however, Castro imposed an increasingly rigid political system on Cuba; by the 1970s, local initiatives had been taken over by a centralizing bureaucracy in an attempt to squelch discontent. Although tactics such as releasing 200,000 refugees to the United States in the early 1980s reduced some of the discontent, Castro found himself challenged by popular unrest and the collapse of the world's socialist economies after 1989.

Legacy

By improving public welfare and reiterating his enthusiasm for socialism, Fidel Castro created a popular regime in Cuba that serves as an international example of socialism's potential—both to improve social welfare and to hinder democracy.

Castro liberated Cubans from the exploitation of traditional elites only to destroy Cubans' potential political rights. After the Revolution Cuban people enjoyed for the first time a free educational and medical system. Castro achieved broad improvements in Cubans' standard of living. Cuba thus served as a model for other socialist nations. However, the price of social welfare was the freedoms of civil society. With the collapse of the socialist economic sys-tem in the Soviet Union after 1989 and the enduring, politically motivated embargo against Cuba by the United States, however, Cubans have suffered enormously and discontent has grown. Castro's words still inspire Cubans, though, because they remind them of the divisions capitalism may bring to Cuba, divisions that encouraged Castro's 1959 revolution in the first place.

Castro also influenced the rest of the world by becoming the most ardent supporter of socialist revolution in the lesser-developed world, much to the chagrin of the United States and Castro's partners in the Soviet Union, who felt upstaged by Castro. In Cuba, socialists could express a passion for revolution that other regimes kept in check. Cuba became a center for those who wished to expand socialism. In the end, Castro knew that the Cuba he created was a small place and subject to the whims of the larger powers. However, he knew as well that with a small amount of encouragement, dedicated socialists could create amazing things, his Cuba being the prime example.

Del Testa

WORLD EVENTS		CASTRO'S LIFE
Russian Revolution	1917	
	1926	Fidel Castro is born
Great Depression	1929–39	
World War II	1939–45	
	1945	Castro enrolls in Havana University
Communist China is established	1949	
	1953–56	Castro launches two failed rebellions
	1959	Castro takes over Cuba
	1961	Bay of Pigs invasion
	1962	Cuban Missile Crisis
Israel defeats Arab nations in Six-Day War	1967	
Vietnam War ends	1975	
	1975–80	Castro sends Cuban troops to Angola to support socialists
	1980–81	Castro permits 200,000 Cubans to leave for United States
Dissolution of Soviet Union	1991	

For Further Reading
Balfour, Sebastian. *Castro*, 2nd ed. Harlow, England: Longman House, 1995.
Quirk, Robert E. *Fidel Castro*. New York: Norton, 1993.

Catherine de Médicis

Queen, Regent, and Queen
Mother in France
1519–1589

Life and Work

An able politician, Catherine de Médicis struggled to maintain the power of the French crown during the upheavals of the Wars of Religion (1562–98). Although her sons failed to carry on the Valois dynasty, Catherine's efforts ensured the survival of the French monarchy.

Catherine was born into the ruling de Medici family of the Italian state of Tuscany on April 13, 1519. Orphaned soon after birth, she was raised in Florence by her extended family, which included Pope Clement VII. Catherine learned politics at an early age, when the Italian peninsula (not yet a unified nation-state) witnessed political conflicts between its many states and the powerful papacy.

In 1533, at age 14, she married Henri (who assumed the throne as Henri II in 1547), the second son of the French King François I, as part of diplomatic negotiations between France and Clement VII. Bright and intellectually curious, Catherine studied Latin, Greek, mathematics, and astronomy, unusual even for noblewomen. At first unpopular because she was Italian and childless, Catherine struggled to gain legitimacy. Her popularity increased after she began producing children, including four sons, all potential heirs to the throne.

When Henri II was killed in a joust in 1559, Catherine's son François II assumed the throne. When he died prematurely in 1561, his younger brother Charles IX succeeded him. Catherine was appointed regent, as Charles IX was too young to reign. Even after he ended the regency in 1563, he was dominated by his mother. The following year she accompanied Charles on a great tour of France, introducing her son to his realm and bolstering royal authority.

As regent, Catherine virtually ruled France. Her major concern was to contain the conflict between Catholics and Protestants. French Protestants, followers of John Calvin known as Huguenots, had gained many adherents among the aristocracy, which politicized the religious conflict. At first Catherine, Catholic but not devout, tried to reconcile the opposing groups. But she could not prevent the outbreak of the Wars of Religion in 1562, which divided France repeatedly in the following decades.

In the context of civil war, Catherine attempted to maintain and extend the authority of the crown. She allied the crown first with the Protestants, led by the House of Navarre, then in 1567 she turned against the Huguenots and formed an alliance with the Catholics, led by the House of Guise. In 1572, another attempt at reconciliation turned tragic. Henry of Navarre, the future HENRY IV and leader of the Huguenots, was to marry Marguerite, Catherine's daughter, in Paris. Days after the ceremony, the Guises led an attack that killed many Huguenot nobles assembled to attend the wedding. Known as Saint Bartholomew's Day Massacre, the Catholics' attacks spread across France, killing thousands of Huguenots. While Catherine did not plot the attack, evidence suggests she may have supported the Guises.

Catherine's influence diminished after the death of Charles IX in 1574. Her third son, Henry III, assumed the throne and resisted his mother's advice. However, she continued to represent the crown in negotiations with Huguenot leaders until her death on January 5, 1589.

Legacy

Catherine de Médicis struggled against many obstacles to bolster the French monarchy, enabling future rulers to rebuild and strengthen royal power. Her efforts to maintain peace between the Catholics and the Huguenots, though largely a failure, did introduce a measure of toleration that lasted over a century.

The retention of royal power and prestige was Catherine's paramount concern. The centuries-old Salic Law in France restricted royal succession to the male line, which prevented Catherine from ruling in her own right. Although an able and energetic leader, she was forced to rule through her sons, which hampered her effectiveness. She lacked the legal and royal authority, and her sons lacked the political acumen, to impose a settlement on the warring religious factions, or to enact reforms for a more efficient administration and judiciary. These reforms were left for the future reigns of Henry IV, Louis XIII, and LOUIS XIV.

The Wars of Religion severely strained royal authority. However, Catherine did not link religious affiliation with loyalty to crown. She spearheaded genuine efforts to reconcile the differences that kept the Huguenots and Catholics at odds. The crown's eventual alliance with the Catholic extremist House of Guise was a decision based on political concerns rather than religious belief. The royal policy of toleration for Huguenots, attempted by Catherine and institutionalized under Henry IV, lasted over a century, and was only revoked in 1685 by Louis XIV.

Catherine's struggle to maintain royal authority, while not a complete success, nevertheless set the stage for the development of absolutism in seventeenth-century France, a process that reached its apogee during the reign of Louis XIV (1643–1715) and ended only with the French Revolution of 1789.

Lemoine

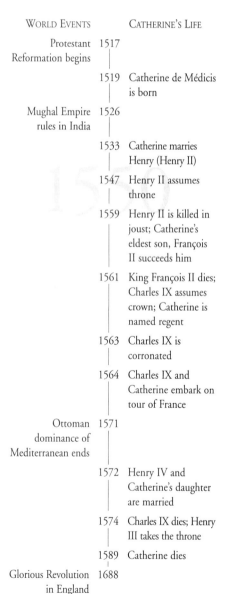

WORLD EVENTS		CATHERINE'S LIFE
Protestant Reformation begins	1517	
	1519	Catherine de Médicis is born
Mughal Empire rules in India	1526	
	1533	Catherine marries Henry (Henry II)
	1547	Henry II assumes throne
	1559	Henry II is killed in joust; Catherine's eldest son, François II succeeds him
	1561	King François II dies; Charles IX assumes crown; Catherine is named regent
	1563	Charles IX is corronated
	1564	Charles IX and Catherine embark on tour of France
Ottoman dominance of Mediterranean ends	1571	
	1572	Henry IV and Catherine's daughter are married
	1574	Charles IX dies; Henry III takes the throne
	1589	Catherine dies
Glorious Revolution in England	1688	

For Further Reading

Knecht, R. J. *Catherine de' Medici.* London: Longman, 1998.

———. *French Renaissance Monarchy: Francis I and Henry II.* London: Longman, 1996.

Catherine II

Empress of Russia
1729–1796

Life and Work

Under the enlightened rule of Catherine II (Catherine the Great) the Russian Empire developed culturally and expanded its territories. At the same time, half of the population sank into a condition of serfdom.

Catherine was born in 1729 as Sophia Augusta Frederika, the daughter of the prince of Anhalt-Zerbst, a small German state. As a German princess she developed a strong interest in the secular arts and, like most educated Europeans of the eighteenth century, learned French. When she was 15 she married the heir to the Russian throne, Peter III. His highly eccentric personality, however, appalled the cultivated Catherine, who turned to her own lovers at court for support. It was one of these, Count Gregory Orlov, who led a revolt against Peter on Catherine's orders in 1762. Catherine was installed as the ruler and Peter was forced to retire to a palace, where, in a drunken brawl several days later, he was murdered.

Catherine's early policies as empress were influenced by an enthusiastic interest in reform. In 1766, for instance, she ordered the creation of a Legislative Commission to prepare a new codification of the laws. Her enthusiasm was dampened in 1773, however, when a massive uprising of peasants led by a cossack named Emile Pugachev (who actually claimed to be Peter III) nearly overthrew her. Thereafter her policies took a conservative turn, and the Legislative Commission was itself ultimately disbanded. In an effort to strengthen the crown's alliance with the nobility, she issued a Charter to the Nobility in 1785. This granted nobles certain rights such as freedom from state service and taxation, as well as greater control over their lands. It was also accompanied by laws that consolidated the nobility's control over peasants. As a result, approximately half of the Russian population was reduced to serfdom.

Diplomatic and military achievements under Catherine, on the other hand, were just short of spectacular. In 1770 Russian ships sank the Turkish fleet at the Bay of Chesme. With the Treaty of Kuchuk-Kainarji in 1774, the Ottoman Empire ceded territory, including the north shore of the Black Sea. In the West, a series of partitions between 1772 and 1795 incorporated eastern Poland into the empire, bringing Russia up to the borders of Prussia and Austria.

Finally, Catherine showed great enthusiasm for bringing European learning and the arts to Russia. She encouraged familiarity with leading philosophers such as Baron de Montesquieu. Her passion for art resulted in the construction of the Hermitage in Saint Petersburg, which assembled one of the greatest art collections in Europe.

Having strengthened Russia and tied its destiny more closely to Europe, Catherine died in Saint Petersburg in 1796.

Legacy

Catherine II's reign influenced the development of Russia and the rest of Europe for more than a century.

Catherine was one of the first European monarchs to apply the principles of the Enlightenment to government. Philosophers such as Voltaire had argued that the government's only legitimate concern is the improvement of the civic order. Catherine applied this teaching to absolutist monarchy. Her policy of enlightened absolutism (as historians call it) failed to substantially improve political institutions during her time. Nevertheless, it offered an example to later rulers who were more committed to improving the social order.

Catherine also contributed to the development of modern Russian culture. Before the late eighteenth century, Russia remained rooted in the Orthodox Christian tradition of the Middle Ages. After Catherine, however, educated society began to embrace secular arts such as literature, painting, and music. This movement flowered particularly during the nineteenth century. The poetry of Aleksandr Pushkin and the prose of Nikolay Gogol would draw upon Western literary tradition. So vital did Russia's native cultural tradition become after Catherine that for the first time the flow of ideas across Europe was reversed. The works of Fyodor Dostoevsky, Leo Tolstoy, Anton Chekhov, and Peter Ilich Tchaikovsky all found their way to Western Europe, and all had a profound impact upon its cultural life before and after World War I.

Finally, Catherine's foreign policy achievements led to the greater integration of Russia and Western Europe. A position on the borders of Prussia and Austria would bring Russia into the wars of the French Revolution, and, in 1812, it would be the Russian army that delivered the fatal blow to NAPOLÉON I. For more than a century afterward Russia was one of the Great Powers of Europe and played a central role in diplomacy. Continuing hostilities with the Ottoman Empire would result in the humiliating defeat of the Crimean War (1854–56), the direct precipitate for ALEXANDER II's Great Reforms. Finally, by occupying the shores of the Black Sea and the frontiers of central Europe, Russia was drawn irresistibly and fatally into World War I in 1914.

Strickland

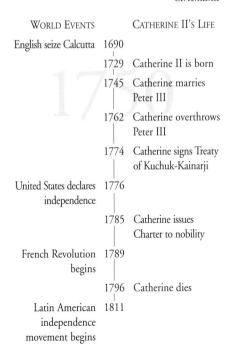

WORLD EVENTS		CATHERINE II'S LIFE
English seize Calcutta	1690	
	1729	Catherine II is born
	1745	Catherine marries Peter III
	1762	Catherine overthrows Peter III
	1774	Catherine signs Treaty of Kuchuk-Kainarji
United States declares independence	1776	
	1785	Catherine issues Charter to nobility
French Revolution begins	1789	
	1796	Catherine dies
Latin American independence movement begins	1811	

For Further Reading
Alexander, John T. *Catherine the Great: Life and Legend.* Oxford: Oxford University Press, 1989.
de Madariaga, Isabel. *Russia in the Age of Catherine the Great.* London: Weidenfeld and Nicolson, 1981.
Maroger, Dominique, ed. *The Memoirs of Catherine the Great.* Translated by Moura Budberg. New York: Macmillan, 1955.

Cavour, Camillo Benso di

Leader of Italian Unification
1810–1861

Life and Work

Italian leader Camillo Benso di Cavour, through his adaptability and diplomatic efforts, led the successful struggle for Italian unification in the nineteenth century.

Cavour was born in Piedmont-Sardinia in northern Italy on August 1, 1810. He graduated from the Royal Military Academy of Piedmont-Sardinia and received a commission in 1826. Although raised as a Roman Catholic monarchist, Cavour admired British liberal political and economic institutions. In 1831, to protest the anti-liberal regime of King Carlo Alberto, Cavour resigned his commission. He founded a newspaper in 1847, *Il Risorgimento* ("the Resurrection," a term later applied to the Italian unification movement), to express his liberal ideology, support Italian unification, and encourage a war of liberation against the Austrian Empire. Before 1861 Italy was not a unified nation-state. It consisted of several independent kingdoms and duchies; the Austrian Empire possessed Lombardy and Venetia in northern Italy; the Pope controlled central Italy, known as the Papal Estates, as well as Rome.

In 1848 widespread Italian and European political and social upheavals launched Cavour into his political career. Certain that a constitutional monarchy and representative government would provide a stable political framework for a unified Italy, Cavour published an article in *Il Risorgimento* urging the king of Piedmont-Sardinia to introduce a constitution. The king agreed, and Cavour was elected to the newly created parliament in 1848. In 1852 Cavour was appointed prime minister. He encouraged economic growth and modernization domestically and negotiated alliances with other European states to gain support for Italian unification.

Cavour understood that Piedmont-Sardinia would need the support of a great power such as France to provide the military aid needed to drive Austria out of northern Italy. Piedmont's alliance with France and Britain in the Crimean War (1854–56) and the peace conference in 1856 gave Cavour the opportunity to transform the "Italian question" into a European issue. In 1859 Napoleon III, then ruler of France, agreed to send French troops to help Piedmont defeat the Austrian Empire. Austria relinquished Lombardy, although Venetia remained in Austrian hands. Piedmont's success against Austria sparked insurrections in the central Italian states of Tuscany, Parma, Modena, and the Legations, a province of the Papal Estates. In March 1860, overwhelming majorities voted for annexation to Piedmont in plebiscites negotiated by Cavour.

Also in 1860, Cavour faced a new challenge in southern Italy when republican revolutionary GIUSEPPE GARIBALDI overthrew the Kingdom of Naples and prepared to invade Rome. Cavour, in the name of supporting the Pope, sent troops to block Garibaldi, but also took control of Umbria and the Marches, two provinces of the Papal Estates. Deciding that Piedmont was Italy's best hope for Italian unification, Garibaldi transferred the Kingdom of Naples to Piedmont. On March 17, 1861, the united Kingdom of Italy was proclaimed, minus Rome and Venetia. Appointed unified Italy's first prime minister, Cavour died on June 6, 1861, only three months after his greatest, yet incomplete, triumph.

Legacy

Camillo Benso di Cavour's skill as a diplomat, his ability to adapt to changing circumstances, and his single-minded determination to see Italy unified under the monarchy of Piedmont-Sardinia led to the creation of a centralized Italian nation-state. Yet, historical, economic, cultural, and linguistic differences between the Italian states, as well as Italy's role in the rise of nationalism in nineteenth-century Europe, presented problems that have afflicted Italy to the present day.

Before 1861, Italian politicians and thinkers had proposed three models of Italian unification: a loose confederation of states with the Pope serving as president; a republic stressing a broad electorate and social reform; a moderate constitutional monarchy. Cavour's leadership ensured that a centralized constitutional monarchy, stressing liberal political and economic institutions, would succeed in uniting the Italian states despite their differences.

Centralization by Piedmontese rulers kept Italy unified, but did not address the problems of social reform or the needs of the poverty-stricken south. To pay for unification, the government imposed new taxes that hurt lower-income Italians. In addition, in 1868, the Church, angered at the loss of papal lands, ordered Italian Catholics to withdraw from national politics. Italy was still divided by religious, regional, and socioeconomic differences.

Cavour was also a leader in the efforts of nineteenth-century moderate and conservative European political leaders to manipulate nationalist and patriotic enthusiasm, with the goal of keeping the monarchies they supported in power. Before the European revolutions of 1848 made it clear that political leaders needed to appeal to a mass constituency, nationalism was seen as a product of the French Revolution, which had destabilized the monarchies of Europe. After 1848, moderate and conservative rulers and politicians saw nationalism as a way to unite their subjects under their respective monarchies, thus avoiding revolution and radical social reform. The conservative turn in nationalism fostered rivalries between the great powers of Europe that eventually led to World War I. Italy's entry into the war in 1915 on the side of the Allies and post-war disappointments were responsible, in part, for the triumph of BENITO MUSSOLINI's fascist movement in 1922.

Lemoine

World Events		Cavour's Life	
French Revolution begins	1789		
	1810	Camillo Benso di Cavour is born	
Latin American independence movement begins	1811		
Congress of Vienna reorganizes Europe	1815		
	1847	Cavour founds *Il Risorgimento*	
	1852	Cavour appointed prime minister of Piedmont-Sardinia	
	1860	Cavour blocks Giuseppe Garibaldi's invasion of Rome; Cavour takes control of Umbria and the Marches	
	1861	Kingdom of Italy proclaimed	
		Cavour appointed first prime minister of unified Italy but dies three months later	
Germany is united	1871		

For Further Reading

Hearder, Harry. *Cavour.* London and New York: Longman, 1994.
Mack Smith, Denis. *Cavour.* London: Weidenfeld and Nicolson, 1985.

Charlemagne

Founder of the First Christian
Empire in the West
c. 742–814

Life and Work

Charlemagne (Charles the Great) created a
Christian empire in western Europe that
existed in various forms for more than 1,000
years. A defender of the papacy and a patron of
learning, he helped lay the foundations for
medieval European civilization.

Charlemagne was born around 742, the
eldest son of Pepin the Short, king of the
Franks, and the grandson of Charles Martel.
The Frankish kingdom was centered on the
Rhineland in northern Europe and was one of
several Germanic states to succeed the ancient
Roman Empire after its collapse during the
fifth century. When Pepin died in 768
Charlemagne was forced to share the throne
with his brother Carloman. The latter's prema-
ture death in 771 enabled Charlemagne to
assume sole authority over the Franks.

During his reign, Charlemagne was occupied
by the perpetual wars waged across Europe. In
774 he rescued Pope Hadrian I by destroying an
army of Lombards that had invaded central
Italy. In the east he fought the Slavic Avars, and
in the west the Spanish Moors. The fiercest conflict occurred in northern Germany against the
pagan Saxons. More than 30 years were needed
to subdue them, and Charlemagne's policies

were at times very brutal. Only in 804 was
peace in the north established.

Having forged an empire across the greater
part of western Europe (excluding Spain and
Britain), Charlemagne was eager to have his
realm recognized and legitimated by the
Church. In 800 he visited Rome and, in a
famous coronation ceremony held on
Christmas Day in Saint Peter's Basilica, was
crowned emperor by Pope Leo III.

As a Christian ruler, Charlemagne spent his
later years improving the administration of the
empire and influencing church affairs. He
built a splendid palace at Aachen (Aix-la-
Chapelle) to serve as a permanent court. He
appointed itinerant inspectors called *missi
dominici* to exercise his will in the provinces,
and he issued laws such as the Programmatic
Capitulary of 802 that sought to apply justice
uniformly to all subjects. Finally, he assembled
a large body of scholars to facilitate religious
learning and copying.

After assuring the succession of his son
Louis I in 813, Charlemagne died in 814.

Legacy

The Carolingian Empire profoundly influenced the history of western Europe and
the Roman Catholic church.

The foundation for the Carolingian Empire
was the Christian church. Charlemagne held
deep religious convictions and intended from
the beginning to apply them to his rule. In
this he was influenced by the example of
JUSTINIAN I and other Byzantine emperors in
the East, who intervened in church affairs and
supported missionary activities. As a result
Charlemagne was remembered by later
medieval statesmen as a proponent of Christian
statecraft and was even called a "second
Constantine" (after the first Christian emperor
CONSTANTINE I).

Charlemagne's most important legacy was
the Carolingian Renaissance. Personally convinced that his empire was threatened by doctrinal ignorance and apostasy, Charlemagne
promoted a revival of learning and copying in
monasteries that was often supported by imperial law. The most brilliant example was the
court school of Aachen, where scholars from
all corners of Europe assembled to write
biographies, histories, and poems. Alcuin, a
scholar from Britain, copied classical Christian

texts, helped to standardize the Catholic
liturgy, and prepared an improved edition of
the Bible. Nearly all ancient Roman works
known in modern times are based upon copies
made during the Carolingian Renaissance.

Not all of Charlemagne's activities had universal benefits for the Roman Catholic church,
however. By the end of the eighth century,
bishops in the East and the West had become
increasingly estranged from one another by
disagreements about church administration.
The eastern bishops supported the Byzantine
emperor as the only legitimate heir to the
emperors of ancient Rome. In the West, however, the Pope claimed supremacy over the eastern bishops and, aware of his isolation, sought
a ruler to defend his claim. Charlemagne's
coronation by the Pope in 800 was a victory for
the papacy, but one that deepened the ecclesi-
astical rift. In 1054 a formal schism resulted
when a papal legate traveled to Constantinople
and excommunicated the eastern bishops, dramatically placing the papal bull upon the altar
of the Church of Hagia Sophia. Christendom
thereafter became divided into the Orthodox
church in the East and the Roman Catholic
church in the West.

Strickland

WORLD EVENTS		CHARLEMAGNE'S LIFE
Islamic expansion into northern Europe is halted at Tours	732	
	c. 742	Charlemagne is born
Battle of Talas halts Islam's north Asian expansion	751	
	768	Charlemagne and brother, Carloman, assume throne at death of Pepin
	771	Charlemagne assumes sole authority at death of Carloman
	774–804	Charlemagne fights numerous wars across Europe
	800	Charlemagne is coronated by Pope Leo III in Rome
	802	Charlemagne issues Programmatic Capitulary
	814	Charlemagne dies
Ethnic Chinese rule is reasserted in northern China	980	

For Further Reading

Chamberlin, Russell. *Charlemagne: Emperor of the Western World*. London: Grafton, 1986.

Collins, Roger. *Charlemagne*. Toronto: University of Toronto Press, 1998.

McKitterick, Rosamund, ed. *Carolingian Culture: Emulation and Innovation*. Cambridge: Cambridge University Press, 1994.

Charles V

Holy Roman Emperor
1500–1558

Life and Work

Charles V ruled one of the largest empires in European history. Although his life was marked by great achievements, his failure to prevent the spread of Protestantism and to unify his realm finally caused him to retire in disappointment.

Charles was born in 1500 to the powerful Habsburg family. His father, Philip I, ruled the Netherlands and his mother, Juana, daughter of King Ferdinand II of Spain, was the heir to the throne of that country. His paternal grandfather Maximilian I was the Holy Roman Emperor in Germany. While Charles was still a boy, the deaths of these relatives made him heir to one of the largest territories Europe had ever seen. His father died in 1506, leaving him the Netherlands; in 1517, Ferdinand II died, and, as his mother was insane and thus unfit for her inheritance, Charles received Spain, Naples, and the territories of New Spain in America. Finally, in 1519 Maximilian I died and Charles inherited Germany. Despite the opposition of HENRY VIII of England and Francis I of France, the 19-year-old boy was elected Holy Roman Emperor and crowned by Pope Leo X in 1520.

The reign of Europe's most powerful ruler was to be unhappy, however. Francis immediately provoked a war with Charles. The object was Italy, to which both rulers had defensible claims. At the Battle of Pavia in 1525, Francis was badly defeated by imperial forces and was taken hostage on the battlefield. After being freed, however, he waged additional wars against Charles in later years.

Conflicts with powers outside Europe generally ended more decisively. In 1521 the Aztecs were conquered for Spain by HERNÁN CORTÉS, as were the Incas by FRANCISCO PIZARRO in 1533. Nearer to home, the Ottoman Empire briefly threatened central Europe, but a siege of Vienna by SULEYMAN I was broken by imperial forces in 1532.

Far more threatening was the spread of Protestantism in Germany. His preoccupation with France left Charles unable to address the Reformation. His impotence was revealed at the Diet of Worms in 1521, where he failed to persuade Martin Luther to submit to Rome. In 1546 he waged a successful war against the Protestant Schmalkaldic League, but victory failed to bring reunion to the church in Germany. In 1555, Charles was forced to concede failure at the Peace of Augsburg. This treaty introduced the famous principle *cujus regio, ejus religio* ("whose region, his religion"), by which Lutheranism gained legitimacy in many of the empire's German principalities.

For the piously Roman Catholic Charles, this failure was nearly unbearable. Frustrated by his powerlessness to defend the faith, he abdicated in 1556 and spent the remainder of his life in the monastery of Yuste in Spain, dying there in 1558.

World Events		Charles V's Life
Columbus sails to Americas	1492	
	1500	Charles V is born
Protestant Reformation begins	1517	
	1520	Charles is elected Holy Roman Emperor
	1521	Charles fails to persuade Martin Luther to submit to Rome at Diet of Worms
	1525	Charles's forces defeat France at Battle of Pavia
Mughal Empire rules in India	1526	
	1532	Turks lay siege to Vienna but are defeated by Charles's army
	1555	Charles concedes at Peace of Augsburg
	1558	Charles dies
Ottoman dominance of Mediterranean ends	1571	

Legacy

Charles V's failure to check the Reformation and to unify his vast territories profoundly influenced the development of modern Europe.

By gathering Spain, the Netherlands, Naples, and Germany under one crown, Charles had hoped to create an immense empire that could dominate Europe and preserve its traditional Roman Catholicism. Instead, foreign wars and neglect of individual territories sapped his strength and enabled Protestants to establish a permanent foothold in northern Europe. By the end of the sixteenth century the division of Europe according to religious confession was virtually complete. Lutheranism dominated northern Germany and Scandinavia; Anglicanism dominated England; and Roman Catholicism dominated Spain, France, Italy, and Poland. What is more, although the Peace of Augsburg had legitimated Lutheranism in Germany, religious conflict would explode there again in the Thirty Years War (1618–48).

Many of the forces that had prevented Charles from preserving Catholic unity also made it impossible for him to create an integrated territorial administration. His decision to divide the realm in half before his retirement was an admission of this fact. Spain and the Netherlands were assigned to his son PHILIP II, while Germany was assigned to his brother Ferdinand I. This division led directly to the rise of two powerful states and indirectly to the rise of a third. Spain, which Charles had always favored, now had the opportunity to develop its American colonies without concern for the affairs of central Europe. For its part, the Holy Roman Empire evolved into a purely central European state ruled by the Habsburg dynasty. Charles was the last Holy Roman Emperor crowned by a Pope, and, in the nineteenth century, the Habsburgs would rename their realm the Austrian Empire. Finally, Charles's decision to include the Netherlands in his bequest to Philip had an indirect impact on that territory. Resenting the dominion of Roman Catholic Spain, Dutch Protestants revolted against Philip in the late sixteenth century and were able to achieve complete independence by the middle of the seventeenth century.

Strickland

For Further Reading

Alvarez, Manuel Fernández. *Charles V: Elected Emperor and Hereditary Ruler.* London: Thames and Hudson, 1975.

Rady, Martyn C. *The Emperor Charles V.* London: Longman, 1988.

Von Habsburg, Otto. *Charles V.* Translated by Michael Ross. New York: Praeger, 1969.

Chiang Kai-shek

Leader of Nationalist China
1887–1975

Life and Work

Between 1920 and 1950, despite facing many enemies, Chiang Kai-shek tried to build a strong, democratic, and unified China.

Chiang was born on October 31, 1887, at Chicow, a village in the mountains of China's central coast. In 1903, he entered a private high school in nearby Ningpo. Early in the twentieth century, revolutionary, anti-foreigner literature circulated in China's schools. Attracted by the messages of this literature and wanting to oppose China's ineffectual imperial government, in 1907 Chiang traveled to a Japanese military school to train as an officer. In Japan, Chiang also attended the lectures of SUN YAT-SEN, an exiled leader of China's most important opposition movement. Chiang soon became one of Sun's followers.

In 1911, the Qing emperor of China abdicated and Sun, ruling through his newly formed Kuomintang ("Revolutionary") Party, declared China a republic. Between 1912 and 1923, Chiang moved between Japan and China, suffering through the changing fortunes of Sun, the Kuomintang, and the Chinese Republic. In 1924, he established the influential Whampoa military academy near Canton, in southern China. With troops trained at Whampoa as well as Chinese communist soldiers newly allied with the Kuomintang, Chiang created a republican army. Between 1924 and 1928, Chiang used this army to assert an uneasy Kuomintang authority over China by destroying many of the warlords who had taken over the country since 1911. Sun's death in 1925 elevated Chiang's position within the Kuomintang, and a 1927 purge of the Kuomintang's communist allies temporarily eliminated the only source of opposition to the Kuomintang's leadership over China. In 1927, Chiang married Mei-ling Soong, whose strong family ties to Asian banks he hoped would help China.

As commander-in-chief, Chiang spent 1927 to 1931 consolidating his rule. His forces captured Shanghai and Nanking in 1927, and Beijing in 1928. With the help of foreigners, Chiang began to improve China's government and economy and to democratize its society. Chiang faced a new threat, however, from Japan, which in 1931 conquered the northeastern province of Manchuria and by 1937 advanced further into Chinese territory. Throughout World War II, Chiang received military aid from the Allies and slowly retook land conquered by Japan. However, after the war, the rank corruption and strong-arm tactics of the Kuomintang pushed many Chinese to support MAO TSE-TUNG's communists. Though technically allied since 1936, Chiang and Mao's forces battled for control of China after 1945. In 1949, Mao forced Chiang to retreat to the island of Taiwan. Chiang remained president of a Nationalist Chinese government on Taiwan until his death in 1975.

Legacy

Chiang Kai-shek preserved China as a single political entity in the face of enemies who wanted to divide and conquer it. In addition, Chiang's dogged defense of China's unity in the late 1930s and 1940s tied up much of Japan's military force, thus dampening Japan's ability to thoroughly conquer Asia during World War II.

Chiang took Sun's vision of a united, independent, republican China and gave it substance through an effective military, political party, and bureaucracy. For Chiang, nationalism could solve all of China's problems, for if the Chinese expelled foreign powers and believed in themselves, they could become strong again. Because of its activist message, many Chinese rallied to the Kuomintang, especially in China's cities. However, the Kuomintang never had any effective central ideology. This lack of motivational ideology created opportunities for corruption and abuse of power.

Chiang imposed a sense of modern nationalism among all of the Chinese people, whether they supported him or not, and he kept China unified politically. At various times, Chiang also successfully rallied his potential enemies, such as the Soviet Union, the United States, and the Chinese communists, behind his vision of a modern, independent, industrial China. However, Nationalist Taiwan and Communist China represent the strongest example of enduring Cold War politics, both sides claiming to represent the government of China and neither willing to negotiate the issue. The stubborn, anti-foreigner nationalism Chiang infused into China in the 1920s, 1930s, and 1940s endures in both Nationalist and Communist China, and makes each the bitter enemy of the other.

Del Testa

WORLD EVENTS		CHIANG'S LIFE
Germany is united	1871	
	1887	Chiang Kai-shek is born
Russo-Japanese War	1905	
World War I	1914–18	
Russian Revolution	1917	
	1924	Chiang founds Whampoa military academy near Canton
	1924–28	Chiang recaptures China from warlords
Great Depression	1929–39	
	1931	Japanese invade Manchuria
	1936–45	Japanese try to conquer China
World War II	1939–45	Chiang recaptures land from Japanese
	1945–48	Civil war between Chiang and Mao
Communist China is established	1949	Chiang retreats to Taiwan
	1950–75	Chiang serves as president of Nationalist China on Taiwan
Israel defeats Arab nations in Six-Day War	1967	
Vietnam War ends	1975	Chiang dies
Dissolution of Soviet Union	1991	

For Further Reading
Chun-ming Chang. *Chiang Kai-shek, His Life and Times*. Abridged English edition. New York: St. John's University, 1981.
Payne, Robert. *Chiang Kai-Shek*. New York: Weybright and Talley, 1969.

Churchill, Winston

British Statesman

1874–1965

Life and Work

Winston Churchill served in the British government for more than half a century. His firm leadership as prime minister during World War II helped an isolated Britain survive the Battle of Britain and ultimately triumph over Nazi Germany.

Winston Leonard Spencer Churchill was born on November 11, 1874, the son of Lord Randolf Churchill, and the grandson of the Duke of Marlborough. His studies at Harrow and Sandhurst were followed by service in the army. Churchill served in India in 1897, witnessed the Battle of Omdurman in the Sudan in 1898, and in 1899 made a daring escape after being captured during the Boer War in South Africa. He published many articles about his adventures and thereby established a reputation at home. He began his political career in 1900 by winning a seat in Parliament.

In the period before World War I, Churchill sponsored progressive legislation and served as undersecretary for the colonies. As first lord of the admiralty during World War I, his promotion of the disastrous Gallipoli Campaign of 1915 risked jeopardizing his reputation. In the years after the war, he maintained a low profile in government as a Conservative. During the 1930s he became a sharp critic of Britain's diplomatic policy of appeasement of ADOLF HITLER, and denounced Prime Minister Neville Chamberlain's participation in the Munich Conference of 1938. When Britain was finally compelled to go to war in 1939, Churchill's prophetic stance was rewarded with a seat in the government, and in 1940 he was elevated to the office of prime minister.

Churchill's greatest service to Britain was given during World War II. His resolute leadership was desperately needed by a nation that found itself fighting Nazi Germany alone after the fall of France in the summer of 1940. Buoyed by his refusal to enter peace negotiations with Hitler, the Royal Air Force managed to preserve air supremacy in the Battle of Britain during the fall of that year. Churchill honored the pilots, saying "never in the field of human conflict was so much owed by so many to so few." When the Soviet Union and the United States entered the war in 1941 on Britain's side, Churchill helped lead the way to victory. He participated in several war conferences, including the Yalta Conference in early 1945, but losses by his Conservative Party in elections during the spring forced him to resign unexpectedly in the midst of the peace negotiations at Potsdam.

Churchill's most memorable action after the war was an address in 1946 in Fulton, Missouri, where he warned that the Soviet Union had lowered an "iron curtain" across the center of Europe. He held the office of prime minister again between 1951 and 1955. His final years were spent warning of the threat of communism and writing books, including a six-volume history of World War II, for which he was awarded the Nobel Prize for Literature in 1953. Having been knighted in Britain and given honorary citizenship in the United States, he died on January 24, 1965.

Legacy

Winston Churchill left a rich political legacy in Britain, and his defiant resistance during the first years of World War II averted an early victory for Germany.

Churchill's many years as a member of Parliament enabled him to influence legislation and governmental policy. A partnership with David Lloyd George before World War I yielded remarkably progressive social and economic programs, including increased taxes on the wealthy. His leadership as prime minister during World War II, however, is his most important legacy. By keeping Britain unconquered for the year between the fall of France in June 1940 and the German invasion of the Soviet Union in June 1941, he prevented Hitler from achieving an early victory.

Churchill also influenced the early development of the Cold War. During the wartime conferences he assumed a sterner position toward JOSEPH STALIN than the more conciliatory FRANKLIN DELANO ROOSEVELT, and his expressed desire for an invasion through the Balkans rather than western Europe in 1942 increased Stalin's suspicions that the Western allies were unreliable. His aggressive stance toward communism after the war, expressed in his "iron curtain" address, only exacerbated the already tense relationship between the United States and the Soviet Union. Long after his death, Churchill's hostility toward Soviet communism inspired conservative politicians in the West who, rightly or wrongly, feared Soviet expansion in Europe and the world.

Strickland

WORLD EVENTS		CHURCHILL'S LIFE
Germany is united	1871	
	1874	Winston Churchill is born
	1898	Churchill witnesses Battle of Omdurman
	1900	Churchill is elected member of Parliament
Russo-Japanese War	1905	
World War I	1914–18	
	1915	Churchill is discredited by his advocacy of Gallipoli campaign
Russian Revolution	1917	
Great Depression	1929–39	
World War II	1939–45	
	1940	Churchill is appointed prime minister
	1945	Churchill is forced to resign
	1946	Churchill delivers "iron curtain" address
Communist China is established	1949	
	1953	Churchill receives Nobel Prize for Literature
	1965	Churchill dies
Israel defeats Arab nations in Six-Day War	1967	

For Further Reading

Blake, Robert. *Winston Churchill.* Phoenix Mill, England: Sutton, 1998.

Gilbert, Martin. *Churchill: A Life.* New York: Holt, 1991.

Manchester, William Raymond. *The Last Lion: Winston Spencer Churchill.* Two volumes. Boston: Little, Brown, 1983–1988.

Clemenceau, Georges

French Politician and Journalist
1841–1929

Life and Work

During his long career in French politics, Georges Clemenceau shaped the domestic policies of republican France and defined Europe's relationship to Germany between the two world wars.

Clemenceau was born to a staunchly republican family in Mouilleron-en-Pareds (in royalist western France) on September 28, 1841. The son of a doctor, he went to medical school, graduating from the University of Paris in 1862. In 1865, Clemenceau immigrated to the United States, but in 1869 he moved back one year before France, then ruled by Napoléon III, went to war with Prussia, the largest German state at the time.

After Napoléon III's defeat by Prussia, the Third Republic was proclaimed on September 4, 1870. Clemenceau moved to Paris, where he was appointed mayor of the Montmartre district in 1870. Elected to the Chamber of Deputies in 1876, he developed the agenda of the republican left in France. In the Chamber and through the newspaper he founded in 1880 (*La Justice*), Clemenceau developed policies favorable to the working class. He also used his talent as a public speaker to make ferocious attacks on his political opponents, earning the nickname "The Tiger."

Clemenceau's implication in the Panama Scandal (which involved bribery of deputies by the nearly bankrupt promoter of the Panama Canal) allowed his many enemies to unify and defeat him in the elections of 1893. For the next nine years, Clemenceau concentrated on journalism, founding another newspaper, *L'Aurore* (*The Dawn*). He returned to the spotlight when he publicly supported Alfred Dreyfus, a Jewish army officer wrongly accused of spying for Germany and sentenced to a life term on Devil's Island. Dreyfus was eventually proven innocent, and Clemenceau returned to politics.

Elected to the Senate, the upper chamber of the French Parliament, in 1902 and serving as premier from 1906 to 1909, he enacted some of the social reform policies he had supported in the Chamber of Deputies and strengthened ties with Great Britain and Russia against Germany. When World War I began, he at first criticized the government's handling of the war effort. In 1917, at France's weakest point in the war, Clemenceau was appointed premier. He adopted ruthless measures such as arresting those he called "pacifists, defeatists and traitors," and established a virtual civilian dictatorship. He also raised morale by touring the front lines and meeting with troops. His strong leadership pulled France through the final year of the war and to victory in 1918. He presided over the Paris Peace Conference of 1919, arguing for reparations and the demilitarization of the border between Germany and France. Defeated in the 1920 election for president, Clemenceau retired from politics, concentrating on journalism and lecture tours. He died on November 24, 1929, after a career spanning approximately 50 years.

Legacy

Georges Clemenceau's impact was both positive and negative. The republican democracy he championed was adopted by much of Western Europe in the twentieth century; however, his virulent anti-German policy during the Paris Peace Conference contributed, ultimately, to the outbreak of World War II.

During his entire career, Clemenceau considered it his duty to ensure the survival and vitality of the Third Republic. He focused his political energies on issues favorable to workers and left-wing republicans—old age and unemployment insurance, nationalizing the railroads and utilities, rights for labor unions, free public education, and so forth—all designed to

increase the power of the Chamber of Deputies, France's most representative government institution. Some of these policies were enacted before his retirement, even more after his death. These reforms contributed to a stable and prosperous France in the twentieth century.

By contrast, Clemenceau's anti-German policies proved to be a disaster for France. Clemenceau sought to eliminate Germany as a threat by crippling that country militarily and economically. During the 1919 Paris Peace Conference, Clemenceau demanded that Germany take full responsibility for the outbreak of the war, pay steep reparations to France and other Allied countries, and demilitarize the Rhineland, a heavily industrialized region in Germany close to the border with France. Enshrined in the Treaty of Versailles, these demands embittered most Germans and gave ADOLF HITLER a powerful platform from which to denounce the Peace of Paris and prepare Germany for war. Only after World War II did France and Germany form an economic and political alliance from which the European Union has emerged.

Lemoine

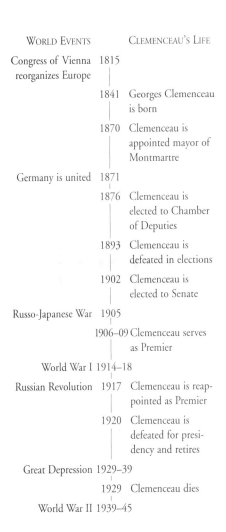

WORLD EVENTS		CLEMENCEAU'S LIFE
Congress of Vienna reorganizes Europe	1815	
	1841	Georges Clemenceau is born
	1870	Clemenceau is appointed mayor of Montmartre
Germany is united	1871	
	1876	Clemenceau is elected to Chamber of Deputies
	1893	Clemenceau is defeated in elections
	1902	Clemenceau is elected to Senate
Russo-Japanese War	1905	
	1906–09	Clemenceau serves as Premier
World War I	1914–18	
Russian Revolution	1917	Clemenceau is reappointed as Premier
	1920	Clemenceau is defeated for presidency and retires
Great Depression	1929–39	
	1929	Clemenceau dies
World War II	1939–45	

For Further Reading
Newhall, David S. *Clemenceau: A Life at War.* Lewiston, N.Y.: Edwin Mellen, 1991.
Watson, D. R. *Georges Clemenceau: A Political Biography.* Plymouth, England: Eyre Methuen, 1974.

Cleopatra VII

Queen of Egypt

69–30 B.C.E.

Life and Work

The last pharaoh, Cleopatra VII preserved Egyptian political and economic independence from direct Roman rule longer than expected. Her defeat brought an end to the 300-year Greek Ptolemaic dynasty in Egypt, introduced Roman imperial rule, and consolidated the rule of Octavian (later called AUGUSTUS) as successor to JULIUS CAESAR.

World Events	Cleopatra VII's Life
	B.C.E.
Overland silk trade between Rome and China begins	c. 121
	69 Cleopatra VII is born
	51 Cleopatra and Ptolemy XIII become co-rulers
Rome's conquest of Gaul completed	50
	48 Cleopatra forced out of Egypt by Ptolemy's faction
	47 Cleopatra forms alliance with Julius Caesar
	46 Cleopatra travels to Rome
	44 Caesar is assassinated; Cleopatra returns to Egypt
	41 Cleopatra meets Marc Antony
	32 Rome declares war on Egypt
	31 Cleopatra and Antony are defeated at Battle of Actium
	30 Antony and Cleopatra commit suicide
Jesus is crucified c. 33 C.E.	

Born in Alexandria in 69 B.C.E., Cleopatra was the daughter of Ptolemy XII Auletes of the Hellenistic, Greco–Macedonian dynasty established by ALEXANDER III (Alexander the Great) 300 years earlier. An intelligent, cultured, and well-educated woman who could speak many languages, Cleopatra learned early from her father the need to manipulate the powerful Romans to maintain Egypt's independence. In Ptolemaic Egypt (of which Alexandria was the capital), daughters of the pharaohs were expected to rule as queens. Cleopatra's father decreed that she rule jointly with her brother, Ptolemy XIII, whom she married at 17 (an ancient Egyptian practice adopted by the Ptolemaic dynasty). However, after taking the throne together in 51, Ptolemy XIII, under the influence of court favorites (companions who often became advisors), drove Cleopatra from power in 48.

At the same time, Rome was embroiled in a civil war. Julius Caesar defeated another Roman leader, Pompey, pursuing him to Egypt. Cleopatra, seeing in Caesar a potential ally, entered his apartments by having herself rolled into a carpet. She convinced Caesar to attack her brother and became Caesar's lover, bearing him a son, Ptolemy Caesarion. In 47 Caesar defeated Ptolemy XIII (who drowned while fleeing a battle) in the Alexandrian War. Cleopatra married her younger brother, now Ptolemy XIV, then traveled to Rome in 46. After Caesar was assassinated in 44, Cleopatra returned to Egypt, murdering her brother–husband so that her son could rule by her side.

Caesar's assassination precipitated a civil war in Rome, pitting the consul Marc Antony against Octavian, a grandnephew whom Caesar had adopted and made his heir. At Tarsus in Asia Minor in 41, Cleopatra met and began a relationship with Antony, bearing him three children. Despite Antony's marriage to Octavia, Octavian's sister, Cleopatra formed an alliance with Antony designed to ensure Egyptian independence and Antony's triumph over Octavian.

In response, Octavian began a propaganda war against Cleopatra in 36, who was portrayed as a "courtesan queen" and a witch. In 32, he publicized a forged will attributed to Antony, purporting to leave all of his wealth to Cleopatra. This incited the Romans to declare war on Egypt. Outnumbered and foiled by Octavian's superior strategy at the Battle of Actium in Greece in 31 (soon after Octavian took Alexandria), Antony

and then Cleopatra committed suicide in 30; Egypt was declared a province of Rome. Octavian's triumph was complete.

Legacy

An ambitious ruler, Cleopatra VII combined political astuteness with her personal charms to save her kingdom; nevertheless, Roman might triumphed and Egypt lost its independence.

Antony and Cleopatra's defeat at Actium marked a turning point in the transformation of Rome from a republic into an empire. Octavian distributed Egyptian treasure to his supporters in Rome, consolidating his victory over Antony and putting an end to the Roman civil wars. Octavian was renamed Augustus, the first emperor of Rome.

Cleopatra was the last pharaoh of an Egyptian monarchy that had lasted 4,000 years. Egypt became a province of Rome, supplying the new empire with agricultural wealth (provided by the Nile River) amounting to approximately five million bushels of grain a year. Rome also took advantage of Egypt's position as a crossroads of trade and culture, situated as it was at the meeting point of three continents—Africa, Asia, and Europe.

Yet Cleopatra, descended from Alexander's Greek general Ptolemy, also provided a model of universal rule that Augustus sought to construct around the Mediterranean. The Hellenistic ideal of peaceful community under one law, which Cleopatra attempted to construct and defend in Egypt, was adopted by Augustus, who adapted the ideal to imperial rule, creating a bureaucracy based in part on the Ptolemaic model. Augustus also adopted the Pharaonic practices of godlike kingship.

Cleopatra's death demoralized the Egyptian people, who lost their independence to foreign rule for the next two millennia. When, in the late third century C.E., the Roman Empire was divided into eastern and western districts, Egypt was administered from Constantinople, the new capital of the East. In 641 it fell under the conquering Muslims spreading out from the Arabian peninsula. Egypt continued to be ruled by succeeding empires until it achieved real independence (from the British) with GAMAL NASSER's coup against the foreign-imposed monarchy in 1952.

Lemoine

For Further Reading

Foreman, Laura. *Cleopatra's Palace: In Search of a Legend.* New York: Random House, 1999.

Foss, Michael. *The Search for Cleopatra.* London: Michael O'Mara, 1997.

Cohn-Bendit, Daniel

Leader of French Student Protest
1945–

Life and Work

Daniel Cohn-Bendit, a prominent leader of the May 1968 student revolts in France, is emblematic of the changes in left-wing politics in the West. Critical of both the status quo of postwar Europe and the traditional communist opposition, Cohn-Bendit has spearheaded the Green movement in Germany and France.

Cohn-Bendit, nicknamed "Danny the Red" both for his red hair and political beliefs, was born in France in 1945 to Jewish parents who had fled Nazi Germany in the 1930s. Although by choice a German national, Cohn-Bendit attended university in France. He majored in sociology at the University of Paris, where he became a student activist late in 1967, protesting against various university policies.

On March 22, 1968, Cohn-Bendit led a demonstration at Nanterre protesting the Vietnam War. The group that emerged, called the "Mouvement du 22 mars" (March 22 Movement) continued its protests, leading to disciplinary action against Cohn-Bendit and five others, which resulted in widespread student revolts. The student revolt in turn sparked a sympathetic national workers' strike, which shut down the French economy for a

number of weeks in May and June. Cohn-Bendit was expelled to Germany by the French government on May 20, 1968.

Opposed both to the conservative government of CHARLES DE GAULLE and the stodgy French Communist Party, Cohn-Bendit proclaimed himself an anarchist. His book, *Obsolete Communism: The Left-Wing Alternative* (1968), called for spontaneous political action to effect radical social and political change, rather than the creation of a vanguard of revolutionaries guiding proletarian revolt, such as was pioneered by VLADIMIR ILICH LENIN in the 1917 Russian Revolution.

In Germany, Cohn-Bendit continued his activism, working for a time as a union organizer of automobile workers and participating in another student movement in 1986. Cohn-Bendit was also one of the founders of the environmentalist German Green Party. He was elected to European Parliament in 1994 by the German Green Party and in 1999 by the French Green Party. In between, in 1996, he served on Frankfurt's city council.

Legacy

Daniel Cohn-Bendit led a student revolt that hastened the end of Charles de Gaulle's era and helped to change social and cultural relations in France and Western Europe.

Although the student revolts that Cohn-Bendit led or participated in operated within a tradition of street protest dating in France from prior to the French Revolution, their impact was felt more in the relations between generations than in the political arena. Young Europeans successfully resisted the discipline and restrictions that had been imposed on previous generations of students. Student revolts remain common in France (large protests occurred in 1986 and 1995), and they are sometimes accompanied by strikes by workers in nationalized sectors such as transportation and utilities.

Through the kind of spontaneous political action Cohn-Bendit favored, much of the youth of Europe continued to challenge their elders and the post–World War II social and political order. The May 1968 revolts contributed to a change in social values toward increased sexual freedom, defense of minorities, and gender equality. They also undermined the authority and legitimacy of government in France and

other European countries, a problem that continues in Europe to the present.

Cohn-Bendit's pioneering efforts on behalf of the fledgling environmental Green Party in Germany and France have resulted in some electoral gains. However, it remains to be seen whether the Green movement effects significant change in European environmental policies. While participating in the European Union's democratic process, Cohn-Bendit continues to challenge the established social and economic order.

Lemoine

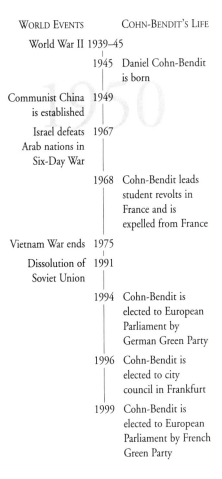

WORLD EVENTS		COHN-BENDIT'S LIFE
World War II	1939–45	
	1945	Daniel Cohn-Bendit is born
Communist China is established	1949	
Israel defeats Arab nations in Six-Day War	1967	
	1968	Cohn-Bendit leads student revolts in France and is expelled from France
Vietnam War ends	1975	
Dissolution of Soviet Union	1991	
	1994	Cohn-Bendit is elected to European Parliament by German Green Party
	1996	Cohn-Bendit is elected to city council in Frankfurt
	1999	Cohn-Bendit is elected to European Parliament by French Green Party

For Further Reading

Caute, David. *The Year of the Barricades: A Journey Through 1968.* New York: Harper & Row, 1988.

Daniels, Robert V. *Year of the Heroic Guerrilla: World Revolution and Counterrevolution in 1968.* New York: Basic Books, 1989

Columbus, Christopher

First European Explorer of
the Americas
1451–1506

Life and Work

By single-mindedly pursuing the goal of finding a westward route from Europe to India, Christopher Columbus inadvertently opened the Americas to European conquest.

On or about September 10, 1451, Cristoforo Colombo was born to a family of wool merchants near Genoa, Italy. Columbus (the Latinized form of his name) turned to the sea early in life, traveling as a teenager to Genoa's colonial possessions in the Mediterranean, the Cape of Good Hope, and, in 1477, to Ultima Thule ("last land," either Iceland or Bristol, England). Although probably skilled in piloting and navigation, Columbus might also have been a master chartmaker, an important skill at the time. In 1478 or 1479, Columbus married well, receiving as a dowry an impressive collection of charts from his seafaring in-laws. These invaluable charts sparked his imagination.

Most learned people since the time of the Greeks and Romans had suspected that the Earth was round, and Arab mathematicians had accurately deduced the circumference of the Earth. However, travel in uncharted waters by ship, especially the relatively small wooden ships of the

day, was a perilous business. From the charts he received in his dowry, however, Columbus guessed that a route, far shorter than around the tip of Africa, must exist to the profitable Spice Islands and India, with which Europeans had only recently begun to trade directly. Throughout the 1480s, Columbus, when not engaged in commercial ventures, tried to find a sponsor for his idea of an expedition westward across the unknown seas to India. Only in 1492 did he find a sponsor in Spain's Queen ISABELLA I.

Queen Isabella ordered the coastal town of Palos to provide Columbus with ships and men for a voyage of exploration. Columbus departed Palos in early August 1492 and reached Watlings, or San Salvador Island, on either October 11 or 12, a voyage of at least 40 days. Columbus landed and took possession of the island and its people, the Guanahaní. He established a small settlement, explored the coasts of Bahamas, Cuba, and Haiti, searched for gold, repaired his vessels, and returned to Spain, arriving on March 4, 1493. Columbus became a European celebrity and was charged by King Ferdinand to return on a second, much larger expedition. In all, Columbus would undertake four voyages.

The second voyage, lasting 1493 to 1496 and funded with money taken from Jews expelled from Spain, traced the outline of Jamaica and Cuba and established a permanent colony in the so-called West Indies. A third voyage, 1498–1500, brought additional colonists to Cuba, but somehow got Columbus in trouble. In a fourth and final voyage, 1502–04, Columbus explored the north coast of Brazil. Until the end of his days, Columbus insisted he had reached India, even if everyone else around him quickly concluded that in fact they had discovered a new land. Columbus died in May 1506.

Legacy

Christopher Columbus unleashed a period of conquest and colonialism by the European nations that lasted almost 500 years and produced some of the greatest triumphs and most terrible moments in human history.

Columbus wanted to reach India and the Spice Islands for one reason: profit. The monopolization of the valuable spice trade by the Arabs and Venetians and the difficulty of traveling around Africa's Cape of Good Hope made looking for a westward route to India a tempting quest, despite the incredible dangers. Columbus recognized that profit alone might not suffice to

find backing for his risky venture. He knew, however, that he might find justification and support for a profit-taking venture in the religious zeal of the Spanish people, who were already busy expelling Jews and Muslims from Spain. He could promise to carry Spain's crusade against nonbelievers to the Indies. Indeed, this zealotry had peaked just as Columbus began his 1492 voyage. In that year, King Ferdinand defeated the remaining Muslims, and the Roman Catholic church's inquisitor-general ordered the conversion or expulsion of Spain's many Jews. In this way, Columbus set a precedent for combining profit and proselytization, by forcing European civilization and the Christian cross on people outside of Europe.

In a larger sense, Columbus sparked an incredible age of discovery, not only of Europeans' discovering the world around them but also of scientific learning. In this environment of discovery, Europeans felt free enough to take risks and could anticipate great rewards if their risks paid off. Shortly after Columbus's death, trade increased enormously between European states and between Europe and the rest of the world. Explorers and early scientists brought back new knowledge of nature and cultures from the New World and Asia and Africa, contributing to a new spirit of investigation, criticism, and, in some cases, toleration for dissent, that had far-reaching social and cultural consequences. It became easier after Columbus to question timeworn religious and philosophical assumptions precisely because so much more evidence had become available to both provoke and support such challenges.

Del Testa

World Events		Columbus's Life
Ming Dynasty reasserts Chinese control of China	1368	
	1451	Christopher Columbus is born
Ottoman Empire conquers Constantinople	1453	
Columbus sails to Americas	1492	Columbus begins first voyage
	1493–96	Columbus engages in second voyage
	1498–1500	Columbus sails on third voyage
	1502–04	Columbus embarks on fourth voyage
	1506	Columbus dies
Protestant Reformation begins	1517	

For Further Reading

Fernández-Armesto, Felipe. *Columbus.* New York: Oxford University Press, 1991.
Rivière, Peter. *Christopher Columbus.* Stroud, England: Sutton, 1998.

Constantine I

First Christian Emperor

c. 274–337

Life and Work

Constantine I (Constantine the Great) ruled the Roman Empire after a century of civil war. By converting to Christianity and building a new capital in the East, he laid the foundation for Rome's successor, the Byzantine Empire.

Constantine (in full Flavius Valerius Constantinus) was born c. 274 in Naissus (in present-day Serbia). He was the oldest son of Constantius, a general in the Roman army, and Helena, an innkeeper's daughter. Helena had converted to the Christian faith and would play an important role in persuading her son to do likewise. When Emperor DIOCLETIAN established the Roman tetrarchy (rule by four men—an emperor in both East and West, and a second-in-command should a replacement be needed) in 293, Constantius was made subordinate to the emperor's joint ruler Maximian in the West. Diocletian retired in 305 and forced Maximian to do likewise. This left the West in the hands of Constantius. During a campaign near York in Britain in 306, however, Constantius died after proclaiming Constantine his successor.

At this point the tetrarchy fell apart, with Maximian returning from retirement and his son Maxentius making claims to power from his position in Rome. In an effort to preserve peace, Constantine married Maximian's daughter, Fausta, in 307. This proved ineffective, however, and in 310 Constantine defeated Maximian in battle and forced him to commit suicide. Maxentius, in order to avenge his father, now issued a challenge from Rome. Marching from Germany, Constantine encountered Maxentius on the Tiber River outside Rome in 312. The same evening he witnessed a vision in the sky that profoundly shaped his subsequent reign. According to one account, a burning cross appeared with the statement *in hoc signo vinces* ("by this sign you will conquer"). Constantine converted to Christianity on the spot and ordered his troops to paint the Greek letters symbolizing the faith on their shields. At the Battle of Milvian Bridge the next day, Constantine was indeed victorious as Maxentius and thousands of his troops were driven into the river and drowned. In 324 Constantine defeated the remaining armies of the tetrarchy and assumed sole rule.

Constantine's most renowned acts as emperor after the Battle of Milvian Bridge were strengthening the Christian faith and establishing a political system that would protect it in the future. To do this he issued his most famous law, the Edict of Milan, in 313. By its terms, the persecution of Christians throughout the empire, which had culminated under Diocletian, was to cease. Furthermore, Christians were for the first time given the legal right to practice their faith. An act of 324 went even further, making Christianity the state religion in all but name. This prepared the way for the Church's first ecumenical council at Nicea in 325, which the emperor presided over himself. Finally, in 330 Constantine dedicated a new capital for the empire, named Constantinople. Built on the site of ancient Byzantium near the Bosphorus straits, the "new Rome" stood at a strategic point between Europe and Asia. Just as important, its Christian architecture symbolized the new goals of Roman statecraft.

Having linked the Roman Empire to Christianity, Constantine died in 337.

Legacy

Constantine I set the Roman Empire on a course of development that would last for centuries. As the state became the protector of the Church, Christianity grew to become Europe's dominant faith.

The Christian statecraft that Constantine pursued after his conversion established a model for subsequent emperors in Constantinople and the rest of Europe. The Edict of Milan had brought an end to nearly three centuries of Christian persecution. In subsequent centuries, Byzantine emperors such as JUSTINIAN I (r. 527–65) would use the resources of the state to preserve and even to help disseminate the faith further. Constantine had set the standard by using the state's resources to build some of Christendom's most important churches. Among these were Saint Peter's Basilica in Rome, the Church of Hagia Sophia in Constantinople, and the Church of the Holy Sepulchre in Jerusalem (over the site where Jesus was said to have been buried). Thereafter, Jerusalem became one of the most important destinations for Christian pilgrimages worldwide. While most of the churches founded under Constantine were ultimately destroyed in their original form, his example would inspire Christian rulers of later centuries to build churches stretching from Spain to Russia.

Constantine's statecraft also facilitated the growth of the Church. The Nicene Council was one of the most important of the early Church's seven ecumenical councils. For the first time, hundreds of bishops were free to gather publicly and make decisions about the unity of doctrine and the threat of heresies such as Arianism (which stated that Christ was not truly God). The Nicene Creed, which was produced by the council, became the standard statement of faith confessed by all believers in the Catholic and Orthodox branches of Christendom. Finally, the freedom of the Church to establish missions and to worship publicly led ultimately to the conversion of millions of people throughout Europe. This proved to be Constantine's greatest legacy and is symbolized by the Orthodox church's later decision to canonize him as Saint Constantine the Apostle–Like.

Strickland

For Further Reading

Eusebius. *Eusebius' Life of Constantine.* Edited by Averil Cameron and Stuart Hall. New York: Oxford University Press, 1999.

Grant, Michael. *The Emperor Constantine.* London: Weidenfeld and Nicolson, 1993.

Jones, A. H. M. *Constantine and the Conversion of Europe.* New York: Collier, 1962.

Pohlsander, Hans A. *The Emperor Constantine.* London: Routledge, 1996.

WORLD EVENTS		CONSTANTINE I'S LIFE
Roman Empire reaches greatest size	117	
	c. 274	Constantine I is born
	305	Diocletian retires
Constantine becomes emperor of Rome	306	Constantius dies, naming Constantine his successor
	310	Constantine defeats Maximian
	312	Constantine converts to Christianity and defeats Maxentius
	313	Constantine issues Edict of Milan
	325	Constantine presides over Council of Nicea
	330	Constantine dedicates Constantinople, new capital of Roman Empire
	337	Constantine dies
Christianity becomes religion of Roman Empire	391	

Cortés, Hernán

Spanish Conqueror of Mexico
1485–1547

Life and Work

Hernán Cortés (also Hernando Cortéz) undertook the daring conquest of the Aztec Empire of Mexico, making Spanish colonization possible, destroying one culture, and creating a new one in its place.

Cortés was born in Medellín, Spain, in 1485. Although little is known of Cortés' early life, some historians believe that he studied law at the University of Salamanca. A *hidalgo* (member of the minor nobility), Cortés sought wealth, status, and power in the New World. In 1504 he sailed to Hispaniola (present-day Haiti and the Dominican Republic) in the Caribbean.

In 1511 he accompanied Diego de Velásquez on his conquest of Cuba. In 1518, Velásquez sent him on an expedition of limited exploration, trade, and Roman Catholic evangelism along the coast of Mexico. Cortés, however, took his small fleet along the coast of Mexico, eventually meeting emissaries of the Aztec ruler, MONTEZUMA II. Learning that the Aztecs possessed large amounts of gold, Cortés decided to head inland (against Velásquez's orders), destroying his fleet to force his reluctant men to follow him.

Forming alliances with the Tlaxcalans and other indigenous enemies of the Aztecs, Cortés marched to Tenochtitlán, the magnificent Aztec capital (present-day Mexico City; its population dwarfed most European cities). In November 1519, Cortés entered Tenochtitlán and took Montezuma hostage for several months.

Velásquez attempted to have Cortés arrested, but Cortés returned to the coast and recruited more men. During Cortés' abscence from Tenochtitlán, Aztec priests and warriors were slaughtered during an Aztec celebration, and Montezuma was killed. Upon returning to Tenochtitlán, Cortés decided to retreat to Tlaxcala, losing many soldiers and much of their plundered gold along the way.

Determined to recapture Tenochtitlán, Cortés spent several months conquering Aztec lands to the east. Meanwhile, smallpox, transmitted by Cortés's men, wiped out much of the Aztec population, contributing to the Spaniards' success. Cortés organized a siege, and in August 1521, the Aztecs surrendered. Tenochtitlán was destroyed.

In 1522, CHARLES V, king of Spain and Holy Roman Emperor, appointed Cortés governor of the new imperial lands. The rest of Cortés' life was spent consolidating his rule and defending his role in the conquest of the Aztecs. Deposed in 1526 by a coalition of his rivals, he traveled to Spain in 1528 to plead his case to the emperor in person. Charles V named him the marquis of the Valley of Oaxaca. He returned to Mexico in 1530, discovering Lower (Baja) California in 1536. He returned to Spain in 1540 and died on his estate near Seville on December 2, 1547.

Legacy

Hernán Cortés' conquest helped to establish the economy and social relations of colonial Mexico; he also destroyed a great civilization and inadvertently introduced devastating European diseases that decimated the indigenous population.

Motivated by a quest for gold and the desire to expand the Christian Empire of Charles V's Spain, Cortés used colonization as the cornerstone of successful conquest. Not finding as much gold as expected, Cortés handed out *encomiendas* (a grant of Amerindians to serve conquistadors) to his troops and founded new communities, which began to transform the culture and social structure of Mexico. His independent, headstrong behavior also prompted the creation of the Council of the Indies, by which the Spanish government sought to control the administration of its new overseas empire. The Kingdom of New Spain was the first colonized territory to obtain a viceroy, whose task was to consolidate, both administratively and territorially, the lands conquered by Cortés.

The momentous contact between two very different cultures produced wide-ranging effects on both societies. One was the rapid decline in the Amerindian population due to European diseases; as much as 90% of the Indian population was wiped out by the end of the sixteenth century. Many of the surviving Indians had European cultural practices imposed upon them: law, technology, and Roman Catholic Christianity. As a result, much of the indigenous culture was destroyed.

Although large deposits of gold were not found, silver was discovered and successfully mined, increasing the money supply in Europe and contributing to a long-lasting inflationary trend in Europe. The introduction of European crops and livestock damaged or destroyed native plant and animal species. The introduction of such crops as tomatoes, beans, potatoes, and maize from the New World to the Old increased the food supply from Ireland to China, providing an increased hedge against famine.

Lemoine

World Events		Cortés' Life
Ottoman Empire conquers Constantinople	1453	
	1485	Hernán Cortés is born
Columbus sails to Americas	1492	
	1504	Cortés sails to Hispaniola
Protestant Reformation begins	1517	
	1518	Cortés begins voyage to coast of Mexico
	1519	Cortés enters Tenochtitlán; takes Montezuma hostage
	1521	Cortés defeats Aztecs
	1522	Cortés is appointed governor of Kingdom of New Spain
Mughal Empire rules in India	1526	
	1528	Cortés returns to Spain; Charles V makes him marquis of Valley of Oaxaca
	1547	Cortés dies in Spain
Ottoman dominance of Mediterranean ends	1571	

For Further Reading
Prescott, W. H. *History of the Conquest of Mexico.* New York: Cooper Square Press, 1999.
Thomas, Hugh. *Conquest: Montezuma, Cortes, and the Fall of Old Mexico.* New York: Simon & Schuster, 1993.

Cromwell, Oliver

Leader of the English Civil War
1599–1658

Life and Work

Oliver Cromwell led the forces of Parliament during the English Civil War.

Cromwell was born in Huntingdon in 1599 to a family that had been enriched by Roman Catholic church lands expropriated by HENRY VIII during the English Reformation. He studied law briefly at Cambridge, and in 1628 he became a member of Parliament. In his thirties he had an intense religious experience that convinced him he was called by God to eliminate the Anglican church's Roman Catholic traditions and to promote greater morality among the people. This form of English Protestantism was known at the time as "Puritanism."

Cromwell felt that the Puritan cause was greatly threatened by King Charles I, who had acceded to the throne in 1625 and who hoped to restore many of the Anglican church's Roman Catholic traditions. In 1640 Cromwell led attacks on the king's religious policies in what is known as the Long Parliament. He also supported the 1641 Triennial Act that would have required the king to summon Parliament every three years. The king resisted, however, and by 1642 the conflict degenerated into the English Civil War (1642–49).

Cromwell immediately distinguished himself as a military leader. At the Battle of Marston Moor in 1644 he defeated a large force of royalists, and, in 1645, he organized a force called the New Model Army, which destroyed the royalist army at Naseby in 1645. In 1647, Charles himself was captured. When Charles refused to accept constitutional limitations on his power, he was publicly beheaded on Cromwell's orders in 1649. England was then declared a commonwealth.

Power, however, remained in the hands of Cromwell, who was named Lord Protector. He promoted Puritanism and suppressed rebellions in Scotland and Ireland. He also declared religious freedom for all but Roman Catholics. In 1653 he accepted an Instrument of Government that both secured his title and assured triennial Parliaments. In practice, however, he chose to rule as a military dictator. He refused the crown, but did appoint his son Richard as successor.

Meanwhile, the English had begun to question the value of the commonwealth. At the time of Cromwell's death in 1658, many were calling for the restoration of the monarchy.

Legacy

Oliver Cromwell was instrumental in destroying the absolute monarchy that had ruled England for centuries. His political actions, however, left a troubled legacy that would not be resolved until the end of the seventeenth century.

Before the seventeenth century, England had been ruled by monarchs who claimed absolute power. Nevertheless, the rising powers of the Parliament, which had played an important role in the sixteenth-century Reformation, presented a political challenge to absolute monarchy. Members of Parliament claimed that the king could not rule without the consent of the people, and that the people's representatives must be regularly convened. During the Restoration (1660–88) following Cromwell's death, this claim was increasingly expressed in demands for a constitution. When Charles II (r. 1660–85) and his brother James II (r. 1685–88) exhibited a renewed commitment to divine right, Cromwell's example of armed opposition was revived. In 1688 a group within Parliament invited Prince William of Orange and his wife Mary (the daughter of Charles II) to come from the Netherlands to replace James. The king, lacking an army, was forced to flee without serious bloodshed. This Glorious Revolution established constitutional monarchy in England. Henceforth, Parliament would be convened regularly and would play the leading role in government.

The Glorious Revolution of 1688 also established Cromwell's model for relations between the church and the state. In the wake of the sixteenth-century Reformation, England had been divided by three main religious parties. Anglicans sought to maintain the religious settlement of ELIZABETH I, Roman Catholics hoped to restore that church's traditions, and Puritans hoped to push toward a more radically Protestant ideal. As Cromwell had realized as Lord Protector, however, conflicts among these parties threatened political stability. He had thus come to believe that religious toleration was necessary to maintain the strength and unity of the country. Protestant leaders of Parliament during the Restoration agreed, especially in light of the fact that the later Stuarts showed a predilection for Roman Catholicism. In fact, it was the Catholic baptism of the male heir in 1688 that immediately provoked an appeal to the Protestants William and Mary. After the Glorious Revolution, religious toleration became a permanent element of the English constitution.

The effects of Cromwell's military campaigns were felt long after the seventeenth century. During the Civil War and afterward, he had used the New Model Army to suppress rebellions in Ireland and Scotland. His actions in Ireland were especially violent, particularly because he regarded the Catholic rebels as enemies of God. After a victorious battle near Drogheda in 1649, he ordered his troops to massacre the town's inhabitants, including every Catholic priest and friar. Memories of Drogheda and other dark moments of English rule would live on among Irish and Scots nationalists for centuries to come.

Strickland

World Events		Cromwell's Life
Ottoman dominance of Mediterranean ends	1571	
	1599	Oliver Cromwell is born
	1640	Cromwell sits in Long Parliament
	1642–49	Cromwell defeats royalists in English Civil War
	1649	King Charles I is executed on Cromwell's orders
	1658	Cromwell dies
Glorious Revolution in England	1688	

For Further Reading

Ashley, Maurice. *The English Civil War.* Rev. ed. Gloucester, England: A. Sutton, 1990.

Gaunt, Peter. *Oliver Cromwell.* Oxford: Blackwell, 1996.

Gregg, Pauline. *Oliver Cromwell.* London: J. M. Dent, 1988.

Cyrus II

Founder of the Persian Empire
c. 600–530 B.C.

Life and Work

Cyrus II (Cyrus the Great) ruled Persia and established an empire that dominated the ancient Near East.

Cyrus was born early in the sixth century B.C., the son of a Persian prince named

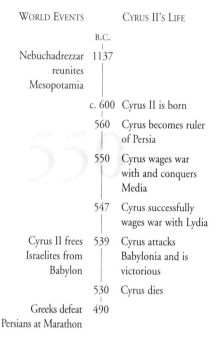

WORLD EVENTS		CYRUS II'S LIFE
	B.C.	
Nebuchadrezzar reunites Mesopotamia	1137	
	c. 600	Cyrus II is born
	560	Cyrus becomes ruler of Persia
	550	Cyrus wages war with and conquers Media
	547	Cyrus successfully wages war with Lydia
Cyrus II frees Israelites from Babylon	539	Cyrus attacks Babylonia and is victorious
	530	Cyrus dies
Greeks defeat Persians at Marathon	490	

Cambyses. At the time Persia was a small kingdom in the region east of the great city of Babylon. Babylon had once been part of the Assyrian Empire, but was now the center of a truncated state called Babylonia. To the north of Babylonia was the more powerful kingdom of Media, and to the west of it the kingdom of Lydia (occupying what is now Turkey).

Ancient sources disagree considerably about the background and youth of Cyrus. One account, favored by Herodotus, claimed Cyrus was the offspring of Cambyses and the daughter of the powerful king of Media, Astyages. Astyages, being warned in a dream that his daughter's offspring would overthrow him, had the infant kidnapped and brought to Media, where he was adopted by a common herdsman and forgotten. After reaching maturity, however, the resentful Cyrus managed to return to Persia, where he claimed his inheritance in 560. Several years later he raised an army and attacked the forces of Astyages, bringing about the downfall of Media in 550.

With Cyrus's expansion westward, conflict with the Lydians was inevitable. In 547 the king of Lydia, Croesus, attacked the Persians with his famous cavalry. Cyrus, knowing that he must destroy this cavalry to win the war, decided to place camels in his front lines. Ancient sources say the Lydian horses were so frightened by the sight of the exotic creatures that they failed to carry their riders, enabling the Persians to win the day. After the collapse of Lydia, Cyrus installed his own government in Asia Minor and turned to new campaigns.

The last remaining challenge to Persian expansion was presented by Babylonia. Its king, Nabunaid, had abandoned the powerful city to campaign against the Egyptians in the west. With the king gone, the Babylonians had come under the administration of a notorious lord named Belshazzar. His drunken orgies and neglect for Babylonian religious rituals such as the festival of the New Year had created deep public resentment. Thus, when the Persian army attacked in 539, it met very little resistance. When Cyrus entered the city of Babylon, he was welcomed as a liberator.

Having conquered the great kingdoms of the Near East, Cyrus was still not satisfied. In 530 he set off on a campaign to the northeast, the goal of which may have been the conquest of nomadic lands on the Eurasian Steppe. Before the end of the year, however, he was killed during a battle with a local tribe.

Legacy

The rise of the Persian Empire influenced the history of the Near East for centuries. In particular, Persian rule brought momentous changes to the Greeks and Jews.

Cyrus II created an empire that had a strong impact on the peoples of the Near East. For the Persians, contact with Mesopotamia resulted in ties that enriched the native language and influenced the development of Zoroastrianism, a religion. In addition, many peoples conquered by Persia were granted religious freedom. In the case of Babylon, Cyrus even ordered the reconstruction of temples that had fallen into disrepair under Belshazzar. Persian rule also recognized the empire's diversity, with administrative positions going to men of non-Persian origin. As a result, the empire played a leading role in near eastern affairs until it was destroyed in the fourth century B.C. by ALEXANDER III.

Cyrus's policy of religious toleration was of special consequence in the case of the Jews. The ancient city of Jerusalem, established in the tenth century B.C. by King DAVID, had been conquered in 586 by the Babylonians under Nebuchadnezzar. With Solomon's Temple burned to the ground, much of the Jewish population had been forced into Babylonian captivity. When Cyrus conquered Babylonia in 539, however, he freed the Jews from the conditions of their exile. Not only were they allowed to return to Jerusalem, they were given funds out of the Persian treasury to begin the reconstruction of the Temple.

Cyrus's rule also had an ominous result. His conquest of Lydia brought Persia into contact with Greek civilization. The Greeks at this time were in the process of building their own empire in Asia Minor, which under PERICLES would constitute a powerful state. Antagonisms between the Greeks and the Persians during the reign of Cyrus were mild, but under his successor, DARIUS I, they would explode into war.

Strickland

For Further Reading

Cook, J. M. *The Persian Empire.* London: J. M. Dent and Sons, 1983.

Dandamaev, Muhammad A., and Vladimir G. Lukonin. *The Culture and Social Institutions of Ancient Iran.* Translated by Philip C. Kohl. Cambridge: Cambridge University Press, 1989.

Olmstead, A. T. *History of the Persian Empire: Achaemenid Period.* Chicago: University of Chicago Press, 1948.

Darius I

Ruler of Ancient Persia
550–486 B.C.

Life and Work

Darius I (Darius the Great) made Persia the largest empire the world had yet known. His rule included the introduction of efficient administrative districts, the construction of roads, and an unsuccessful war with Greece.

The rise of Darius was linked to his marriage with Atossa, the daughter of CYRUS II. Cyrus died in 530 B.C., leaving two sons named Bardiya and Cambyses. The first of these sons died under mysterious circumstances, which allowed Cambyses to rule until his death in 522. However, while Cambyses was still on his deathbed, a usurper by the name of Gaumata rose up in revolt, claiming to be Cyrus's lost son Bardiya. Darius entered the political fray at this point, using the succession crisis to assert his own claim to the throne. Due in part to his marriage, he was able to obtain the support of the Persian nobility and thus defeated the usurper by the end of the year.

Darius's rule was marked by vast military expansion. No sooner had he secured his political position at home than he set off on a campaign to secure the lands of Egypt, which had initially been conquered under Cambyses. In 519 he defeated the pharaoh's armies and incorporated a large part of the ancient kingdom into the Persian Empire. Darius next led

his armies eastward until they reached the Indus River valley, where he built fortresses and consolidated Persian rule. In 514 his army crossed the Black Sea at the Bosphorus Straits using a bridge made of boats. Darius ventured far into eastern Europe, crossing the Danube and seeking battle with the Scythians. He was unable to secure his position, however, and was forced to return to Asia Minor.

Darius's one great mistake was to war with the Greeks. The presence of the Persian Empire in Asia Minor had already exacerbated relations with the Ionian League, an alliance of Greek cities on the Aegean Sea. Gaining the support of powerful Athens, the league revolted against the Persians in 499. Although unsuccessful, this provoked Darius into launching an invasion of the Greek mainland. After an unsuccessful naval voyage in 492, which resulted in shipwreck, the Persians finally landed an army in 490 and forced the Greeks to commit to battle at Marathon. Although the Persians outnumbered the Athenians, they were badly beaten and the survivors were forced to take to their ships and flee back across the Aegean.

An enraged Darius was contemplating yet another invasion of Greece in 486 when he died suddenly.

Legacy

Darius I left behind a powerful Persian Empire. Nevertheless, his military policies set a precedent that ultimately led to disaster.

Many of the reforms and projects of Darius's reign long outlived him. He had a highway called the Royal Road built between the empire's capital Susa and Sardis in Asia Minor, which, along with a canal dug between the Nile and the Red Sea, enabled Persians to increase transportation and communications in subsequent decades. He also introduced a uniform coinage. While some Greeks and Lydians had been using coins issued by civil authorities in the sixth century B.C., Darius was one of the first rulers to mint currency for use in a territory as sprawling as the Persian Empire.

His renovation of the administrative system also strengthened Persian rule. During his reign, Persia was divided into 20 separate provinces ("satrapies"). Each was to provide tribute to the king, offer military service in

time of war, and oversee justice, but in addition regional governors possessed considerable autonomy. One of the strengths of the empire in subsequent centuries was this system of administration, which, when linked to greater communications, allowed Persian rulers to govern their enormous territory more effectively.

Darius also showed himself eager to build palaces and monuments to commemorate his rule. In fact, he is considered to be one of the most historically minded rulers of the ancient world, having made a point of ordering scribes (he was himself illiterate) to produce lists of his campaigns and conquests. The monuments he built, such as the grand palace of Persepolis, not only contributed to the glory of his memory, but survived until modern times as symbols of Persian cultural achievement.

In foreign policy, however, Darius left a destructive legacy. His preoccupation with punishing the Greeks for their defiance of Persia led to similar policies among his successors. In 480, his son Xerxes set out on an expedition to subdue the proud Athenians, and this time the Persian army was devastated. After engagements at Thermopylae and Salamis, the Persian forces were forced to abandon their designs on Greece.

Strickland

For Further Reading

Burn, A. R. *Persia and the Greeks.* New York: St. Martin's Press, 1962.

Cook, J. M. *The Persian Empire.* London: J. M. Dent and Sons, 1983.

Olmstead, A. T. *History of the Persian Empire: Achaemenid Period.* Chicago: University of Chicago Press, 1948.

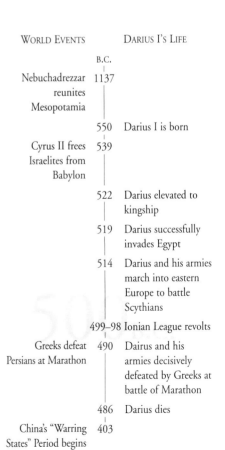

WORLD EVENTS		DARIUS I'S LIFE
	B.C.	
Nebuchadrezzar reunites Mesopotamia	1137	
	550	Darius I is born
Cyrus II frees Israelites from Babylon	539	
	522	Darius elevated to kingship
	519	Darius successfully invades Egypt
	514	Darius and his armies march into eastern Europe to battle Scythians
	499–98	Ionian League revolts
Greeks defeat Persians at Marathon	490	Dairus and his armies decisively defeated by Greeks at battle of Marathon
	486	Darius dies
China's "Warring States" Period begins	403	

David

King of Ancient Israel
c. Tenth Century B.C.

Life and Work

As the greatest king of ancient Israel, David united the Jews and helped to establish the system of religious worship that would shape Jewish life for more than a millennium. All of our knowledge about him comes from the Bible, and there is no consensus among historians about precise dates during which he lived and ruled. It is generally believed that he came to power about 1000 B.C. and ruled for 40 years.

David was born to the family of Jesse and spent his childhood as a shepherd. Although Jesse lived in the obscure town of Bethlehem, his family was selected as the source for a new ruler when Saul, Israel's first king, forfeited his right to rule by neglecting the will of God. According to 1 Samuel, God sent the prophet Samuel to Bethlehem to summon Saul's replacement. Only after Samuel had seen all of Jesse's older sons was David, the youngest, brought forward. The prophet immediately

recognized him as God's chosen ruler and anointed him king on the spot.

David did not begin to rule immediately, however. Saul was naturally loathe to step aside, and so David, who wanted to avoid taking his inheritance by force, humbly assumed a position in Saul's court as a musician. One day when he had accompanied the king out to the battlefield, David demonstrated his valor by defeating an enormous warrior named Goliath in a duel. His victory still did not win the throne, though, and in subsequent years he had to flee Saul's court. Only after Saul died at the battle of Mount Gilboa did David finally take what for several years had rightfully been his.

David's 40-year reign was one of the most momentous periods in the history of the Jews. Not all of Israel's 12 tribes initially recognized David's authority, but under the constant threat of the Philistines and other surrounding peoples, unity was ultimately established. The army was now able to defend the people against invasion and the state was ordered according to Mosaic Law, the laws in the Torah traditionally attributed to Moses. To symbolize these achievements, David established the city of Jerusalem as the capital and had the Ark of the Covenant enshrined within it.

David usually lived a devout life as the God–chosen ruler of Israel, but his seduction of a beautiful married woman named Bathsheba nearly undermined his rule. Having sent her husband to his death in battle, David was confronted by the prophet Nathan and told that his reign would henceforth be scarred by personal misfortune. This was realized when David's son Absalom revolted. These experiences exacted a heavy toll on David, and, reaching the end of life, he sought a successor who would rule more faithfully than he. Before dying, therefore, he called his son Solomon to him and admonished him to rule according to the will of God.

Legacy

David made a major contribution to the development of Judaism and Christianity. His pious statesmanship provided a model for rulers in subsequent centuries.

David's consolidation of a territorial state in Palestine enabled the Jews to build a civiliza-

tion that lasted, with one significant break, until the time of the Romans. Under David's son Solomon, Israel's prosperity reached a high point, and, while later Davidic kings would sometimes rule poorly, the Israelite people began to develop a national self–consciousness that survived political troubles. Thus when Nebuchadrezzar defeated the last Davidic king in 586 B.C., sending the Israelites into the Babylonian captivity, the memory of a national homeland would sustain them until 539, when CYRUS II of Persia allowed them to return. Although physically expelled again by the Romans after the time of Christ, many Jews would continue to regard Palestine as their national homeland. In the nineteenth century A.D. the Zionist movement would be formed by THEODOR HERZL which would result in the foundation of modern Israel in 1948 under King David's namesake, DAVID BEN-GURION.

The religious traditions of Judaism were also deeply influenced by the life of David. David himself contributed to the composition of the Old Testament. Most of the Psalms are attributed to him, and some, such as Psalm 51 (which he wrote after being confronted by Nathan about Bathsheba), reveal the author's deeply religious character. David had been forbidden by God to build a temple in Jerusalem (presumably because of his sins), but Solomon's Temple, built on Mount Zion in Jerusalem during the next reign, established a long tradition of religious ritual and national pilgrimage for the Jews. Thus Jesus, when he conducted his ministry in the first century, centered it upon Jerusalem and the temple.

Finally, Christianity and Christian civilization came to recognize in David the origins of Jesus's family line and a model for religious statecraft. The Gospel of Matthew identifies Jesus as "the son of David," and though Jesus was crucified and did not reestablish the old, worldly kingdom of David, he was recognized by the Apostles as the Messiah who had now established a new, heavenly kingdom. Meanwhile, in medieval Europe political theorists frequently cited David's rule as a model for Christian statecraft. Kings such as CHARLEMAGNE were customarily anointed by a high priest as David had been by Samuel, and they were expected to use their authority to protect the faith.

Strickland

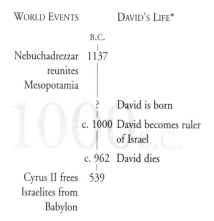

WORLD EVENTS   DAVID'S LIFE*

B.C.

Nebuchadrezzar 1137
reunites
Mesopotamia

? David is born

c. 1000 David becomes ruler of Israel

c. 962 David dies

Cyrus II frees 539
Israelites from
Babylon

* Scholars cannot date the specific events in David's life with accuracy. This chronology is based on the biblical account.

For Further Reading

1 Samuel, 2 Samuel, 1 Kings, 1 Chronicles, Psalms.

Brueggemann, Walter. *David's Truth in Israel's Imagination and Memory.* Philadelphia: Fortress, 1985.

de Vaux, Roland. *Ancient Israel: Its Life and Institutions.* Translated by John McHugh. New York: McGraw Hill, 1961.

Steussy, Marti J. *David: Biblical Portraits of Power.* Columbia: University of South Carolina Press, 1999.

de Beauvoir, Simone

French Philosopher and Feminist
1908–1986

Life and Work

Gifted with a superior intellect, Simone de Beauvoir gradually emerged from the shadow of her life-long companion, the existentialist philosopher Jean-Paul Sartre, to become, by the 1960s, the world's foremost feminist theorist.

Born in Paris in 1908 into a repressive and increasingly impoverished family, de Beauvoir turned inward and toward study as an escape from family troubles. At school, de Beauvoir found she had an unequaled mind for philosophy. Entering the Sorbonne, France's top university, at 16, de Beauvoir took her doctoral exams in 1929 and placed second after Sartre, who took the exams at the same time. (Some suspect that she placed second because her examiners could not tolerate a woman surpassing a man.) De Beauvoir and Sartre became a couple and chose to become teachers to pay for extensive international travel.

Throughout the 1930s, de Beauvoir taught at a *lycee* ("high school") and worked with Sartre on the developing philosophy of existentialism. Although intrigued by its intellectual premises, de Beauvoir never committed herself to existentialism's bleak and pessimistic

tendencies (there is no God, therefore no God-given human nature; man is alone, "condemned to be free"). During the late 1930s and World War II, de Beauvoir began to work on the place of women in society, culminating in her masterwork, *The Second Sex* (1949), an analysis of the status of women. This book revolutionized and reanimated Western feminism by questioning women's inferior position in society and by encouraging women to develop themselves intellectually and politically. "One is not born," she wrote, "but rather becomes, a woman." De Beauvoir became an internationally respected literary figure, a "public intellectual," and an inspiration to millions of women around the world, including Indian Prime Minister Indira Gandhi and Betty Friedan, author of *The Feminine Mystique* (1963). Adding to de Beauvoir's fame was her active participation in France's anti-colonial movement of the late 1940s through 1962, during which time France abandoned its colonies in Indochina and North Africa and granted independence to its sub-Saharan colonies.

During the 1950s and 1960s, de Beauvoir was intellectually productive and began to distance herself somewhat from Sartre and other intellectuals. Beginning with her critical exposé of French intellectual life in *Les Mandarins* (1954), de Beauvoir illuminated, as no one else had done to that point, the meaning and method of women's lives and their relationship to society at large. Although she occasionally lent her support to broader political movements, such as the student revolts of 1968 and the anti–Vietnam War movement, de Beauvoir spent most of her time in scholarly pursuits.

Increasingly withdrawing from public life, de Beauvoir nevertheless remained a profound inspiration to the world's activist feminists of the 1970s. Although deeply associated with Sartre until his death in 1980, de Beauvoir's intellectual achievements began to be taken more and more on their own merits. De Beauvoir died in 1986.

Legacy

Simone de Beauvoir gave the post-war feminist movement a strong and rigorous philosophical basis and inspired women worldwide to seek equality and a higher valuation (and revalorization) of their enormous contributions to society.

Seen in the context of the exclusive, male-dominated intellectual environment existing before World War II, de Beauvoir's intellectual achievements are extraordinary. Often closely linked with Sartre until late in her life, de Beauvoir transcended the open discrimination against women and their intellectual activity to produce a critique of that prejudice—a critique that has remained inspirational to feminists and philosophers to the present day. Her main idea, that society valorized men as normal and that women were therefore "Other," has inspired a wide variety of theoretical and activist philosophies that have had worldwide consequences.

Del Testa

WORLD EVENTS		DE BEAUVOIR'S LIFE
Russo-Japanese War	1905	
	1908	Simone de Beauvoir is born
World War I	1914–18	
Russian Revolution	1917	
	1924	de Beauvoir enters Sorbonne
Great Depression	1929–39	
	1929	de Beauvoir takes doctoral exams
World War II	1939–45	
Communist China is established	1949	*The Second Sex* is published
	1954	*Les Mandarins* is published
Israel defeats Arab nations in Six-Day War	1967	
Vietnam War ends	1975	
	1986	de Beauvoir dies
Dissolution of Soviet Union	1991	

For Further Reading

Bair, Deirdre. *Simone de Beauvoir: A Biography.* New York: Summit Books, 1990.

Brosman, Catharine S. *Simone de Beauvoir* Revisited. Boston: Twayne Publishers, 1991.

De Beauvoir, Simone. *The Mandarins.* Cleveland; New York: World Publishing, 1956.

———. *The Second Sex.* Translated and edited by H. M. Parshley. New York: Knopf, 1953.

Vans, Mary. *Simone de Beauvoir.* London: Sage, 1996.

Debs, Eugene Victor

American Politician and
Labor Activist
1855–1926

Life and Work

By simultaneously promoting democracy and social welfare, Eugene Victor Debs helped the American labor movement through its most difficult period.

On November 5, 1855, Debs was born to immigrant parents of modest means in Terre Haute, Indiana. Debs went to public school through the tenth grade and thereafter studied business at night school. In 1870, Debs found work on the Vandalia Railroad, but was laid off in 1874. Interested in the emerging labor movement, in 1875 Debs joined the Brotherhood of Locomotive Firemen, even though he no longer worked for the railroads. Debs soon became a labor leader, campaigned vigorously for workers in violent 1877 and 1886 railroad strikes, and led the 1888–89 strike against the Burlington-Northern Railroad.

In 1893, Debs formed the influential but short-lived American Railway Union (ARU). He did so in an effort to unite the existing membership of the job-specific railroad unions into a federated association. In its first and last big action, the ARU significantly aided the 1894 national strike against the manufacturer and operator of Pullman sleeping cars. Although the strikes gained widespread sympathy, they lost the strike and seven died during its course. Thereafter, the strikers were extensively black-listed. For supporting the strike, Debs and other labor leaders went to jail for several months for violating a blanket federal injunction against strikes on the nation's railways.

Angered by the bitter strike, Pullman's victory, and his politically motivated imprisonment, in 1897 Debs joined the Socialist Party, seeing it as a way to unite labor reform with political action. Debs's Socialist Party was about populism, or social welfare politics, even if his enemies said his membership indicated Debs's support for violent social revolution. Beginning in 1900, while continuing to support labor activism in many forms, Debs was the Socialist Party's candidate for president. Between 1900 and 1920, Debs would run unsuccessfully five times, but was an increasingly popular candidate. During World War I, Debs supported the sometimes violent International Workers of the World, a popular federative union. In 1918, in retaliation for that support, the federal government sentenced Debs to 10 years in prison for sedition. During the 1920 election, Debs garnered almost a million votes from his jail cell as a presidential candidate. Although still active in labor politics after a 1921 presidential pardon gave him his freedom, Debs was increasingly unwell, and died on October 20, 1926.

Legacy

Eugene Debs's influential amalgam of democracy, collective unity, and labor rights pushed forward the cause of labor reform and made him more effective than any other American labor leader before or since.

Early in his professional life, Debs recognized that the American labor movement suffered from a profound lack of unity despite the strength of its many profession-specific unions. His ability to unify these groups into one coherent force galvanized the labor movement and forever altered it. Debs realized that laborers had great power to make employers respond to their needs if they acted together. Beginning with the 1886 strike and his American Railway Union, Debs strove for reform through unity. Unlike other labor leaders, Debs mixed his quest for reform with support for the United States government, thereby casting labor activism in the United States as a patriotic act. He reached out to millions of workers through speeches and meetings, and could push a labor dispute in workers' favor just by his mere presence.

In addition, Debs tried to unify all workers by bridging the vast racial, ethnic, and religious divides of late nineteenth century America, even if most workers were culturally unprepared for such unity. Because of Debs, America's new industrial employers and employees began to sit down as equal partners in labor negotiations, and labor became a powerful, unified movement.

Debs is partly responsible for the American labor movement adopting, unlike its revolutionary and sectarian European and Asian cousins, a vigorously pro-country, pro-capital stance during the twentieth century. This attitude resulted, up until the 1970s, in a successful and powerful labor movement that was never seriously at odds with American government or business. Debs's formulation ensured, for the most part, a stable work environment in exchange for economic prosperity. However, the American labor movement never entirely overcame its profession-specific structure or racial prejudices, which limited its social effectiveness. In addition, Debs failed to carry his successes in the labor movement forward into the political realm, because socialism was seen as anti-individual and therefore anti-American. Without a leader such as Debs, the American labor movement became politically quiescent and bureaucratized and lost membership, a state from which it has only just begun to recover.

Del Testa

World Events		Debs's Life
Congress of Vienna reorganizes Europe	1815	
	1855	Eugene Victor Debs is born
Germany is united	1871	
	1875	Debs joins Brotherhood of Locomotive Firemen
	1888–89	Debs leads strike against Burlington-Northern Railroad
	1893	Debs forms American Railway Union
	1897	Debs joins Socialist party
	1900	Debs runs for U.S. presidency
Russo-Japanese War	1905	
World War I	1914–18	
Russian Revolution	1917	
	1918	Debs is sentenced to prison for sedition
	1926	Debs dies
Great Depression	1929–39	

For Further Reading

Ginger, Ray. *Eugene V. Debs: A Biography.* New York: Collier Books, 1970.

Salvatore, Nick. *Eugene V. Debs: Citizen and Socialist.* Urbana/Chicago: University of Illinois Press, 1982.

de Gaulle, Charles

French Politician and Military Leader
1890–1970

Life and Work

World War II war hero Charles de Gaulle guided post–war France to political stability and leadership in Europe.

Born in Lille, in northern France, on November 22, 1890, to a family with a long history of military service, de Gaulle enlisted in the army in 1909, entering the prestigious military academy of Saint–Cyr the following year. As a lieutenant, de Gaulle fought in World War I, was wounded three times, and was captured by the Germans in 1916. Despite repeated attempts to escape, he remained a prisoner of war until 1918.

After the war de Gaulle studied military strategy at the Ecole Superieure de Guerre. In his lectures and books, he advocated a highly mobile military made up of professionals, a proposal that went against the established orthodoxy, which emphasized a defensive strategy. Promoted to general early in World War II, de Gaulle was given command of the tank brigade of the Fifth Army. German forces, using a mobile strategy favored by de Gaulle, defeated French forces in three weeks. A new government headed by Marshal Pétain collaborated with Germany, ceding three-fifths of France to Germany. De Gaulle, refusing to concede defeat, fled to Great Britain, where he organized a government–in–exile, the Free French Forces.

De Gaulle entered Paris at the head of the liberation forces in August 1944.

At first leader of the post–war provisional government, he resigned in 1946 because of disagreements over the new constitution. He formed a new party, "Rally of the French People," and built up a following, but stayed out of formal politics until 1958. In that year France faced a strong independence movement in Algeria, one of its oldest and most important colonies. De Gaulle was asked to form a government to resolve the crisis. He abolished the constitution of the Fourth Republic. The new constitution of the Fifth Republic, still in force, gave greater powers to the president, especially in foreign affairs. In 1962 de Gaulle granted independence to Algeria and France's other colonies, and survived assassination attempts by army officers disgruntled by the loss of Algeria.

In the next 10 years, de Gaulle defied the United States on many issues. He pulled French forces out of the North Atlantic Treaty Organization (NATO, the group of Western powers united to prevent the spread of communism after World War II) in 1966, developed a nuclear weapons and energy program, and increased economic cooperation with West Germany and the Common Market in an effort to unify Europe against U.S. economic, political, and military power. In May 1968 student and worker uprisings threatened his power, but an upsurge of support saved his administration. In 1969, a referendum he proposed—Senate reforms and regional decentralization— failed at the polls. He retired shortly thereafter, and died on November 9, 1970.

Legacy

Charles de Gaulle, in part because of his leadership in World War II, brought stability to the French political system after the war, repositioned France from a colonial power to an ally of Third World nations, and ensured that France would play a leading role in unifying European political and economic institutions.

In France, de Gaulle, who firmly adhered to the democratic and republican ideals of the Revolution of 1789, combined the principles of the Revolution with the equally firm tradition of a strong executive authority. This brought a stable framework for French political culture that has lasted to the present.

In colonial matters, de Gaulle came to realize that France had to relinquish its empire and renegotiate its relationship with the new post–colonial nation–states. As a military man and war hero, he was one of the few French politicians who had the legitimacy to grant Algeria its independence in 1962. The process of decolonization largely complete by the late 1960s, de Gaulle developed the policy of support for Third World countries against the perceived imperialistic intentions of the United States so that France would not lose influence among its former territories.

De Gaulle believed in the idea of French grandeur, which promoted France as an international presence beyond its actual economic and military power. His ultimate goal was to unify Europe from the Atlantic to the Ural Mountains in Russia, with France playing a leading role, and to weaken United States influence in Europe. Simultaneously, he supported the United States without reservation against the communist regimes in Eastern Europe. France's combination of support and independence in its foreign policy relationship with the United States also continues to the present.

Lemoine

WORLD EVENTS		DE GAULLE'S LIFE
Germany is united	1871	
	1890	Charles de Gaulle is born
Russo-Japanese War	1905	
World War I	1914–18	
	1916	De Gaulle is captured by German forces
Russian Revolution	1917	
Great Depression	1929–39	
World War II	1939–45	
	1940	De Gaulle forms French government-in-exile movement
	1944	De Gaulle returns as provisional leader
	1946	De Gaulle resigns from government
Communist China is established	1949	
	1958	De Gaulle returns to leadership
	1966	De Gaulle pulls France out of NATO
Israel defeats Arab nations in Six-Day War	1967	
	1969	De Gaulle resigns
	1970	De Gaulle dies
Vietnam War ends	1975	

For Further Reading
Lacouture, Jean. *De Gaulle*. Translated by Patrick O'Brien. 2 vols. New York: Norton, 1990–1991.
Mahoney, Daniel J. *De Gaulle: Statesmanship, Grandeur, and Modern Democracy*. Westport, Conn.: Praeger, 1996.

de Gouges, Olympe

French Political Thinker
1748–1793

Life and Work

Using her fame and commitment to individual liberties, Olympe de Gouges applied the opportunities presented by the French Revolution to campaign for the rights of women.

Olympe de Gouges was born Marie Gouze in Montauban, a town near Toulouse, France, in 1748. Gouze, unlike many of her female peers, received an elementary education in a school run by the Ursuline religious order. At home she spoke Occitan, a romance language spoken in southern France, and, as for many people of the time, French was always a second language.

Gouze's life might have progressed like that of most provincial middle-class women of the time, dominated by marriage, childbearing, and housekeeping. In 1765, against her wishes, Gouze was married to a man she detested, a minor bureaucrat. In 1766, he died during a massive flood of Montauban, but Gouze apparently felt no regrets. She soon fell in love with a wealthy man whose family had a large stake in the transport of military materiel; she followed him to Paris in 1768. Although they did not marry, Gouze received a large annual stipend from him for the rest of her life.

In Paris, Gouze changed her name, in a fashion typical for someone seeking a higher station in life at the time, to de Gouges, giving her simultaneously pretensions to aristocratic and French birth (as opposed to poor and Occitan). She lived the good life, had many affairs, and mixed with people at the peaks of literary, political, and philosophical society. After 1784, de Gouges became involved in the theater, both as an actress and as a playwright. Although a fair actress, it was her plays that made her increasingly well known, especially her 1789 *l'Esclavages des Noirs, ou la Naufrage* (*Slavery of the Blacks, or, the Shipwreck*) a play dealing with the moral problems of slavery.

In 1788, de Gouges began writing political tracts, usually dealing with a need to moderate political extremism while achieving political reforms. After the French Revolution of 1789, de Gouges continued to celebrate moderate reforms through tracts, short plays, and essays, becoming one of the most celebrated female revolutionary writers of the time. Her popularity peaked in 1791 with an essay presented to the National Assembly entitled "*Esprit Français, ou Problème à resoudre sur le labyrinthe de divers complots*" ("The French Spirit, or a Problem to Resolve in Regards to the Maze of Many Plots"), although she is more famous for her September 1791 *Declaration of the Rights of Women.*

Beginning in 1791, de Gouges, building on her popularity and the greater public presence permitted women in the wake of the revolution, began to take more activist stands on issues of the day. She organized women to support or challenge, for example, the imprisonment of certain aristocrats and religious figures, attacks on protesters by the police, and other causes. In 1792, de Gouges made a fatal mistake in plastering Paris with posters denouncing MAXIMILIEN ROBESPIERRE, leader of the most radical faction of the National Assembly and instigator of the Terror (the name given to an effort to purge France of potential enemies of the revolution, that is, of Robespierre).

On July 22, 1793, Robespierre's Committee of Public Safety ordered the imprisonment of de Gouges. This was done in the context of a France under siege at every border and along all its coasts, where such punishment assuaged a real panic among the revolutionary government. In October, the committee charged her with writing against the sovereignty of the people and condemned her to death.

De Gouges was executed by guillotine on November 2, 1793.

Legacy

Olympe de Gouges made women's rights synonymous with revolutionary rights, a union of ideas that has endured since 1789.

As a rich, widowed actress who kept many lovers and moved comfortably between the worlds of art and politics, de Gouges went against many of the social norms of her day in revolutionary Paris. Women in the Paris of the 1780s often took sides politically or supported the French Revolution. However, very few women had the status and credentials of de Gouges. In her lifetime, de Gouges gained a reputation as an ardent supporter of particular issues that revolved around liberty, especially for women and slaves, and she became well known for her careful use of the language of the Enlightenment as a tool for promoting the rights of women. De Gouges called upon the revolutionary government to live up to its promises of liberty and justice for all by extending these promises to *all* of the French. However, telling revolutionary leaders what to do became increasingly dangerous, especially when the Terror began in 1793 and no outspoken citizen was safe from the "Republican Razor."

After her death, de Gouges became a symbol of an early call for women's rights. Her *Declaration of the Rights of Women* mimicked the French Revolution's *Declaration of the Rights of Man and Citizen*, which guaranteed all citizens of France rights to "liberty, property, security, and resistance to oppression." In the context of a Europe that tended to deny equal rights to women and revolutionary movements that tended to codify this denial and give it legal form, through the *Declaration of the Rights of Women* de Gouges bravely asked the French Revolution to follow through on its promises. As with many subsequent revolutions (and female revolutionaries), however, women's rights were neglected or forgotten when women's physical support was no longer needed. Indeed, it took women like SIMONE DE BEAUVOIR, BETTY FRIEDAN, and GLORIA STEINEM to keep activism alive in the face of conservative reactions to women's rights movements in the twentieth century.

Del Testa

WORLD EVENTS		DE GOUGES'S LIFE
English seize Calcutta	1690	
	1748	Marie Gouze is born
	1768	Gouze moves to Paris; while in Paris she changes name to Olympe de Gouges
United States declares independence	1776	
	1784–89	de Gouges dedicates herself to acting and playwrighting
French Revolution begins	1789	
	1791	de Gouges publishes *Rights of Women*
	1793	de Gouges is executed
Latin American independence movement begins	1811	

For Further Reading

Godineau, Dominique. *The Women of Paris and Their French Revolution.* Translated by Katherine Streip. Berkeley: University of California Press, 1998.
Kelly, Linda. *Women of the French Revolution.* London: Hamish Hamilton, 1987.

de Klerk, Frederik Willem

South African Political Leader
1936–

Life and Work

Frederik Willem de Klerk used an impeccable legal career and high social and political position to force white South Africa to end apartheid (formalized racial separation).

Born March 18, 1936, de Klerk enjoyed a privileged upbringing in South Africa, both because of his father's position as a leading politician and as a white person in a country divided by race. He studied at the conservative Pochestroom University, where he received a law degree with honors in 1958. Throughout his secondary and undergraduate education, de Klerk participated in pro-Afrikaner politics as a member of the student wing of the National Party.

After practicing law, de Klerk resumed his participation in politics with the National Party, which had been responsible for tightening South Africa's apartheid laws in 1948. Elected as a member of Parliament in 1972, de Klerk served as minister of various governmental bureaus. In 1986, he was elected as the leader of the House of Assembly. He became the chairman of the provincial committee of the National Party in Transvaal after 1982. Throughout these years, de Klerk focused on the welfare of blacks while not challenging the core of apartheid.

South African President P. W. Botha had a stroke in January 1989 and relinquished the chairmanship of the National Party; the National Party elected de Klerk as its leader in January. He successfully opposed the return of Botha to the presidency and was formally elected president in September. De Klerk immediately accelerated a process of taking South Africa beyond the apartheid system that Botha had begun in 1984 at the start of his term as president. Beyond a belief in improved and equitable white–black relations, de Klerk moved to eliminate apartheid in South Africa because of the economically crippling international embargo on South African goods, a growing threat of guerrilla warfare over apartheid emanating from Namibia, and, after the fall of the Berlin Wall, the disappearance of any threat of Soviet-sponsored communist insurrection among blacks.

In 1990, de Klerk began a series of talks with representatives of the four so-called designated races: whites, blacks, coloureds (mixed-race people), and Asians (essentially Indians). Also in that year, de Klerk ordered the release of all political prisoners, including NELSON MANDELA, and lifted the ban on the African National Congress (ANC) and Pan-African Congress. In 1991, despite right-wing opposition led by the Conservative Party, de Klerk's National Party passed legislation ending laws that discriminated against blacks in health, education, employment, and public amenities.

In 1992, along with Mandela and other black leaders, de Klerk proposed a new constitution that would allow for majority politics, that is, an equal vote for all voters. It aimed at preventing the recent violence between rival power blocs such as the ANC and the Inkatha Freedom Party. In April 1994, the ANC gained a majority in the House of Assembly, and de Klerk joined Mandela's government as its second deputy president.

De Klerk, along with Mandela, was awarded the Nobel Prize for Peace in 1993. He retired from politics in 1997.

Legacy

With a preference for political moderation and with a real desire to make South Africa a functional, multiracial country, Frederik de Klerk provided the political impetus to end apartheid in South Africa.

In 1989, South Africa's white leadership had only two choices: a severe tightening of oppression or a complete relaxation and reconfiguration of the white-dominated state. Given that South Africa might fall into total anarchy if the conflict between whites and blacks continued, de Klerk, mustering all of his carefully built political support, decided to free South Africa from the noose that was choking both blacks and whites to death and to try the approach of accommodation and cooperation.

While de Klerk's actions ended political separation, they could not end the economic divide between the races. De Klerk knew that in a political and economic system the majority may rule, but it must accommodate itself to the minorities who support it. That is why de Klerk decided to turn to moderate leaders such as Nelson Mandela for reform, rather than letting time and frustration bring other, more radical, leaders to the fore. Although South Africa still has many problems, they remain the problems of working on equality rather than enforcing domination.

Del Testa

WORLD EVENTS	DE KLERK'S LIFE
Great Depression 1929–39	
	1936 Frederik Willem de Klerk is born
World War II 1939–45	
Communist China is established 1949	
Israel defeats Arab nations in Six-Day War 1967	
	1972 de Klerk is first elected to Parliament
Vietnam War ends 1975	
	1986 de Klerk becomes leader of House of Assembly
	1989 de Klerk is elected president
	1990 de Klerk orders release of South African political prisoners
Dissolution of Soviet Union 1991	
	1993 de Klerk is named co-recipient of Nobel Prize for Peace
	1997 de Klerk retires from politics

For Further Reading
De Klerk, F. W. *The Last Trek: A New Beginning: The Autobiography.* London: Macmillan, 1998.
Welsh, Frank. *A History of South Africa.* London: HarperCollins, 1998.

Deng Xiaoping

Leader of China, 1978–1997

1904–1997

Life and Work

Deng Xiaoping was the most important leader of China following the death of MAO TSE-TUNG.

Deng was born Deng Xiansheng in China's southwest province of Sichuan on August 22, 1904. He attended high school in the provincial capital of Chongqing, and in 1920 he took the unusual step of traveling to France, both to work and to study. Disillusioned, he joined the Communist Youth League. Increasing police harassment in Paris prompted Deng to go to Moscow in 1926. In Soviet Russia Deng attended Sun Yat-sen University and officially joined the Chinese Communist Party (CCP), changing his first name to Xiaoping ("Little Peace").

Deng returned to China late in 1926 to participate in an ongoing revolution being waged by an alliance between the CCP and the nationalist Kuomintang Party (KMT). The alliance fell apart the following year when CHIANG KAI-SHEK, leader of the KMT, led an attack on CCP members. Deng continued to work for the CCP in the 1920s and 1930s, rising to increasingly important positions and participating in the Long March (1934–35), a trek undertaken by Chinese communists that saved the movement from destruction by the KMT. From 1937 to 1945, during the war against the Japanese occupation, Deng worked as a political commissar of communist armies. In 1945 he was elected member of the CCP Central Committee.

At the end of the civil war between the CCP and the KMT, which resulted in the triumph of the Communist Party in China in 1949, Deng was firmly associated with CCP leader Mao Tse-tung. Deng was appointed secretary-general of the Central Committee in 1954, vice premier in 1954, and member of the Politburo of the Central Committee in 1955. He at first supported Mao's Great Leap Forward (1958–60), which stressed steel production and collectivized agriculture. When millions died in the resulting famine, Deng stifled Mao's influence.

Mao returned to power when he launched the Cultural Revolution in 1966. Deng was criticized as a "capitalist roader" who was betraying the communist revolution. In 1967 he was removed from all party appointments; in 1970 he was sent to be "re-educated" by working in a factory. Recalled in 1973, only to be arrested again following massive demonstrations against the Cultural Revolution in 1976, Deng was definitively reinstated in 1977, after Mao's death in 1976.

In 1978 Deng, now chief party leader, began reforms designed to increase economic growth and international trade. He focused on the "Four Modernizations" (in agriculture, industry, science and technology, and defense). Collective farms were phased out and free trade was allowed to expand. China's economy grew enormously in the 1980s and 1990s.

However, Deng was not prepared to allow much political or cultural liberalization, which might have undermined the CCP's monopoly of power. In 1989, troops violently suppressed pro-democracy student demonstrations in Beijing's Tiananmen Square and elsewhere. After 1989, Deng went into semi-retirement, resigning from all posts in 1990. He continued to advise his successors until his death on February 19, 1997.

Legacy

Deng Xiaoping guided Communist China away from Mao's radical reforms toward more pragmatic economic policies. However, the lack of corresponding political reforms threatens to hamper future economic growth and create uncontrollable nationalism.

Deng's economic reforms increased the wealth of many ordinary Chinese. However, inequalities of wealth emerged between the predominantly rural interior and the coastal cities where much international trade was conducted. Other problems emerged as the economy outgrew the country's financial, judicial, and administrative institutions, and strained its environment. It became increasingly clear that the CCP could no longer completely control economic development in China.

The Communist Party had better success repressing demands for political liberalization. Deng feared that if the CCP sanctioned a more open political culture, communism in China could possibly suffer the same fate as the now-dissolved Soviet system.

Deng oversaw the transformation of Communist China from a heavily-politicized, inward-looking nation, into one that has opened itself to international trade and cultural contacts. Paradoxically, the rise of the Chinese economy and the increase in per capita income has accompanied a rise in nationalism, as China began to assert itself in the sphere of international geopolitics, especially in its relations with the United States.

Lemoine

WORLD EVENTS		DENG'S LIFE
Germany is united	1871	
	1904	Deng Xiaoping is born
Russo-Japanese War	1905	
World War I	1914–18	
Russian Revolution	1917	
	1926	Deng joins Chinese Communist Party
Great Depression	1929–39	
World War II	1939–45	
	1945	Deng is elected to CCP Central Committee
Communist China is established	1949	
	1955	Deng is elected to Politburo
Israel defeats Arab nations in Six-Day War	1967	Cultural Revolution; Deng is criticized
Vietnam War ends	1975	
	1977	Deng becomes leader of China
	1989	Deng orders suppression of Tienanmen Square protests
	1990	Deng resigns
Dissolution of Soviet Union	1991	
	1997	Deng dies

For Further Reading

Evans, Richard. *Deng Xiaoping and the Making of Modern China.* New York: Viking Penguin, 1997.

Yang, Benjamin. *Deng, A Political Biography.* Armonk, N.Y.: M. E. Sharpe, 1998.

Diocletian

Roman Emperor

c. 243–312

Life and Work

Diocletian rescued the Roman Empire from civil war and enacted administrative reforms that enabled it to survive for another century.

Diocletian (in full, Gaius Aurelius Valerius Diocletianus) was born with the name Diocles in Illyricum, a region of the Roman Empire located on the Balkan peninsula. He entered the Roman army and advanced to the rank of general within a relatively short time. In 284 he was accompanying the imperial entourage as it approached the city of Nicomedia when Emperor Numerian, who had come to power only the previous year, was murdered by Aper, a general in the elite Praetorian Guard. Aper's intention was to seize control of the empire himself, an act consistent with the character of Roman politics for nearly a century. On this occasion, however, the assassin was seized and a hastily convened military council decided to make Diocles emperor instead.

Diocles now assumed the name Diocletian and, after defeating the army of a rival named Carinus at the Battle of Margus River in 285, he was able to claim the most important symbol of imperial rule, the title of Augustus. He realized, however, that the civil wars and assassinations dominant in Roman politics must be prevented if he was to retain power. His first act as emperor was therefore to alter the administration of the empire. In 286 he bestowed the title of Augustus upon a comrade named Maximian and gave him jurisdiction in the west. In 292 he added a third man, subordinate to himself and Maximian, with his own territory to administer, creating a system of government known as the tetrarchy. The new administrative system enabled the government to respond more rapidly in times of crisis, and thus helped Roman armies defeat the barbarians in 290 and the Persians in 298.

Diocletian's interest in strengthening the state also led him to issue laws about economic and religious life. To increase tax revenue, a census was conducted in 294 and the tax system revised. Innovative price controls on foods and services were introduced, though with mostly disappointing results. Finally, believing that state loyalty demanded allegiance to Rome's official forms of paganism, Diocletian launched a massive persecution of the Christian church in 303.

Satisfied that he had secured a lasting future for the Roman Empire, Diocletian retired from office in 305. He spent the remainder of his life in his native region of Illyricum, where he built a palace on the Adriatic Sea. He died in 312.

Legacy

Diocletian's rule enabled the Roman Empire to restore control over sprawling territories in Europe, Asia Minor, and Africa. His persecution of the Christian church, however, failed to have the desired effect.

Diocletian ended the civil wars that had weakened Roman government since the death of MARCUS AURELIUS. Much of the intervening period had been dominated by what historians call the "barracks emperors," unprincipled military adventurers who used bribery and murder to secure power. These emperors were often overthrown by violence in turn, and, during the 50 years that preceded Diocletian no fewer than 20 emperors succeeded one another. Diocletian's policies restored security to the office of the emperor, and, while assassination did not disappear, in later years its role in shaping the political system was greatly diminished.

Diocletian's most celebrated act of statecraft was the creation of the tetrarchy. By the end of the third century the Roman Empire possessed vast territories that were extraordinarily difficult to administer and defend. Since the time of AUGUSTUS these had usually been ruled from the traditional capital of Rome, and, although a few emperors had experimented with employing joint rulers, policy decisions and military leadership often depended upon the activities of an emperor residing in that city. Diocletian's tetrarchy offered a solution to the problems of ruling the vast territories. It not only divided the empire into western and eastern halves, but included reforms designed to strengthen the emperor's control over them. Provincial governors, who had often supported the rebellions of the third century, now found their military powers greatly reduced. A new administrative unit called a diocese was introduced that gave the emperor more control in raising armies and collecting revenue. In subsequent years, these administrative reforms strengthened the empire and enabled it to withstand the assaults of enemies on the northern and eastern frontiers.

Some of Diocletian's actions, however, had unintended results. The tetrarchy itself, for instance, came to have a long-term weakening effect upon the imperial administration. Diocletian always maintained unrivaled authority over the entire empire, but by assuming direct control only of its eastern half and residing in the city of Nicomedia there, Rome and the western half of the empire began to decline in status. The decline was encouraged by Diocletian himself, who visited the traditional capital for the first time only in 303. The empire's next great emperor, CONSTANTINE I, would formalize this development by building a new capital in the east called Constantinople.

Diocletian's aggressive religious policies also failed to unify the empire. His persecution of the Christian church after 303 was one of the most brutal in the history of ancient Rome and resulted in the martyrdom of thousands of believers. However, the persecution not only failed to diminish the strength of Christianity, it may have elevated Christianity's status among many of the common people. What is more, with the conversion of Emperor Constantine himself only a decade later, it proved to be the last major persecution of the Christians in Europe until the rise of regimes such as that of VLADIMIR ILICH LENIN in modern times.

Strickland

For Further Reading

Barnes, Timothy. *The New Empire of Diocletian and Constantine.* Cambridge, Mass.: Harvard University Press, 1982.

Ricciotti, Giuseppe. *The Age of the Martyrs: Christianity from Diocletian to Constantine.* Translated by Anthony Bull. Milwaukee, Wis.: Bruce, 1959.

Williams, Stephen. *Diocletian and the Roman Recovery.* London: B. T. Batsford, 1985.

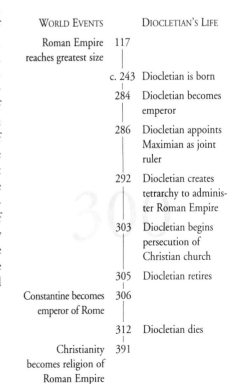

WORLD EVENTS		DIOCLETIAN'S LIFE
Roman Empire reaches greatest size	117	
	c. 243	Diocletian is born
	284	Diocletian becomes emperor
	286	Diocletian appoints Maximian as joint ruler
	292	Diocletian creates tetrarchy to administer Roman Empire
	303	Diocletian begins persecution of Christian church
	305	Diocletian retires
Constantine becomes emperor of Rome	306	
	312	Diocletian dies
Christianity becomes religion of Roman Empire	391	

Disraeli, Benjamin

British Politician and Leader
of the Conservative Party
1804–1881

Life and Work

British politician and novelist Benjamin Disraeli transformed the Conservative Party in Great Britain into a mass party, ensuring its survival into the twentieth century.

Born in London, December 21, 1804, the eldest son of a Jewish family, Disraeli was baptized as an Anglican at his father's behest. Disraeli did not attend university; he was tutored in law and became a clerk in an attorney's office in London in 1821. Although Disraeli was a very ambitious social climber and aspiring writer, success eluded him in the early years; he was beset by poor health and financial problems. Through contacts he cultivated in London's high society, Disraeli began a career in politics that would last until 1880.

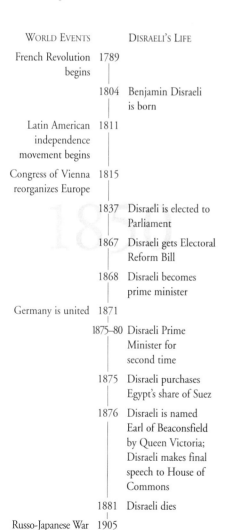

World Events		Disraeli's Life
French Revolution begins	1789	
	1804	Benjamin Disraeli is born
Latin American independence movement begins	1811	
Congress of Vienna reorganizes Europe	1815	
	1837	Disraeli is elected to Parliament
	1867	Disraeli gets Electoral Reform Bill
	1868	Disraeli becomes prime minister
Germany is united	1871	
	1875–80	Disraeli Prime Minister for second time
	1875	Disraeli purchases Egypt's share of Suez
	1876	Disraeli is named Earl of Beaconsfield by Queen Victoria; Disraeli makes final speech to House of Commons
	1881	Disraeli dies
Russo-Japanese War	1905	

In 1837 he was elected to Parliament as a member of the Conservative Party (Tories), which represented the interests of large landowners. Disraeli joined Young England, an informal group of Tories who criticized free trade and liberalism and expressed a paternal concern for the plight of the working class. He elaborated his ideas in three political novels, *Coningsby* (1844), *Sybil* (1845), and *Tancred* (1847).

In Parliament, Disraeli broke with the Conservative Party leadership by opposing the repeal of the Corn Laws in 1846 (these laws imposed tariffs on most imported grains, which increased their price). By 1849, he had assumed the leadership of the Tories in the House of Commons (the lower house of the Parliament). In 1867 he obtained the votes needed to pass an Electoral Reform Bill, which extended the right to vote to many male urban workers, more than doubling the number of voters. Ironically, workers voted for the Liberals in 1868, and Disraeli, prime minister briefly before the election, resigned his premiership.

In 1875, prime minister once again, Disraeli, as he stated, to "gain and retain for the Conservatives the lasting affection of the working classes," passed bills legalizing strike picketing and breaches of contract by strikers. He also concentrated on promoting the British Empire and international interests, understanding that this bolstered national pride among all Britons. In 1875 he purchased the Egyptian ruler's share in the Suez Canal; in 1876 he had Queen Victoria proclaimed Empress of India. He also opposed Russian advances in the Balkans, which threatened British access to its colonial possessions, and took control of the island of Cypress in 1878, which increased British influence in the eastern Mediterranean.

In 1876 Queen Victoria named Disraeli Earl of Beaconsfield. That same year he made his final speech to the House of Commons before moving to the House of Lords (where only aristocrats were allowed to take a seat). Defeated again by the Liberal opposition in 1880, Disraeli retired from politics. He died on April 19, 1881.

Legacy

Benjamin Disraeli successfully reconciled conservatism and modern democratic politics, which transformed the Conservative Party into a mass party acceptable to the newly enfranchised working class.

Disraeli crafted his parliamentary agenda to appeal to English national pride, working-class interests, and pro-imperial policies, and to reflect the social unity and support for the monarchy that characterized the attitudes of many Britons, regardless of class or social origin. He succeeded in making the Conservative Party appeal both to wealthy landlords and to the urban working class, anticipating the nationalist politics of the twentieth century.

Unlike many Conservatives, who feared that working-class participation in political life would result in anarchy, Disraeli understood, and convinced other Conservatives, that authority and stability could be maintained by cultivating the support of the nonradical working class. Only by modern political manipulation of a broadened electorate could the Conservatives achieve their goals and keep the Liberal Party elite in check. This allowed the Conservative Party to weather the political repercussions of World War I, which virtually destroyed its rival, the Liberal Party.

Disraeli transformed the Conservatives into a national party, which ensured its survival and dominance in British politics during much of the twentieth century. His tactics have been imitated elsewhere, for example, by American Republicans such as President Richard M. Nixon, who based his support on the so-called "silent majority" of hardworking, law-abiding citizens. MARGARET THATCHER, Conservative Party leader and prime minister throughout the 1980s, can also be seen as a descendant of Disraelian conservatism.

Lemoine

For Further Reading
Smith, Paul. *Disraeli: A Brief Life.* New York: Cambridge University Press, 1999.
Vincent, John. *Disraeli.* Oxford: Oxford University Press, 1990.

Edward I

King of England
1239–1307

Life and Work

Although King Edward I's forces were often at war to subdue the Scots and Welsh, his rule was marked by legal and administrative reforms that weakened feudalism and set the groundwork for a cooperative parliamentary system.

Born in June 1239 to King Henry III and Queen Eleanor of Provence, Edward grew up in a prosperous England and in a court full of intrigue. He received a classical education, learning French and Latin, music and mathematics. In 1254, Edward traveled to England's possessions in western France to meet his future bride, Eleanor of Castile. At his marriage, Edward became independent, receiving numerous lands as his personal domain and an annual stipend.

By accepting the crown of Sicily, Edward's father, Henry III, became enmeshed in an ugly struggle in 1254 between the Pope and the Holy Roman Empire. In 1258, the cost of supporting this and other adventures forced Henry III to turn to the English barons for money. The barons, led by Henry's brother-in-law Simon de Montfort, took the opportunity to reassert the conditions of the Magna Carta of 1215, which had forced English kings to hold a parliament with nobles and commoners (Old French *parlement*, or "speaking"). The agreement that the barons forced upon Henry in 1258 was called the Provisions of Oxford; when Henry later repudiated the agreement, de Montfort and other barons rebelled and fought the king in what became known as the Barons' War (1263–67). Although initially their hostage until his escape in 1265, Edward eventually raised an army and defeated the barons. De Montfort was killed in 1265 at the battle of Evesham, waged against the barons by Edward with the help of Welsh forces.

For the next three years, Henry and Edward governed England peacefully, trying to heal the wounds of the earlier conflict. Edward and Queen Eleanor of Castile left on a crusade (the eighth) in 1270, which accomplished little. When his father died in 1272, Edward felt secure enough in his position to take two years to return from the Continent to England to receive the crown. Made king on August 2, 1274, Edward set about stabilizing the political and financial situation of England and England's possessions in France. As a token of his good faith and as an indication of his constant need for money, Edward convened Parliament twice a year for advice and support for the remainder of his reign.

Beginning in 1275, with the help of his chief clerk Robert Burnell, Edward surveyed his possessions for the worth of its produce, both to clarify the tax due to the crown and to eliminate rampant corruption. He also conquered Wales as a way to increase England's tax base. In 1290, driven in part by a need for money to finance his endless campaigns against the Scots and Welsh, Edward expelled some 12,000 to 16,000 of England's Jews, and confiscated their wealth. In 1292, Edward secured the allegiance of the Scots, but after 1302 faced mounting opposition from highland chieftains, culminating in the revolt of William Wallace in 1307. En route to Scotland to suppress yet another Scots uprising (this one led by Robert Bruce), Edward died July 7, 1307. He is buried in Westminster Abbey.

Legacy

King Edward I extricated England from the financial and diplomatic mess into which it had fallen during the reign of his father and, in doing so, bureaucratized and, to some degree, democratized the country's administration.

The instability of Henry III's reign—marked by foreign entanglements on behalf of his French friends and allies—affected Edward's leadership later in life, for he felt obligated to eliminate foreigners from his court, pay greater attention to domestic English affairs, and involve himself less in Continental politics. Edward also learned a lesson, by negative example, from his father: English kings could no longer rule arbitrarily if they wanted to manage England's resources efficiently. This is why Edward turned to his clerks for financial, legal, and administrative reforms and turned to the Parliament for political stability. These choices realigned England with the values set down in the 1215 Magna Carta, reluctantly signed by his grandfather, King John, and allowed England to gradually evolve, until the Great Revolution of 1688, into a parliamentary system ruled by a strong monarchy. Edward's disaffection with foreign powers influencing England encouraged him to distance Britain from the Roman Catholic church, a trend that many subsequent rulers continued to amplify until Henry VIII separated the English church from the Roman Catholic church in 1588.

In a broader context, despite some domestic consolidation, Edward was the monarch of Europe with the widest worldview. Just as the king of France and the German emperor became involved in difficult internal conflicts and turned away from international cooperation, Edward expanded English rule into Wales through a ruthless conquest, solidified English dominance over Scotland through a lengthy and costly pacification, and strengthened the English presence in western France. This contributed to 200 years of heavy English participation in rich Continental commerce and promoted England's growing prosperity and stability.

Del Testa

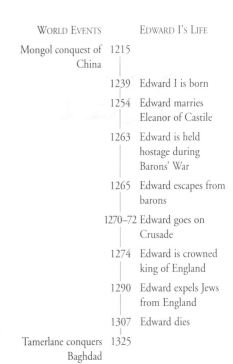

World Events		Edward I's Life
Mongol conquest of China	1215	
	1239	Edward I is born
	1254	Edward marries Eleanor of Castile
	1263	Edward is held hostage during Barons' War
	1265	Edward escapes from barons
	1270–72	Edward goes on Crusade
	1274	Edward is crowned king of England
	1290	Edward expels Jews from England
	1307	Edward dies
Tamerlane conquers Baghdad	1325	

For Further Reading

Chancellor, John. *The Life and Times of Edward I.* London: Weidenfeld and Nicolson, 1981.

Prestwich, Michael. *Edward I.* New Haven, Conn.: Yale University Press, 1997.

Eisenhower, Dwight David

Thirty-Fourth President of the
United States
1890–1969

Life and Work

Using impressive leadership skills, General Dwight David Eisenhower coordinated the 1944 Normandy invasion that helped end World War II. As president of the United States in the 1950s, Eisenhower used these same leadership skills to keep the country on a steady course as the Cold War intensified and anticommunist sentiment became a dangerous threat in the United States.

Eisenhower was born October 14, 1890, to a poor family in Denison, Texas. After high school, Eisenhower passed the entrance exams for West Point, entering in 1911. Commissioned in 1915, Eisenhower was made a trainer at army bases during growing U.S. involvement in World War I. In 1918, he was made commandant of the army's

World Events		Eisenhower's Life
Germany is united	1871	
	1890	Dwight David Eisenhower is born
Russo-Japanese War	1905	
	1911	Eisenhower enters West Point
World War I	1914–18	
Russian Revolution	1917	
Great Depression	1929–39	
	1935–40	Eisenhower serves under Gen. MacArthur in Philippines
World War II	1939–45	
	1942	Eisenhower made commander, Allied forces in Europe
Communist China is established	1949	
	1953–61	Eisenhower serves as president of United States
Israel defeats Arab nations in Six-Day War	1967	
	1969	Eisenhower dies
Vietnam War ends	1975	

new training facility for tanks, an extraordinary assignment for someone so young.

Throughout the 1920s and early 1930s, Eisenhower continued to receive important staff assignments, including postings to the army's Panama Canal base, the Command and General Staff School, and the War College. After 1935, Eisenhower served General Douglas MacArthur in the Philippines, an American protectorate. By 1936, Eisenhower was widely considered to be the best officer in the army. During World War II, Eisenhower rose from colonel in 1940 to a general managing America's beleaguered Far East theater in 1942. In mid-1942, Eisenhower was made commander of Allied forces in Europe.

Eisenhower always believed in attacking Nazi Germany through France and got his chance in 1944. As supreme commander of the Allied invasion of Normandy, Eisenhower controlled the largest amphibious assault force ever assembled. His caution, exceptional organizational and diplomatic abilities, and close relationship with the average soldier helped make the invasion successful. In 1945, Eisenhower returned to the United States a hero. In 1952, Eisenhower ran as the Republican candidate for President of the United States and won. Taking office as president in 1953, he sought to keep the economy steady, restrained military expansionism in the face of a supposedly expansionist Soviet Union, enforced court-ordered desegregation, and balanced his own restrained anticommunism against the rabid tendencies of men such as Senator Joseph McCarthy. After completing two terms as president in 1961, Eisenhower served as advisor to subsequent presidents. He died after a brief illness in 1969.

Legacy

Dwight Eisenhower was the greatest all-around military leader since Napoleon. However, the qualities that enabled Eisenhower to lead successful military invasions also reflected his limitations.

In leading men or delegating authority, Eisenhower made sure that military ability met appropriately with strategic task. In addition, because he focused on one goal and was not arrogant, Eisenhower was one of the few officers who worked successfully with both his British and French counterparts while simultaneously handling the burdens of waging war.

Although the Soviet Union deserves much credit for defeating Nazi Germany, without Eisenhower's leadership, the war would have lasted longer and cost more lives.

As president, however, Eisenhower emphasized the military's limits. Decrying the threat of the military–industrial complex to civil society, and noting that every bomber built deprived thousands of children of new schools, Eisenhower kept the U.S. military to a strategic minimum despite vigorous calls for enormous expansion. Although forced by belief and politics to check aggressive acts of communist expansion, Eisenhower avoided strategies that might trigger a world-ending nuclear apocalypse.

The qualities that made Eisenhower such a good general, however, made him a slightly less effective president. No racist himself, in order to ensure the support of the army's numerous racist generals and, later, racist Southern voters, Eisenhower had always refused to deal with racism head-on. When Arkansas's governor resisted court-ordered desegregation of schools in 1957, Eisenhower sent in federal troops not so much to support racial equality but to ensure that the rulings of federal courts were not defied. Had Eisenhower been more active in promoting racial rights, he might have prevented the violence that ripped the United States apart in the 1960s and early 1970s. Eisenhower also did not want to alienate political support around a popular issue by too harsh treatment of vicious anticommunists in government. Consequently, terrible damage was done to many people's lives during the Red Scare of the early 1950s.

Del Testa

For Further Reading

Ambrose, Stephen E. *Eisenhower: Soldier and President.* New York: Simon & Schuster, 1990.
Perret, Geoffrey. *Eisenhower.* New York: Random House, 1999.

Eleanor of Aquitaine

Medieval Queen and
Patron of Culture
1122–1204

Life and Work

Eleanor of Aquitaine used marital alliances to become one of the most important women in medieval Europe. Deeply disappointed by her married life, she nonetheless exercised great influence on the development of culture in her day.

Eleanor was born to William X, duke of Aquitaine, in 1122. Her father's lands, richer than even those of the king of France in the north, made Aquitaine one of the most coveted territories in Europe. As Eleanor had no surviving brothers and only two younger sisters, she became the heir apparent. She was raised to appreciate the chivalric literature that was beginning to gain popularity among the knights and ladies of courtly society. Her life of reading was interrupted in 1137, however, by the death of her father. Fearing for the security of her inheritance, the 15-year-old duchess hastily accepted the marriage proposal of Louis, the heir to the French throne. They married soon after, and by the time she reached Paris her new husband had acceded to the throne as King Louis VII. A year that had begun by orphaning her thus ended by making her the queen of France.

Eleanor's experiences with Louis were troubled from the beginning. For a young woman who had spent her youth reading courtly romances, the monkish Louis, who had been raised for the priesthood, was a disappointment. Her thirst for adventure was quenched briefly in 1147 when she was permitted to accompany Louis on the Second Crusade (1147–49). This proved short-lived and abortive, however, and back in France she began to seek an annulment. In 1152 her wishes were fulfilled, and in the same year she remarried. The new bridegroom was the handsome heir to Anjou and Normandy, Henry Plantagenet. In 1154 he successfully claimed the throne of England and became King HENRY II (r. 1154–89). Eleanor was again a queen.

Her second marriage proved even more of a failure. Henry was habitually unfaithful; his infidelities caused Eleanor to become deeply estranged from him over the years. In 1173, resentment and a strong attachment to her son RICHARD I led her to support an unsuccessful rebellion against Henry. Imprisoned in France for this, she obtained release only upon Henry's death in 1189.

Eleanor's final years witnessed the reigns of two of her sons, her favorite Richard I (r. 1189–99) and the much less lovable John (r. 1199–1216). Eleanor managed the realm while Richard was away on the Third Crusade (1189–92) and thwarted John's efforts to usurp the throne. In 1194 she raised and delivered the ransom needed for Richard's release from captivity in Austria. After Richard's death she did her best to support John, but his careless management of the realm appalled her. On April 1, 1204, with John in danger of losing Aquitaine to France, Eleanor died at Fontevrault.

Legacy

Although Eleanor rarely had the opportunity to impose her will in politics, she had significant impact upon the diplomatic and cultural history of medieval Europe.

The territory Eleanor brought to the English throne was highly valued by Henry's successors. Richard, who was duke of Aquitaine before becoming king in 1189, was compelled to wage repeated wars against the feudal knights of the duchy to maintain royal control. An even greater threat arose from Louis VII, whose marriage to Eleanor prompted him to claim the territory for France. Later French kings would war repeatedly against England for these lands and, after the exhausting Hundred Years War (1337–1453), would finally triumph.

Eleanor made brilliant contributions to European culture. Her own court was considered one of the most cultivated of the day, and her example inspired other rulers. This was especially noticeable among her children. Richard, who had been taught by her to compose poetry and sing songs, became a model of chivalry for medieval poets. Countess Marie of Champagne, Eleanor's daughter, became a leading patron of the arts, supporting the work of such literary figures as Chrétien de Troyes. Chretien's most notable compositions treated the Arthurian legend, and it has been suggested by scholars that Eleanor served him as a model for Queen Guenevere.

Finally, the fact that one of the greatest supporters of medieval culture was a woman cannot be separated from the new status that women had begun to enjoy in the twelfth century. Courtly romances celebrated women as the object of knightly veneration and moral respect. While such a standard imposed its own burden upon noblewomen, historians note that it served to alleviate some of the degradation of women. Perhaps this is the most fitting legacy for a woman who did not hesitate to march on a Crusade, to provoke uprisings against her husband, or to travel across Europe to negotiate the release of her son from captivity.

Strickland

WORLD EVENTS		ELEANOR OF AQUITAINE'S LIFE
Timbuktu influential throughout west central Africa	c. 1100	
	1122	Eleanor is born
	1137	Eleanor accedes to duchy of Aquitaine and marries shortly thereafter; is crowned queen of France
	1152	Eleanor has marriage to Louis annulled; Eleanor marries Henry Plantagenet
	1154	Eleanor is crowned queen of England
	1173	Eleanor supports rebellion by sons against Henry
	1173–89	Eleanor is imprisoned in France
Saladin takes Jerusalem for Islam	1187	
	1194	Eleanor carries ransom to Austria for Richard
	1204	Eleanor dies
Mongol conquest of China	1215	

For Further Reading

Kelly, Amy Ruth. *Eleanor of Aquitaine and the Four Kings.* Cambridge, Mass.: Harvard University Press, 1950.

Meade, Marion. *Eleanor of Aquitaine.* New York: Hawthorn Books, 1977.

Owen, D. D. R. *Eleanor of Aquitaine: Queen and Legend.* Oxford: Blackwell, 1993.

Elizabeth I

Queen of England
1533–1603

Life and Work

Elizabeth I came to power in England amid domestic religious conflict and foreign military threats. At the end of her long reign, however, the country enjoyed great stability and strength.

Elizabeth was born in 1533 to Anne Boleyn and King HENRY VIII, who was succeeded after his death in 1547 first by Elizabeth's younger half-brother Edward VI (r. 1547–53) and then by her Roman Catholic half-sister Mary (r. 1553–58). Conflict between England's Protestant and Roman Catholic parties raged during this time; Elizabeth, raised as a Protestant, was imprisoned by Mary in the Tower of London.

When Elizabeth succeeded Mary in 1558, she moved immediately to restore the Protestant legislation of Henry VIII and Edward VI. In 1559 a new Act of Supremacy made her the supreme governor of the church, and she gave positions of influence at court to leading Protestants. Nevertheless, she made it clear that Roman Catholics would also have a stake in the English state. In an effort to win their support, she pursued a policy of toleration and even embraced some Roman Catholic practices. Efforts at reconciliation were shaken, however, when the Roman Catholic queen of Scotland, Mary

Stuart, sought asylum in England in 1568. Mary became the center of renewed Catholic conspiracies, and in 1587 Elizabeth reluctantly had her executed. Despite such strains, Elizabeth succeeded in restoring order to the English church. In 1563, Parliament passed the Thirty-Nine Articles, which established the basic principles of the Anglican church, and in subsequent years the religious conflict that Elizabeth had inherited began to subside.

Elizabeth's cautious domestic policies were in contrast to a series of aggressive actions against Spain. Spain was Europe's greatest military power at the time and was ruled by a staunch defender of Catholicism, PHILIP II. Eager to expand English naval strength and reduce the power of her rival, Elizabeth encouraged privateers such as Sir Francis Drake to plunder Spanish ships sailing between Europe and the New World. Even more brazenly, when the Protestant provinces of the Netherlands revolted against Spanish rule in 1572, she began to send money and soldiers in support. In 1588 Philip responded by sending his navy, the famed Spanish Armada, against England. England was saved by a miraculous "Protestant wind" that drove the Armada into confusion and allowed the English fleet to sink a part of it.

When Elizabeth died in 1603, England had recovered from a century of domestic conflict to resume its place as one of Europe's leading powers.

Legacy

The religious policies and naval expansion of Elizabeth I helped make England one of the most prosperous states in Europe.

Between 1558 and 1563 Elizabeth had overseen the restoration of Protestantism in England. The Anglican church however, retained many features of Roman Catholicism; by combining Protestantism with these traditions, the Elizabethan Settlement established the Anglican church upon what church historians call the *via media,* or middle course. In later centuries the Anglican church (and in the United States its affiliate the Episcopal church) would often serve to bridge the distance between the two branches of Western Christendom. At times, this bridge collapsed. For instance, in the seventeenth century extreme Protestants (Puritans) would seek to "purify" the church of its Roman Catholic heritage. Nevertheless, the inclusive perspective

fostered by the *via media* would enable Anglicans to play a prominent role in the twentieth-century ecumenical movement seeking to restore unity to Christendom.

Elizabeth also affected the relationship between church and state in England. By the end of the seventeenth century the tolerant attitude she exhibited emerged in an England once again torn by religious conflict. The English Civil War (1642–49) witnessed divisions among Anglicans, Roman Catholics, and Puritans, despite efforts by OLIVER CROMWELL to introduce religious toleration. Only after the Glorious Revolution of 1688 did a Bill of Rights (1689) secure religious toleration in England.

Elizabeth's foreign policy was also influential down the centuries. England established close relations with the Netherlands when it finally gained independence from Spain in the seventeenth century. Her energetic thrust toward the New World resulted in increased exploration and, in 1607, the founding of the English colony at Jamestown. By the end of the eighteenth century, England would have the largest colonial empire in the world, protected by the most powerful navy.

Finally, Elizabeth's patronage of the arts contributed to the flowering of English culture. The riches of the Italian Renaissance were appropriated and given native expression in the music of Thomas Morley and the poetry of Sir Philip Sidney. Elizabethan drama attained the greatest brilliance, developed as it was by writers such as Christopher Marlowe and William Shakespeare.

Strickland

World Events		Elizabeth I's Life
Mughal Empire rules in India	1526	
	1533	Elizabeth is born
	1558	Queen Mary dies; Elizabeth becomes queen of England
	1559	Act of Supremacy makes Elizabeth head of church in England
Ottoman dominance of Mediterranean ends	1571	
	1587	Elizabeth has Mary Stuart executed
	1588	Elizabeth witnesses destruction of Spanish Armada
	1603	Elizabeth dies
Glorious Revolution in England	1688	

For Further Reading

Hibbert, Christopher. *The Virgin Queen: The Personal History of Elizabeth I.* London: Viking, 1990.

Somerset, Anne. *Elizabeth I.* London: Weidenfeld and Nicolson, 1991.

Weir, Alison. *Elizabeth the Queen.* London: Jonathan Cape, 1998.

Franco, Francisco

Spanish General and Dictator
1892–1975

Life and Work

Francisco Franco used his forceful personality, his dedication to political conservatism, and the respect he had earned among Spain's conservative elites to establish a dictatorship that ruled over Spain for more than 35 years.

Franco was born Francisco Paulino Hermenegildo Teódulo Franco Bahamonde on December 4, 1892, into a devout Roman Catholic family. In 1898, the morale of the Spanish people reached its lowest point after the humiliating loss of most of its colonies to the United States. The decline affected Franco and he joined the army. He graduated from the Toledo officers' academy in 1910 and was immediately posted to garrison duty. Franco volunteered for combat when a war broke out in Spanish Morocco.

Franco arrived in Spanish Morocco in February 1912 and was immediately put in command of Moroccan troops serving under the Spanish. For five years, Franco led his men to repeated victories; he was promoted to major and received many of Spain's highest military awards. In 1917, with no post available for an officer of his rank in Morocco, Franco was sent to northern Spain, where he became infamous for dealing harshly with striking workers.

Franco spent the 1920s climbing still higher in Spain's military. In 1931, a republic replaced the military dictatorship that had ruled Spain since 1923, and its leaders initiated extensive land, educational, and military reforms to shatter the power of Spain's traditional elites. Franco disliked the republic but remained obedient. On February 16, 1936, a leftist coalition known as the Popular Front won Spain's general election; on February 17, 1936, Franco demanded that the prime minister hand over power to the army.

Between 1936 and 1939, Franco waged a slow and unrelenting campaign of unified Nationalists against the politically fragmented Republican Loyalists. Franco received aid from both BENITO MUSSOLINI and ADOLF HITLER, while the Loyalists received support from JOSEPH STALIN. The Loyalists, however, lost because its leaders could not decide on a common goal. Madrid surrendered on March 27, 1939; in August, Franco declared himself *caudillo*, or supreme leader.

During World War II, Franco played his cards carefully, never declaring war, alienating neither the Axis nor the Allies. Internally, Franco initiated a popular but ruthless Roman Catholic authoritarianism, imprisoning or even executing anyone suspected of leftism or freemasonry (Free Masons are a secret, fraternal society dedicated to free thinking).

After World War II, as a result of its neutrality, Spain suffered commercial and political isolation until the 1950s, when the political expediency of having Franco as an ally outweighed the earlier actions of his regime, which still bore the marks of the right-wing authoritarian states the Allies had gone to war to defeat. Gradually, though maintaining rigid political control and censorship, Franco began to occupy himself with his succession, arranging that King Juan Carlos and a republic should follow his death. Growing agitation among the youth of Spain and general dissatisfaction with the stunted economy was met with repression. By the 1970s a frail Franco relied increasingly on his aides; he died on November 20, 1975 and was succeeded by King Juan Carlos and a democratic constitutional monarchy.

Legacy

Francisco Franco revealed the power of the deep and enduring conservatism embedded in Spain's ruling classes and the difficulty of suppressing democracy and social justice in a country that desires them.

Spain, which in previous centuries had encompassed a powerful empire, emerged from the nineteenth century a defeated and impoverished nation. Franco built on the malaise that gripped Spain's middle classes and Roman Catholic peasantry during the first 35 years of the century; these groups wanted prosperity but not the social and cultural ideas that often accompanied modernization. He promised order based on traditional norms and forms, and he delivered—but at a terrible cost. Tens of thousands died in the Spanish Civil War of 1936–39, and many thousands more were made political prisoners.

Franco's legacy is also one of the larger, cynical world of international politics. Beginning with the Spanish Civil War, the Western democracies did little to oppose Franco's ascent to power because they were opposed to giving Nazi Germany and fascist Italy any excuse to push for a wider war. The Western democracies also had reason to fear that if Spanish anarchists and communists defeated Franco's forces, their ideologies might become attractive to those beleaguered by the Great Depression and thereby threaten democratic control of Western Europe and the United States. After World War II, the democracies tolerated Franco because, in the black-and-white, either/or ideological struggle of the early Cold War, it was essential to the stability of the western Mediterranean for the NATO (North Atlantic Treaty Organization) nations to tolerate, even support, a virulent anti-communist in control of an oppressive Roman Catholic dictatorship. (For instance, the NATO wanted a base on Spanish soil and got one.) Post-Franco Spain has proven to be just as stable as it was under Franco, except that the Spanish avidly support democracy and international organizations designed to preserve peace and promote prosperity.

Del Testa

WORLD EVENTS		FRANCO'S LIFE
Germany is united	1871	
	1892	Francisco Franco is born
Russo-Japanese War	1905	
	1910	Franco graduates from Toledo Military Academy
	1912–17	Franco commands troops in Spanish Morocco
World War I	1914–18	
Russian Revolution	1917	
Great Depression	1929–39	
	1936–39	Franco fights Spanish Civil War
	1939	Franco takes power
World War II	1939–45	Franco keeps Spain neutral during World War II
Communist China is established	1949	
Israel defeats Arab nations in Six-Day War	1967	
Vietnam War ends	1975	Franco dies; King Juan Carlos takes throne two days later
Dissolution of Soviet Union	1991	

For Further Reading

Ellwood, Sheelagh. *Franco*. New York: Longman, 1994.

Preston, Paul. *Franco: A Biography*. London: HarperCollins, 1993

Franklin, Benjamin

American Philosopher and
Revolutionary Patriot
1706–1790

Life and Work

Benjamin Franklin used his natural intelligence, boundless energy, endless curiosity, and belief in Enlightenment principles to help advance the cause of science as well as encourage the intellectual development and political freedom of the United States.

Born on January 17, 1706, in Boston, Franklin quickly distinguished himself among his peers as a smart and precocious child. At eight, Franklin started grammar school, to which his parents could afford to send him for only two years. Realizing that his son needed to find a way to support himself, Franklin's father apprenticed him in 1718 to his brother, James, a printer. At his brother's press, Franklin mastered the printing trade and began to contribute anonymously to a satirical newspaper published there. Soon, however, Franklin found his brother overbearing, and in 1723 fled to Philadelphia, where he was hired by another press. In Philadelphia, Franklin became so well respected as a printer that the

governor of Pennsylvania sent him to England in late 1724 to buy equipment to start a government press. Finding no financial support in England, Franklin worked there for two years until he could return to Philadelphia, in 1726.

Between 1730 and 1760, with a large income from successful printing shops and a newspaper, Franklin dedicated himself to educating himself and others. Franklin invented many useful things, including an efficient fireplace and the lightning rod. He sponsored the Philadelphia Fire Company and started the University of Pennsylvania. He engaged in many scientific experiments, the most famous of which involved demonstrating the effects of electricity in 1752, and published his results along with other useful knowledge in popular books, such as the annual *Poor Richard's Almanack,* begun in 1732.

Beginning in 1747, Franklin became involved in politics when he organized a militia to drive pirates from the Delaware River. In 1756, Franklin led a troop that defended Pennsylvania's western borders from marauding French and Indian soldiers. Throughout the 1750s and 1760s, Franklin served as a representative for several of the colonies in England and he was charged with airing the complaints of the Americans to often indifferent British officials. In 1766 he convinced the British Parliament to repeal the Stamp Act, a law the colonists had found unduly burdensome. These missions also brought him into contact with many European scientists and many French officials sympathetic to the American colonies' complaints against Britain. In 1775, Franklin returned to Philadelphia, where he established an efficient and profitable postal system after the Continental Congress named him Postmaster General.

Abandoning hope of negotiated peace with Britain, Franklin signed the Declaration of Independence in 1776 and traveled to France to seek military support there. In 1781, Franklin negotiated independence for America's 13 colonies in Britain, and signed an official peace in 1783. Returning to the United States, Franklin continued experimenting and corresponding with friends and admirers as best he could, but found himself slowed by various illnesses. He died peacefully on April 17, 1790.

Legacy

Benjamin Franklin connected the United States to Europe's Enlightenment, estab-

lishing the United States as an intellectual and political force.

Franklin influenced others with his very personality. He represented the ideal man of the Enlightenment. He was rational, pragmatic, and optimistic, and he encouraged people to be the same. He was curious about the world and tried to make it a better place to live every day. His inventive spirit and accomplishments inspired others and his inventions paved the way for further scientific inquiry. Franklin, however, did not hoard his knowledge or his considerable wealth, but deployed them to help others learn and improve themselves. This altruism, combined with his considerable achievements and personable nature, made him perhaps the most popular and admired figure in the Western world during the latter half of the eighteenth century. His person and actions stood for the emerging United States, a country that represented Enlightenment values.

Franklin used his fame, connections, and ability to reason carefully to help shape America's independence movement at home as well as to influence political policy in Britain and France. At first he tried to get the British to relax their tightening grip on the 13 colonies by evoking the image of reasonable government. When negotiation failed, he appealed to another Enlightenment value, freedom from tyranny to rally support for the struggling colonies from places, such as France, where people were sympathetic to such values. Franklin symbolized a young nation and an ideal that has rarely been achieved since.

Del Testa

World Events		Franklin's Life
English seize Calcutta	1690	
	1706	Benjamin Franklin is born in Boston
	1723	Franklin moves to Philadelphia
	1732	Franklin compiles first *Poor Richard's Almanack*
	1756	Franklin leads volunteers to defend Pennsylvania
	1766	Franklin testifies against Stamp Act in London
United States declares independence	1776	Franklin signs Declaration of Independence
	1783	Franklin signs treaty of peace with Britain
French Revolution begins	1789	
	1790	Franklin dies
Latin American independence movement begins	1811	

For Further Reading
Ambler, Louise Todd. *Benjamin Franklin, a Perspective.* Cambridge, Mass.: Harvard University Press, 1975.
Jennings, Francis. *Benjamin Franklin, Politician.* New York: W. W. Norton, 1996.

Frederick I

Holy Roman Emperor
c. 1123–1190

Life and Work

Frederick I (Frederick Barbarossa) expanded the territory of the Holy Roman Empire and became one of its greatest rulers. Although frequently at odds with the Pope, he proved his devotion to the Church by leading a fatal Crusade to the Holy Land.

Nicknamed "Barbarossa" for his red beard, Frederick I was born to the Hohenstaufen duke of Swabia about 1123. When his father abdicated in 1147 to enter a monastery, Frederick inherited the duchy. Frederick's ambitions to be elected Holy Roman Emperor were initially challenged by the Welf duke Henry the Lion of Saxony, but in 1155 he was able to obtain Pope Hadrian IV's blessing and was crowned in Rome.

Frederick, however, soon fell afoul of the papacy. The conflict was centered upon the northern region of Italy known as Lombardy. Referring to the precedent of earlier emperors such as OTTO I, Frederick claimed Lombardy as an imperial possession. In 1158 he launched an invasion of the region and in 1162 his soldiers sacked Milan. The new Pope, Alexander III, promptly condemned these actions; Alexander's own position in Italy was tenuous and he was wary of the ambitious emperor, having excommunicated him in 1160 for supporting a rival Pope. Alexander sponsored a military alliance called the Lombard League to eject Frederick. At the Battle of Legnano near Milan in 1176, Frederick's imperial army was finally destroyed. Frederick was forced to renounce his claim to Lombardy. After a ceremony in which the humbled emperor was compelled to kiss the feet of Alexander, however, he was accepted back into the Church.

In other areas of Europe Frederick was more successful in expanding imperial territory. In 1156 he married the Burgundian Princess Beatrix, enabling the Hohenstaufens to claim large territories in Burgundy and Provence. An invasion of Poland in the following year forced the Polish duke to pledge fealty. Finally, a marriage Frederick arranged between his son and the heiress to the kingdom of Sicily ensured that southern Italy would one day become an imperial possession.

In 1189, Frederick decided to go on a Crusade. By joining forces with Philip Augustus of France and RICHARD I of England, he hoped to serve the Church and demonstrate the empire's leadership in European diplomacy. He obtained a vow from Henry the Lion not to usurp the throne in his absence, and then set out for the Holy Land at the head of a huge army. Even to Arab armies of SALADIN it appeared as though this Third Crusade (1189–92) might be a success. However, while Frederick was fording a river in Asia Minor in 1190, his horse stumbled and he drowned.

Legacy

Although Frederick I left an enlarged Holy Roman Empire to his successors, it was one that lacked integration. Nevertheless, his martial image lived on for centuries among the German population.

Although Frederick's wars in Lombardy ultimately failed to bring northern Italy under imperial rule, he was successful in acquiring other important territories in Europe. Parts of Burgundy, Poland, and Denmark were claimed for the empire and the dynastic marriage of Frederick's son also brought the rich lands of Sicily and southern Italy into the empire. These territorial possessions sometimes brought greater security and strength but sometimes had a weakening effect. This was especially true in southern Italy. Under Frederick's grandson FREDERICK II (r. 1215–50), control over this territory would become extremely costly and threaten the very survival of the empire. Frederick II's wars in Italy provoked revolts among his vassals, a revival of the Lombard League, and another papal bull of excommunication. Indeed, Frederick I's namesake was considered such a threat to the papacy that a crusade was launched to rid the empire of him. In the long run, the Italian commitments made by Frederick I weakened the empire.

Frederick's internal policies also had an important impact upon the later history of the Holy Roman Empire. With the exception of Henry the Lion (who, after violating his promise not to revolt, was finally stripped of his lands), Frederick generally tolerated the autonomous power of his dukes. As a result he failed to create a stable state bureaucracy that could administer his ever-growing territories. This weakness was exacerbated by later emperors, who followed Frederick's example, and allowed themselves to be lured away from Germany by the wealth of Italy. By the thirteenth century this feudal system of administration had weakened Germany in the face of the emerging monarchies of France and England. Germany would remain divided politically until the Prussian statesman OTTO VON BISMARCK united it in the nineteenth century.

Strickland

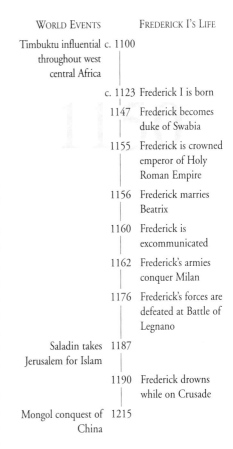

WORLD EVENTS		FREDERICK I'S LIFE
Timbuktu influential throughout west central Africa	c. 1100	
	c. 1123	Frederick I is born
	1147	Frederick becomes duke of Swabia
	1155	Frederick is crowned emperor of Holy Roman Empire
	1156	Frederick marries Beatrix
	1160	Frederick is excommunicated
	1162	Frederick's armies conquer Milan
	1176	Frederick's forces are defeated at Battle of Legnano
Saladin takes Jerusalem for Islam	1187	
	1190	Frederick drowns while on Crusade
Mongol conquest of China	1215	

For Further Reading

Fuhrmann, Horst. *Germany in the High Middle Ages, c. 1050–1200.* Translated by Timothy Reuter. Cambridge: Cambridge University Press, 1986.

Munz, Peter. *Frederick Barbarossa: A Study in Medieval Politics.* Ithaca, N.Y.: Cornell University Press, 1969.

Pacaut, Marcel. *Frederick Barbarossa.* Translated by A. J. Pomerans. New York: Scribners, 1970.

Frederick II

King of Prussia
1712–1786

Life and Work

Frederick II (Frederick the Great) overcame a troubled childhood to become the most effective ruler in Prussian history. He guided his domestic policy by the ideals of the Enlightenment and his foreign policy by sheer cunning.

Frederick was born in Berlin in 1712, the son of Frederick William I. His father had expanded the Prussian army into one of Europe's finest. A great disciplinarian, he expected his son to conform to the strict norms of military life while still a boy. When Frederick was 18, he fled his father with the aid of a friend. Seized immediately and imprisoned, he was forced to see his friend beheaded as an accomplice. Thereafter Frederick obeyed his father, but in 1734 he moved to a palace in Rheinsberg where he and his wife, Elisabeth Christine, supported a circle of enlightened cultural figures. Frederick took a special interest in freemasonry and embraced its ideal of a secular state. He also took up the flute and wrote a number of compositions for the instrument.

Frederick succeeded his father as king in 1740, the same year MARIA THERESA of Austria came to power. Austria traditionally dominated Germany, but the accession of a female heir had required diplomatic approval of a document called the Pragmatic Sanction. Frederick William I had signed this document, but Frederick, sensing his rival's political weakness, decided before the end of the year to attack Austria and seize its rich manufacturing province of Silesia. The resulting War of Austrian Succession (1740–48) brought the province under Prussian control. In 1756 Frederick again attacked Austria, this time provoking a major Continental conflict known as the Seven Years War. Although aided somewhat by England, he was forced to fend almost entirely for himself against a coalition of Austria, France, and Russia. When the war ended in 1763, however, Prussia's strength had been greatly increased. Subsequent years witnessed additional gains in the regions of Franconia and Poland.

Frederick's was guided by the Enlightenment in his domestic governance. Believing that the state should be subjected to natural reason, he pursued reforms he believed prudent. He introduced projects to improve agriculture, to protect Prussian manufacturing, and to facilitate freedom of expression. He also built a magnificent palace at Potsdam called Sans Souci, where he debated with the French philosophe Voltaire and wrote works on statecraft, morals, and art.

He died at Sans Souci on August 17, 1786.

Legacy

Frederick II made Prussia the dominant power of northern Germany. During the century that followed his death, Prussia would have a great impact upon the political, diplomatic, and military history of Europe.

Frederick considered himself an enlightened ruler free from the prejudices and ignorance of his predecessors. His correspondence with Voltaire revealed a genuine desire to apply natural reason to statecraft and, in many cases, he succeeded. He ordered the abolition of torture, for instance, and promoted religious toleration. But he was largely unable to disseminate the ideals of the Enlightenment among the common people, who remained illiterate, poor, and isolated in the countryside. As a result, Prussia did not develop strong institutions of civil law and participatory government during the decades that followed his reign. Instead, the class of wealthy landowners known as Junkers, whom Frederick had used for military leadership, remained dominant in Prussian society. Their ascendancy and the priority given to military service fostered a highly conservative social order that lasted well into the nineteenth century.

Meanwhile, Prussia found itself increasingly involved in European politics and diplomacy. The Seven Years War proved to be a diplomatic turning point. Formerly, Austria had dominated Germany and had frequently warred with France to the west. Frederick's alliance with England, however, had pushed the Austrians into the arms of their traditional enemy. Furthermore, when Prussia emerged victorious from the conflict, it was the dominant power in northern Germany. In later years nationalists seeking to unite the many territories of Germany would therefore look increasingly to Prussia, not Austria, for leadership. This question of leadership was debated during the revolutions of 1848; in 1866 another Austro-Prussian War would finally settle in Prussia's favor. In 1871, Frederick's Hohenzollern heir William I of Prussia became the first ruler of a united Germany.

Strickland

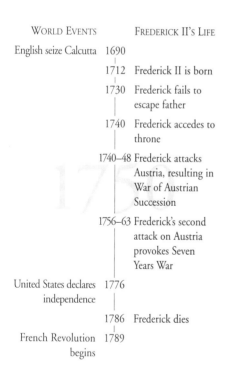

WORLD EVENTS		FREDERICK II'S LIFE
English seize Calcutta	1690	
	1712	Frederick II is born
	1730	Frederick fails to escape father
	1740	Frederick accedes to throne
	1740–48	Frederick attacks Austria, resulting in War of Austrian Succession
	1756–63	Frederick's second attack on Austria provokes Seven Years War
United States declares independence	1776	
	1786	Frederick dies
French Revolution begins	1789	

For Further Reading

Asprey, Robert. *Frederick the Great: The Magificent Enigma.* New York: Ticknor and Fields, 1986.

MacDonogh, Giles. *Frederick the Great: A Life in Deed and Letters.* London: Weidenfeld and Nicolson, 1999.

Showalter, Dennis. *The Wars of Frederick the Great.* London: Longman, 1996.

Friedan, Betty

Feminist Leader
1921–

Life and Work

In 1963, Betty Friedan wrote *The Feminine Mystique*, a best-selling book that castigated male-dominated society for hobbling women's creativity and freedom. In so doing, she sparked a worldwide movement demanding women's equality with men.

Betty Naomi Goldstein was born on February 4, 1921, into a middle-class household in Peoria, Illinois. Goldstein was always an excellent student, which helped her get into Smith, a prominent women's college. She majored in psychology and graduated *summa cum laude,* in 1942. She then traveled to the University of California–Berkeley to begin a prestigious graduate fellowship but found wartime Berkeley unbearable. In 1944, she fled to New York City, where she worked as a writer for liberal press services.

Three subsequent events catalyzed Friedan's growing belief that society oppressed women. In 1947, she married and began a stormy 25-year relationship with Carl Friedan, an advertising executive. In 1952, concerns over her desires for a second maternity leave caused Friedan to leave her job. And, in 1955, she and her family moved to the suburbs.

Although she remained an active participant in the communities in which she lived and continued working as a freelance writer, Friedan found suburban life numbing and the demands placed on a housewife stultifying. Friedan used her fifteenth college class reunion as a chance to distribute a detailed questionnaire to graduates to gauge their level of satisfaction with their personal and professional lives. The results formed the basis of *The Feminine Mystique.* The book argued that society encouraged even the most talented women to crave the "feminine mystique," a state in which women sublimated their intellectual creativity and personal desires into raising children and domesticity. The book sparked a furious debate in the United States.

In the mid-1960s, Friedan made feminism a household word and assumed leadership of groups that sought women's rights. In 1966, along with other activists, Friedan created the National Organization for Women (NOW), which was one of the first broad-based women's rights groups. Using the 1964 Civil Rights Act as a springboard for legal action, Friedan and other women's rights leaders often succeeded in ending overt discrimination against women in employment and wages. In 1970, the women's movement achieved its greatest success with the adoption by the United States House of Representatives of the ultimately defeated Equal Rights Amendment. After 1970, Friedan quickly lost her leadership in the women's rights movement as younger, more radical women came to the fore. By 1973, she turned to writing and individual support of women's causes. In 1981, Friedan published *The Second Stage,* an evaluation of the women's movement.

Legacy

Betty Friedan launched a worldwide women's rights movement whose impact continues to expand every day.

Friedan identified the source of women's oppression as the raising of children and keeping house. When her audience embraced the tenet that women needed satisfaction outside of the home, they challenged millennia of social norms. In the context of social upheaval, social activism, and a redefinition of racial and political relationships during the 1960s, the women's rights movement found widespread support. Many women activists had found the super machismo of most 1960s political movements disturbing. For example, during the occupation of and strike against Columbia University by its students in 1968, many women protesters were delegated to subservient positions in the movement.

Friedan received a favorable international reception, and she addressed international gatherings of women throughout the late 1960s and early 1970s. However, feminism for Friedan had limits, which in the context of the inclusive and radical tendencies of social activists by 1970 made her less and less popular. She argued forcefully that the mixture of issues diluted the potency of the women's movement, and her refusal to consider race, class, or sexual preference as integral to women's rights put her out of step with her younger collaborators. Friedan's stance ultimately changed the leadership and face of the feminist movement. Although always acknowledged as the original post–World War II American feminist, Friedan was increasingly criticized, though her image has been somewhat rehabilitated since the 1980s. After 1972, she broke with NOW and the leadership of GLORIA STEINEM and Bella Abzug.

Del Testa

WORLD EVENTS		FRIEDAN'S LIFE
Russian Revolution	1917	
	1921	Betty Naomi Goldstein is born
Great Depression	1929–39	
World War II	1939–45	
	1942	Goldstein graduates Smith College, enters University of California–Berkeley
	1947	Goldstein marries Carl Friedan
Communist China is established	1949	
	1963	Friedan writes *The Feminine Mystique*
	1966	Friedan and others create National Organization for Women (NOW)
Israel defeats Arab nations in Six-Day War	1967	
Vietnam War ends	1975	
	1981	Friedan publishes *The Second Stage*
Dissolution of Soviet Union	1991	

For Further Reading

Hennessee, Judith. *Betty Friedan, Her Life.* New York: Random House, 1999.

Horowitz, Daniel. *Betty Friedan and the Making of the Feminine Mystique.* Amherst: University of Massachusetts Press, 1998.

Gandhi, Mohandas

Indian Nationalist; Spiritual Leader
1869–1948

Life and Work

Mohandas Gandhi (Mahatma Gandhi) pioneered the strategies of nonviolent civil disobedience to achieve national independence and social reform for India.

Gandhi was born on October 2, 1869, the son of the prime minister of Purbandhar, a small, western Indian state. Gandhi was married at 13, then sent to England by his family in 1888 to study law. In 1893, Gandhi moved to South Africa. There he developed his political skills fighting against white South African policies of discrimination against Indians and conceiving of

WORLD EVENTS		GANDHI'S LIFE
Congress of Vienna reorganizes Europe	1815	
	1869	Mohandas Gandhi is born
Germany is united	1871	
	1893	Gandhi goes to South Africa to practice law
Russo-Japanese War	1905	
World War I	1914–18	
	1914	Gandhi returns to India
Russian Revolution	1917	
	1920	Gandhi launches first nationwide *satyagraha*
	1922	Gandhi is imprisoned
Great Depression	1929–39	
	1930	Gandhi encourages mass defiance of British salt monopoly
World War II	1939–45	
	1942	Gandhi is arrested for obstructing war effort
	1946	British announce their withdrawal from India
	1947	India gains independence
	1948	Gandhi is assassinated
Communist China is established	1949	

the methods of nonviolent civil disobedience, known as *satyagraha*, which stressed the moral force of passive resistance.

Gandhi returned to India in 1914, just as World War I began. Many Indians, Gandhi included, supported the British war effort, sending over one million troops to the Western Front, but also felt the British should accord home rule to Indians in exchange. After the war the British suppressed nationalist agitation in India. In April 1919 British troops fired on an outlawed demonstration in Amritsar, killing hundreds of unarmed Indians. This event, known as the Amritsar Massacre, transformed the struggle for independence into a national mass movement.

In August 1920, in response to the massacre, Gandhi launched his first nationwide *satyagraha*, calling on Indians to paralyze British rule by resigning from all government posts, schools, and institutions. He also joined the Indian National Congress, becoming its president in 1925. Gandhi was arrested for sedition in 1922 and sentenced to six years in prison but was released after two because of ill health. He continued his campaign of civil disobedience, defying the British salt monopoly in 1930 by encouraging local salt production.

Discouraged after several years of activism that produced few results and more riots and arrests, Gandhi resigned his presidency of the Indian National Congress in 1934 and began devoting his energies to helping the poor. He resumed his campaign with the outbreak of World War II, refusing cooperation with the British without a promise of independence for India. He was arrested once more in 1942, but released when his wife, Kasturbai, also arrested, died in prison in 1944.

In 1946 the British decided to give India full independence. Muslim Indians demanded that a Muslim state (Pakistan) be established. Gandhi opposed the division of Indian territory according to religion and refused to participate in negotiations on the partition. When violence erupted between Hindus and Muslims in 1946 and just after Indian and Pakistani independence became effective on August 15, 1947, Gandhi fasted and traveled across the country in an effort to quell the violence. On January 10, 1948, after attending negotiations between Hindus and Muslims, Gandhi was shot and killed by a Hindu extremist who objected to Gandhi's inclusive philosophy.

Legacy

Mohandas Gandhi created one of the most powerful nonviolent movements for independence and social reform. His example inspired both other independence movements in European colonies and social reform movements in the United States and elsewhere.

Gandhi formulated the principle of *svaraj*, or self–rule, which to Gandhi meant not only political independence but a moral regeneration that would achieve unity among Indians of all religions and an end to untouchableness and the low status of women. Gandhi emphasized what he saw as the unique spiritual potential of India with its various religious traditions such as Hinduism, Islam, and Buddhism. With this message Gandhi turned the Indian National Congress into a mass movement stressing inclusiveness.

Gandhi's movement for national liberation inspired other colonized peoples in Asia and Africa. In the 20 years following Indian independence, most of the European overseas colonies had gained their independence, some as or even more peacefully than had India.

Much of Gandhi's vision did not become a reality. Yet his protege JAWAHARLAL NEHRU, helped to carry it on and sustain India as the world's largest democracy. Gandhi's methods were also adopted by other social reform movements, most notably the African–American civil rights movement, led by MARTIN LUTHER KING, JR., in the 1950s and 1960s.

Lemoine

For Further Reading

Copley, Antony. *Gandhi, Against the Tide.* London: Basil Blackwell, 1987.

Nanda, Bal Ram. *Mahatma Gandhi: A Biography.* Boston: Beacon Press, 1958.

Payne, Robert. *The Life and Death of Mahatma Gandhi.* New York: Dutton, 1969.

Garibaldi, Giuseppe

Nineteenth-Century Leader of
Italian Unification
1807–1882

Life and Work

Italian nationalist Giuseppe Garibaldi, along with GIUSEPPE MAZZINI and CAMILLO BENSO DI CAVOUR, led the struggle for Italian unification in the nineteenth century. Leading a band of guerrilla fighters, Garibaldi overthrew the monarchy in Naples, allowing the proclamation of the Kingdom of Italy.

Garibaldi was born on July 4, 1807, in Nice (now in France). Sailing the Mediterranean, Garibaldi learned of Italian nationalist organizations, including Young Italy, an organization founded by Mazzini and dedicated to the unification of Italy. Late in 1833, after meeting with Mazzini, Garibaldi joined Young Italy. The following year, Garibaldi took part in a failed insurrection led by Mazzini in Genoa against the kingdom of Piedmont-Sardinia. Garibaldi was sentenced to death in absentia and fled to South America, where for 14 years he fought for republican causes, learning the techniques of guerrilla fighting and the tactics of popular revolt.

In 1848, Garibaldi returned to Italy to take part in the revolutions that had erupted along the entire peninsula. He participated in a number of skirmishes and, most notably, led the defense of the newly established Roman Republic against French forces sent to restore the Pope in 1849. The Italian uprisings all failed, and Garibaldi was exiled again. However, his struggles inspired support for unification among many Italians.

In 1859, the process of Italian unification (known as the Risorgimento) began when Cavour, prime minister of Piedmont-Sardinia, negotiated an alliance with Napoleon III of France to drive the Austrians from the northern Italian provinces of Lombardy and Venetia. Returning from exile, Garibaldi was given command of Italian volunteers assigned to engage the Austrians in the Alps. Piedmont took the province of Lombardy from Austria, and Garibaldi was hailed as a hero.

In May 1860 Garibaldi sailed to Sicily with about 1,000 volunteers. There they led a popular and successful insurrection against Francis II, ruler of the kingdom of Naples, of which Sicily was a part. Triumphant, Garibaldi headed for Naples on the mainland, where he defeated royal forces and deposed the king.

Garibaldi then made preparations to march on Rome. To prevent revolution from spreading north, Cavour sent troops to block him. Garibaldi, who wanted above all else to see Italy unified, handed Naples over to Piedmont-Sardinia. On March 17, 1861, the Kingdom of Italy was proclaimed.

Although most of Italy was unified, Garibaldi continued plotting to invade Rome. In 1862, Italian troops stopped his invasion; in 1867, France, which, under Napoleon III, considered itself a protector of the papacy, sent in troops to halt another attempt. Garibaldi remained active in politics until 1874, when he retired on the island of Caprera. He died on June 2, 1882.

Legacy

Giuseppe Garibaldi brought the issue of national unification to the forefront of Italian society in the nineteenth century. Garibaldi was a charismatic leader and romantic revolutionary who inspired similar nationalist movements in the nineteenth and twentieth centuries.

Garibaldi began his political life as a follower of Mazzini; he saw the republic as the ideal form of government for a nation-state. Garibaldi believed that the best way to achieve the dual goals of national unification and revolution was through the use of small, dedicated guerrilla bands. Although very spiritual, Garibaldi was an avowed enemy of the Roman Catholic church. His repeated attempts to conquer Rome and depose the Pope reflect his desire to eliminate the influence of the church in Italian political life. Italian liberals have continued this struggle into the twentieth century.

Garibaldi ultimately accepted a constitutional monarchy under the leadership of Piedmont-Sardinia. He played a crucial role in the unification of Italy with his conquest of Sicily and Naples and with his willingness to hand the southern lands over to the Piedmontese. His great personal popularity among the Italian people contributed to the legitimacy of the new nation-state. On June 2, 1946, Garibaldi's dream was realized when Italy officially became a republic; Garibaldi was celebrated as a founding father.

In the twentieth century Garibaldi was still regarded as a hero in nations as disparate as Great Britain, Uruguay, and the former Soviet Union. Revolutionary movements on the right and the left have claimed Garibaldi as a heroic ancestor. Italian fascists led by BENITO MUSSOLINI applauded Garibaldi's dedication to the nationalist cause and the fact that, before turning Naples over to Piedmont, he ruled it as a dictatorship. Garibaldi believed in dictatorship as a strictly temporary measure, however, and considered himself an internationalist and democrat. Italian communists were inspired by Garibaldi, yet he was not a totalitarian; he cherished liberal ideals of freedom and humanitarianism.

Lemoine

WORLD EVENTS		GARIBALDI'S LIFE
French Revolution begins	1789	
	1807	Giuseppe Garibaldi is born
Latin American independence movement begins	1811	
Congress of Vienna reorganizes Europe	1815	
	1834	Garibaldi participates in failed uprising and flees to South America
	1849	Garibaldi defends Rome against French forces
	1860	Garibaldi and followers take control of kingdom of Naples
	1861	Garibaldi marches on Rome, but is blocked by Cavour
	1862	Italian troops repel Garibaldi's attempted invasion of Rome
	1867	French troops repel Garibaldi's second attempt to invade Rome
Germany is united	1871	
	1882	Garibaldi dies
Russo-Japanese War	1905	

For Further Reading

Hibbert, Christopher. *Garibaldi and His Enemies.* London: Penguin Books, 1987.
Ridley, Jasper. *Garibaldi.* New York: Viking Press, 1976.
Smith, Denis Mack. *Cavour and Garibaldi 1860.* Cambridge: Cambridge University Press, 1954.

Genghis Khan

Founder of the Mongol Empire
1162–1227

Life and Work

Conquering the peoples of Central Asia, China, and Persia, Genghis Khan created one of the most powerful empires in the world.

World Events		Genghis Khan's Life
Timbuktu influential throughout west central Africa	c. 1100	
	1162	Genghis Khan is born
	c. 1175	Genghis Kahn's father dies and Genghis Khan is banished
Saladin takes Jerusalem for Islam	1187	
	1206	Genghis Khan proclaimed leader of Mongols
	1213	Mongols invade northern China
Mongol conquest of China	1215	
	1220	Genghis Khan orders armies to invade Persia which is conquered
	1223	Genghis Khan invades Rus
	1227	Genghis Khan dies
Tamerlane conquers Baghdad	1325	

Genghis Khan was born in 1162 with the name Temujin. His father was a Mongol chief whose death in c. 1175 left the young boy unable to manage the affairs of tribal rule. Opposed by a rival clan, Temujin was banished along with his mother to a remote region of the Steppe, where it was hoped he would perish. He showed great tenacity, however, and with his charisma managed to build a large following. After recovering his authority with his own tribe, he gradually expanded his influence over others. This frequently led to conflict with rivals, and, on more than one occasion, he was the target of assassination. In one case, his enemies plotted to kill him during his betrothal feast. He narrowly escaped, and returned later with an army to avenge himself. By 1206, he had established himself as the undisputed ruler of all the Mongol tribes, a status that earned him the name Genghis Khan ("Universal Ruler").

Historians are unsure what provoked Genghis Khan to launch his mounted campaigns of imperial expansion after 1206. In any case, his first target was an ambitious one. China, which had been ruled by the Song dynasty for nearly three centuries, was eastern Asia's greatest power. In 1213, Mongol forces burst through the Great Wall and immediately set upon the major cities of the north. In 1215 Peking fell to the ruthless army, and by 1234 all of northern China lay under Mongol rule. Almost at the same time, Genghis Khan ordered his armies to march on Persia, which itself fell in 1220. The Russians were next. In 1223, Genghis Khan led an expeditionary force across the Steppe to southern Rus, only to pull back before a serious engagement was possible. He made effective use of his position, though, by descending upon the Central Asian khanates of Bukhara and Samarkand. In these and other cities he ordered all of the civilian survivors executed, with the exception of those who would make suitable slaves.

Genghis Khan might have turned upon yet another great civilization, but on August 18, 1227, he died in a riding accident. Even his funeral was a testament to his character, for during the ceremony scores of horses and young women were led out to his grave and slaughtered.

Legacy

Genghis Khan created an empire whose boundaries and administration were still insecure at the time of his death. His successors continued his brutal policies of expansion but failed to preserve an integral mongol state.

In the east his grandson, Kublai Khan, continued to expand Mongol rule over southern China, and, by 1271, he was able to proclaim the beginning of the Yuan dynasty there. In the west, another grandson, Hulagu, sacked and burned the city of Baghdad, killing the Islamic caliph. Further north, another relative, Ogodei, and his armies marched all the way to the plains of Hungary and might have continued on to Vienna when death brought his rampage to a sudden end.

The brutality of Genghis Khan's rule left a baneful legacy for subsequent Mongol rulers and, in the end, their subjects. By employing tactics of terror in battle, especially against besieged cities, Genghis Khan established a practice that would have devastating results on subject populations and sow the seeds for future revolt. When his successors in the north, for instance, continued his campaign against the Russians in 1240, they sacked the great city of Kiev, burning it to the ground. Subsequent generations of Russians would remember this brutal disgrace, feeling with time a greater sense of unity in the face of the detested Mongol yoke.

Genghis Khan's failure to establish a lasting form of state administration in the realms he conquered also undermined the authority of future Mongol rulers. His generals and elites came to depend upon military glory and tribute for their livelihood, preventing a stable regime during peacetime. Thus, as soon as Genghis Khan died, rivals for the succession divided the empire into various personal realms. In China the Yuan dynasty of Kublai Khan would rule without attention to greater Mongol interests. Its lack of regard for Chinese interests would bring its overthrow in less than a century. In the lands of Rus, the Golden Horde (the Mongol successor state) would establish control over the resentful Christian Orthodox population, but would constitute little more than an armed band that gathered tribute until finally repudiated in 1480 by Ivan III, who refused to make any further tribute payments.

Strickland

For Further Reading

Chambers, James. *The Devil's Horsemen: The Mongol Invasion of Europe.* New York: Atheneum, 1979.
Hoang, Michael. *Genghis Khan.* Translated by Ingrid Cranfield. London: Saqi, 1990.
Morgan, David. *The Mongols.* Oxford: Blackwell, 1986.

Gladstone, William Ewart

British Politician and Leader
of the Liberal Party
1809–1898

Life and Work

Leader of the British Liberal Party during much of the nineteenth century, William Ewart Gladstone governed Great Britain by putting into effect many of the principles of liberalism during the reign of Queen Victoria.

Gladstone was born on December 29, 1809, in Liverpool, England. At Oxford University he excelled in his studies and joined the debate club. Debating was an excellent preparation for a career in Parliament, and in 1832, the year after his graduation, Gladstone was elected to Parliament as a member of the Conservative Party (Tories). Appointed president of the Board of Trade in 1843, Gladstone became convinced of the economic importance of free trade.

He began to identify himself more with the Liberal Party (Whigs) in 1846, after the controversial Corn Laws, which had imposed tariffs on most imported grains since the twelfth century, were repealed. Gladstone supported repeal, which had divided the Conservative Party. In 1847 he was elected member of Parliament for Oxford University. In the years to follow, Gladstone also accepted ministry portfolios of increasing importance.

In 1867 he assumed the leadership of the Liberal Party; in 1868 he became prime minister, a post he held until 1874. Under his leadership, Parliament passed bills that expanded the civil service and state support for education, adopted secret ballots in elections, abolished the purchase of military commissions, and eliminated religious tests for Oxford and Cambridge universities. Prime minister again from 1880 to 1885, Gladstone also pushed through a third Reform Act (1884); the first two, passed in 1832 and 1867, extended the franchise to the middle classes, giving the vote to all male taxpayers—about two-thirds of all adult males.

Gladstone also sought to curb British imperialism. He granted independence to the Transvaal in South Africa, yet sent troops to occupy Egypt in 1882 after a nationalist revolt there. Gladstone's hope was to remove the troops quickly; however, they remained until 1956.

The "Irish problem" concerned Gladstone more than any other issue; each time he was prime minister he introduced bills to Parliament favorable to Irish Roman Catholics. Prime minister for the last time from 1892 to 1894, Gladstone introduced two bills that would have extended home rule in Ireland, but both failed. Embittered by this defeat, Gladstone retired in 1894, after 61 years of government. He died four years later, on May 19, 1898.

Legacy

Combining strong religious and moral convictions with a willingness to adapt to changing circumstances, William Ewart Gladstone provided effective political leadership in Victorian Britain. His principles defined the Liberal Party in the nineteenth century and anticipated many important twentieth-century issues.

For Gladstone, government's responsibility was to oppose privilege, injustice, and inhumanity. Yet he believed in individual responsibility for employment, social mobility, and accumulation of wealth. Individuals needed such freedom and liberty; Gladstone's various reform bills reflected this philosophy.

Although he held deep religious convictions, Gladstone came to see that the Anglican church could not maintain its privileged place in British society. Sympathizing with the plight of Roman Catholic Ireland, he proposed bills in Parliament to give the Irish more autonomy

and championed a bill disestablishing the Irish church (an offshoot of the Church of England). Among Gladstone's many reforms designed to alleviate Irish rural poverty, he sponsored bills that attempted land reform favorable to tenant farmers in Ireland, provided fair rent, and restricted eviction by landowners.

Gladstone's Christian and Liberal Party views also affected foreign policy at a time of British international supremacy. In his electoral campaign of 1880 he criticized the foreign policy of Benjamin Disraeli, his Conservative predecessor and parliamentary rival. His sense of justice and support for liberty underlay his ambivalence toward British imperialism. He believed in self-government for colonists and showed a measured respect for the existing indigenous population.

Gladstone's guiding principles were effective in Britain until 1930s, when the Great Depression destroyed the Liberal Party. These principles continued to inspire both the Labour and Conservative Parties in the twentieth century. Gladstone's policies anticipated important currents of British political thought in the twentieth century, such as liberty, equality of opportunity, justice for Ireland, and anti-imperialism.

Lemoine

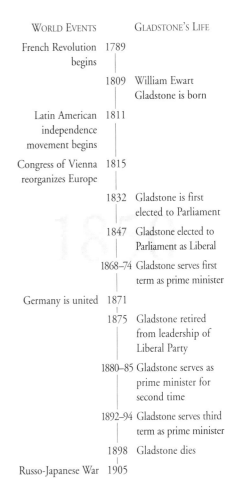

WORLD EVENTS		GLADSTONE'S LIFE
French Revolution begins	1789	
	1809	William Ewart Gladstone is born
Latin American independence movement begins	1811	
Congress of Vienna reorganizes Europe	1815	
	1832	Gladstone is first elected to Parliament
	1847	Gladstone elected to Parliament as Liberal
	1868–74	Gladstone serves first term as prime minister
Germany is united	1871	
	1875	Gladstone retired from leadership of Liberal Party
	1880–85	Gladstone serves as prime minister for second time
	1892–94	Gladstone serves third term as prime minister
	1898	Gladstone dies
Russo-Japanese War	1905	

For Further Reading
Matthew, H. C. G. *Gladstone, 1809–1874.* Oxford: Clarendon Press, 1986.
Ramm, Agatha, and William Ewart. *Gladstone.* Cardiff: University of Wales Press, 1989.
Stansky, Peter. *Gladstone: A Progress in Politics.* Boston: Little, Brown, 1979.

Gorbachev, Mikhail

Last Soviet Leader

1931–

Life and Work

Mikhail Gorbachev came to power in a Soviet Union suffering from long-term economic and political problems. Dedicated to strengthening the communist system, his reforms inadvertently provoked its collapse.

Gorbachev was born on March 2, 1931, in the village of Privolnoe, north of Caucasia. In 1950 he entered Moscow State University, where he met and married Raisa Titorenko. Graduating with a law degree in 1955, he soon devoted himself to the Communist Party. By 1980 he had become a member of its top body, the Politburo, and upon the death of LEONID BREZHNEV in 1982 he emerged as a leading proponent of reform.

In 1985 he was elevated to the post of general secretary of the Party and immediately launched a program called *perestroika* ("restructuring"). His goal was to strengthen the Soviet Union's stagnant economy by enacting a series of reforms. To create a climate for these reforms, and to counter the strength of his conservative opponents in the Politburo, he simultaneously introduced a policy called *glasnost* ("openness"). This was designed to encourage public discussion of the communist system's problems. The explosion of a nuclear power station at Chernobyl in 1986 served only to highlight these problems, and this, along with a growing economic crisis, eroded Gorbachev's popular support.

Meanwhile, his conservative opponents were preparing a putsch. On August 18, 1991, in the wake of demands by Lithuanian nationalists for secession from the Soviet Union, a group of neo-Stalinists led by Boris Pugo declared a state of emergency and demanded the removal of Gorbachev. By this time hostility to the communist system had become too great, however, and a mass outpouring of democratic opposition led by Russian President BORIS YELTSIN derailed the scheme. As the army sided with Yeltsin, the putsch failed and the Communist Party was banned. Yeltsin's creation of a Commonwealth of Independent States (CIS) in early December finally doomed the Soviet Union and Gorbachev's leadership of it. On December 25, 1991, Gorbachev resigned, and the Soviet Union was formally dissolved.

Thereafter a private citizen, Gorbachev spent the remainder of the decade organizing a Gorbachev Fund for international cooperation and supporting Russia's peaceful transition to democracy. He remained true to his highly humanistic principles by criticizing both the intolerant Communist Party revivalists and the aggressive capitalists who had succeeded them in managing the Russian economy. In 1996 he entered the race for the Russian presidency, but failed to unseat Yeltsin. The man who had made a peaceful transition to democracy in Russia possible received scarcely one percent of the people's vote.

Legacy

Gorbachev's reforms made the collapse of communism in the Soviet Union possible. Due in a large part to his devotion to human rights, this tumultuous event proved to be one of the most peaceful revolutions in history.

Gorbachev's decision to share the responsibilities of reform with Soviet society was fate-

ful. *Glasnost* enabled Soviet citizens to begin exploring (often for the first time) the shortcomings of Soviet history and of communist rule. Thus as televisions and newspapers began to broadcast evidence of massive ecological destruction, grave social problems, and brutal police repression, popular loyalty to the system simply dissolved.

Gorbachev's commitment to the peaceful and democratic reform of communism had important effects throughout the world. In China it helped inspire the democratic protest on Tiananmen Square in 1989, though repression by conservative communists under DENG XIAOPING resulted in the deaths of approximately 3,000 people. In Eastern Europe, Gorbachev's example had a happier outcome. Declaring a "new course" in Soviet diplomacy, Gorbachev formally revoked the Brezhnev Doctrine in 1989, thereby assuring that political reform in communist Eastern Europe would not bring Soviet military intervention. By the end of the year, communism there was swept away in a series of democratic revolutions such as those under VACLAV HAVEL in Czechoslovakia and LECH WALESA in Poland. All of this offered yet more inspiration to radical forces back in the Soviet Union.

Gorbachev's humanistic vision of communism, then, died amid a struggle between radical democrats and conservative communists. His greatest legacy, perhaps, is that the revolution that he made possible occurred so peacefully.

Strickland

World Events	Gorbachev's Life
Great Depression 1929–39	
	1931 Mikhail Gorbachev is born
World War II 1939–45	
Communist China 1949 is established	
	1950 Gorbachev enters Moscow State University
Israel defeats 1967 Arab nations in Six-Day War	
Vietnam War ends 1975	
	1980 Gorbachev becomes member of Politburo
	1985 Gorbachev becomes general secretary of Communist Party and launches reforms
	1989 Gorbachev revokes Brezhnev Doctrine
Dissolution of 1991 Soviet Union	Gorbachev resigns

For Further Reading

Gorbachev, Mikhail S. *Perestroika: New Thinking for Our Country and the World.* New York: Harper & Row, 1987.

Hosking, Geoffrey. *The Awakening of the Soviet Union.* Cambridge, Mass.: Harvard University Press, 1990.

Kaiser, Robert G. *Why Gorbachev Happened.* New York: Simon & Schuster, 1992.

Lewin, Moshe. *The Gorbachev Phenomenon: A Historical Interpretation.* Berkeley: University of California Press, 1991.

Guevara, Ernesto

Marxist Revolutionary and
Guerrilla Leader
1928–1967

Life and Work

Ernesto (Ché) Guevara organized a revolutionary movement throughout Latin America that combined Marxist theory and guerrilla warfare. His success in helping to overthrow the government of Cuba was followed by a disastrous campaign in Bolivia.

Ernesto Guevara was born in Argentina to middle-class parents on June 14, 1928. He developed a deep concern for the poor as a youth, and a journey through several Latin American countries in the early 1950s revealed such repression and impoverishment that he abandoned his original plans for a career in medicine. Believing that only a fundamental reordering of society could bring lasting benefits, he began to read KARL MARX. In 1954, after witnessing the American-sponsored overthrow of the leftist regime of Jacobo Arbenz Guzmán in Guatemala, he dedicated himself to the life of a revolutionary.

In 1955 he became aquainted with FIDEL CASTRO and joined efforts to overthrow the authoritarian regime of Fulgencio Batista in Cuba. In 1956, he organized a heroic invasion of the island from the ship *Granma*, but was forced, along with his accomplices, to take to

the hills as a guerrilla for nearly two years. In 1959 forces under his command seized Havana and installed Castro as the head of a new communist regime. Guevara was appointed minister of industry in 1961, but failed to achieve the levels of industrialization he desired. He soon fell out with Castro, mainly because of his criticisms of the Soviet Union, Cuba's communist patron. Increasingly isolated and dissatisfied, he left Cuba to pursue revolutionary activities in other parts of the nonindustrial world.

After an unsuccessful campaign in Africa in 1965, he returned to Latin America. In 1960 he had written a book entitled *Guerrilla Warfare,* and he now applied its teaching by organizing a network of Marxist guerrilla bands. In 1967 his forces became surrounded in Bolivia, however, and with no response from Castro to pleas for assistance, Guevara was forced to surrender. On October 9, 1967, he was executed by the Bolivian government.

Legacy

Ernesto Guevara left a unique example of revolutionary activity that grew in influence after his death. His daring military exploits and concern for the poor produced a cult that inspired revolutionaries for the remainder of the century.

Guevara's goal from an early stage had been to overthrow Latin America's many authoritarian states and to replace them with a unified workers' state resembling, to some extent, Communist Soviet Union. At this time Latin America already shared the Roman Catholic faith and (with the exception of Brazil) the Spanish language. It was to these elements of unity that SIMÓN BOLÍVAR had appealed without success when seeking to build a unified political order early in the nineteenth century. Guevara's Marxist vision, however, emphasized social justice and economic self-determination. As a result of the revolution in Cuba, for instance, property was redistributed and programs to develop a native industrial economy were introduced. These priorities appealed to twentieth-century revolutionaries who hoped both to incite mass insurrection and free their lands from the threat of intervention by the United States. Guevara's application of guerrilla warfare in the revolutionary struggle

offered hope that the revolutionaries could build sufficient support among the peasantry to overpower governmental forces. Guevara's method was employed in the late twentieth century by the Shining Path movement of Peru, whose use of guerrilla warfare and terrorism against the government sparked a civil war in 1980 that, while failing to alter the social order, claimed approximately 25,000 lives.

Guevara also influenced later revolutionaries by means of a cult that formed around his memory. The bearded image of the late revolutionary, along with his nom de guerre, Ché, became a symbol for spontaneous insurrection throughout the world. It was seen during the Cultural Revolution of MAO TSE-TUNG in China and during the worldwide student insurrections of 1968.

Strickland

WORLD EVENTS		GUEVARA'S LIFE
Russian Revolution	1917	
	1928	Ernesto (Ché) Guevara is born
Great Depression	1929–39	
World War II	1939–45	
Communist China is established	1949	
	1954	Guevara turns to life of revolutionary
	1956	Guevara leads guerrilla forces to Cuba
	1959	Guevara is one leader of Cuban Revolution
	1960	Guevara sees publication of *Guerrilla Warfare*
	1965	Guevara leads unsuccessful guerrilla movement in Africa
Israel defeats Arab nations in Six-Day War	1967	Guevara is executed in Bolivia
Vietnam War ends	1975	

For Further Reading

Anderson, Jon Lee. *Che Guevara: A Revolutionary Life.* New York: Grove, 1997.

Castaneda, Jorge G. *Compañero: The Life and Death of Che Guevara.* Translated by Marina Castaneda. New York: Knopf, 1997.

Sinclair, Andrew. *Guevara.* London: Fontana, 1970.

Gustavus Adolfus

King of Sweden
1594–1632

Life and Work

Gustavus Adolphus transformed Sweden from a remote kingdom into a powerful European empire. He fought successful wars around the Baltic and his intervention in the Thirty Years War helped to preserve Protestantism.

Gustavus was born in Stockholm in 1594. His father, King Karl IX, had usurped the Swedish throne after the former king, Sigismund, abandoned it to become the king of Roman Catholic Poland. In 1611 Gustavus acceded to the throne but was immediately confronted by nobles demanding political concessions. In the following year he appointed Count Axel Oxenstierna as his chancellor and was able to settle the crisis by signing a document known as the Constitutional Charter.

Concurrently, Gustavus was faced with a military crisis. Denmark had attacked Sweden shortly before his accession; only in 1613 was peace gained through the Treaty of Knäred. Another war with Russia followed, and was concluded in Sweden's favor in 1617. The Treaty of Stolbova granted Finland and Livonia to Sweden, thereby making it an empire. In 1621 war with Poland erupted, lasting until 1629. Gustavus's greatest military struggle occurred in central Europe, however. Since 1618 the forces of the Catholic League led by the Holy Roman Empire had been inflicting heavy losses on Protestant forces in Germany. Although the ruler of a Protestant power, Gustavus had at first resisted pleas to intervene on the side of the desperate Germans. In 1630, however, he changed his mind and marched at the head of his troops to Stettino on the Baltic, which he captured in 1631. He then relieved the Protestants at Magdeburg in Germany. When the Swedish forces arrived, they found a fallen city and thousands massacred. Gustavus exacted revenge later the same year at the Battle of Breitenfeld, where his innovative use of infantrymen laid waste to opposing forces. In the following year near the River Lech, Gustavus used a floating bridge and relentless cannonades to destroy the Catholic League's army.

Gustavus now seemed to have an open road to Vienna. But the Catholic League was able to organize a new force; in 1632, at the Battle of Lützen, Gustavus's illustrious life of war was ended by a stray musket ball.

Legacy

When he was killed at Lützen, Gustavus Adolphus left behind a transformed Swedish state and a military tradition that would alter the course of European history.

Gustavus's tireless wars in the Baltic region greatly enhanced the power of Sweden. What had formerly been a kingdom limited to Scandinavia now became the major imperial power of eastern Europe. Both Poland and Russia would have to face Swedish armies later in the seventeenth century. In the case of Russia, Sweden would launch an invasion under Charles XII (r. 1697–1718) that would nearly destroy PETER I (Peter the Great). Sweden had also been strengthened by Gustavus's administration. Oxenstierna ruled wisely while the king was campaigning, introducing tax and legal reforms that increased the power of the central government.

Gustavus defended Protestantism—historians regard his victory at Breitenfeld as a turning point in the Thirty Years War. In addition to saving Protestantism at a moment of crisis, Gustavus bears partial responsibility for the general destruction of Germany during the course of the war. While he had been unable to prevent the tragedy at Magdeburg in 1631, his campaigns kept the war going much longer than would have been possible without him. By defeating the Catholic League, he also prevented Germany from being united under Roman Catholic imperial rule. As a result, Germany would remain divided until the nineteenth century.

Finally, Gustavus contributed to a military revolution. A devout Christian, he insisted that his troops conduct themselves in what he considered an honorable manner, disavowing acts of torture and rapine; however, he was one of the first rulers to rely upon conscription. His well-planned attacks included arranging his infantry in tightly grouped parallel lines where the careful timing of the discharge and reloading of their muskets enabled them to direct almost continuous fire upon the enemy. Common foot soldiers and cavalry, which had formed the core of European armies since the early Middle Ages, now gave way to these trained infantry lines. What is more, since a great deal of discipline was essential for volley tactics, the role of the state in training armies and conducting drills increased. Thus by the end of the century King LOUIS XIV of France would deploy professional armies modeled on those of Gustavus, and the infantry line would remain a centerpiece of the modern army until the invention of the machine gun before World War I.

Strickland

For Further Reading
Asch, Ronald G. *The Thirty Years War: The Holy Roman Empire and Europe, 1618–1648.* New York: St. Martin's Press, 1997.
Roberts, Michael. *Gustavus Adolphus.* 2nd ed. London: Longman, 1992.
———. *The Swedish Imperial Experience, 1560–1718.* Cambridge: Cambridge University Press, 1979.

Hadrian

Emperor of Rome
76–138

Life and Work

Hadrian continued the reforms his cousin and predecessor, Emperor Trajan, had begun in 96, and in so doing, helped ensure Rome one of its longest periods of peace and prosperity.

Caesar Traianus Hadrianus Augustus, commonly known as Hadrian, was born Publius Aelius Hadrianus on January 24, 76, probably in Rome. He was schooled in Rome. In 86, after his father's death, Hadrian was entrusted to Trajan, a high government official. In 90, Hadrian traveled to and spent several years at his family's ancestral home in Spain. He joined a military college in Seville. After 95, Hadrian acted as a tribune, or civilian military commander, of the Legion II Adiutrix in Germany.

After Emperor Nerva's death in 98, Trajan ascended to the throne. Trajan ensured that Hadrian served in posts that earned him rank and respect within the Roman administration. Between 101 and 106, Hadrian assisted Trajan as a magistrate and secretary and in successful military campaigns against the kingdoms of Dacia (modern Romania) and in the province of Arabia. In 108, he served as governor of Lower Pannonia (modern Hungary and Serbia). Between 109 and 112, Hadrian lived in Athens, becoming an Athenian citizen and serving as a magistrate. In 113, Hadrian joined Trajan in a campaign against the Parthians, who held lands claimed by the Romans to the east of contemporary Armenia and Turkey.

Trajan adopted Hadrian just a day before he died in 117. Although facing much anger for initially ordering the assassination of potential opponents, Hadrian quickly established his power base and began a series of popular reforms. He decreed a tax amnesty, organized important legal and administrative reforms, and encouraged learning and the arts. Over the next 17 years, Hadrian spent much time away from Rome, either campaigning against the Germans, Britons, and Parthians between 121 and 124, brutally putting down the Jews of Judea in about 132–135, or peacefully touring provinces such as Africa in 127. After 135, Hadrian spent more time in Rome, ordering the construction of baths and theaters for the public and enjoying the prosperity for which he was partly responsible. Following the death of his appointed heir, Lucius Aelius, in 136, Hadrian adopted another heir, Antonius Pius, who in turn adopted two heirs of his own, MARCUS AURELIUS and Lucius Verus. All three served as emperors over the next 44 years and carried on Hadrian's program of reforms. Hadrian died on July 10, 138.

Legacy

Hadrian promoted a Golden Age by ordering administrative reforms and patronizing the arts. Ironically, the methods used to achieve this legacy encouraged a slow ossification of the empire that later emperors could not reverse.

To promote universal peace and prosperity, Hadrian worked hard to enhance reforms begun by preceding emperors. Hadrian is chiefly remembered for adding force to Trajan's efforts to both give more authority to and lighten the burden on the provinces. Like Trajan, Hadrian wanted to make the provinces just as dynamic as Rome itself and thus make the empire a whole of integrated, mutually supporting regions. To ensure that provincial governments actively carried out reforms that favored integration and provided for the welfare of the masses, Hadrian visited almost all of the provinces at least once. Hadrian's personal touch also extended to his relations with the military. To improve the soldiers' efficiency and discipline, Hadrian set an example by living in the field with his troops for long periods and by abolishing luxury from military encampments.

Although wise in the short term, Hadrian's reforms took the empire in a disadvantageous, though perhaps unavoidable, direction. Hadrian reinforced a subtle switch of authority from Rome to provincial centers, perhaps in response to the political influence of Rome's provincial armies or Hadrian's own provincial origins. Although making the empire function more smoothly and accentuating peace and prosperity, the switch of administrative responsibility to the provinces and use of "nationally" specialized militaries made the development of autonomous, anti–Rome regional powers more likely. Hadrian's efforts to defend the empire more effectively from advanced provincial bases led him to freeze the provincial, and thus the empire's, boundaries. Part of the empire's military dynamism had originated in its undetermined northern, southern, and eastern boundaries. With Hadrian, fixed fortifications, such as Hadrian's Wall in Britain, made Rome a geographically and defensively frozen state. Over the next 300 years, despite expeditions by Hadrian and some of his immediate successors to conquer Dacia, Armenia, and Mesopotamia, Roman armies gradually spent themselves in part by trying to recapture lost fortresses and fight off more mobile "barbarian" armies. These barbarian invasions were among the many other factors that led to the collapse Rome's authority, the disintegration of the empire, and the coming of the Dark Ages.

Del Testa

World Events	Hadrian's Life
Jesus is crucified c. 33	
	76 Hadrian is born
	90 Hadrian attends military college in Seville
	95 Hadrian is tribune in Germany
	101–106 Hadrian assists Emperor Trajan's administration
Roman Empire reaches greatest size	117 Hadrian succeeds Trajan as emperor
	121–135 Hadrian wars with Germans, Britons, Parthians, and Jews
	138 Hadrian dies
Constantine becomes emperor of Rome	306

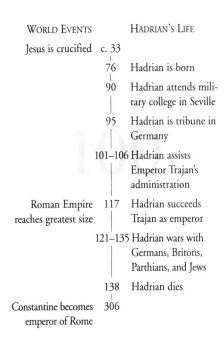

For Further Reading

Birley, Anthony B. *Hadrian: The Restless Emperor.* New York: London, 1997.

Perowne, Stewart. *Hadrian.* New York: W. W. Norton, 1961.

Hammurabi

Sumerian King

c. 1820/1810–c. 1750 B.C.E.

Life and Work

Hammurabi united the independent city-states of Mesopotamia and formed the political foundations of one of humankind's first great civilizations.

World Events	Hammurabi's Life
B.C.E.	
Indus Valley civiliza- c. 2000 tion flourishes	
	c. 1820 /1810 Hammurabi is born
	1792 Hammurabi becomes king
	1764 Hammurabi forms defensive coalition, attacks Larsans
	1762 Hammurabi begins military campaign to east
	1761 Hammurabi begins military campaign to north
First signs of 1760 organized civilization in China	Hammurabi defeats Larsans and subsequently resettles them on Babylonian land
Hammurabi unites c. 1750 Mesopotamia	Hammurabi dies
Minoan civilization c. 1425 is destroyed	

Born sometime between 1820 to 1810 B.C.E., Hammurabi was the son of King Sinmuballit of Babylon, then a small city-state and rival of the hundreds of other small city-states that made up ancient Sumeria and Mesopotamia. Very little about his early life and his reign are known. Before he became king upon his father's death in 1792, Hammurabi had held some administrative posts as a form of training. Although still young when he became king, Hammurabi quickly became known as an effective leader.

Initially, Hammurabi engaged in building or restoring temples, dedicating worship objects to the deities, and overseeing the construction of the all-important irrigation canals. However, Hammurabi also built up his military forces, which he turned against rival city-states in 1787.

Hammurabi wanted to make Babylon, with its strategic position and strong military, the premier city-state in the region. Hammurabi struck first down the Euphrates River toward King Rim-Sin of Larsa. Although Babylon made modest gains in territory at the expense of Larsa, this military adventure taxed Hammurabi's ability to wage aggressive warfare, and between 1784 and 1769 he did not mount another campaign of conquest.

In 1764, Hammurabi arranged a coalition with neighboring kingdoms to assure access to the metal-producing areas of Persia and prevent an unfriendly coalition from building against him. With his security assured, Hammurabi once again moved against King Rim-Sin of Larsa, this time utilizing the most terrifying weapon of the day—a temporary dam of the Euphrates that either denied life-giving waters to the Larsans or destroyed them in a sudden release of its waters. King Rim-Sin was defeated in a final siege of Larsa itself. After 1760, Hammurabi resettled the Larsans on his own lands.

In 1762, Hammurabi struck east, and in 1761 he struck north. By 1755 the eastward campaigns, quite costly given the necessity of long sieges, had brought the eastern Sumerian kingdoms under Hammuabi's control but exposed Babylon directly to the Kassites of Persia, a war-like people who would conquer Babylon 160 years later. The northern campaigns were also successful, bringing a former ally, King Zimrilin of the Mari, under Babylonian control. These campaigns were fought for better control of the Euphrates or control of valuable trade routes to the north of Babylon.

Old and sick, with many of his duties already taken over by his son Samsuiluna, Hammurabi died sometime around 1750.

Legacy

Hammurabi took Babylon out of its relative isolation by conquering important sources of trade and water and prepared a legal foundation for a strong state—the Code of Hammurabi—but in so doing exposed Babylon to forces that even its newfound power could not contain.

Prior to the kingship of Hammurabi, Babylon was a creatively rich yet economically disadvantaged backwater. Cities farther to the south, such as Larsa, or to the north, such as Kirsi, enjoyed many more economic advantages. Hammurabi's grandfather and his father had tried without great success to conquer those city-states. Hammurabi succeeded because of his natural talents to lead and organize effectively and because he made careful diplomatic and military preparations. Thus, Babylon, though not long under the sway of Hammurabi's descendants, became the center of Mesopotamian affairs. Although Hammurabi's descendants did not rule Babylon for very long, Hammurabi permanently recentered the focus of Mesopotamian politics and culture to Babylon.

Hammurabi is often credited for greatness because of the Code of Hammurabi, which laid down the rule of administrative and judicial regularity as well as the state management of resources and ritual. His centralizing effort should be seen as a plan rather than the actual state of affairs, because transforming such a ritualistic society must have been difficult at best. Even the Code of Hammurabi may have had less influence than historians once thought, for archeologists have discovered many other codes from around the same time or earlier. However, despite its potential lack of originality and limited scope, the Code of Hammurabi did strengthen Hammurabi's state by eliminating the most arbitrary aspects of the law under which common people lived. The citizens of Babylon could therefore trust their ruler and his rule more thoroughly because it was predictable and established with the interests of society in mind.

Del Testa

For Further Reading

Oppenheim, A. Leo. *Ancient Mesopotamia: Portrait of a Dead Civilization.* Chicago: University of Chicago Press, 1964.
Reade, Julian. *Mesopotamia.* Cambridge, Mass.: Harvard University Press, 1991.

Hatshepsut

Female Pharaoh

c. 1522–1458 B.C.E.

Life and Work

Through careful political maneuvering and deft manipulation of ancient Egypt's cultural values, Queen Hatshepsut became one of Egypt's greatest sovereigns.

Hatshepsut was born sometime about 1522 B.C.E., in the XVIII dynasty, the eldest daughter of King Thutmose I. Thutmose I had worked continually to improve Egypt, embarking on extensive building projects and conquering the lands beyond Upper Egypt, in Nubia (present-day Sudan). All of his children had received an excellent courtly education. When her father died, Hatshepsut married her half-brother, Thutmose II, and in 1512 she became his queen. Thutmose II was frequently away on military expeditions, using rebellions in frontier areas as an excuse to expand Egypt's control into Palestine and Libya. Meanwhile, Hatshepsut remained in Egypt, clearly subsidiary to Thutmose II but fully engaged in imperial administration. When Thutmose II died after only three years as king, Hatshepsut became co-regent with Thutmose III, the son of her husband and a consort, Isis.

It was almost unprecedented for Hatshepsut to promote herself as king, but Thutmose III was much younger than she and Egypt was in such need of steady leadership that she was gradually accepted as sole ruler in 1472. In addition, Hatshepsut had so much experience, and had linked herself so carefully with Egypt's ruling elites during her husband's many absences that making her leader may have seemed appropriate. In order to rule, Hatshepsut had to assume the role of a man, sporting an artificial beard at official ceremonies and using the "Five Great Titles" appropriate for a king.

To show her respect for the religious system that guaranteed her right to rule, Hatshepsut ordered the construction of many religious monuments and frequently consulted with religious authorities in order to assure their loyalty. To safeguard the frontiers, and perhaps with Hatshepsut hoping that he would perish in battle, Thutmose III was sent by Hatshepsut on no fewer than 17 military campaigns in Asia, Palestine, and the Middle East. Hatshepsut led armed conquests of her own, raiding the kingdom of Punt, probably in the location of modern Eritrea, for tropical products and treasures.

At the height of her reign, Hatshepsut took a lover, Senenmut, a military officer of low birth, who nearly destroyed her. As she had done for many of a humble background, Hatshepsut promoted Senenmut within the imperial bureaucracy, determining that he had the abilities necessary to advance many of Egypt's causes. Senenmut manipulated Hatshepsut's growing reliance on him to make himself a king in all but name. This was particularly dangerous because a small but influential group of powerful Egyptians had never approved of the idea of a woman ruling over men. Hatshepsut's infatuation with Senenmut ended suddenly in about 1465 when she discovered that he had replaced her name on the inner portals of her tomb, then under construction, with his own. He was instantly stripped of power and died under mysterious circumstances.

After 20 to 30 years of successful if intrigue-filled rule, Hatshepsut died of natural causes sometime in February of 1458.

Legacy

What makes Hatshepsut's legacy special is that she ruled over a glorious period of New Kingdom Egypt, characterized by prosperity, peace, and expansion. What makes it almost unique is Hatshepsut's sex. (Egypt had had two other female kings—CLEOPATRA VII being one.)

Part of Hatshepsut's success originated with how she used Egypt's cultural traditions to defy social limitations that kept women from ruling. The eldest child of a popular king whose designated heir had died suddenly, Hatshepsut, obviously a supremely intelligent and political individual, claimed that *maat*, or the divine mandate of rule, had passed to her. By donning the clothes of a king and ruling effectively, there were no outward signs that she in fact had not inherited *maat*. Practicalities probably also encouraged a general acceptance of Hatshepsut's rule. At the time, Egypt had finally begun to enjoy prosperity after a long period of foreign domination, and no one wanted to disturb a carefully cultivated stability. In addition, Hatshepsut had ensured that, with Thutmose III absent on military campaigns, she had authority over the day-to-day bureaucratic duties that earned her the loyalties of the civil service. She also insisted on bringing up humble men of talent into positions of power, generating a kind of "cult of personality" based on loyalty and reciprocity. The prosperity engendered by the stability of Hatshepsut's reign produced a second Golden Age for Egypt that lasted for the next 300 years.

During Hatshepsut's rule, no one challenged her directly (although Senenmut came close to doing so), most likely because she reinforced traditional values and encouraged agricultural and commercial prosperity to such a degree that detractors could find no basis on which to criticize her. Hatshepsut took seriously the adage "clothes make the man": she "wore" her kingship and disproved the notion that rulership had to pass through males alone. Although disparaged after her death as a cultural rebel, Hatshepsut stood out as a very early symbol of someone who promoted talent over sex as a criterion for leadership.

Del Testa

WORLD EVENTS	HATSHEPSUT'S LIFE
B.C.E.	
Hammurabi unites c. 1750 Mesopotamia	
	c. 1522 Hatshepsut is born
	c. 1512 Hatshepsut marries half-brother Thutmose II and becomes Queen
	c. 1472 Hatshepsut becomes sole leader
	c. 1465 Hatshepsut dismisses Senenmut
	1458 Hatshepsut dies
Minoan civilization c. 1425 is destroyed	

For Further Reading

Tyldesley, Joyce. *Hatchepsut: The Female Pharaoh.* New York: Viking, 1996.

Wells, Evelyn. *Hatshepsut.* Garden City, NY: Doubleday, 1969.

Havel, Vaclav

Writer and President of
the Czech Republic
1936–

Life and Work

Once a playwright and political dissident imprisoned by Czechoslovakia's communist regime, Vaclav Havel played a leading role in the 1989 "Velvet Revolution" in Czechoslovakia. His moral authority guided the Czech Republic through its transformation

from a one-party communist state into a peaceful pluralistic democracy.

Havel was born on October 5, 1936, in Prague, the capital of Czechoslovakia, the son of a prosperous restaurant owner. His family's property was confiscated when the Communist Party took control of the Czechoslovak government in 1948. Because of his family's bourgeois background, Havel was initially denied access to higher education; Havel, however, did obtain a university degree by taking night classes.

Interested in theater, Havel took a job as a stagehand in 1959, and by 1968 he was writing his own plays. Havel participated in the "Prague Spring" of 1968, when reformists inside and outside the government sought increased independence from the Soviet Union. The Soviets soon crushed this rebellion with tanks and armed troops, and Havel's plays were banned. He continued to work for human rights, writing essays that coalesced into Charter 77, a manifesto for human rights signed by more than 200 dissidents. He was repeatedly arrested and imprisoned in the following decades, the longest for four years from 1979 to 1983, with the last sentence imposed as late as January 1989.

Later in 1989, the Soviet Union loosened its tight control of the Eastern European states, and a series of revolutions spread across the region, toppling most of the communist regimes. In Czechoslovakia, Havel took a leading role in the large demonstrations that took place in November, led by the opposition group Civic Forum; in December the communist government agreed to form a coalition government with Civic Forum. In what became known as the "Velvet Revolution" for its nonviolent transfer of power, Havel was elected interim president and reelected in July 1990.

In 1992 Havel resigned from office to oppose the separation of Slovakia from the Czech lands. He was subsequently elected to the presidency of the new Czech Republic in 1993. Despite deteriorating health, Havel was reelected in 1998 and continues as head of state of the Czech Republic.

Legacy

Vaclav Havel's political dissent and struggle for freedom and human rights enabled him and his artistic and intellectual colleagues to guide Czechoslovakia into a democratic and pluralistic society.

Through Civic Forum, Havel constructed a new legitimate and democratic system that could step in and quickly replace the discredited communist government.

Havel's effort to create an open and honest political culture was shaken by the many difficulties surrounding the legacies of the communist system. For instance, the debate about appropriate treatment of communist era collaborators and informants resulted in many innocent people being charged with collaboration and forced out of government jobs. In addition, Havel opposed the withdrawal of Slovakia from the federation but could not prevent the Slovaks from voting to secede from the federation.

Havel helped to guide the Czech Republic through the difficult transition from a state-controlled economy to a free-market economic system. Havel's rivalry with Vaclav Klaus, prime minister from 1992 who sought a quick transition to a free-market system within a centralized state structure, forced Havel to clarify his vision of a post-communist democracy and capitalist economy built on a healthy civil society based on mutual respect.

Because Havel committed himself so ardently to peaceful coexistence with other European states, he helped to keep extreme nationalism under control in central Europe. Havel ensured that the Czech and Slovak Republics separated peacefully. Keeping the Czech Republic stable and peaceful enabled Havel to guide his country into the North Atlantic Treaty Organization in 1999, using the diplomatic functions of the presidency to do so. Despite some errors of judgment, Havel has provided a model of conduct for newly democratizing nation-states.

Lemoine

World Events	Havel's Life
Great Depression 1929–39	
	1936 Vaclav Havel is born
World War II 1939–45	
	1959 Havel begins career in theater
Communist China 1949 is established	
Israel defeats 1967 Arab nations in Six-Day War	
	1968 Havel participates in "Prague Spring"
Vietnam War ends 1975	
	1977 Havel helps draft and signs Charter 77, calling for human rights
	1979–83 Havel is imprisoned
	1989 Havel takes leadership of Civic Forum, becomes interim president of Czechoslovakia
	1990 Havel is elected president of Czechoslovakia
Dissolution of 1991 Soviet Union	
	1992 Havel resigns after partition of Czechoslovakia
	1993 Havel is elected president of Czech Republic
	1998 Havel is reelected to presidency

For Further Reading

Keane, John. *Václav Havel: A Political Tragedy in Six Acts.* London: Bloomsbury, 1999.
Krisoeova, Eda. *Václav Havel: The Authorized Biography.* Translated by Caleb Crain. New York: St. Martin's Press, 1993.

Henry II

King of England

1133–1189

Life and Work

Henry II was one of England's most ambitious kings. He amassed enormous territories on the European continent, enacted far-reaching legal reforms, and waged a daring struggle against the privileges of the clergy.

Henry was born in 1133 in the French town of Le Mans. His father, Geoffrey Plantagenet, was the count of Anjou and his mother, Mathilda, was the daughter of Henry I of England. By the time Henry succeeded his father in 1151, the duchy of Normandy had been added to the Plantagenet inheritance. In the following year Henry increased his lands further by winning the hand of ELEANOR OF AQUITAINE, former wife of the king of France and heir to the richest territory of southern France. Henry next turned to England and arranged a treaty by which he would inherit the English throne upon the death of King Stephen (successor to Henry I). Thus at the time of his ascension in 1154 Henry controlled an empire stretching from the Scottish highlands to the Pyrenees.

In England, Henry pursued ambitious policies that yielded very mixed results. Important legal reforms succeeded in introducing juries in royal courts and laid the foundations for a system of common law. Efforts at subordinating the Church to royal control, however, were a disaster. Hoping to make Church leadership submissive, Henry in 1162 had appointed Thomas à Becket, a personal friend and the former royal chancellor, as archbishop of Canterbury. In 1164 he then issued an edict called the Constitutions of Clarendon, placing the clergy under the jurisdiction of royal courts for criminal offenses. To Henry's great dismay, Becket rose as the leader of opposition to the edict. With the archbishop threatening to bring all of England under interdict if the Constitutions were not revoked, Henry appealed in a fit of rage to his knights for a violent solution to the impasse. Accordingly, on December 29, 1170, four knights entered Canterbury Cathedral in battle dress to murder the defiant archbishop. To everyone's astonishment, he did not resist. In the wake of the martyrdom, as popular outrage soared and Pope Alexander III ordered Becket's canonization (1173), Henry was forced to withdraw the Constitutions. In 1174 he was publicly flogged on the streets of Canterbury and forced to do penance at the shrine of Saint Thomas à Becket recently installed in the cathedral.

The greatest disappointment of Henry's reign was not Becket's victory from beyond the grave, however, but the treachery of his own family. In 1173 Eleanor had inspired a revolt by her sons, for which Henry permanently imprisoned her. In 1188 his son Richard again revolted in alliance with King Philip Augustus of France, and Henry, now chronically weakened by a bleeding ulcer, was finally forced to surrender to their demands the following year in Normandy. Carried from the peace conference on a litter, he died only three days afterward.

Legacy

Henry II had a great impact upon the development of English diplomacy and law in later centuries. What is more, his conflict with Becket impressed generations of Europeans up through modern times.

Although Henry was following the example of WILLIAM I (William the Conqueror), the acquisition of vast continental territories presented a great burden to successors. Wars to defend these territories from France required Henry's son King RICHARD I (r. 1189–99) to abandon England for most of his reign and his other son King John (r. 1199–1216) to raise taxes so high that a revolt by the nobility was provoked (which, in turn, led to the famous Magna Carta). Persistent English claims to European territory would culminate in the Hundred Years War (1337–1453). Only this unmitigated disaster brought an end to Henry's territorial legacy.

England's legal tradition, on the other hand, benefited greatly from Henry's rule. Juries brought a higher standard of justice to the realm; when trial by ordeal was banned by the Church in the thirteenth century, the role of juries was expanded even further. The replacement of baronial courts with royal courts made Henry the father of English common law. In subsequent centuries, property disputes and criminal cases were settled according to laws that applied to all subjects. Thus, by the end of the Middle Ages, England had already developed rudimentary forms of some of the most important institutions of modern jurisprudence.

Finally, Henry's struggle to subordinate the Church to royal power lived on in the memory of both the clergy and the laity of Europe. The papacy was able to prevent Henry's successors from undertaking similar measures for centuries. Saint Thomas à Becket's shrine became one of the most popular destinations for pilgrims in England (depicted famously in Geoffrey Chaucer's *The Canterbury Tales*) and on the Continent knowledge of his martyrdom was widely disseminated among commoners. Becket thus came to serve as a symbol of the medieval Church's supremacy over the secular state. Nevertheless, the independence of the clergy was finally reduced in the sixteenth century by Henry's equally headstrong namesake HENRY VIII, who broke from Rome and declared himself the head of the English church.

Strickland

WORLD EVENTS		HENRY II'S LIFE
Timbuktu influential c. 1100 throughout west central Africa		
	1133	Henry is born
	1152	Henry marries Eleanor of Aquitaine
	1154	Henry accedes to English throne
	1164	Henry issues Constitutions of Clarendon
	1170	Henry instigates murder of Thomas à Becket
	1174	Henry does penance at shrine of Saint Thomas
Saladin takes Jerusalem for Islam	1187	
	1188	Henry's son, Richard, revolts
	1189	Henry dies in Normandy
Mongol conquest of China	1215	

For Further Reading

Appelby, John T. *Henry II: The Vanquished King*. London: G. Bell and Sons, 1962.

Barlow, Frank. *Thomas Becket*. London: Weidenfeld and Nicolson, 1986.

Warren, W. L. *Henry II*. Berkeley: University of California Press, 1973.

Henry IV

King of France
1553–1610

Life and Work

Henry IV (Henry of Navarre) ended the Wars of Religion that had plagued France in the sixteenth century. He then reconstructed the French economy and royal finances.

Henry was born into two royal families on December 13, 1553. He was the son of Antoine de Bourbon, of the French royal family, and Jeanne d'Albret, of the kingdom of Navarre, in modern southwestern France. Henry grew up at a time of increasing religious tensions stemming from the Protestant Reformation, which had split France into two opposing factions of Catholics and Huguenots (French Protestants). Henry's family was itself split by the Reformation. In 1560 his mother proclaimed her adoption of Protestantism. The same year, Henry was sent from his native Navarre to live with his father (who remained Catholic) at the royal court in Paris. During his years at court,

Henry learned statecraft, witnessing the outbreak of the Wars of Religion in 1562. In 1567 Jeanne escaped with her son to join Huguenot forces, waging war until 1570, when the crown and the Huguenots signed the Peace of Saint–Germain, which accorded the Huguenots a measure of official toleration.

To cement the peace, a marriage was arranged between Henry and Marguerite, sister of King Charles IX. The 1572 ceremony was a prelude to more civil war. Only days after the ceremony fanatical Catholics slaughtered the Huguenots gathered in Paris to celebrate the marriage. Known as the Saint Bartholomew Day's Massacre, it spread to the rest of France, and thousands of Protestants were killed. Henry was detained by royal authorities and forced to convert to Catholicism or be killed. Henry complied, but fled Paris in 1576, renouncing Catholicism and rejoining Huguenot forces.

In 1584 (King Charles IX had died in 1574) King Henry III's younger brother, the Duke d'Alençon, died, making Henry of Navarre the next in line for the throne. This sparked a crisis in France, as most Catholics would not accept a Protestant king. Henry III formed an alliance with Henry, Duke de Guise (the House of Guise led the Catholics in France), against Henry of Navarre. Following the "War of Three Henrys," Henry of Navarre took the throne in 1589 and became Henry IV.

To gain acceptance by Catholics, in 1593 Henry IV again converted to Catholicism. In 1598 he promulgated the Edict of Nantes, which accorded the Huguenots a certain amount of autonomy and negotiated the Treaty of Vervins with Spain. These actions put an end to the religious wars in France.

The wars over, Henry restored the French economy, which helped to fill the treasury's empty coffers. Public works, such as roads, canals, and buildings, were begun, and overseas colonies were encouraged. To solidify the new Bourbon dynasty, Henry's first (childless) marriage was annulled. Henry married Marie de' Medici, who immediately produced an heir, the future Louis XIII. Henry was assassinated by a fanatical Catholic, François Ravaillac, on May 14, 1610.

Legacy

Henry IV's chief accomplishment was bringing lasting peace to France after

nearly 40 years of civil and religious war. Royal authority had nearly collapsed during the war years, with both Catholics and Protestants questioning the power and prerogatives of royal rule. Henry succeeded in negotiating, through his conversion to Catholicism and the Edict of Nantes, a compromise between the belligerents that put an end to open warfare and restored confidence in the crown. However, his reign did not eliminate aristocratic challenge to royal authority. His descendants suppressed recurring revolts, LOUIS XIV most successfully. The Bourbon dynasty he founded ruled France, with one major interruption, until 1830.

Henry IV's compromise with the Huguenots, while ending the war, did not solve the problem of two faiths in a nation where the king embodied and defended only one (Catholic) faith. Henry's descendants, Louis XIII and Louis XIV, resolved the issue by choosing to weaken, then eliminate, rather than tolerate, the Huguenot presence in France. The Roman Catholic church retained enormous power and influence in French politics and society into the nineteenth century.

The economic growth promoted by the stable social and political order Henry constructed enabled France to finance its military rivalry with the Habsburg dynasty (especially the branch ruling Spain) in the seventeenth century. By the start of the eighteenth century, France had triumphed, replacing the Habsburg monarchy in Spain with a Bourbon king. The resulting geopolitical shifts elevated France to its status as a great power in the seventeenth and eighteenth centuries.

Lemoine

WORLD EVENTS		HENRY IV'S LIFE
Mughal Empire rules in India	1526	
	1553	Henry of Navarre is born
	1560	Henry leaves Navarre to reside at Paris court
	1567	Jeanne and Henry join Huguenots
Ottoman dominance of Mediterranean ends	1571	
	1572	Henry marries Marguerite, sister of King Charles IX
	1574	King Charles IX dies; his brother Henry III is crowned
	1589	Henri IV accedes to throne
	1593	Henry IV converts to Catholicism
	1598	Henry IV signs treaty with Spain and issues Edict of Nantes
	1610	Henry IV is killed
Glorious Revolution in England	1688	

For Further Reading
Bevan, Bryan. *Henry IV.* London: Rubicon, 1994.
Seward, Desmond. *The First Bourbon: Henri IV, King of France and Navarre.* Boston: Gambit, 1971.

Henry VIII

King of England
1491–1547

Life and Work

Henry VIII ruled England at a time when the Protestant Reformation challenged the authority of the Roman Catholic church. Although religiously conservative, his desire for a marriage annulment led him to break relations with Rome and launch the Reformation in England.

Henry was born in Greenwich in 1491, the second son of Henry VII. The death of Henry VII's first son, Arthur, who had been married to Catherine of Aragon, enabled Henry VIII to accede to the throne in 1509. Henry immediately married Arthur's widow, whose marriage had never been consummated.

In his early years as king, Henry VIII increased English power through wars with France and Scotland. His chancellor, Cardinal Wolsey, helped him to finance these wars by raising taxes and extracting money from England's many Roman Catholic monasteries. Henry also issued denunciations of Martin Luther's Protestant ideas, for which he was named "Defender of the Faith" in 1521 by Pope Leo X. By 1529, however, Henry's concerns had shifted to domestic affairs. Catherine had failed to produce a male heir to the throne. Henry came to fear that the Tudor dynasty was in danger and to this was added his sudden conviction that marriage to his brother's widow had offended God and would therefore never yield an heir. He sent Wolsey to Rome to appeal for a marriage annulment. When the Pope demurred, Henry made the audacious decision to defy Rome. In 1533 he dismissed Catherine and married a courtesan named Anne Boleyn. The following year he then compelled a subservient English Parliament to issue the Act of Supremacy, by which the monarch himself was now declared the "supreme head of the church of England."

Henry's break from Rome in 1534 outraged many English Christians. Sir Thomas More, for instance, who had replaced Wolsey as chancellor in 1530, refused to comply with the Act of Supremacy. As a result, he was beheaded for treason and replaced by Thomas Cromwell, who proved utterly loyal to Henry. Under him all Roman Catholic monasteries were dissolved in 1538 and their lands given to the state. With the acquisition of this wealth Cromwell was able to distribute rewards to members of Parliament who continued to pass legislation supporting Henry. Ironically, like former chancellors, Cromwell was ultimately unable to satisfy his temperamental master and in 1540 he was sent to the executioner's block.

Nor was Henry's family life without its own grim irony. Failing to produce a male heir herself, Anne Boleyn was beheaded in 1536, as was another in a succession of no fewer than six wives. Henry died in 1547.

Legacy

The reign of Henry VIII had an enormous impact upon England. His violent behavior toward court and family had repercussions among his successors, while his moderate religious settlement contributed to the formation of the Anglican tradition.

Henry had opposed the radical positions of many contemporary Protestant reformers; when Henry broke from Rome in 1534, he had sought to retain many of the traditions of the Roman Catholic church. Under King Edward VI (r. 1547–53), Protestant church leaders gained control of the Parliament and passed a series of acts placing the English church more firmly within the Protestant camp.

Under Queen Mary (r. 1553–58), Protestants were dealt a harsh but ultimately ineffective blow by Roman Catholics, of whom the new queen was one. Mary hoped to undo the Reformation and, like Henry, was prepared to use violence. Although the epithet "Bloody Mary" later applied to her tends to obscure the violent deeds of her Protestant predecessors, she oversaw a new phase of persecutions and executions.

Only under ELIZABETH I (r. 1558–1603), Henry's daughter by Anne Boleyn and the last of the Tudor monarchs, did the violent process of reform unleashed in 1534 subside. Elizabeth followed her father's example by assuring that much of the Roman Catholic heritage was retained in the church's theology and liturgy. At the same time, she facilitated efforts to make independence from Rome even more explicit. The results of this "Elizabethan Settlement" were expressed in a document called the Thirty Nine Articles, passed by Parliament in 1571. The institution of the papacy was rejected along with monasticism and the veneration of saints, but the Catholic mass and the apostolic succession of the clergy were maintained. In subsequent centuries the Anglican church (and its sister branch the Episcopal church in the United States) would uphold this *via media*, or middle course, between Protantism and Catholicism.

Strickland

World Events		Henry VIII's Life
Ottoman Empire conquers Constantinople	1453	
	1491	Henry is born
Columbus sails to Americas	1492	
	1509	Henry accedes to throne; marries Catherine of Aragon
Protestant Reformation begins	1517	
Mughal Empire rules in India	1526	
	1533	Henry marries Anne Boleyn
	1534	Henry breaks with Rome
	1538	Henry and Thomas Cromwell dissolve monasteries
	1540	Henry orders execution of Cromwell
	1547	Henry dies
Ottoman dominance of Mediterranean ends	1571	

For Further Reading

Gwyn, Peter. *The King's Cardinal: The Rise and Fall of Thomas Wolsey.* London: Barrie and Jenkins, 1990.

Richmond, Hugh M. *King Henry VIII.* Manchester, England: Manchester University Press, 1994.

Solt, Leo F. *Church and State in Early Modern England, 1509–1640.* Oxford: Oxford University Press, 1990.

Henry the Navigator

Portuguese Prince and Patron
of Exploration
1394–1460

Life and Work

Henry the Navigator was a patron of navigation and discovery at a time when Europe was seeking new trade links with Africa and Asia. Because of him Portugal took the lead in maritime exploration and began a process of global expansion.

Henry was born in Oporto in 1394, the fifth child of King John of Portugal. As he was not destined for the throne, he was given the opportunity as a young man to pursue interests unrelated to statecraft. The greatest of these was navigation, a science that was making important advances during the late Middle Ages. Historians debate whether Henry's interest in navigation was spontaneous or merely sparked by his desire to expand Portugal's naval, commercial, and crusading power. Whatever the case, he consistently exercised royal influence to advance it. Although he usually held only minor positions of responsibility during the reigns of other family members, he led an important naval campaign in 1415 that captured the port of Ceuta on the coast of North Africa. This victory prompted the Portuguese to pursue exploration and conquest in the Atlantic and along the west coast of Africa during and after his lifetime.

Henry played a leading role in this expansion. Made the grand master of the Order of Christ in 1420 for his crusading zeal, he assigned Portuguese naval power a key role in the *reconquista*, the policy of reconquest of Christian lands lost to the Muslims during the eighth century. A strong navy also enabled Portugal to protect her ports from Moorish pirates. Finally, maritime exploration of the African coast resulted in strategic trading links for Portugal. Knowledge of the West African coast remained very rudimentary, and no European had ever ventured beyond a dreaded point known as Cape Bojador. To enable Portuguese sailors to reach this point and beyond, Henry established a school of navigation and built an observatory at his palace in Sagres. Then, beginning in 1421, he sent annual voyages of exploration down the African coast.

The results of his patronage were impressive. In 1418 a fleet discovered the Atlantic island of Madeira, and the discovery and colonization of the Azores soon followed. A psychological breakthrough occurred in 1434 when a bold admiral under Henry's orders finally sailed past Cape Bojador. Additional voyages brought the Portuguese as far south as Sierra Leone before Henry died at Sagres on November 13, 1460.

Legacy

Henry the Navigator was the most important force behind maritime navigation and reconnaissance in fifteenth-century Europe. As a result of the studies and voyages he supported, Portugal became a global power.

Henry's navigational school at Sagres helped the Portuguese become some of the best sailors of the contemporary world. By employing the latest navigational methods and exploiting the recently developed caravel (a deep-water sailing ship), they were able to expand into the Atlantic and along the African coast earlier than any other European power. Once they established trading ports and fortresses, they were in a position to exercise greater control over trade in gold and spices. Before Henry's time gold especially was supplied overland from the Sudan through Timbuktu. By establishing a strong fortress on the Gold Coast in 1482, Henry's successors were able to secure more direct access to the gold trade, whose wealth came to exceed any other source of royal income. In the same year, an expedition was mounted up the Congo River basin, and finally, in 1488, Bartolomeu Dias rounded the Cape of Good Hope and opened eastern Africa and the Indies to Portuguese trade. Only with CHRISTOPHER COLUMBUS's discovery of the New World in 1492 under the patronage of the Spanish Queen ISABELLA I was Portuguese preeminence challenged.

Knowledge of overseas routes to Africa, the Indies, and Latin America enabled the Portuguese to build one of the world's largest commercial empires. With the Treaty of Tordesillas in 1494, Portugal accepted a compromise with rival Spain by which Portugal renounced any territories west of a line running through the eastern part of South America (whose geography was still unknown to Europeans). After the discovery of Brazil in 1500, this treaty entitled Portugal to claim a large part of the New World as its own. In the sixteenth century, Portuguese colonists also began to expand to the east. Forts such as Goa, built on the west coast of India in 1510, became important trading posts and naval stations. In later centuries some of these would be lost in wars with other European states, and ultimately in the twentieth century the empire would cease altogether. Portuguese civilization, however, would leave a significant legacy among the nearly 200 million people around the world who spoke Portuguese at the end of the twentieth century.

Strickland

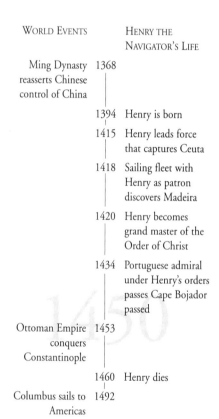

WORLD EVENTS		HENRY THE NAVIGATOR'S LIFE
Ming Dynasty reasserts Chinese control of China	1368	
	1394	Henry is born
	1415	Henry leads force that captures Ceuta
	1418	Sailing fleet with Henry as patron discovers Madeira
	1420	Henry becomes grand master of the Order of Christ
	1434	Portuguese admiral under Henry's orders passes Cape Bojador passed
Ottoman Empire conquers Constantinople	1453	
	1460	Henry dies
Columbus sails to Americas	1492	

For Further Reading

Fisher, Leonard Everett. *Prince Henry the Navigator*. New York: Macmillan, 1990.
Fritz, Jean. *Around the World in a Hundred Years: From Henry the Navigator to Magellan*. New York: Putnam, 1994.
Russell, P. E. *Prince Henry the Navigator: The Rise and Fall of a Cultural Hero*. Oxford: Oxford University Press, 1984.

Herzl, Theodor

Founder of Zionism

1860–1904

Life and Work

During a time of rising anti-Semitism in Europe, Theodor Herzl founded the modern Zionist movement. His vision of an independent homeland for Jews and his work to realize it yielded a powerful movement by the beginning of the twentieth century.

Theodor Herzl was born on May 2, 1860, in the Hungarian city of Pest (which was later united to Buda to become Budapest). His father, an assimilated Jew, was in banking. As a youth, Herzl showed every sign of conforming to the life of an assimilated Jew and in 1878 enrolled as a law student at the University of Vienna. With a strong interest in literature, however, he could not help coming into contact with the anti-Semitism that was growing in central Europe during the late nineteenth century. In 1885 he received his degree but soon after chose to accept the position of literary correspondent with the Viennese newspaper *Neue Freie Presse* in Paris. Here also he was struck by anti-Semitism, which could be directed even against assimilated Jews like himself who conformed to the dominant culture. His alienation reached a peak in 1895 when Alfred Dreyfus, an assimilated French officer of Jewish descent, was convicted of

espionage on highly dubious evidence. The Dreyfus Affair led Herzl to conclude that only the physical withdrawal of Jews from Europe could protect them from injustice. In his book, *The Jewish State,* published in 1896, he advocated the founding of a Jewish state.

In the years that followed he formed the Zionist movement to realize his goal. Although he briefly considered territories in Africa, his followers soon considered Palestine (with its capital of Jerusalem) the only viable location. Herzl traveled to Constantinople in 1896 in the hope of negotiating an agreement with the Ottoman sultan but was completely unsuccessful. He also failed to win support for his movement from the wealthy Jewish Rothschild family in Europe. Nevertheless, in 1897 the First Zionist Congress was held in Switzerland. Marking the foundation of the World Zionist Organization, it represented the culmination of Herzl's lifelong work.

Herzl died on July 3, 1904.

Legacy

Theodor Herzl left behind a movement that would culminate in the founding of modern Israel. While this event fulfilled his dream, it also provoked enormous conflict in the Middle East.

After Herzl's death, the World Zionist Organization actively promoted Jewish settlement in Palestine. The increased repression of Jews in twentieth-century Eastern Europe, which exploded during the Holocaust under ADOLF HITLER, convinced many leaders that immediate resettlement was essential for the survival of Jewry. Herzl himself had warned that any settlement of Palestine must receive the authorization of the political powers concerned. After the Ottoman Empire collapsed during World War I (1914–18), Britain began to administer Palestine according to a League of Nations mandate. Zionist leaders were able to obtain a promise from the British for the increased settlement of Jews. In 1917 the British had issued the Balfour Declaration, promising a future "Jewish homeland" in Palestine. This apparent victory, however, was soon threatened by protests among the Arab population of Palestine. As demonstrations and riots broke out, the British reversed their commitment and cut the quotas of Jews allowed to

settle. The Arab Revolt of 1936 further undermined hopes that the British would fulfill their promise. But when the Holocaust killed nearly six million European Jews, Zionist demands regarding Palestine became difficult to resist. As Britain surrendered its mandate to the territory, an independent Israel was declared by DAVID BEN-GURION and other Jews on May 14, 1948.

Immediately thereafter, the Arab countries surrounding Israel took up the Palestinian cause and attacked the new state. Israel survived this first Arab–Israeli War (1948), the Six-Day War (1967), and the Yom Kippur War (1973), but its existence was then challenged by the Palestinians themselves. In 1964 the Palestinian Liberation Organization (PLO) was created under YASIR ARAFAT to organize an armed struggle for the destruction of Israel. While the organization became considerably more moderate after 1994, a terrorist group calling itself the *Hezbollah* ("Party of Allah") and an insurrection known as the *intifada* ("shaking-off") continued to trouble Israeli–Palestinian relations at the beginning of the twenty-first century.

Strickland

WORLD EVENTS		HERZL'S LIFE
Congress of Vienna reorganizes Europe	1815	
	1860	Theodor Herzl is born
Germany is united	1871	
	1885	Herzl receives law degree
	1896	Herzl publishes *The Jewish State*
	1897	Herzl, among others, founds World Zionist Organization
	1904	Herzl dies
Russo-Japanese War	1905	

For Further Reading

Beller, Steven. *Herzl.* London: Weidenfeld and Nicolson, 1991.

Kornberg, Jacques. *Theodor Herzl: From Assimilation to Zionism.* Bloomington: Indiana University Press, 1993.

Schoeps, Julius H. *Theodor Herzl and the Zionist Dream.* Translated by Annemarie and Francis Clark-Lowes. London: Thames and Hudson, 1997.

Hirohito

Emperor of Japan
1901–1989

Life and Work

Hirohito exerted a strong moral influence on Japan's pre–World War II leaders and formed the stable center of Japanese politics and society throughout his life.

Born April 29, 1901, Hirohito grew up in Tokyo's Imperial Palace, steeped in tradition, ceremony, and military training. He attended a special palace school, the Peers' School, until he was in his early teens, and received more advanced education through tutorials from experts after that. This background guided Japan's supreme leader into modern, pro-Western learning while preserving respect for those aspects of Japan's culture that bound it together in relative social harmony for 300 years.

WORLD EVENTS		HIROHITO'S LIFE
Germany is united	1871	
	1901	Hirohito is born
Russo-Japanese War	1905	
World War I	1914–18	
Russian Revolution	1917	
	1921	Hirohito visits Europe as Crown Prince
		Hirohito becomes regent for his father
	1926	Father dies; Hirohito becomes emperor
Great Depression	1929–39	
	1931	Japan takes over Manchuria in China
World War II	1939–45	
	1945	Hirohito abandons direct rule
Communist China is established	1949	
Israel defeats Arab nations in Six-Day War	1967	
Vietnam War ends	1975	Hirohito visits United States
	1989	Hirohito dies
Dissolution of Soviet Union	1991	

In mid-1921, Hirohito toured Europe and confirmed Japan's equality with the great powers by meeting with the leaders of England, France, Belgium, the Netherlands, and Italy. After 1922, because his father, the "Taisho" emperor Yoshihito, was no longer able to perform his tasks as leader, Hirohito began to assume the powers of emperor as regent (individual who rules in someone else's place). In 1926, Hirohito became Japan's 124th emperor. While his ministers, military officials, and the elected parliament governed Japan, Hirohito, who was considered divine, could sway official opinion. He mixed the Japanese emperor's traditional roles (e.g., approving legislation, leading the armed forces, and watching over the state Shinto religion) with deep intellectual curiosity.

Hirohito walked a delicate line between the forces of democracy and militarism during the 1920s and 1930s, foiling a coup in 1936 by personally ordering the rebels to desist. He kept abreast of Japan's military expansionism in China during the 1930s and into Southeast Asia and the Pacific in the 1940s, intervening over his commanding generals on occasions. Upon Japan's surrender at the end of World War II in 1945, Hirohito was prepared to bear responsibility for Japan's military disaster and whatever punishment the Allies might mete out. However, the United States, which wanted a conservative leader in Japan around which a demilitarized, democratic state could grow, chose to retain Hirohito, stripped of his status as divine. After 1945, Hirohito continued to serve as a moral center for Japan and became its chief agent of post-war reconciliation, culminating with a visit to the United States in 1975. He died January 7, 1989, and was succeeded by his son, Akihito.

Legacy

Throughout his life, Hirohito used his traditional moral power to mediate between Japan's often conflicting political forces and to moderate the extremism that marked Japanese society. This mediation, however, often resulted in compromises that Hirohito may not have intended.

In order to modernize Japan's society and economy and defend Japan against Western encroachment, Hirohito's grandfather the Meiji emperor had established the emperor system, which introduced representative democracy but also concentrated power in the hands of the emperor, who coordinated Japan's resources for modernization.

No longer benefiting from the novelty of modernization or economic growth after World War I, the Japan Hirohito governed after 1921 experienced periods of great economic, political, and social upheaval, contained only by rigid militarization of Japanese society and Japan's economy between 1937 and 1945. Hirohito had to balance political forces that sought to return Japan to the conservative, class-bound society it had been before Japan ended its self-imposed isolation in 1868. Hirohito had a reputation as a peace lover, beginning in 1921 with his expressions of horror at seeing Europe's World War I battlefields. However, Hirohito balanced his love of peace with the practicalities of Japan's unstable political environment and Japan's desire to expand in Asia as a colonial power as co-equal European nations had already done. Although never condoning particularly aggressive behavior by Japan's military, such as Japan's takeover of Manchuria and northern China beginning in 1931 or the surprise attack on the United States naval base at Pearl Harbor in December 1941, Hirohito always supported victory once the military made its decisions. In addition, Hirohito's knowledge of morally reprehensible military activities, such as the testing of gruesome bacteriological and chemical agents on human subjects or the systematic raping and pillage of the residents of China's capital, Nanking (Nanjing), in 1937, places into doubt either his absolute authority or morality. His rock-steady disapproval of real extremes—such as returning to the social and political order of pre-1868 Japan advocated by some military officers, of the advancement of communism after 1945—kept Japanese society from destroying itself, irrespective of the aggressive actions taken by Japan's military during World War II. Hirohito appears more as an "invisible hand" in Japanese government between 1920–45, guiding but never forcing Japanese government.

After 1945, the Allies stripped Hirohito of his role in government and religion, paring down his role to one of symbol. In this capacity, Hirohito proved an excellent leader. The stability and hard work shown by Hirohito after World War II certainly had a mollifying effect on Japan's domestic politics and its ability to become an economic superpower after 1945.

Del Testa

For Further Reading

Bix, Herbert P. *Hirohito and the Making of Modern Japan.* New York: HarperCollins, 2000.
Hoyt, Edwin Palmer. *Hirohito: The Emperor and the Man.* New York: Praeger, 1992

Hitler, Adolf

Ruler of Nazi Germany
1889–1945

Life and Work

As the founder of National Socialism, Adolf Hitler subjected Germany to a cruel dictatorship and directly caused World War II.

Adolf Hitler was born in Branau, Upper Austria, on April 20, 1889. He joined the German army when World War I broke out in 1914. After Germany was defeated in 1918, he organized the National Socialist German Workers' Party, or Nazis, to overthrow the liberal Weimar Republic. In 1923 he led an unsuccessful uprising in Bavaria known as the Beer Hall Putsch, for which he was imprisoned nine months. During this time he wrote an autobiography, *Mein Kampf* (*My Struggle*), that set forth his nationalistic ideology and outlined his political goals. After his release he exploited severe discontent with the Weimar economy to win over voters and, in 1932, to obtain the largest percentage of seats for the Nazis in the German Reichstag. On January 30, 1933, he was appointed chancellor and on March 23 an Enabling Act gave him dictatorial powers.

Hitler created a totalitarian system that he called the Third Reich. In 1935 his fanatical anti-Semitism produced the Nuremberg Laws, which deprived Jews of civil rights. His totalitarian goals also extended into the sphere of culture, where a propaganda apparatus headed by Joseph Goebbels and yearly mass rallies at Nuremberg presented him as a demigod. He sought to replace Christianity with a secular cult defined by his own racist and nationalistic ideology.

Hitler directly incited World War II, which he saw as an opportunity to increase German power, expand to the east, and eliminate Europe's Jewish population. After invading Poland on September 1, 1939, his armies took over France in 1940 and scored stunning victories against the Soviet Union in 1941. However, Hitler's fanaticism produced a false conviction that Germany was invincible. After heavy losses inflicted by the Soviet army at Stalingrad (1942–43), the German army became unable to sustain its operations in eastern Europe. Hitler further depleted Germany's resources by ordering a systematic campaign of murder against the Jews, which came to be known as the Holocaust. By the summer of 1944 the Soviet army had crossed into eastern Germany, and Britain and the United States had landed armies in northern France.

A fanatic to the end, Hitler refused to accept the hopelessness of the situation. Only on April 30, 1945, with the Soviet army fighting its way through Berlin, did he acknowledge the enormity of his mistake. Withdrawing to the private rooms of his bunker, he shot himself through the head, and was found with his wife, Eva Braun, who had died from poisoning.

Legacy

Although he ruled only 13 years, Adolf Hitler swept away much of traditional Germany, overthrew numerous governments, and caused the deaths of approximately 40 million people.

When Hitler came to power in 1933, Germany was already in a state of crisis with mass unemployment and inflation, cultural traditions under siege, and weakened religious communities. The Nazi regime accelerated the collapse of these institutions by subjecting them to totalitarian power. It introduced a state-managed economy that, while strengthening industrial capitalism, displaced the ideal of free enterprise enshrined in nineteenth-century liberal economics. By politicizing elements of traditional art such as realism and heroism, it transformed them and served to delegitimate them among intellectuals. Finally, it accelerated the decline of religion among Germans by appropriating religious ritual and promoting secular goals for German civilization. After the war, the Federal Republic of Germany in the west and the German Democratic Republic in the east inherited a radically different civilization than had existed in 1933. What is more, in seeking to rebuild Germany, each consciously avoided many of the traditional institutions found in the pre-Nazi past.

The "new order" that Hitler sought to impose on Europe also brought destruction to many of the countries surrounding Germany. Among the states overthrown during the war were the Third Republic of France (replaced by the puppet Vichy regime), Poland, and the Kingdom of Yugoslavia. Although occupied eastern European states were liberated by the Soviet army at the end of the war (with the exception of Yugoslavia), they were soon transformed into communist regimes modeled upon that of JOSEPH STALIN in the Soviet Union. As for the Soviet Union, successful resistance to the German invasion gave the communist regime a prestige that helped it to survive until 1991.

The death toll in Europe during World War II is Adolf Hitler's darkest legacy. Nearly every European power sacrificed large numbers of soldiers and civilians, with the Soviet Union suffering a staggering 27 million dead. At the center of this tragedy was two-thirds of the Jewish population of Europe, nearly six million in all, who were slaughtered by the Nazis during the Holocaust.

Strickland

For Further Reading

Bullock, Allen. *Hitler: A Study in Tyranny.* New York: Harper and Row, 1952.

Fest, Joachim C. *Hitler.* Translated by Richard and Clara Winston. New York: Harcourt Brace Jovanovich, 1974.

Kershaw, Ian. *Hitler.* London: Longman, 1991.

WORLD EVENTS		HITLER'S LIFE
Germany is united	1871	
	1889	Adolf Hitler is born
Russo-Japanese War	1905	
World War I	1914–18	
	1914	Hitler joins German army
Russian Revolution	1917	
	1923	Hitler leads unsuccessful Beer Hall Putsch
Great Depression	1929–39	
	1933	Hitler is made dictator with Enabling Act
	1935	Hitler enacts Nuremberg Laws
World War II	1939–45	
	1945	Hitler commits suicide
Communist China is established	1949	

Ho Chi Minh

Vietnamese Revolutionary Leader
c. 1890–1969

Life and Work

In 1954, Ho Chi Minh led Vietnam to independence from the French, who had occupied the country since 1858, and supported a second independence movement that in 1975 led to the unification of North and South Vietnam.

Around 1890, Ho was born Nguyen Tat Thanh in the province of Nghê-An to peasant intellectuals who opposed French occupation. After briefly teaching at a primary school in 1911, Ho wandered the globe, taking jobs on a French ship, in the United States, and in England.

In 1917, Ho moved to Paris and began his active political life, culminating in demands for Vietnam's independence from France at the post–World War I Paris Peace Conference. When the Allies rebuffed him, Ho dedicated himself to the cause of colonized peoples everywhere. In 1920, Ho became a charter member of the French Communist Party; he had turned to communism because it espoused liberation and social welfare. In 1923, the Soviet Union became Ho's patron, and he moved to Moscow. Over the next 17 years, Ho worked to establish a communist independence movement in his country. At the start of World War II the Japanese virtually took control of Vietnam from the French. In 1940–41 Ho secretly returned to Vietnam and launched an armed movement, the Viet Minh, that by 1945 controlled much of Vietnam's countryside.

The Allies defeated Japan in 1945; during the course of World War II, Japan had devastated the French in Vietnam. Accordingly, Ho was able to declare Vietnam independent on September 2, 1945, but the French tried to reimpose their authority in December 1945. In 1954, after the final defeat of the French at the Battle of Dien Bien Phu, an agreement signed in Geneva divided the country and Ho was left in charge of a Communist North Vietnam.

Ho guided North Vietnam's early development and had great successes, including mass literacy and public health campaigns, and great failures, including a disastrous land reform program and rigid political oppression. To carry out a forced reunion of north and south, Ho agreed in 1959 to permit guerrilla activity against South Vietnam and the forces of its chief ally, the United States. By the mid-1960s, Ho's failing health limited his ability to participate directly in government, but his patriotic image inspired those still seeking reunification and independence under the communist flag.

Ho died in Hanoi on September 3, 1969. In his honor, in 1975 the communist Vietnamese renamed Saigon, Vietnam's southern capital, Ho Chi Minh City.

Legacy

Ho Chi Minh's legacy rests on the real and symbolic value of his ejection of the French from Vietnam and the start of reunification between north and south.

Before 1954, no other colonized people had successfully ejected a colonial occupier

through violence; in addition, between 1959 and 1975, the communist Vietnamese were the first group to successfully resist the military might of the United States. Ho's successes against the French inspired many rebel leaders, including Ahmed Ben Bella and his National Liberation Front in Algeria and YASIR ARAFAT and the Palenstine Liberation Organziation, to try to end the colonial occupation of their nations through violence. Ho showed other rebels, such as FIDEL CASTRO, that socialism could successfully unify people in less developed nations against corrupt regimes. The successes of Ho, Ben Bella, and Castro forced the United States and the Soviet Union to take the Cold War out of Europe and into Africa, South America, and Asia, often with tragic results, such as in Vietnam in the 1960s and 1970s, Chile in the 1970s and 1980s, and Afghanistan in the 1980s. The two superpowers, however, often misinterpreted what leaders such as Ho wanted from communism, and turned nationalist social welfare regimes into battlefields between good and evil.

Ho's charismatic power emanated from his personal austerity and his unwavering support of anti-colonial activities in Vietnam and the rest of the world. Unfortunately, the way his followers interpreted Ho's communism sometimes led to extremism that made scapegoats or victims of certain members of Vietnamese society, such as landowners, non-Vietnamese highland peoples, and Chinese who lived in Vietnam.

Del Testa

World Events		Ho Chi Minh's Life
Germany is united	1871	
	c. 1890	Ho Chi Minh is born
Russo-Japanese War	1905	
World War I	1914–18	
Russian Revolution	1917	Ho moves to Paris
	1920	Ho becomes charter member of French Communist Party
Great Depression	1929–39	
World War II	1939–45	
	1941–45	Ho founds Viet Minh movement
	1945	Ho declares Vietnam's independence
Communist China is established	1949	
	1959	Ho authorizes guerrilla activity to reunite North and South Vietnam
	mid-1960s	Ho retires from active political life
Israel defeats Arab nations in Six-Day War	1967	
	1969	Ho dies
Vietnam War ends	1975	

For Further Reading

Duiker, William J. *Ho Chi Minh*. New York: Hyperion, 2000.

Neumann-Hoditz, Reinhold. *Portrait of Ho Chi Minh: An Illustrated Biography*. Translated by John Hargreaves. New York: Herder and Herder, 1972.

Huayna Capac

Incan Emperor
c. 1480–1527

Life and Work

Building on the successes of previous Incan kings, by 1525 Huayna Capac had extended the Incan Empire, known as *Tahuantinsuyu*, or "land of four quarters," to its greatest extent.

The historical record for the Inca is very sketchy. It is known, however, that Huayna was the son of the TOPA INCA YUPANQUI, an Incan king who expanded the Inca Empire beyond the borders of contemporary Peru and Chile into the Amazon forests of present-day Bolivia. Huayna came from a very small ethnic group, the Inca, that, since the early 1400s, had conquered or allied with rival ethnic groups in the Andes and along South America's western coastal plain to assemble a great empire. As a child, Huayna received the education of an Incan prince, which included four years of training in Quechua, the Incan lingua franca; use of the string abacus, or *quipu*; Incan religion; and Incan history. At the death of his father in 1493 and amid court intrigues, Huayna came to power suddenly and fairly young (Huayna means, roughly, "boy-king"). He immediately set about strengthening his position so that no similar struggle over succession would affect his rule or that of his own heir.

As was customary among new Incan rulers, Huayna spent the first few years of his reign touring the various provinces of the empire. Then he embarked on a solidification of Inca rule that his father had begun. To ensure his power, Huayna launched five initiatives. First, he tried to assert absolute imperial control into the area of Lake Titicaca over the Inti people. In this effort he failed, although the Inti agreed to closer collaboration. Second, he tried to send armies to the east of the Andes to conquer the tropical forests of the western Amazon, rich in luxury goods such as feathers and aromatic woods. In this he also failed, because of the humid climate and guerrilla warfare waged by the local peoples. Third, Huayna insisted on a greater Incan orthodoxy among con-quered peoples, forcing them to use the Quechua language and schooling local leaders in Incan ways. In this he was successful. Fourth, he began to insist on his own divinity to a degree, turning the traditional role of the Incan emperor from one of facilitator of the worship of the Sun into the receptacle of that worship and the Sun's power. This transformation of the status of the Incan leader upset many within the Incan Empire and sowed the seeds for a future rebellion against the increasing arrogance of the Incan kings. Finally, in about 1513, Huayna marched against rebels in the area presently known as Ecuador, slaughtering in an unprecedented fashion the communities engaged in revolt. In addition, he decided that Quito, the regional capital, was more suitable than Cuzco as a residence.

In 1522, after concluding campaigns along the Pacific coast and into the Amazon, Huayna prepared to retire to Quito. However, in 1523, the Chiriguana people of present-day Paraguay conducted a raid into the Incan territory and temporarily captured some border fortresses. While the Inca quickly recaptured the lost territory, they also caught smallpox from renegade Spaniards among the fleeing Chiriguana. This disease quickly ravaged the Incan Empire. In 1527, Huayna died suddenly, probably of disease of a European origin spreading southward from Central America. His two heirs, Huascar and Atahualpa, inherited different parts of the empire and immediately fell to attacking one another, destroying the unity Huayna had worked hard to maintain.

Legacy

Huayna Capac kept the Incan Empire strong in the face of growing internal divisions and external threats.

Indeed, had his sons not destoryed this unity by battling one another for supremacy after Huayna's death, the Incan Empire, with its mighty resource base and efficient bureaucracy, might have withstood the onslaught of the Spaniards. During his reign, Huayna continued the practice of imposing Incan culture on conquered peoples, which bound people to the Inca and ensured a regional indigenous identity based on one of two local languages that persists to the present.

However, unity is a function of economic and political development as much as linguistic homogenization. Huayna alienated many local leaders by using wholesale slaughter of local rebels rather than subjecting them to the traditional punishment, in which the rebels received a ritual punishment, involving chatisement or stylized blows in the context of a performance, rather than being subjected to physical violence. In addition, he did nothing to improve economic conditions, and increasingly assumed ceremonial and religious functions himself, depriving others of purpose and pride. Unequal economic development ensured that the Spaniards found eager allies ready to dispose of the Inca. However, those who collaborated with the Spanish against Incan rulers soon found they had only traded one master for another, and even today, those native peoples not related to Europeans in some way do less well economically than those who are more closely associated with a European background.

Del Testa

WORLD EVENTS		HUAYNA CAPAC'S LIFE
Ottoman Empire conquers Constantinople	1453	
	c. 1480	Huayna Capac born in Cuzco
Columbus sails to Americas	1492	
	1493	Huayna comes to power at death of his father
	1513	Huayna invades Ecuador
Protestant Reformation begins	1517	
	1523	Huayna puts down Chiriguana people
Mughal Empire rules in India	1526	
	1527	Huayna dies
Ottoman dominance of Mediterranean ends	1571	

For Further Reading

Canseco, Rostworowski de Diez. *History of the Inca Realm.* Translated by Harry B. Iceland. New York: Cambridge University Press, 1999.

Hyams, Edward, and George Ordish. *The Last of the Incas: The Rise and Fall of an American Empire.* New York: Simon & Schuster, 1963.

Hung Hsiu-ch'üan

Leader of the Chinese Taiping Rebellion

1814–1864

Life and Work

Hung Hsiu-ch'üan's Taiping Rebellion posed the most serious threat to the Manchu Qing dynasty during the nineteenth century, increasing the influence of the West on Chinese society and hastening the decline of the Chinese imperial government.

Hung was born in 1814, in the Guandong province, a member of an ethnic minority called the Hakka. Hung repeatedly failed the government's rigorous civil service exam that would have allowed him to enter the Chinese government bureaucracy and ensured financial

WORLD EVENTS		HUNG'S LIFE
Latin American independence movement begins	1811	
	1814	Hung Hsiu-ch'üan is born
Congress of Vienna reorganizes Europe	1815	
	1849	Hung amasses 10,000 military followers
	1850	Hung's army defeats Qing army
	1853–64	Hung's Taipings invade and rule Nanjing
	1864	Hung dies, possibly by suicide
Germany is united	1871	

security and a higher status for his family. Moving to Guanzhou to continue studying for the exams, Hung encountered Protestant missionaries distributing religious tracts. Failing the exams again, Hung had a mental breakdown and experienced strange dreams. As he read the tracts, he began to believe that he was the younger brother of Jesus Christ, a life-long belief that spurred him to form a rebellion against the Manchu "devils." Manchus were the ethnic group of the ruling Qing dynasty.

He began to preach openly against Confucianism, Taoism, and Buddhism. The group he formed was both Christian and anti-Manchu, and it quickly developed into a military organization. By 1849 he had amassed nearly 10,000 followers determined to destroy the repressive Qing government.

In 1850, Hung declared himself the Taiping (shortened from Heavenly King of Taiping Tianguo, which means "Heavenly King of Great Peace"). The Taiping Rebellion, begun that same year, scored military successes as it moved north all the way to Nanking (Nanjing), where the triumphant Taiping troops, now numbering more than 60,000, took the city, systematically killing all the Manchus living there. There, Taiping forces established their own authoritarian and utopian "Heavenly Kingdom," which ruled for 11 years (1853–64).

The movement was Christian and ascetic; women could hold positions of authority; an exam system based on the Bible and Hung's religious revelations (which he had written down) was established; egalitarian land reforms, a "common treasury," and military conscription were also established.

After the success of Nanking, Hung failed to seize the initiative and take advantage of anti-Manchu sentiment to push on to Beijing and topple the Qing dynasty; he also fostered resentment in the countryside because of the taxes needed to maintain his huge armies. The Qing dynasty enlisted the support of the Western powers (especially the British and the Americans), who sent military forces to help defeat the Taiping. Chinese officials stayed loyal to the Manchus because the Christian Taiping attacked traditional Chinese values. They mounted local resistance to the Taiping movement, which was defeated in 1864. Hung died (he may have committed suicide) in 1864, and provincial officials organized armies to defeat the remnants of the Taiping. The

Taiping and other violent anti-Qing rebellions that occurred among the Muslim population of China at that time resulted in a massive death toll—perhaps 30 million or more by 1873.

Legacy

Hung Hsiu-ch'üan and his cohorts unleashed over a century of turmoil in China. Hung's Taiping Rebellion gravely damaged the central authority of the already weakened Qing dynasty. In the twentieth century, Hung's movement inspired anti-Manchu nationalists such as SUN YAT-SEN and Chinese communists such as MAO TSE-TUNG.

Although the Qing managed to save their dynasty, Hung's rebellion strengthened the authority of provincial governments that had spearheaded the military defeat of the Taiping. The regional governors-general took the initiative to rebuild after the wars of rebellion and sought to modernize the military and industrial infrastructure according to Western methods. However, the so-called dowager empress, Cixi (also spelled Tz'u Hsi), who ruled as regent when her son the emperor was still a child, resisted Westernizing reforms.

Hung's rebellion also opened the way to other defeats and rebellions. In 1894, the Chinese realized how little their reforms had accomplished when they were defeated by the Japanese in a war over Korea. Chinese humiliation and increased Western intrusion in Chinese affairs ignited what has become known as the Boxer Rebellion of 1900. The uprising had the support of the court at first, but was ruthlessly repressed by an international force, which remained in the capital, Beijing, even after the rebellion had been quashed.

Hung's egalitarian principles inspired political thinkers, including the founders of the Nationalist and Chinese Communist Parties. Among many Chinese, including army officers, loyalty was shifting away from the dynasty to the new Nationalist and anti-Manchu movement led by Sun Yat-sen, considered the father of the Chinese republican revolution. A military uprising forced the last emperor, a child named P'UI, to abdicate in 1912. A republic was proclaimed, but China faced internal turmoil until 1949, when Mao Tse-tung's Chinese Communist Party triumphed over the nationalists.

Lemoine

For Further Reading

Jen Yu-wen. *The Taiping Revolutionary Movement.* New Haven, Conn.: Yale University Press, 1973.

Weller, Robert P. *Resistance, Chaos and Control in China: Taiping Rebels, Taiwanese Ghosts and Tiananmen.* Seattle: University of Washington Press, 1994.

Hussein, Saddam

Iraqi Political Leader
1938–

Life and Work

By combining populism, pan-Arab nationalism, and authoritarianism, Saddam Hussein led Iraq from a shattered democracy in the 1960s to an internationally unpopular state in the twenty-first century.

Born on April 28, 1938, to a peasant family in Tikret, central Iraq, Hussein spent the first years of his life shuttled between abusive relatives. In 1956, an uncle sent Hussein to a secondary school in Baghdad. Attracted to its mixture of Arab nationalism and socialism, in 1957 Hussein joined the Ba'th Party, a pan-Arab political organization that sought to reunite the countries of the Arab world. He became a Ba'th activist, raising money for the party in high school.

Hussein was forced to flee Iraq in 1961 after helping in a failed assassination attempt on Iraq's leader, 'Abd al-Karim Qasim. In Cairo, Egypt, Hussein graduated from high school and then went to law school. In 1963, Hussein returned to Iraq when the Ba'th Party took power, but was arrested in 1964 when the military took over the country. The Ba'th took power again in 1968, and Hussein was made head of Iraq's security services, where he gained a reputation as an effective behind-the-scenes player.

Throughout the 1970s, and often following political murders, men aligned with Hussein

slowly replaced Iraq's government officials and military officers. The negative popular opinion of the military and government, generated by their failure to squelch rebellions in Iraq, made it easier for violent "replacements" to occur without inspiring protest. Although already long the de facto leader of Iraq, Hussein was not proclaimed president until September 11, 1979.

During the 1970s, Hussein had steered Iraq's growing oil revenue toward bettering the quality of life for Iraqis, especially by improving education, rights, and services for women. He also equipped and trained an enormous military. On June 17, 1980, Iraq invaded Iran to forestall the growth of Iranian religious influence in Iraq and the related threat to the power of Hussein and the Ba'th Party. The war would last until 1988, when Iran, exhausted and facing shrill internal divisions over the war, agreed to a cease-fire.

Although Western powers and Arab nations—afraid of Iran's religious fundamentalism—had given Iraq enormous sums of money to conduct the war, Iraq still ended up $30 billion in debt. When Hussein, facing a rebellious and war-weary population, could not convince the Saudis and Egyptians into paying his war debt, he decided to invade Kuwait in order to exploit Kuwait's oil reserves. Iraqi forces invaded Kuwait on August 1, 1990, and annexed the country, after looting it, a week later. This annexation destabilized the region and convinced the United States and Saudi Arabia to demand, through the United Nations, that Hussein withdraw from Kuwait. After a long military build-up, a coalition of international forces under the banner of the United Nations, led by the United States, invaded Iraq on January 16, 1991. The Allied Coalition quickly destroyed much of Iraq's military and infrastructure.

Although he agreed to the terms set by the United Nations in a cease-fire agreement, Hussein has spent the past decade trying to avoid United Nations sanctions while keeping control of the Iraqi people, which he does only through increasingly brutal means.

Legacy

Saddam Hussein's efforts to make Iraq a powerful regional symbol of Arab strength have failed, largely because of his invasion of Kuwait, the resulting military response by the United States and its United Nation allies, and his iron-fisted rule of the Iraqi people.

Hussein's misguided attempt to annex Kuwait and reap economic benefit from its oil wealth led to disaster for Iraq, resulting in a severe weakening of the Iraqi economy. This weakening was largely the result of the stranglehold that U.N. cease-fire agreement sanctions placed on Iraqi exports.

Beyond the boundaries of Iraq, Hussein's aggressive tactics against neighboring countries have destabilized the region. His reputation as an Arab leader has been discredited and weakened by his brutal oppression of his own people. Rather than proving himself to be a capable ruler with vision and moral authority, Hussein's actions have engendered mistrust in his fellow Arab leaders and resulted in the opposite of Hussein's original pan-Arab ambitions.

Del Testa

WORLD EVENTS	HUSSEIN'S LIFE
Great Depression 1929–39	
	1938 Saddam Hussein is born
World War II 1939–45	
Communist China 1949 is established	
	1957 Hussein joins Ba'th Party
	1961 Hussein flees to Egypt
	1963 Hussein returns to Iraq
	1964 Hussein is arrested
Israel defeats Arab nations in Six-Day War 1967	
	1968 Hussein made head of security services after Ba'th take power in Iraq
Vietnam War ends 1975	
	1979 Hussein proclaimed president of Iraq
	1980–88 Hussein is embroiled in Iran–Iraq War
	1990 Hussein orders invasion of Kuwait, precipitating Persian Gulf War
Dissolution of 1991 Soviet Union	

For Further Reading
Karsh, Efraim. *Saddam Hussein: A Political Biography.* New York: Free Press, 1997.
Stefoff, Rebecca. *Saddam Hussein.* Brookfield, Conn.: Millbrook Press, 1995.

Ignatius of Loyola

Founder of the Society of Jesus
1491–1556

Life and Work

In a period of religious upheaval, Ignatius of Loyola abandoned a secular career to serve the Roman Catholic church. The Society of Jesus (the Jesuits) that he created became one of the most important Roman Catholic orders.

Ignatius was born Iñigo López de Recalde in the Basque region of Spain in 1491. Raised in his family's ancestral castle at Loyola, he developed a taste for courtly life and the romantic tales of knightly heroes. He entered the army as a youth and in 1521 was wounded in a battle against the French at Pamplona. He had a protracted and excruciating convalescence. As he recovered, he read books, including lives of the saints. He was so impressed by their example that he renounced his military career and pledged to make a pilgrimage to Jerusalem. In 1523 he made his way to the Holy Land, barefoot and begging along the way. Returning to Spain the following year, he was arrested and jailed by the Inquisition for unauthorized preaching. Dismayed by such a reaction to his missionary work, he studied at the universities of Barcelona, Alcalá, and Paris, where in 1535 he received his master's degree.

During his university years Ignatius, as he had now come to be known, sought the companionship of fellow students who had a similar calling to missionary work. With the Protestant Reformation sweeping through northern Europe, he believed Roman Catholic preachers were needed who were especially well trained in theology. In Paris he assembled a group of other students, among whom was Francis Xavier (1506–52). Gathering together at the cathedral of Montmartre on August 15, 1534, they vowed to travel to Rome for the Pope's blessing and from there to Jerusalem. When Ignatius arrived at the outskirts of Rome in 1537, however, he experienced a vision of Jesus that dissuaded him from his pilgrimage. Inspired by a new understanding of his mission, he drew up a rule for a religious order "for the propagation of the faith" anywhere in the world the Pope might command. This rule was approved by Pope Paul III in 1540. In the following year Ignatius was elected general of what was now the Society of Jesus.

Ignatius spent the remainder of his life in Rome. Much of his time was occupied in writing works such as the *Spiritual Exercises* (1548) and his *Autobiography* (1555). Continuing to experience visions until the end, he died on July 31, 1556, in Rome. He was canonized a saint in 1622.

Legacy

Ignatius of Loyola established a religious order that would influence religious life and politics for centuries.

The Society of Jesus had been designed to serve the Pope in a time of intense religious upheaval. The Protestant Reformation launched by Martin Luther in 1517 had attacked the papacy and the institutional structure of the Roman Catholic priesthood. Jesuits, as members came to be known, pursued a number of activities designed to reverse the Reformation. Committed mainly to teaching and debating, some members even helped administer the Spanish Inquisition, which earned the order the enmity of many later observers such as Voltaire.

Many Jesuits were not involved with the Counter–Reformation, however, but in missionary work around the globe. This had been the explicit purpose of the Society, and, during the centuries after Ignatius's death, Jesuit missionaries converted enormous numbers of people outside Europe. The greatest success was in the New World, where the great majority of the native population gradually became Roman Catholic after the arrival of Jesuit and other missionaries in the sixteenth century. Other members of the Society traveled to Asia. Francis Xavier was sent in 1541 to India, where he established a missionary school at Goa and translated the Nicene Creed into local tongues. There he also deployed the powers of the Portuguese Inquisition against European merchants who were oppressing native converts. His most remarkable achievement was the conversion of large numbers of Japanese after 1549. Within a generation hundreds of thousands were converted, with Nagasaki becoming a predominantly Christian city. These successes were perceived as a threat to the new government established by Tokugawa Ieyasu in 1600, however, and Japan was closed to foreigners. Finally, in China the Jesuit Matteo Ricci (1552–1610) made extraordinary efforts to convert the imperial court. His tolerance for some Confucian practices such as ancestor veneration sparked the Rites Controversy in Rome, however, and he failed ultimately to convert the Chinese. Nevertheless, his writings about Chinese civilization profoundly influenced political philosophers such as Montesquieu during the eighteenth-century Enlightenment.

The Society of Jesus was often regarded in Europe with suspicion and, during the late eighteenth century was banned by virtually all governments except, ironically, Protestant England and Orthodox Russia. Pope Pius VII revived it in 1814, however, and it immediately resumed its missionary and educational work. By the late twentieth century members of the order were some of the most vocal proponents of social justice in Latin America. In El Salvador the Society's stand against injustice provoked a government death squad to the murder of the Jesuit priest Rutilio Grande in 1977, an event that would profoundly influence the career of Oscar Romero.

Strickland

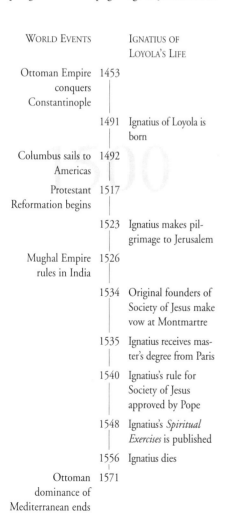

World Events	Ignatius of Loyola's Life
Ottoman Empire conquers Constantinople — 1453	
	1491 Ignatius of Loyola is born
Columbus sails to Americas — 1492	
Protestant Reformation begins — 1517	
	1523 Ignatius makes pilgrimage to Jerusalem
Mughal Empire rules in India — 1526	
	1534 Original founders of Society of Jesus make vow at Montmartre
	1535 Ignatius receives master's degree from Paris
	1540 Ignatius's rule for Society of Jesus approved by Pope
	1548 Ignatius's *Spiritual Exercises* is published
	1556 Ignatius dies
Ottoman dominance of Mediterranean ends — 1571	

For Further Reading

Barthel, Manfred. *The Jesuits: History and Legend of the Society of Jesus.* New York: Morrow, 1984.

Idigoras, J. Ignacio Tellechea. *Ignatius of Loyola: The Pilgrim Saint.* Translated by Cornelius Michael Buckley. Chicago: Loyola University Press, 1994.

Letson, Douglas, and Michael Higgins. *The Jesuit Mystique.* London: HarperCollins, 1995.

Isabella I

Queen of Spain
1451–1504

Life and Work

Isabella I (Isabella the Catholic) ruled Spain in partnership with her husband, Ferdinand II, and helped make it one of the most powerful states of early modern Europe. She promoted ambitious policies of state centralization, religious crusading, and overseas exploration.

Isabella was born in 1451 to King Juan II of Castile. She was not raised to rule but to provide dynastic security through marriage. In 1454 Juan died, and was succeeded by Isabella's half-brother Enrique, who ultimately fell out with Isabella, and when Enrique was informed about her intentions to marry Ferdinand, heir to the kingdom of Aragon, he forbade the union. Isabella persevered, however, and married Ferdinand in 1469. It was now clear that she intended to succeed Enrique, despite his efforts to have his daughter Juana proclaimed heir. When Enrique died in 1474 Juana received the support of the king of Portugal. In 1476 Ferdinand defeated the Portuguese army at the Battle of Toro. Isabella's throne was thus secured; in 1479, Ferdinand succeeded his father to the throne of Aragon. Aragon and Castile were now united under the joint rule of Ferdinand and Isabella, though each territory retained a considerable degree of autonomy.

Isabella's marriage to Ferdinand was a happy one, and Ferdinand supported most of her policies. Because of the conflict accompanying her rise to power, she was eager to impose a more centralized form of government and promote the integration of Spanish territories under her rule. The *cortes* ("parliaments") of Castile and Aragon were weakened, and new responsibilities for administration were given to low-ranking noblemen and even to commoners. Isabella also wanted to complete the centuries-old *reconquista*, or reconquest of the Iberian peninsula for Christianity. Muslim Moors, who had expanded into Spain in the eighth century, still held the southern state of Granada. On January 2, 1492, Granada fell to an army led by Ferdinand and accompanied by Isabella. The religious fervor and intolerance that inspired the completion of the *reconquista* also led Isabella to turn against Spain's Jews. In 1492, she had already received Pope Sixtus IV's reluctant permission to appropriate the Inquisition in her efforts to root out *conversos* (converts who had relapsed to Judaism), but on March 31, 1492, she and Ferdinand also ordered all Jews who refused baptism to leave Spain. Finally, in the same momentous year, the monarchs gave their approval to CHRISTOPHER COLUMBUS to lead an expedition in search of a western sea route to the Indies. On October 12, 1492, Columbus landed at what is today San Salvador in the Caribbean. Isabella died on November 26, 1504.

Legacy

While Isabella I's reign strengthened Spain and led to the rise of its seaborne empire, her policies of religious persecution left a bitter legacy.

Seeking to unify the Iberian peninsula under a single crown and a single faith, Isabella and Ferdinand laid the foundation for the Spanish national state. Their policies of centralization enabled the crown to reduce the powers of the nobility. The result was to create a more powerful state that in 1512 was able to annex Navarre and thus complete the integration of modern Spain. Having taken the first steps at colonizing the New World under Isabella, Spain also became the richest state in Europe, and under PHILIP II would threaten to dominate other powers such as England. What is more, expansion in the New World brought virtually all of Latin America under Spanish influence. Despite a rapacious desire for silver, a brutal colonial administration, the enslavement of natives, and a catastrophic loss of life, Latin America would emerge from the wars of independence in the nineteenth century as a predominantly Spanish-speaking and Roman Catholic civilization.

Isabella's policies toward non-Christians, while helping to unify the nation and protect the Roman Catholic church, also contributed to a tradition of intolerance that would be a curse to Europeans in later centuries. The Spanish Inquisition was especially brutal under Tomás de Torquemada; in the sixteenth century it would even harass IGNATIUS LOYOLA and Teresa of Ávila. The Inquisition would become synonymous with religious fanaticism, providing modern intellectuals such as Voltaire and Fyodor Dostoevsky with fuel for their attacks on Roman Catholicism. Finally, the expulsion of Spain's 200,000 Jews under Isabella uprooted lives, deprived the state of considerable talent, and contributed indirectly to the terrible fate of European Jewry in the twentieth century. Since England and France had also issued orders of expulsion two centuries earlier, many Jews were compelled after 1492 to seek residence in Eastern Europe, the very region in which ADOLF HITLER would let loose the Holocaust.

Strickland

WORLD EVENTS		ISABELLA I'S LIFE
Ming Dynasty reasserts Chinese control of China	1368	
	1451	Isabella is born
Ottoman Empire conquers Constantinople	1453	
	1469	Isabella marries Ferdinand
	1479	Castile and Aragon are united under Isabella and Ferdinand
Columbus sails to Americas	1492	Isabella and Ferdinand's forces reclaim Granada, order expulsion of Jews, and commission Columbus's voyage
	1504	Isabella dies
Protestant Reformation begins	1517	

For Further Reading

Fernadez-Armesto, Felipe. *Ferdinand and Isabella*. New York: Taplinger, 1975.

Kamen, Henry Arthur Francis. *The Spanish Inquisition: An Historical Revision*. London: Weidenfeld and Nicholson, 1997.

Rubin, Nancy. *Isabella of Castile: The First Renaissance Queen*. New York: St. Martin's Press, 1991.

Ivan III

Medieval Russian Tsar
1440–1505

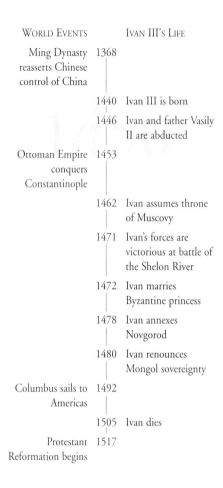

WORLD EVENTS		IVAN III'S LIFE
Ming Dynasty reasserts Chinese control of China	1368	
	1440	Ivan III is born
	1446	Ivan and father Vasily II are abducted
Ottoman Empire conquers Constantinople	1453	
	1462	Ivan assumes throne of Muscovy
	1471	Ivan's forces are victorious at battle of the Shelon River
	1472	Ivan marries Byzantine princess
	1478	Ivan annexes Novgorod
	1480	Ivan renounces Mongol sovereignty
Columbus sails to Americas	1492	
	1505	Ivan dies
Protestant Reformation begins	1517	

Life and Work

Ivan III (Ivan the Great; in full, Ivan Vasilyevich) vastly expanded the power of fifteenth-century Muscovy and established the political foundations of the Russian Empire.

Ivan was born in 1440 in the kingdom of Muscovy, a state centered upon the city of Moscow that had suffered for centuries from civil wars. His political character was shaped at an early age when in 1446 he and his father Vasily II, having set out on a pilgrimage, were seized by a rival to the throne and held for ransom. The six-year-old Ivan was finally released through the mediation of an Orthodox bishop, but not before his captor had gouged out the eyes of his father, causing him to be known thereafter as Vasily the Blind. The young Ivan never forgot the terror and humiliation of this experience, and, when he succeeded his father to the throne in 1462, he devoted his energies to increasing the power of the Muscovite ruler and his state.

Ivan's reign constituted the final stage of what historians traditionally call "the gathering of Rus." Set in motion by earlier Muscovite rulers, this was a process of territorial expansion that culminated under Ivan with the integration of virtually all Russian-speaking lands occupying the eastern limits of Europe. Ivan showed that he was prepared to use diplomacy to achieve this goal but just as often resorted to force of arms. Such was the case with the republic of Novgorod, a prosperous commercial power to the west of Muscovy that had supported Ivan's boyhood abduction. In 1471 the resentful prince defeated Novgorod's army at the Battle of the Shelon River; in 1478 the republic was added to a growing list of conquests.

In a symbolic act aimed at unifying his expanding Russian territories, in 1472 Ivan married the niece of the last Byzantine emperor, who had perished on the walls of Constantinople when it fell to the Muslim Turks in 1453. Following the defeat of Novgorod, Ivan became occupied with another traditional goal of his predecessors, the renunciation of Mongol sovereignty. Led by GHENGIS KHAN, the Mongols had invaded the Eurasian Steppe in 1223 and soon reduced the Russian states they found there to a condition of vassalage. By the end of the fifteenth cen-tury, divisions within the Mongol Empire had reduced its power over these Russian states considerably. In 1480 Ivan took the historic step of publicly renouncing all tribute obligations, finally freeing Muscovy from the dreaded Mongol yoke. He died in 1505.

Legacy

Ivan III's territorial expansion influenced the course of history through two major developments: the elimination of all rival Russian states in eastern Europe and the formation of an autocratic system of government. This dual legacy both increased the power of Ivan's successors and limited their flexibility in times of political crisis.

Ivan's commitment to "the gathering of Rus" created a single national state that was integrated by a common language and religion. The Russian-speaking lands of eastern Europe had accepted Orthodox Christianity as early as 988, but internecine strife and Mongol domination during the centuries that followed had prevented political leaders from achieving unification. Ivan's symbolic marriage in 1472 elevated Muscovy in the eyes of the Orthodox church and in subsequent years some Russians would even claim that Russia represented the "Third Rome," a Christian empire with a mission to protect the Orthodox faith throughout the world.

Ivan's achievements also yielded a system of government that would both assist and plague Russian leaders in later centuries. Ivan was the first ruler to call himself *tsar*. This title, which was derived from *caesar*, reflected a principle of rule called autocracy whereby no legal restrictions were placed upon the ruler's authority. Autocracy enabled Russian tsars such as PETER I (r. 1682–1725) to mobilize national defenses in time of war and to promote reforms designed to strengthen the state. Autocracy also created severe problems. It repeatedly permitted the tsar's power to be exercised in an arbitrary and oppressive way, as in the extreme case of IVAN IV (r. 1547–84). It also made solutions to political challenges depend solely upon the abilities of the tsar. In the case of NICHOLAS II (r. 1894–1917), for instance, the tsar's abilities would prove tragically inferior to his challenges.

Strickland

For Further Reading

Crummey, Robert O. *The Formation of Muscovy, 1304–1613.* London: Longman, 1987.

Fennell, J. L. I. *Ivan the Great of Moscow.* London: Macmillan, 1963.

Ostrowski, Donald. *Muscovy and the Mongols: Cross-Cultural Influences on the Steppe Frontier, 1304–1589.* Cambridge: Cambridge University Press, 1998.

Ivan IV

Ruler of Russia
1530–1584

Life and Work

Ivan IV (Ivan the Terrible; in full, Ivan Vasilyevich) created the Russian Empire and pursued major reforms of its administrative and legal system. Despite extraordinary energy and vision, however, he succumbed in later years to fits of paranoia and cruelty that so destabilized his government that many of his early achievements were negated.

Ivan was born in 1530 as heir to the kingdom of Muscovy. When his father Vasily III died in 1533, Ivan's mother ruled as regent, but after her death in 1538 a group of noblemen known as *boyars* usurped power for themselves. The violent character of their rule was resented by the young Ivan, who was frequently insulted and beaten in his Kremlin palace. At the age of 13 he was able finally to bring *boyar* rule to an end by having the chief usurper arrested and executed. Then, in 1547, Ivan became the first Russian ruler to crown himself with the title of tsar.

His reign is usually divided into two periods. The first witnessed promising domestic reforms and military victories. After marrying Anastasia, a member of the Romanov family, a month after his coronation, he organized an inner circle of advisors called the Chosen Council to assist him in reforming the Muscovite state. With it he oversaw the creation of a written code of laws in 1550 called the *Sudebnik*. He was then able to launch a series of successful military campaigns that included the conquest of the Muslim state of Kazan in 1552.

The second period of Ivan's reign saw the degeneration of his mental condition and with it his rule. Always suspicious of court intrigues, when his beloved Anastasia died in 1560 he feared a renewed *boyar* conspiracy. In subsequent years he had virtually every member of the Chosen Council arrested or executed, often condemning their family members along with them. In 1564 his paranoia became so strong that he fled Moscow and abdicated his throne. He returned the following year with plans for a new institution called the Oprichnina. This strange entity became the center of a campaign against his supposed enemies, and on one chilling occasion he personally observed as 100 *boyars* and others were tortured and executed in a public square. Nevertheless, out of a sense of religious obligation he would sometimes donate large sums of his own money to the church for the repose of his victims' souls.

In 1584 he died in Moscow.

Legacy

Ivan IV's reign severely weakened the Russian Empire. While some achievements survived him, civil unrest and political instability troubled it for another generation.

Ivan did much to strengthen the system of autocracy he inherited from his Muscovite predecessors. The legal code he introduced increased the power of the tsar and created a more efficient system of regional administration. He was also able to oversee reforms in church administration that benefited the state. In this he can be compared to his contemporary King Henry VIII, who oversaw the reform of the church in England. In 1551, for instance, Ivan watched as a church council called the Stoglav Council reformed church life and restricted the amount of land that monasteries and other religious institutions could possess. This enabled the tsar to exercise greater control over the clergy and prepared the way for more drastic church reforms under Peter I. State power was also increased by spectacular military conquests. In addition to the conquest of Kazan, the western part of Siberia was annexed in 1582. It was the acquisition of these and other non-Russian territories that marked the foundation of a multinational and multireligious empire.

Nevertheless, the devastating experience of Ivan's reign led to civil upheavals and military reversals that threatened the empire with collapse. The Oprichnina, which never ruled more than half of the land, was directed more by Ivan's paranoia than for the good of the state. As its black-uniformed officials moved through central Russia terrorizing the population, civilians fled and foreign armies took advantage of the situation to seize territory in the west. In the end, Ivan's activities even threatened the survival of his dynasty. During a fit of rage in 1581, he beat his eldest son in the head with a staff so severely that he died several days later. When Ivan himself died in 1584, the heir to the throne was Fyodor, a frail imbecile. When he subsequently proved unfit to rule, the empire collapsed in a civil war known as the Time of Troubles (1598–1613). The central government collapsed, insurrections raged, and an invasion by Poland threatened the very existence of Russia. Only with the ascension of Michael Romanov as tsar in 1613 was stability finally restored.

Strickland

For Further Reading
Payne, Robert, and Nikita Romanoff. *Ivan the Terrible.* New York: Thomas Y. Crowell, 1975.
Platonov, S. F. *Ivan the Terrible.* Edited and translated by Richard Hellie. Gulf Breeze, Fla.: Academic International Press, 1974.
Yanov, Alexander. *The Origins of Autocracy: Ivan the Terrible in Russian History.* Translated by Stephen Dunn. Berkeley: University of California Press, 1981.

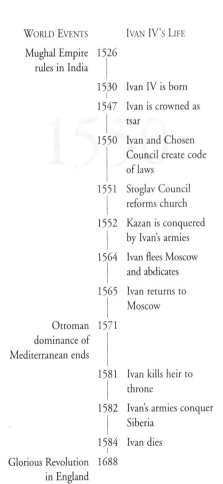

WORLD EVENTS		IVAN IV'S LIFE
Mughal Empire rules in India	1526	
	1530	Ivan IV is born
	1547	Ivan is crowned as tsar
	1550	Ivan and Chosen Council create code of laws
	1551	Stoglav Council reforms church
	1552	Kazan is conquered by Ivan's armies
	1564	Ivan flees Moscow and abdicates
	1565	Ivan returns to Moscow
Ottoman dominance of Mediterranean ends	1571	
	1581	Ivan kills heir to throne
	1582	Ivan's armies conquer Siberia
	1584	Ivan dies
Glorious Revolution in England	1688	

Jaurès, Jean

French Socialist and Politician
1859–1914

Life and Work

Jean Jaurès, founder of the modern French Socialist Party, was one of the first and most successful socialists to work within the parliamentary system. As an internationalist, he worked to reduce hostility between France and Germany, anticipating their economic and political cooperation after World War II.

Born in Castres, in southern France, on September 3, 1859, to a family of modest means, Jaurès displayed his intellectual potential at a young age. He was educated at the Ecole Normale Superieure, an elite institution of higher education in Paris. His success in school resulted in a teaching post at Toulouse University in southern France. A talented public speaker who was attracted to republican politics, Jaurès was elected at age 26 to the Chamber of Deputies, making him the youngest deputy in the French parliament. During his first term (1885–89) he quickly became disillusioned by the moderate leadership then controlling the Chamber. After his defeat in the 1889 elections, he briefly retired from politics, resuming his teaching duties in Toulouse.

At this time he took an interest in socialist theory, voraciously reading the works of LOUIS BLANC, KARL MARX, and others. Contact with workers solidified his commitment to socialism, and he became a spokesman for coal miners striking in the southern French city of Carmaux in 1892. Running as an independent socialist, Jaurès was elected deputy again, serving from 1893 to 1898 and 1902 to 1914. As leader of the socialists in the Chamber of Deputies, Jaurès struggled to unify the socialist movement, then split into six competing factions, and transform it into a parliamentary power.

During his time out of office, Jaurès focused his energies on journalism and support for Alfred Dreyfus, a Jewish army officer wrongly accused in 1894 of spying for Germany and sentenced to life in prison. Dreyfus was eventually proven innocent. The Dreyfus case brought a left-of-center coalition into power, including the socialists. In 1902 Jaurès, deputy once again, founded the French Socialist Party. He also was elected vice president of the Chamber of Deputies and worked hard to maintain the coalition government. This effort failed in part due to the decision by Socialist Party leaders, meeting at the congress of the Socialist International in Amsterdam in 1904, to prohibit socialists from participating in "bourgeois" cabinet ministries in Europe. Although he remained a deputy, Jaurès withdrew from the coalition government.

Jaurès actively opposed nationalistic militarism and worked to prevent conflict in Europe, where tensions between the Great Powers (France, Britain, Germany, Austria, and Russia) raised the threat of war. He sought reconciliation between France and Germany after the assassination of the Austrian archduke Franz Ferdinand, the event that ultimately sparked World War I. Jaurès was assassinated by a fanatical French nationalist on July 31, 1914, on the eve of the war that he had worked so hard to avoid.

Legacy

The founding father of twentieth-century French socialism and an antiwar activist, Jaurès was a model of parliamentary conduct for future French and European socialists and social democrats.

Part of his influence stems from his support for workers, expressed in the socialist newspaper he founded in 1904 (*L'Humanité*) and in his book, *Socialist History of the French Revolution* (published 1901–1904), and his belief that socialism could be established in free elections and through gradual reforms, rather than by violent revolution. His humanitarianism made him acceptable in mainstream politics. Under his leadership the socialist political movement flourished in France. He organized and unified, as best he could, the various French socialist factions, giving the left a stronger role in the Chamber of Deputies.

Many socialists and communists opposed participation in parliamentary politics, espousing instead revolutionary activities outside formal politics, or even outside the law. Jaurès's dedication, both to socialism and to participation in the formal political institutions of France, provided a model for future socialists in Europe and other nations, an alternative to the extra-legal tactics practiced by Russian communists and their followers.

Jaurès was also a forerunner of future efforts to foster cooperation among European states, especially between France and Germany. Although many socialists opposed nationalism in favor of international class loyalties, Jaurès accepted the reality of nation-states and sought to foster cooperation and the construction of a coherent world order. Thus, he was one of the most vocal opponents of a European war. Zealous nationalism overwhelmed his and others' efforts for peace before World War I. It would take another world war for Europeans to begin the cooperation that would result in the creation of the European Union.

Lemoine

WORLD EVENTS		JAURÈS'S LIFE
Congress of Vienna reorganizes Europe	1815	
	1859	Jean Jaurès is born
Germany is united	1871	
	1885–89	Jaurès serves first term in Chamber of Deputies
	1893–98	Jaurès serves second term in Chamber of Deputies
	1894	Dreyfus Affair begins
	1901–04	Jaurès publishes *Socialist History of the French Revolution*
	1902–14	Jaurès serves three terms in Chamber of Deputies
	1902	Jaurès founds French Socialist Party
	1904	Jaurès founds newspaper *L'Humanité*
		Congress of Socialist International prohibits socialists from taking part in "bourgeois" governments
Russo-Japanese War	1905	
	1914	Jaurès is assassinated on July 31, three days before start of World War I
World War I 1914–18		

For Further Reading

Goldberg, Harvey. *The Life of Jean Jaurès*. Madison: The University of Wisconsin Press, 1962.

Weinstein, Harold Richard. *Jean Jaurès: A Study of Patriotism in the French Socialist Movement*. New York: Octagon Books, 1973.

Jefferson, Thomas

Third President of the United States
1743–1826

Life and Work

Thomas Jefferson was the chief writer of the Declaration of Independence. As a leader of the early republic, he founded the Democratic Party and facilitated the western expansion of the nation.

Jefferson was born in Albemarle County, Virginia, on April 13, 1743. He entered the College of William and Mary at age 17, graduating in 1762. He began his law practice in 1767. Jefferson was elected to the Virginia House of Burgesses, serving from 1769 to 1774, when he began to oppose British policies toward the American colonists.

Elected to the Continental Congress in 1775, Jefferson chaired the committee that drafted the Declaration of Independence, which he presented to the Congress on July 2, 1776. He served as governor of Virginia (1779–81) during the war for independence (1775–83). Jefferson was elected as a Virginia delegate to Congress in 1783 and became U.S. minister to France in 1785. He served as secretary of state (1790–93) in GEORGE WASHINGTON's first administration.

Jefferson opposed the financial measures designed by Secretary of the Treasury Alexander Hamilton because they benefited wealthy northern merchants at the expense of southern and western farmers. In 1798 he also opposed the Alien and Sedition Acts, which made it easier to deport foreigners and to prosecute those who criticized the federal government. Jefferson, with JAMES MADISON, composed the Kentucky and Virginia Resolutions, which upheld the right of states to determine the constitutionality of federal policy. His opposition to Federalist policy led him to form the Democratic–Republican Party, which coexisted with the Federalist Party represented by Washington's administration.

Jefferson became vice president in John Adams's administration (1797–1801), and was elected president in 1801, serving until 1809. During his tenure he purchased the Louisiana Territory from France in 1803 and promulgated the Embargo Act (1807, though repealed in 1809), which prohibited trade with Britain and other belligerents in the Napoleonic Wars.

Jefferson retired to Monticello, his Virginia farm, in 1816. He founded the University of Virginia in 1819, whose campus he designed. He died on July 4, 1826.

Legacy

The Declaration of Independence established the idea that a nation's sovereignty existed within the people rather than a monarchy and stipulated that equality was the key to civil government. Ever since, citizens of the United States and others around the world have relied on these principles to expand human rights and self-determination and to define their political principles.

Thomas Jefferson's anti-Federalist position led to the formation of the Democratic–Republican Party, forerunner of the present-day Democratic Party. Jefferson's arguments were used by southern Democrats to justify secession on the basis of states' rights during the Civil War and opposition to the civil rights movement during the 1950s and 1960s. Present-day Democrats assert that Jefferson's egalitarian principles form the basis of the party's social welfare platform. Republicans today, whose party was formed in 1854, also claim Jefferson as a philosophical ancestor because he sought to restrain the powers of the federal government.

Jefferson believed that the new republic should be based on an agricultural economy made up of small farmers, and sought new lands for them to cultivate. Thus he purchased the Louisiana Territory, a vast expanse between the Mississippi River and the Rocky Mountains.

The Louisiana Purchase, which doubled the size of the United States, encouraged immigration westward, a virtually unstoppable "manifest destiny," that within a century almost totally destroyed the Native American way of life.

As a southern plantation owner, Jefferson owned numerous slaves, yet in principle he opposed the institution of slavery, a paradoxical attitude that characterized American political life for the next 50 years. The Northwest Ordinance, passed at Jefferson's instigation in 1787, prohibited slavery in territories north of the Ohio River. His generation's inability to resolve the contradictions between the founding ideals of the republic and the reality of slavery eventually led to the outbreak of the Civil War in 1861.

Jefferson's ideals expressed in the Declaration of Independence inspired leaders such as Abraham Lincoln to extend that definition to groups previously excluded. Because of Jefferson's leadership, the United States has also maintained a balance between a strong national government and a relatively decentralized democracy.

Lemoine

WORLD EVENTS		JEFFERSON'S LIFE
English seize Calcutta	1690	
	1743	Thomas Jefferson is born
United States declares independence	1776	Jefferson helps draft Declaration of Independence
	1783	Jefferson elected as a Virginia delegate to Congress
	1785	Jefferson represents United States as minister to France
French Revolution begins	1789	
	1790	Jefferson is appointed secretary of state
	1797	Jefferson becomes vice president
	1801–09	Jefferson serves as president of United States
	1803	Jefferson purchases Louisiana Territory
Latin American independence movement begins	1811	
Congress of Vienna reorganizes Europe	1815	
	1826	Jefferson dies
Germany is united	1871	

For Further Reading

Elkins, Stanley, and Eric McKitrik. *The Age of Federalism.* Oxford: Oxford University Press, 1993.

Ellis, Joseph J. *The American Sphinx: The Character of Thomas Jefferson.* New York: Knopf, 1997.

Risjord, Norman K. *Thomas Jefferson.* Madison, Wis.: Madison House, 1994.

Joan of Arc

Defender of France and Roman
Catholic Saint
1412–1431

Life and Work

Joan of Arc emerged from obscurity to lead the French army to victory during the Hundred Years War. Although convinced that she had been called by God, she was burned at the stake as a heretic in 1431.

Joan of Arc was born in 1412 to a family of peasants in the northern French village of Domrémy. During her childhood France and England were locked in the Hundred Years War, a conflict that had been fought intermittently since 1337 and that took a dangerous turn for France in 1415 at the Battle of Agincourt. The situation was made more desperate by the fact that the Burgundians had recently given their support to the English and had assisted in the capture of Paris, the traditional capital. After the death of the mad King Charles VI in 1422, the dauphin (eldest son of the king and heir to the throne) Charles hoped to rally French forces in the south and then march north to Reims in order to be crowned king. He was ambivalent about a campaign to recover Paris, however. In the meantime, the war took its toll on the French, and Domrémy was pillaged by the English in 1425.

That very year the 13-year-old Joan had the first of many visions. This and later encounters with saints and angels led her to believe she had been called by God to defend the French. She took her visions very seriously, and, after an encounter with the Archangel Michael, even made a vow to preserve her virginity.

In 1429 she obtained the help of a local official to be taken to Charles in Chinon. There she amazed the dauphin by her ability to identify him among other princes despite a disguise. After she was rigorously examined about the orthodoxy of her faith, Charles gave the 17-year-old girl a suit of armor and sent her at the head of an army to lift an English siege at Orléans. To the surprise of both the English and the French, she relieved the city on April 29, 1429. She was then able to accompany the dauphin to Reims, where in her presence on July 17 he was crowned King Charles VII. In September she turned to the recovery of Paris, but when the ambivalent king failed to send relief she was forced to withdraw. Joan's disappointment was followed by disaster in 1430 when she was captured by the Burgundians. Handed over to their English allies, she was then placed on trial as a witch and heretic.

Joan's trial began in 1431 and was heavily rigged against her. Not offered counsel, she ultimately failed to defend herself against charges that were as concerned with her male dress as they were with her religious orthodoxy. She made a sincere effort to cooperate with the judges, but in the end was found guilty. On May 30, 1431, she was taken to the marketplace in Rouen and burned at the stake, crying "Jesus!" until the flames finally consumed her.

Legacy

Doubted by Charles and disgraced by the English, Joan of Arc became a heroine of France and a saint of the Roman Catholic church. Her memory fueled popular legend and inspired the works of later artists such as William Shakespeare, Voltaire, Mark Twain, and Peter Tchaikovsky.

Joan's leadership of the French army in a time of military crisis is considered by historians to be the turning point in the Hundred Years War. Before her relief of Orléans, the English had enjoyed near-constant ascendancy. The war had been fought almost entirely on French soil and, by the beginning of the fifteenth century, domestic turmoil threatened to bring final defeat to France. The English, whose motives for war included claims upon French territory and the French throne, were on the verge of destroying the last stronghold of resistance when they besieged the strategic city. That they were driven away from it by Joan (who was thereafter nicknamed the Maid of Orléans) assured continued French resistance. Patriotism was kindled among soldiers who looked upon Joan as a common Frenchwoman sent to them by God himself. After her death, French victories mounted under Charles, and in 1453 England was finally forced to sue for peace. Thereafter English claims to the French throne ceased, and lands that had been held in France since the time of WILLIAM I (William the Conqueror) were surrendered. In later centuries Joan became an important symbol of French national pride.

Joan also had significant impact in religious matters. While the clergy had played an important role in her trial, the expulsion of the English brought a reconsideration of the court's verdict. Church leaders were impressed by Joan's actions—among them the expulsion of blasphemers and prostitutes from her army. While the question of her visions was not addressed, her readiness to cooperate with Church officials was considered a sign that she had been judged unfairly. In 1455, then, the Church ordered a reexamination of the trial and in the following year a priest publicly exonerated Joan on the very site of her execution. In modern times, her simple but orthodox faith in Roman Catholic Christianity became a model of common piety for the Church, and in 1920 Pope Benedict XV made her a saint.

Strickland

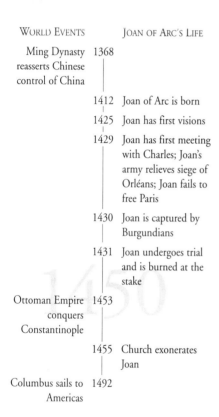

WORLD EVENTS		JOAN OF ARC'S LIFE
Ming Dynasty reasserts Chinese control of China	1368	
	1412	Joan of Arc is born
	1425	Joan has first visions
	1429	Joan has first meeting with Charles; Joan's army relieves siege of Orléans; Joan fails to free Paris
	1430	Joan is captured by Burgundians
	1431	Joan undergoes trial and is burned at the stake
Ottoman Empire conquers Constantinople	1453	
	1455	Church exonerates Joan
Columbus sails to Americas	1492	

For Further Reading

Gies, Frances. *Joan of Arc: The Legend and the Reality.* New York: Harper and Row, 1981.
Sumption, Jonathan. *The Hundred Years War.* London: Faber and Faber, 1990.
Warner, Marina. *Joan of Arc: The Image of Female Heroism.* New York: Knopf, 1981.

Joseph, Chief

Chief of the Nez Percé
c. 1840–1904

Life and Work

Even though Chief Joseph's efforts to flee the oppressive Indian reservation system of the United States were unsuccessful, he became an inspiration for those Americans who demanded greater respect for the native peoples of the United States.

Chief Joseph, a Native American leader of the Nez Percé people, was born In-mut-too-yah-lat-lat ("Thunder Rolling in the Mountains") in the Oregon Territories in the 1840s. Like many Nez Percé (French, "pierced nose"), Chief Joseph's father had converted to Christianity, and Joseph himself attended a mission school where he received a primary academic education. The Nez Percé had enjoyed some of the friendliest relationships with settlers who began to colonize the fertile Oregon lands in the 1840s.

After 1846, with the Oregon Territories definitively brought under the domain of the United States, the federal government encouraged the Nez Percé and other native peoples of the Northwest to settle on small, unproductive reservations while nonlocal settlers took over the best lands. Some Nez Percé, such as Chief Joseph, questioned the plans of the U.S. government and also questioned, because of the unconfirmed authority of the signatories, the 1863 and 1871 treaties that had secured the move of the Nez Percé to the reservations.

In 1877, because of the demands of settlers for higher-quality lands, the federal government demanded that Joseph, his family, and his small following remove themselves from the Wallowa Valley, Oregon, to a reservation at Laprew. On June 17, 1877, Chief Joseph and his followers, acting on a plan previously agreed upon, began a flight toward Canada. For three months, Joseph and his group, numbering 200 to 300 warriors and their families, trekked over 1,000 miles across Oregon, Washington, Idaho, and Montana, chased by more than 2,000 federal troops. The U.S. army never caught up with Joseph, and Joseph's warriors defeated the army in several engagements. Despite the conflicts, Chief Joseph earned a reputation as a humane leader, always buying supplies from farmers and ranchers and always treating prisoners carefully.

On September 30, 1877, 40 miles from the Canadian border, Joseph and his band found themselves trapped by the U.S. army in the Bear Paw mountains of Montana. Rather than face a bloodbath, Joseph, with great sorrow and dignity, surrendered to General Nelson A. Miles. Chief Joseph and his group were exiled to the Indian Territory, now known as Oklahoma, until 1885, when they received permission to return to Washington state (although the government forbade them from occupying their ancestral home).

In 1903, Chief Joseph made a trip to Washington, D.C., to meet with President THEODORE ROOSEVELT in order to plead, fruitlessly, for the right to return to their ancestral homes.

Chief Joseph died on September 21, 1904.

Legacy

Chief Joseph protested in words, and then by flight, the pitiless treatment received by the native people of the United States, made all the more horrible because the Nez Percé were a peaceful people.

It is a fact of American history that the white settlers' greed for land practically destroyed the Native American cultures. What is little known is the accommodation that many Native Americans, such as Chief Joseph, tried to reach with the newly arrived immigrants, and how much they valued an exchange of knowledge and beliefs. Also little discussed is how colonizing societies, such as the United States, consistently imposed social orders on native societies that warped their systems of leadership and corrupted efforts at accommodation that might have otherwise produced friendly and mutually beneficial relationships. Chief Joseph's negotiations with whites over the issue of reservation—calling into question the authority of those natives who had negotiated for him without forming a community consensus—and his flight to Canada as a protest against the policies of the United States brought into sharp focus the failure of the treaty system and relations with native peoples in general.

As a consequence of Chief Joseph's flight, many whites became aware, through the extensive coverage of the event in the newspapers, of the plight of Native Americans. In many places, whites began to advocate some recompense to native peoples, and some small gains were made in restoring Native Americans to at least some small remnant of their original lands, especially in the West. During the 1880s and 1890s, however, this growing sympathy for and response to the plight of Native Americans was damaged by new ideas, such as "scientific" racism, that wrecked positive relations between dominant white society and Native Americans and challenged the ability of Native Americans to preserve their culture. The period from the turn of the century through the 1960s marked a second onslaught against native people, this time not attacking them physically, but destroying their cultures through forced assimilation into "the American Way."

Del Testa

WORLD EVENTS		CHIEF JOSEPH'S LIFE
Congress of Vienna reorganizes Europe	1815	
	c. 1840	Chief Joseph is born
Germany is united	1871	
	1877	Chief Joseph flees toward Canada and is captured
	1885	Chief Joseph and his people return to Oregon
	1903	Chief Joseph visits Washington, D.C., to meet with President Theodore Roosevelt
	1904	Chief Joseph dies
Russo-Japanese War	1905	

For Further Reading
Howard, Helen Addison. *The Saga of Chief Joseph.* Lincoln: University of Nebraska Press, 1978.
Nez Percé Chief Joseph. *Chief Joseph's Own Story.* Billings, Mont.: Council for Indian Education, 1983; 7th printing, 1994.

Justinian I

Byzantine Emperor
482–565

World Events		Justinian I's Life
Western Roman Empire collapses	476	
	482	Justinian I is born
Height of Toltec Civilization in Central America	c. 500	
	527	Justinian becomes emperor at the death of his uncle
	533	Justinian orders invasion of Africa
	534	Final edition of *Corpus juris civilis* is completed
	535	Justinian orders invasion of Italy
	548	Empress Theodora, Justinian's wife, dies
Byzantine Empire regains Italy	553	
	565	Justinian dies
China's disparate states are reunified	606	

Life and Work

Justinian I (Justinian the Great) was one of history's most visionary rulers. He drew upon a Christian faith to renew the legal, territorial, and religious foundations of the Byzantine Empire.

Justinian hailed from the region of Illyricum on the Balkan peninsula. Little is known about his early life, but after the elevation of his uncle Justin I to the Byzantine throne in 518, he was unexpectedly made joint ruler. In 527 he was proclaimed emperor upon Justin's death. Justinian was assisted for much of his reign by his wife, Theodora, a former actress whose fortitude proved crucial in suppressing the Nika Riots of 532 that destroyed the Church of Hagia Sophia and left a large part of Constantinople in ashes. To his great sorrow, Theodora died in 548.

One of Justinian's earliest and most ambitious acts was the codification of Roman law. Justinian had a body of works, called the *Corpus juris civilis,* assembled; the final edition was completed in 534. This assemblage provided a standard for civil law in subsequent centuries. Justinian was also ambitious in foreign policy. In 533 he ordered his general, Belisarius, to clear northern Africa of the barbarian Vandals, and in 535 he ordered the invasion of Italy. Within years Justinian managed to bring most of the territories of the former Roman Empire into his realm. He then turned to the matter of establishing a universal Christian civilization centered upon Constantinople.

As unity of faith was fundamental to his vision, he convened the Church's Fifth Ecumenical Council in 553 to settle issues concerning the person of Christ and heresy. He also issued laws affecting the clergy and used the state's resources to finance missionary activities. Perhaps his most memorable contribution to Christian civilization was the reconstruction of the Church of Hagia Sofia. This expensive project was an expression of his desire to integrate government and Church life in the manner of CONSTANTINE I or even King DAVID, whose son Solomon had built the ancient Jewish Temple of Jerusalem. Justinian was said to have been so impressed by Hagia Sophia's new design (which included an enormous central dome) that on the day of the consecration in 562 he exclaimed, "Solomon, I have outdone you!"

Having completed this testament to his rule, he died in 565.

Legacy

While the Byzantine Empire ultimately failed to retain the territories reconquered by Justinian I in the west, the ideal of a close relationship between Church and state survived for nearly a millennium.

Justinian was the last Byzantine emperor to maintain control over the western territories of the former Roman Empire. The stunning victories achieved by Belisarius during the sixth century were ultimately reversed, and in 800 the west came under the rule of CHARLEMAGNE. Later Byzantine emperors accommodated themselves to ruling only in the east, where, with the thriving commerce of Constantinople, a strong and vibrant civilization continued to develop.

Justinian's involvement in Church life, following the example of fourth-century rulers such as Constantine I (r. 312–37) and Theodosius I (r. 379–95), left a much deeper legacy than his foreign policy. Later emperors issued laws affecting the clergy, personally financed missionary activities, and occasionally convened Church councils. Results were sometimes divisive. In the eighth century Emperor Leo III (r. 717–41), a militant iconoclast, would order the destruction of all the Church's icons in the belief that they invited idolatry. Although motivated by the same piety and desire for doctrinal purity that guided Justinian, Leo's actions precipitated the Iconoclastic Controversy and upset Church life for more than a century. On the other hand, the power of the ruler often benefited the Church. In the lands of tenth-century Rus, for instance, Grand Prince Vladimir (r. 980–1015), after being converted by Byzantine missionaries, used his authority to order the baptism of the entire Russian people. Thereafter, Russian rulers such as IVAN III Vasilyevich acted to protect and expand eastern Christianity even after its former patron state, the Byzantine Empire, fell to the Islamic Turks in 1453.

Strickland

For Further Reading

Browning, Robert. *Justinian and Theodora.* 2nd ed. New York: Thames and Hudson, 1987.

Evans, J. A. S. *The Age of Justinian: The Circumstances of Imperial Power.* London: Routledge, 1996.

Moorhead, John. *Justinian.* London: Longman, 1994.

Norwich, John Julius. *Byzantium.* 3 vols. New York: Knopf, 1988–95.

Kennan, George F.

U.S. Diplomat and Scholar
1904–

Life and Work

One of the leading post–World War II U.S. diplomats, George F. Kennan formulated the policy of containment employed against the Soviet Union during the Cold War.

Kennan was born in Milwaukee, Wisconsin, on February 16, 1904. After attending military school he went to Princeton University, graduating in 1925, and then joined the U.S. Foreign Service. Kennan soon began to specialize in Russian affairs, serving at posts in the then-independent Baltic republics of Latvia, Lithuania, and Estonia, and helping to open the first U.S. embassy in Moscow, where he served from 1933 to 1936. Posted to Berlin in 1937, Kennan was interned by Germany after war was declared on the United States in December 1941.

Released in 1942, Kennan was again posted to the U.S. embassy in Moscow in 1944. He opposed the alliance with the Soviet Union during World War II and, as a political realist, advocated the division of Europe into spheres of influence between the United States and the Soviet Union even before the end of the war.

With the war against Germany won, Kennan concentrated on designing the policy of containment against the Soviet Union. His 1946 "long telegram" to the State Department and a 1947 article ("The Sources of Soviet Power"), published anonymously in the journal *Foreign Affairs,* warned of Soviet expansionism and proposed the policy of geopolitical containment to counter Soviet tactics. He did, however, oppose the militarization of the policy of containment. In 1947 Kennan was named leader of the State Department Policy Planning Staff (PPS), serving Secretary of State GEORGE MARSHALL—and helping to define the Marshall Plan—until 1949, after which he joined the Institute for Advanced Studies at Princeton University. In 1952 he was named ambassador to the Soviet Union, but returned the following year after the Soviets expelled him for making negative comments about their political system.

Kennan retired permanently from diplomatic duty in 1963. In his career as a scholar and public historian Kennan has criticized aspects of American foreign policy, including the war in Vietnam, and, more recently, U.S. foreign policy following the end of the Cold War.

Legacy

George F. Kennan's policy of containment was applied not only against the Soviet Union but also worldwide during the 40 years of the Cold War, thus leading to the expansion of U.S. political and military global presence.

Kennan exerted the most influence during the formative years of U.S. postwar foreign policy. He helped to frame the antagonistic policy toward the Soviet Union, which led to the start of the Cold War in Europe. Kennan envisioned a more political, economic, and diplomatic, rather than a strictly military, approach to relations with Europe and the Soviet Union. His vision was reflected in the Marshall Plan and other economic aid, implemented in part to combat the communist influence in Europe through increased economic ties with the United States.

However, Kennan's policies also resulted in a military buildup, including the permanent stationing of U.S. troops in Western Europe. In 1949 the North Atlantic Treaty Organization (NATO) was organized to provide for the collective defense of Western European countries and the United States against the Soviet bloc. In addition to the deployment of conventional military forces, nuclear weapons continued to be developed by both the United States and the Soviet Union.

The Cold War policy of the United States toward the Soviet Union was also applied in Asia after the Chinese Communist Party took control of China in 1949. Kennan convinced U.S. policy makers to make Japan the linchpin of American actions in East Asia, providing Japan with economic assistance similar to that provided to Western Europe. When Communist North Korea invaded South Korea in 1950, the United States, in conjunction with the United Nations, sent troops to stop what was seen as an attempt on the part of the Soviet Union to spread communism worldwide. U.S. involvement in Vietnam also resulted from the application of the concept of containment in Asia.

Kennan, when explaining the policy of containment, predicted that the Soviet Union would eventually break up. His policy, though Kennan believed it was often misapplied, played a role in the dissolution of the Soviet Union. In both Europe and East Asia, Kennan's policies structured U.S. foreign policy for the duration of the Cold War.

Lemoine

WORLD EVENTS		KENNAN'S LIFE
Germany is united	1871	
	1904	George F. Kennan is born
Russo-Japanese War	1905	
World War I	1914–18	
Russian Revolution	1917	
	1925	Kennan joins U.S. Foreign Service
Great Depression	1929–39	
	1933	Kennan helps open first U.S. embassy in Moscow
World War II	1939–45	
	1947	Kennan writes "anonymous" article published in *Foreign Affairs*
	1949	Kennan resigns from Foreign Service
	1963	Kennan retires from government service
Israel defeats Arab nations in Six-Day War	1967	

For Further Reading

Miscamble, Wilson. *George Kennan and the Making of American Foreign Policy, 1947-1950.* Princeton, N.J.: Princeton University Press, 1992.

Russell, Richard L. *George Kennan's Strategic Thought: The Making of an American Political Realist.* Westport, Conn.: Praeger, 1999.

Stephanson, Anders. *Kennan and the Art of Foreign Policy.* Cambridge, Mass.: Harvard University Press, 1989.

Kenyatta, Jomo

First President of Kenya
c. 1891–1978

Life and Work

Jomo Kenyatta emerged as the undisputed leader of Kenya's independence movement, guiding the new East African nation into and through a period of economic growth and political stability.

Jomo Kenyatta (a name he later adopted) was born Johnstone Kamau Ngengi about 1891, in Ngenda, Kikuyuland, British East Africa. He received his primary education at a Church of Scotland Mission, following his hospitalization there at age 10 for a serious illness. In 1922 he joined the Young Kikuyu Association, a nationalist organization formed by the Kikuyu tribe, the largest in the British East African colony. It soon

WORLD EVENTS		KENYATTA'S LIFE
Germany is united	1871	
	c. 1891	Jomo Kenyatta is born
Russo-Japanese War	1905	
World War I	1914–18	
Russian Revolution	1917	
Great Depression	1929–39	
	1931–46	Kenyatta resides in Great Britain
World War II	1939–45	
	1946	Kenyatta returns to British East Africa, becomes president of Kenya African Union
Communist China is established	1949	
	1952–59	Kenyatta is arrested and imprisoned
	1963	Kenya gains independence from Britain
	1964	Kenyatta is elected president of Kenya
Israel defeats Arab nations in Six-Day War	1967	
Vietnam War ends	1975	
	1978	Kenyatta dies in office
Dissolution of Soviet Union	1991	

merged with the East African Association to form the Kikuyu Central Association; Kenyatta was elected its general secretary in 1928.

Devoting all his energies to Kenyan independence, Kenyatta often went to different European nations both to study and to demand increased self-government for Kenya. From 1931 to 1946 he remained in Great Britain. There he furthered his education and continued nationalist activity with other Africans residing in Britain. In 1945 he organized the Fifth Pan-African Congress (regular meetings where Africans and African Americans debated ways in which to promote African independence, unity, and cultural heritage). Kenyatta returned to British East Africa in 1946, assuming leadership of the Kenya African Union, a new organization esposing a more militant nationalism than previous organizations.

Meanwhile, Mau Mau, a rural guerrilla resistance movement against white rule, stepped up acts of violence against white settlers. In 1952, the British blamed nationalist leaders and arrested Kenyatta (though he was not a leader of the Mau Mau). He was sentenced to seven years of hard labor and was released in 1959 to restricted house arrest. In 1960 Kenyatta was elected president of the newly formed Kenya African National Union, which became the ruling party when Kenya gained independence from Britain on December 12, 1963.

In 1964 Kenyatta was elected Kenya's first president. He would be reelected in 1969 and 1974. As president, Kenyatta pursued a policy of reconciliation with whites, who were persuaded to sell their rich lands to Africans and develop nonagricultural businesses. Kenyatta followed a policy of economic modernization, social welfare, and expanded education.

Although Kenyatta was generally pro-Western, he kept Kenya "nonaligned," that is, he did not take sides with the United States or the Soviet Union during the Cold War.

Kenyatta died in office on August 22, 1978, in Mombasa, Kenya.

Legacy

Jomo Kenyatta achieved an appreciable level of modernization in Kenya, providing a model of effective leadership for newly independent African states in the twentieth century.

Kenyatta possessed the prestige and abilities of a leader who could unite the disparate peoples of Kenya into a relatively stable nation-

state. His widespread popularity as a national hero and his adoption of popular social programs as the first president of independent Kenya meant that the one-party state he constructed was not as repressive as other postcolonial African states. The institutions of a thriving civil society, such as a free press and debate in parliament, were allowed. However, the final years of his regime were marred by corruption at high levels, the result of Kenyatta's firm grip on power.

Kenyatta's economic policies, which involved attracting foreign aid and investment along with redistribution of formerly white-owned agricultural land to Africans, led eventually to economic growth. As a result, Kenya developed its industrial sector, became self-sufficient in the production of food, and began to export coffee and tea. A small middle class started to emerge in the 1970s, a remarkable achievement for a post-colonial society.

Kenyatta's immediate successor, Daniel arap Moi, continued his policies and made an effort to end some of the corruption. However, Kenya could not completely escape the vulnerability of most African states to fluctuations in the world market prices of agricultural commodities, especially coffee and tea. Economic woes led arap Moi to resort to authoritarian measures to suppress unrest, measures made easier to employ because of Kenyatta's decision to create a one-party state. International pressure in the 1990s brought about the creation of a multiparty system in the 1990s but intimidation of opposition leaders continues.

Lemoine

For Further Reading

Assensoh, A. B. *African Political Leadership: Jomo Kenyatta, Kwame Nkrumah, and Julius K. Nyerere.* Melbourne, Fla.: Krieger, 1998.
Miller, Norman, and Rodger Yeager. *Kenya: The Quest for Prosperity.* 2nd ed. Boulder, Colo.: Westview, 1994.

Kerensky, Alexander

Prime Minister of Russia
1881–1970

Life and Work

During the Russian Revolution of 1917, Alexander Kerensky directed the policies of the provisional government but was unable to prevent the Bolshevik Party from seizing power by the end of the year.

Kerensky was born on April 22, 1881, in the Russian town of Simbirsk. In 1899 he moved to St. Petersburg to enroll in the law school at the university. In 1905 he witnessed a revolution against tsarist authority that resulted in the establishment of a representative assembly known as the Duma. He was especially influenced during this revolution by Bloody Sunday, an event in which a crowd of peaceful workers in St. Petersburg was fired upon by the tsarist police. Kerensky witnessed part of the march that resulted in the massacre, and afterward he spent time assisting the families of its victims. His outrage culminated in his decision to enter revolutionary politics that year. He was thereafter arrested, but family connections enabled him to return to public life quickly. After 1905 he devoted his law career to promoting social justice in Russia and, in 1912, was elected as a reformist deputy to the Fourth Duma.

After Tsar NICHOLAS II was toppled on March 8, 1917 (February 26, according to the Old Style, Julian calendar then in use in Russia), Kerensky was appointed minister of justice in Russia. He failed, however, to consolidate the revolutionary forces that brought him to power. In May, Kerensky became the minister of war. He maintained Russia's commitment to fighting World War I, going so far as to lead a disastrous summer offensive in Galicia. Kerensky became prime minister of Russia's provisional government in July. Under his leadership, the provisional government expressly deferred substantial economic reforms until a democratically elected constituent assembly could be convened to give them legal authorization. In the meantime, the disruptions of the war prevented the speedy election of such an assembly. By the end of 1917, popular discontent with Kerensky and his regime had become so great that on November 7 (October 25 Old Style) the Bolshevik Party was able to step in and seize power for itself. This takeover was referred to as the October Revolution. As VLADIMIR ILICH LENIN put it at the time, "we found power lying in the street and merely picked it up."

Kerensky narrowly escaped arrest during the Bolshevik coup and was later forced to flee the country. In 1940 he finally settled in the United States. There he spent the remainder of his life trying to organize anticommunist emigre societies and serving as a scholar at Stanford University. He managed to produce several books about the Russian revolution and in them tried to defend his tragic role. At times he feared suffering the fate of LEON TROTSKY, who, as another exile from Soviet communism, was killed in Mexico City on JOSEPH STALIN's orders. But on June 11, 1970 Kerensky died of natural causes in New York City, never having returned to his native land.

Legacy

Alexander Kerensky's failure to consolidate the Russian Revolution after March 1917 constitutes his chief historical legacy. It was this failure that enabled the Bolsheviks to seize power by the end of the year and transform Russia into a socialist society.

When Kerensky was elevated to power in early 1917, Russian society was being torn apart by war and revolution. Kerensky was a socialist aligned with the popular Socialist Revolutionary Party. As he himself embraced a relatively moderate political ideology, he was able at first to create a bridge between radical socialists, who dominated a workers and soldiers' council called the Petrograd Soviet, and conservative liberals, who dominated the provisional government. Unfortunately, as the world war continued and fundamental reforms were delayed, workers, soldiers, and peasants became increasingly critical of Kerensky's position and began to favor the radical alternative offered by the Bolshevik Party.

Kerensky's failure to consolidate power reflected the failure of Russia to shape the 1917 revolution around a moderate political ideology. He supported a series of laws that granted free speech and political amnesty, but he insisted that Russians await the constituent assembly to enact more fundamental social and economic reforms. This approach to reform was based on the liberal tradition of representative and constitutional government. Failing utterly to answer the pressing demands of the Russian people during this time of crisis, this approach was rejected by more radical political leaders. Thus Lenin could claim that the October Revolution answered the demands of the people. In fact, the demands of most Russians during the Russian Revolution were cruelly disappointed by the communist dictatorship that, in the words of Leon Trotsky, would consign all other political forces such as Kerensky to "the dustbin of history."

Strickland

WORLD EVENTS		KERENSKY'S LIFE
Germany is united	1871	
	1881	Alexander Kerensky is born
	1899	Kerensky begins to study law
Russo-Japanese War	1905	Revolution shakes tsarist system; Duma is created
	1912	Kerensky elected to Fourth Duma
World War I	1914–18	
Russian Revolution	1917	February: Russian Revolution and formation of provisional government
		June–July: Kerensky leads failed summer offensive in Galicia; Kerensky is elevated to prime minister
		October: Kerensky flees after Bolshevik seize power
Great Depression	1929–39	
World War II	1939–45	
	1940	Kerensky arrives in United States
Communist China is established	1949	
Israel defeats Arab nations in Six-Day War	1967	
	1970	Kerensky dies
Vietnam War ends	1975	

For Further Reading

Abraham, Richard. *Alexander Kerensky: The First Love of the Revolution.* New York: Columbia University Press, 1987.

Kerensky, Alexander. *Russia and History's Turning Point.* New York: Duell, Sloan and Pearce, 1965.

Pipes, Richard. *The Russian Revolution.* New York: Alfred A. Knopf, 1990.

Khomeini, Ruhollah

Iranian Religious Leader
1902–1989

Life and Work

Ruhollah Khomeini (known as Ayatollah Khomeini) formed a political movement that energized many Iranians who felt oppressed by the institutionalization of Western values in Iran and the exclusion of most people from the country's enormous wealth.

Khomeini was born on September 24, 1902, to a wealthy family of clerics and merchants. Khomeini received his education in religious institutions, eventually moving, in 1922, to Persia's (now Iran's) most holy city, Qom.

In Qom, Khomeini began a prodigious writing career, commenting on Islamic ethics and law and the characteristics of the good Muslim family. During this time, Khomeini began to attract a following, and by the 1950s had gained the title of ayatollah, or religious leader. Above all, Khomeini stressed a rigid interpretation of Islamic social codes and called for a theocracy, or government by religious leaders.

World Events		Khomeini's Life
Germany is united	1871	
	1902	Ruhollah Khomeini is born
Russo-Japanese War	1905	
World War I	1914–18	
Russian Revolution	1917	
	1922	Khomeini goes to Qom to study
Great Depression	1929–39	
World War II	1939–45	
Communist China is established	1949	
	1964	Shah exiles Khomeini; he settles in Iraq
Israel defeats Arab nations in Six-Day War	1967	
Vietnam War ends	1975	
	1978	Khomeini is exiled from Iraq
	1979	Khomeini becomes leader of Iran
	1989	Khomeini dies
Dissolution of Soviet Union	1991	

In 1962 and 1963, Shah Mohammad Reza Pahlavi, the authoritarian leader of Iran from 1941 to 1978, confiscated lands owned by religious institutions and began a series of reforms to liberate women. Khomeini spoke out against the confiscations and reforms. The shah imprisoned Khomeini for a year, which provoked large-scale antigovernment rioting. On November 4, 1964, the shah exiled Khomeini, who settled in neighboring Iraq, where he called for the shah's overthrow.

Khomeini remained in Iraq until October 6, 1978, when Iraq's leader, SADDAM HUSSEIN, distrustful of the movement growing around Khomeini, exiled him. Khomeini settled briefly in a Paris suburb, from which he sent religious messages to Iran, calling for the shah's overthrow. These tape-recorded messages provoked the Iranian people to protest in massive numbers, forcing the shah to leave Iran on January 16, 1979. Khomeini returned to Iran on February 1, 1979, and issued a new constitution that made Iran an Islamic republic. Khomeini became Iran's political and religious leader for life.

Khomeini ensured that his interpretation of the Islamic social code, or *sharia*, was enforced. Clerics dictated most of the new government's policy, which was enforced by revolutionary guards. The *sharia* required that women wear the veil, that unmarried men and women associate separately, and banned both alcohol and Western music. Thousands of officials from the shah's regime and other "counterrevolutionaries" were executed. Hundreds of thousands of Iran's middle class—including much of the educated elite—left the country.

With his power assured, Khomeini began an active campaign against the West, beginning with holding the staff of the American embassy as hostages from November 4, 1980, until January 16, 1981, and exporting the revolution to the countries around Iran. Iran also fought a long and bloody war against secular Iraq—which had invaded Iran on June 17, 1980—that did not end until 1988. Although the regime provided a moral model for many, an enormous economic decline and cultural "brain drain" marked Khomeini's entire regime. The ayatollah died on June 4, 1989.

Legacy

Ruhollah Khomeini led a political movement in Iran that was centered on Islam.

Onto this movement Khomeini stamped his own opposition to the West and Western values.

Khomeini tried to live such a pure and holy existence, and made such persuasive and elegant interpretations of Islam, that he could not have helped but attract attention, at least within religious circles. He advocated a theocratic government, however, that was as tyrannous as the shah's but had its foundation in a traditional code of morality. Khomeini had an orthodox interpretation of Islam, whose classic tolerance for outsiders was almost completely ignored by him. People flocked to Khomeini because the mosques were the only large institution the shah tolerated besides the government and the army.

To many Iranians in the 1960s and 1970s, the shah was simultaneously selling out the country to the West and trying to make Iran a Western country. Iran's large and morally conservative peasant population and its urban poor, who had not benefited from the economic development undertaken by the shah but had been forced to pay for it through higher taxes, found Khomeini's message attractive and followed him in great numbers. Khomeini provided a way for the people left behind by or alienated by the shah's modernization efforts to protest and to take the power denied to them into their own hands. In addition, in the context of the Cold War, the West supported the shah, probably for too long, because he represented a centrist, putatively democratic regime along the southern border of the Soviet Union. In addition, Iran was a good source of oil for the West.

Del Testa

For Further Reading

Amjad, Mohammed. *Iran: From Royal Dictatorship to Theocracy.* New York: Greenwood Publishing, 1989.
Moin, Baqer. *Khomeini: Life of the Ayatollah.* New York: I. B. Tauris, 1999.

Khrushchev, Nikita

Soviet Leader and Reformer
1894–1971

Life and Work

Nikita Khrushchev succeeded JOSEPH STALIN as the leader of the Soviet Union and was committed to reforming the totalitarian system he inherited. His ambitious projects ultimately failed, however, and he was forced to retire in disgrace.

Khrushchev was born on April 17, 1894, in the Russian village of Kalinovka, near the Ukrainian frontier. His father was of peasant stock; poverty forced him to work in coal fields part of the year. Receiving little formal education, Khrushchev began to work at factories while still a boy and participated in his first strike in 1912. Joining the Bolsheviks in 1918 during the civil war, he personally witnessed the war's hardships when his first wife died in the resulting famine of 1922. He was later given responsibility for overseeing construction of the Moscow Metro. The turnover in personnel that occurred during Stalin's purges of the 1930s led to his appointment in 1938 as a member of the Politburo.

Upon Stalin's death in 1953, Khrushchev was able to outmaneuver a chief rival, Georgii Malenkov, and became the Communist Party's general secretary. He then launched a series of bold economic programs such as the 1954 virgin lands campaign in which millions of acres of Central Asian desert were converted to agriculture. Khrushchev's boldest step in establishing power was his denunciation of Stalin in a speech delivered secretly to a party congress on February 25, 1956. By accusing Stalin of subverting communism through terror and a personality cult, Khrushchev created the political atmosphere he needed to broaden his ambitious reforms. He also traveled to the United States in 1959 in an effort to enhance Soviet prestige abroad.

Reform was never popular among a party elite that depended upon the Stalinist system for its privileges. Although Khrushchev managed to survive the political turmoil that accompanied the Hungarian uprising of 1956, his activities increasingly alienated the party elite. After the

humiliating Cuban missile crisis of 1962, when the United States forced the Soviet Union to remove nuclear missiles from the Caribbean, Khrushchev introduced a plan to reform the Communist Party by dividing it into two halves. At this point opposition finally boiled over, and while he was away on vacation on the Black Sea in 1964, a Politburo putsch led by LEONID BREZHNEV removed him from office. Denounced for subjecting the Soviet Union to "hare-brained schemes," of reform, Khrushchev passed his remaining years peacefully studying agriculture and writing his memoirs. He died in Moscow on September 11, 1971.

Legacy

Nikita Khrushchev enacted significant reforms of the Communist system that constituted a process historians call "destalinization." The failure of his economic reforms and his highly eccentric methods of rule, however, provoked a conservative reaction that lasted for more than 20 years.

Khrushchev had the secret police redesigned to prevent the sort of unrestrained terror that had existed under Stalin. Being renamed the KGB (Committee of State Security) to reflect the change, it would never again conduct mass arrests and executions. Furthermore, although Khrushchev was careful never to allow the text of his secret speech to be published, his efforts to exorcise Stalin's ghost resulted in the decline of the Stalin cult in public life. In 1961, this was given symbolic expression when the dictator's body was removed from its place in Lenin's Tomb on Red Square. Intellectual life even experienced a brief "thaw," as writers such as Boris Pasternak and Alexander Solzhenitsyn (who had been sent by Stalin to Siberia) began to offer challenges to the ideological uniformity of the Stalin years. Destalinization was a major step toward Khrushchev's goal of creating a more beneficent socialist society, and its impact was felt long after he was forced into retirement.

His failure to achieve permanent improvements in economic performance, however, weakened his reform program and left the Soviet Union unable to adapt to new economic and technological circumstances in the second half of the twentieth century. The virgin lands campaign, for instance, while initially celebrated as a great success, actually became a fail-

ure that in 1963 contributed to the humiliating need to purchase grain from capitalist Canada. By favoring what critics called "economic miracles," and avoiding systemic reforms, Khrushchev assured that agriculture would remain the Achilles' heel of the Soviet economy well into the 1970s and 1980s.

Strickland

WORLD EVENTS		KHRUSHCHEV'S LIFE
Germany is united	1871	
	1894	Nikita Khrushchev is born
Russo-Japanese War	1905	
World War I	1914–18	
Russian Revolution	1917	
	1918	Khrushchev joins Bolshevik Party
Great Depression	1929–39	
	1938	Khrushchev becomes member of Politburo
World War II	1939–45	
Communist China is established	1949	
	1953	Khrushchev becomes Communist Party's general secretary on Stalin's death
	1954	Khrushchev launches virgin lands campaign
	1956	Khrushchev decounces Stalin in a speech to a party congress
	1959	Khrushchev visits United States
	1964	Khrushchev is removed from office
Israel defeats Arab nations in Six-Day War	1967	
	1971	Khrushchev dies
Vietnam War ends	1975	

For Further Reading

Crankshaw, Edward. *Khrushchev: A Career.* New York: Viking, 1966.

Khrushchev, Nikita. *Khrushchev Remembers.* Boston: Little, Brown, 1970.

Medvedev, Roy A., and Zhores A. Medvedev. *Khrushchev: The Years in Power.* New York: Columbia University Press, 1976.

Tompson, William J. *Khrushchev: A Political Life.* New York: St. Martin's Press, 1995.

King, Martin Luther, Jr.

U.S. Civil Rights Leader
1929–1968

Life and Work

The leading advocate of nonviolent civil disobedience to combat racial injustice, Martin Luther King, Jr., and the protest movement he led ended overt segregation in the American South and expanded civil rights for African Americans in the United States.

Martin Luther King was born in Atlanta, Georgia, on January 15, 1929, by which time the South had adopted Jim Crow laws that segregated blacks and whites. The son of a Baptist minister, King graduated from Morehouse College in Atlanta at the age of 19. In 1951 King entered Crozer Seminary in Pennsylvania as a divinity student, then moved on to graduate school at Boston University. During his studies, King adopted the philosophy of nonviolent civil disobedience as advocated by MOHANDAS GANDHI and Henry David Thoreau. One year before completing his dissertation in 1955, King was appointed to the pastorship of the Dexter Avenue Baptist Church in Montgomery, Alabama.

WORLD EVENTS		KING'S LIFE
Russian Revolution	1917	
Great Depression	1929–39	
	1929	Martin Luther King, Jr. is born
World War II	1939–45	
Communist China is established	1949	
	1955	King leads bus bocott
	1957	King organizes Southern Christian Leadership Conference
	1963	King leads March on Washington
	1964	King awarded Nobel Prize for Peace
Israel defeats Arab nations in Six-Day War	1967	
	1968	King assassinated
Vietnam War ends	1975	

On December 1, 1955, a black woman, Rosa Parks, was arrested after refusing to give up her seat on a bus to a white passenger. Her arrest sparked a boycott of the bus system in Montgomery, led by King, which was eventually successful in ending segregation on city buses. The victory propelled King to national prominence.

In 1957 King and others organized the Southern Christian Leadership Conference (SCLC) to help expand the new protest movement throughout the country. As leader of the SCLC, King struggled to maintain unity among African Americans, who began to divide over the aims and methods of the civil rights movement. In Birmingham, he helped to organize boycotts and demonstrations. King was arrested, and there he wrote his famous "Letter from a Birmingham Jail" (1963).

In 1963, King also led a mass march on Washington, D.C., where he made his now-famous "I Have a Dream" speech. The Kennedy administration responded to the march by increasing support for the Civil Rights Act then being debated in Congress. In 1964 King was awarded the Nobel Prize for Peace. He continued his civil rights work, both in the South and the North, and began to speak out against the Vietnam War and the economic problems that most African Americans, and poor people in general, faced throughout the United States.

King was assassinated in Memphis on April 4, 1968. His death was followed by violent protests in more than 100 cities across the United States.

Legacy

Martin Luther King, Jr., led the effort to end segregation, to pass federal civil rights legislation, and to extend voting rights in the American South. The African-American civil rights movement influenced other protest movements in the last decades of the twentieth century.

King helped end the daily humiliation and brutality of segregation and unpunished racial violence in the South. Through great struggle, African Americans gained equal access to public services and public accommodations; educational opportunities were expanded and blacks were integrated into previously all-white universities. Many African Americans obtained well-paying, high-status jobs once monopolized by

whites. Furthermore, desegregation improved the economy for both blacks and whites through increased investment and modernization. African Americans also increased their political power, serving in elected positions from local sheriff to mayor, governor, and congressman.

However, King's violent death convinced some militants of the failure of non-violent protest, leading to increased calls for violent action in the so-called Black Power movement. King's own organization, the SCLC, lost its influence not long after King's death.

Beyond the United States, King's identification of the American civil rights movement with the struggle for national liberation among the colonized peoples led to a change in U.S. policy toward racist regimes in South Africa and Rhodesia (now Zimbabwe), both of which have evolved into majority-rule democracies. In the 1980s South African churches took the lead in using nonviolent methods to break down the system of apartheid, leading to the election of NELSON MANDELA in 1993. King's example also inspired nonviolent protest movements in Ireland and Eastern Europe, where nearly all of the communist regimes were toppled with very little violence at the end of the twentieth century.

King's vision of a just and racially integrated society inspired many Americans and bolstered the ideals of American democracy. Other ethnic minorities, such as Hispanics and Native Americans, as well as women, adopted aspects of King's strategy and vision. His birthday is a national holiday, celebrated on the third Monday in January.

Lemoine

For Further Reading

Fairclough, Adam. *Martin Luther King, Jr.* Athens: University of Georgia Press, 1995.

Harding, Vincent. *Martin Luther King: The Inconvenient Hero.* Maryknoll, N.Y.: Orbis Books, 1996.

Oates, Stephen B. *Let the Trumpet Sound: The Life of Martin Luther King, Jr.* New York: Mentor, 1982.

Kokhba, Bar

Jewish Rebel Leader
d. 135 C.E.

Life and Work

Bar Kokhba took up arms against Roman troops and Roman efforts to destroy Jewish culture in the Middle East and is remembered in Jewish history as one of its greatest martyrs.

There is almost no information on the background and upbringing of Bar Kokhba, born Simeon Bar Kosba. As a young adult, he may have been a bandit. Sometime around 130 C.E., Bar Kokhba began to attract a following of Jews who opposed the Roman occupation of Judea. At this time, he transformed his name into Bar Kokhba ("Son of the Star," a reference to Jacob, the third Jewish patriarch) and accepted the titles of "prince" and "Messiah" in order to lend an aura of holiness to his campaign. The titles also lent Bar Kokhba the authority to declare a Jewish state.

Why did Bar Kokhba revolt against the Romans? The Roman province of Judea, brought under direct Roman rule in 6 C.E., had always been a rebellious place—its Jewish majority refusing to worship Roman gods, although cooperating with the Romans to generate common prosperity. Between 66 and 70, the Roman emperor Titus had waged a terrible and punitive war against Jews who had revolted against Rome's authority. He eventually dispersed Judea's Jews, conquered Jerusalem, and destroyed the Temple of Solomon, the center of Jewish religious life.

In 132, Bar Kokhba rose against the Romans specifically because in 131 the Roman emperor Hadrian had decreed a Hellenization (the imposition of Greco–Roman culture) of Judea in order to destroy Jewish culture and its tendency to independence. Hadrian had ordered the construction of a new city, Aelia Capitolina, on the site of the ruined Jerusalem and the construction of a temple to the Roman god Jupiter on the site of the destroyed Jewish temple. For at least a year, Hadrian ignored signs of the brewing revolt, the fortification of Judea against the Romans, and the skirmishing of Jewish raiders with Roman troops. But in 133, when Bar Kokhba captured Hadrian's Aelia Capitolina,

nearly destroying an entire legion in the process, and began to mint coins, and when, as a result, Jews throughout the Roman Empire became restless, Hadrian decided to crush the revolt.

Hadrian ordered his best general, Julius Severus, the governor of Britain, to Judea, with 35,000 troops. In Judea, Severus delayed a frontal attack and instead turned to concentrating Jews in prison camps and laying siege to Bethar, Bar Kokhba's stronghold near Jerusalem. The siege and occupation of Judea was very costly to the Romans, and even more costly to the Jews, who lost almost 600,000 soldiers and sympathizers. Finally, in 135, Bar Kokhba was captured and killed while trying to escape Bethar, the rebellious Jews were scattered to the four corners of the Roman Empire, and Judea was "pacified" through utter destruction.

Legacy

Bar Kokhba's rebellion effectively ended any hopes of Jewish political dominance of Judea during the Roman era but reinforced an already indomitable cultural sensibility that had maintained Jewish civilization in the face of systematic persecution.

Bar Kokhba did not rebel against the Romans because of their political and military domination of Judea and its Jewish population—Jews had a long experience with the Romans and knew that no power equaled their might. Rather, Bar Kokhba decided he could not allow Jewish culture to be overwhelmed by Rome. While the Jews of Judea had long appreciated Greek values and philosophy, making them the *dominant* cultural values challenged the continued existence of a Jewish cultural, and perhaps even national, identity.

Bar Kokhba's failed revolt and the related Roman oppression of Jews would seem to have spelled the doom of Jewish culture. However, with a cultural identity reinforced by the brutal treatment they had received at the hands of the Romans, the remaining Jews maintained a separate identity while accommodating themselves to the laws of the lands in which they lived. This cultural significance grounded in legal accommodation endured for centuries and ensured the survival of the Jews despite pogroms, exile, and genocide.

In the long term, Bar Kokhba also reinforced the existence of a culturally distinct

people and land in Judea, and once Jews had gained civil rights and a sense of modern nationalism during the late nineteenth century the recapture of their homeland from occupation became important. Like the rebels who held the fortress of Masada against the Romans in 73 C.E., Bar Kokhba's defense of Bethel became a fertile source of inspiration to Jews who faced enemies in Palestine after 1948.

Del Testa

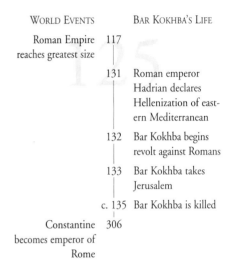

World Events		Bar Kokhba's Life
Roman Empire reaches greatest size	117	
	131	Roman emperor Hadrian declares Hellenization of eastern Mediterranean
	132	Bar Kokhba begins revolt against Romans
	133	Bar Kokhba takes Jerusalem
	c. 135	Bar Kokhba is killed
Constantine becomes emperor of Rome	306	

For Further Reading

Rosenthal, Monroe. *Wars of the Jews: A Military History from Biblical to Modern Times.* New York: Hippocrene, 1990.

Yidal, Yigael. *Bar-Kokhba: The Rediscovery of the Legendary Hero of the Last Jewish Revolt against Imperial Rome.* London: Weidenfeld and Nicolson, 1971.

Kollontai, Aleksandra

Russian Socialist Feminist
1872–1952

Life and Work

Aleksandra Kollontai entered the women's liberation movement in Russia at a time of revolutionary change. Although she served in the Soviet government during its early years, her radical ideals ultimately left her isolated.

Aleksandra Mikhailovna Kollontai (née Domontovich) was born in St. Petersburg in 1872 to a noble father and a woman who had left her husband to live with him. Her mother considered herself a "new woman," free from the restraints of traditional morality. Against her mother's advice, Aleksandra married an engineer named Vladimir Kollontai in 1893 and soon after gave birth to a son. She found married life and the duties of motherhood dreary, however, and spent much of her time studying social issues. In 1896, she turned to socialism. Increasingly restless, she abandoned her family in 1898 to pursue an education in

WORLD EVENTS		KOLLONTAI'S LIFE
Germany is united	1871	
	1872	Aleksandra Kollontai (née Domontovich) is born
Russo-Japanese War	1905	
World War I	1914–18	
	1915	Kollontai joins Bolshevik Party
Russian Revolution	1917	Kollontai is appointed commissar of public welfare
	1918	Kollontai helps write revolutionary divorce and abortion laws
	1921	Kollontai supports Workers' Opposition and is demoted
Great Depression	1929–39	
World War II	1939–45	
Communist China is established	1949	
	1952	Kollontai dies
Israel defeats Arab nations in Six-Day War	1967	

Switzerland. Upon her return to Russia, her growing revolutionary reputation made it necessary for her to flee the country in 1908. In 1915 she joined the Bolshevik Party after meeting VLADIMIR ILICH LENIN. In 1917 she returned to Russia and supported the Bolshevik Revolution in November.

Kollontai was made commissar of public welfare by the new regime and soon distinguished herself as one of its most radical members. An outspoken opponent of the Orthodox church, she ordered the seizure of the famous Alexander Nevsky Monastery in 1918 that resulted in the shooting of many unarmed priests. Describing herself as a "Bolshevik Antichrist," she also sought to undermine the church's strength by supporting a law separating church and state for the first time in Russian history. Even more ambitious were her efforts to increase the rights of women. In 1918 she helped draft a law granting women the right to abortion and divorce. That year she also published *The New Morality and the Working Class,* in which she prophesied the "withering away of marriage" in the new socialist society. As head of the Zhenotdel (Women's Section) in 1920, she pursued policies designed to replace nuclear families, which she considered retrograde, with voluntary associations in which adults could enter sexual relations freely with the resulting children being raised collectively.

In 1921 Kollontai's influence went into irreversible decline, however, when she supported a democratic party faction known as the Workers' Opposition. Denounced at the tenth party congress that year, she was dismissed from her office and in 1922 sent to Norway as a diplomat. For the remainder of her life she served as a diplomat in several countries and returned permanently to the Soviet Union only in 1945. She died in Moscow in 1952.

Legacy

Alexsandra Kollontai's example in the Soviet government and her many writings continued to inspire the women's movement in the Soviet Union. Her ability to unite the ideals of feminism with socialism offered an alternative to the liberal feminism dominant in the West.

After her appointment to the Soviet embassy in Norway, Kollontai virtually ceased to play a role in Soviet family policy. Even the laws that she had helped write were ultimately watered down or altogether replaced. To a large extent this was a result of the rise of JOSEPH STALIN in 1928. In the 1930s he abolished the right to abortion outright and placed heavy restrictions on the right to divorce. Nevertheless, the Soviet Union remained one of the world's most progressive societies measured by the standard of women's rights. Women continued to possess equal political status with men, and the state supported social programs designed to improve women's lives. The communist government encouraged women to enter the workforce and to maintain professional careers. As a result, women in the Soviet Union came to dominate important professions such as medicine that remained largely the domain of men in the West.

Kollontai's vision of a new Soviet woman unencumbered by marriage and children, however, went unrealized. The revolutionary ideals that consumed intellectuals such as herself during the 1920s were redirected under Stalin and finally died out in the 1960s. Her radical experiments in family policy and sexual behavior were rejected by most women in favor of social relations that she would have described with dismay as "bourgeois."

Nevertheless, Kollontai's intellectual legacy survived as one of the most influential expressions of socialist feminism. In Western Europe and the United States, twentieth-century feminism became primarily concerned with the rights and interests of female individuals. This tradition can be called liberal feminism because of its origins in the larger tradition of economic and political liberalism of the nineteenth century. Exponents as varied as Virginia Woolf and SIMONE DE BEAUVOIR shared an interest in assuring a woman's freedom from all external authority and in maximizing her self-determination. Drawing upon the class analysis of KARL MARX, Kollontai labeled such concerns "bourgeois feminism." She argued instead for a definition of women's rights that emphasized the interests of the larger community of the working class. This collective definition of women's freedom, then, offered an alternative approach for feminists during the twentieth century.

Strickland

For Further Reading

Clements, Barbara Evans. *A Bolshevik Feminist: The Life of Aleksandra Kollontai.* Bloomington: Indiana University Press, 1979.

Farnsworth, Beatrice. *Aleksandra Kollontai: Socialism, Feminism, and the Bolshevik Revolution.* Palo Alto, Calif.: Stanford University Press, 1980.

Stites, Richard. *The Women's Liberation Movement in Russia: Feminism, Nihilism, and Bolshevism, 1860–1930.* Princeton, N.J.: Princeton University Press, 1978.

Las Casas, Bartolomé de

Roman Catholic Missionary and
Opponent of Slavery
1474–1566

Life and Work

Bartolomé de las Casas accompanied the earliest Spanish settlers to the New World. After becoming a priest he attacked the abuses of Spanish rule and influenced the policies of Emperor CHARLES V.

Las Casas was born in Seville, Spain, in 1474. His father was a merchant who sailed with CHRISTOPHER COLUMBUS on his second voyage to the Americas in 1493. Las Casas's imagination was fired by the sight of the departing ships, and he decided to travel to the New World as a settler when he came of age. In 1502 he obtained permission to travel with the Spanish governor to the island of Hispaniola. There he became a planter, and, after assisting the suppression of an Indian uprising, he was awarded an *encomienda*, or grant of land and Indian laborers. His venture failed, however, and in 1506 he returned to Europe. He was ordained a priest either in Rome or back in the New World after 1512. Nevertheless, he continued to participate in the colonial system, assisted another pacification campaign, and received another *encomienda*. In 1514, however, he experienced a moral conversion while reading the Bible and afterward renounced his *encomienda* holdings. Thereafter he devoted his life to the relief and protection of the Indians.

After obtaining royal support from Madrid, he led an investigative commission to the New World in 1515 to examine the *encomienda* system and its abuses. Believing that enslavement of the Indians was the chief evil, he promoted a plan to use Spanish settlers in Venezuela. When this plan failed in 1521, he briefly turned to the idea of substituting the Indian slaves with black slaves transported from Africa, whom he thought physically better able to withstand the tropical sun. He later rejected this idea, and when colonists began to act on a similar plan he emerged as an opponent of black slavery also. In 1542 he persuaded Charles V to issue the New Laws banning Indian slavery. This apparent victory, however, was negated when Spanish settlers refused to comply. As a result, las Casas never saw the actual abolition of slavery.

In the field of missionary work he was more successful. In addition to seeking the amelioration of the Indians' social condition, he made a number of evangelical journeys in Guatemala and elsewhere that yielded large numbers of converts. In 1544, however, he was run out of Chiapas by Spanish settlers enraged at his threat to withhold the sacrament of extreme unction to slave owners. He spent the last years of his life in Spain writing books about Spanish colonial repression and publicly challenging others who continued to tolerate it. He died in Seville on July 31, 1566.

Legacy

Bartolomé de las Casas influenced European attitudes toward slavery in the New World and helped expand Roman Catholicism.

Las Casas's attack on slavery and oppression in the New World was an unusual challenge to his contemporaries. Accustomed to the militancy that had driven the fifteenth-century *reconquista* of ISABELLA I, Spaniards were one of Europe's most self-confident and racially condescending peoples. During the early sixteenth century Europeans debated the question of whether Indians in the New World possessed the faculty of reason and souls. Las Casas had been compelled to dispute this issue at length with a priest named Juan Sepúlveda before the king himself. In 1533 Pope Paul III, responding in part to las Casas's campaign, issued an encyclical stating categorically that Indians are indeed as fully human as the Spaniards.

Nevertheless, during the centuries that followed both Spaniards and Europeans in general continued to regard non-Europeans as inferior. Slavery was abolished in the European empires during the nineteenth century; however, the values that had supported it since the time of las Casas persisted and even reached a peak in the late nineteenth century when scientific racism came to influence the secular theories of Social Darwinists.

Las Casas's missionary activities, on the other hand, were more fruitful in the short term. The Roman Catholic mission in the New World was a stunning success during the first century of Spanish and Portuguese colonization, despite the institution of slavery and the horrendous loss of life suffered by Indians infected by European diseases. Hundreds of thousands of Mexican Indians were baptized during the first years alone; by the end of the seventeenth century, Roman Catholicism had become the dominant religion of the Western hemisphere south of Rio Grande. Catholicism gave rise to a rich native religious tradition, including saints such as Martín de Porres (d. 1639), whose care for the poor inspired later native priests such as OSCAR ROMERO. Native Catholicism also inspired the political development of Latin America. The Virgin of Guadalupe, an image of the Virgin Mary revealed to a converted Indian boy in 1510, became the symbol of the Mexican independence movement in the early nineteenth century.

Strickland

World Events		Las Casas's Life
Ottoman Empire conquers Constantinople	1453	
	1474	Bartolomé de las Casas is born
Columbus sails to Americas	1492	
	1502	Las Casas makes first journey to Americas
	1512	Las Casas is ordained
	1514	Las Casas renounces *encomienda*
Protestant Reformation begins	1517	
Mughal Empire rules in India	1526	
	1542	Las Casa persuades emperor to enact New Laws banning Indian slavery
	1544	Las Casas is driven from Chiapas
	1566	Las Casas dies
Ottoman dominance of Mediterranean ends	1571	

For Further Reading

Hanke, Lewis. *Bartolomé de las Casas: Bookman, Scholar, and Propagandist*. Philadelphia: University of Pennsylvania Press, 1952.

Simpson, Lesley Byrd. *The Encomienda in New Spain: Forced Labor in the Spanish Colonies, 1492–1550*. Berkeley: University of California Press, 1929.

Wagner, Henry. *The Life and Writings of Bartolomé de las Casas*. Albuquerque: University of New Mexico Press, 1967.

Lawrence, Thomas Edward

British Soldier and Writer
1888–1935

Life and Work

Writer and soldier Thomas Edward Lawrence (Lawrence of Arabia) played a leading role in the Arab Revolt against Turkish rule during World War I, ultimately paving the way for Arab independence.

Born in Wales on August 16, 1888, Lawrence was one of five illegitimate sons of an Anglo-Irish nobleman and the governess of his children. Lawrence considered himself a misfit, striking out on his own intellectual pursuits and physical challenges. He was educated at Oxford University, majoring in history. Lawrence was fascinated with medieval art and architecture, which eventually drew him to the Middle East in 1909 to study the forts constructed during the Crusades.

Intrigued by the Arabic language and Arab customs, Lawrence returned to the Middle East two years later to participate in an archaeological project in Syria. At this time, much of the Arab world was ruled by the Turkish Ottoman Empire. In 1908 a nationalist organization, Young Turkey, took power, initiating some modernizing reforms and imposing Turkish culture and language on non-Turkish subjects. The effort at "Turkification" fostered resentment among the Arab population, which turned into a nationalist revolt with the outbreak of World War I in 1914. Lawrence was swept into the Arab Revolt as a British army officer.

He had joined British Military Intelligence in Cairo late in 1914, by which time Turkey had entered into the war on the side of the Central Powers (German and Austria-Hungary). The British began talks with Hashemite grand sharif Ibn Ali Hussein of Mecca, a prominent Arab leader, who then declared independence from the Ottoman Empire in June 1916. Lawrence was sent to advise Faisal, son of Ibn Ali Hussein and the military leader of the Arab Revolt.

In an effort to ingratiate himself with the Arabs, Lawrence adopted the clothing and practices of the Bedu, the ethnic group that made up the majority of the fighters in the Arab Revolt. From 1916 to 1918 he led guerrilla attacks on the Hejaz Railway, which linked Damascus (Syria) with Medina (Arabia) and supplied the Ottoman troops. He also participated in the capture of Aqabah (1917) and led the Arab forces that joined the British in the conquest of Damascus (1918).

The war over and the Ottoman Empire defeated, Lawrence, along with Faisal, attempted to defend Arab interests at the Paris Peace conference in 1919. During the war, Britain and France, in the secret Sykes-Picot Agreement (1916), had agreed to divide the Middle East between them, betraying the promises of independence they had made to the Arabs. Lawrence and Faisal failed to secure Arab self-rule, and the Arab regions became mandates administered by Britain and France for the newly formed League of Nations.

Despite this failure, Lawrence became a celebrity. He wrote several well-received books about his adventures, most notably *The Seven Pillars of Wisdom* (1922). In 1921 he worked in the Middle East division of the British colonial office, then withdrew from the public spotlight, rejoining the military under a pseudonym. He died in a motorcycle accident in 1935.

Legacy

In the Middle Eastern theater of World War I, Thomas Edward Lawrence developed strategies and tactics of guerrilla warfare that were adopted by regular armies in the decades to follow. His leadership in the Arab Revolt, and the accounts he published afterward, although initially failing to win the Arabs independence, contributed to the establishment of independent Arab nation-states after World War II.

World War I is known chiefly as a time when outdated military tactics and strategy resulted in millions of deaths on the Western Front in France and Belgium. By contrast, Lawrence, thrust somewhat reluctantly into his role as military advisor and leader, learned the strengths and the weaknesses of the tough Bedu rebels under his command and developed a strategy in which a small band of the most dedicated fighters infiltrated behind enemy lines to destroy infrastructure and communications and conduct surprise attacks. These methods were adopted as the model for irregular warfare and commando units in the following decades.

Lawrence sought to reward the Hashemite dynasty for its leadership in the Arab Revolt. He encouraged the colonial office to offer Faisal the Iraqi throne and some measure of self-rule. Faisal's brother, Abdulla, was granted the throne of Trans-Jordan (now the Kingdom of Jordan). Although the Hashemite dynasty failed to maintain its rule in Arabia (where Ibn Saud gained power), and lost the throne in Iraq (1958), the Hashemites continued to rule in Jordan, where King Hussein followed a pro-Western policy.

Lawrence initially supported British imperialism, but later became one of the first Westerners to actively support Arab independence. Although he knew of the Sykes-Picot Agreement during the war, he urged Faisal and the Arab leadership to demand independence. Rather than help the Arabs to gain immediate independence, however, Lawrence unwittingly facilitated British involvement in the Middle East. Nonetheless, his efforts contributed to the emergence of Arab nationalism in the twentieth century, a movement that shaped the organization of the Middle East into nation-states.

Lemoine

WORLD EVENTS		LAWRENCE'S LIFE
Germany is united	1871	
	1888	Thomas Edward Lawrence is born
Russo-Japanese War	1905	
	1909	Lawrence travels to Middle East
	1911	Lawrence returns to Middle East for archaeological expedition
World War I	1914–18	
	1914	Lawrence joins British Army
Russian Revolution	1917	
	1918	Arab forces under Faisal and Lawrence enter Damascus
	1919	Lawrence's and Faisal's proposals for Arab independence rejected
	1921	Lawrence joins British colonial office's Middle East division
	1922	*Seven Pillars of Wisdom* first published
Great Depression	1929–39	
	1935	Lawrence dies in motorcycle accident
World War II	1939–45	

For Further Reading
Asher, Michael. *Lawrence, the Uncrowned King of Arabia.* London: Viking, 1998.
Lawrence, T. E. *Seven Pillars of Wisdom: A Triumph.* New York: Doubleday, 1991.

Lenin, Vladimir Ilich

Founder of Soviet Communism
1870–1924

Life and Work

With fanatical devotion and indefatigable energy, Vladimir Ilich Lenin created the Russian Communist Party and brought it to power during the revolution of 1917.

Lenin was born in the Siberian town of Simbirsk on April 22, 1870. His family name was Ulyanov, but he adopted Lenin as a revolutionary nom de guerre after his brother Alexander was hanged in 1887 for conspiring to assassinate Tsar Alexander III. Lenin earned a coveted law degree from the University of Saint Petersburg in 1891, but decided against any professional activities not devoted to the overthrow of the autocratic government of Alexander's successor, NICHOLAS II. Inspired by the ideas of KARL MARX, he believed that a violent confrontation between Russia's workers and their capitalist masters was inevitable, despite the fact that the country's population was overwhelmingly peasant, not industrial laborers.

Fleeing Russia after a period of Siberian exile, Lenin attended a congress of Russian Marxists in Brussels in 1903 and formed an independent faction called the Bolsheviks. Living in Swiss exile when the tsarist regime finally collapsed under the strains of World War I in March 1917, Lenin

obtained German assistance to return to Russia. Upon his arrival he issued a statement, the "April Theses," in which he called upon Russians to overthrow the democratic provisional government of ALEXANDER KERENSKY and establish a workers' state based upon the network of workers' soviets, or councils, that had begun to proliferate throughout Russia. By the end of the year the Bolshevik slogan "All Power to the Soviets!" had captured the support of many common people, especially peasants who equated revolution with sweeping land reform. Thus on November 7 he and LEON TROTSKY were able to orchestrate the October Revolution, so called because it occurred on October 25 according to the old style Julian calendar then in use.

Lenin then directed the formation of the Soviet Union under a dictatorship of the Bolshevik Party, which now adopted the name Communist. Because Lenin insisted that his party rule alone, non-communist forces called "Whites" arose to fight what became the deadliest civil war in European history. After order was restored in 1921, Lenin maintained unrivaled leadership of the party until a series of strokes beginning in 1922 forced his removal from the government. Having lost the power of speech in his final months, he looked on in silence as JOSEPH STALIN took his first steps toward succession. Lenin died on January 21, 1924.

Legacy

In the years after 1917, the Communist Party brought innumerable improvements to Russia. Nevertheless, the uncompromising political tradition established by Vladimir Ilich Lenin led to gross abuses of power.

Dedicated to improving the standard of living for the common people, the communists initiated a series of reforms after 1917 that yielded impressive results. Within years, the Soviet people enjoyed a program of universal education, state-supported programs for health care, and new opportunities for women. It is probable that these and other reforms would have been sought by the other revolutionary parties proscribed after 1917, but they remain one of the twentieth century's most remarkable achievements.

By retaining what Lenin had called a "dictatorship of the proletariat," however, democ-

racy and free speech suffered because the government refused to tolerate dissent. What is more, as Lenin had given the Communist Party a highly centralized character, democratic procedures became impossible. Decision making was restricted to a small body called the Politburo at the top of an ever-growing bureaucratic pyramid. Finally, with his model of personal leadership, Lenin facilitated the rise of Stalin's dictatorship after 1928.

Lenin's fanatical application of Marxist doctrines to Russia (where Marx had not thought the first proletarian revolution likely) also established a destructive ideological tradition. Russia in 1917 was a country dominated by the plow, not the factory, and most of the population was deeply religious. Citing the writings of Lenin himself, Soviet leaders sought to direct, often by violent means, the transformation of Russia into a "modern" society based upon an industrial economy and secular values. The costs of this transformation were extraordinarily high, however, and were paid especially by bearers of the traditional order such as the peasantry and the Orthodox church. What is more, while the regime was mistreating and sometimes even killing its ideological opponents, it propagated a vision of the Soviet experience that blatantly misrepresented the truth (*pravda* in Russian). One of the best expressions of this was the official Communist Party newspaper entitled *Pravda*, which so distorted historical reality through the years that when the Soviet public finally gained access to a free press under MIKHAIL GORBACHEV during the 1980s, a massive repudiation of communism resulted.

Strickland

WORLD EVENTS		LENIN'S LIFE
Congress of Vienna reorganizes Europe	1815	
	1870	Vladimir Lenin is born
Germany is united	1871	
	1891	Lenin earns law degree
	1903	Lenin forms Bolshevik Party
Russo-Japanese War	1905	
World War I	1914–18	
Russian Revolution	1917	Lenin delivers "April Theses"; October Revolution establishes communist dictatorship
	1922	Lenin suffers first stroke
	1924	Lenin dies
Great Depression	1929–39	

For Further Reading

Malia, Martin. *The Soviet Tragedy: A History of Socialism in Russia, 1917–1991.* New York: Free Press, 1994.

Meyer, Alfred G. *Leninism.* Cambridge, Mass.: Harvard University Press, 1957.

Ulam, Adam. *The Bolsheviks: The Intellectual, Personal, and Political History of the Triumph of Communism in Russia.* New York: Macmillan, 1965.

Volkogonov, Dmitri. *Lenin: A New Biography.* Translated and edited by Harold Shukman. New York: Free Press, 1994.

Leopold II

King of Belgium and Colonial Ruler
1835–1909

Life and Work

Leopold II became king of Belgium at a time when industrial expansion and diplomatic rivalry threatened to upset the traditional order of Europe. His efforts to create a colonial empire in Africa increased Belgian power and produced one of the most brutal regimes in the world.

World Events		Leopold II's Life
Congress of Vienna reorganizes Europe	1830	
	1835	Leopold is born
	1865	Leopold accedes to throne
Germany is united	1871	
	1876	Leopold sponsors founding of International African Association
	1879	Leopold commissions expedition of Henry Stanley
	1882	Founding of International Association of the Congo
	1885	Congo Free State established; Leopold is its ruler
Russo-Japanese War	1905	
	1908	Leopold cedes government of Congo Free State to Belgian Parliament
	1909	Leopold dies
World War I 1914–18		

Leopold was born on April 9, 1835, to the first king of Belgium, Leopold I. As a youth he became conscious that the kingdom he would inherit occupied an extremely vulnerable position within Europe. Created only four years before his birth, Belgium was surrounded by powerful states and its social order had been greatly altered by industrialization and secularization. Leopold came to believe that by establishing overseas colonies, as other European powers were doing, Belgium could secure its position within Europe and inspire patriotic loyalty among a population drifting away from the traditional influence of the Roman Catholic church.

In 1865 he acceded to the throne and immediately set the kingdom on a course of overseas expansion, particularly in Africa. In 1876 he sponsored the founding of the International African Association, whose stated goal was to promote exploration of the Congo River basin and to work toward the elimination of slavery there. Its implicit goal, however, was the annexation of the entire Congo region, which the empire-hungry Leopold described as a "magnificent African cake." Leopold sponsored a reconnaissance expedition by the famous explorer Henry Morton Stanley in 1879, and a new organization, the International Association of the Congo, was founded in 1882 with the goal of achieving complete annexation. At the Berlin Conference of 1885 the Congo Free State was recognized as a Belgian possession.

From the start, Africans were subjected to immense brutality by the Congo Free State's government, which, unlike Belgium, was under Leopold's personal rule. Congolese tribes were at the mercy of the army, which continued after 1885 to conquer and annex new territories. Many of the conquered were subjected to a form of labor resembling slavery—flight from this condition was punishable by bodily mutilation. Slowly, news of the atrocities began to reach Europe and the United States, carried in many cases by Christian missionaries opposed to colonial exploitation. Leopold finally appointed an investigative commission that, to his dismay, issued a scathing attack upon the system in 1905. In 1908 the aging king was forced to cede control of the Congo to the Belgian Parliament, which had never fully supported his colonial adventures. Leopold died the following year, largely estranged from his people.

Legacy

Leopold II's persistent efforts to build a Belgian Empire had a profound impact upon both Belgium and Africa.

When Leopold inherited the throne from his father in 1865, Belgium was a constitutional monarchy. A Parliament was elected regularly and possessed the power to restrain the monarch's activities. When the Congo Free State was founded in 1885, for instance, many parliamentary representatives threatened to refuse the king's request for personal control over the territory. Leopold's authoritarian efforts to build an empire, however, while calculated to strengthen Belgian unity, served, in the end, to undermine it. Parliament became divided between his supporters and his opponents, and only after the Congo Free State was wrested from him in 1908 was unity restored. The result was a Belgian political system more committed to limiting the powers of the king.

Leopold's legacy in Africa also had consequences contrary to his intentions. The brutality of his regime served to undermine his claims that European rule benefited Africa. Leopold believed along with the English poet Rudyard Kipling that a "white man's burden" obligated Europeans to spread their civilization throughout the world. As a result, the continent of Africa, which had been mostly free of Europeans when Leopold came to power, was almost entirely annexed by them during the late nineteenth century. Leopold played an important role in this "scramble for Africa," as historians call it, but the misery his rule brought to the Congo region mostly served to undermine the belief in European beneficence.

In the end Africans threw off European rule in a wave of independence movements that followed World War II, with the Congolese forming the state of Zaire in 1960. Appropriately, one of the only remnants of European rule in Africa after its collapse was Christianity, due in part to the resistance Christian missionaries had offered to the regimes of Leopold and others. By 1990 the continent had become home to an estimated 150 million Christians.

Strickland

For Further Reading

Chamberlin, Muriel Evelyn. *The Scramble for Africa*. London: Longman, 1974.

Emerson, Barbara. *Leopold II of the Belgians: King of Colonialism*. New York: St. Martin's Press, 1979.

Hochschild, Adam. *King Leopold's Ghost: A Story of Greed, Terror, and Heroism in Colonial Africa*. Boston: Houghton Mifflin, 1998.

Lincoln, Abraham

Sixteenth President of
the United States
1809–1865

Life and Work

Considered by many to be the greatest president in the history of the United States, Abraham Lincoln guided the Union (North) to a hard-fought victory over the Confederacy (South), preserving the unity of the nation and putting an end to slavery in the United States.

Lincoln was born in Kentucky, on February 12, 1809. His father, a farmer, moved the family to Indiana in 1816. Lincoln was largely self-educated. He moved to Illinois in 1830, settling in New Salem, where he taught himself law, became an attorney, and soon took an interest in politics. Lincoln was elected to the Illinois legislature in 1834, serving until 1837. Elected to the U.S. House of Representatives in 1847, he served only two years, then withdrew from politics, disillusioned with Congress's inability to resolve the problem of slavery in the country's new states.

Lincoln reentered politics to oppose the Kansas–Nebraska Act (1854), which threatened to extend slavery beyond boundaries decreed by the Missouri Compromise of 1820. Lincoln led the effort to form the Republican Party in 1856. In his subsequent, unsuccessful campaign for the U.S. Senate, he engaged in debates with Stephen Douglas that established him as a national anti-slavery spokesperson.

In 1860 Lincoln was nominated by the Republican Party as its candidate for president. His victory was followed by the secession of the Southern states, starting with South Carolina on December 20, 1860, and the formation of the Confederate States of America. Civil war faced Lincoln from his first day in office.

Conducting the Union's Civil War effort was Lincoln's greatest accomplishment. The Union Army was initially ill equipped and unprepared, and Lincoln had to contend with generals who were ineffectual and reluctant to engage the Confederate forces in decisive battles. Lincoln eventually took the difficult but necessary steps to defeat the Confederacy.

With no clear end to the war in sight, Lincoln escalated the war into a total one—incurring heavy casualties on both sides. After a crucial victory at the Battle of Antietam (1862), Lincoln issued the Emancipation Proclamation, which freed all rebel-state slaves as of January 1, 1863. Two months later he initiated conscription. In July, Union soldiers inflicted a major defeat of Confederate forces at Gettysburg, and General Ulysses S. Grant defeated a Confederate army at Vicksburg, Mississippi. In 1864 Atlanta fell to General William Tecumseh Sherman, who brought the full force of the war deep into the Confederacy.

Despite opposition from some members of his own party, Lincoln was reelected in 1864. Not long after his inauguration in 1865 the war ended with Confederate General Robert E. Lee's surrender to Grant at Appomattox on April 9, 1865. Only days later, on April 15, Lincoln was assassinated by John Wilkes Booth at Ford's Theater in Washington, D.C.

Legacy

In what some historians call the "Second American Revolution," Abraham Lincoln's victory over the Confederacy shifted political power to the North and redefined the relationship between the federal government and the states. His Emancipation Proclamation also established the federal government as a positive power for the extension of individual liberty.

Lincoln's immediate impact was the abolition of slavery and the defeat of the Confederate States of America. The Thirteenth Amendment, ratified on January 31, 1865, after hard lobbying by Lincoln, banned slavery in all of the states. This, plus the Fourteenth Amendment, which

guaranteed civil rights to former slaves, laid the constitutional foundation that would help African Americans to embark on the civil rights movement in the twentieth century. The Civil War also destroyed the political and economic power of the South, and its influence was diminished for several decades.

The Civil War resulted in a shift from a negative idea of rights (that is, freedom *from* government intrusion) to a positive view of the role of the federal government in extending rights. Thus, the federal government, rather than state governments, was seen as the guarantor of citizenship rights and protector of individual liberty. The end of Reconstruction (1865–77), a period of postwar adjustment and political reintegration, restored state power to a certain extent. Yet the principle of extended federal power was applied by future administrations in times of crisis, as with FRANKLIN DELANO ROOSEVELT's New Deal programs instituted to counter the Great Depression and with federal action to support the civil rights movement of the 1950s and 1960s.

Lemoine

WORLD EVENTS		LINCOLN'S LIFE
French Revolution begins	1789	
	1809	Abraham Lincoln is born
Latin American independence movement begins	1811	
Congress of Vienna reorganizes Europe	1815	
	1834	Lincoln is elected to Illinois legislature
	1847	Lincoln is elected to U.S. House of Representatives
	1856	Lincoln helps form Republican Party
	1861	Lincoln is inaugurated as president; Southern states begin to secede
	1863	Lincoln issues Emancipation Proclamation
	1864	Fall of Atlanta; Lincoln is reelected
	1865	Confederacy surrenders; Lincoln is assassinated
Germany is united	1871	

For Further Reading

McPherson, James M. *Abraham Lincoln and the Second American Revolution.* Oxford: Oxford University Press, 1990.

Oates, Stephen B. *With Malice Toward None: A Life of Abraham Lincoln.* New York: Harper Perennial, 1994.

Peterson, Merrill D. *Lincoln in American Memory.* Oxford: Oxford University Press, 1994.

Livingstone, David

Scots Missionary and Explorer
1813–1873

Life and Work

David Livingstone emerged from a working-class family to become an early British explorer of southern Africa, opening the way to future colonization of a region rich in natural resources.

Livingstone was born in poverty on March 19, 1813, in Blantyre, Scotland. Put to work in a cotton mill at age ten, Livingstone took advantage of every educational opportunity and studied in his spare time. He decided to become a doctor and a missionary, initially wanting to work in China. In 1836 he started medical school at Anderson's College in Glasgow; in 1838 he was admitted to the London Missionary Society and finished his medical studies in London. Warfare in China prevented missionary work there (the first of the Opium Wars, between Britain and China, lasted from 1839 to 1842), so Livingstone applied to go to Africa instead. His great passion for exploration began when he moved to the southern tip of the continent, the interior of which was still a mystery to Europeans in the early nineteenth century.

During the 1840s Livingstone concentrated on missionary work, founding three missions. From 1849 to 1852 he undertook three journeys along Lake Ngami and the Zambezi River; from 1853 to 1856 he traversed southern Africa from Angola on the west coast to Mozambique on the east. Later he discovered Victoria Falls (which he named after Britain's Queen Victoria). He was careful to note the abundant natural resources of the regions he explored.

In 1856 he returned to Britain and published a book, *Missionary Travels and Researches in South Africa* (1857), which made him famous. After a lecture tour, he was given government support for an expedition up the Zambezi River. Resigning from the London Missionary Society, Livingstone began an expedition in 1858 that proved to be a failure—many became ill or died from tropical diseases. Hopes that the Zambezi River would be a navigable route into the interior of southern African were dashed. Livingstone returned to Britain in 1864.

Undaunted, Livingstone returned to Africa in 1866 with the stated intention of combating the African slave trade and to discover the source of the Nile. He made more discoveries, yet he compromised his health and never found the Nile watershed. He died of malaria on May 1, 1873, in Zambia.

Legacy

David Livingstone helped to end the slave trade in east and central Africa, yet his expeditions opened the African interior to future British colonization.

Livingstone, an idealistic humanitarian, believed that the best way to end the slave trade was by promoting increased commerce in goods. His descriptions of the lands he explored, however, gave those who followed him a clearer understanding of their geography and thus a road map for colonization. After Livingstone's death British colonialists began to expand into the African interior in earnest. Christian missionaries and anti-slavery activists followed in Livingstone's footsteps, giving the British government justification to declare a "protectorate" over many African regions in order to see to their safety. Rebellions were subdued with military force; Africans thus lost control of their own lands.

The moral overtones of Livingstone's work and exploration also provided convenient cover for British economic interest in the resources of southern and central Africa. In 1876 the Livingstonia Central Africa Company was founded (later changing its name to the Africa Lakes Corporation) to exploit the natural wealth of the region. The new industrial capitalist economy Livingstone had hoped for was indeed established, but for the benefit of the British. Africans lost their best land, and other resources such as gold and diamond fields, to the colonizers.

Livingstone's concern for the well-being of the African population was disregarded by future colonialists, such as CECIL RHODES. The British South Africa Company (BSAC), founded by Rhodes, was associated with the Africa Lakes Corporation. Although the slave trade was abolished when Britain appropriated the region, the BSAC charged African residents the so-called Hut Tax, which forced subsistence farmers to grow cash crops to pay it. Europeans also used forced labor, which damaged the indigenous economy and destroyed the African Iron Age of highly skilled iron workers and subsistence farmers. Livingstone's goal of improving the lives of Africans through "civilization, Christianity and commerce" was subverted to the needs of the British Empire, creating bitter resentments between Africans and white settlers that persist to the present.

Lemoine

WORLD EVENTS		LIVINGSTONE'S LIFE
Latin American independence movement begins	1811	
	1813	David Livingstone is born
Congress of Vienna reorganizes Europe	1815	
	1838	Livingstone is admitted to London Missionary Society
	1849–56	Livingstone embarks on several journeys
	1857	Livingstone publishes *Missionary Travels and Researches in South Africa*
	1858	Livingstone returns to Africa
	1864	Livingstone returns to Britain
	1866	Livingstone begins search for source of Nile
Germany is united	1871	
	1873	Livingstone dies
Russo-Japanese War	1905	

For Further Reading

Holmes, Timothy. *Journey to Livingstone: Exploration of an Imperial Myth.* Edinburgh: Canongate Press, 1993.
Livingstone, David. *Life and Explorations of David Livingstone: The Great Missionary Explorer in the Interior of Africa.* Philadelphia: John E. Potter, 1874.

Louis XIV

King of France
1638–1715

Life and Work

During his long reign Louis XIV, known as the "Sun King," personified absolute monarchy and transformed France into the greatest European power of his era.

Louis XIV was born in Saint-Germain-en-Laye, outside of Paris, on September 5, 1638. When his father, Louis XIII, died in 1643, his mother, Anne of Austria, was appointed regent. She and her chief advisor, Cardinal Jules Mazarin, carefully groomed young Louis, who was a quick learner, for the throne, allowing him to attend councils of state to observe the process of government decision making.

The regency was a fragile time for royal authority. Several disparate groups, including members of the nobility, the Parlement of Paris (the top law court in France), and even common townspeople, attempted a revolt known as the Fronde in 1648, which forced Louis and his mother to flee Paris. This was a formative experience for Louis, as he became determined to maintain the social order under the firm guidance of the king.

In 1654, when he was only 16, Louis ended the regency with his coronation. In 1661 Mazarin died and Louis shocked the court by declaring that he would be his own first minister, choosing advisors based on merit rather than on aristocratic seniority. He was determined to control every important aspect of the royal government. He and Jean-Baptiste Colbert, a commoner who rose to be a chief advisor to Louis, codified the laws, developed the nation's infrastructure and economy, encouraged North American colonies, patronized the arts, and reorganized the military to create a standing army.

Louis made every effort to cultivate the mystique of royalty. He based the legitimacy of his rule on the concept of divine right (in which God had chosen the Catholic king to rule, and all of his subjects were to conform to Catholicism). In 1685 Louis revoked the Edict of Nantes promulgated by his grandfather HENRY IV in 1598, thus ending the policy of official toleration of French Protestants. He built the magnificent palace of Versailles (completed in 1682) to impress foreigners and his subjects. To control the aristocracy, he had them stay at Versailles, which was very expensive, and attend to every detail of his daily life.

Part of the king's mystique stemmed from the success of his military campaigns. From 1654 onward, Louis involved France in more than 50 years of warfare, usually invading the countries on France's eastern and northern borders to expand French territory and power in Europe. After early success, Louis faced military defeat later in his reign in the War of the Spanish Succession (1702 to 1714), severely straining royal finances in the process.

Louis XIV, a much less popular king at the end of his reign than at the beginning, died in 1715, and was succeeded by his great-grandson, Louis XV.

Legacy

Louis XIV's reign marked the high point of absolute monarchy and the elevation of France to supreme power in Europe. However, absolute monarchy was increasingly challenged by the forces of change that resulted in the French Revolution, which abolished the monarchy in 1792.

Like his predecessors, Louis XIV believed that the sovereignty of the state was embodied in the king. The nobility, and sometimes commoners, had challenged this idea in the past. Louis XIV firmly established the centralization and bureaucratization of the royal government, haltingly begun in the sixteenth century and developed by Cardinal ARMAND-JEAN DU PLESSIS RICHELIEU during the reign of Louis XIII. The bureaucratic and centralizing reforms were carried on by the French republics that replaced the monarchy in France.

Louis XIV elevated France to the top position in European power politics, which it did not fully relinquish until the defeat of NAPOLÉON I in 1815. France's chief opponents in these struggles, Spain and the Netherlands, great powers in the sixteenth and seventeenth centuries, sank to the second tier in the eighteenth, replaced by England and the German state of Prussia. Joined later by Russia and the Austrian Empire, these powers formed the alliances that shaped European history until the outbreak of World War I in 1914.

Absolutist government became increasingly unworkable in the decades following Louis's reign. During the eighteenth century the ideas of the Enlightenment challenged the basic principles of absolutist rule. Future kings needed strength of will and political flexibility to make the system work. In 1789 Louis XVI, a king with limited capacities, could not resolve the political, financial, and cultural crises facing the crown, crises whose origins were to be found in Louis XIV's reign. The fall of the monarchy during the French Revolution ushered in the modern era.

Lemoine

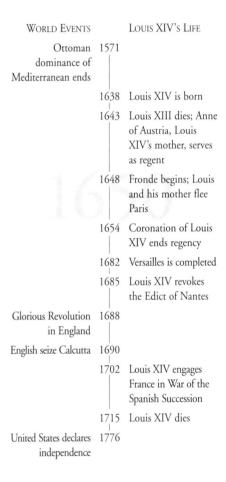

World Events		Louis XIV's Life
Ottoman dominance of Mediterranean ends	1571	
	1638	Louis XIV is born
	1643	Louis XIII dies; Anne of Austria, Louis XIV's mother, serves as regent
	1648	Fronde begins; Louis and his mother flee Paris
	1654	Coronation of Louis XIV ends regency
	1682	Versailles is completed
	1685	Louis XIV revokes the Edict of Nantes
Glorious Revolution in England	1688	
English seize Calcutta	1690	
	1702	Louis XIV engages France in War of the Spanish Succession
	1715	Louis XIV dies
United States declares independence	1776	

For Further Reading

Milford, Nancy. *The Sun King*. New York: Viking Penguin, 1995.

Sturdy, David J. *Louis XIV*. New York: MacMillan, 1998.

Luxemburg, Rosa

German Radical Socialist
1871–1919

Life and Work

From an early age, Rosa Luxemburg was a political activist who encouraged socialist revolution as a way to improve the life of the average person and bring an end to divisions between people based on race, class, or religion.

Born on March 5, 1871, in Zamosch, Polish Russia (before 1795 and after 1918, an independent Poland), into a family of lower-middle-class Jews, Luxemburg moved with her family to Warsaw in 1874. A good student, Luxemburg began studying at a gymnasium, or academic high school at age 10. Immediately after high school, she began to participate in secret anti-Russian, pro-worker movements. In 1889, she moved to Switzerland to study rather than face almost certain arrest in Polish Russia. In Zurich, like many radicals, she studied law and political economy, earning a doctorate in 1898.

Highly influenced by an orthodox interpretation of Marxism, Luxemburg railed against the reformism, or gradual improvement of the existing political system, that she believed pervaded the Russian and Polish socialist parties. With a like-minded colleague, Leo Jogisches, she founded the revolutionary, anti-nationalist Kingdom of Poland Social Democratic Party. Like Jogisches, Luxemburg opposed the primacy given to nationalism among established Polish socialists and supported by the top Russian socialist, VLADIMIR LENIN. She believed nationalism distracted people from the true goal of revolutionary international socialism that knew no political frontiers.

In 1898, Luxemburg married Gustav Lübeck in order to obtain German citizenship and the ability to travel to Berlin to work with Europe's largest socialist party, the Social Democrats. In 1905, Russia experienced its first revolution when protests by Russian peasants forced Tsar NICHOLAS II to grant political reforms. In 1906, Luxemburg traveled to Warsaw in order to agitate for revolution, and was promptly imprisoned by Russian authorities. While in prison, Luxemburg began to support the idea of revolutionary mass action, in which a loosely structured socialist party would coordinate a general strike of the workers. Although the general strike had an appeal for revolutionary socialists, Luxemburg faced stiff criticism from Russian socialists for not promoting a hierarchical party structure that employed a tiny, dictatorial elite to control the course of a workers' revolution.

In 1907, after release from prison, Luxemburg returned to Berlin and, until 1914, taught at the Social Democratic Party School. During these years, she theorized in pamphlets, books, and lectures about the motivations for capitalist imperial expansion and continued to stress the need for worker radicalism. When World War I began in 1914, Luxemburg, along with radical socialist Karl Liebknecht, went into opposition and formed the revolutionary Spartacus League. Throughout the war, Luxemburg was repeatedly arrested for sedition. From prison, she called for an immediate proletarian revolution and the formation of a strong International, a world socialist coordinating body.

At the end of the war in November 1918, Luxemburg and Liebknecht were released from prison and immediately began to organize for a socialist revolution. In the political and social chaos of Berlin, Luxemburg, Liebknecht, and the Spartacus League did battle with right-wing forces for control of the city. The Social Democratic Party and its leader, Eduard Bernstein, still strong and influential among many Germans, resisted the call to revolution. Luxemburg's establishment of the German Communist Party in December 1918 attracted few followers. Because Luxemburg refused to adopt the Russian Bolshevik emphasis on agrarian over industrial development, national

over international politics, vanguard versus democratic leadership, and terror over conversion politics, the German Communist Party received little substantive international support and foundered quickly.

On January 15, 1919, right-wing extremists murdered Luxemburg and Liebknecht.

Legacy

Rosa Luxemburg challenged European socialists to live up to the revolutionary aspects of socialism that she believed had dissolved in the face of nationalism and reformism.

Luxemburg found the idea of a workers' revolution attractive because it supported universal equality and an end to class differentiation. However, she found that the socialism of the day had turned away from revolution toward accommodating capitalism and nationalism, the two forces that she felt distracted workers from achieving their right to rule.

Luxemburg was a female political activist who was highly respected by Europe's great revolutionary socialist leaders at a time when women in general did not participate in politics and certainly did not receive the attention of the major socialists. However, her strident activism, especially in the context of other outstanding activists of the day such as EMMELINE PANKHURST, ALEXANDRA KOLLONTAI, and Emma Goldman, showed that women had a broad and powerful role to play in politics, and that socialism, especially radical socialism, might provide a path to liberation for women in Europe and abroad.

Del Testa

WORLD EVENTS		LUXEMBURG'S LIFE
Congress of Vienna reorganizes Europe	1815	
Germany is united	1871	Rosa Luxemburg is born
	1898	Luxemburg receives doctorate
Russo-Japanese War	1905	
	1906	Luxemburg returns to Poland to promote revolution and is imprisoned
	1907	Luxemburg begins teaching in Berlin
World War I	1914–18	Luxemburg is imprisoned repeatedly
Russian Revolution	1917	
	1919	Luxemburg is murdered
Great Depression	1929–39	

For Further Reading
Ettinger, Elzbieta. *Rosa Luxemburg: A Life.* Boston: Beacon Press, 1986.
Shepardson, Donald E. *Rosa Luxemburg and the Noble Dream.* New York: P. Lang, 1996.

Madison, James

Fourth President of the United States
1751–1836

Life and Work

One of the most active and influential participants in the American Revolution and early republic, James Madison shaped the framework U.S. government that has endured to the present.

Born on March 16, 1751, in Port Conway, Virginia, Madison grew up the son of a wealthy plantation owner. Madison was educated by tutors before entering the College of New Jersey (later known as Princeton University), where he took a special interest in political theory. Graduating in 1771, he soon became involved in the movement for American independence from Great Britain. In 1776 he was elected a delegate to Virginia's Provincial Convention, where he earned a reputation for intellectual thoroughness.

Although Madison served in the Continental Congress from 1780 to 1783, his major accomplishment took place as a result of his involvement in the Constitutional Convention (1787). The new constitution was designed to appeal to and to represent as many interest groups as possible to create a truly national government. Madison also helped to draft the Bill of Rights (adopted in 1791), which stated the rights of individuals (freedom of press, speech, religion, assembly, etc.).

To secure the ratification of the new constitution, Madison, with Alexander Hamilton and John Jay, wrote *The Federalist Papers,* a series of essays to explain the new constitution and advocate its ratification, which was achieved in 1788. From 1789 to 1797 Madison served in the U.S. House of Representatives, where he eventually became a leader of the Democratic–Republican Party, the loyal opposition to the Federalist Party, represented by GEORGE WASHINGTON's administration.

Although Madison favored a strong national government, he soon opposed the doctrines of the Federalists because they encroached on individual rights and state governmental power. He opposed the financial measures designed by Federalist Hamilton, President Washington's secretary of the treasury, because they created a national financial structure that benefited wealthy northern merchants at the expense of southern and western farmers. In 1798 he also opposed the Alien and Sedition Acts, which made it easier to deport foreigners and to prosecute those who criticized the federal government. In response, Madison composed the Virginia Resolutions, which upheld the right of states to determine the constitutionality of federal policy.

In 1801 Madison was appointed secretary of state in THOMAS JEFFERSON's administration, and succeeded him as president in 1809. His administration waged a successful war against Britain (1812–14) over the issue of American neutrality in the Napoleonic Wars. Madison served two terms as president, retiring to his Virginia estate in 1817. He served as rector of the University of Virginia until his death on June 28, 1836.

Legacy

James Madison's chief legacy is his crucial contribution to the drafting and ratification of the United States Constitution, which he did much to define and defend while serving the federal government in many capacities.

Madison's priorities in constructing a workable constitution influenced the political culture of the United States in many ways. Madison realized that conflict based on opposing interests was inevitable, so he devised a constitutional republic that would permit an open and public forum in which to reconcile these competing interests. He combined a deep concern for individual liberty, including freedom of religion and the separation of church and state, with the need for a strong central government—a balance in government responsibilities and restraints still evident in American politics today.

Under Madison's leadership, the new Constitution accorded powers to a central federal government at the expense of the states, but also provided for "checks and balances" between the three branches of the federal government (executive, legislative, and judicial) and the state governments, making the enlarged government less inclined to turn tyrannical or oppressive. Madison also opted for a representative government rather than a direct democracy, which contributed to the stability and moderation of the American political system.

Madison's legacy extends to his government service following ratification of the Constitution. His anti-Federalist position led to the creation of the Democratic–Republican Party, which attracted the loyalty of southern and western interests. This split established the early stages of the two party system, which endures to the present.

As president, Madison avoided defeat at the hands of the British in the War of 1812, confirming U.S. sovereignty. His ability to conduct the war without major changes to the Constitution set a precedent for future chief executives facing similar wartime conditions. Madison also supported projects to build roads and canals, establish a national university and a new national bank, which encouraged economic growth and facilitated the Industrial Revolution in the United States.

Madison's genius resulted in a document that continues to guide and to define the U.S. government. Further, the Constitution, with its balance of powers and the political stability it has afforded the United States through many crises, has served as a model for countless nation-states formed in the nineteenth and twentieth centuries.

Lemoine

For Further Reading

Elkins, Stanley, and Eric McKitrik. *The Age of Federalism.* Oxford: Oxford University Press, 1993.

Rakove, Jack N. *James Madison and the Creation of the American Republic.* Glenview, Ill.: Scott, Foresman/Little, Brown Higher Education, 1990.

Rutland, Robert Allen. *James Madison: The Founding Father.* New York: Macmillan, 1987.

WORLD EVENTS		MADISON'S LIFE
English seize Calcutta	1690	
	1751	James Madison is born
United States declares independence	1776	
	1780–83	Madison serves in Continental Congress
	1787	Madison is delegate to Constitutional Convention
French Revolution begins	1789	
	1798	Madison opposes Alien and Sedition Acts
	1801	Madison is appointed secretary of state
	1809	Madison becomes fourth president
Latin American independence movement begins	1811	
Congress of Vienna reorganizes Europe	1815	
	1836	Madison dies
Germany is united	1871	

Malcolm X

African-American Political and
Religious Leader
1925–1965

Life and Work

One of the most important figures in the African-American struggle for social justice, Malcolm X helped to instill a sense of pride among African Americans and influ-enced the militant black nationalist movement from the 1960s to the present.

Malcolm X was born Malcolm Little in Omaha, Nebraska, on May 19, 1925. His father, a Baptist minister, was a frequent target of the local Ku Klux Klan because he was a follower of black nationalist Marcus Garvey. His father was later killed, possibly by another racist group, in 1931, throwing the family into poverty and disorder. In 1939 Malcolm went to live in a home for juvenile delinquents; in 1940 he moved in with his half-sister in Boston.

In Boston, and later in New York City, Malcolm became involved in the criminal underground. In 1946 he was arrested and convicted of theft and sentenced to prison. During his incarceration, Malcolm resumed his education, interrupted after his move to Boston, and took an interest in the Nation of Islam (NOI), an American version of the Islam that considered black people to be Allah's favorites and whites to be the devil. The movement also called for the establishment of a separate state for African Americans. Its leader, Elijah Muhammad, eventually became a father figure to Malcolm.

Malcolm joined the NOI after his release from prison in 1952, dropped his "slave name," Little, and adopted the surname "X" to symbolize the African identity stolen by white slave owners. Active and energetic, Malcolm X rose in the ranks, and was appointed minister of the NOI temple in New York City. There he and the NOI attracted the attention of the national media, which portrayed the organization as preaching hatred and violence. Malcolm X replied that African Americans had the right to defend themselves "by any means necessary" if attacked.

A gifted speaker, Malcolm X soon became the voice of the Nation of Islam, gaining national prominence. However, he began to develop doubts about the conservative nature of the Nation and its lack of political activism. Muhammad began to turn against Malcolm X. In 1964 Malcolm X left the NOI to form his own organization, Muslim Mosque, Inc. That same year he voyaged to Mecca, where he encountered Muslims of all races worshiping peacefully together, which modified his attitude toward whites.

He returned to the United States as El-Hajj Malik El-Shabazz and founded the Organization for Afro-American Unity to promote black independence. On February 21, 1965, Malcolm X was assassinated, possibly by Nation of Islam operatives.

Legacy

Malcolm X inspired many African Americans to reject the sense of inferiority that many of them had internalized through centuries of slavery and discrimination. His criticism of the liberal integrationist approach to race relations has endured to the present.

Like MARTIN LUTHER KING, JR., Malcom X evoked a sense of pride among many African Americans. His ability to speak to any audience, enabled him to reach a wide spectrum of the population.

Malcolm X's strident views on whites and advocacy of black separatism, and particularly his call for blacks to renounce nonviolence, contrasted with King's nonviolent civil disobedience. King's advocacy of passive resistance was more acceptable to the white establishment, thus, perhaps contributing to some of the successes of the early civil rights movement.

In the last years of his life Malcolm X modified his position on black separatism, advocating the development of African-American economic, political, and cultural institutions rather than a separate black nation. Many African-American activists embraced this view in the years after Malcolm X's death. The Black Power movement that arose in the late 1960s, including the Black Panthers (formed in 1966), saw him as a chief inspiration. In the 1970s, 1980s, and 1990s, African-American studies programs on college campuses and community control organizations pushing for more political and economic power in black neighborhoods also claimed to be promoting Malcolm's ideas.

Because Malcolm X's beliefs were undergoing change in the year before his death, many different groups, such as Afrocentrists (who postulate an African origin of Western civilization and promote radical black nationalism), the relatively moderate Rev. Jesse Jackson, and many of the nation's African-American youth, hail him as a hero. It remains to be seen in which direction they take Malcolm X's legacy.

Lemoine

WORLD EVENTS		MALCOLM X'S LIFE
Russian Revolution	1917	
	1925	Malcolm Little is born
Great Depression	1929–39	
World War II	1939–45	
	1940	Malcolm Little moves to Boston
	1946	Malcolm Little is jailed
Communist China is established	1949	
	1952	Malcolm X is released from prison, joins Nation of Islam
	1964	Malcolm X leaves Nation of Islam, makes pilgrimage to Mecca and takes the name El-Hajj Malik El-Shabazz
	1965	Malcolm X is assassinated
Israel defeats Arab nations in Six-Day War	1967	

For Further Reading

Franklin, Robert Michael. *Liberating Visions: Human Fulfillment and Social Justice in African-American Thought.* Minneapolis, Minn.: Fortress Press, 1990.

Malcolm X with Alex Haley. *The Autobiography of Malcolm X.* New York: Grove Press, 1966.

Perry, Bruce. *Malcolm: The Life of a Man Who Changed Black America.* Barrytown, N.Y.: Station Hill Press, 1991.

Mandela, Nelson

President of South Africa,
Human Rights Leader
1918–

Life and Work

Nelson Mandela led the effort to end apartheid in South Africa. As father of a new South Africa, he encouraged reconciliation between blacks and whites and provided the stability needed to maintain a pluralistic democracy.

Born Rolihlahla Mandela on July 18, 1918, he was the son of a counselor to the chief of the Thembu clan, part of the Xhosa, the largest ethnic group in the Transkei in South Africa's Eastern Cape Province. He adopted the first name Nelson in elementary school. In 1938 Mandela began attending Fort Hare College, but was expelled in 1940 for leading a student strike. He then fled to Johannesburg to escape an arranged marriage and finished his education at the University of Witwatersrand, obtaining a law degree in 1942.

Mandela joined the Youth League of the African National Congress (ANC) in 1944 and rose to a leadership role 1949. By this time the white racist Nationalist Party had taken control of the government and began to institute the policy of apartheid, which segregated the white, black, coloured (mixed race), and Asian (Indian and Pakastani) populations and established separate "homelands" for each group, to the detriment of the non-white population. The government also established an oppressive

police state to enforce the provisions of apartheid, and Mandela soon became a target of this security apparatus. On trial for treason from 1956 to 1961, Mandela was acquitted.

After the Sharpeville Massacre of 1960, in which the police opened fire on a peaceful protest, killing 69 black demonstrators and wounding about 190 others, the government banned the ANC. Mandela made the difficult decision to abandon the ANC's policy of nonviolence. On trial again in 1964 for sabotage, treason, and conspiracy in what became known as the Rivonia Trial, Mandela was sentenced to life imprisonment, most of which he served on Robben Island off the coast of Cape Town.

In 1990 Mandela, whose imprisonment had become an international cause celebre, was released by order of President FREDERIK WILLEM DE KLERK. The following year Mandela was elected president of the ANC. In 1994 he was elected president of South Africa, representing the ANC in South Africa's first all-race national elections. As president, Mandela implemented social, political, and economic measures to improve the standard of living for the impoverished masses of black South Africans.

Mandela retired from public office in June 1999. As a private citizen Mandela continues to promote peace in Africa through his nonprofit Nelson Mandela Foundation.

Legacy

Nelson Mandela maintained stable and cordial relations with the white minority while creating a new political and social structure for a post-apartheid South African society.

Upon his release from prison in 1990, Mandela used his stature as an uncompromised liberation leader to force concessions from the white government, making a peaceful transition to majority rule possible. As president, Mandela focused on nation-building rather than partisan politics—dismantling the South African police state of the apartheid era and encouraging a free press and vibrant civil society. South Africa has so far achieved the transition to a multiparty democracy without widespread violence or civil war.

Mandela's policy of reconciliation with the white minority—he has even gone so far as to court members of extremist white nationalist organizations—has made him vulnerable to accusations of being too concerned with the needs of the white minority over the problems

of economic development for the black majority. Some have asserted that Mandela's moderate leadership prevented more radical social and economic reforms. South Africa's crime rate has soared, foreign investment (following the lifting of international sanctions) was lower than had been hoped, and economic problems proved daunting and difficult to address.

Despite these problems, Mandela's prestige has remained high among both white and black South Africans. However, he has discouraged the creation of a cult of personality, making stability and continuity more likely for South Africa in the future. His promotion of racial harmony rather than divisiveness and revenge has been the key to the peaceful transition to majority rule in South Africa.

Lemoine

WORLD EVENTS		MANDELA'S LIFE
Russian Revolution	1917	
	1918	Nelson Mandela is born
Great Depression	1929–39	
World War II	1939–45	
	1944	Mandela joins African National Congress (ANC)
Communist China is established	1949	
	1960	Mandela abandons nonviolence in wake of Sharpeville massacre
	1964	Mandela is sentenced to life imprisonment for treason and conspiracy
Israel defeats Arab nations in Six-Day War	1967	
Vietnam War ends	1975	
	1990	Mandela is released from prison
Dissolution of Soviet Union	1991	Mandela is elected president of ANC
	1994	Mandela elected president of South Africa
	1999	Mandela retires from public office

For Further Reading

Meer, Fatima. *Higher Than Hope: The Biography of Nelson Mandela.* London: Hamish Hamilton, 1990.

Meredith, Martin. *Nelson Mandela: A Biography.* London: Hamish Hamilton, 1997.

Mansa Mūsā

Emperor of Mali
d. 1337

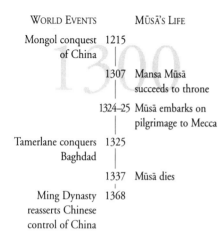

World Events		Mūsā's Life
Mongol conquest of China	1215	
	1307	Mansa Mūsā succeeds to throne
	1324–25	Mūsā embarks on pilgrimage to Mecca
Tamerlane conquers Baghdad	1325	
	1337	Mūsā dies
Ming Dynasty reasserts Chinese control of China	1368	

Life and Work

Mansa (meaning "king") Mūsā, also known as Kankan Musa, united, centralized, and expanded Mali, transforming it into a prosperous trading empire

Very little is known of Mūsā's early life. A descendant of Sundiata, the founder of the Mali Empire in the thirteenth century, Mūsā succeeded to the throne around 1307. Most of his immediate predecessors had been weak rulers, leaving Mali disunited. Mūsā's first task was to subdue his provincial governors and restore central authority.

With political stability restored, Mūsā promoted trans-Saharan trade based on Mali's enormous wealth in gold mines located in present-day Guinea. He established trade and cultural relations with Morocco and helped make trans-Saharan trade routes more secure from bandit clans. Trade with North Africa increased the prosperity of his empire, which stretched from the Atlantic coast across half of West Africa to encompass present-day Mali, Senegal, Gambia, and parts of Mauritania.

Mūsā, a Muslim, like most of West Africa's ruling and merchant elite, is most famous for his pilgrimage to Mecca in 1324. (The pilgrimage to Mecca, known as the *hajj*, is an act of devotion that every Muslim is supposed to undertake, if possible, at least once in life.) Stopping in Cairo for a number of weeks, Mūsā distributed so much gold that Egypt suffered increased inflation and depressed gold prices for twelve years.

After returning from the *hajj* in 1325, Mūsā encouraged more orthodox Islamic practices, built many mosques, sent scholars to Morocco, and set up centers for Koranic studies, most notably in Timbuktu. However, many of his subjects, who practiced local animist religions, resisted these efforts.

Mansa Mūsā died in 1337.

Legacy

By promoting trade, and ensuring the security of trade routes, Mansa Mūsā solidified the prosperity and unity of Mali, which reached its height of power during his reign.

Mūsā created a strengthened empire that withstood external and domestic attacks for many years and was one of the largest empires in its time, rivaled only by the Mongol Empire of Central Asia. However, the wealth of Mali attracted raiders from both north and south who, when the empire suffered from weak rulers, plundered the region. Although Mūsā was a strong leader, he was unable to secure an orderly succession for his dynasty, and after his death civil war broke out between royal houses competing for the throne.

Mūsā's pro-Islam policies, while fostering a long-lasting tradition of religious learning in Timbuktu, alienated many subjects, who broke away from Mali at the first opportunity. Important regions, especially the gold-rich area near the Niger River, began to break away to form their own states. One of these states, Songhay, eventually displaced Mali, though Mali remained a strong state into the fifteenth century.

Mali's enormous wealth in gold also gained the attention of Europeans, who were just beginning to explore the west coast of Africa in search of an ocean route to the wealth of Asia. Mūsā's travels and contacts with North Africans gained him a reputation among fourteenth-century Europeans as the "richest king in Africa." From that time forward, Europeans attempted to reach Mūsā's kingdom to trade for gold and other resources. In the sixteenth century, European travelers began to set up trading posts in the region to obtain some of the wealth of West Africa, which eventually led to the slave trade and colonization in the region.

Lemoine

For Further Reading
Levitzion, Nehemia. *Ancient Ghana and Mali.* London: Methuen, 1973.
Thobhani, Akbarali. *Mansa Musa: The Golden King of Ancient Mali.* Dubuque, Iowa: Kendall/Hill Publishing, 1998.

Mao Tse–tung

Chinese Communist Leader
1893–1976

Life and Work

Mao Tse–tung created a powerful, popular movement that, at a great cost in human lives, unified China and liberated its people from external oppression.

Born on December 26, 1893, in China's Hunan province, Mao rebelled against rural family life by taking up politics. He joined anti–foreigner nationalist associations that appeared in China around the time it became a republic in 1912. In early 1918, Mao traveled to Beijing, where he discovered Marxist communism while serving as a university librarian; in 1921, Mao became a founding member of the Chinese Communist Party (CCP).

The CCP was founded at a propitious moment, because its members had allied the nationalist Kuomintang Party, which, under the leadership of CHIANG KAI-SHEK, was in the process of reconstructing a republic in China after 10 years of chaos that followed the revolution of 1911. The alliance, however, was full of conflict. It resulted in several attacks by Chiang on the CCP, one of which occurred in 1934 on the so–called Jiangxi Soviet, a laboratory for many of Mao's ideas on empowerment of the peasantry. Following this 1934 assault, Mao led a long fighting retreat, called the "Long March," which saved the CCP and made him a legend.

The Japanese invasion of China in 1937 and the reunification of the Kuomintang and CCP enabled Mao to make the communists a patriotic force, with new recruits from China's peasantry and working classes. After the end of the war with Japan in 1945, Chiang turned on the CCP again, but lost mainland China to Mao in 1949. Mao now became chairman of the new People's Republic of China.

After 1949, Mao ordered a significant land reform that lasted through mid–1955, when it was succeeded by a program of intense collectivization of peasant lives and land. Falsely convinced of his initiatives' success, in 1956 Mao launched the Hundred Flowers Movement, followed in 1958 by the Great Leap Forward, which aimed to make industry and communal living a part of everyday life. Both were disastrous, the former exposing hundreds of thousands of intellectuals to arrest, and the latter causing nearly 30 million Chinese to die of starvation.

In the early 1960s, severely criticized because of the Great Leap Forward's failure, Mao sought a power base outside the CCP and turned to provincial leaders, the army, and students through the Cultural Revolution, which became a monstrous attack against entrenched CCP figures and those intellectuals and experts who had survived the Hundred Flowers Movement. The ensuing chaos reaffirmed Mao's power over the people, but cost him the support of the army and much of the government. By 1969, faced with a near civil war in China and with no friends abroad, Mao quietly turned toward rapprochement with the United States—culminating in the visit of President Richard Nixon in 1972—and a reaffirmation of the need for economic growth and social stability. In 1972, Mao essentially retired from politics, although he remained an important and powerful figure behind the scenes until his death on September 7, 1976.

Legacy

Mao Tse–tung forced, at a terrible cost, the greatest social and political reorganization of a people and country the world has ever known, in essence redistributing wealth, and therefore power, from an entrenched elite to China's long–suffering common people.

Mao's political beliefs originated in a combination of Leninist Marxism, which stressed communist revolution from above, and his own ideas about a "Chinese" communism, in which

the peasantry became revolutionaries. Mao's amalgam conflicted with orthodox Marxism, which viewed the working classes as having a vanguard role. Mao's popularity with many Chinese came from a belief that he valued transformation over destruction, respect for the strongly moralistic tone of his messages and conduct, and the importance government initiatives gave to peasants and agriculture. Mao's strength remained in the peasantry throughout his rule. However, he increasingly made decisions and set off powerful social forces in the interest of his own vision of a Communist China rather than what China actually needed to achieve lasting social and economic reform.

Mao often launched programs, such as the 1956–57 Hundred Flowers Movement or the 1965–72 Cultural Revolution, in the name of strengthening China, but covertly used them to root out his ideological opponents. Despite its tragic excesses, Maoism, with its emphasis on peasant activism and party populism, united the Chinese people, paved the way for China's current success, and served as an important model for countries across Asia, such as Cambodia, and across Africa, such as Tanzania, into the 1980s.

Del Testa

WORLD EVENTS		MAO'S LIFE
Germany is united	1871	
	1893	Mao Tse–tung is born
Russo-Japanese War	1905	
World War I	1914–18	
Russian Revolution	1917	
	1921	Mao and others form Chinese Communist Party (CCP)
Great Depression	1929–39	
	1934–35	Mao leads "Long March"
World War II	1939–45	
Communist China is established	1949	CCP takes over China
	1958–61	Mao initiates Great Leap Forward
	1966–72	Mao governs during Cultural Revolution
Israel defeats Arab nations in Six-Day War	1967	
Vietnam War ends	1975	
	1976	Mao dies
Dissolution of Soviet Union	1991	

For Further Reading

Breslin, Shaun. *Mao*. Profiles in Power. London: Addison, Wesley, Longman, 1998.

Terrill, Ross. *Mao: A Biography*. Rev. and expanded ed. Palo Alto, Calif.: Stanford University Press, 1999.

Marcus Aurelius

Roman Emperor and Philosopher
121–180

Life and Work

Marcus Aurelius preserved Rome's Golden Age by defending the empire against multiple invasions and enforcing a personal discipline and magnanimity that inspired those he led.

On April 16, 121 Marcus Aurelius (in full, Caesar Marcus Aurelius Antoninus Augustus) was born Marcus Annius Verus in Rome, to a family that had earned respect and wealth in Rome's western provinces. By the 100s,

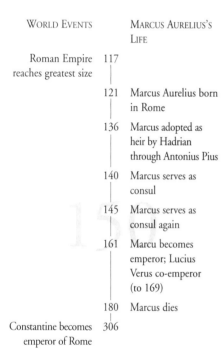

WORLD EVENTS		MARCUS AURELIUS'S LIFE
Roman Empire reaches greatest size	117	
	121	Marcus Aurelius born in Rome
	136	Marcus adopted as heir by Hadrian through Antonius Pius
	140	Marcus serves as consul
	145	Marcus serves as consul again
	161	Marcu becomes emperor; Lucius Verus co-emperor (to 169)
	180	Marcus dies
Constantine becomes emperor of Rome	306	

Marcus's family was an integral part of the colonial elite that helped govern the empire from Rome. Tutors specialized in Greek, Latin, and oratory gave Marcus an excellent education, and he developed a profound love of philosophy. Emperor HADRIAN, who was close to Marcus's grandfather, showed special favor to young Marcus and ensured that he joined organizations, such as the Salian Order of priests, that gained him connections and respect. In 136, Hadrian adopted the future emperor Antonius Pius as his heir, and forced Pius to adopt both Marcus and Lucius Verus, another favorite. When Pius took the throne in 138, Marcus was appointed to various offices appropriate to his position as heir apparent, acting as consul, or chief magistrate, in 140 and 145. Unlike most men in his position, Marcus never commanded troops in the field as a youth, which had a serious effect on his ability to lead later in life.

In 161, upon the death of Antonius Pius, Marcus became emperor and asked that Lucius serve with him as co-emperor. Marcus curried favor by distributing large amounts of money to Rome's citizens and soldiers. Trouble soon disturbed the peace, however. Parthia, an empire east of present-day Turkey, conquered Armenia, one of Rome's client states, and then defeated two Roman legions sent to retake it. Marcus sent Lucius, who had good military training, with a large force to retake Armenia, which he did in 164. Unfortunately, Lucius's troops returned with a virulent form of plague, which devastated Rome's military and threatened the empire's population. In addition, beginning in 162, German tribes occupied Roman provinces along the Danube River, destroying several legions in the process. Subduing these tribes and bringing them under Rome's control was difficult because of Marcus's military inexperience, the death of Lucius in 169, the rashness of the German tribes, the reformulation of the military after the plague, a weakening of Rome's financial position (which had necessitated a sale of imperial property), and a rebellion in Egypt in 175. Exhausted, Marcus died peacefully on March 17, 180.

Legacy

Marcus Aurelius's primary legacy was to have preserved the Roman Empire's Golden Age in the face of terrible adversity. In addition, he unintentionally bequeathed to the world, in the form of his *Meditations*, a substantial and influential corpus of philosophy.

As emperor, Marcus began his reign by improving the legal and administrative reforms begun under his predecessors, Hadrian and Trajan. He set a careful personal example by limiting the imperial household's consumption of luxuries and by keeping the usual scandals of the throne to a minimum. Marcus's careful administration kept the empire on a steady course despite great challenges, and his example of integrity reassured the Roman people, allowing the creative and commercial energies of the previous 60 years to continue while Marcus mounted an effective defense against the Germanic invaders.

Although he preserved the integrity of an empire under terrible duress, the plague and the invasion of the Germanic tribes forced Marcus to make choices that had long-term consequences for the composition and course of the empire. Although eventually reconquering the lands lost to the German tribes, Marcus had to draft non-Italians into the legions and compromise with some of the German tribes by absorbing them into the empire. Rome was unprepared for a sudden shift away from its Italian elites and their cultural dominance. As a result of this shift, along with subsequent German invasions, poor imperial leadership, religious strife, and the increased intervention of the military into political affairs, Rome began a slow slide into anarchy and disintegration. Marcus's reign marks the zenith of Roman civilization, the high point from which it later declined.

During Marcus's lifetime, philosophy was not as highly regarded as oratory—the ability to speak and convince. Therefore, although Marcus's allegiance to the Stoic school, which emphasized self-reliance, self-control, and altruism, was personally inspirational to him, and created a reserved personality that was a good example to the Roman people, his studies of philosophy were not widely appreciated during his lifetime. However, his philosophical reflections, collected in a book called *Meditations*, profoundly influenced early Christian and Enlightenment philosophers and remains inspirational to students of philosophy to the present day.

Del Testa

For Further Reading

Birley, Anthony. *Marcus Aurelius: A Biography.* London: B. T. Batsford, 1987.

Grant, Michael. *The Roman Emperors: A Biographical Guide to the Rulers of Imperial Rome, 31 BC–AD 476.* New York: Scribner's, 1985.

Maria Theresa

Empress of Austria
1717–1780

Life and Work

Maria Theresa ruled the Habsburg Austrian Empire during a time of grave military and political crisis. Her tenacity enabled the state to defend its territories and to enact important reforms that brought strength in future years.

Maria Theresa was born in 1717 to Emperor Charles VI of Austria. Charles, who lacked a male heir, feared that the succession of Maria Theresa after he died would invite treachery among the surrounding powers. He therefore issued a document known as the Pragmatic Sanction that identified his daughter as the heir. After considerable negotiations, his neighbors accepted the succession. When he died in 1740, the succession appeared to be assured.

FREDERICK II (Frederick the Great), who had himself just come to power in Prussia, rejected the Pragmatic Sanction and invaded the Austrian province of Silesia in the very year of Maria Theresa's ascension. The situation was grave, but the new empress rose to the occasion. Her energetic leadership and the resilience of the army enabled Austria to weather the War of Austrian Succession (1740–48). At the Peace of Aix-la-Chapelle, Maria Theresa was forced to concede the loss of Silesia, but her rule was assured through recognition of her husband,

Francis I, as emperor. In later years the constant threat of Prussian attacks led Maria Theresa to forge an alliance with France, which helped her defend the realm again during the Seven Years War (1756–63).

Fear of military threats inspired Maria Theresa to experiment with internal reforms. She oversaw a professionalization of the army and ordered new taxation practices that tapped the country's wealth more efficiently than ever. She also promoted higher productivity in manufacturing and agriculture, and even sought to eliminate the blight of serfdom. A new system of courts and governmental administration introduced in 1749 facilitated the centralization of her sprawling realm. Furthermore, conscious of the dangers associated with a lack of heirs, she produced no fewer than 16 children (including Marie Antoinette). She took care to train her eldest son, Joseph, for succession. Finally, the loss of Silesia was partly compensated during the last years of her reign when she annexed the eastern territories of Galicia and Bukhovina.

Having strengthened Austria and assured its continued survival, Maria Theresa died in 1780.

Legacy

Maria Theresa left a revitalized Austria that would influence European affairs throughout the nineteenth century.

Maria Theresa's successors followed her example in reforming and strengthening the Austrian state. Joseph II (r. 1780–90) continued to give close attention to economic affairs. He abolished serfdom altogether and promoted schooling that would prepare his subjects to staff an expanded state bureaucracy. He promoted freedom of religion (something the devoutly Roman Catholic Maria Theresa had shunned) and favored freedom of the press. Finally, his support of enlightened culture in the capital of Vienna laid the foundation for a century of artistic brilliance. He was a patron of Wolfgang Amadeus Mozart, and during the nineteenth century Vienna would become the musical capital of Europe.

By standing strong in the face of Prussia's repeated attacks from the north, Maria Theresa left a large empire to her heirs. Her military reforms were taken up by her immediate successors, which helped prepare Austria for the exhausting Napoleonic Wars. Although the

Austrian army would be beaten on the field in early engagements, by 1815 Austria was an important power in the coalition that destroyed the Napoleonic Empire. Austria hosted the victorious Congress of Vienna in that year; and for nearly half a century following, the Austrian statesman KLEMENS VON METTERNICH would dominate European diplomacy.

The territories acquired by Maria Theresa in Galicia and Bukhovina gave the Austrian Empire an increasingly multinational character that would ultimately trouble domestic politics. Joseph continued her policies of centralization in the belief that incorporating distant territories into a uniform bureaucracy was essential for survival. Many of the eastern territories, however, resisted centralization, which was often accompanied by the imposition of the German language. Hungary revolted against efforts to introduce a new and more uniform system of administration. In 1848 nationalist revolts would nearly tear the empire apart. By 1914 nationalism had become so destabilizing that a Serbian terrorist would take the life of the heir, Austrian Franz Ferdinand, in Sarajevo. This event provoked the World War I, which ultimately destroyed the Austrian Empire.

Strickland

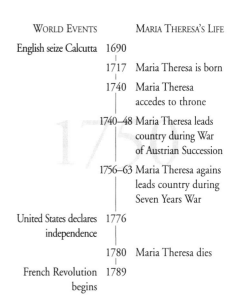

WORLD EVENTS		MARIA THERESA'S LIFE
English seize Calcutta	1690	
	1717	Maria Theresa is born
	1740	Maria Theresa accedes to throne
	1740–48	Maria Theresa leads country during War of Austrian Succession
	1756–63	Maria Theresa agains leads country during Seven Years War
United States declares independence	1776	
	1780	Maria Theresa dies
French Revolution begins	1789	

For Further Reading

Berenger, Jean. *A History of the Habsburg Empire.* Translated by C. A. Simpson. London: Longman, 1994.

Crankshaw, Edward. *Maria Theresa.* New York: Viking, 1969.

Pick, Robert. *Empress Maria Theresa: The Early Years, 1717–1757.* New York: Harper and Row, 1966.

Marshall, George

U.S. Soldier and Diplomat,
Drafter of the Marshall Plan
1880–1959

Life and Work

Often compared to GEORGE WASHINGTON for his personal integrity, George Marshall, as chief of staff of the U.S. Army, contributed greatly to the U.S. victory in World War II; his development of the Marshall Plan facilitated the political and economic recovery of Western Europe after World War II.

WORLD EVENTS		MARSHALL'S LIFE
Germany is united	1871	
	1880	George Catlett Marshall is born
Russo-Japanese War	1905	
World War I	1914–18	
Russian Revolution	1917	
	1917–18	Marshall serves in World War I
Great Depression	1929–39	
World War II	1939–45	Marshall serves as army chief of staff during World War II
	1947	President Harry Truman appoints Marshall secretary of state; Marshall designs Marshall Plan
Communist China is established	1949	
	1950	Truman appoints Marshall secretary of defense
	1953	Marshall awarded Nobel Prize for Peace
	1959	Marshall dies
Israel defeats Arab nations in Six-Day War	1967	

George Catlett Marshall was born on December 31, 1880, in Uniontown, Pennsylvania. Marshall entered Virginia Military Institute in 1897; graduating in 1901 at the top of his class, he was commissioned in the U.S. Army in 1902. An able organizer, Marshall was one of the first Americans sent to France to plan complex military operations when the United States declared war on Germany in 1917.

After the war he held a number of different positions in the army, until named chief of staff in 1939, a post he held until 1945. A top military advisor to President FRANKLIN DELANO ROOSEVELT, Marshall oversaw the reorganization and creation of the largest military in U.S. history. He also helped to devise the overall strategy for a global war fought in numerous theaters. Although he retired in November 1945, President HARRY S. TRUMAN called him out of retirement a few days later to serve (ultimately unsuccessfully) as a mediator in the Chinese civil war between CHIANG KAI-SHEK's Nationalists and MAO TSE-TUNG's Communists. Truman named Marshall secretary of state in 1947.

That same year, Marshall designed the European Recovery Act, better known as the Marshall Plan, to help Europe recover from World War II and to keep the communists in Western Europe from gaining power. After resigning in 1949, he was again called back by Truman in 1950 to become secretary of defense, taking part in the decision to send troops to Korea. In 1951 Senator Joseph McCarthy attacked Marshall (and many others) for being "soft on communism." Marshall, disgusted by McCarthy's tactics and suffering from health problems, resigned, this time for good, shortly thereafter. He was awarded the Nobel Prize for Peace in 1953 for his work on the Marshall Plan. He died in Washington, D.C., on October 16, 1959.

Legacy

As army chief of staff, George Marshall prepared the United States to enter and win a two-front global conflict. The Marshall Plan contributed to the postwar European economic recovery and the eventual political and economic unity of Europe through the European Union.

Displaying strategic vision, Marshall, as chief of staff from 1939 to 1945, persuaded Congress (then favoring an isolationist policy) to expand the hitherto underfunded military. As a result, the United States entered World War II more prepared than it would have been otherwise. Marshall's support of the "Germany first" policy, the policy to put ground, air, and naval forces in a combat theater under a single command, and other strategic decisions, helped the Allies win the war. His military reforms, especially the creation of the Joint Chiefs of Staff, endure to the present, and were well suited to the Cold War era.

In 1947 Marshall successfully urged support for anticommunist governments in Greece and Turkey, a policy (later known as the Truman Doctrine) in which the United States took on the responsibility for aiding non-communist regimes defeat foreign or domestic communist opponents. This policy was later extended, with uneven success, to include nations outside of Europe, such as Korea, Vietnam, and various Latin American countries.

The Marshall Plan, which poured billions of dollars into war-ravaged Western Europe, provided the economic and psychological boost needed to embark on 30 years of unprecedented economic growth and political stability. The plan forced participating European nations to work together to allocate the funds that the United States provided in a lump sum. Western European unification was thus fostered and grew into the European Union in the decades to follow.

Both the Truman Doctrine and the Marshall Plan led the way to the formation in 1949 of the North Atlantic Treaty Organization (NATO), which established a permanent presence for U.S. armed forces in Europe during the Cold War and gave Western Europe a measure of security against the perceived threat from the Soviet Union. However, these policies accelerated the Cold War division of Europe, confirming the creation of a "bipolar" world of superpowers.

Marshall's success in pushing the United States toward a policy of engagement rather than isolationism is part of the reason that Western Europe remains wealthy and prosperous and continues to solidify the European Union. Eastern Europe, being under Soviet control, did not benefit from the Marshall Plan and could not keep up with the West economically. Its communist governments were abolished after the fall of the Berlin Wall in 1989. In 1999 Eastern European nations such as Poland, the Czech Republic, and Hungary joined NATO and are making other efforts to integrate into the West's economic system.

Lemoine

For Further Reading

Cray, Ed. *General of the Army: George C. Marshall, Soldier and Statesman.* New York: Norton, 1990.
Stoler, Mark A. *George C. Marshall: Soldier-Statesman of the American Century.* Boston: Twayne, 1989.

Marx, Karl

Revolutionary Socialist
1818–1883

Life and Work

Karl Marx entered socialist politics and developed a revolutionary philosophy that would ultimately influence millions.

Marx was born on May 5, 1818, in the Prussian city of Trier. His family's Jewish background imparted to him the perspective of an outsider. This was given an intellectual foundation in 1836 when he encountered a radical school of philosophers known as the Left Hegelians at the University of Berlin. Marx embraced their atheistic claims that man alone is the source of good; after receiving a doctorate in philosophy in 1841 Marx was rejected for a professorate because of his radical views. He then turned to journalism.

Marx took a special interest in the revolutionary movement of the time. In 1843 he moved to Paris and met Friedrich Engels. Entering into immediate collaboration in revolutionary journals, the two were commissioned by a group of workers to write a pamphlet summarizing their views. The resulting *Communist Manifesto* (1848) presented Marx's view of history, the new industrial economy, and the future of the revolutionary movement. Claiming that "all history is the history of class struggle," it articulated Marx's claim that human behavior is

motivated solely by material concerns. It appeared at precisely the moment when the revolutions of 1848 erupted throughout Europe. When governments remained in place, however, Marx was forced to flee to London, where he lived in poverty for the remainder of his life. He made regular visits to the British Museum to research his massive study of capitalism, *Das Kapital.* He also remained active in revolutionary politics and helped to found the International Working Men's Association in 1864. His brutally intolerant opinion of rival philosophers drove the Russian anarchist MIKHAIL BAKUNIN out of the association in 1872, and it collapsed soon after.

Self-confident about his philosophy to the end, Marx died in London exile in 1883.

Legacy

One of the most important intellectuals of the nineteenth century, Karl Marx altered the course of philosophy and established a revolutionary movement that would transform the world in the twentieth century.

Marx's philosophy came to be known as dialectical materialism. Dismissing religion as "the opiate of the people," Marx claimed that human existence is determined by material (or economic) forces, and political change and revolution can only occur dialectically, that is, as a result of economic transformation and class conflict. Marx claimed that the contemporary rise of industrial capitalism in Europe and America signaled the final stage in history and a violent struggle between the two great economic classes of the age, the bourgeoisie and the proletariat.

Marx's vision of a historically inevitable triumph over exploitation fueled the minds of revolutionaries and intellectuals in the West for more than a century. Frustrated by the failure of other nineteenth-century socialist revolutionaries, they embraced Marxism for several reasons. First, dialectical materialism was highly sophisticated. Not only did it enclose the whole of human experience (the nature of man, the structure of society, the course of history itself) within a single system, but it offered new perspectives on a range of philosophical topics, from economics to aesthetics. It also offered a secular explanation for human suffering during an age when most intellectuals had abandoned the

teachings of traditional religion. Its vision of economic alienation throughout the ages, and its scientifically supported prophecy that a cataclysmic event will inevitably occur at the end of history to restore mankind to a condition of unity, offered a secular variation on the Christian understanding of universal salvation. Finally, Marxism proved to be one of the most effective ways of approaching revolutionary politics.

Thus Marxism came to dominate the thinking of the Social Democratic Party in industrial Germany before World War I. It also gained ascendancy, ironically, in precisely those countries that Marx himself considered economically backward and therefore unprepared for revolution. Russia, which had industrialized only partly and possessed a minuscule proletariat, constituting some 5% of the population, became in 1917 the first country in which Marxism actually triumphed. Its success was attributable to the organizational skills and militancy of the Communist Party under VLADIMIR ILICH LENIN. After the Russian Revolution, however, the communists applied Marx's prescription for an industrial economy by launching a massive and ultimately catastrophic plan to transform the economy under JOSEPH STALIN. Revolutionaries in other traditional societies throughout the world also sought to couple social justice and industrial transformation. MAO TSE-TUNG (China), JOSIP TITO (Yugoslavia), and FIDEL CASTRO (Cuba) each established a communist regime in his country, and other revolutionaries such as ERNESTO GUEVARA sought unsuccessfully to do likewise in other parts of the world.

With the collapse of the Soviet Union in 1991, Marxism finally lost the status that had made it the dominant philosophy of revolution of the twentieth century.

Strickland

WORLD EVENTS		MARX'S LIFE
Congress of Vienna reorganizes Europe	1815	
	1818	Karl Marx is born
	1841	Marx receives doctorate in philosophy
	1848	Marx and Friedrich Engels publish *Communist Manifesto*
	1864	Marx helps found International Working Men's Association
Germany is united	1871	
	1883	Marx dies
Russo-Japanese War	1905	

For Further Reading

Berlin, Isaiah. *Karl Marx: His Life and Environment.* 4th ed. Oxford: Oxford University Press, 1996.

Kolakowski, Leszek. *Main Currents of Marxism: Its Rise, Growth, and Dissolution.* 3 vols. Translated by P. S. Falla. Oxford: Oxford University Press, 1978.

Raddatz, Fritz J. *Karl Marx: A Political Biography.* Translated by Richard Barry. Boston: Little, Brown, 1978.

Mazzini, Giuseppe

Nineteenth-Century Italian
Nationalist
1805–1872

Life and Work

Although Giuseppe Mazzini did not play a direct role in the Risorgimento (the process of Italian unification), he popularized and propagated the idea of national unification in nineteenth-century Italy.

Mazzini was born in Genoa, in the Kingdom of Piedmont-Sardinia, on June 22, 1805. At that time, Italy was not a unified nation-state; it consisted of several independent kingdoms and duchies—the Austrian Empire possessed Lombardy and Venetia in northern Italy, and the Pope controlled central Italy, known as the Papal Estates, as well as Rome. Mazzini enrolled at the age of 14 in the University of Genoa, where he studied history, literature, philosophy, English, and German. There he became a nationalist, opposing Austrian control of Lombary and Venetia.

Believing that popular insurrection, revolution, and guerrilla warfare were the best ways to achieve Italian unification and social reform, Mazzini sought to unify the Italian peninsula

World Events		Mazzini's Life
French Revolution begins	1789	
	1805	Giuseppe Mazzini is born
Latin American independence movement begins	1811	
Congress of Vienna reorganizes Europe	1815	
	1831	Mazzini founds Young Italy; exiled from Piedmont-Sardinia
	1848	Mazzini takes part in Lombard revolt against Austria; rules Roman Republic as part of governing triumvirate
	1866	Mazzini is elected to parliament, but Italian government nullifies his election
Germany is united	1871	
	1872	Mazzini dies
Russo-Japanese War	1905	

through a democratic "revolution from below." He developed a strong belief in the power of the populace to effect radical change. "God and the People" became his motto. Although considered a radical left-wing revolutionary by moderate and conservative Italian nationalists, he shared their conviction that the struggle for national unity could overcome class and social antagonisms.

In 1831 Mazzini founded Young Italy, an organization that aimed to establish an Italian republic through revolution. Exiled from Piedmont for his politcal beliefs, Mazzini edited a Young Italy journal in France and traveled widely in Europe advocating nationalist revolutions. In 1837, exiled from France, he moved to England, where he established a boys' school for Italian exiles and gathered around him a following of dedicated revolutionaries.

In 1848, Mazzini returned to Italy to participate in numerous social and political upheavals. Fighting first in the Lombard revolt against Austrian rule, he later ruled the new Roman Republic (established after Pope Pius IX fled Rome following widespread anti-papal demonstrations) as part of a governing triumvirate. By 1850 both the Lombard revolt and the Roman Republic, weakened by internal divisions between monarchists and republicans, had been crushed.

In the eyes of moderate Italians the failures of these insurrections discredited Mazzini's concept of unification through popular revolt. Instead, many turned to the idea of unification under a constitutional monarchy, proposed by Camillo Benso di Cavour, a prime minister of Piedmont-Sardinia. Italy achieved unification in 1861 through the efforts of Cavour and Giuseppe Garibaldi, leaving a disillusioned Mazzini on the sidelines.

Although Mazzini had been repudiated by many Italians, he was elected to the Italian parliament twice in 1866, but the new Italian government perceived him as a dangerous radical and annulled the elections. Retiring from politics, Mazzini continued to publish his opinions in *La Roma del Popolo*, a republican paper he founded in 1871, until his death in Pisa on March 10, 1872.

Legacy

Although Giuseppe Mazzini's unique vision was rejected by most Italians, his efforts helped to bring the issue of national unification to the forefront of Italian society in

the nineteenth century and anticipated nationalist movements in the following century.

Mazzini embraced seemingly contradictory ideals and principles—he was a republican who encouraged revolutionary action by ordinary people, yet accepted that all classes, including elite Italians, had a role to play in national life. Although an ardent nationalist, Mazzini respected all nationalities—national identity was but a bridge to a common sense of humanity. He had a devoted core of followers, yet lost many more who disagreed with one aspect or another of his beliefs. Republicanism, partly as a result of this disunity, did not gain widespread legitimacy in Italy until the twentieth century.

Although failing to spark insurrections among ordinary Italians, Mazzini inspired others, including Garibaldi, to take direct action in the struggle for Italian unification. Unified Italy began as a constitutional monarchy, yet many Italians continued to hope for an Italian republic. Mazzini's dream became a reality on June 2, 1946, when Italy officially became a republic—after 21 years of rule by the fascist dictator Benito Mussolini and the convulsions of World War II. More than 70 years after his death, Mazzini was celebrated as a founding father of the new Italian republic.

Mazzini was also a forerunner of the leaders of national liberation movements in the twentieth century. While perhaps not acknowledging Mazzini by name, revolutionaries in China, Cuba, Vietnam, South America, and other regions adopted the tactics of guerrilla warfare and popular insurrection that Mazzini had advocated.

Lemoine

For Further Reading
Mack Smith, Denis. *Mazzini.* New Haven, Conn.: Yale University Press, 1994.
Sarti, Roland. *Mazzini: A Life for the Religion of Politics.* Westport, Conn.: Praeger, 1997.

Mehmed II

Ottoman Sultan
c. 1432–1481

Life and Work

Mehmed II (Mehmed the Conqueror), considered the true founder of the Ottoman Empire, consolidated Turkish Ottoman rule of the eastern Mediterranean and established the political and cultural character of an empire that was to last until the twentieth century.

Born Mehmed Celebi on March 30, probably in 1432 (some sources cite 1429, 1430), the third son of Sultan Murad II was raised to be a ruler. In 1444 Murad set off to counter Christian forces crusading in Ottoman territory, leaving Mehmed in charge. When he returned Murad abdicated in favor of Mehmed, who had become heir to the throne after the death of his elder brother. Murad returned to the throne in 1446, however, acknowledging that Mehmed was not yet ready to rule. In 1451, Murad II died, and Mehmed definitively took the Ottoman throne. He had his remaining brother drowned to prevent dynastic opposition to his reign, a practice he later codified into law to provide for an orderly succession.

Mehmed spent the rest of his reign consolidating and expanding the Ottoman Empire. Mehmed called for a holy war against the remnants of the Christian Byzantine Empire. Using the new technology of the cannon, Mehmed laid siege to the Byzantine capital, Constantinople, capturing the city in 1453, then putting an end to a weakened empire that had been a world power since it was founded in 330 by the Roman Emperor CONSTANTINE I (Constantine the Great).

Mehmed continued westward into Europe; from 1454 he began his campaign to conquer Serb territory and other lands on the Balkan Peninsula, further consolidating Ottoman dominion. He then unsuccessfully laid siege to Belgrade. Wounded in the attack, he returned to Constantinople, redirecting his invasion of Europe toward Greece. In 1458 he conquered Athens, then returned to the conquest of Serbia in 1459.

Mehmed fought against Venice from 1463 to 1479, continued the conquest of Greece, and conquered the Crimea (1475) and Albania (1476). He faced opposition from Muslim rulers to the east, however, especially Prince Uzan Hasan, who controlled Karaman in southeastern Anatolia. Mehmed defeated Hasan's forces in 1473, bringing Karaman under Ottoman control. After concluding a favorable peace treaty with Venice (1479), he invaded southern Italy, raiding cities on the Italian peninsula in 1480. However, Mehmed, now known as "the Conqueror," was not successful in besieging the Aegean island of Rhodes.

Because Mehmed acknowledged the local traditional and religious practices of the non-Muslim territories he had conquered and allowed them to continue, these conquests influenced the Ottoman legal and political structure. Mehmed codified these policies in the Book of Laws. He also strengthened and centralized administration and taxation by exercising greater control over hitherto autonomous provincial government officials.

Mehmed died on May 3, 1481, while preparing a military campaign against the sultan of Egypt.

Legacy

Mehmed II's conquests made the Ottoman Empire a major power in Europe as well as in Asia Minor.

Mehmed established the Ottoman Turks as leaders within the Muslim world, a role that expanded under future sultans who had the strength and vision to build on his success. Mehmed consolidated the authority of the sultanate, turning Constantinople into the capital of the empire, and creating a magnificent palace and mosque complex. His policy of killing all claimants to the throne except the designated heir created deadly competition among the sons vying for parental favor, but also encouraged them to learn how to govern their allocated provinces effectively.

In newly conquered lands Mehmed established a multireligious social structure, allowing non-Muslims a measure of self-government. He organized each religious group into a legal category called millets, which governed according to the laws and precepts of their respective religious heritages. This policy of religious toleration continued into the late nineteenth century.

Mehmed's conquests temporarily sealed off the Eastern Mediterranean lands and the Black Sea from Europe, blocking the land routes used for trading with the East. This sparked increased exploration of sea routes south of the African coast and westward across the Atlantic Ocean, leading to the European discovery of the Americas and the beginnings of European overseas empires.

Mehmed's capture of Constantinople put an end to the Byzantine Empire, the last relic of the Roman Empire and Hellenic (Greek) culture. However, the Ottoman policy of religious toleration permitted the survival of the Eastern (Greek) Orthodox church. Russia now took the lead in the Orthodox Christian church, providing it with a justification for future involvement in Balkan and Turkish affairs, especially in the nineteenth century.

Lemoine

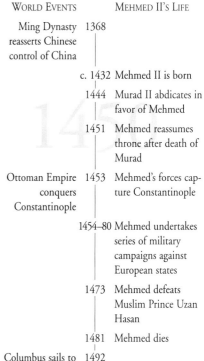

WORLD EVENTS		MEHMED II'S LIFE
Ming Dynasty reasserts Chinese control of China	1368	
	c. 1432	Mehmed II is born
	1444	Murad II abdicates in favor of Mehmed
	1451	Mehmed reassumes throne after death of Murad
Ottoman Empire conquers Constantinople	1453	Mehmed's forces capture Constantinople
	1454–80	Mehmed undertakes series of military campaigns against European states
	1473	Mehmed defeats Muslim Prince Uzan Hasan
	1481	Mehmed dies
Columbus sails to Americas	1492	

For Further Reading

Babinger, Franz. *Mehmed the Conqueror and His Time*. Translated by Ralph Manheim. Princeton, N.J.: Princeton University Press, 1978.

Kritovoulos. *History of Mehmed the Conqueror*. Translated by Charles T. Riggs. Westport, Conn.: Greenwood Press, 1970.

Menelik II

Ethiopian Emperor
1844–1913

Life and Work

Menelik II was emperor of Ethiopia at the turn of the nineteenth century. His modernization efforts, as well as his resistance to Italian invasions, made him one of the greatest Ethiopian rulers of modern times.

Menelik II, born on August 19, 1844, as Sahle Maryam, was the son of Haile Manakot, king of the Showa people who occupied southern Ethiopia. Manakot gave his son the formal name of Menelik to recall the glorious son of King Solomon and the Queen of Sheba. The Showa were a semi-independent people under the nominal protection of the emperor of Ethiopia. Between 1813 and 1847, Manakot's predecessor, Sahle Selassie, had made Showa the stable center of an Ethiopia divided by civil war. As a boy, Menelik received the education of a prince from tutors.

World Events		Menelik II's Life
Congress of Vienna reorganizes Europe	1815	
	1844	Menelik II is born
	1855	Menelik taken hostage by Tewodros II
Germany is united	1871	
	1889	Menelik becomes Emperor Menelik II
	1896	Menelik defeats Italians at Battle of Adowa
Russo-Japanese War	1905	
	1913	Menelik dies
World War I 1914–18		

In 1855, the self-proclaimed emperor of Ethiopia, Tewodros II, after unifying the north, invaded and conquered Showa as part of his efforts to consolidate his power and stabilize Ethiopia. Tewodros took young Menelik captive and held him for 10 years; although a captive, Menelik was given an excellent academic and military education. Menelik also observed Emperor Tewodros's restless efforts to modernize and expand Ethiopia and learned many important lessons in how to rule.

By the 1870s, Ethiopia no longer faced serious internal troubles, but was challenged by even more dangerous pressures from European powers seeking to dominate the whole of Africa. Tewodros, who did not understand the European diplomatic norms to which he had tacitly agreed in negotiations with the British, imprisoned several British subjects who he believed were plotting against him. This move caused Britain to attack him in 1867–68 in order to free the prisoners. Subsequently, Yohannes IV, a noble from Tigré province claimed the emperor's crown, but allowed Menelik to return to rule Showa as king.

His rule was brief, for in 1872, Yohannes asserted his right to rule over Showa, and Menelik was forced into a temporary retirement. Yohannes repulsed repeated attempts by the Italians to make Ethiopia a colony; he died on the battlefield in 1889. At Yohannes's death, Menelik came to the throne. He negotiated the Treaty of Ucciali, which temporarily ended hostilities between Italy and Ethiopia; specific terms in the treaty actually renewed tensions, however, and in 1896 the Italians again attacked Ethiopia, only to be soundly defeated by Menelik's troops at the Battle of Adowa in 1896.

After the decisive defeat of the Italians, Menelik turned toward the modernization of his country so that it would no longer face external aggression. He modernized the army, provided new schools and hospitals throughout Ethiopia, built a railroad between Addis Ababa, the capital, and the coast, and defined Ethiopia's borders in a way that endured until Eritrea's independence in 1993. Under Menelik the export of excellent Ethiopian coffee began, resulting in a generalized prosperity during the 1920s.

Menelik died December 12, 1913, in Addis Ababa.

Legacy

Menelik II's modernization efforts and resistance to Italy's colonial aggression set Ethiopia on a firm foundation as an independent nation. Perhaps more importantly, these efforts and their broader, symbolic meaning influenced many other Africans during the colonial period.

Menelik's primary legacy centers on his thwarting of Italian designs on Ethiopia. Indeed, besides the Japanese, the Thai, and the Afghans, the Ethiopians were the only people to resist efforts by Europeans to colonize an Old World region. Further, Ethiopia is one of only two African countries (Liberia is the other) to retain its independence after 1900. Menelik was successful because he promoted modernization and consistently focused on developing a single Ethiopian identity that would unify divided peoples into a powerful whole. Besides the European nations, only the Ethiopians, Vietnamese, Armenians, and Japanese can be said to have had a modern sense of nationalism before the colonial period.

Menelik's victories also severely challenged the bogus racial theories deployed by Europeans in order to make themselves seem superior to other peoples and enabled many people to recognize that, with a sense of unity and modern weaponry, Africans could defeat invading Europeans and develop modern nations in the process.

Del Testa

For Further Reading

Marcus, Harold G. *The Life and Times of Menelik II: Ethiopia 1844–1913.* Oxford: Clarendon Press, 1975.
Taylor, R. Bingham. *Menelik of Ethiopia.* London: Longman, 1978.

Menes

Egyptian Pharaoh
c. 2925 B.C.E.

Life and Work

Bringing order to a patchwork of petty principalities and free cities, the king (or kings) known as Menes united Upper and Lower Egypt into a single kingdom.

Very little is known about Menes, and, indeed, according to some scholars, his name may be a combination of the names of several Egyptian kings—named "Scorpion," Narmer ("catfish with chisel"), and Aha—each of whom accomplished a particular task that historians have credited entirely to Menes as a person.

If we accept that Menes was indeed a single person, it appears that he was born in Thinis, a province in Upper (that is, farther from the Mediterranean) Egypt, and became that province's king sometime about 2925 B.C.E. Menes initiated a series of administrative reforms and military preparations that eventually allowed him to unite Upper and Lower Egypt, culturally similar but politically distinct entities, into one country. Indeed, one of the rare images supposedly of him shows Menes wearing a dual crown of red and white, the colors, respectively, of Upper and Lower Egypt.

In addition to unifying Egypt, Menes established a new capital at Memphis (near present-day Cairo), at approximately the point along the Nile River where Lower Egypt ended and Upper Egypt began. Even today, Memphis shows the powerful architectural legacy of Menes. The whole process of consolidation of Upper and Lower Egypt involved de-emphasizing the power of individual towns and replacing it with a loyalty to a single king.

As legend has it, after ruling for 62 years as king, Menes was trampled to death by a hippopotamus.

Legacy

Menes paved the way for the stability that allowed individual Egyptian leaders to effectively utilize all of the rich agricultural, mineral, and human resources of the Nile Valley and inaugurated 3000 years of creativity and greatness.

At the time of Menes, the world's great cultures had just begun to solidify in the Nile Valley, Mesopotamia, the Indus River Valley, and along the Yangtze River (in present-day China). The unification of Upper and Lower Egypt allowed the Egyptian state to muster much greater resources than individual states. This essential transformation of local allegiances to a larger state occurred first in Egypt; however, the consolidation of Upper and Lower Egypt created considerable administrative responsibilities, and it can be assumed that Menes had to occupy himself to a very great degree with creating an effective bureaucracy.

In addition, Menes imposed a single culture over Egypt, where a plurality once existed. This creation of a "national" culture led to an artistic style that blossomed especially following the reign of Menes. However, the kings who came after Menes followed the cultural styles established in his time very rigidly and did not always adapt to changing needs and new ideas. This created the potential for popular revolts against the Egyptian kings based on how distant the backward-looking ideas of the kings seemed from the needs of people.

Del Testa

For Further Reading

James, T. G. H. *A Short History of Ancient Egypt: From Predynastic to Roman.* London: Cassell, 1995.

Wilkinson, Toby A. H. *Early Dynastic Egypt.* New York: Routledge, 1999.

Metternich, Klemens von

Austrian Diplomat
1773–1859

Life and Work

Klemens von Metternich constructed a new, more conservative European order after Napoleon's defeat in 1815.

Klemens Wenzel Nepomik Lothar von Metternich was born into the social milieu of European high diplomacy in Koblenz in 1773. He began his education at the University of Strasbourg in eastern France. Disturbed by the mob violence he witnessed there during the revolution of 1789, he transferred to the university in Mainz, now part of Germany. He and his family fled to Vienna in 1794, after France invaded present-day Belgium (then part of the Austrian Empire) and the western German principalities.

In Vienna, Metternich joined the diplomatic service, rising quickly to the post of for-eign minister in 1809. He understood that for the Austrian Empire to retain a measure of independence from France, he had to collaborate with NAPOLÉON I. He arranged a marriage between Napoléon and Marie-Louise, daughter of Austria's Emperor Francis I. He also allied Austria with France for the invasion of Russia in 1812. However, Metternich retracted Austria's alliance when it became apparent that Napoléon had been defeated in Russia.

When Napoléon was definitively defeated at Waterloo (south of Brussels) in 1815, Metternich saw the opportunity to bring the victorious powers to the table and negotiate a new European order. At the Congress of Vienna (1814–15), Metternich established a European system designed to suppress democratic reform movements. To ensure that traditional government would not topple, this "Concert of Europe" intervened in countries troubled by revolutionary insurrection: Naples in 1821, Spain in 1823, and the Papal States in 1830.

Metternich also engineered the creation of the German Confederation to maintain Austrian leadership and influence over German states. The confederation, under his leadership, issued the Karlsbad Decree (1819), aimed at suppressing revolutionary movements.

In 1848, however, the Austrian Empire, like much of Europe, was shaken to its core by national, popular, and liberal insurrections. By this time Metternich was viewed as the embodiment of repression. He fled Austria and lived in Great Britain for three years. The failure of the 1848 revolutions and the restoration of the Austrian monarchy allowed Metternich to return to Vienna, where he died on June 11, 1859.

Legacy

The "Metternich System" maintained a balance among the great powers of Europe that prevented the outbreak of a continent-wide war until World War I in 1914.

Metternich supported traditional and legitimate monarchies that ruled over a social hierarchy and upheld the law with the help of able advisors and an efficient civil service. Metternich's contemporaries and recent scholars have accused him of being a reactionary, bent on repressing civil liberty and suppressing revolution, whether national or liberal. Others have pointed out that

Metternich was trying to keep the tensions straining Europe at the time from tipping the continent into upheaval or war.

Metternich's combination of legitimate rule and good government was designed to prevent the kind of social and political upheavals seen in the French Revolution. With few exceptions, domestic insurrections were suppressed until 1848. Yet, Metternich's repressive measures and anti-national stance heightened resentment among Austrian and German liberals and radicals. The revolutions in Austria and the German states were characterized by a bitterness and intensity that had gained strength from long years of repression.

Metternich also wanted to prevent another major war involving most or all of the European states, and in this his success outlasted his tenure in office. Long after Metternich's forced resignation in 1848, the Metternich System maintained a balance of power between the five strongest states in Europe—Great Britain, France, Austria, Germany, and Russia—that ensured peace for a century. It also, however, suppressed liberal and national development in central and eastern Europe in the name of preserving the Austrian monarchy and empire. As a result, Austria did not develop politically or economically, which allowed Prussia to lead the other German states into unification in 1871. Although severely strained on occasion, Metternich's diplomatic system survived him for another half century before crumbling during World War I.

Lemoine

World Events		Metternich's Life
English seize Calcutta	1690	
	1773	Klemens von Metternich is born
United States declares independence	1776	
French Revolution begins	1789	
	1809	Metternich appointed foreign minister of Austrian Empire
Latin American independence movement begins	1811	
	1814–15	Metternich participates in Congress of Vienna
Congress of Vienna reorganizes Europe	1815	
	1819	Metternich instrumental in Karlsbad Decree
	1848	Metternich flees Austria during revolutions in Europe
	1859	Metternich dies
Germany is united	1871	

For Further Reading

Billinger, Robert D., Jr. *Metternich and the German Question: States' Rights and Federal Duties, 1820–1834.* Newark: University of Delaware Press, 1991.

May, Arthur James. *The Age of Metternich: 1814–1848.* Rev. ed. New York: Holt, Rinehart and Winston, 1963.

Milne, Andrew. *Metternich.* London: Rowman and Littlefield, 1975.

Montezuma II

Aztec Leader
c. 1466–1520

Life and Work

Montezuma II tried to accommodate the aggressive conquistador HERNÁN CORTÉS, ultimately failing to defend his empire against the Spaniards.

In approximately 1466 (dates vary, from 1466 to 1480), Montezuma ("he who angers himself") was born the eighth son of the Aztec emperor Axayatacl. At the time, the Aztecs managed an extensive and rich empire in central Mexico, that included 400 independent cities, many of whose inhabitants despised Aztec rule. Montezuma received an education typical of the nobility, attending a special school that emphasized cosmography and mathematics as well as the performing and military arts. Montezuma was known for his skillful use of tactics, for his supreme courtesy, and for his occasional brutality. When his uncle Ahuitzotl died in 1502, Montezuma assumed the throne, becoming the Aztec Empire's supreme political, military, and religious figure. He engineered several significant conquests early in his reign and attended to the welfare of his people.

Beginning in 1518, reports of white men who walked on water reached Tenochtitlán (present-day Mexico City and the administrative center of the Aztec empire). These were Spaniards who had stopped off the coast of Veracruz to resupply and repair their vessel while searching for additional islands in the Caribbean. The tardiness of this group had provoked Hernán Cortés, then in Cuba, to mount a large search party. Reaching Veracruz, Cortés learned of the interior empire of the Aztecs and decided to strike out for Tenochtitlán to meet with the emperor. Cortés sent a message to Montezuma asking to meet so that Cortés might deliver a letter of greetings from the king of Spain.

Montezuma refused, because he had heard that the foreigners lusted only after gold and were capable of great violence, and because the Aztec calendar divined a bad omen during the year of Cortés's arrival. In addition, Cortés vaguely resembled the image of an Aztec god, Quetzalcóatl, who was white and was to return to Earth to judge the Aztecs.

The Aztecs and their allies fought the invaders. However, the psychological impact of the mounted Spaniards (the Aztecs had never seen horses), the Spaniards' use of cannon, and the relatively disorganized fighting style of the Aztecs impaired their ability to resist. Having failed to prevent Cortés from crossing the high mountain passes that led to the Valley of Mexico, Montezuma received the Spaniards in mid-November 1519. Montezuma gave the Spaniards a great deal of freedom, so much that they eventually made him a captive. By intimately associating himself with the conquistadors, Montezuma lost all authority. With the subject states siding with the Spaniards against the Aztecs and with much of the Aztec aristocracy wiped out in a Spanish massacre, Montezuma had no hope; indeed, when he finally called for a revolt in early 1520, Montezuma was killed by stones thrown by the Aztec public.

Legacy

Montezuma II appears to have been an ineffective leader in the face of aggressive foreign invaders. However, Montezuma may have softened Spanish attitudes to some degree and allowed the peoples of Mexico some time to prepare for the coming of the Spaniards by hosting the conquistadors for several months, rather than simply ordering their destruction.

Montezuma faced enormous pressure and confusion upon hearing of the appearance of foreigners. He had to both acknowledge that the timing of Cortés's arrival and his physical appearance did not bode well for the Aztecs and had to ensure extra Aztec courtesy for potential gods. He also knew that the foreigners possessed incredible new weapons and that people subject to the Aztecs, such as the Tlaxacan, would not hesitate to ally with the newcomers. By trying to put off the Spaniards and by then hosting them, Montezuma did his best to slow their influence, anticipating that intemperate action might provoke a more violent response.

Montezuma did indeed keep Cortés in relative isolation in Tenochtitlán for nearly half a year, trying to limit political divisions caused by the presence of a new actor. At the time, however, Aztec society was beginning to unravel, because of the heavy demands the Aztecs placed on their subject peoples and the increasing competition for resources caused by population growth throughout Mexico. Montezuma could

not anticipate the intense scheming of Cortés, nor how new, unseen enemies, such as smallpox, brought by the Europeans, would devastate the people of Mexico. In the end, Montezuma sacrificed himself by showering the Spaniards with everything that was Aztec, ultimately losing all, including his authority as a ruler.

Del Testa

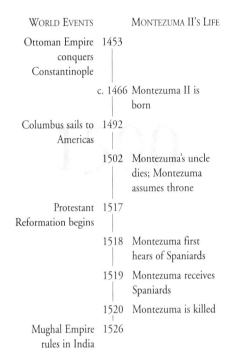

World Events		Montezuma II's Life
Ottoman Empire conquers Constantinople	1453	
	c. 1466	Montezuma II is born
Columbus sails to Americas	1492	
	1502	Montezuma's uncle dies; Montezuma assumes throne
Protestant Reformation begins	1517	
	1518	Montezuma first hears of Spaniards
	1519	Montezuma receives Spaniards
	1520	Montezuma is killed
Mughal Empire rules in India	1526	

For Further Reading
Collis, Maurice. *Cortés and Montezuma.* London: R. Clark, 1994.
Thomas, Hugh. *Conquest: Montezuma, Cortés, and the Fall of Old Mexico.* New York: Simon & Schuster, 1993.

Mu'āwiyah I

Founder of the Umayyad Dynasty
c. 605–680

Life and Work

Mu'āwiyah I (in full, Mu'āwiyah ibn Abi Sufyan) rose from a clan that had opposed the rise of Islam to become the founder of its first dynasty, the Umayyad.

Little is known about Mu'āwiyah's early life. He was born to Abi Sufyan, a prosperous trader and farmer of Medina and head of the Umayya, one of two clans in control of much of the trade that flowed across the Arabian

World Events		Mu'āwiyah I's Life
Byzantine Empire regains Italy	553	
	c. 605	Mu'āwiyah I is born
China's disparate states are reunified	606	
Muhammad conquers Mecca	630	Mu'āwiyah's family converts to Islam
	639	Mu'āwiyah is appointed governor of Syria
	657	Mu'āwiyah challenges Ali ibn Abi Talib at Battle of Siffin
	660	Mu'āwiyah proclaims himself caliph
	680	Mu'āwiyah dies
Islamic expansion into northern Europe is halted at Tours	732	

peninsula. Sufyan had opposed the rise of Islamic power in Medina under the prophet Muhammad, but in 630 he converted, along with his family, to Islam. This conversion, along with the military exhaustion of the Byzantine and Persian Empires that claimed Arabia, enabled Muhammad to unite all Arabs under Islam. Mu'āwiyah probably received schooling from tutors and certainly received practical training from his father's clan in commerce, agriculture, and the military arts. He briefly served as Muhammad's secretary between 630 and the prophet's death in 632.

In 639, an outbreak of plague killed thousands in Syria, including its governor. Umar, the first caliph of Islam, installed Mu'āwiyah as a replacement. Mu'āwiyah proved an able governor, building and professionalizing a large army, promoting trade, and solidifying Islamic rule. By innovating and spreading the faith, Mu'āwiyah gained a reputation both as a good administrator and good Muslim.

In 656, the third caliph, Uthman, a fourth cousin of Mu'āwiyah, was murdered at his home in Medina, and Ali ibn Abi Talib, the son-in-law of Muhammad, claimed the caliphate for himself. However, much of Islam refused to follow Ali, and civil war brewed throughout the Middle East. Mu'āwiyah, still governor of Syria, refused to recognize Ali as caliph unless Uthman's assassins were punished. In 657, Mu'āwiyah traveled to Iraq to challenge Ali at the Battle of Siffin. After months of skirmishes, Mu'āwiyah and Ali clashed but were so horrified at the sight of Muslim-on-Muslim violence that they agreed to on-site arbitration. The arbitration committee determined that both men should end their claims to the caliphate, a decision that in essence informed Ali he was not worthy of the post. Ali left in disgust and was murdered shortly thereafter. In May 660, Mu'āwiyah declared himself caliph, and by 661 ruled an Islamic empire that stretched from Morocco to the edge of India.

As caliph, Mu'āwiyah dedicated his rule to three tasks: solidifying his rule in the east, expanding his rule in the west, and improving the internal commerce of the Umayyad Empire's center. In the east, he appointed a tough lieutenant to break the will of those who remained loyal to the late Ali; in the west, he sent another lieutenant to attack the Berbers and push Islam into Spain; in the center, he

attacked the Christian Byzantine Empire relentlessly, as much to break the Byzantines' control of Mediterranean trade as to rescue local people from leaders he considered "Unbelievers."

Mu'āwiyah died in April 680; immediately thereafter those who remained loyal to Ali rose in revolt in Iraq.

Legacy

By carefully manipulating traditional values, Mu'āwiyah I formed the first Islamic dynasty out of disparate groups and interests.

Establishing enduring rule in a region of fractured loyalties took a great deal of skill. Mu'āwiyah knew that Islam would bind people together in a common identity. The transformation of that identity into a cohesive domain, however, was more challenging. In addition to political genius and great piety, Mu'āwiyah understood how to play traditions off of one another to achieve political goals. For example, in terms of blood, Mu'āwiyah's claim to the caliphate was tenuous compared to that of Ali, so he turned to pre-Islamic Arab traditions to legitimate his leadership. These traditions held that ability and seniority mattered more than heredity. Mu'āwiyah, as the better ruler, made his claim to clan leaders throughout Arabia, and they turned massively in his favor.

However, in the name of short-term stability, Mu'āwiyah named his feckless son, Yezid, as successor. While ensuring a smooth transfer of power, it damaged Mu'āwiyah's claim to respect for traditions. Mu'āwiyah also aggravated two great and enduring divisions in the Arab world. First, he did nothing to reconcile the various sects of Islam. Indeed, despite relative mercy shown to the followers of Ali, Mu'āwiyah did not tolerate dissent within Islam and did much to repress those not of the majority Sunni sect. This repression led to sectarianism that still divides the various Arab nations from one another despite a strong sense of political nationalism among modern Arabs. Second, Mu'āwiyah promoted his clan, the Umayya, over the Hashimites, the clan of Muhammad. The rivalry between clans provided another enduring source of division within Islam in the centuries after Mu'āwiyah's death.

Del Testa

For Further Reading

Hawting, G. R. *The First Dynasty of Islam: The Umayyad Caliphate, AD 661–750.* London: Croom Helm, 1986.
Madelung, Wilferd. *The Succession to Muhammad: A Study of the Early Caliphate.* Cambridge: Cambridge University Press, 1997.

Mugabe, Robert

President of Zimbabwe
1924–

Life and Work

From a humble beginning, Robert Mugabe helped transform a white-dominated Rhodesia into a black-dominated Zimbabwe.

Mugabe was born on February 21, 1924, in Kutama, Southern Rhodesia, which was then a self-governing British colony. Mugabe had the good fortune to attend a Roman Catholic village school, where his ability earned him a place at University College in Fort Hare, South Africa. At Fort Hare, Mugabe became deeply involved in nationalist politics and vowed to end the domination of Southern Rhodesia's blacks by a small minority of white settlers. In 1960, Mugabe returned to Southern Rhodesia to work with the leaders of the newly formed National Democratic Party (NDP), who were trying to negotiate a more equitable relationship between whites and blacks. When this effort failed, the NDP split. In 1961, Mugabe and Ndabanigi Sithole founded the Zimbabwe African National Union (ZANU), a more radical alternative to the other splinter of the NDP, Joseph Nkomo's Zimbabwe African People's Union (ZAPU).

While serving as leader of the ZANU, Mugabe was arrested for subversive speech, and spent 10 years in prison. While in prison, he continued his pro-black activism and earned several law degrees through correspondence courses. Released from prison in 1975, Mugabe

aligned with Joseph Nkomo and immediately began to lead a guerrilla war against the white ruling minority in Rhodesia. Mugabe and Nkomo's Patriotic Front of Zimbabwe fought for four years, ultimately forcing the white minority government to negotiate in 1979. In 1980, British-sponsored elections were held, and Mugabe and his party won in a landslide. Southern Rhodesia became Zimbabwe, the name for ancient stone fortresses built by Africans of the region.

Mugabe immediately turned to a government of reconciliation, allowing the remaining whites ample representation in Parliament, supporting the remaining white farmers and businessmen on whose shoulders Zimbabwe's economy rested, and forming a coalition with Nkomo's ZAPU. However, by 1984, Mugabe had edged Nkomo out of the coalition, and sparked ethnic tension between the ZAPU, dominated by the Shona people, and the Mugabe's ZANU, whose membership was mainly composed of the historically dominant Ndebele people. Mugabe revealed his secret designs to transform Zimbabwe into a one-party socialist state by uniting, in 1987, all of Zimbabwe's parties into a single ZANU–Popular Front (PF) and having himself elected as both first secretary of the ZANU–PF and first executive president of the country.

Under Mugabe's absolute rule, Zimbabwe quickly went from being one of Africa's richest countries to one of its poorest. Although reelected in 1990 against weak opposition, Mugabe's popularity declined. In 1999, he began to make claims against the white landholders that held 30% of Zimbabwe's arable land, and forced them to return about half of that land to Zimbabwe's black people. This move was not as popular as it might sound, however, because those who claimed land had no equipment or other means to make it productive.

Legacy

Robert Mugabe's dedication to independence and the destruction of white privilege brought about black domination in Zimbabwe. However, this destructive authoritarianism and rigidity has caused much recent suffering in Zimbabwe.

The white government of the former Rhodesia was unwilling to compromise on its hold on power in the country, and unbending on the exclusion of the black majority in its prosperity and government. From a moderate

position, Mugabe, influenced by the revolutionary tactics and politics of Vietnamese communist leader HO CHI MINH and the black radicalism of the American MALCOLM X, evolved into a fierce opponent of compromise. Mugabe successfully forced white Rhodesia to become multiracial Zimbabwe.

Initially, Mugabe reconciled with the country's remaining whites in order to maintain economic strength and prevent civil strife. However, he made sure to avoid the appearance of coddling the whites by emphasizing the economic development of rural black Zimbabwe, whose people often lived on marginal lands with little modern equipment. Accordingly, the situation of black farmers improved somewhat, especially as Mugabe's government paid more for black-raised crops than the white government had done and made sure that the black farmer did not have as far to travel to transport crops to market. However, Mugabe's autocratic streak, originating in his years as a rebel leader and in his belief in a hard-line socialism, has led to economic decline; his recent seizure of white-owned lands is just an example of his increasingly autocratic leadership.

Del Testa

WORLD EVENTS		MUGABE'S LIFE
Russian Revolution	1917	
	1924	Robert Mugabe is born
Great Depression	1929–39	
World War II	1939–45	
Communist China is established	1949	
	1960	NDP is formed
	1961	Mugabe and Ndabanigi Sithole form ZANU
	1965–75	Mugabe is imprisoned
Israel defeats Arab nations in Six-Day War	1967	
Vietnam War ends	1975	Mugabe becomes rebel leader
	1980	Mugabe wins elections; Rhodesia becomes Zimbabwe
	1984	Mugabe unites factions into one party
Dissolution of Soviet Union	1991	
	1999	Mugabe begins seizure of white-held lands

For Further Reading

Davidson, Basil. *Modern Africa: A Social and Political History.* 3rd ed. New York: Longman, 1994.

Worth, Richard. *Robert Mugabe of Zimbabwe.* Englewood Cliffs, N.J.: J. Messner, 1990

Mussolini, Benito

Italian Dictator and Founder of the
Fascist Movement
1883–1945

Life and Work

Italian dictator Benito Mussolini introduced the first self-proclaimed fascist government, inspiring ADOLF HITLER and others in the decades to follow.

Mussolini was born on July 29, 1883, in Romagna, a region in east-central Italy. Mussolini exhibited violent impulses at an early age and was expelled from a Roman Catholic boarding school for stabbing another student. At first a socialist, Mussolini worked as a schoolteacher and journalist, jobs obtained through connections with other socialists.

In 1912 Mussolini became the editor-in-chief of *Avanti!*, an Italian socialist newspaper. His success as a propagandist made him the de facto leader of the Socialist Party. Mussolini was

World Events		Mussolini's Life
Germany is united	1871	
	1883	Benito Mussolini is born
Russo-Japanese War	1905	
World War I	1914–18	
	1915	Mussolini serves Italy in World War I
Russian Revolution	1917	
	1919	Mussolini founds Fascist Party
	1922	Mussolini leads fascist March on Rome; Mussolini is appointed prime minister
Great Depression	1929–39	
World War II	1939–45	
	1940	Mussolini involves Italy in World War II
	1943	Mussolini is arrested, but rescued by Germans
	1945	Mussolini is executed
Communist China is established	1949	

expelled from the Socialist Party in 1914, however, because he opposed Italy's neutrality during World War I. In May 1915, Austria declared war on Italy, and Mussolini immediately enlisted in the army. Seriously wounded during training, he was discharged in June 1917 and returned to his job as editor of *The People of Italy*, the pro-war newspaper he had founded.

In March 1919 Mussolini formed a new political party, the *Fasci di Combattimento* ("fighting leagues"), and created a militia of black-shirted youths dedicated to attacking socialists and communists. Many conservatives, fearing a communist revolution, shared power with the fascists in the Parliament in 1921. In October 1922 Mussolini staged the fascist March on Rome to seize power, and was named prime minister by King Victor Emmanuel III.

The 1924 assassination by fascists of a socialist politician, Giacomo Matteotti, helped Mussolini create a dictatorship. By 1928 all political parties, except the fascists, were outlawed, freedom of the press was rescinded, and a secret police agency was created.

In 1936, Mussolini formed an alliance with Nazi Germany and declared war on the Allies in June 1940. In 1941, Italy suffered humiliating defeats in Greece and Africa, forcing Germany to intervene. In July 1943, after the Allies had invaded Sicily, the king had Mussolini removed from office and arrested; in September 1943, the Germans rescued Mussolini and installed him as ruler of German-occupied northern Italy. When Allied forces pushed the Germans out, Mussolini was captured by Italian resistance fighters and executed on April 28, 1945.

Legacy

The most important figure in the rise of fascism after World War I, Benito Mussolini's tactics were imitated by Adolf Hitler and others; he introduced a new form of politics to Europe and the world.

Mussolini took advantage of the upheaval caused by World War I to introduce fascism to Italy. Mussolini's fascist state was both conservative and revolutionary, advocating violence, discipline, aggressive imperialism, and war. Mussolini employed carefully crafted theatricality to develop the cult of the leader, both as totalitarian ruler and symbol of the all-powerful state.

Many of Mussolini's policies and tactics inspired Hitler, who formed his own fascist party in the 1920s, naming it the National Socialist Workers' (Nazi) Party. In the Munich putsch of 1923, Hitler attempted a March on Berlin similar to Mussolini's March on Rome. After it failed Hitler changed tactics and decided, like Mussolini, to seize power through the democratic system, which he destroyed when taking power in 1933. Like Mussolini, Hitler used squads of violent thugs, the brown-shirted SA (*Sturmabteilung*, or "storm troops"), who physically attacked and intimidated their opponents.

The defeat of Italy and Germany in World War II completely discredited fascism; in the war's aftermath, Italy's monarchy was replaced by a parliamentary republic. The effort to prevent another dictatorship or a communist takeover and domination by the Soviet Union characterized Italy's government after World War II and led to the creation of a weak executive under the dominance of Parliament.

However, vestiges of Mussolini's policies remain in Italy. Postwar governments retained a high level of management of the economy, and much of the fascist state apparatus remained in place. Economic growth was partly based on Mussolini's economic modernization under the policy of corporatism.

More generally, Mussolini's regime created what some have called the "fascist mentality," an authoritarian tendency that favors the rule of the strongman over individual liberties. Long years of fascist propaganda had created a lack of confidence in parliamentary democracy that made republican government more difficult in postwar Italy.

Lemoine

For Further Reading

Mack Smith, Denis. *Mussolini*. London: Weidenfeld and Nicolson, 1981.

Ridley, Jasper. *Mussolini*. London: Constable, 1997.

Napoléon I

Emperor of France
1769–1821

Life and Work

Napoléon I (Napoléon Bonaparte) conquered most of Europe in the first decade of the nineteenth century. Although ultimately defeated, Napoléon changed the face of Europe.

Napoléon was born on August 15, 1769, on Corsica, one year after France obtained possession of that Mediterranean island. In 1779 he began attending military school on the French mainland and was commissioned as a lieutenant in 1785. In 1795 he defeated a royalist insurrection against the revolutionary government with, as he described it, "a whiff of grape-shot," referring to the clusters of small cast-iron balls shot from cannons.

Napoléon was given command of the army of Italy formed to invade the Italian peninsula. In 1796, he waged a brilliant campaign against the Italians and the Austrians, who controlled part of northern Italy. In 1798 he invaded Egypt with the goal of damaging Great Britain's trade interests and imperial ambitions. Although unsuccessful in Egypt, Napoléon returned to France a hero. He overthrew the revolutionary government and created the Consulate, a triumvirate (three-man rulership), with himself as first consul. In 1804, he proclaimed himself emperor of a new ruling dynasty in France.

From then on, Napoléon's authority as a leader was tied to his success on the battlefield. After stabilizing the government and enacting wide-ranging domestic reforms, Napoléon scored a stunning series of victories that redrew the map of Europe: he defeated Austria at Austerlitz (1805), the powerful German state of Prussia at Jena and Auerstedt (1806), and Russia at Friedland (1807). By 1807 Napoléon controlled most of Europe and used his authority to introduce political and administrative reforms in Germany, Italy, the Netherlands, and other parts of the Continent. Russia agreed to form an alliance with France. Great Britain, across the English Channel, remained the only undefeated enemy.

In 1806 Napoléon instituted the Continental System, which established a boycott of British goods. To enforce the boycott Napoléon invaded first Portugal and Spain in 1808, and Russia in 1812; these proved to be his greatest military blunders. Napoléon's army, forced to retreat in 1813 during the harsh Russian winter, was devastated. All former allies turned on the French. Napoléon retreated to France, where in 1814 he abdicated and was exiled to the Mediterranean island of Elba.

While the coalition of victorious powers were negotiating the peace, Napoléon escaped and returned to Paris. In what became known as the Hundred Days, Napoléon once again became ruler of France. In June 1815, however, he was decisively defeated at Waterloo by a combination of British and Prussian forces. He was exiled again, this time to the tiny island of St. Helena in the South Atlantic, where he wrote his memoirs. Badly treated by the British, he died, most likely of stomach cancer, on May 5, 1821.

Legacy

Through his military conquests, Napoléon I spread the principles of the French Revolution throughout much of Europe, thereby transforming the political landscape for the next two centuries.

Napoléon considered himself a man of the Enlightenment, an eighteenth-century philosophical movement that, among other tenets, questioned the divine right of monarchs to embody the sovereignty of the state. Unlike many French army officers, Napoléon approved of the French Revolution; Napoléon supported the most radical faction of revolutionaries who had overthrown the monarchy, executed King Louis XVI, and proclaimed France a republic.

In the European lands under his direct control, Napoléon introduced political, legal, and administrative reforms (known as the Napoleonic Code), including legal equality, religious toleration, economic freedom, property rights, and civil marriage and divorce. He also centralized government administration, taxation, and education. Napoléon helped to develop liberal traditions in Europe, elements of which have survived in France and other European countries to the present.

In central Europe, the number of sovereign German states were reduced from 234 to 40. Napoléon's defeat of the Austrians led to the dissolution in 1806 of the Holy Roman Empire, which had controlled German lands since 962, and to its replacement by the Confederation of the Rhine. French occupation, however, sparked a sense of national identity among many Germans, who refused foreign rule and fought to drive Napoléon and the French out of German lands.

Although a product of the French Revolution, Napoléon also drew on royal traditions. He declared himself emperor, restored the old aristocracy, and created kingdoms in conquered territories, putting family members on their thrones. He divorced his first wife to marry a princess of the Austrian dynasty in order to produce an heir for his new dynasty. Some historians argue that Napoléon was the last enlightened despot in European history.

Lemoine

World Events		Napoléon I's Life
English seize Calcutta	1690	
	1769	Napoléon Bonaparte is born
United States declares independence	1776	
	1785	Napoléon becomes French army officer
French Revolution begins	1789	
	1795	Napoléon suppresses Paris royalist uprising
	1796	Napoléon appointed commander of army of Italy
	1799	Napoléon takes over government of France
	1804	Napoléon proclaims himself emperor
	1808–12	Napoléon invades Portugal, Spain, and Russia
Latin American independence movement begins	1811	
	1814	Napoléon abdicates
Congress of Vienna reorganizes Europe	1815	Napoléon again becomes ruler, is defeated at Waterloo, and is exiled
	1821	Napoléon dies
Germany is united	1871	

For Further Reading

Chandler, Daniel. *The Campaigns of Napoleon: The Mind and Method of History's Greatest Soldier.* New York: Macmillan, 1966.

Dufraisse, Roger. *Napoleon.* Translated by Steven England. New York: McGraw-Hill, 1992.

Tulard, Jean. *Napoleon: The Myth of the Savior.* Translated by Teresa Waugh. London: Weidenfeld and Nicolson, 1984.

Nasser, Gamal Abdel

President of Egypt
1918–1970

Life and Work

As leader of the military junta that ousted Egypt's corrupt pro-British monarchical regime, Gamal Abdel Nasser led the Arab nationalist movement and opened the Middle East to Soviet influence during the Cold War, altering the geopolitical dynamics of the region in the following decades.

Nasser was born in Alexandria, Egypt, on January 15, 1918, to a lower-middle-class family. The British had dominated Egypt since 1882, ruling indirectly through the Egyptian monarchy, to the growing resentment of many Egyptians. As a youth Nasser became involved in anti-British activities, joining Young Egypt, a radical nationalist group. Nonetheless, he applied and was accepted to the Royal Military Academy in 1936, and was commissioned in 1938.

WORLD EVENTS		NASSER'S LIFE
Russian Revolution	1917	
	1918	Gamal Abdel Nasser is born
Great Depression	1929–39	
	1938	Nasser graduates from Royal Military Academy
World War II	1939–45	
	1948–49	Nasser fights in first Arab-Israeli War
Communist China is established	1949	
	1952	Nasser and Free Officers depose King Farouk
	1953	Republic is proclaimed in Egypt
	1954	Nasser is named prime minister
	1956	Nasser is elected president and nationalizes Suez Canal; Britain, France, and Israel invade Egypt
Israel defeats Arab nations in Six-Day War	1967	Nasser tenders resignation in wake of Six-Day War
	1970	Nasser dies
Vietnam War ends	1975	

During World War II Nasser and his fellow officers, humiliated at Egypt's capitulation to British dominance, resolved to gain independence, naming themselves the "Free Officers." Nasser was elected president of their executive committee after his leadership in the Arab–Israeli War of 1948–49. Blaming the corrupt monarchy for Egypt's poor performance in the war, the Free Officers planned a coup.

On July 23, 1952, the Free Officers deposed King Farouk and dissolved Parliament, replacing it with the Revolutionary Command Council under Nasser's leadership. They declared a republic in 1953. The following year Nasser was named prime minister, and in 1956 he was elected president of a one-party state.

Nasser challenged Western influence in the Middle East, negotiating an arms deal with the Soviet Union. This provoked the World Bank to refuse Egypt funds for the construction of the Aswan High Dam. In retaliation, Nasser nationalized the Suez Canal (still controlled by the British) in July 1956. Britain, France, and Israel then together took over the Sinai Peninsula and Suez Canal. This proved a humiliating diplomatic failure for the invaders, who were condemned by the international community and soon withdrew their forces. Nasser emerged a hero in the Arab world.

His popularity at a high point, Nasser implemented economic reforms that benefited millions of poor Egyptians. He nationalized foreign-owned companies and industrial enterprises, creating a mixed economy through a five-year plan guided by a National Planning Committee. The Aswan Dam, built with Soviet funding, generated hydroelectric power and increased irrigation.

Internationally, Nasser embraced the non-alignment movement, in which developing countries avoided alliances with either Cold War superpower. Nasser promoted Arab nationalism by uniting Egypt with Syria in the United Arab Republic (UAR) in 1958; the UAR was dissolved when Syria withdrew in 1961.

Humiliated by another Arab defeat in the Six-Day War with Israel in 1967, Nasser attempted to resign but was forced to rescind his resignation by popular demand. He died suddenly on September 28, 1970, of a heart attack.

Legacy

Although many of Gamal Abdel Nasser's domestic and international policies were not carried on by his successors, he did succeed in making Arab concerns an international priority in the Cold War era.

In the domestic sphere, Nasser's policies, while providing economic and educational opportunities to more Egyptians than before, resulted in a bureaucracy that grew enormously with its vast new responsibilities, but eventually became inefficient and unresponsive. The one-party state became more coercive, relying increasingly on repressive mechanisms, such as press censorship and arbitrary arrests, to control the public debate. The slow-moving bureaucracy and police state atmosphere eventually gave birth to an Islamic fundamentalist movement hostile to the regime.

Nasser's economic policies did not, in the end, make much of a dent in the deeply entrenched poverty in Egypt. Nasser's successor, ANWAR AS-SADAT, turned away from state control of the economy, introducing liberal economic reforms. He also negotiated closer political and economic ties to the West, particularly the United States, raising the specter of dependency that Nasser and his officers had wanted to eliminate in their struggles against the British and the corrupt monarchy.

Nasser's pan-Arab policies also failed to establish Arab unity under the dominance of Egypt. His efforts to rid the Middle East of the monarchies and other regimes established after World War I destabilized the region, igniting civil wars in Lebanon, Jordan, Iraq, and Yemen in the 1950s and 1960s. The frontiers created by the post–World War I League of Nations mandates stubbornly remained in place, despite their imposition by the European-dominated league. Nasser's influence in the Arab states, coupled with his establishment of close ties with the Soviet Union, helped to push the United States into an alliance with Israel, affecting the geopolitical strategies of the Cold War. The humiliating defeat of the Six-Day War motivated Nasser's successors to reverse his policies and seek peace with Israel. The Gulf War of 1991, in which the United States and its allies declared war against Iraq and its supporters, tore to shreds the remnants of pan-Arab nationalism in 1991.

Yet, Nasser's Arab nationalism gave the Arab states a way to voice their diplomatic, military, and economic concerns to the international community, providing the unity needed to dissolve the remnants of Western colonial rule in the Middle East.

Lemoine

For Further Reading
Mikdadi, Faysal. *Gamal Abdel Nasser.* Westport, Conn.: Greenwood, 1991.
Woodward, Peter. *Nasser.* London: Longman, 1992.

Nehru, Jawaharlal

First Prime Minister of India
1889–1964

Life and Work

Jawaharlal Nehru led India during its transformation from a British colony into the world's largest democracy. He also led the Cold War nonalignment movement in which many developing nations steered a middle path between the United States and the Soviet Union.

Nehru was born on November 14, 1889, in Allahabad, India, the son of Motilal, an Indian nationalist leader. Although opposed to British rule in India, the wealthy Nehru family adopted a British lifestyle and sent their son to England to be educated at Cambridge. Despite his elite background, Nehru felt like an outsider in England, which stirred nationalist feelings in him for the first time.

He returned to India in 1912 to practice law, joining the nationalist movement in 1919 and supporting MOHANDAS GANDHI's *satyagraha* (campaign of nonviolent civil disobedience). In 1920 he helped to create a mass base for the hitherto elite Indian National Congress. In 1921 Nehru was arrested by the British and imprisoned for four months. He was later elected general secretary of the Congress Party, and in 1929 was elected president of the Congress Party. In 1927 Nehru had declared, in a Congress Party statement, that India sought independence from Britain. Nehru was arrested again after his participation in Gandhi's cam-

paign to oppose the government's salt monopoly in 1930. The pattern of protest and imprisonment continued through the end of World War II, when Nehru was released to negotiate the withdrawal of the British from India.

During the negotiations, which lasted until August 15, 1947, when Britain granted India independence, conflict between Hindus and Muslims erupted into violence. Nehru reluctantly concluded that British India had to be partitioned into Muslim Pakistan and mostly Hindu India, even though he, like Gandhi, supported a pluralistic society. In 1947, Nehru, who became India's first prime minister, had to declare martial law to contain the violence that had resulted in over a million deaths.

Nehru began the task of nation-building. He believed in a democratic political structure, yet he also embraced centralized economic planning as the best way to generate economic growth for his country. In 1951, Nehru unveiled India's first Five Year Plan, stressing increased agricultural productivity. Nehru's popularity remained high, and he was reelected in 1957 and 1962. He died of a stroke in 1964; his daughter, Indira Gandhi, and grandson Rajiv, both ruled India for many years after his death.

Legacy

As one of India's founding fathers, Jawaharlal Nehru emphasized both democracy and socialist state planning, showing other developing nations in Africa and Asia that democracies can function in the post-colonial era. His nonalignment movement also provided an alternative to Cold War alliances with either the United States or the Soviet Union.

Nehru was a democratic socialist who helped to establish and legitimize a multiparty parliamentary system in India. Nehru sought a mixed economy, where established industries, farms, and commerce remained in private hands, but where the state played a role in economic development. The state assumed ownership of new industries such as steel mills, public utilities, and irrigation projects guided by the National Planning Commission, which decided how to develop India in a manner best suited to its population, made up largely of poor farmers. The system was not coercive, as in the Soviet Union, but worked with incentives for poor farmers to cooperate in exchange for funds that improved their standard of living. The combination of representative democracy and socialist economic

policies largely succeeded, though widespread poverty remained. Secular democracy was threatened in India with the rise of a Hindu fundamentalist party, the Baharatiya Janata Party.

Building a new nation-state during the Cold War presented Nehru with another dilemma—to which he devised a creative solution. Not wanting to lead India into a neocolonial relationship with either the United States or the Soviet Union, Nehru formulated the policy of nonalignment. An effort to steer a middle course between the two superpowers, the policy, in practice meant that India would play both superpowers against each other when it came to technological aid or arms purchases. In 1962, a territorial dispute with China turned into war. When Indian troops were defeated and Indian resistance began to collapse, Nehru, fearing an invasion, appealed to the United States for military assistance. Despite the limitations of nonalignment, many other developing nations adopted similar policies as a way to preserve their political and economic independence.

Lemoine

WORLD EVENTS		NEHRU'S LIFE
Germany is united	1871	
	1889	Jawaharlal Nehru is born
Russo-Japanese War	1905	
	1912	Nehru returns to India and practices law
World War I	1914–18	
Russian Revolution	1917	
	1919	Nehru joins Mohandas Gandhi in nationalist movement
	1921–47	Nehru is arrested repeatedly
Great Depression	1929–39	
	1929	Nehru is elected president of Indian National Congress
World War II	1939–45	
	1947	Nehru is appointed first prime minister
Communist China is established	1949	
	1951	Nehru launches India's first Five Year plan
	1964	Nehru dies
Israel defeats Arab nations in Six-Day War	1967	

For Further Reading

Judd, Denis. *Jawaharlal Nehru.* Cardiff, Wales: GPC Books, 1993.

Misra, Kashi Prasad. *Nonalignment Movement: India's Chairmanship.* New Delhi: Lancers Books, 1987.

Nicholas II

Last Tsar of Russia
1868–1918

Life and Work

Few statesmen in world history have had as tragic and memorable a life as Nicholas II of Russia. A man of kind and pious disposition, he found his modest political talents overwhelmed by the crisis of the tsarist regime at the dawn of the twentieth century.

WORLD EVENTS		NICHOLAS II'S LIFE
Congress of Vienna reorganizes Europe	1815	
	1868	Nicholas II is born
Germany is united	1871	
	1891	Nicholas survives assassination attempt in Japan
	1894	Nicholas assumes throne
Russo-Japanese War	1905	Nicholas creates constitutional monarchy; Nicholas issues October Manifesto and creates the Duma
World War I	1914–18	
	1915	Nicholas assumes direct command of Russian army
Russian Revolution	1917	Nicholas is overthrown by revolution
	1918	Nicholas and his family killed by communists
Great Depression	1929–39	

Nicholas was born to the Romanov dynasty on May 18, 1868. Although the heir apparent, he received very little training for his future responsibilities apart from the reactionary instruction of Constantine Pobedonostsev, a layman who presided over the Holy Synod created by PETER I. Unlike Peter, Nicholas had little ambition to rule and spent his youth enjoying social pursuits in Saint Petersburg and traveling to Japan, where in 1891 he survived an attempt on his life. When his strong-willed father, Alexander III, died in 1894, he found himself the ruler of Europe's largest and most unstable Great Power.

Upholding the reactionary views of his tutor, Nicholas announced to a gathering of noblemen upon assuming the throne that any hopes entertained by his subjects for political reforms that might compromise the principle of autocracy were "senseless dreams." A revolution sparked by a war with Japan in 1905, however, forced him to reverse this position. In the wake of a general strike that year he issued the October Manifesto, which promised a constitutional government and a representative assembly called the Duma.

For nearly a decade afterward, Nicholas was able to steer a stable course that included free political debate and much-needed agriculture reform. When Orthodox Serbia appealed for military support to fight Austria and Germany in 1914, however, Nicholas, heedless of the lessons of 1905, reluctantly gave it. As World War I began to consume his empire, he insisted on imitating the example of his Muscovite ancestors by traveling to the front in 1915 to lead the war personally. This placed political authority back in the capital in the hands of his wife, Alexandra. Concerned mainly about the welfare of the hemophiliac heir to the throne Alexei, she all but handed it on to a bizarre mystic named Rasputin.

As educated society grew increasingly disgusted by Alexandra's incompetence in the capital and Nicholas's failures on the front, war shortages provoked a bread strike on March 8, 1917 (February 23 according to the old style Julian calendar) that quickly became a revolution. Toppled from power, Nicholas and his family were ultimately sent by the Bolshevik government of VLADIMIR LENIN to a town in the Ural Mountains named Ekaterinburg. There, on July 17, 1918, Nicholas II, his wife,

their five children, and the servants were taken to the basement of the house in which they were being detained and shot. Russia's long tsarist tradition expired with them.

Legacy

The failure of Nicholas II to preserve the Russian monarchy in the early twentieth century had an enormous impact upon his own and subsequent generations of Russians.

Committed to preserving the principle of autocracy, Nicholas prevented the Russian monarchy from exhibiting the dynamic qualities it had shown under predecessors such as Peter I and ALEXANDER II. Nicholas was fearful that the slightest compromise with liberalism would weaken his regime, and indeed his grandfather Alexander II had been assassinated after enacting reforms such as the liberation of the serfs. Nevertheless, by refusing to work with leaders of liberal opinion who sought to strengthen the monarchy, he undermined all but the most reactionary of his loyal supporters. Thus, by 1905, moderate reform had become impossible and Nicholas was compelled to offer much more to revolutionaries in that year than had been requested by noblemen in 1894.

Yet Nicholas continued to resist the political concessions he had made under duress in 1905. As a result, the leaders of many political parties became critical of the constitutional monarchy. This was true especially in the Duma during World War I. Virtually all the deputies welcomed Nicholas's declaration of war and offered their loyalty to the tsar. However, as he interfered with the military leadership and prevented liberal deputies from organizing an autonomous war effort, he was increasingly seen as an obstacle to victory. In one dramatic case, a liberal deputy named Paul Miliukov rose on the Duma floor late in 1916 to summarize Nicholas's shortcomings. At the end of each point, he asked the same frustrated question: "Is this stupidity, or is this treason?" When Nicholas was overthrown in 1917 it was deputies from the Duma who formed a provisional government headed by ALEXANDER KERENSKY. Nicholas II had convinced too many political minds in Russia that monarchy was unsuitable for the country in the twentieth century.

Strickland

For Further Reading

Lievan, Dominic. *Nicholas II: Emperor of All the Russias.* London: John Murray, 1993.

Lincoln, Bruce W. *In War's Dark Shadow: The Russians before the Great War.* New York: Simon and Schuster, 1983.

Massie, Robert K. *Nicholas and Alexandra.* New York: Atheneum, 1967.

Warth, Robert D. *Nicholas II: The Life and Reign of Russia's Last Monarch.* Westport, Conn.: Praeger, 1997.

Nightingale, Florence

Pioneer of Modern Nursing
1820–1910

Life and Work

Inspired to improve health care in England and repulsed by the condition of British military hospitals during the Crimean War, Florence Nightingale created the modern nursing profession and, as a result, radically reduced the mortality of the sick and injured.

Born on May 12, 1820, in Florence, Italy, to a wealthy British family, Nightingale received an advanced and classical education and was expected to use that education as a way to attract a suitable husband. In 1837, however, she claimed that God had spoken her saying that she had a mission; thinking this mission was related to health, Nightingale dedicated herself to learning how to care for the sick. To this end, she attended, after 1850, the Institution of Protestant Deaconesses in Kaiserswerth, Germany.

Returning to Britain from Kaiserswerth in 1853, Nightingale took a position at London's Harley Street nursing home, where she made radical reforms in the care of the sick. While working there, she determined that the major fault of health care was the insufficient training of nurses.

In 1854, the Crimean War broke out between the Russian Empire and a coalition of British, French, and Turkish forces. Hearing about the appalling conditions of sick and injured British troops, Nightingale organized a unit of 38 female nurses and traveled to Scutari, Turkey. Finding the conditions abysmal, she used money brought from Britain to introduce new standards of hygiene and improved medical equipment. As a result, the mortality rate at the Scutari hospital declined from 42% to 2% between 1854 and 1855.

Nightingale became an instant celebrity. When she returned to London in 1856, however, she shunned all publicity and became a veritable hermit, advocating health care from her home. A testimonial fund was collected for her services in the Crimea, and in 1860 she used the money to establish the Nightingale School and Home for nurse training at St. Thomas Hospital in London. In 1857, Nightingale wrote *Notes on Matters Concerning the Health, Efficiency, and Hospital Administration of the British Army*, which comprehensively addressed military medical issues and procedures, and in 1859 followed it with *Notes on Nursing*. In 1907 she became the first woman to be given the British Order of Merit.

Nightingale died in London on August 13, 1910.

Legacy

Florence Nightingale's legacy rests on the improvements she made to the medical conditions of the British military and to her professionalization of nursing and the modernization of it through the application of hygiene. In addition, despite her retreat from public life after 1856, she became an example for women throughout the world.

The two books Nightingale completed following her service in the Crimean War combined empirical evidence and first-hand experience to advocate for strict hospital hygiene and attention to the needs of the sick. Prior to Nightingale, nursing had often been left to the untrained and indiffrent. Her establishment in 1860 of the nursing program at London's St. Thomas Hospital and at the Army Medical College institutionalized her hygienic and compassionate methods, whose impact is felt on a daily basis down to the present.

The formalization of nurses' training and improvement of sanitary conditions in medical and hospital settings that Nightingale instituted especially benefited the British military. Despite indifference, and sometimes outright opposition by the male-dominated military establishment, her efforts to improve medical care in the military improved the plight of British soldiers across the globe. After her return, in 1858, her ideas were instituted in British military efforts in India during the Indian Mutiny (1857–58). The introduction of new standards in military medical care eventually led, in 1868, to the establishment of the Sanitary Department in the India Office.

In addition, at a time when women rarely gained an extensive education, rarely avoided marriage, and rarely engaged in a public role in society, Nightingale stretched the tolerance for women in charitable roles and made some forms of professional activity for women acceptable. The link of rigorous education, professional comportment, and a nurturing role that she demonstrated helped pave the way for the entry of women into the medical, teaching, and scientific professions later in the nineteenth century.

Del Testa

For Further Reading
Huxley, Elspeth. *Florence Nightingale*. New York: Putnam, 1975.
Woodham-Smith, Cecil. *Florence Nightingale, 1820–1910*. New York: McGraw-Hill, 1951.

WORLD EVENTS		NIGHTINGALE'S LIFE
Congress of Vienna reorganizes Europe	1815	
	1820	Florence Nightingale is born
	1837	Nightingale receives instructions from God
	1854	Nightingale travels to Turkey as nurse in Crimean War
	1856	Nightingale returns to Britain
	1857	Nightingale writes *Notes on Matters Concerning the Health, Efficiency, and Hospital Administration of the British Army*
	1859	Nightingale writes *Notes on Nursing*
	1860	Nightingale institutes nursing programs at two health facilities
Germany is united	1871	
Russo-Japanese War	1905	
	1907	Nightingale receives British Order of Merit
	1910	Nightingale dies
World War I	1914–18	

Nkrumah, Kwame

Leader of Ghana
1909–1972

Life and Work

Kwame Nkrumah established the model for new African states by leading Ghana's pioneering independence movement in the 1950s and championing Pan-Africanism.

Nkrumah was born on September 21, 1909, in the British Gold Coast Colony of West Africa. His father, a goldsmith, and his mother, a rice trader, provided their precocious son with an education. Nkrumah excelled in school and, in 1926, began university training at Achimota College, graduating in 1930. In 1935 he traveled to the United States and attended university in Pennsylvania, encountering the ideas of American black nationalists such as W. E. B. Du Bois and Marcus Garvey. In 1945 Nkrumah moved to Britain, where he organized the Fifth Pan-African Congress and began studies at the London School of Economics.

Returning to the Gold Coast in 1947, Nkrumah became the general secretary of the United Gold Coast Convention, a party founded to demand self-rule from Britain; he broke with it the following year and formed the more radical Convention People's Party (CPP) in 1949. Demands for independence became more strident, and when Nkrumah was arrested by the British in 1950 he became a popular hero. The CPP won the 1951 British-organized elections, and in 1952 Nkrumah was appointed prime minister. In 1957 he led the Gold Coast to independence, renaming it Ghana after an eleventh-century West African kingdom. The people of Ghana, by a 1960 popular vote, established the country as a republic and elected Nkrumah its president.

As leader of the first sub-Saharan colonial territory to gain independence, Nkrumah sought to modernize the economy through public works, including a hydroelectric dam on the Volta River. Nkrumah also supported liberation movements in all of Africa and Pan-Africanism, which stressed the solidarity of all peoples of the continent across borders drawn during the colonial era. In 1963 he participated in the founding of the Organization of African Unity (OAU).

Despite his international prestige, Nkrumah faced insurmountable problems at home. Frustrated by provincial opposition to centralized government control, Nkrumah undermined Ghana's parliamentary democracy by curbing free speech and political dissent, using the police and the army to break workers' strikes and creating a one-party state. He also appointed himself president for life and allowed the creation of a cult of personality centered on the glorification of his every word and deed.

By the mid-1960s political repression and worsening economic conditions tied to the decrease in the price of cocoa (the country's chief export) destroyed Nkrumah's popularity. The police and the army conspiring together overthrew Nkrumah's government on February 24, 1966. In exile in Guinea-Conakry, Nkrumah devoted his time to reading and writing a manual on guerrilla warfare. He died of cancer in Bucharest, Romania, on April 27, 1972.

Legacy

Kwame Nkrumah's legacy exemplifies both the achievement and failures of Africa in the post-colonial era. Ghana's example was important to other Africans, and its national unity within colonial boundaries set the model for future African states. Nkrumah's vision of Pan-African unity, though less than successful, remains a goal for some African diplomats who seek an end to regional wars and the creation of an African trading bloc similar to the European Union. His failure to achieve a stable democracy and real economic independence from the West was repeated in many other African countries.

Nkrumah fought for general African political and economic independence, with the result that within a few years of Ghana's independence, most of Africa had achieved at least some degree of political liberation from Western colonialism. Nkrumah's cultivation of a distinctly Ghanaian sense of national (as opposed to tribal or regional) identity established the model for other states, which maintained the boundaries drawn by colonial powers during the late nineteenth century.

Nkrumah met with less success promoting the concept of Pan-Africanism. He sought to cultivate a sense of African unity across the continent through the OAU, just as he had unified Ghana under one central government, with the ultimate goal of a "United States of Africa." Although African unity has proven difficult to achieve, African leaders such as JULIUS NYERERE and NELSON MANDELA have worked to mediate inter-African conflicts. However, the OAU has not been very effective in promoting its goal of an African economic community.

Nkrumah's undemocratic domestic policies highlight the problem in Africa of "Big Man" politics, which emphasizes loyalty to the often self-proclaimed great leader in place of adherence to the rule of law and the constitutional framework underpinning a democratic republic. Nkrumah, at first venerated as the hero of independence, was by 1966 vilified and blamed for all of Ghana's political and economic troubles. Successive regimes in Ghana, both military and civilian, have been unable to solve Ghana's economic problems. Other African leaders, such as Mobutu Sese Seko of Zaire, established similar dictatorships.

Nkrumah's reputation and influence rose somewhat when his warnings about neocolonialism (a term he coined) proved true. Although politically independent, many African states continue to be economically dependent on the West, exporting raw materials and importing finished goods from industrialized nations, while depending on the financial aid of rich donor nations for development projects, such as the Volta River project, of often dubious value to the local African population.

Lemoine

World Events		Nkrumah's Life
Russo-Japanese War	1905	
	1909	Kwame Nkrumah is born
World War I	1914–18	
Russian Revolution	1917	
Great Depression	1929–39	
World War II	1939–45	
Communist China is established	1949	Nkrumah founds Convention People's Party (CPP)
	1951	Nkrumah's CPP wins first Gold Coast general election
	1957	Nkrumah renames Gold Coast Ghana at independence
	1960	Ghana becomes republic; Nkrumah is elected first president
	1966	Nkrumah is overthrown in coup
Israel defeats Arab nations in Six-Day War	1967	
	1972	Nkrumah dies
Vietnam War ends	1975	

For Further Reading

Assensoh, A. B. *African Political Leadership: Jomo Kenyatta, Kwame Nkrumah, and Julius K. Nyerere.* Melbourne, Fla.: Krieger, 1998.

Birmingham, David. *Kwame Nkrumah: The Father of African Nationalism.* Rev. ed. Athens: Ohio University Press, 1990.

Nyerere, Julius

First Leader of Independent
Tanzania
1922–1999

Life and Work

Called *Mwalimu* ("teacher") by his fellow Tanzanians, Julius Nyerere forged a unified nation-state after Tanzania won independence from Great Britain in 1961. He combined Marxism with local tribal customs to create a unique form of African socialism.

Nyerere was born in March 1922, one of 26 children of Burito Nyerere, chief of a small tribe in the northwestern corner of the East African territory then called Tanganyika. At age 12, Nyerere was sent to boarding school and then to a secondary school in Tabora, where he flourished. In 1943 he graduated and went on to Makerere College in nearby Uganda. In 1949 he went to Edinburgh University in Scotland, the first Tanganyikan to attend a British university. Upon graduation in 1952, Nyerere returned to Tanganyika, where he immediately joined the independence movement.

In 1954 Nyerere, having become a leader of the independence movement, founded the Tanganyika African National Union (TANU) to demand self-government and liberation from Great Britain. Adopting an inclusive, nonracial platform, TANU achieved full independence for Tanganyika by December 1961. Nyerere was appointed the new nation's first

prime minister, only to resign several weeks later for reasons that he never made clear. Nyerere ran for president in Tanganyika's first post-independence elections, winning by a landslide in 1962. In 1964 Tanganyika and the nearby Indian Ocean island of Zanzibar merged to form the new state of Tanzania.

As president, Nyerere set out to construct a uniquely African economic system, based on the 1967 Arusha Declaration, which decreed government control of the economy. Agriculture was collectivized around the village unit and major industries nationalized in an effort to create a self-sufficient economy. These policies, however, were gradually abandoned by the 1990s because of worsening economic conditions stemming from high foreign debt and inefficiencies in the system of collectivized agriculture.

After leaving office in 1985, Nyerere led diplomatic missions as a mediator for peace in Central and East Africa, especially in Burundi. He also encouraged the creation of a multiparty political system to replace the benign one-party state he had led for 24 years. Nyerere died of leukemia on October 14, 1999, in London.

Legacy

Julius Nyerere created a peaceful and unified nation-state and provided a model for other African states of national and party leadership based on a clearly defined code of ethics and a flexible decision-making style.

As president, Nyerere united more than 120 tribes into a cohesive nation-state whose citizens identify themselves first as Tanzanians. Nyerere's egalitarian policies resulted in a more even income distribution than in many other post-colonial African states. Primary and secondary education and literacy improved, as well as basic health care and water supplies. Although Nyerere established Tanzania as a one-party state during his presidency, he also encouraged a broad-based party membership, fielding more than one candidate in parliamentary elections. Furthermore, Nyerere, unlike his counterparts in many other African states, left office willingly, allowing a peaceful transfer of power to his successor rather than establishing a dictatorship.

Nyerere's dedication to civil rights and racial equality for the whites and Asians who remained in Tanzania after independence influenced other African leaders. A key figure in the Pan-African movement and a founder of the Organization of

African Unity, Nyerere offered vital support to black majority movements in the white-dominated southern African states. Like Nyerere, NELSON MANDELA as the first black president of South Africa enacted a policy of reconciliation with the white minority population.

The failure of Nyerere's economic policies of self-sufficiency and collectivization taught Tanzanians that socialist methods did not always work in Africa. Individual incentive was unwittingly discouraged, and subsistence farmers were often moved against their will to collectivized villages with essential services not yet in place. Many Asian business owners left the country, and production of the major cash crops fell. Economic aid from donor countries was stolen or misused; a war waged against Idi Amin's Uganda in 1979 also strained Tanzania's resources to the breaking point. To his credit, Nyerere did not attempt to retain these economic policies when it appeared that they were not working.

Nyerere, unlike many other post-colonial African leaders, maintained the flexibility to adapt when necessary, which fostered stability in a region that has experienced civil war and chaotic conditions in recent years. In 1992, with Nyerere's encouragement, Tanzania shifted to a multiparty system.

Lemoine

WORLD EVENTS		NYERERE'S LIFE
Russian Revolution	1917	
	1922	Julius Nyerere is born
Great Depression	1929–39	
World War II	1939–45	
Communist China is established	1949	
	1954	Nyerere founds TANU
	1961	Tanganyika achieves independence; Nyerere is appointed its first prime minister
	1962	Nyerere resigns as prime minister and is later elected president
	1964	Tanganyika and Zanzibar merge to form Tanzania
Israel defeats Arab nations in Six-Day War	1967	
Vietnam War ends	1975	
	1985	Nyerere retires from presidency
Dissolution of Soviet Union	1991	
	1999	Nyerere dies

For Further Reading

Assensoh, A. B. *African Political Leadership: Jomo Kenyatta, Kwame Nyerere, and Julius K. Nyerere.* Melbourne, Fla.: Krieger, 1998.

Graham, Shirley. *Julius K. Nyerere: Teacher of Africa.* New York: Messner, 1975.

Osei Bonsu

Ruler of African Asante Kingdom
c. 1779–1824

WORLD EVENTS		OSEI BONSU'S LIFE
United States declares independence	1776	
	c. 1779	Osei Bonsu is born
French Revolution begins	1789	
	1800	Osei Bonsu assumes throne
	1806–16	Osei Bonsu leads battles against Fante
Latin American independence movement begins	1811	
Congress of Vienna reorganizes Europe	1815	
	1824	Osei Bonsu defeats British in Battle of Nsamankow; Osei Bonsu dies
Germany is united	1871	

Life and Work

The greatest of the Asante warrior-kings, Osei Bonsu defeated the British in a key battle that forestalled British domination of the Gold Coast of West Africa for several decades.

Osei Bonsu was born Osei Asibe about 1779, in the West African Asante Empire, roughly corresponding to present-day Ghana. Asante possessed a considerable amount of wealth in gold, which made it a desirable trading partner for European merchants on the coast. Osei Asibe succeeded his eldest brother Osei Kwame (who was overthrown because he converted to Islam) in 1800, acceding to the Golden Stool, the sacred symbol of Asante rule, and changing his name to Osei Tutu Kwame. He first crushed a rebellion by Muslim subjects in the northwest who wanted to reinstall the pro-Muslim Osei Kwame. After his victory, Osei Bonsu tolerated the Muslims, appointing some as advisors, and followed a similar policy of alternating military force with conciliatory diplomacy in his relations with other African states and with the British.

The next conflict began in 1806 with the Fante, who controlled coastal territory. The Fante wanted to profit from the trade between the British and the then-interior state of Asante by acting as middlemen. The Fante provoked war with the Asante by harboring two tribal leaders who had broken Asante laws and had fled the kingdom to escape justice. Osei Bonsu himself led a disciplined and highly trained army of possibly up to 200,000 men into several battles (one of which involved the British at their trading fort on the coast) that resulted in total defeat of the Fante by 1816. It was at this point that he adopted the name Bonsu, meaning "whale," or "king of the ocean."

After absorbing the Fante state into the Asante Empire, Osei Bonsu reluctantly went to war with the British because they had repudiated a treaty signed in 1817 that had recognized Asante sovereignty over coastal areas where British merchants had established fortress trading stations. The British also provoked the Asante by contemptuously rejecting the many overtures of peace Osei Bonsu had offered. In 1824, in a campaign characterized by British arrogance and incompetence (British troops received boxes of macaroni rather than the ammunition they were expecting), Osei Bonsu defeated a British force in the Battle of Nsamankow, in which the British commander was killed. The Asante did not immediately follow up on this victory because Osei Bonsu died shortly after the battle.

Legacy

Osei Bonsu maintained a strong centralized state and promoted a peaceful trading relationship with the British. Although he prevented the immediate conquest of the region by the British, he could not prevent the eventual victory of the British later in the nineteenth century.

During his reign Osei Bonsu put down rebellions, conquered nearby states, and created an efficient, centralized bureaucracy and communication system to make Asante the most powerful state in West Africa in the early nineteenth century. His conciliatory policy also promoted peace in previously rebellious territories, especially the Muslim northwest. As a result, Islam extended its influence in the Asante kingdom. Osei Bonsu also expressed interest in Western education and architecture, commissioning a "Palace of Culture" modeled on English architecture. Future rulers followed his policies, which made possible Asante resistance to the growing power of the British on the coast.

Osei Bonsu's defeat of British forces in 1824 kept Great Britain from extending its African imperial territory in the Gold Coast region for another 75 years. Yet his early victory may have led to the idea that improvements in military technology were not needed. Asante's strength as an imperial state enabled it to resist conquest by the British, but its lack of industrialization and development of military technology made the empire no match for the increasingly industrialized British. By the end of the nineteenth century the British were employing prototype machine guns, while the Asante still used the same flintlock muskets their ancestors had used against the British generations earlier. In 1902 Asante was declared a British colony.

Lemoine

For Further Reading
Edgerton, Robert B. *The Fall of the Asante Empire: The Hundred-Year War for Africa's Gold Coast.* New York: Free Press, 1995.

Otto I

Founder of the Holy Roman Empire
912–973

Life and Work

Otto I (Otto the Great) restored unity to the eastern half of the Carolingian Empire after more than a century of disunity. The new Holy Roman Empire that he created brought Germany into close contact with the medieval papacy.

Otto was born in 912 in Saxony, one of five German duchies that had been part of the Carolingian Empire of CHARLEMAGNE (r. 771–814). His father, Henry the Fowler, had been named king over these duchies only with the greatest difficulty and lacked the power to integrate them into a centralized monarchy. When Otto succeeded him in 936, he too was faced with a divisive political situation. The following year a revolt broke out in Bavaria, which Otto put down quickly; however, others soon followed. Most were led by dukes who hoped to retain control over their territories. In 953 even Otto's own son, Liudolf, revolted but was forced to surrender the following year.

These civil wars ended just in time to allow Otto to prepare for a foreign war in the east. In 955 the Hungarians invaded Germany and threatened to destroy it. Otto, having recovered from Liudolf's revolt with remarkable speed, led an army to meet them; at the Battle of Lechfeld near Augsburg, he led the charge

that brought victory. This, combined with campaigns against the Slavs in Poland, secured Germany's eastern border from further attack.

Italy was another theater for battle. In 951 its deposed Queen Adelaide sent an appeal to Otto for support in restoring her to the throne. Otto responded swiftly by crossing the Alps and overthrowing Adelaide's tormentor, a usurper named Berengar. As a reward, Adelaide married Otto, thus making him king of Italy as well as of Germany. Once the newlyweds had returned to the north, however, Berengar again usurped the throne, provoking another invasion in 961. Having settled the conflict decisively by 962, Otto was crowned Holy Roman Emperor by Pope John XII in Rome.

The remaining decade of Otto's life was occupied mainly by efforts to consolidate the empire and obtain recognition for it from the powerful Byzantine emperor in Constantinople. A series of minor military clashes between the two Christian powers was settled in 972 when Otto's son Otto II married a Byzantine princess.

Having recovered a large part of the Carolingian inheritance, Otto died in 973.

Legacy

The creation of the Holy Roman Empire under Otto I left a powerful German monarchy that would influence European politics and religion for centuries.

From an early age Otto's goal had been to restore the empire that Charlemagne had established in 800, which had all but disappeared in the wake of the Treaty of Verdun of 843. By reuniting its eastern duchies and obtaining the imperial crown from the Pope, Otto revived a Roman Catholic imperial vision for medieval Western Europe.

The Holy Roman Empire thereafter relied upon the Church to maintain political order. The civil wars of Otto's time led his successors to favor bishops rather than dukes in administering the realm. This offered the German bishops more influence in state affairs, but it also assigned the emperors a greater role in investing them with their office. This intrusion of secular power into Church affairs ultimately provoked the eleventh-century Investiture Controversy, a struggle by Pope Gregory VII against Emperor Henry IV to ban the lay investiture of bishops. Henry's humiliating submission to the Pope, symbolized by his

famous journey to Canossa in 1077 seeking forgiveness, revealed the emperor's political dependence upon the papacy.

The specifically German character of the Holy Roman Empire also influenced and sometimes complicated diplomacy in later years. Emperors were expected to serve the interests of the German princes, but many such as FREDERICK I followed Otto's example by pursuing conquests in Italy. Like the issue of lay investiture, this foreign policy commitment often served to aggravate relations with the papacy. Nevertheless, the Church continued to look to the empire as its secular patron. In the sixteenth century Emperor CHARLES V would use his resources in an unsuccessful struggle against the Protestant Reformation. Although finally dissolved by NAPOLÉON I (Napoléon Bonaparte) in 1806, the Holy Roman Empire would live on in the memory of Germans who supported the creation of a second German Empire in 1871 under OTTO VON BISMARCK.

Strickland

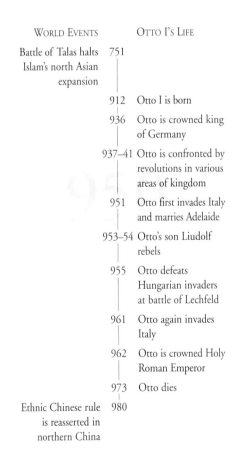

WORLD EVENTS		OTTO I'S LIFE
Battle of Talas halts Islam's north Asian expansion	751	
	912	Otto I is born
	936	Otto is crowned king of Germany
	937–41	Otto is confronted by revolutions in various areas of kingdom
	951	Otto first invades Italy and marries Adelaide
	953–54	Otto's son Liudolf rebels
	955	Otto defeats Hungarian invaders at battle of Lechfeld
	961	Otto again invades Italy
	962	Otto is crowned Holy Roman Emperor
	973	Otto dies
Ethnic Chinese rule is reasserted in northern China	980	

For Further Reading

Baum, Franz H. *Medieval Civilization in Germany, 800–1273.* New York: Praeger, 1969.

Leyser, Karl. *Rule and Conflict in Early Medieval Society: Ottonian Saxony.* London: E. Arnold, 1979.

Reuter, Timothy. *Germany in the Early Middle Ages, c. 800–1056.* London: Longman, 1991.

Owen, Robert

Utopian Visionary
1771–1858

Life and Work

Robert Owen, a successful factory owner himself, attacked the exploitation of workers and established model factory communities.

Owen was born in 1771 in Newtown, England. The son of a minor artisan, he began working in a London factory as a boy and by 1788 had amassed sufficient capital to start his own enterprise in the burgeoning factory town of Manchester. He chose cotton spinning because this industry was dramatically expanding due in part to the invention of the steam engine. Owen's venture in Manchester ultimately failed, and he found employment with a large firm, the Chorlton Twist Company, that, impressed by his management skills and ambition, sent him to manage its interests in the town of New Lanark, Scotland. In 1799, he found himself in a position to purchase the cotton mills and in 1813 formed a partnership with the renowned utilitarian philosopher Jeremy Bentham.

By this time Owen had become highly critical of the factory system as it was emerging in indus-

trial Britain. Drawing upon the traditions of Enlightenment rationalism and Christian charity, he wrote a book, *A New View of Society*, in 1813 that envisioned an industrial society united by cooperation rather than exploitation. He sought to apply this vision to his factories in New Lanark—shortening hours, building housing, providing education, and establishing stores that offered subsidized goods at prices that the workers could afford. The experiment was so novel in a society where the competitive practices of economic liberalism predominated that the community attracted thousands of curious visitors every year. Owen used his considerable fortune to establish similar factory communities elsewhere, most notably at New Harmony, Indiana. He also toured extensively, propagating his model of cooperative capitalism in public lectures. In 1833 he formed the Grand National Consolidated Trades Union, the first labor union in England.

Despite his energy and wealth, however, none of his communities flourished and most followed the example of New Lanark, which failed in 1829. Nevertheless, Owen remained optimistic that his vision would some day triumph. He died in 1858.

Legacy

Robert Owen established a vital movement that sought to redress the problems of England's early industrial society. Although his projects proved impractical, his vision of social justice provided inspiration to the socialist movement of the nineteenth century.

Owen is often described by historians as a utopian thinker. Drawing upon Thomas More's visionary book *Utopia* from the sixteenth century, he and contemporaries such as Charles Fourier and Henri Saint-Simon objected to the demeaning and repressive effects of the capitalistic free market on workers. Owen himself had grown up in the home of an artisan, and the decline of a system of manufacturing in which the family works together at home seemed to him a baneful and unnecessary effect of industrialization. Referring vaguely to the teaching of the New Testament about loving one's neighbor and sharing property in common, Owen elaborated a mostly rationalistic argument for reorganizing the factory system around the principle of mutual benefits among the employers and

the employed. The many books and pamphlets he left behind, however, lacked a sophisticated analysis of the economic problems of capitalism and the policies required to solve them. His thought possessed a strong idealism that frequently took the place of clarity; in Bentham's words, it "begins in vapour and ends in smoke." His ideas therefore quickly fell into disuse, and only at the end of the century was there a mild revival of interest in them among the socialistic English Fabians.

If Owen's writings had little long-term influence, his example profoundly affected the generations of socialists who followed him. He had been one of the first intellectuals to address the injustices arising from industrial capitalism. His efforts to understand these injustices and to mobilize other factory owners, the government, and workers themselves to eliminate them inspired many contemporaries. The United States Congress, for instance, asked him to address a joint session in 1829. By the middle of the nineteenth century, the Owenite movement had begun to merge into the socialist movement that came finally to be dominated by the followers of Karl Marx. Marx, who considered himself a "scientific socialist" by virtue of his devotion to empirical research, felt only contempt for the utopian visionary. But Marx's chief collaborator, Friedrich Engels, stated in the *Communist Manifesto* (1848) that Owenite utopianism was "full of the most valuable materials for the enlightenment of the working class."

Strickland

World Events		Owen's Life
English seize Calcutta	1690	
	1771	Robert Owen is born
United States declares independence	1776	
	1788	Owen launches Manchester factory
French Revolution begins	1789	
	1799	Owen purchases cotton mills in New Lanark
Latin American independence movement begins	1811	
	1813	Owen completes *A New Vision of Society*
Congress of Vienna reorganizes Europe	1815	
	1829	Collapse of New Lanark
	1833	Owen forms Grand National Consolidated Trades Union
	1858	Owen dies
Germany is united	1871	

For Further Reading

Cole, G. D. H. *The Life of Robert Owen.* 3rd. ed. London: F. Cass, 1965.

Harrison, J. F. C. *Quest for the New Moral World: Robert Owen and the Owenites in Britain and America.* New York: Scribner's, 1969.

Royal, Edward. *Robert Owen and the Commencement of the Millennium: A Study of the Harmony Community.* Manchester, England: Manchester University Press, 1998.

Pachacuti Inca Yupanqui

Founder of the Incan Empire
c. 1408–c. 1474

Life and Work

Pachacuti Inca Yupanqui prevented the collapse of the tiny Incan state, subsequently expanded the Incan Empire over much of western South America, and prepared an effective administrative structure for that vast empire.

Very little is known of Pachacuti's early life. He was born the disfavored son of Inca Virococha, an Incan king who had begun the process of securing the isolated and relatively backward Incan people against unfriendly neighbors. As a prince, Pachacuti would have attended a special palace school, studying the Incan language, religion, and military arts for at least four years. He also would have studied the regional accounting system based on the *quipu*, a kind of string abacus and ledger combined.

Pachacuti established himself through a particularly brave and perhaps foolhardy resistance against apparently unbeatable odds. Throughout the fourteenth and fifteenth centuries, interethnic warfare in the Andes had intensified greatly, probably over access to scarce arable land and mineral resources for an expanding population. In this tense environment, Pachacuti's father, who controlled only an area around Cuzco (in modern Peru), sought allies and protection against the surrounding tribes. Although the Inca succeeded in forging bonds with several neighboring groups, the aggressive Chanca people began conducting raids against the Inca. In 1438, having waited until Virococha was elderly, the Chanca tribe attacked Cuzco from the north, and Virococha and his designated heir, Inca Urcon, fled in the face of certain defeat. Along with two old generals, Vicaquirau and Maita, Pachacuti rallied the remaining Incan troops and called for the aid of the Incas' allies, beating the Chanca in a fantastic battle in which, according to legend, even the stones became Incan soldiers. With the heir, his brother, in disgrace, Pachacuti declared himself king.

Over the next 25 years, Pachacuti embarked on a series of strategic conquests, taking a swath of land equal to the southern half of modern Ecuador and the northern third of modern Bolivia. In 1463, Pachacuti turned over military command to his son, TOPA INCA YUPANQUI, and Topa extended the empire even farther north and south, well into modern Ecuador and throughout Bolivia and northern Chile. For his part, Pachacuti turned his attention to perfecting the governance of the Incan Empire, ensuring a regular and predictable administration, extensive transportation infrastructure and commercial regulation, and a way for conquered peoples, even those who were not of Incan descent, to wield some power.

Pachacuti turned over his kingship to his son Topa in 1471 so he could pursue a life of contemplation. He died shortly after his abdication.

Legacy

Pachacuti Inca Yupanqui preserved the Incan people against destruction and expanded the empire across western South America, ensuring a vibrant regional empire and strong ethnic identity among indigenous peoples that endures to this day.

After defeating the Chanca and expanding the Incan domain, Pachacuti worked hard to give the empire an imperial infrastructure, the most important component of which was an effective administration. Under Pachacuti, the Inca organized all of the empire's peoples, thus ensuring that the Inca had not only an effective accounting of all of the members of the empire but also a ready source of labor and low-level positions of responsibility in which the leaders of conquered peoples could serve. The manipulation of resources made the Inca a powerful nation and allowed them to take care of the public welfare of millions in a way that had not been possible before.

Although brutal to those groups who resisted the imposition of Incan administration or turned against the Inca once they were included in the empire, the Inca generally adopted people into the empire rather than enslaving people to imperial will. In addition, Pachacuti recognized the limits and needs of administration, setting geographical limits to imperial expansion and forbidding his troops from pillaging and plundering (traditional "rights" enjoyed by victorious forces). Indeed, he ordered the execution of one of his own sons who had returned with the wealth of conquered peoples after a military campaign. To make local administration particularly effective, Pachacuti ordered that *curacas*, non-Incan leaders, had to receive training in the Incan capital in Cuzco in the national language, Quechua, thus encouraging the gradual "Incanization" of the empire's leadership and elite. This cultivated unity ensured at least some effective resistance to aggressive outside groups, such as the Spanish, and ensured an enduring regional identity in which many indigenous peoples still take pride.

Del Testa

WORLD EVENTS		PACHACUTI'S LIFE
Ming Dynasty reasserts Chinese control of China	1368	
	c. 1408	Pachacuti is born
	1438	Pachacuti successfully defends Cuzco, becomes Incan king
	1438–63	Pachacuti expands Incan empire
Ottoman Empire conquers Constantinople	1453	
	1463	Pachacuti turns over Incan military to son, Topa
	1471	Pachacuti turns over empire to Topa
	c. 1474	Pachacuti dies
Columbus sails to Americas	1492	

For Further Reading

Hyams, Edward, and George Ordish. *The Last of the Incas: The Rise and Fall of an American Empire.* New York: Simon & Schuster, 1963.

Rostworowski de Diez Canseco, Maria. *History of the Inca Realm.* Translated by Harry B. Iceland. New York: Cambridge University Press, 1999.

Pankhurst, Emmeline

Leader of Women's Suffrage
Movement in Great Britain
1858–1928

Life and Work

Emmeline Pankhurst led the suffrage movement in Great Britain, inspiring other women's rights movements in Europe and the United States.

Emmeline Pankhurst (née Goulden) was born on July 14, 1858, in Manchester, England, the daughter of anti-slavery and reform-minded parents. While attending boarding school in Manchester, she began to take part in the movement for women's suffrage. In 1879 Goulden married Richard Marsden Pankhurst, an attorney who supported women's rights. While starting a family and struggling to support it, Richard Pankhurst remained active in the movement, promoting the Married Women's Property Bill of

1882 giving wives the right to control their own income. In 1889 the Pankhursts formed the Women's Franchise League to demand the right of women to vote in local elections

In 1903 Pankhurst, enlisting the support of her daughter Christabel (1880–1958), founded the Women's Social and Political Union (WSPU), whose motto was "Deeds, Not Words." The WSPU gained attention by staging protests at Liberal Party gatherings and opening-day sessions of Parliament. In 1906 Pankhurst was arrested following a demonstration, a pattern often repeated in the years to follow.

By 1909 Pankhurst, daughter Christabel, and the WSPU, frustrated at the lack of reform, resorted to acts of violence, prompting more arrests, hunger strikes in jail, and forced feeding. Pankhurst also embarked on foreign tours to raise money for the cause, including several trips to the United States. In 1912 Pankhurst was arrested for breaking a window in the prime minister's residence and sentenced to nine months in prison. However, she was soon released after beginning a hunger strike and violently resisting forced feeding. She and Christabel continued attacks against public and private property. Arrested again, Pankhurst nearly died during another hunger strike.

Pankhurst suspended her activities with the outbreak of World War I in 1914, devoting her energies to the war effort. In 1916, in recognition of women's support of the war effort, the British Parliament granted women over 30 the right to vote. In 1918 Pankhurst moved to Canada; she campaigned against venereal disease; she returned to Great Britain in 1926. In 1928 Parliament lowered the voting age to 21, the same age at which men were qualified to vote. Pankhurst died not long after the passage of the second enfranchisement bill, on June 14, 1928, while campaigning for a seat in Parliament.

Legacy

Emmeline Pankhurst's single-minded dedication breathed new life into the cause of women's suffrage in Great Britain and elsewhere. Her militancy was imitated by later generations of women's rights activists.

Pankhurst inspired movements in other countries, especially the United States. National Woman's Party founder Alice Paul, who was influenced by Pankhurst while studying in England, was a leading advocate of her aggressive style of protest in the United States. Pankhurst

herself spoke to large groups in American cities such as Boston and New York, spurring efforts to extend the franchise to women in the individual states and to lobby Congress to pass a constitutional amendment to extend the vote to all women in the United States. American women gained the franchise through the Nineteenth Amendment, which took effect in 1920. By 1945, nearly all European and North American countries, along with Australia and New Zealand, had granted women the right to vote.

Although Pankhurst's militant and sometimes violent tactics also engendered fear and hostility toward the women's rights movement, many of the feminists who followed in her footsteps employed her tactics of civil disobedience. The Women's Liberation Movement that emerged in the 1960s in Europe and North America used many imaginative militant strategies, such as street demonstrations, to attract public attention.

Like Pankhurst, later feminists framed their demands within the context of the political and legislative process. Politicians, learned to cultivate the women's vote by promoting issues important to women, such as equal pay, abortion rights, and the punishment of sexual harassment. Winning the vote also allowed women to run for elective positions. Women now serve at every level of government in many countries. In Great Britain, MARGARET THATCHER became the first woman prime minister in 1979. However, as a member of the Conservative Party, Thatcher also reduced funding for social programs designed to help women become more self-supporting.

Lemoine

WORLD EVENTS		PANKHURST'S LIFE
Congress of Vienna reorganizes Europe	1815	
	1858	Emmeline Goulden is born
Germany is united	1871	
	1879	Emmeline Goulden marries Richard Pankhurst
	1903	Pankhurst founds Women's Social and Political Union
Russo-Japanese War	1905	
	1912	Pankhurst is arrested, and begins hunger strike in jail
World War I	1914–18	Pankhurst suspends suffrage activity during WWI
	1916	Britain grants suffrage to women over 30
Russian Revolution	1917	
	1928	Women granted full and equal suffrage in Great Britain; Pankhurst dies
Great Depression	1929–39	

For Further Reading
Kamm, Josephine. *The Story of Emmeline Pankhurst.* New York: Meredith Press, 1961.
Wingerden, Sophia A. *The Women's Suffrage Movement in Britain, 1866–1928.* New York: St. Martin's Press, 1999.

Pericles

Ruler of Ancient Athens
c. 495–429 B.C.

Life and Work

Pericles ruled Athens during a time of political division, imperial expansion, and impending war. Nevertheless, he succeeded in establishing one of the most creative and dynamic civilizations of the ancient world.

In the fifth century before Christ, Athens was rivaled only by Sparta in its leadership of Hellenic Greece. Born around 495 B.C., Pericles came from a family without substantial wealth. Nevertheless, he was able to obtain a very liberal education under the tutoring of leading Sophist philosophers such as Anaxagoras. Especially important in his childhood training was the art of rhetoric, which would become crucial to his political career.

Pericles also distinguished himself in the Athenian military. Athens was expanding its empire, and the ambitious Pericles won wide popularity as a naval commander. He realized that to rise to power in Athens he would need to overthrow the power of the city's oligarchs, who were entrenched in an assembly called the Areopagus. His principal opponent in this was a man named Cimon who, in addition to favoring an elite system of rule, sought to maintain close military ties with Sparta. Pericles thus decided to use democracy and an expansionist foreign policy to gain a political base. Leading a popular campaign against Cimon and the power of the Areopagus, he was able in 461 to defeat his rivals and establish a popular dictatorship.

Once in power, Pericles launched a program of city construction designed to express patriotism and elevate Athenian power. The city's sacred hill of temples, the Acropolis, had been burned to the ground during the Persian Wars (500–449). Pericles rebuilt a number of temples and added new ones. The greatest of them all was the Parthenon, a temple dedicated to Athena, the city's patron goddess, built at the summit of the Acropolis by 438.

Pericles also promoted the expansion of the empire, knowing that ultimately this would bring Athens into conflict with Sparta. He believed, however, that as long as Athens dominated the large alliance of Greek cities called the Delian League, which included Sparta, Athenian power would remain secure. His advocacy of establishing overseas colonies, however, brought the rivalry with Sparta to a crisis. When war finally came in 431, he was convinced that Athenian arms would prevail.

Instead of ending in a quick Athenian victory, however, the Peloponnesian War (431–404) dragged on for 27 years. At first, Pericles rallied Athenians around a patriotic devotion to their city. Before long, however, the armies of both sides succumbed to starvation and disease. Such was the fate of Pericles himself, who in 429 perished along with a third of the Athenian population during an outbreak of the plague.

Legacy

For twenty five years after the death of Pericles, Athens would continue fighting the destructive war that he had done much to provoke. Nevertheless, his rule of Athens is remembered by historians for positive contributions to democracy and high culture.

The Peloponnesian War was the most traumatic event in the history of Hellenic Greece. After defending themselves in a mutual alliance against the mighty Persian Empire, Athens and Sparta dissipated their wealth and power. A turning point in the war came when the Athenians lost their fleet near the Italian port city of Syracuse. When Persia finally entered on the side of Sparta, Athens was forced to accept a humiliating peace. The war that Pericles had invited thus destroyed Athenian diplomatic leadership.

Such was not the case in politics. While the Peloponnesian War caused the civil order created by Pericles to crumble, in subsequent centuries Western civilization would look back to Periclean Athens as a model of enlightened government. By the time the Roman republic was transformed by JULIUS CAESAR, for instance, it had absorbed much that Greece and its successor Hellenistic states had to offer, including a belief that civic loyalty is one of the highest of human virtues. In modern times, Pericles's challenge to oligarchic elites and his belief that humanity is free to shape the political order without reference to the divine order would appeal to democratic politicians and proponents of secularized statecraft.

In the sphere of culture Pericles's rule established an example of civic consciousness that had lasting consequences. The Parthenon, completed in 432 B.C., was only the most beautiful of many temples on the Acropolis that celebrated civic identity. In subsequent centuries its fluted Doric columns and triangular pediments would be reproduced in countless examples of state architecture from imperial Rome to revolutionary France. The other arts of Athens were less directly influenced by the political ideals of Pericles, but contemporary Athenian playwrights such as Aristophanes, Aeschylus, Sophocles, and Euripides frequently employed civic themes in their works. These had a direct influence upon European authors such as William Shakespeare. Perhaps the most memorable monument to the political vision of Pericles was left by Thucydides in his *History of the Peloponnesian War*. Although bitterly disillusioned by the war, he eloquently acknowledged the high ideals of Periclean statecraft in a famous account of Pericles's funeral oration. Delivered to the survivors of the first wave of casualties, its confidence in the future example of Athens is unmistakable. Athenians do not "copy the laws of neighboring states," Pericles announced bravely, "we are rather a pattern to others."

Strickland

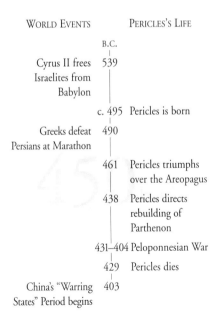

World Events		Pericles's Life
	B.C.	
Cyrus II frees Israelites from Babylon	539	
	c. 495	Pericles is born
Greeks defeat Persians at Marathon	490	
	461	Pericles triumphs over the Areopagus
	438	Pericles directs rebuilding of Parthenon
	431–404	Peloponnesian War
	429	Pericles dies
China's "Warring States" Period begins	403	

For Further Reading

Buckley, Terry. *Aspects of Greek History, 750–323*. London: Routledge, 1996.

Kagan, Donald. *Pericles of Athens and the Birth of Athenian Democracy*. New York: Macmillan, 1991.

Podlecki, Anthony J. *Pericles and His Circle*. London: Routledge, 1998.

Perón, Eva Duarte de

Argentinean Populist
1919–1952

Life and Work

Eva Duarte de Perón (née Maria Eva Duarte) rose from a humble background to become one of Argentina's most notable political figures. She worked to build a stable political order and to improve the lives of the poor.

Perón was born on May 7, 1919, in the village of Los Toldos, Argentina. Her parents were unmarried at the time, and she was prevented from taking the name of her respected father. Instead, she lived with a poor mother who, according to a humiliating rumor, had been traded to her landowning father for a horse and a buggy. Perón suffered from the social stigma attached to her birth and, in 1935, decided to leave her home and move to Buenos Aires to pursue a career as an actress. It was at this time that she received the affectionate name Evita.

World Events		Perón's Life
Russian Revolution	1917	
	1919	Eva Duarte de Perón (née Maria Eva Duarte) is born
Great Depression	1929–39	
	1935	Duarte moves to Buenos Aires to pursue acting career
World War II	1939–45	
	1945	Duarte marries Juan Perón
	1946	Juan Perón becomes president
	1947	Eva Perón is instrumental in obtaining the vote for women
Communist China is established	1949	Eva Perón forms Perónista Feminist Party
	1952	Eva Perón dies
Israel defeats Arab nations in Six-Day War	1967	

In 1944 she attended a benefit for earthquake victims where she met Colonel Juan Perón, Argentina's secretary of labor and social affairs. She soon became his mistress. In 1945 the populist Juan Perón was arrested by leaders of the military but was released after a massive show of support by workers known as the "shirtless ones." In the aftermath of this experience, Juan and Eva were married. With support for Juan at an all-time high, he was able to win the presidential elections in 1946. As his wife, Eva now possessed a respected name and an opportunity to enter Argentina's political life.

Perón's activities after 1946 included support for her husband in the face of further conspiracies, political mobilization, and relief for the nation's poor. She unwaveringly supported her husband and rallied workers behind him. As a result, she was despised by military elites and, when a plan to have her named vice president in 1951 was announced, was forced by them to withdraw. Nevertheless, she continued to offer service to the Perónist Party through unofficial channels. In part through her urging, for instance, women were given the right to vote in 1947, and two years later formed the Perónista Feminist Party. She often made visits to factories and working-class neighborhoods to rally the poor. Her most famous achievements, in fact, concerned the "shirtless ones." She established an Eva Perón Foundation that grew to become a massive welfare organization offering extensive support.

Argentina's poor were the first to join her husband in grieving when cancer prematurely took her life on July 26, 1952.

Legacy

Eva Duarte de Perón's work directly helped to improve the lives of thousands of common Argentineans, and her energy and charisma galvanized support for her husband and strengthened her husband's regime. To this day, Perónism and its ideas are powerful political forces in Argentina and Latin America.

Argentina lacked a stable political system during the Great Depression (1929–39) and World War II (1939–45). Juan Perón himself had contributed to this instability by participating in military coups in 1930 and 1943. After winning the elections of 1946, he sought to establish a stable and authoritarian political

system that would outlast his tenure as president. Eva Perón's origins among the poor and her indefatigable efforts to rally support for the Perónist regime enabled him and his successors to rule with greater self-confidence. He was forced to flee Argentina in 1955 after supporting a violent attack upon the Roman Catholic church, but his party survived and he was able to return to be reelected president in 1973. What is more, Perónism lived on beyond his death in 1974, offering an ideology that linked the interests of the state with those of the working class and its trade unions. Carlos Menem, who was elected president in 1989, declared himself a moderate Perónist. After a decade of military rule and human rights abuses in Argentina, Menem succeeded in reintroducing democracy and improving the economy during the 1990s.

Eva Perón's support for the poor had a more short-term effect. By the time of her death the foundation had overseen the construction of nearly 1,000 schools, hundreds of homes, and scores of hospitals for the needy. Nevertheless, many of these facilities fell into disrepair in the years that followed. The greatest obstacle to improving the living conditions of the poor were, after all, beyond its control. The Argentinean economy, which had been one of the wealthiest at the beginning of the twentieth century, experienced a continual decline that lasted into the 1990s. Nevertheless, memory of Evita among the Argentineans remained vivid and offered encouragement to successive generations of workers and underprivileged.

Strickland

For Further Reading
De Perón, Eva Duarte. *My Mission in Life.* Translated by Ethel Cherry. New York: Vantage Press, 1953.
Frazer, Nicholas. *Evita.* New York: Norton, 1991.
Ortiz, Alicia Dujovne. *Eva Peron.* Translated by Shawn Fields. New York: St. Martin's Press, 1996.

Peter I

Reformer of the Russian Empire
1672–1725

Life and Work

Peter I (Peter the Great) transformed the Russian Empire into a modern bureaucratic state.

Peter was born in 1672 in Moscow. He acceded to the throne in 1682 but was immediately challenged by a rival faction, including a sickly half-brother, Ivan, and an ambitious half-sister, Sophia. While the 10-year-old Peter helplessly looked on, these rivals had several of his supporters put to death. He was thereafter forced to reside in a village outside of Moscow; left to his own devices, he developed a passion for military organization and Western knowledge. Only in 1689 did his rivals finally fall from power, leaving him with sole authority.

A man of sharp intellect and great physical strength, Peter was committed to the expansion of Russia's military power. He was convinced that Western technology was essential for this, and so in 1696 he traveled under a pseudonym throughout Germany, the Netherlands, and England in search of practical knowledge about modern warfare and statecraft. Back in Russia he gave priority to military reforms. Between 1700 and 1721 Russia fought the Great Northern War against Sweden. Peter not only modernized and expanded the army during this time, but founded the Russian navy.

Civil reforms were enacted to facilitate military reforms. In 1717 Peter created a bureaucratic system of government organized into Colleges, which were then topped by a body called the Senate. In 1722 he established a system of state service called the Table of Ranks, whereby all governmental officials were able to obtain promotion according to talent rather than noble ancestry. Peter himself set a standard for state service by adopting the Western title of "emperor," a reform that symbolized his belief that the ruler is merely a servant (albeit the highest) of the state. In return, he expected complete devotion from his subjects. Effective limits were placed upon the freedoms of the nobility by the Table of Ranks, for instance, and the burdens on the peasantry were increased in 1718 with the introduction of a head tax.

Peter died in 1725, having transformed the Russian Empire.

Legacy

Peter I's impact upon history is difficult to underestimate. His reforms not only transformed the character of Russian life, they enabled subsequent generations of Russians to influence the development of European civilization.

Peter's military victories and administrative reforms were generally successful in elevating Russia's status within Europe. After defeating the Swedish army at Poltava in 1709, Russia acquired valuable new territories along the Baltic Sea that allowed it to expand trade with the West and put an end to centuries of isolation. It was here that, in 1703, Peter built a new capital named Saint Petersburg. For the next two centuries the city became Russia's "window on the West," providing a cultured, Western milieu for rulers such as CATHERINE II and artistic figures such as Aleksandr Pushkin, Fyodor Dostoevsky, and Rimsky-Korsakov. Peter also succeeded in enforcing the use of the Western system of recording dates since the birth of Christ rather than the creation of the world. Western dress and education were also imported. Peter's passion for Western manners was so strong, in fact, that he compelled his officials to have their beards shaved and their teeth inspected for cavities, sometimes by the emperor himself. By the time he died, Russia's destiny had been inseparably linked to Europe's.

Yet the methods he used to achieve his reforms were often brutal and in almost all cases impaired the ability of Russians to exercise political autonomy. During Peter's reign, Russian political life took a very different turn than it did in England, where the Glorious Revolution of 1688 placed power in the hands of Parliament. Peter's reign was more comparable to that of LOUIS XIV, but he extended royal absolutism far beyond the limits of his French contemporary. Inheriting the tradition of Muscovite autocracy from predecessors such as IVAN III, Peter regarded any limits upon the ruler' authority as a threat to the state. He thus treated potential rivals ruthlessly. For example, when his eldest son, Alexei, appeared to defy him in 1718 by withholding support for his reforms, he had him imprisoned, tortured, and killed.

In a decision even more fateful for Russian history, Peter prevented the Russian Orthodox church from replacing its patriarch in 1700, and then abolished the office altogether in 1721. In its place he established a body called the Holy Synod, which was designed in principle to increase the efficiency of church administration. In practice it subordinated the church to the state, preventing the Orthodox clergy from exercising autonomous leadership in Russia until 1917, when a much more repressive system of church–state relations was adopted by the Bolsheviks.

Strickland

For Further Reading

Anisimov, Evgenii V. *The Reforms of Peter the Great: Progress through Coercion in Russia.* Translated by John T. Alexander. Armonk, N.Y.: M. E. Sharpe, 1993.

Hughes, Lindsey. *Russia in the Age of Peter the Great.* New Haven, Conn.: Yale University Press, 1998.

Marshall, William. *Peter the Great.* London: Longman, 1996.

World Events		Peter I's Life
Ottoman dominance of Mediterranean ends	1571	
	1672	Peter I is born
	1682	Peter accedes to throne
Glorious Revolution in England	1688	
	1689	Peter assumes absolute authority
English seize Calcutta	1690	
	1700–21	Peter engages in Great Northern War against Sweden
	1703	Peter builds new capital, Saint Petersburg
	1722	Peter introduces Table of Ranks
	1725	Peter dies
United States declares independence	1776	

Philip II

King of Spain
1527–1598

Life and Work

At a time when Europe was divided by the Protestant Reformation, Philip II increased Spanish power and advanced the interests of the Roman Catholic church.

Philip was born in Valladolid, Spain, in 1527. His father was the illustrious Habsburg emperor CHARLES V, who ruled Germany, Spain, the Netherlands, parts of Italy, and Spanish America. With the exception of Germany, Philip inherited these territories when Charles retired in 1556. As Italy was claimed by the Valois king Henry II of France also, Philip found himself at war almost immediately. He was well served by the Spanish infantry at the Battle of St. Quentin in 1557, and in 1559 he dictated the Treaty of Cateau-Cambrésis, ending the long Habsburg–Valois Wars. Another military threat was posed by the Turks, who had begun to expand up the Balkan Peninsula. In 1560 they sunk a Spanish–Italian armada. In 1571, however, Philip financed another expedition that destroyed the Turkish fleet near Lepanto. This important battle signaled the beginning of the end of Turkish naval power in the Mediterranean.

Philip's military experiences in northern Europe were less successful. In 1566 Protestants went on a rampage in the Netherlands, destroy-

ing all of the Roman Catholic churches they found. Philip, deeply committed to Catholicism, sent an army under the ruthless duke of Alva to suppress the disorders. This only provoked greater resistance among the Dutch, and when Protestant England under ELIZABETH I began supporting the Protestant provinces north of Antwerp, Phillip lost effective control of them. Furious with England for its intervention and harried by privateers such as Sir Francis Drake (who in 1587 attacked the Spanish port of Cádiz), Philip sent his armada into the English Channel. When the armada arrived in 1588, however, unexpected storms and English harassment led to its near complete destruction. All hope for restoring Roman Catholicism in the Netherlands was now lost.

Philip's rule in Spain itself was a mixture of success and frustration. His vision of a deeply pious Roman Catholic nation was expressed in El Escorial, a grand palace with a cathedral built near Madrid, where the king's bedchamber was fitted with a window opening onto the altar. Philip also used the Spanish Inquisition begun by his great-grandmother ISABELLA I to repress religious dissent. He succeeded in putting down a revolt by Moriscos (converted Moors) in 1570, and in 1580 he expanded the Spain's territory by annexing Portugal. Despite such achievements, however, recurring bankruptcies threatened to undermine Spanish power during the last years of his reign.

At dawn on September 13, 1598, after an attack of gout that had left him bedridden for nearly two months, Philip died at El Escorial.

Legacy

Although Philip II built one of the greatest powers in contemporary Europe, his successors failed to prevent the decline of Spain during the following century.

Philip's wars established Spain as the dominant military power in Europe. The Spanish infantry was almost invincible, and though the armada of 1588 had been destroyed, Spanish naval power soon recovered. Philip's military commitments placed enormous burdens upon the state treasury, however. Shipments of silver and other forms of wealth from the New World proved insufficient to forestall the series of dangerous financial crises that occurred during his reign. What is more, his relative indifference to domestic commerce and manufacturing left

Spain economically weak in relation to emerging commercial powers such as England and the Netherlands. For its part, the Spanish aristocracy neglected new opportunities for investment, and the middle class remained small. Finally, his emphasis upon religious uniformity, while helping to protect the Roman Catholic church, fostered a climate of intellectual isolation. The result was a decline in Spanish influence and power during the seventeenth century. Philip's namesake Philip IV (r. 1622–65), for instance, failed to alter the character of the Spanish economy, and his renewal of war against the Netherlands and France greatly weakened the state. By the beginning of the eighteenth century, Spain had ceased to be a dominant power.

Philip also contributed unintentionally to growing hardships among the population of Spanish America. Large numbers of Amerindians had already been subjugated by Spanish conquerors under Charles V, but Philip's policies had a deep impact upon the organization of the colonial empire in later years. Philip's attitude about the treatment of Amerindians vacillated between the compassionate missionary views of BARTOLOMÉ DE LAS CASAS (1474–1566) and those of rapacious colonists who regarded the native population only as an instrument of enrichment. An Ordinance on Discoveries in 1573 banned further conquests and urged a policy of protection rather than exploitation, but it was not energetically enforced from Madrid. As a result, Amerindians continued to suffer for another two centuries at the hands of colonial administrators and settlers.

Strickland

WORLD EVENTS		PHILIP II'S LIFE
Mughal Empire rules in India	1526	
	1527	Philip II is born
	1556	Philip accedes to throne
	1559	Philip dictates terms of treaty of Cateau-Cambrésis
Ottoman dominance of Mediterranean ends	1571	Philip finances critical Battle of Lepanto against Turks
	1573	Philip signs Ordinance on Discoveries
	1580	Philip annexes Portugal
	1598	Philip dies
Glorious Revolution in England	1688	

For Further Reading

Kamen, Henry. *Philip of Spain.* New Haven, Conn.: Yale University Press, 1997.

Lynch, David. *The Spanish World in Crisis and Change, 1598–1700.* London: Blackwell, 1992.

Parker, Geoffrey. *The Grand Strategy of Philip II.* New Haven, Conn.: Yale University Press, 1998.

Pizarro, Francisco

Spanish Conqueror of Peru

c. 1470–1541

Life and Work

A distant cousin of HERNÁN CORTÉS, Francisco Pizarro conquered the Incas of Peru, expanding the Spanish overseas empire and contributing to the transformation of South American and European societies.

Pizarro was born about 1470 in Trujillo, Extremadura province, Spain, the illegitimate son of a *hidalgo* ("minor aristocrat"). Never acknowledged by his father, he did not receive a formal education and remained illiterate. Trained as a soldier, he joined the exodus of *hidalgos* in 1502 seeking wealth and power in the New World, settling first in Hispaniola (present-day Haiti and Dominican Republic). In 1509 he accompanied Alonso de Ojeda's exploration of the coast of Colombia, then served as Vasco Núñez de Balboa's chief lieutenant in the expedition that discovered the Pacific Ocean (1513). Pizarro settled in present-day Panama City, serving as the new town's governor and magistrate.

Enriched by his offices, Pizarro sought to increase his fortune by exploring Peru, center of the wealthy Inca civilization. In 1527 he made port at Tumbes (Peru) and was welcomed by an Inca nobleman. Encouraged, Pizarro, back in Panama, resolved to return to Spain in 1529 to ask royal permission to continue. Given full command, Pizarro returned with his half-brothers and approximately 180 soldiers.

In 1532 they reached Peru, and in November they arrived at Cajamarca, home of the Inca ruler, Atahualpa. The Spaniards massacred Atahualpa's men and he was taken hostage and later executed. The conquistadors went on to capture the capital, Cuzco. Already weakened by civil war and smallpox (introduced by the Spaniards), the Inca Empire collapsed.

In 1533 Pizarro ruled as governor of Peru, indirectly through Atahualpa's half-brother, Manco Capac. Pizarro consolidated his conquest, founding many cities, including Lima, and establishing *encomiendas* (a system of forced labor) to distribute among the conquistadors.

The Inca attempted a rebellion but were defeated. A former partner but now rival of Pizarro's, Diego de Almagro, seized the opportunity to take power for himself and waged a civil war against Pizarro and his brothers. He too was defeated and executed. Pizarro himself was assassinated by Spaniards in the name of Almagro, on June 26, 1541.

Legacy

Francisco Pizarro's conquest, motivated by lust for gold and silver, led to the Spanish colonization of South America and the wholesale remaking of that continent's culture.

The original band of conquistadors ruled municipalities newly formed after the conquest, such as the new capital, Lima. The endless feuds among Spaniards and the search for gold and silver also fueled continued exploration and conquest in the Americas and set the stage for colonization throughout South America and north to the present-day southwestern United States.

European diseases such as smallpox, measles, and influenza, along with the forced-labor policies, killed the majority of Amerindians and destroyed Inca culture. Africans were imported as slaves to make up for loss of the indigenous population. Spanish social and cultural practices were introduced to the New World. Many Amerindians who survived the epidemics adopted European practices, obtaining university educations and converting to Roman Catholicism.

Immigration, though controlled by the government, accelerated in the seventeenth century. The initial lack of European women created mixed-blood children, called *mestizos*, who later became the majority ethnic group in Latin America.

Foodstuffs such as potatoes, corn, tomatoes, and chocolate, among others, vastly increased the variety and quality of the European and Asian diets, spurring a rise in world population in the seventeenth century. In exchange, Europeans brought wheat, coffee, sugar-cane, cows, pigs, sheep, and other commodities to the New World, which wreaked havoc on some indigenous plant and animal species.

Pizarro's desire to establish a permanent government in the territory he conquered led to the creation of the Kingdom of Peru, the Council of the Indies, and the office of viceroy to control the actions of the conquistadors and to channel efficiently the riches of South America to Spain. More important for Spain and Europe generally, the silver discovered in the region was carried in fleets of ships back to Spain. The increased supply of bullion in Europe led in part to the price revolution, characterized by steady inflation throughout the sixteenth century.

The wealth pouring in from the American colonies, encouraged the Spanish crown to seek total domination in European affairs, sparking large-scale military conflicts with other European states. Yet even the riches of the New World could not cover the war's enormous expenses, and by the late sixteenth century Spain faced repeated bankruptcies. Furthermore, Spain's European rivals, especially France, Britain, and the Netherlands, began to found their own overseas empires, challenging Spanish control in the Americas.

Pizarro was assassinated before much of this transformation took place. Yet his rapid conquest of the Inca opened the floodgates to the European dominance of South America. These initial European overseas conquests eventually led to European domination of the globe through colonialism, which reached its peak in the late nineteenth century.

Lemoine

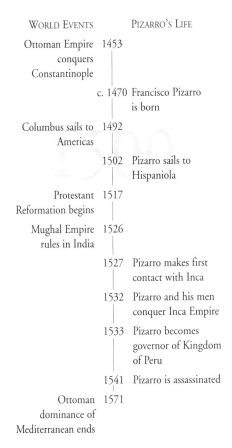

WORLD EVENTS		PIZARRO'S LIFE
Ottoman Empire conquers Constantinople	1453	
	c. 1470	Francisco Pizarro is born
Columbus sails to Americas	1492	
	1502	Pizarro sails to Hispaniola
Protestant Reformation begins	1517	
Mughal Empire rules in India	1526	
	1527	Pizarro makes first contact with Inca
	1532	Pizarro and his men conquer Inca Empire
	1533	Pizarro becomes governor of Kingdom of Peru
	1541	Pizarro is assassinated
Ottoman dominance of Mediterranean ends	1571	

For Further Reading

Lockhart, James. *The Men of Cajamarca: A Social and Biographical Study of the First Conquerors of Peru.* Austin: University of Texas Press, 1972.

Prescott, W. H. *History of the Conquest of Peru.* New York: Cooper Square Press, 1999.

Pol Pot

Cambodian Political Leader

c. 1925–1998

Life and Work

Pol Pot led an extremist communist state and facilitated the deaths of over one million people.

Pol Pot was born Saloth Sar to a wealthy peasant family in Prek Sbauv, a village in north central Cambodia, then a protectorate of France, in either 1925 or 1928. In the 1940s, Pol Pot attended secondary and vocational schools in Phnom Penh and Paris. After World War II, Pol Pot became a leftist political activist, and while in Paris between 1949 and 1953, he adopted stringent Marxism. After returning to Cambodia in 1953, just in time for its independence from the French, Pol Pot became a primary school teacher and clandestine political operative for communist political groups.

In 1963, anticommunist repression begun by King Norodom Sihanouk, Cambodia's leader from 1942 to 1970, forced Pol Pot and his closest allies into eastern Cambodia's wilderness. There, Pol Pot joined the camps of Vietnamese guerrillas fighting for the reunification of North

and South Vietnam under the communist flag. Working with and receiving aid from the communist Vietnamese for five years, Pol Pot established his leadership over a Cambodian Communist Party (the Khmer Rouge). He gradually drifted away from North Vietnam's support and toward an alliance with Communist China.

During the early 1970s, Pol Pot began to take over Cambodia. When Phnom Penh fell to Pol Pot's Khmer Rouge on April 17, 1975, Pol Pot, through his lieutenants, initiated a complete transformation of Cambodian society based on an extreme form of Maoism. Emptying the cities, collectivizing all aspects of life, and celebrating the peasantry, Pol Pot's new political machine searched for internal enemies and demanded expression of people's patriotism through unrelenting manual labor. In reaction to cross-border attacks on its citizens, in 1979 the Vietnamese invaded Cambodia and ended Pol Pot's reign of terror. He fled to far western Cambodia, where he directed a clandestine regime until his supporters, in 1998, turned on him in order to regularize their relations with a new, democratic regime formed in Phnom Penh after the departure of the Vietnamese in 1989. Pol Pot died on April 16, 1998.

Legacy

Pol Pot transformed Cambodia into a radical experiment whose devastating impact endures in Cambodia's people and politics.

The immediate legacy of Pol Pot's life is the one million murders, one seventh of Cambodia's 1975 population, that were perpetrated by his followers. Pol Pot had deemed about 150,000 morally corrupt; members of some of these groups were summarily executed in order to eliminate any potential opposition to Pol Pot. About 900,000 people, mostly former city dwellers, were simply worked to death in order to make Cambodia into a "peasant paradise." Many deaths were stretched out over weeks by vicious torture. In order to accomplish such atrocities, Pol Pot successfully manipulated, through his soothing utopian visions and charismatic personality, the social and racial tensions and jealousies within Cambodia. Country folk attacked city folk, Cambodian attacked Vietnamese, and the uneducated attacked the educated.

Pol Pot wanted to create his vision of a mythologized thirteenth-century Cambodian

empire in the twentieth century and, after "purification," dominate Indochina through a rich, collectivized, agricultural state. The Cambodian people, unfortunately, were vulnerable to Pol Pot's promises: after enduring the corruption and cronyism of the French colonial occupation from 1862 to 1953 and Sihanouk's state from 1953 to 1970, as well as the presence of communist Vietnamese from 1959 to 1975 and bombing by the United States from 1970 to 1974, many Cambodians found the peaceful and prosperous vision offered by Pol Pot inspirational. To avoid any suspicion of insufficient enthusiasm that might put their own dedication and lives in peril, Pol Pot's lieutenants often enforced his purification orders with notorious zeal. Pol Pot's regime retains an image as the apogee of horror and beyond the limits of even calculated terror.

In addition, Pol Pot revealed the cynicism of the struggle between the communist states and the Western democratic states after the end of the Vietnam War and revitalized the idea of genocide as a tool of politics. By late 1976, most of the major world governments knew genocidal activities were taking place in Cambodia. Yet Pol Pot enjoyed four years of domestic security and enormous foreign aid because no government wanted to upset Communist China, Cambodia's chief ally, or support the pro-Soviet Vietnamese, who opposed Pol Pot's regime, or challenge the anti-Vietnamese Thai, who were benefitting financially by trading with Pol Pot's government. Meanwhile, Pol Pot perpetrated an enormous human tragedy.

Del Testa

World Events		Pol Pot's Life
Russian Revolution	1917	
	1925 or	Pol Pot is born
	1928	Saloth Sar in north central Cambodia
Great Depression	1929–39	
World War II	1939–45	
Communist China is established	1949	
	1953	Pol Pot returns to Cambodia from Paris as political activist
Israel defeats Arab nations in Six-Day War	1967	
Vietnam War ends	1975	Pol Pot and Khmer Rouge take Phnom Penh
	1975–79	Pol Pot transforms Cambodian society
	1979	Pol Pot flees after Vietnam invades Cambodia
Dissolution of Soviet Union	1991	
	1998	Pol Pot dies

For Further Reading

Chandler, David. *Brother Number One: A Political Biography of Pol Pot.* Rev. ed. Boulder, Colorado: Westview Press, 1999.

Kiernan, Ben. *The Pol Pot Regime: Race, Power, and Genocide in Cambodia under the Khmer Rouge, 1975-1979.* New Haven, Conn.: Yale University Press, 1996.

P'u-i

Last Emperor of China
1906–1967

Life and Work

Throughout his life, P'u-i (Henry P'u-i) was a pawn, but one who wanted enlightened and modern rule for China in the context of its age-old imperial system.

On February 7, 1906, P'u-i (also spelled Pu Yi), nephew of China's contemporary emperor, was born into an atmosphere of intrigue in Beijing's Forbidden City. P'u-i and most of the imperial leadership were Manchus, sinicized Mongolians who had taken over China from the ethnic Chinese in 1644 and founded the Qing dynasty. Since the 1870s, Cixi (also spelled Tz'u Hsi), the Dowager Empress, had ruled China from behind the scenes, going so far in 1898 as to have the reigning emperor, Kuang Hsu, placed under house arrest when he initiated reforms that threatened China's existing political and social structures. In 1908, on her deathbed, Cixi had P'u-i made emperor under the regency of his father after having Kuang Hsu again placed under house arrest. P'u-i grew up entirely within the bounds of Beijing's 250-acre Forbidden City, which he would not leave until 1924. Utterly spoiled and yet controlled by tradition, P'u-i received a classical education until age 13, when Reginald Johnson, a member of the British embassy, began to teach him the English language and "modern" subjects.

In 1911, China was transformed from an empire into a republic by SUN YAT-SEN and his allies, and in 1912 P'u-i abdicated in the face of threats to his safety. After 1912, China fell into a period of political and social chaos, although life for P'u-i remained essentially unchanged. In 1917, a warlord conquered Beijing and had P'u-i declare himself emperor again. However, this reign ended after 12 days in the face of a counterattack by rival warlords and Nationalist Chinese forces. In 1924, P'u-i abandoned Beijing in the face of another attacker and traveled to Tientsin, on the coast of China, where he engaged in an elaborate court social life and plotted to get his throne back under Japanese protection.

In 1931, the Japanese invaded and occupied Manchuria, in northeastern China. P'u-i and his entourage immediately moved there, hoping that the Japanese would enthrone him. In 1934, they did so, and P'u-i acted as the puppet ruler of Manchuria, renamed Manchukuo, until August 1945, when it was taken over by the Soviets. P'u-i was captured by the Soviets and kept as a pampered guest until he was unceremoniously returned to China in 1950, which had become communist under MAO TSE-TUNG in 1949. P'u-i then spent nine years in a reeducation camp; after his release in 1959, he became a gardener and librarian, dying of cancer in 1967.

Legacy

P'u-i's legacy is primarily symbolic, for he himself never ruled over anyone but his household staff. His life reveals much more about the incredible importance of authenticity in the increasingly nationalistic struggles of the twentieth century than about great leadership or innovation.

It is important to remember that China's last emperor was not Chinese at all, but descended from the Manchu people of northeastern Asia who had taken over the leadership of China around 1644. In the growing anti-foreigner movement that became powerful and influential among the Chinese, especially after the Boxer Rebellion of 1900 and the growing exploitation of China by foreigners, the Manchus were not particularly popular as rulers, both because of their refusal to adapt to modern thinking and their ethnic origins. P'u-i was a representative of a "foreign occupation" and faced increasingly vigorous opposition from within China after the establishment of the republic in 1911. However, the Japanese chose P'u-i to rule over occupied Manchuria in 1934 precisely because of his origins and dynastic lineage; they expected that P'u-i as a figurehead would confer upon Japan the legitimacy necessary to justify their illegal occupation of Chinese territory before and during World War II. P'u-i certainly understood that he was being used as a puppet, but hoped throughout that he could mollify the Japanese and improve the lives of Manchurians.

Twice more did P'u-i's background serve the needs of others. During the late 1940s, the Soviets held him as a privileged hostage, hoping to use his claim as leader of China to disrupt China if Mao Tse-tung did not gain power. In 1950, when the Soviets delivered P'u-i to the Chinese communists, Mao used him to demonstrate his mastery over both China's past and its many nationalities. Indeed, Mao had P'u-i wed a Chinese woman in 1962, the first time a Manchu ruler had ever married someone other than another Manchu. In the end, P'u-i was more symbol than sovereign, but his life's path reveals how important the symbolism of leadership can be.

Del Testa

WORLD EVENTS		P'U-I'S LIFE
Russo-Japanese War	1905	
	1906	P'u-i is born
	1908	P'u-i is made emperor under regency of father
	1912	P'u-i abdicates in wake of establishment of Chinese Republic
World War I	1914–18	
Russian Revolution	1917	P'u-i is emperor again for 12 days
	1924–31	P'u-i lives in Tientsin
Great Depression	1929–39	
	1934	P'u-i is named emperor of Manchuokuo by Japanese
World War II	1939–45	
Communist China is established	1949	
	1950	P'u-i is returned to China from Russia
	1959	P'u-i is granted amnesty by Mao Tse-tung and released from reeducation
Israel defeats Arab nations in Six-Day War	1967	P'u-i dies
Vietnam War ends	1975	

For Further Reading

Neville, John Iröns. *The Last Emperor: The Life of the Hsüan-t'ung Emperor Aisin-Gioro P'u-yi, 1906–1967.* London: House of Fans, 1983.

Brackman, Arnold C. *The Last Emperor.* New York: Scribner's, 1975.

P'u-i. *From Emperor to Citizen: The Autobiography of Aisin-Gioro Pu Yi.* Translated by W. J. F. Jenner. Oxford and New York: Oxford University Press, 1987.

Rama IV

King of Siam (Thailand)
and Modernizer
1804–1868

Life and Work

Rama IV was born Mongkut to Rama II, the crown prince of Siam (the name of Thailand before 1940), on October 18, 1804. Mongkut enjoyed all the rights and privileges of the heir apparent of Siam, receiving an edu-

WORLD EVENTS		RAMA IV'S LIFE
French Revolution begins	1789	
	1804	Rama IV is born Mongkut
Latin American independence movement begins	1811	
Congress of Vienna reorganizes Europe	1815	
	1824	Mongkut begins monastic life
	1837	King Rama III appoints Mongkut abbot
	1851	Rama IV becomes king
	1855	Rama IV signs first treaties with Western countries
	1868	Rama dies and is succeeded by his son Chulalongkorn
Germany is united	1871	

cation based on ancient Buddhist and Hindu texts and rites, and in the military arts. In addition, he spent several months in a monastery. At 20, he discovered a calling to Buddhism and spent seven years at Wat Samorai as a humble monk.

At Samorai, Mongkut studied and learned so quickly that in three years he became the temple's chief examiner. He produced criticisms of lax religious practices and compiled a history of Siam. In 1837, his half-brother, then king, Rama III, appointed Mongkut as the abbot of Wat Pawaraniwea, where he became a renowned religious scholar. He also became a friend of many Europeans living in or traveling through Siam, and endeavored to learn from them as much of Western culture as possible, including English. When he became king in 1851, he was already admired by European governments for his learning and his respect for modern knowledge. Indeed, Rama IV became known as something of an America-lover, and carried on extensive correspondence with U.S. Presidents Franklin Pierce, James Buchanan, and ABRAHAM LINCOLN.

Rama IV became king on May 15, 1851. Recognizing that the European powers coveted Siam as a protectorate or colony and would go to any lengths to gain the right to conduct trade and do business there, Rama initiated a series of reforms to build a base on which a modern Siam might prosper and yet remain independent. He signed a series of treaties beginning in 1855 that granted Europeans and Americans the rights they expected in Asia, such as commerical access and the right to be tried for crimes committed in Siam under the laws of their country of origin (extraterritoriality). He issued a standardized coinage, reduced import duties, and challenged slavery. He allowed Siamese royal ambassadors to travel abroad, rather than being limited to only receiving missions. Further, he reoriented the economy toward export of its vast rice reserves, which generated capital for future modernization projects.

To bring about the reforms he knew his country desperately needed, Rama had to introduce them slowly. Government officials and other important persons feared losing their jealously guarded rank and privileges. Rama spent much of his time negotiating with unwilling, resistant officials and ensuring that his son, the Crown Prince Chulalongkorn, would be prepared to become king. Chulalongkorn succeeded his father upon Rama's death on October 1, 1868.

Legacy

Rama IV developed a keen interest in learning and his own country, and became a popular and respected king who prepared Siam to resist the encroachment of foreign powers and to prepare for a prosperous independence.

The most important single reform Rama made was to make himself accessible to his people. For hundreds of years, the Siamese kings had walked as gods on Earth and remained aloof. Terrible punishments awaited those who looked directly at the king or did not bow in the right way. Rama humanized himself by acting as a normal monk who had direct relations with average people whom he permitted to look upon him. He reinstated a lapsed right by which average people could petition the king to redress grievances. In creating this accessibility, he not only earned popular respect but could act as the people's moral advocate, a position that has helped Thai kings maintain stability during times of adversity ever since. When, in 1981, Thailand's Queen Sirikit denounced a military coup, she did so in part as the pinnacle of Thai society and partly as an appeal to popular support of the royal family begun under Rama.

Rama ensured that Siam would at least have the opportunity to remain independent during the era of European colonial expansion. Between 1850 and 1910, European powers made colonies of Burma, Cambodia, Laos, Malaysia, and Vietnam, and the threat to Siam remained strong until after World War I. However, in an impulse resembling that of the Japanese, Rama decided that Siam needed internal reforms and modernization in order to hold out successfully against European interference. He also realized that the people of Siam could favor no particular country or they would risk being overwhelmed by it. Rama began a tradition of paying attention to all foreign visitors and taking from each something useful. Thus began the process of preparing Siam to become one of the most successful economies in Southeast Asia, especially after World War II. After many periods of crisis, Thailand became one of the most vibrant democracies in Southeast Asia, and serves as a social and economic model for its neighbors.

Del Testa

For Further Reading

Moffat, Abbot Low. *Mongkut, the King of Siam.* Ithaca, N.Y.: Cornell University Press, 1961.
Wyatt, David K. *Thailand: A Short History.* New Haven, Conn.: Yale University Press, 1984.

Ramses II

Egyptian Pharaoh
d. 1213 B.C.E.

Life and Work

Ramses II, sometimes known as Ramses the Great, pushed the borders of Egypt to their greatest extent while simultaneously ensuring badly needed internal peace in Egypt.

Although the details of his childhood remain unclear, it is known that Ramses' family, of nonroyal origin, had risen up the ranks of the Egyptian leadership during the reign of Amenhotep IV (1353–1336 B.C.E.), and that Ramses II's father, Seti I, came to power after the death of Amenhotep's successor, Tutankhamen. During the reign of Amenhotep and Tutankhamen, the Egyptian Empire, earlier covering all of what is today considered Egypt and much of Palestine and Syria, had suffered many military reversals. Seti I brought rebellious Palestine and Syria back firmly under Egyptian control, although he could not make headway against the Hittites, who had set up impregnable fortresses along the Orontes River in northern Syria.

During Ramses' childhood, Seti I gave his son a very special education by according him, at the age of 10, the rank of captain and having him accompany military campaigns against the Hittites and Libyans. In addition, Seti also granted his son a special status as regent, or heir to the throne, also at age 10, to assure that the

reins of power would pass smoothly into the hands of his chosen successor.

When he came to power in 1279, Ramses immediately moved to cement the loyalty of the Egyptian people. First, he traveled to the southern capital of Thebes to receive the appropriate religious blessings from the special deities worshiped there. Second, he had a lovely capital built in the Nile Delta, named Per-Ramses, in an area between Egypt's possessions along the Upper Nile and its outposts in Syria. Ramses also undertook great projects of religious architecture, placing in stone his commitment to the heavens. Ramses II left more monuments than any other pharaoh.

Between 1276 and 1275, Ramses succeeded where his father could not. He attacked the Hittites along the Orontes River at Qadesh and achieved a great tactical advantage there, although neither side could declare a decisive victory. However, Ramses continued to hold firm against the Hittites, who in 1258 signed a treaty with Ramses, sealing it with the marriage of Ramses to the daughter of the Hittite king. Between the attack on the Hittites and the conclusion of the treaty with them, Ramses spent a great deal of time and energy defending Egypt against raiding nomads, especially from Libya and Palestine.

Ramses died in 1213.

Legacy

During his reign, Ramses II began a great period of consolidation and unification of Egyptian lands that strengthened the empire against foreign encroachment and gave its people the time to prosper and pursue renewed artistic endeavors for at least a few decades.

Ramses was successful because of his own natural abilities and his defense of Egypt, and because he paid attention to the various factions within the empire. Not only did he pay homage to the priests and support the military, he made his mark wherever he went through the construction of monuments.

Curiously, the internal peace and broad expanse of Egypt created by Ramses had an undermining effect on the Egyptian state and society. Growing Egyptian prosperity at this time had enriched Egypt's nomadic and settled neighbors, and their populations increased accordingly. The wealth and prosperity of Egypt became increasingly attractive

to outside peoples, and, throughout his reign, Ramses found himself involved in more and more border conflicts. It cost Egypt increasing amounts to defend its borders; adding to the obvious difficulties, the Egyptian gold mines were exhausted of their ore during the reign of Ramses. In addition, increased trade brought more and more foreigners and foreign ideas into Egypt. During the reign of Ramses, for example, the worship of Asiatic gods became more prevalent, turning some of the people away from their loyalty to Egyptian cultural symbols. After Ramses II, Egypt gradually fell into a period of prolonged chaos because no central authority could remain dominant in Egypt.

Del Testa

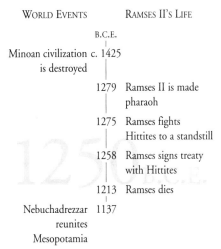

World Events		Ramses II's Life
	B.C.E.	
Minoan civilization	c. 1425	
is destroyed		
	1279	Ramses II is made pharaoh
	1275	Ramses fights Hittites to a standstill
	1258	Ramses signs treaty with Hittites
	1213	Ramses dies
Nebuchadrezzar	1137	
reunites		
Mesopotamia		

For Further Reading

Kitchen, K. A. *Pharaoh Triumphant: The Life and Times of Ramesses II, King of Egypt.* Warminster, England: Aris & Phillips, 1983.

Velikovsky, Immanuel. *Ramses II and His Time.* Garden City, N.Y.: Doubleday, 1978.

Rashid, Hārūn ar-

Caliph of Abbasid Empire
766–809

Life and Work

From a long line of gifted caliphs, Hārūn ar-Rashid emerged as the greatest leader of the Abbasid Caliphate, or dynasty, as well as its most sumptuous and charitable ruler.

Sometime in February 766, in Khorasan, Iran, Hārūn ar-Rashid (the Arabic form of Aaron) was born; Hārūn ar-Rashid was the great-grandson of Saffah, who had overthrown the Umayyad Caliphate in 749 and founded the Abbasid Caliphate; the usurpation was the culmination of an anti-Umayyad movement that had grown up around the descendants of the prophet Muhammad's uncle Abbas. By the time of Hārūn ar-Rashid's birth, the Abbasids ruled an empire that stretched from Morocco to India, and from the Caucasus to Upper Egypt. His childhood was one long tutelage, with three great thinkers appointed to watch over him to ensure that he learned not only about philosophy and the Koran, but also science and statecraft. He had "apprenticeships" as governor of Armenia and Azerbaijan and in military campaigns against Christian Byzantium in the late 770s and early 780s.

In 785 Hārūn ar-Rashid's father died and was replaced by Hadi, his first son. Hadi, however, proved an unpopular ruler, and was assassinated. On September 14, 786, Hārūn ar-Rashid became caliph, that is, the spiritual and civil leader of Islam. He immediately set about rectifying some of the doubt Hadi had created about the ability of the Abbasids to rule, ordered a stiffening of Koranic law so that no imperial subject doubted under whose authority he or she was held. He also began preparations for an enormous campaign against Byzantium, with the hope his forces might capture Constantinople and break Christianity. Finally, Hārūn ar-Rashid sponsored lavish celebrations in Baghdad, his capital, and throughout the empire. Recorded in the Arabic fantasy *The Thousand and One Nights,* the opulence of Hārūn ar-Rashid's court had no equal. Examined more critically, the endless celebrations probably served to widely and personally redistribute wealth and seal personal bonds of loyalty. The wealth resulted from an efficient tax system and tariffs drawn from a profitable trading empire that had grown over the previous 100 years.

Wealth, however, was shared only with those with access to court or other high government posts. Protest against increasingly heavy and arbitrary taxation, encouraged by the appearance of "anti-Abbassid" religious sects, caused unrest throughout the empire. He also faced palace intrigues, which caused him to seek malleable rather than able men for his advisors. Hārūn ar-Rashid's empire was not weak, however, and he raised two military campaigns, in 779 and 781, against the faltering Byzantium Empire. Curiously, he sent and received emissaries from CHARLEMAGNE, the Holy Roman Emperor, because both wanted to see the Umayyad dynasty in Spain destroyed, and both had an interest in weakening Byzantium.

Hārūn ar-Rashid spent the remainder of his reign quelling minor disturbances and fostering trade and learning. He died on March 24, 809.

Legacy

Despite constant infighting and intrigue, Hārūn ar-Rashid maintained a peace throughout his reign that brought enormous material and intellectual prosperity to millions of people while unknowingly sowing the seeds for disunity and collapse throughout the Near and Middle East.

During his entire reign, Hārūn ar-Rashid shrewdly took steps to ensure that the Abbasid dynasty tolerated no external or internal enemies and enjoyed internal prosperity. He dealt sharply with those who opposed his rule, and generously rewarded loyalty. The more he lashed out, however, the more enemies he made, provoking seething tensions that pushed him further into seclusion and ceremony that set a pattern for many reclusive rulers who followed him. To maintain the sumptuous wealth of his time, fueled by trade and production, the empire needed smooth and honest internal governance from local rulers. After Hārūn ar-Rashid, the Abbasid rulers fell into a pattern similar to the Chinese dynasties, in which military expenditures grew so high that taxation became unbearable to the peasantry, who in turn fled the land, depriving the emperor of enough wealth to defend the empire. Gradually, the Abbasid dynasty broke up and was later replaced by Muslim empires based in Constantinople (Istanbul, present-day Turkey) and Persia (present-day Iran) rather than Baghdad.

Hārūn ar-Rashid became, however, the inspiration for 1,200 years of leadership in the Near and Middle East, and legends of his luxurious court informed Western notions of Arab culture as exotic, fantastical, and decadent. He accepted the appeals of Charlemagne to open a dialogue with the Christian West, touching off in both the Abbasid Near East and Umayyad Spain an exchange of scholars and trade that formed the basis of Europe's intellectual revival in the Middle Ages. This cultural exchange reflected a broad tolerance for those with different religious or cultural, but not political, views, for which the Near and Middle East remained known for a millennium after Hārūn ar-Rashid. However, the opulence, sensuality, and "conspicuous consumption" of Hārūn ar-Rashid's court also became a model, in a negative way, that continued down to Reza Pahlavi, the last shah of Iran, who surrounded himself with jewels and gold while his people starved—a provocation that sparked the rise of Islamic fundamentalism.

Del Testa

World Events		Hārūn ar-Rashid's Life
Battle of Talas halts Islam's north Asian expansion	751	
	766	Hārūn ar-Rashid is born
	779	Hārūn ar-Rashid's first military campaigns against Byzantium
	786	Hārūn ar-Rashid becomes caliph
	809	Hārūn ar-Rashid dies
Ethnic Chinese rule is reasserted in northern China	980	

For Further Reading

Clot, André. *Harun al-Rashid and the World of the Thousand and One Nights.* Translated by John Howe. London: Saqi Books, 1986.

Glubb, John Bagot. *Haroon al Rasheed and the Great Abbasids.* London: Hodder and Stoughton, 1976.

Rhodes, Cecil

British Administrator in South Africa
1853–1902

Life and Work

Cecil Rhodes combined a successful diamond and gold mining business and a political career in an effort to create an "English-speaking empire," transforming society in both southern Africa and in Europe.

Cecil John Rhodes was born in Hertfordshire, England, on July 5, 1853, the son of an Anglican minister who came from a family of successful merchants. He received an ordinary education in the local schools, but was determined to further his education at Oxford University. However, he first sought his fortune in South Africa.

He arrived in Natal in 1870 and soon moved to the diamond fields near Kimberley in the Orange Free State, establishing the De Beers Mining Company in 1881. He was also elected to the British Cape Colony Parliament in 1881, forming an alliance with the Boers (Dutch settlers) at the expense of the indigenous Africans. (By 1881 he had also received a degree from Oxford, after entering in 1873.)

Rhodes worked to expand the British Empire north into Bechuanaland (accomplished in 1884) and was appointed deputy commissioner for the territory (now part of Botswana). In 1889 he formed the British South Africa Company (BSAC) and obtained a Royal Charter from the British government, giving the BSAC the authority to negotiate with African rulers. The same year BSAC negotiated a treaty with King Lobengula of the Ndebele to secure the mineral rights in his kingdom in exchange for modern rifles. This territory was eventually renamed Rhodesia.

Simultaneously, Rhodes's mining company had gained control of 90% of the world production of diamonds by amalgamating the mining companies in Kimberley. The company also expanded into gold mining.

With the commercial and financial power of two wealthy enterprises to support him, Rhodes pursued "The Dream" of an expanded British Empire that would reabsorb the United States and include British domination of eastern Africa, symbolized by a railroad that stretched from the Cape to Cairo, Egypt (then also part of the British Empire). His dream also motivated the establishment of the Rhodes Scholarship to Oxford University, which targeted American students in an effort to create a new Anglo-Saxon elite for the new empire.

From 1890 to 1896 Rhodes also served as prime minister of the Cape Colony. In 1894 he passed the Glen Gray Act, which segregated Africans into districts that lacked representation in the Cape Colony Parliament. His goal was the creation of a South African federation that included the Boers and British settlers, but not the indigenous population.

Rhodes's string of successes came to an end with an error in judgment. In an effort to overthrow the independent Boer Republic of Transvaal, Rhodes supported a raid by British police into the Transvaal in 1895. The raid was a failure, and Rhodes resigned his premiership (1897). He died of heart disease in 1902.

Legacy

A key figure in the so-called mining revolution of the nineteenth century, Cecil Rhodes played a crucial role in the social, political, and economic transformation of southern Africa that had repercussions in Europe.

Rhodes's most important legacy was the expansion of British control over a greater amount of African territory. The 1895 raid was directly responsible for the Boer War (1899–1902) between Britain and the Afrikaner (descendants of the Boers) settlers. After bitter fighting that featured the first appearance in history of concentration camps (introduced by the British), the Boer Republics of the Orange Free State and Transvaal lost their independence and were included in the Union of South Africa. In Europe, nationalist enthusiasm was heightened by the colonial conquest of Africa that Rhodes did much to promote. The colonial powers of the late nineteenth century—Britain, France, Germany, the Netherlands, among others—became involved in a frenzied "scramble" for those lands not yet under European control. Colonial rivalry brought the European powers to the brink of war several times. When World War I erupted in 1914, the belligerent nations drew heavily on the natural and human resources of their African possessions.

The colonialists' largely dismissive and exploitative attitude toward black Africans, which Rhodes shared with other Europeans, gave rise to African nationalist liberation movements after World War I. These movements gained momentum after World War II, leading to the independence of nearly every African colony by 1980.

Even Rhodes's beloved Cape Colony, which he saw as one of the anchors of Britain's worldwide empire, declared independence as part of the Union of South Africa in 1961. The new state used his Glen Grey Acts as the basis of the system of apartheid, a system of legalized racial segregation that was abolished in 1994. The Rhodes Scholarship program continues to exist, outliving its founder by more than a century.

Lemoine

World Events		Rhodes's Life
Congress of Vienna reorganizes Europe	1815	
	1853	Cecil Rhodes is born
	1870	Rhodes goes to southern Africa
Germany is united	1871	
	1881	Rhodes forms De Beers Mining Company
		Rhodes elected to Cape Colony Parliament
	1889	Rhodes forms British South Africa Company
	1890–96	Rhodes serves as prime minister of Cape Colony
	1894	Rhodes passes Glen Grey Act
	1897	Rhodes resigns
	1902	Rhodes dies
Russo-Japanese War	1905	

For Further Reading
Roberts, Brian. *Cecil Rhodes: Flawed Colossus.* London: Hamish Hamilton, 1987.
Rotberg, Robert I. *The Founder: Cecil Rhodes and the Pursuit of Power.* Oxford: Oxford University Press, 1988.

Richard I

King of England and Leader of the
Third Crusade
1157–1199

Life and Work

Richard I (Richard the Lion Heart) ruled England in a time of incessant war. He lived by the principles of chivalry, fought a crusade in the Holy Land, and died near a French battlefield.

Richard was born in 1157 to King HENRY II of England and ELEANOR OF AQUITAINE. Although not the oldest son, Richard developed strong ambitions to succeed his illustrious father while still a boy. In 1172 he obtained the duchy of Aquitaine (in France), one of the realm's richest lands, and used it as a basis for developing his military skills. In the following year Eleanor, estranged from Henry, instigated a revolt by Richard and his brothers. Henry put down the rebellion and imprisoned Eleanor, but allowed Richard to retain Aquitaine. The subsequent deaths of Richard's older brothers, Henry and Geoffrey, increased

WORLD EVENTS	RICHARD I'S LIFE
Timbuktu influen- c. 1100 tial throughout west central Africa	
1157	Richard I is born
1172	Richard becomes duke of Aquitaine
1173	Richard first revolts against Henry II
Saladin retakes 1187 Jerusalem for Islam	Muslims defeat Christian forces at Battle of Hattin
1189	Richard crowned king of England
1191	Richard and allies capture Acre
1193	Richard is captured and imprisoned in Vienna
1199	Richard dies
Mongol conquest 1215 of China	

his chances of being selected heir, but his father continued to avoid promises and even showed a preference for Richard's younger and only remaining brother, John.

Meanwhile, Richard's attention was distracted by the revival of Arab power in the Holy Land. In 1187 SALADIN annihilated the Christian army at Hattin in Palestine, conquered Jerusalem, and, in an act that appalled all of Europe, seized possession of a fragment of the true cross of Christ. On the morning after receiving news of these events, Richard entered the cathedral of Tours and made a solemn vow to lead a crusade.

His vow could not be fulfilled, however, until after the death of Henry in 1189, which was precipitated in part by another rebellion against his father by Richard and his temporary ally King Philip Augustus of France. Having finally obtained the crown, Richard now left the realm in the hands of his brother John and set off on what historians call the Third Crusade (1189–92). Allied with Philip and FREDERICK I of Germany, he conquered Acre in 1191 but was unable to wrest Jerusalem from the Arabs.

With the return of Philip and the death of Frederick, Richard soon began to have second thoughts about the crusade. Receiving news that John had begun conspiring with Philip back in England, Richard began a return journey that took him through the Holy Roman Empire. To his dismay, the duke of Austria seized him in Vienna in 1193 and held him for ransom. After a huge sum finally arrived the following year Richard returned to England. He obtained a new oath of fealty from John and then set off to France to deal with Philip. The remainder of his reign was spent there fighting campaigns. During the siege of a castle at Chalus, he received an arrow wound and died from infection on April 6, 1199.

Legacy

While Richard I's colorful life embodied many of the ideals of the age of chivalry, his predilection for combat and indifference to the responsibilities of government had largely negative consequences.

Richard's code of chivalry made a strong impression upon generations of Europeans. Under the influence of his mother, he had

been raised to appreciate the arts and even composed and sang the songs of a troubadour. In military affairs he also made a heroic figure. He always fought at the head of his troops and rarely lost a battle. His image as a noble warrior was kept alive among later generations of medieval Europeans and served as a basis for the legend of Robin Hood, which in the nineteenth century would inspire Walter Scott's romantic novel *Ivanhoe.*

Nevertheless, historians in modern times have tended to note the negative effects of Richard's rule. In an age of unremitting feudal conflict Richard can hardly be condemned for fighting wars, and indeed many of the wars he fought in France were entirely defensive. But some of his campaigns were marred by cruelty, especially when fighting the Arabs in the Holy Land. In the most notorious case, he ordered the massacre of a large number of Arab hostages when Saladin failed to honor a peace treaty. The effect of such acts was to make the crusades more brutal than they already were, and to plant the seeds of Christian–Muslim animosity even deeper. What is more, Richard's capture of Acre and other cities enabled the Crusader nations to retain their position in the Holy Land for another century; in 1291, they were finally driven out.

Richard's lack of involvement in domestic affairs while king of England, ironic in light of his fierce struggle to win the throne in the early years, also had a negative effect upon his immediate successor John (r. 1199–1216). Richard had scarcely spent six months in England during the decade of his rule and this encouraged John to begin the abuses that would nearly ruin the kingdom after Richard's death. As the king, John ruled England tyrannically and, although no military hero, became absorbed in expensive wars on the Continent. The result was the loss of most of the realm's continental possessions and a policy of stifling taxation that provoked an uprising among barons at Runnymede in 1215. John was forced to sign the famous Magna Carta, which compelled the king to obey certain legal customs such as those concerning taxation. This document helped bring England closer to the constitutional monarchy that was finally secured during the Glorious Revolution of 1688–89.

Strickland

For Further Reading

Bridge, Antony. *Richard the Lionheart.* London: Grafton, 1989.

Gillingham, John. *Richard Coeur de Lion: Kingship, Chivalry, and War in the Twelfth Century.* London: Hambledon, 1994.

Runciman, Steven. *A History of the Crusades.* 3 vols. Cambridge: Cambridge University Press, 1951–54.

Richelieu, Armand-Jean du Plessis

Royal Advisor to King Louis XIII
1585–1642

Life and Work

Armand-Jean du Plessis Richelieu shaped the French monarchy into an administrative model that set the stage for LOUIS XIV's absolute monarchy in the late seventeenth century.

Richelieu was born in Paris on September 9, 1585, to a provincial noble family loyal to the monarchy. As the third son of the family, he was destined at first for military service. Instead, in 1606 he became the bishop of Luçon, a post that provided the family some income. Ambitious, Richelieu was determined to rise to prominence in the royal government.

In 1614 he was elected to the Estates-General, comprised of the three estates of France (the clergy, the aristocracy, and commoners). There he ingratiated himself to the queen mother, Marie de Médicis who was regent for the young king Louis XIII, and was appointed cardinal in 1622. Louis XIII eventually came to rely on his guidance, appointing him chief minister in 1624.

Richelieu controlled much of the domestic and foreign policy of France, though he always carefully consulted with the king. He worked to tame the often fractious and scheming members of the nobility. Aristocratic revolts were suppressed, some-

For Further Reading
Bergin, Joseph. *The Rise of Richelieu.* New Haven, Conn.: Yale University Press, 1991.
Knecht, Robert. *Richelieu.* London: Longman, 1991.

times with arrests and executions. Richelieu also appointed officials, known as *intendants*, to centralize certain government functions previously controlled by nobles.

Another challenge came from French Protestants, known as Huguenots. They were accorded a measure of religious toleration by Henry IV, Louis XIII's father, which Richelieu respected. Yet Richelieu sought to destroy the political and military independence many noble Huguenots still maintained. In 1628 the crown laid siege to the western port city of La Rochelle, a Huguenot stronghold. The capitulation of La Rochelle the following year led to the defeat of Huguenots all over France.

Richelieu's influence with the king created enemies at court. Marie de Médicis and her allies, who disapproved of Richelieu's foreign policy, attempted to have him dismissed in 1630. On November 11, known as the Day of Dupes, Louis XIII sided with the cardinal. Marie de Médicis was banished from the court, as were all her allies.

As in his domestic policies, Richelieu's foreign policy sought to increase the king's power. This meant rivalry with the Habsburg dynasty, two branches of which ruled the Holy Roman Empire (encompassing the German states) and Spain. In 1635 Richelieu involved France in the Thirty Years' War, a central European conflict involving the Habsburgs. Initial defeats plagued the war effort. But crucial French victories came after Richelieu's death in 1642.

Legacy

Although it is debatable how far-reaching and visionary Armand-Jean du Plessis Richelieu's reforms actually were, his efforts made possible the future triumph of absolute monarchy in France.

For Richelieu the interests of the state, represented by the crown, were paramount. The king ruled by "divine right" and embodied the state. Reacting to aristocratic revolts, Richelieu did much to destroy the vestiges of the nobility's sense of sovereignty, a remnant of the medieval feudal order. He used the concept of *lèse-majesté*, insult to the sovereign, as a pretext to arrest nobles. "One king, one law, one faith" was the motto by which Richelieu justified limiting the nobility's power. Louis XIII's successor, Louis XIV, carried on the process until he had almost completely subjugated the nobility at his court in Versailles.

For similar reasons Richelieu endeavored to weaken Huguenot power in France. The successful military campaigns waged against Huguenot strongholds gave the crown the opportunity to weaken the provisions of the Edict of Nantes, a truce between Roman Catholics and Protestants signed by HENRY IV in 1598, which accorded the Protestants special political privileges that enabled them to the practice of their faith without persecution. Richelieu's policies removed the Protestants' political protection, making it easier for Louis XIV to revoke the Edict of Nantes in 1685.

Richelieu also set the stage for Louis XIV's future military triumphs and the transformation of Europe's balance of power. By embroiling France in the Thirty Years' War, Richelieu weakened the power of the Habsburg monarchy, especially the branch ruling Spain. This facilitated Spain's decline during the reign of Louis XIV, when the Habsburgs in Spain were replaced by a branch of the French Bourbon dynasty.

The reign of Louis XIII, which Richelieu did so much to shape, was a turning point in French and European history, when the role of the king was more clearly defined, the state turned against religious plurality, and France's international status was on the rise. These issues increased in importance during the reign of Louis XIV, and beyond into the nineteenth century.

Lemoine

WORLD EVENTS		RICHELIEU'S LIFE
Ottoman dominance of Mediterranean ends	1571	
	1585	Armand-Jean du Plessis Richelieu is born
	1606	Richelieu is appointed bishop of Luçon
	1622	Richelieu is appointed cardinal
	1624	Richelieu is appointed chief minister to Louis XIII
	1630	Louis XIII sides with Richelieu against mother
	1635	Richelieu embroils France in Thirty Years' War
	1642	Richelieu dies
Glorious Revolution in England	1688	

Robespierre, Maximilien

French Revolutionary and Leader
of the Radical Jacobin Club
1758–1794

Life and Work

Maximilien Robespierre, a committed and egalitarian democrat, led the most radical phase of the French Revolution, known as the Reign of Terror, which was a forerunner of twentieth-century war economies and totalitarian governments.

Born in Arras in northern France on May 6, 1758, Robespierre was the son of a lawyer who deserted his family, reducing it to poverty. Nonetheless, Robespierre, a diligent and hardworking student, received a scholarship to the College Louis-le-Grand, an elite boys' school in Paris. Having obtained his law degree from the University of Paris in 1780, Robespierre moved back to Arras to practice law. Only two years later he was appointed judge in the episcopal court in Arras. Robespierre resigned from the episcopal court rather than hand down a death sentence in a case, though he continued his own practice, increasingly defending poor clients.

In 1788 King Louis XVI, facing financial disaster, called for elections to the Estates-General, a sort of consultative parliament that had not been convened since 1614. Robespierre was elected to the Third Estate (made up of commoners, the vast majority of the population) in 1789 and moved back to Paris. In defiance of the monarchy and nobility, the Third Estate declared itself the National Assembly, asserted its sovereignty over the king, and established a constitutional monarchy. Robespierre joined the most radical group of the Revolution, the Jacobin Club, and quickly rose to prominence. His championing of the poor and working classes and his clean reputation gained him the admiration of the Parisian artisans (known as the *sans-culottes*), who nicknamed him "the Incorruptible."

Meanwhile, Louis XVI and his family attempted to flee to Austria in 1791. They were captured and eventually imprisoned. The moderate faction in the Assembly (known as the Girondins) declared war on Austria and Prussia to unify the nation against these hostile monarchies mobilizing their troops on the border. Robespierre opposed this move because he believed it would lead to military dictatorship. In September 1792 the Parisian *sans-culottes*, with the tacit support of Robespierre, overthrew the monarchy, proclaiming a republic and universal male suffrage. Robespierre was elected to the National Convention; when the convention put Louis XVI on trial for treason, Robespierre voted to execute the king, which occurred in January 1793.

Concurrently, the war with Austria and Prussia, despite some victories, was going badly for the French, discrediting the Girondins. After a bitter struggle, Robespierre triumphed over the moderates and gained control of the government through his leadership on the Committee of Public Safety in the fall of 1793. Thus began the bloody year called the Reign of Terror. Robespierre argued that the threat to the revolution posed by the war, and a civil war in France itself, justified the creation of a police state. Nearly 20,000 people, suspected of treason, were executed by guillotine, including Robespierre's enemies to the right and to the left.

When the war began to turn in favor of the French, public opinion began to turn against the Terror, symbolized by Robespierre and the Committee of Public Safety. Other members of the convention, fearful they would be guillotined next, engineered Robespierre's defeat. On July 28, 1794 he was arrested and guillotined. His death marked the end of the most radical phase of the French Revolution.

Legacy

More than any other single individual, Maximilien Robespierre exemplifies the two faces of modern revolution: the democratic and the totalitarian. He was a fervent democrat who believed that the working classes had a place in the remaking of the political institutions of society. Yet, the methods of the Reign of Terror, which he justified by wartime emergency, foreshadowed the totalitarian governments of the twentieth century.

Robespierre and the Committee of Public Safety were forerunners of both the European war economies of the two world wars and the totalitarian governments of Nazi Germany and Stalin's Russia. Through a tightly knit national network of Jacobin Clubs, the Committee imposed wage and price controls, economic self-sufficiency, mass conscription, and a draconian law against those suspected of counter-revolution. Robespierre and his cohorts operated as a vanguard. They were elite revolutionaries who guided the rest of the population in the creation of a "republic of virtue," a method and ideology of rule adopted and expanded by Vladimir Lenin and the Bolsheviks in the Russian Revolution and civil war (1917–22).

Yet, Robespierre and the Jacobins saw their dictatorial government as a temporary measure "until the peace." They advocated liberty, democracy, universal male suffrage, equality under the law, and some economic measures favorable to the disadvantaged. Many of these ideals, revolutionary in the late eighteenth century, are now fully accepted in liberal democracies.

Finally, Robespierre played an important role in the establishment of what has become known as the "Revolutionary Tradition," which kept open the questions and issues raised by the French Revolution and influenced future democratic republicans and socialists in Europe and its colonies.

Lemoine

World Events		Robespierre's Life
English seize Calcutta	1690	
	1758	Maximilien Robespierre is born
United States declares independence	1776	
	1780	Robespierre obtains a law degree from University of Paris
French Revolution begins	1789	Robespierre elected to Estates-General
	1792	Robespierre is elected to new National Convention
	1793	Louis XVI is executed; Robespierre is appointed to Committee of Public Safety; Reign of Terror begins
	1794	Robespierre is arrested and guillotined
Latin American independence movement begins	1811	

For Further Reading

Hampson, Norman. *The Life and Opinions of Maximilien Robespierre.* London: Duckworth, 1974.
Jordan, David P. *The Revolutionary Career of Maximilien Robespierre.* New York: Free Press, 1985.

Romero, Oscar

Roman Catholic Archbishop
of El Salvador
1917–1980

Life and Work

Oscar Romero assumed leadership of the Roman Catholic church in El Salvador during a time of increasing poverty and governmental repression. Reversing his initial opposition to the clergy's involvement in politics, he became a leading critic of the rightwing regime and in the end was murdered.

Oscar Arnulfo Romero was born in Ciudad Barrios on August 15, 1917, the son of a poor telecommunications worker who was an atheist. As a boy Romero came under the influence of a neighborhood priest and at the age of 13 entered a seminary in San Miguel. In 1937, Romero decided to enroll in a Jesuit seminary in San Salvador, the capital. He next traveled to Rome, where he was ordained in 1942. Back in El Salvador he distinguished himself with pastoral care for the nation's peasantry, and in 1967 he was made a bishop. Generally critical of the clergy's role in organizing opposition to the country's military government, he won the support of the church hierarchy and was made archbishop of El Salvador in 1977.

When Rutilio Grande, a Jesuit priest, was ambushed and killed by a government-supported death squad in 1977, Romero abandoned his conservative position. He established

a church committee to investigate political violence by the government and in 1978 issued a pastoral letter, *The Church, Political Organizations, and Violence,* which defended the rights of Salvadoran peasants to oppose the regime. Supporters of the government, now threatened Romero and placed him under a "sentence of death." He continued, however, using sermons and the diocesan newspaper *Orientación* to challenge the regime.

At the same time, his international reputation grew. In 1980 he was awarded an honorary doctorate from a French university and was nominated for the Nobel Prize for Peace. Conscious of his influence, he even penned a letter to U.S. president Jimmy Carter pleading for an arms embargo against the Salvadoran government. On March 24, 1980, he appeared at the Chapel of Divine Providence in San Salvador to celebrate Mass. As he was saying a prayer an assassin fired a single shot at him, piercing his chest and killing him instantly.

Legacy

Oscar Romero's support for the poor and the circumstances of his death made him a martyr in the eyes of many contemporaries. His martyrdom contributed to growing political unrest in El Salvador and influenced the policies of the Roman Catholic church in Latin America.

Before Romero became archbishop the political system of El Salvador had been dominated by a repressive military regime. It was supported by an oligarchy consisting of no more than 14 individual families who owned most of the country's coffee plantations. After Romero's murder by supporters of this regime, political opposition exploded. The archbishop's funeral service at San Salvador Cathedral was itself a political event that drew over 100,000 outraged Salvadorans. In the following days, the nation's leftist opposition parties formed an alliance called the National Liberation Front (FMLN) to press for a fundamental reordering of the country's political and economic system. The government's military, however, which had been strengthened by years of support from the United States, reacted swiftly and violently. The result was a civil war that came to an end only in 1992 with the Arias Peace Plan for Central America, sponsored by President OSCAR ARIAS SÁNCHEZ of Costa Rica. While elections in

1994 showed continued divisions, with the government and the opposition still winning large support, El Salvador remained mostly peaceful as the century came to a close.

Romero's example was also closely linked to the activities of the Roman Catholic clergy throughout Latin America. In 1968 a group of bishops convened a conference on social justice in Medellín, Colombia. The bishops, along with other theologians, developed what came to be known as liberation theology, a doctrine calling for clerical leadership in leftist political movements seeking the elimination of class oppression. Drawing upon the revolutionary thought of KARL MARX, it affirmed the need for a radical redistribution of wealth and accepted the principle of violent political activity in certain cases. Although Romero was at first critical of liberation theology, he increasingly accepted its ideals after the killing of Father Grande; his own death in 1980 added even greater prestige to the doctrine. Nevertheless, with the accession of John Paul II to the papacy in 1978 liberation theology came under increased criticism, in part because Romero's example had, however unintentionally, contributed to the outbreak of a violent civil war in El Salvador. Liberation theologians such as the Brazilian Leonardo Boff were silenced by the Vatican, which called upon priests to maintain a more restrained approach to politics.

Strickland

WORLD EVENTS		ROMERO'S LIFE
World War I	1914–18	
	1917	Oscar Romero is born
Great Depression	1929–39	
World War II	1939–45	
	1942	Romero is ordained
Communist China is established	1949	
Israel defeats Arab nations in Six-Day War	1967	
Vietnam War ends	1975	
	1977	Romero named archbishop of El Salvador
	1978	Romero publishes *The Church, Political Organizations, and Violence*
	1980	Romero is nominated for Nobel Prize; Romero is murdered
Dissolution of Soviet Union	1991	

For Further Reading

Brockman, James R. *Romero.* New York: Orbis, 1989.

Keogh, Dermot. *Romero: El Salvador's Martyr.* Dublin: Dominican Publications, 1981.

Lynch, Edward A. *Religion and Politics in Latin America: Liberation Theology and Christian Democracy.* New York: Praeger, 1991.

Roosevelt, Eleanor

American Political Activist and
First Lady
1884–1962

Life and Work

Despite a privileged and sheltered background, Eleanor Roosevelt became, both independently and because of her husband, one of the twentieth century's greatest social activists and an important symbol of post-1945 international cooperation.

Born Anna Eleanor Roosevelt on October 11, 1884, in New York City to a distinguished American family long active in commerce, banking, and politics, Roosevelt had every comfort except that of constant emotional support from her parents, who had both died by the time she was 10. Placed in the charge of a guardian, Roosevelt was sent to Britain in 1899 to attend Allenswood, a private girls' boarding school. After graduating at 17, Roosevelt returned to the United States and found that she preferred social work to society parties. Roosevelt's life changed completely in 1905 when she married FRANKLIN DELANO ROOSEVELT, a distant cousin. Roosevelt had six children to tend to by 1916. In addition, as her husband's political ambitions grew, so did Roosevelt's duties as a political wife, culminating in an endless series of social affairs she had to host, especially while her husband was assistant secretary of the navy from 1913 to 1920.

In 1921, Franklin Roosevelt contracted polio. Oddly enough, her husband's crippling bout with polio thrust Eleanor Roosevelt back into public life, for his ambitions never waned. Roosevelt acted as her husband's spokesperson, despite their physical estrangement because of affairs he had had during World War I. From 1924 to 1928, Roosevelt was an active member of the women's division of New York state's Democratic Party, and thereafter was considered by many to be the leader of women in the Democratic Party. After her husband was elected to the presidency, Roosevelt became a powerful proponent for the rights of women, workers, and minorities. Her involvement in these causes culminated in 1939 when Roosevelt quit the Daughters of the American Revolution, whose members had refused to permit Marian Anderson, an African-American singer, to give a concert in Washington, D.C.'s Constitution Hall.

After her husband's death in 1945, Roosevelt continued her social activism without pause, especially when President HARRY S. TRUMAN named her a delegate to the United Nations. The pinnacle of her activist career came on December 10, 1948, when the United Nations adopted the international declaration on human rights she had helped author. Throughout the 1950s and early 1960s, she continued to press for civil rights and labor legislation, eventually serving as the leader of President John Kennedy's Commission on the Status of Women. She died on November 7, 1962.

Legacy

In a time of economic and social strife, Eleanor Roosevelt made sure that disenfranchised Americans and unpopular causes were heard in government, and that Americans without hope had a place to turn for help.

Roosevelt worked tirelessly to promote social justice as a way for people to overcome obstacles that held them back. Perhaps because of her own life long desire for acceptance—she always found herself unattractive and rigid—Roosevelt avoided the cold paternalism that typified the charity of her social class. Instead, she turned toward movements that meant face-to-face contact, such as reformist homes for the impoverished in the early 1900s, and that produced tangible results, such as pressing for a minimum wage for women in the early 1920s.

More important perhaps than her activism was Roosevelt's openness to all people regardless of their race, religion, or national origin. During the first half of the twentieth century, race relations had reached an extreme low point in the United States; Roosevelt, however, promoted without qualification the rights of African Americans and the cause of Europe's pre-1939 refugee Jews. At a time, especially during the 1930s and 1940s, when the world seemed on the road to either anarchy or totalitarianism, Roosevelt was a symbol of democratic reform. Indeed, as she got older, her concern for humanity only grew broader. During and after World War II, Roosevelt was a world symbol of what righteousness, justice, and activism could accomplish. Besides blazing an activist path that was an important model for women after World War II, she also provided subsequent first ladies with a model for social activism and advocacy.

Del Testa

World Events	Roosevelt's Life
Germany is united 1871	
	1884 Eleanor Roosevelt is born
	1899– Roosevelt attends
	1902 Allenswood School in England
Russo-Japanese War 1905	Roosevelt marries Franklin Delano Roosevelt
World War I 1914–18	
Russian Revolution 1917	
	1924–28 Roosevelt is active in women's division of New York state's Democratic Party
Great Depression 1929–39	
World War II 1939–45	
	1939 Roosevelt resigns from Daughters of American Revolution
	1945 Roosevelt is appointed member of U.S. delegation to United Nations
	Roosevelt helps write declaration on human rights
Communist China 1949 is established	
	1962 Roosevelt dies
Israel defeats 1967 Arab nations in Six-Day War	

For Further Reading
Cook, Blanche Wiesen. *Eleanor Roosevelt*. New York: Viking, 1992.
Roosevelt, Eleanor. *The Autobiography of Eleanor Roosevelt*. Cambridge, Mass.: Da Capo Press, 2000.

Roosevelt, Franklin Delano

Thirty-Second President of the
United States
1882–1945

Life and Work

Despite a debilitating illness, Franklin Delano Roosevelt became one of the most popular presidents of all time, successfully leading the United States through the trials of the Great Depression and World War II.

Roosevelt was born on January 30, 1882, into an established, wealthy New York family. He studied at prestigious primary and secondary schools, Harvard University, and Columbia University's Law School. After marrying distant cousin ELEANOR ROOSEVELT in 1905, Roosevelt joined an important law firm in 1909, specializing in admiralty (maritime) law.

Bored by the legal profession and intrigued by politics, Roosevelt ran for the New York state Senate in 1910, and was elected as a Democrat on November 8, 1910. As a state senator, Roosevelt showed a patrician concern for land conservation and agricultural issues. In 1913, Democratic President WOODROW WILSON asked Roosevelt to serve as assistant secretary of the navy, a post he would hold for eight years. During this time, Roosevelt matured politically, learning much about patronage politics and government administration.

After joining a losing vice-presidential campaign in 1920, Roosevelt returned to the law. In 1921, Roosevelt contracted polio, depriving him of the full use of his legs. He spent seven years in rehabilitation, but never regained complete mobility. During this trying time, Roosevelt maintained his spirits and his political ambitions, going from the unpaid position of New York state parks commissioner in 1925 to being elected governor of New York in 1928. As governor, he gained a reputation as a reformer and a strong believer in social justice. Roosevelt used his reputation as the basis for his run for the presidency in 1932, which he won in a landslide against the detested incumbent, Herbert Hoover. Surrounding himself with a so-called "brain trust" of experts, and inspiring the downtrodden with his legendary smile and impressive oratory, Roosevelt created controversial new government programs and proposed new legislation, collectively called the New Deal, to address the Great Depression. Programs such as the Civilian Conservation Corps (CCC) provided work to the unemployed, and new labor legislation gave workers the right to organize. Roosevelt also improved the lives of rural Americans through land reclamation and electrification projects, and reformed banking to the benefit of average citizens. His programs gave the average person hope, but earned Roosevelt the enmity of the rich and influential, who called him a class traitor.

Although trouble was brewing in Europe and Asia throughout the 1930s, Congress and the American people kept Roosevelt focused on domestic affairs. ADOLF HITLER's 1940 invasion of France and Japan's 1941 attack on Pearl Harbor in Hawaii gave Roosevelt acceptable reasons to break the United States' isolation. Although no brilliant tactician himself, Roosevelt assembled the best American military minds to lead the country to victory over Japan, Germany, and Italy in five years. He also engaged in personal diplomacy with Allied leaders, first Britain's WINSTON CHURCHILL, and then the Soviet Union's JOSEPH STALIN, mediating between the two and moderating their extreme visions of the post-war world. Unfortunately, Roosevelt did not live to savor the victory he made possible. He died in office on April 13, 1945, after being elected to an unprecedented fourth term in 1944.

Legacy

Franklin gave Americans the hope, if not always the means, to overcome the greatest challenges to the United States since the Civil War, namely the Great Depression and World War II, and thus changed the relationship of Americans to their government, forever.

Roosevelt's political tendencies gradually evolved from the time he served as a New York state senator in 1910 to his death in office as president in 1945. He had become increasingly conscious of the forces that exploited the common person for profit and used legislation and government to better conditions for laboring Americans. When the Great Depression began in 1929, Roosevelt was appalled that big business and the federal government did not try to alleviate people's suffering. Before Roosevelt, the federal government was relatively small and had been responsible mainly for defense, taxation, currency, interstate commerce, and legislation. After 1932, as president, Roosevelt made the federal government a large institution that became the great guarantor of American public welfare, a role it has maintained and Americans have expected, in different forms, ever since. He also laid the groundwork, intentionally or otherwise, for a revision of race relations in the United States by including African Americans in New Deal policies, for labor and agricultural reforms that encouraged great increases in productivity, and for federal involvement in the everyday lives of all Americans.

Roosevelt was enormously influential in the international arena as well. Although forced to ignore most international relations during much of the 1930s, Roosevelt tried to hold a firm line after 1937 against the Japanese who had brutally invaded northeastern and eastern China; he used the preservation of democracy as the reason for the Allied powers to remain united against Germany during World War II, despite internal bickering. Roosevelt's influence in the arena of international cooperation extended long after his death in such institutions as the United Nations, which he believed to be superior to punitive measures for solving the world's problems.

Del Testa

WORLD EVENTS		ROOSEVELT'S LIFE
Germany is united	1871	
	1882	Franklin Delano Roosevelt is born
Russo-Japanese War	1905	
	1910	Roosevelt is elected New York state senator
	1913–20	Roosevelt serves as assistant secretary of the navy
World War I	1914–18	
Russian Revolution	1917	
	1921	Roosevelt contracts polio
	1928	Roosevelt is elected governor of New York
Great Depression	1929–39	
	1932	Roosevelt is elected president of the United States
World War II	1939–45	
	1944	Roosevelt is elected to unprecedented fourth term
	1945	Roosevelt dies in office
Communist China is established	1949	

For Further Reading

Burns, James MacGregor. *Roosevelt: The Lion and the Fox.* New York: Smithmark Publishers, 1996.
Morgan, Ted. *FDR: A Biography.* New York: Simon & Schuster, 1985.

Roosevelt, Theodore

Twenty-Sixth President of the
United States
1858–1919

Life and Work

Theodore Roosevelt, president in a time of growing national strength, brought progressive reforms in government and a greater American presence abroad.

Roosevelt was born on October 27, 1858, in New York City, the son of a successful banker. He graduated from Harvard University in 1880, and decided to pursue a political career. Between 1882 and 1884 he served as a New York state representative, where he distinguished himself as a progressive member of the Republican Party. His love for adventure led him to organize a volunteer cavalry regiment in 1898 called the Rough Riders, which he led up San Juan Hill in Cuba during the Spanish–American War. Having established popularity at home through military service, he returned to win election as governor of New York in 1899. In 1900 he was selected, despite considerable opposition, to run as vice president alongside William McKinley. After winning, he suddenly found himself elevated to the presidency when McKinley was assassinated in 1901.

Roosevelt distinguished himself by supporting political reform and expanding the powers of the presidency. His authority was greatly enhanced when he won the presidency in 1904. In an effort to subject big business to public control, he supported antitrust actions against the Northern Securities Company, among others. He also used the federal government to regulate and monitor economic life. In 1906 he oversaw the formation of the Interstate Commerce Commission and the passage of the Pure Food and Drug Act, and used the presidency to conserve national forests.

Roosevelt also acted boldly in what became an increasingly interventionist foreign policy. His experience in Cuba had made him more conscious of Latin America, and in 1904 he issued the so-called Roosevelt Corollary to the Monroe Doctrine whereby the United States declared it had a special status in the supervision of diplomatic affairs in the Western hemisphere. Accordingly, in 1903, he supported Panamanian independence from Colombia and used American influence to purchase rights to the Panama Canal Zone. During the Russo–Japanese War, he mediated the Peace of Portsmouth in 1905, for which he was awarded the Nobel Prize for Peace the following year.

Honoring a campaign promise, Roosevelt did not seek reelection in 1908. Leaving Washington, he traveled to Africa on safari. He was unable to resist running against fellow Republican William Howard Taft in 1912, however, though his formation of a rival Progressive Party, dubbed the Bull Moose Party, split the Republicans and led to the election of Democratic candidate WOODROW WILSON, who refused to allow him to organize another volunteer force for service in the World War I (1914–18). Roosevelt died on January 6, 1919.

Legacy

During his eight years in office, Theodore Roosevelt introduced new responsibilities to the American presidency. Following him, presidents were more active in sponsoring governmental reform and in expanding the nation's international influence.

The governmental institutions created under Roosevelt brought a wide variety of benefits to American society. Meat inspection authorities reduced the spread of disease, pharmaceuticals were made safer for consumers, and big businesses were more restrained in the practice of unfair marketing strategies. The authority that evolved into the National Forest Service prevented the loss of large areas of land during the remainder of the century, which would inspire a conservationist movement and the establishment of national parks such as Yellowstone Park in Wyoming. Roosevelt's example of presidential leadership in the legislative process likewise influenced his successors. His relative FRANKLIN DELANO ROOSEVELT, for instance, would use the presidency to promote an economic recovery program called the New Deal during the Great Depression (1929–39).

Finally, Roosevelt's presidency marked an expansion of American foreign policy interests and commitments. His policy in Panama was followed by repeated interventions by the United States in Latin America. Later in the twentieth century, American forces conducted operations in Mexico, Guatemala, and Colombia. Roosevelt's legacy was especially visible under John F. Kennedy, who used both military intervention and economic enticements to pursue American interests. Kennedy's most memorable act of intervention was the failed invasion of Cuba in 1961 known as the Bay of Pigs incident, designed to overthrow the communist leader FIDEL CASTRO. Outside the Americas, Roosevelt's example of expanded diplomatic activity was also followed. Though he himself had urged Wilson to enter World War I without success during its early stages, Wilson found it necessary to bring the United States into the European war in 1917. Although a return to American isolation from Europe followed the conclusion of the war in 1918, Franklin D. Roosevelt was likewise compelled to enter World War II (1939–45) after the bombing of Pearl Harbor in 1941. With President HARRY S. TRUMAN assuming diplomatic leadership in Europe during the Cold War that followed 1945, the United States finally made a seemingly irreversible commitment to the interventionist policies of Roosevelt.

Strickland

WORLD EVENTS		ROOSEVELT'S LIFE
Congress of Vienna reorganizes Europe	1815	
	1858	Roosevelt is born
Germany is united	1871	
	1899	Roosevelt is elected governor of New York
	1900	Roosevelt is elected vice president
	1901	Roosevelt sworn in as president after assassination of William McKinley
	1904	Roosevelt elected president
Russo-Japanese War	1905	
	1908	Roosevelt declines to run for presidency
	1912	Roosevelt unsuccessfully runs for president as Progressive Party Candidate
World War I	1914–18	
Russian Revolution	1917	
	1919	Roosevelt dies
Great Depression	1929–39	

For Further Reading

Burton, David Henry. *Theodore Roosevelt, American Politician: An Assessment.* Madison, N.J.: Fairleigh Dickinson University Press, 1997.

Miller, Nathan. *Theodore Roosevelt.* New York: Morrow, 1992.

Roosevelt, Theodore. *Theodore Roosevelt: An Autobiography. 1913.* Reprint, New York: Da Capo Press, 1988.

Sadat, Anwar as-

President of Egypt
1918–1981

Life and Work

As GAMAL ABDEL NASSER's successor, Anwar as-Sadat took Egypt in new directions, away from state control of the economy and Soviet influence and toward lasting peace with Israel.

Sadat was born Muhammad Anwar as-Sadat on December 25, 1918, to an Egyptian father and a Sudanese mother in a small village on the Nile Delta. Sadat attended the Royal Military Academy and was commissioned in 1938.

Nominally independent since 1922, Egypt in reality was still dominated by Britain, a fact made more obvious during World War II, when the British used the territory to fight German forces in North Africa. In 1942, Sadat was arrested for contacting agents of the German army in North Africa. He escaped in 1944, only to be arrested again in 1946 for his role in the assassination of a pro-British government official. He spent two more years in prison, but was released and eventually reinstated in the army.

Joining the Free Officers, a group of nationalist army officers led by Nasser, Sadat participated in the coup that overthrew the pro-British monarchy in 1952. In 1953 he founded a newspaper, *The Republic*, which became the organ of Nasser's one-party state. He loyally served Nasser's regime, rising to the post of vice president in 1964. Sadat

became president of Egypt when Nasser died in 1970.

Sadat at first followed Nasser's policies, especially regarding Israel. In 1973, assuming the posts of prime minister and military governor-general, Sadat launched a surprise attack against Israel in October to avenge the Arab defeat by Israeli forces in the Six-Day War of 1967. Initial success was mitigated by an Israeli counterattack. American and Soviet diplomats negotiated a cease-fire, allowing Sadat to exploit the war as a strategic victory.

Paradoxically, the war provided an avenue to closer ties with the United States. Sadat had expelled Soviet advisors in 1972 in frustration over Soviet delays in weapons shipments, and in 1976, shifted to a pro-Western policy. He liberalized the economy, and encouraged private and foreign investment. In addition, he reduced press censorship, limited police coercion, and released some political prisoners.

In November 1977, Sadat made a historic journey to Jerusalem, meeting with Israeli Prime Minister MENACHEM BEGIN to negotiate a peace settlement. In 1978, he and Begin went to Camp David in the United States (at then-President Jimmy Carter's invitation) to finalize the negotiations. The difficult transition from belligerence to resolution earned Sadat and Begin the Nobel Prize for Peace later that year.

Sadat's peace initiative isolated Egypt from other Arab states and angered many Egyptians, who were also frustrated by slow economic growth. Sadat was assassinated by Islamic fundamentalists while reviewing troops in Cairo on October 6, 1981.

Legacy

Anwar as-Sadat's courageous decision to establish diplomatic relations with Israel set a precedent that other Arab states followed two decades later. His death marked the rise of Islamic fundamentalism, which was hostile to secular government and peace with Israel.

Although the peace agreement isolated Egypt from other Arab states, Sadat laid the foundation for the continuation of the Middle East peace process. In the 1980s and 1990s, Israel successfully engaged in peace talks with Jordan, Morocco, and Tunisia.

Sadat's establishment of closer ties with the United States, predicated on the peace agreement, did result in increased military and economic aid to Egypt. However, increased

reliance on the United States did not produce the expected economic benefit. Beginning in the 1980s, economic problems related to its policy of subsidizing food items forced Egypt to request international loans. Lending agencies demanded an end to the subsidies; when this was attempted, rioting broke out.

Egypt's economic woes were linked to government corruption and inefficiency, problems that Sadat's regime never adequately addressed despite its efforts to democratize its political culture. Not only radical Islamic fundamentalists, but also moderate opponents of the regime found themselves harassed by security forces and political show trials. The bureaucracy, greatly expanded under Nasser, and slow and unresponsive under Sadat, has not fundamentally improved under his successor, Husni Mubarak.

Lemoine

WORLD EVENTS		SADAT'S LIFE
Russian Revolution	1917	
	1918	Anwar as-Sadat is born
Great Depression	1929–39	
	1938	Sadat graduates from Royal Military Academy
World War II	1939–45	
	1946	Sadat is imprisoned for role in political assassination
Communist China is established	1949	
	1952	Sadat participates in coup that deposes monarchy
Israel defeats Arab nations in Six-Day War	1967	
	1970	Sadat is appointed president
	1973	Sadat launches surprise attack on Israel (October War)
Vietnam War ends	1975	
	1977	Sadat meets with Israili prime minister
	1978	Sadat negotiates agreement with Israel
	1981	Sadat is assassinated
Dissolution of Soviet Union	1991	

For Further Reading
Hirst, David, and Irene Besson. *Sadat*. London: Faber and Faber, 1981.
Israeli, Raphael. *Man of Defiance*. New York: Barnes and Noble, 1985.

Sakharov, Andrei

Soviet Nuclear Weapons
Researcher and Political Dissident
1921–1989

Life and Work

In the opening years of the Cold War, Andrei Sakharov designed the Soviet Union's first hydrogen bomb. His later disillusionment with nuclear weaponry, however, led him to issue fundamental criticisms of the Soviet regime.

Andrei Dmitrievich Sakharov was born in Moscow, the son of a scientist, on May 21, 1921. Raised to follow in his father's footsteps, he graduated in 1942 from Moscow State University with a degree in physics. With World War II (1939–45) raging against Nazi Germany, he worked in the armaments industry, contributing to the victory of the Red Army in 1945. As the Cold War erupted with the United States, however, the Soviet Union feared that

the American monopoly of nuclear weapons would prevent it from maintaining military parity. Sakharov was therefore commissioned along with the physicist Igor Tamm to develop a nuclear weapons arsenal. The team's work enabled the Soviet Union to detonate its first hydrogen bomb in 1953 (a weaker atomic bomb had been developed in 1949). In recognition of his achievement, Sakharov was elevated to the Soviet Academy of Science the same year.

Soon after, however, Sakharov turned away from the military establishment when the moral implications of his work began to trouble him. By 1963 he emerged as a maverick supporter of the first Nuclear Test Ban Treaty. In 1968 he also took the bold step of publishing abroad a criticism of communist politics entitled *Progress, Coexistence, and Intellectual Freedom,* for which he was severely reprimanded. The breach had become irreparable, however, and in the 1970s he became even more outspoken against what he considered the neo-Stalinist government of LEONID BREZHNEV. Following his 1979 protest of the Soviet decision to invade Afghanistan, he was exiled to the city of Gorky in 1980. There he lived under KGB surveillance with his wife and fellow human rights activist Elena Bonner until 1986, when MIKHAIL GORBACHEV released him. He returned to Moscow in 1986 and in 1989 won a seat to the democratic Congress of People's Deputies. Popular among many Soviet liberals and intellectuals, he died on December 14, 1989, after participating in a vigorous Congress debate.

Legacy

Andrei Sakharov's work in nuclear physics brought great military strength to the Soviet Union. Ironically, however, his activities as a dissident ultimately contributed to its collapse.

With the nuclear technology developed by Sakharov and Tamm, the Soviet Union was able in a single decade to achieve military parity with the United States. The development of bomb-carrying missiles, made possible by the successful launching of *Sputnik* in 1957, enabled the military to develop weapons that could deliver great destruction. At first only short- and medium-range missiles were capable of carrying nuclear bombs, leading to an effort by NIKITA KHRUSHCHEV to build Soviet missile bases in Cuba. When this plan fell to pieces in the Cuban Missile Crisis of 1962, military scientists were

ordered to develop long-range missiles that could be launched from Soviet soil. This plan, the most dramatic result of Sakharov's military legacy, was completed in 1965 with the deployment of the 25-megaton SS-9 intercontinental ballistic missile (ICBM). The Soviet Union now had an arsenal that assured any potential enemy that the Soviet Union, if attacked, would have the power to deliver an overwhelming response.

However, the development of this costly weapons system contributed to an economic decline, and Sakharov's daring attacks on communism undermined the Soviet regime's political legitimacy. Having lauded him highly, the government could not denounce him as easily as it could other dissidents such as writer Alexander Solzhenitsyn. Sakharov's demand for intellectual freedom and other human rights inspired many intellectuals in Moscow and other cities to organize human rights watch groups and to circulate subversive underground publications such as *The Chronicle of Current Events.* His objection to the Afghan War also inspired common people who were losing loved ones in a conflict as seemingly futile as the Vietnam War had been for the United States. Finally, as the Soviet Union's most celebrated dissident, his support of BORIS YELTSIN and his actions in the Congress of People's Deputies in 1989 further undermined communism at a critical moment. After millions of Russians rallied behind Yeltsin and the principle of political liberty to oppose the neo-Stalinist putsch of August 1991, the communist regime with which Sakharov had broken in the 1960s finally collapsed.

Strickland

WORLD EVENTS		SAKHAROV'S LIFE
Russian Revolution	1917	
	1921	Andrei Sakharov is born
Great Depression	1929–39	
World War II	1939–45	
	1942	Sakharov is awarded degree in physics
Communist China is established	1949	
	1953	Sakharov and Igor Tamm contribute to detonation of first Soviet hydrogen bomb
Israel defeats Arab nations in Six-Day War	1967	
	1968	Sakharov publishes *Progress, Coexistence, and Intellectual Freedom*
Vietnam War ends	1975	
	1980	Sakharov is exiled to Gorky
	1986	Sakharov is released from exile
	1989	Sakharov is elected to Congress of People's Deputies; Sakharov dies
Dissolution of Soviet Union	1991	

For Further Reading

Bailey, George. *The Making of Andrei Sakharov.* London: Allen Lane, 1988.

Bonner, Elena. *Alone Together.* Translated by Alexander Cook. New York: Knopf, 1986.

Hosking, Geoffrey. *The Awakening of the Soviet Union.* 2nd ed. Cambridge, Mass.: Harvard University Press, 1991.

Saladin

Muslim Military and Political Leader
1137–1195

Life and Work

Saladin rallied the Muslim world in defense against Christian aggressors while earning a reputation for piety and honor throughout the Middle East, North Africa, and Europe.

Saladin (Salah "who honors religion") Abu 'l-Muzaffer Yusuf ibn Ayyub ibn Shadi was born the son of the gifted Abbasid governor of Tikrit, Najm ad-Din Ayyub, in present-day Iraq. The Abbasids controlled an empire that stretched from the Sinai to Persia, challenged mainly by the Christian European (called "Frankish") kingdom of Palestine, the Muslim Seljuks of Central Asia, and the Christian Byzantine Empire of Asia Minor. Saladin was educated in Damascus (in present-day Syria), where his family had relocated for political reasons, studying the Koran, military arts, and Aramaic, Arabic, and Turkish.

In 1153, at 16, Saladin began a meteoric rise in the ranks of the regional governments of the Abbasids, who governed from Baghdad. After an apprentice posting to the government of Aleppo, he returned to Damascus as the deputy military governor in 1155. Between 1164 and 1167, Saladin served as a quarter-master general of armies sent to wage war on the Christian Franks and the Muslim leaders of Egypt. In 1170–71, after mutually destructive political and military struggles between the triumphant Abbasids and the defeated Egyptians, Saladin was made commander-in-chief of armies raised in Egypt, which now included both traditional Syrian and newly loyal Egyptian troops. By 1175, Saladin helped to govern an empire that stretched from Tunis to the Tigris River.

Saladin gained the loyalty of Egyptians by purging the country of potential enemies and embarking on a large public works program. In 1174, he assumed political and military command of Egypt and Syria, but rivals who disliked the power Saladin had gained opposed him in Baghdad. Rather than strike back, Saladin worked hard at improving the lives of his subjects and let the success of his rule (reducing taxes, improving trade, and initiating other public works) speak for itself.

After 1178, Saladin faced a number of crises that threatened the area he had so laboriously brought under his control. Much of the coastal area of the Holy Land had been under the control of Europeans ("Franks") since the late 1080s. Their presence, along with the invasion of northern Iraq by the Seljuk Turks around the same time, had upset the delicate series of alliances that kept the Muslim world of the Near and Middle East and eastern North Africa under the control of the Abbasid caliph, his allies, and his army. In 1187, however, the Franks were battling each other over the right to control the lands and cities of the Holy Land, and Saladin took the opportunity to mount a large army against them. On July 4, 1187, drawing the Franks into a huge battle in the desert near Tiberias (at Hattin), in present-day Israel, Saladin destroyed their army and reoccupied the Christianized cities of Acre, Antioch, Ascalon, and, in October of the same year, Jerusalem.

In response to Saladin's victories, in 1191 the Roman Catholic church called for a Third Crusade, and European leaders of the day, including RICHARD I (Richard the Lion Heart) of England, Philip Augustus of France, and FREDERICK I of the Holy Roman Empire, raised a large army and marched on the Holy Land. Saladin had a very difficult time raising troops to defend recent conquests from new European assaults, and the Crusaders recaptured Acre and several other cities, which they held for the next 100 years. Rather than face disaster, Saladin consented to these conquests and permitted Christians access to Jerusalem through a treaty in 1192; the Franks, who had lost over 100,000 troops in the reconquest of some of the Holy Land, had no stomach for further bloodshed, and abandoned their campaign as well.

Exhausted by years of military campaigns, Saladin died in Damascus on March 4, 1195.

Legacy

Saladin defended the Muslim world against Christian expansion and earned the respect of the European invaders, becoming the stuff of legend.

Saladin campaigned tirelessly for the expansion of Islam, which he believed was the salvation of man. Saladin turned the loyalty he had accrued through his good works and exemplary living into a powerful force to resist the colonization of the Middle East by the Christians of Western Europe. European rulers fervently desired to capture and hold the Holy Land, both because of the religious significance of Jerusalem and also because of the enormously profitable trade that passed through the Middle East and the ports of the eastern Mediterranean coast. The Muslim troops could not hope to overpower the heavy cavalry of the Europeans; Saladin, however, drew the Christian forces into the deserts where they were gradually worn down by thirst and constant harassment.

Saladin impressed Europeans with his fairness and sense of honor. He usually released captured soldiers who had fought honorably, executing only those who had given up Islam to side with the Europeans, and Christian leaders who would not negotiate. For this mercy, Saladin became famous and remains a symbol of the noble opponent, strong of purpose, brutal in war, and fair in peace.

Del Testa

World Events	Saladin's Life
Timbuktu influential throughout west central Africa — c. 1100	
	1137 Saladin is born
	1153 Saladin serves government apprenticeship in Aleppo
	1164–67 Saladin wages war in Egypt
	1170–71 Saladin is commander-in-chief of Abbasid armies in Egypt
Saladin retakes Jerusalem for Islam — 1187	Saladin defeats Europeans at Hattin
	1191 Third Crusade begins
	1192 Saladin signs treaty to end Third Crusade
	1195 Saladin dies
Mongol conquest of China — 1215	

For Further Reading
Newby, P. H. *Saladin in His Time.* Boston: Faber and Faber, 1983.
Regan, Geoffrey. *Saladin and the Fall of Jerusalem.* New York: Croom Helm, 1987.

San Martín, José de

South American Revolutionary
1778–1850

Life and Work

Through exemplary leadership and organizational talents, José de San Martín liberated three countries from Spanish colonial rule, transforming them into republics that endure to this day.

San Martín was born in Yapeyú in present-day Argentina on February 25, 1778, son of the lieutenant governor of the northern department of Yapeyú. In 1781 his father resigned and moved the family first to Buenos Aires and then, in 1783, to Spain. San Martín was educated to become an officer in the Spanish army, joining in 1789, at age 11, and witnessing his first battle at age 13. He took part in numerous battles and was captured three times. He served until 1811, by which time NAPOLÉON I had invaded Spain and installed his brother Joseph on the Spanish throne. In response, the South American colonies rebelled, and San Martín returned to his homeland to take part in the struggle for independence.

Arriving in 1812, San Martín, whose nationalism was based on resentment of Spanish prejudice toward Creoles (those of Spanish descent

born in the colonies), went to the Rio de la Plata in Argentina to assist the struggling revolution. In October he led a military coup under the slogan "Independence, Constitution, Democracy" and was named commander of the army of the north in now-independent Argentina. He decided to expand the struggle for independence into Chile and Peru.

While rebuilding an army demoralized by recent Spanish gains, San Martín devised a bold and original strategy to defeat the Spaniards. He requested the governorship of Cuyo both to disguise his plans and to provide an economic base for his operation. In 1817, after raising an army, San Martín crossed the Andes toward Chile. In the Battle of Chacabuco, San Martín took Spanish troops by surprise, defeating them and liberating Chile. Although celebrated as a hero, San Martín, not personally ambitious, refused promotion and monetary reward. Instead, he planned an attack from the sea against Spanish forces in Lima, Peru.

In 1821 San Martín entered Lima with his triumphant troops and reluctantly became protector of Peru until a new government could be formed. In 1822 he met with SIMÓN BOLÍVAR in an unsuccessful effort to form an alliance. San Martín resigned his post, leaving the final liberation of Peru to Bolívar. He spent the rest of his life in voluntary exile in France, where he died on August 7, 1850, believing that the revolution in South America was not yet complete.

Legacy

The greatest South American soldier of the liberation period, José de San Martín used his considerable strategic and organizational talents to help the new South American nations to develop their own political institutions.

Because San Martín was not, and had no ambition to be, a politician, he offered no defense against his rivals, who cast suspicion on his motives. Reviled and rejected at first, then forgotten, long after his death San Martín became a symbol of Argentine nationalism. Argentina, after a period of instability, settled down and began to develop its economy, increasing both its wealth and its national pride.

Like Simón Bolívar, another revolutionary leader and liberator of South America, San Martín supported open and democratic governments. He also recognized, however, that a heterogeneous population consisting of a plurality of Indians and minorities of blacks, *mestizos* (those

of mixed Spanish–Indian blood), and whites, combined with a lack of political consensus and democratic traditions, made the implementation of liberal constitutions unlikely in the immediate future. San Martín agreed that the population was not yet ready for full democracy and would first need a benevolent dictatorship and a period of education and training. However, strong governments rapidly turned into dictatorships of terror in Argentina and in other parts of South America, causing periodic political and social uprisings well into the twentieth century. The struggle for democracy and freedom also endured into the twentieth century.

With independence assured by San Martín, Argentina's land-owning elites divided into rival factions: the unitarians and the federalists, who argued over the status of Buenos Aires as an autonomous city and about whether to integrate Argentina into international trade regimes or to retain provincial autonomy. Juan Manuel de Rosas, the dictatorial Argentine president from 1835 to 1852 ruled in favor of the cattle ranchers, who supported free trade. Thus, Rosas combined a rule of terror with enrichment of a favored economic elite, a development San Martín would have opposed.

As in other parts of South America, Britain took the lead in controlling import–export markets and in financing the development of Argentina's infrastructure. Throughout the nineteenth and twentieth centuries, Argentina continued to suffer from political repression and from overreliance on the export of raw materials to Europe and the United States, which discouraged domestic industrial development and limited Argentina's sovereignty.

Lemoine

WORLD EVENTS		SAN MARTÍN'S LIFE
United States declares independence	1776	
	1778	José de San Martín is born
French Revolution begins	1789	
	1789–1811	San Martín serves in Spanish army
Latin American independence movement begins	1811	
	1812	San Martín participates in Argentine liberation movement
Congress of Vienna reorganizes Europe	1815	
	1817	San Martín leads army into Chile
	1821	San Martín enters Lima, Peru, in triumph
	1850	San Martín dies in France
Germany is united	1871	

For Further Reading

Nicholson, Irene. *The Liberators: A Study of Independence Movements in Spanish America.* New York: Praeger, 1968.
Roche, David. *Argentina, 1516-1982: From Spanish Colonization to the Falklands War.* New York: Oxford, 1988.

Sa'ūd, Abd al-Aziz ibn

Creator of Modern Saudi Arabia
c. 1876–1953

Life and Work

During the first half of the twentieth century, Abd al-Aziz ibn Sa'ūd (Ibn Sa'ūd) unified and pacified the peoples of the Arabian peninsula and turned their energies toward the creation of wealth and a modern state.

Sa'ūd was born into a family of minor notables of the Arabian peninsula who had fled their homes after an attack by the Egyptians. Sa'ūd grew up under the protection of the Kuwaiti people in an environment of intrigue and revenge, magnified by the growing interests of various powers, local and European, in Arabia. As a youth, he had the training appropriate for the potential leader of an important Arabian family of the time, including horseback riding, marksmanship, and certain aspects of agriculture. In 1890, Sa'ūd also began informal lessons in Arabic and the Koran. His natural intelligence and impressive physical presence marked him as a leader in the making.

Sa'ūd made it his life goal to seek vengeance against the Rashidi, the family that took over the Sa'ūds' possessions after 1891. In 1902, using some modern weaponry and tactics learned from British agents, Sa'ūd took Riyadh, the present-day capital of Saudi Arabia, from the Rashidi and installed himself as governor. From this base, Sa'ūd began 30 years of gradually consolidating the people of Arabia under his leadership, beginning with the settlement of the Bedu people in agricultural and garrison colonies. Aided by the material support of the 1915 Anglo–Arabian Cooperation Treaty, Sa'ūd, through a mixture of patronage, cajoling, and conquest, brought all of what is today Arabia under his control. Consolidation efforts essentially ended in 1929, when Sa'ūd subdued the powerful Dumish and Utaiba clans.

On September 23, 1932, Sa'ūd declared a kingdom, called Saudi Arabia, and began to consolidate his revenue and administration. Earlier, Sa'ūd's finances had been precarious at best. In addition, the Great Depression had diminished the taxes paid to Sa'ūd by devoted Muslims for the *hajj*, the pilgrimage Muslims are supposed to make at least once in their lives to Mecca, a city then under Sa'ūd's control. Sa'ūd's financial prospects changed in the 1930s, when he invited engineers (most of them American) to survey Arabia to locate its known oil deposits. In late 1939, Saudi Arabia began its first commercial oil exports, starting 50 years of revenue growth for the country.

During World War II, Sa'ūd faced many crises, including a war-induced famine and threats from neighboring Yemen, who sympathized with the Axis powers (Germany, Italy, Japan). In March 1945, Sa'ūd met with United States President FRANKLIN DELANO ROOSEVELT during Roosevelt's return from the Allied conference at Yalta. Roosevelt and Sa'ūd discussed expanding Saudi oil exports to the United States, as well as growing Arab tension over the Jewish settlement in Palestine. Through this conversation, Sa'ūd and the Saudis earned a reputation as leaders of the Middle East. After World War II, with oil revenues mounting, Sa'ūd began to provide his kingdom with modern infrastructure, including schools, hospitals, roads, and electricity, and to build a modern army to resist the threats of his sometimes hostile neighbors. On November 9, 1953, Sa'ūd died after a short illness.

Legacy

Abd al-Aziz ibn Sa'ūd guided Arabia's people as a benevolent tribal leader but infused his own administration with modern ideas and methods, producing a powerful base on which post–World War II Saudi Arabia could grow as a modern state.

For at least 500 years before his rule, rival clans had controlled the different parts of the Arabian Peninsula as fiefdoms, each with different interests and prerogatives, uniting only occasionally to oppose common enemies. Leadership was managed by very strict forms of protocol and behavior, with many interlocking alliances and vendettas. After establishing his own local leadership in Riyadh, Sa'ūd used a combination of traditional leadership and his impressive reputation in order to unite the people of Arabia. He was both forward- and backward-looking, and was always governed by a keen desire to promote modern ideas while preserving what he believed to be the heart of the Arabian people—conservative Islam. Without Sa'ūd, Arabia might have been carved up among many rivals.

Sa'ūd's mixture of progressive and conservative values had many consequences, the most important of which centered on Arabia's vital export of oil to Europe and the United States. After World War II, Saudi Arabia became disproportionately powerful relative to its overall population because of its control of huge reserves of crude oil. Sa'ūd viscerally opposed the creation of Israel, and might have acted to prevent it had he and his heirs not been diverted by long-running political debates with Egypt, Jordan, and Yemen, and had they not followed an orthodox, and thus at heart tolerant, version of Islam. Sa'ūd created a Saudi Arabia that brought Arabs and others together in cooperation, remaining conservative and powerful, and not afraid to use wealth and power subtly to achieve its ends.

Del Testa

WORLD EVENTS		SA'ŪD'S LIFE
Germany is united	1871	
	c. 1876	Abd al-Aziz ibn Sa'ūd is born
	1902	Sa'ūd takes Riyadh
Russo-Japanese War	1905	
World War I	1914–18	
	1915	Treaty of Anglo-Arabian Cooperation is signed
Russian Revolution	1917	
Great Depression	1929–39	
	1929	Sa'ūd pacifies Dumish and Utaiba clans
	1932	Sa'ūd declares Saudi Arabian Kingdom
World War II	1939–45	
	1939	Sa'ūdi Arabia, under Sa'ūd's direction, ships first commercial oil exports
Communist China is established	1949	
	1953	Sa'ūd dies
Israel defeats Arab nations in Six-Day War	1967	

For Further Reading
McLoughlin, Leslie. *Ibn Saud: Founder of a Kingdom.* New York: St. Martin's Press, 1993.
Armstrong, H. C. *Lord of Arabia: Ibn Saud.* New York: Kegan Paul, 1998.

Schuman, Robert

Architect of European Unity

1886–1963

Life and Work

Robert Schuman developed a universal vision of Europe inspired by the Roman Catholic church. After World War II he used his training in economics and his influence in politics to make this vision a reality.

Robert Schuman was born to a Roman Catholic family in Luxembourg on June 29, 1886. His native land contained a mixture of French and Germans and bordered the territory of Alsace–Lorraine, which had recently been torn away from France by Germany in the Franco-Prussian War (1870–71). Schuman was raised in an environment of nationalistic rivalry where a powerful Germany under OTTO VON BISMARCK was challenged by a humiliated France calling for "*Revanche!*" ("revenge"). As a youth, he found an alterna-tive political ideal in the teaching of the Roman Catholic church, which had been attacked by the increasingly secularized French and German governments. The church con-demned the secular nationalism of the age and called upon Europeans to revive a universal (or "catholic") spiritual basis for their civilization.

He refused to serve in the German army during World War I and was jailed as a result. The Treaty of Versailles in 1919 returned Alsace–Lorraine to a victorious France, and Schuman entered the French National Assembly. His training in economics enabled him to serve on the numerous financial committees strug-gling with the problems of postwar reconstruc-tion. In 1940 Germany invaded France and Schuman fell into the hands of the Gestapo. In 1942 he managed to escape, and joined the Resistance until France was liberated in 1944.

In that year he helped found the Christian Popular Republican Movement (MRP), whose basis in liberalism and Roman Catholicism mir-rored the newly created Christian Democratic Union of Germany under KONRAD ADENAUER. Schuman was elected to the new French National Assembly in 1945 and became finance minister in 1946. He assumed the office of for-eign minister from 1948 to 1952.

With peace restored, Schuman sought to reconstruct Europe in such a way that national-ism and war would never again divide it. His most influential act was the introduction in 1950 of what came to be known as the Schuman Plan, though it had, in fact, originated with the economist Jean Monnet. The plan called for the creation of a Common Market in European coal and steel. Although it was rejected as a threat to national sovereignty by the English and CHARLES DE GAULLE, it was immediately accepted by Adenauer across the Rhine. The result was the creation of the European Coal and Steel Community in 1951. After fighting two devastating wars against each other, France and Germany now joined their economies in peace, and Europe took a tentative step toward unity.

Schuman retired from government in 1952. On September 4, 1963, he died in the town of Metz in Alsace-Lorraine.

Legacy

Because of its focus on economics, Robert Schuman's vision of a united Europe was realized to a greater and greater degree during the second half of the twentieth century.

Schuman's political ideals were shaped pri-marily by his Roman Catholic faith. He real-ized, however, that a specifically religious model of European civilization was not viable. He believed that industrial capitalism could provide his generation with the necessary basis for unity. This was ironic, of course, for capi-talism, with its principle of free market compe-tition, defied many of the church's teachings about the moral value of economic life. Nevertheless, with the shadows of eastern European communism and American capital-ism falling across the economic map of Western Europe, the idea of unity gained influence. Above all, liberal politicians and business lead-ers sought to prevent another war, which the Schuman Plan of 1950 had promised to make "physically impossible."

The European Coal and Steel Community created by Schuman became the core institu-tion of economic union in Europe during the second half of the twentieth century. In 1957 the Treaty of Rome created the European Economic Community (EEC) that went beyond coal and steel to integrate the entire economies of member states—France, Germany, Italy, Belgium, the Netherlands, and Schuman's native Luxembourg. In subsequent years Denmark, Ireland, Greece, Spain, Portugal, and Britain also joined. Tariff barri-ers within the group were gradually elimi-nated, sparking a period of economic growth lasting through the 1960s.

What is more, economic unity inspired greater political unity. This had been a long-term dream of Schuman's. During the 1970s, new institutions such as a European Parliament and a European Court of Justice were created. To reflect these changes, the Common Market was renamed the European Union (EU) with the Maastricht Treaty of 1991. Although a resurgent ethnic nationalism and new hard-ships for workers forced to adapt to the free market continued to limit the implementation of the Maastricht Treaty, the end of the twenti-eth century saw Schuman's universal vision coming still closer to realization.

Commending his legacy and Schuman's religious faith, Pope John Paul II beatified Schuman in 1995.

Strickland

WORLD EVENTS		SCHUMAN'S LIFE
Germany is united	1871	
	1886	Schuman is born
Russo-Japanese War	1905	
World War I	1914–18	
Russian Revolution	1917	
Great Depression	1929–39	
World War II	1939–45	
	1942–44	Schuman fights in French Resistance
	1944	Schuman helps found Popular Republican Movement
	1945	Schuman is elected to French National Assembly
	1948–52	Schuman serves as French foreign minister
Communist China is established	1949	
	1950	Schuman introduces plan for creation of Common Market
	1957	Treaty of Rome creates European Economic Union
	1963	Schuman dies
Israel defeats Arab nations in Six-Day War	1967	

For Further Reading

Diebold, William. *The Schuman Plan: A Study in Economic Cooperation, 1950–1959.* New York: Praeger, 1959.

Heater, Derek. *The Idea of European Unity.* London: Leicester University Press, 1992.

Trachtenberg, Mark. *A Constructed Peace: The Making of the European Settlement, 1945–1963.* Princeton, N.J.: Princeton University Press, 1999.

Senghor, Léopold Sédar

Writer and Leader of Senegal
1906–

Life and Work

The first president of the independent African nation of Senegal, Léopold Sédar Senghor based his policies on the philosophy of negritude, a definition of the African personality. He created a stable, relatively democratic regime that endures to the present.

Senghor was born in Joal, Senegal, then a French colony, on October 9, 1906. In 1914, he was sent to a Roman Catholic mission school by his father, a prosperous farmer who wanted him exposed to French culture. At first interested in joining the Roman Catholic priesthood, he decided instead to become a teacher, moving to Paris in 1928 to obtain the necessary education. By 1935 Senghor had passed the rigorous exam to obtain a teaching post in France. While in France he also met fellow Africans and other representatives of France's colonized peoples and began to embrace his African identity despite years of immersion in French culture and learning.

In the years that followed, Senghor developed the philosophical concept of *negritude* (best translated as the "African personality"), which defined the unique spiritual identity of black Africans as distinct from the materialist

orientation of white Europeans. In 1939 Senghor was drafted into the French army and was captured by the Germans when they invaded France in 1940. Released two years later, Senghor joined the French Resistance. In 1945, Senghor was elected to the French National Assembly representing Senegal; in 1955 he was appointed to the French cabinet and helped draft the constitution of the French Fifth Republic in 1958.

In 1960 Senghor was elected president of the newly independent nation of Senegal and served until 1981. He created a relatively democratic one-party state and constructed a mixed economy in which large-scale industries were nationalized, yet free enterprise was allowed to exist. Senghor also sought to create a federation of West African states, joining Senegal to a short-lived union with Mali, Benin, and Burkina Faso (1959–60). This effort, however, met with failure and the former colonies of Africa achieved independence by retaining the boundaries created during the era of European colonial conquest. Senghor continued to publish poetry and essays during his time in office, retiring in 1981 to devote more time to writing. In 1984 he was elected member of the prestigious French Academy.

Legacy

Léopold Sédar Senghor, philosopher, poet, and national leader, helped to renew African culture and created a stable West African nation while maintaining ties to France, Senegal's former colonial ruler.

Senghor attempted, with mixed success, to combine the best that African and Western cultures had to offer. He cultivated close political and economic ties with France, a relationship that endures to the present. His belief that African states based on old colonial boundaries would diminish the region's economic prospects and keep Africa politically weak has proved to be correct, yet Senghor's repeated attempts to create a viable federation of West African states have all failed.

Like many African states, Senegal's economy suffers from overreliance on a single cash crop (peanuts), dependency on rich Western nations, a lack of economic development, rising fuel costs, and decreasing prices for agricultural products. In an effort to promote economic growth, Senghor began to abandon

nationalization, liberalizing the economy and introducing free-enterprise reforms.

Although many African states have suffered from political instability, Senegal under Senghor enjoyed a measure of stability, despite an attempted coup by Prime Minister Mamadou Dia in 1962. Senghor became the first African leader to leave office voluntarily in 1981. His successor, Abdou Diouf, continued policies of political and economic liberalization, and proved to be a more efficient administrator. Although Senegal faces many economic problems, Senghor established a more stable base for development than leaders of other African nations have done.

Lemoine

World Events		Senghor's Life
Russo-Japanese War	1905	
	1906	Léopold Sédar Senghor is born
World War I	1914–18	
Russian Revolution	1917	
	1928	Senghor travels to France to continue education
Great Depression	1929–39	
World War II	1939–45	
	1945	Senghor is elected member of French National Assembly
Communist China is established	1949	
	1960	Senghor is elected president of Senegal
Israel defeats Arab nations in Six-Day War	1967	
Vietnam War ends	1975	
	1981	Senghor retires from presidency
	1984	Senghor is elected to French Academy
Dissolution of Soviet Union	1991	

For Further Reading
Hymans, Jacques Louis. *Léopold Sédar Senghor: An Intellectual Biography.* Edinburgh: Edinburgh University Press, 1971.
Markovitz, Irving Leonard. *Léopold Sédar Senghor and the Politics of Negritude.* New York: Atheneum, 1969.
Spleth, Janice. *Léopold Sédar Senghor.* Boston: Twayne Publishers, 1985.

Shaka

Zulu Ruler

c. 1787–1828

Life and Work

Shaka, the founder of the Zulu nation, created a centralized and militaristic state that fostered a long-lasting sense of national pride among South African Zulus, though his military conquests caused a disruptive migration of peoples that has affected the populations of southern and central Africa to the present.

Shaka was born around 1787, the son of Senzangakhona, ruler of the small state of Zulu, of the Nguni people, in southeastern Africa. Shaka's mother, Nandi, did not get

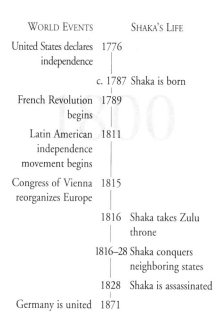

WORLD EVENTS		SHAKA'S LIFE
United States declares independence	1776	
	c. 1787	Shaka is born
French Revolution begins	1789	
Latin American independence movement begins	1811	
Congress of Vienna reorganizes Europe	1815	
	1816	Shaka takes Zulu throne
	1816–28	Shaka conquers neighboring states
	1828	Shaka is assassinated
Germany is united	1871	

along well with his father and she and the young Shaka were exiled by him. Bullied by other children, Shaka grew up a troubled, yet fearless, fighter for Dingiswayo, the chief of Ndwandwe people.

When his father died in 1816, Shaka defeated his rivals and assumed his father's throne, his military genius already obvious. Shaka fashioned and refined the Zulu military system, consisting of regiments organized by age. The ethnic identity of the troops, many of whom came from defeated peoples, was ignored in favor of Zulu national unity, resulting in a well-trained and disciplined army.

Shaka devised the very successful military tactics of deploying troops in flanking maneuvers designed to envelop the opposing army and using short-handled spears for stabbing the enemy in close contact. From 1816 to 1828 the Zulu nation defeated neighboring tribes and expanded its territory. These wars of expansion forced many neighboring peoples to flee in an episode of depopulation and forced migration known as the *Mfecane* ("the crushing").

With a charismatic yet troubled personality, Shaka was a powerful and feared ruler. When his mother died in 1827, a bereaved Shaka declared a period of mourning that included massacres and prohibitions on sexual activity and planting for the next harvest. After Shaka ordered his army on another campaign, two of his half-brothers murdered him on September 12, 1828. The population, exhausted by Shaka's dynamic yet unpredictable ways, was relieved by his assassination.

Legacy

Shaka's successful conquests fostered a sense of national identity able to withstand the white supremacist governments of the twentieth century and survive to the present. However, the disruptions of the *Mfecane* changed the ethnic make-up of much of southern and central Africa and also facilitated European migration into previously populated territories.

The tribes and ethnic groups fleeing the Zulu invasions profoundly changed the population distribution in South Africa. To the north of Zululand new states, such as Swazi, Ndebele, and Gaza, emerged from the fleeing population, pushing other tribes north

in a ripple effect that extended as far as Lake Victoria in Central Africa and east to the Kalahari Desert.

Natal, adjacent to Zululand, was largely emptied of the indigenous population because of Shaka's raids. In 1836, Boers, the descendants of Dutch settlers who had arrived in the seventeenth century, left the British-controlled Cape Colony seeking (in what became known as the Great Trek) new lands outside British domination. They were immediately drawn to empty Natal, which brought them into conflict with the Zulu. Shaka's half-brother, Dingane, not nearly as talented as Shaka, could not maintain a strong Zulu state in the face of pressure from both the Boers, followed by the British, who annexed Zululand after a long series of battles between 1879 and 1888.

However, because of Shaka's military success, Zulus and neighboring tribes retained a sense of national identity. This ethnic pride contributed to resistance among Zulus to conquest and domination by Europeans. In twentieth-century South Africa, Zulu nationalism posed a problem for the African National Congress, which sought the unity of all South African peoples to oppose white oppression during the apartheid era. In 1975, Zulu politician Gatsha Mangosuthu Buthelezi founded the Inkatha Party (later renamed the Inkatha Freedom Party), which soon became the dominant Zulu political party. The post-apartheid era has seen rising tension between the ruling African National Congress and the Inkatha Freedom Party.

Lemoine

For Further Reading

Omer-Cooper, J. D. *The Zulu Aftermath: A Nineteenth-Century Revolution in Bantu Africa.* Evanston, Ill.: Northwestern University Press, 1966.

Parsons, Neil. *A New History of Southern Africa.* 2nd ed. London: Macmillan, 1993.

Shih Huang-ti

Unifier of Ancient China
c. 259–210/209 B.C.E.

Life and Work

Shih Huang-ti, born Chao Cheng, was the emperor of the Ch'in dynasty and established the first cohesive Chinese empire.

Chao Cheng was born around 259 B.C.E. to Chuang Hsiang and his wife, the former concubine of a wealthy merchant. The merchant, Lü Pu-wei, found a way to install his former concubine's new husband on the throne of the state of Ch'in, at the time East Asia's most powerful state, even though Chuang Hsiang was not in the line of formal succession. At the death of Chuang Hsiang in 246, 13-year-old Cheng came to the throne, when the Ch'in state was already the most powerful of the states in the area known as China today. After taking the throne, Cheng became known as Shih Huang-ti (modern spelling Shi Huangdi).

The Ch'in state already possessed a strong military and organized bureaucracy, which Shih Huang-ti set about fortifying. He also planned the expansion of Ch'in beyond its mountainous borders. However, he had some household business to take care of first. During the period between ascending to the throne in 246 and gaining his majority in 238, Shih Huang-ti's mother, whose political support for her son came under suspicion, had taken a lover who had been provided to her by Lü Pu-wei. Shih Huang-ti's first act was to execute his mother and exile Lü. Thereafter, Shih Huang-ti embarked on a ruthless expansion and, by 217, through bribery, espionage, and astounding military strategy, conquered all of the states that made up the area now known as China, including Han, Chao, Wei, Ch'u, Yen, and Ch'i. Shih Huang-ti thus created the first recognizable incarnation of the China that exists today.

In 221, Shih Huang-ti issued a series of edicts that would solidify his rule over all of the Ch'in possessions (where Europeans got the name for China). He promulgated a unified code of law, standardized the currency, the written language, and weights and measures, and set up a nonhereditary bureaucracy loyal to a central state. In addition, he commissioned the building of roads and added to the Great Wall in order to repel invasions from barbarian outsiders. Not content with northern China, Shih Huang-ti sent troops to conquer southern China and northern Vietnam in 217.

To solidify his vast holdings, Shih Huang-ti engaged in enormous labor drafts to lengthen and strengthen the Great Wall. He built a new capital in the Wei Valley named Hsienyang, and built new roads of a uniform width. He would have been remembered more affectionately except that he was brutal to his opponents and scornful of the past. Indeed, in 213 Shih Huang-ti sanctioned burning of all books not related to law or technology.

Shih Huang-ti was assassinated in either 210 or 209.

Legacy

Shih Huang-ti contributed to Chinese history in a profound and enduring way by defining the approximate limits of the Chinese state and by expanding Chinese cultural influence.

Shih Huang-ti demarcated the new limits of the Chinese state with walls in the north and garrisons in the south, and by imposing standardization everywhere in between. The roots of a Chinese nation are traced to these actions. Shih Huang-ti's amalgamation of power over so many people and resources became simultaneously a model and a warning to future rulers—he appears greedy by later standards and harsh to his people while simultaneously confirming his right to rule through victorious campaigns and the consolidation of internal power.

The negatives of Shih Huang-ti's rule overpower his accomplishments. Shih Huang-ti mobilized the masses for national goals through cruel labor drafts, pushed his armies to the geographical limits of ancient conquest, and "purified" his state by burning much of the written record of the past. Although his conquests overawed friend and enemy alike, Shih Huang-ti did not live up to the broader ideal of a just ruler. Instead, he ruled by force and maintained order through a minute policing of all of his subjects. This kind of careful definition of the state's duties and subject's responsibilities became known as legalism, a philosophical movement to which some Chinese rulers would turn over the next 2,000 years but that was generally considered too rigid for effective and just leadership. Shih Huang-ti proved that a ruler could only govern if he has people to rule; in the end, the people deserted Shih Huang-ti and refused to cooperate in his rule.

Del Testa

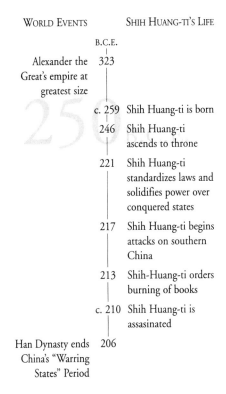

World Events	Shih Huang-ti's Life
B.C.E.	
Alexander the Great's empire at greatest size	323
	c. 259 Shih Huang-ti is born
	246 Shih Huang-ti ascends to throne
	221 Shih Huang-ti standardizes laws and solidifies power over conquered states
	217 Shih Huang-ti begins attacks on southern China
	213 Shih-Huang-ti orders burning of books
	c. 210 Shih Huang-ti is assasinated
Han Dynasty ends China's "Warring States" Period	206

For Further Reading

Cotterell, Arthur. *The First Emperor of China*. London: Macmillan, 1981.

Fuang, Wilson V. Z. *Chin Shih Huang*. Taipei, Taiwan: China Printing, 1971.

Spartacus

Leader of Roman Slave Rebellion
d. 71 B.C.

Life and Work

Spartacus led one of the greatest slave rebellions in ancient Rome. By the time it was quelled, thousands had been killed and the Roman Republic was badly shaken.

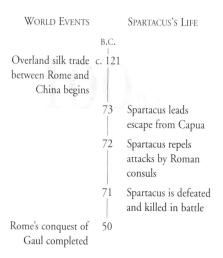

WORLD EVENTS		SPARTACUS'S LIFE
	B.C.	
Overland silk trade	c. 121	
between Rome and		
China begins		
	73	Spartacus leads escape from Capua
	72	Spartacus repels attacks by Roman consuls
	71	Spartacus is defeated and killed in battle
Rome's conquest of	50	
Gaul completed		

The origins of Spartacus are obscure. He appears to have joined the Roman army while a young man living in Thrace, then a Roman province on the Balkan Peninsula. Perhaps because of disloyalty, he was enslaved at some point during the first half of the first century before Christ. Sold in the city of Rome, he was sent to the leading training school for gladiators of the day at Capua. There he came into contact with a large number of slaves, many of whom were from distant lands and spoke different languages. Roman slave policy was to mix slaves of different tongues and races in order to reduce communication and therefore the possibility of organized revolt. Nevertheless, Spartacus was able to effect at least a limited degree of solidarity among his comrades at the school, perhaps through a charismatic personality.

In 73 B.C. Spartacus organized an escape from Capua that included as many as 70 other slaves. The band sped directly for the mountain of Vesuvius, where they established a fortified base. From there they began to conduct raids in the neighborhood for provisions. During the course of one of these they happened upon a wagon train bearing gladiatorial equipment, and the swords and shields they seized gave them the means of resisting the Roman army. As they awaited an attack, news of their escape circulated in the region. Before long their number was increased to hundreds and then thousands, as communities of slaves likewise revolted and came to Vesuvius to form a united army.

When the Roman legions finally did arrive, Spartacus distinguished himself by repulsing them more than once. So successful was his leadership that the ruling Roman consuls themselves were finally dispatched to the region in 72, though the rebel position still held. It was nonetheless clear that time would ultimately favor the authorities. Spartacus seems to have planned a rapid march north over the Alps and then onward to safety in Gaul, but his large army proved too unwieldy for such an escape. In the end the decision was made to march south. When Spartacus's forces failed to find a haven, the Roman general Crassus was sent with 10 legions to bring an end to the rebellion. At a battle near the Silarus River in 71, Crassus surrounded Spartacus's army and by the end of the day the slave leader had fallen and his army was defeated. Spartacus died in the battle but his body was never found.

As Crassus returned to Rome in triumph, 6,000 slaves were crucified on the Capua road as a warning to Rome's slave population.

Legacy

Although ultimately unsuccessful, Spartacus's desperate rebellion lived on in the memory of Roman politicians and modern revolutionaries.

Rome in the first century was a society dependent upon slave labor. The republic's conquest of territories led to the enslavement of a large number of foreign subjects and captured soldiers. While some of these men and women lived under conditions that were no worse than those of many free citizens, many more were treated harshly. And as the republic acquired more territories, it acquired more slaves. By the time of Spartacus's revolt as much as 30% percent of the Roman population were slaves. The broad response to his rebellion among the slave population showed the authorities in Rome the dangers of this social order. Rather than take measures to ameliorate the problem, however, Roman leaders treated the issue of slavery in an even more repressive manner. By the time the Roman Empire was formed nearly a generation later under JULIUS CAESAR (who himself patronized the gladiatorial schools), slavery had become even more deeply ingrained in the Roman social and economic fabric.

In modern times, Spartacus has come to represent the struggle of the oppressed against political authority. This was especially true among Marxist revolutionaries in the twentieth century. In the most explicit revival of Spartacus's image, a radical faction within the German Social Democratic Party, which called itself the Spartacus League, revolted against the Weimar regime in 1919 A.D. Calling upon workers to overthrow the capitalist order, the Spartacists found immediate inspiration in the Bolshevik Revolution of 1917 in Russia. Unlike the Bolsheviks, however, and resembling more its ancient Roman namesake, the Spartacist revolt quickly failed. Leaders such as ROSA LUXEMBURG were later hunted down by reactionary German militants and murdered.

Strickland

For Further Reading

Bradley, Keith R. *Slavery and Rebellion in the Roman World, 140 B.C.–70 B.C.* Bloomington: Indiana University Press, 1989.
Brunt, P. A. *Italian Manpower, 225 B.C.–A.D. 14.* Oxford: Oxford University Press, 1971.
Harris, William V. *War and Imperialism in Republican Rome, 327–70 B.C.* Oxford: Oxford University Press, 1979.

Stalin, Joseph

Soviet Dictator
1879–1953

Life and Work

Joseph Stalin transformed the Soviet Union into a modern industrial and military power. His brutal methods of rule, however, caused the deaths of millions of Soviet people.

Stalin was born on December 9, 1879, in the Georgian town of Gori, then a part of the Russian Empire. His family name was Dzhugashvili and his father was a cobbler. Throughout his life he remained uncomfortable with his non-Russian and non-proletarian roots. Abused by his father and doted on by his mother, he entered a seminary in 1894 but abandoned a religious career after discovering Marxism.

In 1903 he joined the Bolshevik Party of VLADIMIR ILICH LENIN and was assigned the task of organizing bank robberies to help raise funds. Arrested in 1913, he was exiled to Siberia; by this time he had adopted the name Stalin (meaning "man of steel"). After the revolution of March 1917, he traveled to Petrograd (formerly St. Petersburg), where he played a minor role helping Lenin and LEON TROTSKY seize power in the October Revolution. He was made commissar of nationalities in the new government, but did little to distinguish himself. Nevertheless,

through a series of cunning political maneuvers, including his appointment in 1922 as general secretary of the governing Politburo, Stalin was able successively to demote his rivals in the years after Lenin's death in 1924.

By 1928 he began his "revolution from above," a government-directed transformation of the Soviet Union from an agricultural to an industrial economy. A ruthless program of agricultural collectivization resulted in the arrest and deportation of hundreds of thousands of peasants and the starvation of millions. Stalin, eager to establish a reputation as unrivaled party leader, also launched a campaign of terror in 1934 that resulted in the execution of all his real and imagined enemies. By 1939, when war in Europe loomed, he was left alone with a circle of followers in the Politburo who regularly lauded him as the heroic successor to Lenin.

When ADOLF HITLER attacked the Soviet Union in 1941, Stalin's dictatorship was briefly threatened. But as the Soviet people bravely withstood the German assault at the cost of 27 million lives, Stalin remained in power and after the war even lived long enough to oversee the expansion of communism into Eastern Europe. Historians believe he was preparing yet another purge early in 1953, but a stroke on March 5 of that year finally brought an end to his devastating rule.

Legacy

Joseph Stalin created an industrial economy that played a crucial role in strengthening the Soviet Union as a world power. Nevertheless, the political system he created ultimately diminished his achievements.

Stalin's "revolution from above" irreversibly transformed the Russian economy to include an industrial base and a large working class, two factors required for a true proletarian revolution, according to KARL MARX. This proved to be significant—for without heavy industries, victory over Nazi Germany by 1945 would have been nearly impossible. What is more, during the years of the Cold War, the industrial economy, along with great advances in scientific development, provided modern armaments such as nuclear missiles that enabled the Soviet Union to match and in some ways sur-

pass the military strength of the United States. Finally, the peaceful potential of this economy was tapped by Stalin's more benevolent successors, who genuinely sought to improve the people's standard of living by providing modern consumer goods and social services.

Stalin's contribution to Soviet political traditions was unambiguously negative. Not only did he use violence in a despotic and irrational way, surpassing by far his medieval predecessor IVAN IV (Ivan the Terrible), but he oversaw the consolidation of a totalitarian system of rule. While historians disagree over the scope of its success, the communist totalitarian system consisted of four essential elements: a single party dictatorship, a secret police force, a command economy, and enforced ideological uniformity. Some of these elements were already in place before Stalin rose to power, but he made them a systemic part of Soviet communism. So central did they become that subsequent leaders such as NIKITA KHRUSHCHEV could not alter them without threatening their own power. Only MIKHAIL GORBACHEV proved daring enough to initiate reform. Yet, as the four main elements of the totalitarian system were undermined in the years before 1991, so was the Soviet Union itself.

Strickland

For Further Reading

Conquest, Robert. *Stalin: Breaker of Nations.* London: Penguin, 1991.

Tucker, Robert C. *Stalin as Revolutionary, 1879–1929: A Study in History and Personality.* New York: Norton, 1973.

———. *Stalin in Power: The Revolution from Above, 1928–1941.* New York: Norton, 1990.

Volkogonov, Dmitri. *Stalin: Triumph and Tragedy.* Edited and translated by Harold Shukman. London: George Weidenfeld, 1991.

WORLD EVENTS		STALIN'S LIFE
Germany is united	1871	
	1879	Joseph Stalin is born
	1903	Stalin joins Bolshevik Party
Russo-Japanese War	1905	
	1913	Stalin is arrested and exiled to Siberia
World War I	1914–18	
Russian Revolution	1917	Stalin participates in October Revolution
	1922	Stalin is named general secretary of Politburo
	1928	Stalin launches "revolution from above"
Great Depression	1929–39	
	1934	Stalin begins campaign of terror
World War II	1939–45	
Communist China is established	1949	
	1953	Stalin dies
Israel defeats Arab nations in Six-Day War	1967	

Steinem, Gloria

Feminist Activist and Writer
1934–

Life and Work

In the late 1960s, Gloria Steinem dedicated to the cause of feminism her enormous energy, unending concern with social justice, society connections, and a fashionable mystique that had grown up around her, and in so doing, made the women's movement much more inclusive and activist in nature than it had been.

Born on March 25, 1934, to a lower middle–class family, Steinem showed a keen intelligence and beauty from an early age. In school, Steinem did well, despite often having to take care of her parents. In 1952, Steinem entered Smith, a prestigious private college for women, where she established an excellent scholastic record and graduated in 1956 Phi Beta Kappa. In addition, Steinem befriended the daughters of some of America's elite families. After traveling to India as a student fellow and serving as a delegate to international youth meetings, Steinem, beginning in 1960, worked

World Events	Steinem's Life
Great Depression 1929–39	
	1934 Gloria Steinem is born
World War II 1939–45	
Communist China 1949 is established	
	1956 Steinem graduates from Smith
	1960 Steinem works as writer in New York City
	1966 National Organization for Women founded
Israel defeats Arab nations in Six-Day War	1967
	1972 Steinem helps found *Ms.* Magazine
Vietnam War ends 1975	

as a freelance writer in New York, preparing short pieces for magazines such as *Help!*, *Esquire, Show,* and *Glamour* and writing scripts for television shows. During the early 1960s, because of her popular look and her relationships with the well connected, Steinem became a national symbol of the "cool" young woman. In 1963, Steinem became additionally famous for her magazine expose of the treatment of women in the New York City Playboy Club and for *The Beach Book*, a frivolous reflection on what to do at the beach.

Rather than simply leveraging her popularity into wealth and a life of leisure, Steinem instead followed the path she first traced in her expose of the Playboy Club. She became increasingly active in politics. In 1967, Steinem traveled to Washington, D.C., to join the women's strike for peace, an anti–Vietnam War protest, and befriended Bella Abzug, a longtime feminist and political activist. She helped support the 1969 United Farm Workers strike and, after 1970, pushed for the Equal Rights Amendment. Beginning in 1969, Steinem became involved in the leadership of the National Organization for Women (NOW), founded in 1966, but increasingly opposed its domineering moral leader, BETTY FRIEDAN. Eventually, Friedan stepped away from NOW and Steinem became identified as its leader.

In 1972, Steinem helped found *Ms.*, a magazine by and for women. It was popular but always had financial difficulties. After the mid-1970s, Steinem continued to support NOW, *Ms.*, and various political struggles, but also moved onto new struggles, including the right of women to have abortions and her own successful battle against breast cancer. She was a supporter of Bill Clinton's 1992 presidential campaign, and remains politically active.

Legacy

Gloria Steinem opened the American women's movement to a very wide constituency, expanding American feminism to encompass many political issues related to women.

Before becoming a star of the feminist movement, Steinem had been a star of the chic set as well as a respected professional writer. She knew how to handle fame, her own image, and business. Although perhaps counter to the philosophy of the American women's movement that giving credence to notions such as

style and beauty made women complicit in their own oppression, Steinem used her attractiveness and open-mindedness to involve more kinds of women in the women's movement than had ever been involved before. Steinem made the community of women larger by validating all issues—including sexual preference, economic status, and race—that made up women's identities. Hundreds of thousands of women during the 1970s felt empowered by Steinem to agitate for their rights. They felt that they had something in common with each other and women around the world, another idea Steinem pushed very hard.

However, the charge Friedan had always leveled against Steinem's kind of inclusive movement, that issues beyond political and economic empowerment took away from the force of the woman's movement, perhaps had some truth in it. During the mid–1970s, the women's movement, after great successes and at a very critical moment, atomized its strength into many separate and particular issues, including the abortion rights debate, the rights of women workers to equal pay, and so on. These issues, such as the civil rights of lesbians, were often based around sexual or political identities with which most Americans were unprepared to deal. By the late 1970s, Steinem's women's movement, pushing hard for the Equal Rights Amendment, ran into a mounting conservative backlash that had not existed before the mid–1970s but that had rallied around opposition to the feminist movement's more extreme ideas and that tried to make feminism a bad word.

Del Testa

For Further Reading
Heilbrun, Carolyn G. *The Education of a Woman: A Life of Gloria Steinem.* New York: Dial Press, 1995.
Stern, Sydney Ladensohn. *Gloria Steinem: Her Passions, Politics, and Mystique.* Secaucus, N.J.: Carol Publishing Group, 1997.

Suharto

Indonesian Political Leader
1921–

Life and Work

In 1965, Suharto restored order to an Indonesia wracked by political unrest and economic collapse. Although he maintained his power through questionable means, he made Indonesia safe for investment and thus made average Indonesians more prosperous.

Suharto, who, following Indonesian custom, only identified himself with a given name, was born in a poor farming village near Yogyakarta, Java, on June 8, 1921. He attended primary school and joined an Islamic youth organization but could not afford to go beyond middle school. With an average education and without connections, he found it difficult to find a permanent job. His fortunes changed in mid-1940 when he was allowed to enlist in the Royal Netherlands Indies Army. Indonesia was a Dutch colony at the time and kept order with the help of a large local military staffed by Dutch officers.

Suharto found his calling in the military and was quickly promoted to sergeant. In 1942, the Japanese, as part of their Pacific offensive during World War II, took Indonesia from the Dutch and declared much of it a Japanese colony. Along with terrible economic exploitation, the Japanese promoted Indonesian nationalism in order to prepare the people to defend their homeland (and the Japanese) against the inevitable Allied counterattack. In late 1942, after initially opposing the Japanese, Suharto joined the Japanese-sponsored Defense Army of Indonesia, known by the acronym PETA. He rose quickly, but, like many of his fellow soldiers, he became interested in a growing independence movement. On August 15, 1945, when Suharto heard the news of the Japanese surrender, he rushed to Yogyakarta, Java's second city, where he joined a new nationalist army. He showed himself a capable leader by capturing weapons from the remaining Japanese and by preparing defenses against the returning Dutch.

Between 1945 and 1949, Lieutenant-Colonel Suharto distinguished himself as a field commander, leading both regular and guerrilla attacks against the Dutch and their Indonesian supporters. When the Dutch granted Indonesia independence in 1949, which followed Indonesia's declaration of independence in 1945, Suharto continued his field command until he was made a staff officer in 1956. Thereafter, he attended staff college; SUKARNO, Indonesia's president, made him leader of a 1962 invasion of Irian Jaya, a part of extreme eastern Indonesia retained by the Dutch. By this time, General Suharto and many others in the armed forces had become uncomfortable with Sukarno's political radicalism, especially his call to invade Malaysia and his apparent alignment with communists. On September 30, 1965, Suharto, with the support of the military and Islamic politicians, initiated a coup d'état, deposed and then arrested Sukarno. He also encouraged the slaughter of more than 300,000 communists throughout Indonesia. Suharto was made president for life in 1968.

Between 1965 and 1995, Suharto made economic development Indonesia's top priority, using it as the excuse to limit political rights. By the mid-1990s, most Indonesians would no longer tolerate political repression, had learned about the extensive corruption centered on Suharto's family, and had suffered greatly from the economic downturn of 1994. Facing angry student opposition and waning support from his army, Suharto was deposed in 1998 and placed under house arrest.

Legacy

Suharto contributed to the independence of Indonesia from the Dutch in 1945 and, from 1965 on, he imposed stability on an Indonesia almost shattered by President Sukarno's radical politics. Suharto achieved both independence and stability through a mixture of skill, careful political preparation, and elaborate rewards for those who worked with him.

Throughout his life, Suharto sought to preserve Indonesia from disruption and make it more prosperous. Joining the colonial army provided the opportunity for him to share in the protection and prosperity of Indonesia. This pattern repeated itself, with Suharto's involvement in the Japanese-sponsored army and the postwar independence army. Each organization allowed Suharto to fight on the side that promised change without radical revolution. This became important in 1965 when he engineered a return to stability and prosperity by deposing Sukarno and his radical political agenda and dispatching Indonesia's communists, who Suharto expected would limit the wealth of Indonesia's people.

The prosperity and stability Suharto imposed on Indonesia in 1965 returned the country to the mainstream of international politics, including membership in ASEAN (Association of Southeast Asian Nations) in 1967 and an opening to vast foreign investment. Average Indonesians enjoyed improved health, education, transportation, and general welfare. However, to perpetuate stability in a country constantly at odds with itself, Suharto had to ensure that chief political and military leaders benefitted financially. Indonesia's elites, from Suharto on down, received billions of dollars illicitly. Increasingly intolerant of the cronyism that kept the majority of Indonesians from advancing in their jobs and lives beyond a certain level, stung by the 1994 Asian economic crisis, and wanting the right to free expression, Indonesians rebelled against Suharto in 1998—not out of frustration with economic and political stability, but with the limits on opportunity that that had been artificially imposed.

Del Testa

WORLD EVENTS		SUHARTO'S LIFE
Russian Revolution	1917	
	1921	Suharto is born
Great Depression	1929–39	
World War II	1939–45	
	1940	Suharto joins Dutch colonial military
	1942	Japan invades Indonesia and Suharto joins Japanese-sponsored military
	1945–49	Suharto leads anti-colonial nationalist forces; Indonesia gains independence
Communist China is established	1949	
	1962	Suharto leads invasion of Irian Jaya
	1965	Suharto deposes Sukarno
Israel defeats Arab nations in Six-Day War	1967	
	1968	Suharto is made president for life
Vietnam War ends	1975	
Dissolution of Soviet Union	1991	
	1998	Suharto is forced to resign

For Further Reading
Lidsker, William. *Suharto Finds the Divine Vision: A Political Biography.* Honolulu, Hawaii: Semangat Press, 1990.
Vatikiotis, Michael R. J. *Indonesian Politics under Suharto: The Rise and Fall of the New Order.* New York: Routledge, 1998.

Sukarno

Indonesian Political Leader
1901–1970

Life and Work

Sukarno helped Indonesians achieve independence from the Dutch, kept independent Indonesia united, and gave the nation an international political role it was unable to fulfill.

Sukarno was born on June 6, 1901, into a middle-class family in eastern Java. In 1921, he was admitted into the colony's University of Technology, and married the daughter of Tjokroaminoto, Indonesia's great nationalist leader. Sukarno was offered a post at the university in 1926, but had already decided to make a career of the struggle for independence from the Dutch. He attended nationalist and communist lectures, and was part of the upper circles of Indonesia's anti-colonial movement.

By the late 1920s, Sukarno was an important leader in the nationalist movement. At this

World Events	Sukarno's Life
Germany is united 1871	
1901	Sukarno is born
Russo-Japanese War 1905	
World War I 1914–18	
Russian Revolution 1917	
1921	Sukarno begins studies at university
1929–41	Sukarno is in prison or exile repeatedly
Great Depression 1929–39	
World War II 1939–45	
1941	Sukarno returns from exile
1945	Sukarno declares independence
Communist China 1949	Dutch withdraw from Indonesia; Sukarno is made president
is established	
1960	Sukarno dismisses parliament
1965	Sukarno is deposed by army
Israel defeats 1967	
Arab nations in	
Six-Day War	
1970	Sukarno dies
Vietnam War ends 1975	

time, he began to introduce his "organic" style of politics, which rejected Western models of governance and sought to build on local traditions of consensus politics. Sukarno's leadership was short-lived, however. The Dutch colonial authorities arrested him for conspiracy in December 1929, and he was in prison or in exile repeatedly until 1941. Sukarno threw himself at the Japanese when they took over Dutch Indonesia, seeing fellow Asians as liberators in 1942 in the middle of World War II. He was frustrated and disillusioned, however, by the imposition of a regime many times harsher than that attempted by the Dutch. The absence of effective Allied authority in Indonesia permitted Sukarno to declare national independence on September 17, 1945.

Both a civil war between rival political factions and a war of reconquest by the Dutch raged in Indonesia throughout the late 1940s. During this time, Sukarno worked to unify opposing factions by focusing on getting rid of the Dutch. Due to pressure from the United States, the Dutch withdrew from Indonesia in late 1949. Sukarno then became president and ruled over a unified Indonesia. He pushed for local economic development and nationalized foreign investments; both efforts were disasters. In March 1960, Sukarno dismissed parliament and replaced its members with individuals he had handpicked. Thereafter, he pushed for a new political movement, dubbed NASAKOM, which stood for nationalism, *agana* ("religion"), and communism, to oppose the forces of neocolonialism, which he said were bent on enslaving the entire developing world. He helped create the nonaligned movement at the Bandung Conference of 1955 in the Jawat Barat province of Indonesia that rejected the destructive tensions caused by the Cold War. However, as a result of his political radicalism, including his call to invade Malaysia and his alliance with communists, Sukarno was toppled in a coup d'état on September 30, 1965. He was placed under house arrest and died lonely and isolated on July 20, 1970.

Legacy

Sukarno prevented Indonesia from disintegrating into many ethnic and religious components while leading the country to independence from the Dutch. However, his authoritarian style and corruption resulted in his replacement by the more traditional strong-arm leader, SUHARTO.

From an early age, Sukarno believed in respect for and a mixture of religion and political ideas and had a strong tendency toward populism. This blend of ideas enabled him to unite opposing political factions, and his populism enabled him to appeal to broad sectors of Indonesia's fractious society. This was especially important during the tumultuous years between 1945 and 1949, when Indonesia could have destroyed itself from within. Throughout his life, Sukarno tried to formalize his beliefs, beginning in the 1920s with *marhaenism*, or the politics of the common man, and culminating in the 1960s with NASAKOM, in which social justice, social peace, and social unity would oppose the evil of exploitative capitalism.

Sukarno's politics were based on compromise, and compromise became increasingly difficult in the 1950s as he turned away from groups that opposed him. In international relations, although his call for lesser-developed countries to unite with him against the destructive competition of the Cold War won much support, it cost him the international financial support Indonesia needed for future development. In addition, during the 1960s, Sukarno faced mounting resistance from the army, which did not like his vague support for the communists, his watered-down allegiance to Islam, his moral decadence, and his rejection of foreign military aid. By 1965, Sukarno's economic policies had lost popular support, and the army removed him. His downfall showed once again that a leader must provide the basis for peace at home before embarking on complex international initiatives.

Del Testa

For Further Reading

Legge, J. D. *Sukarno: A Political Biography.* London: Allen & Unwin, 1985.
Penders, C. L. M. *The Life and Times of Sukarno.* London: Sidgwick and Jackson, 1974.

Suleyman I

Ottoman Sultan
c. 1494–1566

Life and Work

Continuing the conquests and reforms begun by his predecessors, Suleyman I transformed the Turkish Ottoman Empire into a major world power, yet sowed the seeds of its future decline.

Suleyman (also Suleiman, Sulayman) was born either in November 1494 or September 1495 in Trebizond on the Black Sea. Sultan Selim I, Suleyman's father, had conquered Syria and Egypt and had begun a campaign against the Persians before his death in 1520. Suleyman succeeded him, but before continuing on this path of conquest, he had to suppress rebellion among his own Muslim subjects in Syria, Egypt, and Anatolia, the Turkish heartland.

Like his predecessors, Suleyman was determined to wage a traditional holy war (*jihad*) against Christendom and to conquer more territory for the empire. In 1521, profiting from European disunity caused by the Protestant Reformation, Suleyman conquered Belgrade, a key European defense against the Turks. He then moved on to take the Crusader outpost on the island of Rhodes. A 1526 campaign against Hungarian forces also resulted in victory and Turkish domination of Hungary for 150 years. In 1529, Suleyman laid siege to Vienna, capital of the Habsburg dynasty; the siege marked the deepest penetration of Europe by the Ottoman Turks, and terrified many Europeans, who saw "the infidel" having advanced so far into Europe.

Border disputes with Persia (present-day Iran) forced Suleyman to shift his attention eastward. In 1534–35 he occupied Iraq, (then under Persian dynastic control) and captured Baghdad, neutralizing the Persians and allowing Suleyman to build up his naval fleet for a new attack on North Africa and to regain total control of the eastern Mediterranean. At war for many years with the Persians, he finally concluded peace with them in 1555, obtaining the territories of Georgia, Azerbaijan, and Kurdistan.

In addition to expanding Ottoman territory, Suleyman enacted reforms designed to administer a large and diverse empire. He was also an enthusiastic patron of literature, the arts, and monumental architecture; during his rule, Constantinople became an international center of literature, arts, and architecture.

Suleyman died on September 6, 1566, in Hungary during another campaign against the Habsburgs. By the time of his death, the Ottoman Empire had reached its greatest extent, having doubled in size during his reign.

Legacy

The Ottoman Empire reached its peak under Suleyman I, who established the structure of government that would endure until the constitutional reforms of the late nineteenth and early twentieth centuries. The governmental innovations he instituted, however, would lead to future weakness in the face of European economic, technological, and military advances.

Suleyman encouraged an open, religiously tolerant society, as well as trade and other commercial activities among the subject peoples and foreigners, making the Ottoman Empire the center of a thriving network of international trade routes between East and West.

Suleyman also organized the *ulema* ("clerical class") in a hierarchical order; they, in turn, created a coherent body of laws. These religious leaders, however, later tried to block all reforms that threatened their power, leading to a conservative policy that sapped the innovative approach needed to counter the future threat from industrializing European nations in the eighteenth and nineteenth centuries.

Suleyman's goal of creating a universal monarchy based on Islam, along with the military might he controlled, terrified the Europeans, who saw the Ottomans as unstoppable. The Ottoman threat to the West, most pronounced in the siege of Vienna, sparked more aggressive military and economic behavior by Europeans, who were determined to defend Christendom. To encourage trade with the West, in 1536 Suleyman began to issue capitulations (trade agreements) to European states, which exempted European traders from Ottoman taxation and from certain strictures of Islamic law. This policy opened up economic opportunity for European powers, but discouraged the development of domestic industry in Ottoman lands, as Western manufactured goods were increasingly imported. Other domestic problems dating from Suleyman's reign included rural depopulation, court intrigues, and undue influence of the sultan's harem (where the heirs to the throne were raised). Over time, these weaknesses reduced the financial, economic, and political independence of the Ottoman Empire and increased its reliance on trade with the West—a dependence that reached crisis proportions in the nineteenth century.

Suleyman's very success as a conqueror contributed to his empire's subsequent long-term decline. Having conquered the lands within the geographical limits of his huge army, Suleyman could go no farther. The era of conquest largely ended after his death; subsequent Ottoman sultans were thus denied new lands and other resources with which to reward their troops. The Ottoman administration did not attempt to reform the economy to reflect this new "era of limitations" or to counter the rise of European economic success. The lack of real reform led to an increasingly corrupt administration and military, and to weak and ineffective sultans. When capable sultans occasionally assumed the throne, however, they were able to rely on the administrative framework built by Suleyman to restore the strength of the empire, forestalling complete European dominance.

Lemoine

For Further Reading

Bridge, Antony. *Suleiman the Magnificent: Scourge of Heaven.* London: Granada, 1983.

Clot, André. *Suleiman the Magnificent: The Man, His Life, His Epoch.* Translated by Matthew J. Reisz. London: Saqi Books, 1989.

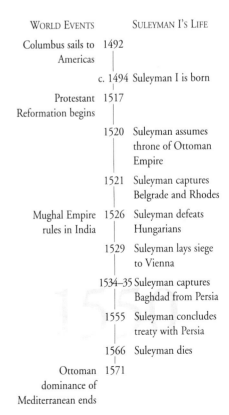

WORLD EVENTS		SULEYMAN I'S LIFE
Columbus sails to Americas	1492	
	c. 1494	Suleyman I is born
Protestant Reformation begins	1517	
	1520	Suleyman assumes throne of Ottoman Empire
	1521	Suleyman captures Belgrade and Rhodes
Mughal Empire rules in India	1526	Suleyman defeats Hungarians
	1529	Suleyman lays siege to Vienna
	1534–35	Suleyman captures Baghdad from Persia
	1555	Suleyman concludes treaty with Persia
	1566	Suleyman dies
Ottoman dominance of Mediterranean ends	1571	

Sunni Ali

Ruler of Songhay Empire

c. 1440–1492

Life and Work

Sunni Ali ruled the Songhay Empire in fifteenth-century Africa. Reputed never to have lost a battle, he extended his realm throughout the western Sudan and captured the famous city of Timbuktu on the edge of the Sahara Desert.

Sunni Ali was born about 1440 as the heir to the Songhay Empire, then a rising power in the western Sudan. His father Sunni Madawu was a Muslim, but his mother retained the animistic faith and practices of her native Soninke ancestors. As a result, Sunni Ali's nominal adherence to Islam was infused with a belief in magic that alienated the empire's Muslim minority but created support among its animistic majority.

In 1464 Madawu died, and Sunni Ali succeeded him as ruler. A highly charismatic warrior, he immediately set Songhay on a course of territorial expansion. In doing so he faced two hostile powers in the region, the Mossi in the south and the Berbers in the north. Since the Niger River served as the Sudan's most important waterway, Sunni Ali concentrated his resources first upon building a large river navy. In time he had as many as 400 boats afloat, and in subsequent years used them with great effectiveness to fight his enemies. He also used sorcery to instill awe in his troops. He was reputed to have the power to make them invisible and to transform himself into a vulture.

In 1468 Sunni Ali attacked the great northern city of Timbuktu with a powerful army. Although it fell with scarcely a fight, he had many of its Muslim scholars executed and many of its buildings destroyed. This and other acts of savagery earned Sunni Ali the reputation of a godless tyrant among contemporary Arabs. In 1473 he put his navy to good use in attacking the river city of Jenné. Soon after he took the desert city of Walata. Hoping to integrate it better into his military state, he proposed building a 200-mile canal between it and the Niger. This plan was frustrated, however, when conflict with the Mossi arose.

When Sunni Ali was traveling home from battle along the Koni River in 1492, his horse, badly overburdened with booty from his latest conquest, lost its footing and collapsed in the water. Before the great warrior's attendants could intervene, he was swept over the falls and drowned.

Legacy

The territorial empire that Sunni Ali created dominated northwestern Africa in later years and influenced the development of global trade.

In the centuries that preceded Sunni Ali's capture of Timbuktu, the Sudan had given rise to the empires of Ghana and Mali. Sunni Ali incorporated much of the territory from these earlier states and established a strong native state at a time when Arabs and Europeans were penetrating south into the African heartland. For more than a century after his death, the Songhay Empire remained the dominant state in this region.

Sunni Ali's charismatic status as a warrior and sorcerer survived his death and served subsequent rulers with an important royal legacy. This was assured even by his son Sunni Baro, who had Sunni Ali's body disemboweled and his intestines preserved in honey for posterity. Although Sunni Baro was overthrown by a Muslim general named Askia, the state continued to develop upon the foundation established by Sunni Ali and soon became even stronger. Only in 1591 did an army of Berbers manage to overthrow the Songhay Empire.

By consolidating a powerful state in the Sudan, Sunni Ali also made a great impact upon trading relations during the fifteenth century and later. Prior to the expansion of Portuguese trading routes along the west coast of Africa by HENRY THE NAVIGATOR, the Sudan had been the center of trade between Africans, Arabs, and Europeans. The trans-Saharan route exchanged African gold and slaves for goods from North Africa and Europe. Control over this lucrative trade, assured by Sunni Ali's capture of Walata and Timbuktu, greatly enriched the later Songhay Empire. It also encouraged Europeans such as ISABELLA I of Spain to follow Henry's example and seek alternative sources of gold overseas. With the rise of European seaborne empires in the sixteenth century, the trans-Saharan route declined in importance and with it the Songhay Empire's power.

Nevertheless, the name of Sunni Ali continued to inspire Africans for centuries. His son's elaborate effort to preserve his memory was paralleled by popular legends that emphasized his magical powers and military acumen. In modern times, some historians have even compared his military genius to that of NAPOLÉON I and his political achievements to those of CHARLEMAGNE. Finally, historical memory about Africa's great native conqueror inspired twentieth-century Ghanian nationalists such as KWAME NKRUMAH.

Strickland

World Events		Sunni Ali's Life
Ming Dynasty reasserts Chinese control of China	1368	
	c. 1440	Sunni Ali is born
Ottoman Empire conquers Constantinople	1453	
	1464	Sunni Ali accedes to Songhay throne
	1468	Sunni Ali captures Timbuktu
	1473	Sunni Ali captures Jenné
Columbus sails to Americas	1492	Sunni Ali dies

For Further Reading

Arkell, A. J. *A History of the Sudan.* 2nd ed. London: Athlone, 1961.

Hale, Thomas A. *Scribe, Griot, and Novelist: Narrative Interpretations of the Songhay Empire.* Gainesville, Fla.: University of Florida Press, 1990.

Saad, Elias N. *Social History of Timbuktu: The Role of Muslim Scholars and Notables, 1400–1900.* Cambridge: Cambridge University Press, 1983.

Sun Yat-sen

Founder of Chinese Republic
1866–1925

Life and Work

Observing the weakness of China in the face of foreign exploitation, Sun Yat-sen (Sun Yixian) dedicated his intelligence and nationalist fervor to transforming his country from a conservative empire to a progressive republic.

Sun was born on November 12, 1866, to a poor farming family in a village near Canton. Sun traveled to Hawaii in 1879, where he joined a brother who was a prosperous farmer. His brother paid Sun's tuition at a Christian boarding school, where he was a good student and converted to Christianity. In 1883, Sun returned to China and spent much of his time railing against the backwardness of the Chinese government. He was banished in 1884.

In 1884, Sun began his higher education in Hong Kong, then a British colony, and in 1887 began medical school. He also joined various secret revolutionary organizations that sought to overthrow China's ruling Ch'ing dynasty. Sun graduated in 1892, practiced medicine in Macao until he was exiled for political activities, and thereafter became a dedicated nationalist.

Following a particularly shameful attack on China by Japan in 1895, Sun organized his first failed uprising, in Shanghai. For the next 16 years, Sun traveled the world, gathering support for his revolutionary organization, the

Revive China Society, and studying revolution in various countries. In 1896 in London, he became famous after being kidnapped by the Chinese embassy and held for two weeks. From 1905 to 1909, Sun worked to foment revolution in China. Success finally came in 1911 when a revolt staged by Sun's allies failed, but inspired other Chinese to rebel against the Ch'ing; the revolt led to the abdication of the emperor and the establishment of China as a republic. Sun returned to China, reaching Shanghai on January 1, 1912, in time to be named provisional president. However, Sun and other leaders agreed that Yüan Shih-k'ai, who had support from the army and former government officials, should act as president. Yüan turned out to be a despot who feared rivals, and Sun had to flee to Japan following an attempt to oust Yüan in 1913.

Sun knew that Yüan might fail and had refused to fully support him. In 1912, Sun had founded the Kuomintang, or "Revolutionary Party," a political organization loyal only to him, which he used to help overthrow the supporters of Yüan and return to power in 1917. In 1918, the Chinese parliament made him generalissimo, or dictator, and Sun tried to stabilize China, which had split into numerous petty states. He transformed the Kuomintang into a popular party that borrowed heavily from the contemporary fascist and communist models of the time. To garner additional support, in 1923 Sun allowed the Chinese Communist Party to cooperate with the Kuomintang. He also imported advisors from wherever he could find support, mainly the Soviet Union and Germany. By mixing elements of many popular political movements and importing expertise, Sun prepared the foundation of his protégé CHIANG KAI-SHEK to reunite Nationalist China under the nationalist flag. Sun died suddenly on March 12, 1925.

Legacy

As a legacy, Sun Yat-sen laid the foundation for a modern Chinese state and for national politics in China.

Sun's unrelenting assault against the Chinese imperial system evolved from his exposure to foreign systems of government that worked and in which average people had a natural political stake. He also recognized how foreign powers were taking advantage of

China's weaknesses and the empire's inability to protect itself from exploitation. His ability to work with many different interest groups, Chinese and foreign, and to attract people to the cause of Chinese nationalism permitted him to slowly gather support. He also encouraged stability within change by acknowledging progressive ideas, such as democracy and progressive thinking, and by incorporating older forms of Chinese governance, such as local control and a fair distribution of wealth. The power of Sun's message of national liberation is evident in how often countries that had hosted him exiled him within a few months or years. For example, the French colonial government in Indochina actively supported Sun until his ideas began to inspire the Vietnamese to rally against the French; it exiled him in 1909.

In addition, Sun put his ideas into practice by setting up an activist political party that carried out his ideas at the local level. Sun encouraged local activism, yet managed it through strong state control and involved people in government directly through the branches of the Kuomintang party. The Kuomintang, led by Chiang Kai-shek after Sun's death, created unity and a semblance of peace—or at least relative order—in China and might have made China into a lasting republic if not for the turmoil caused by the Japanese invasion of 1937 and the never-ending problem of corruption within the regime.

Del Testa

World Events		Sun's Life
Congress of Vienna reorganizes Europe	1815	
	1866	Sun Yat-sen is born
Germany is united	1871	
	1887–92	Sun attends medical school in Hong Kong
Russo-Japanese War	1905	
	1911	Ch'ing emperor abdicates; Chinese Republic declared
	1912	Sun cedes presidency to Yüan Shih-k'ai
	1913	Sun tries to oust Yüan, then flees to Japan
World War I	1914–18	
Russian Revolution	1917	
	1917–18	Sun returns to China and is declared generalissimo
	1925	Sun dies
Great Depression	1929–39	

For Further Reading

Bergère, Marie-Claire. *Sun Yat-sen.* Translated from the French by Janet Lloyd. Palo Alto, Calif.: Stanford University Press, 1998.

Chen, Stephen, and Robert Payne. *Sun Yat-sen: A Portrait.* New York: John Day, 1946.

Suryavarman II

Cambodian King and Builder of
Angkor Wat
1098–c. 1150

Life and Work

After a long period of strife and internecine warfare, Suryavarman II defeated several opponents and ascended to the Cambodian throne, inaugurating the greatest period of premodern Cambodian cultural production and imperial expansion.

World Events	Suryavarman II's Life
First Crusade begins 1095	
	1098 Suryavarman II is born
Timbuktu influential throughout west central Africa c. 1100	
	1113 Suryavarman ascends to throne, begins work on Angkor Wat soon after
	1115 Suryavarman attacks Champa
	c. 1150 Suryavarman II dies
Saladin retakes Jerusalem for Islam 1187	

Born in July 1098, Suryavarman was the grandnephew of two kings who had ruled during an earlier period of Cambodian unity that had ended in the 1060s. He came to the throne after defeating a rival prince in a large battle in 1113. Cambodia in the twelfth century was a theocracy, a form of government in which the supreme ruler is a god (or gods), usually served by a priesthood. A new Cambodian king showed that the gods had chosen him to rule by acting in a godlike fashion, that is, by showing a profound respect for intricate religious ritual, instituting wise rule, and completing heroic acts.

Suryavarman's wise rule included the expansion of Cambodian territory in 1115 at the expense of the Champa, a people who were heavily influenced by India and the Hindu religion and who once occupied what is now southern Vietnam; the transmission for the first time in 300 years of tribute, or material objects that showed homage and symbolic submission, to the Chinese emperor; and the establishment of a strong and efficient administration. The conquest of new land brought slaves and spoils into the Cambodian economy; tribute to China stimulated trade; and effective administration enabled Cambodia to produce enough rice to feed its people and to export for profit. With peace, priests expanded Cambodia's vast network of irrigation works to their greatest extent, ensuring agricultural bounty, effective state control, and widespread prosperity.

Suryavarman's heroic act was to begin constructing Angkor Wat, the enormous addition to the famous temple complex at Angkor. Angkor Wat, starting early in his reign, served as a Hindu temple, tomb, and observatory, and was dedicated to the god Vishnu. Its miles of bas-relief carvings and its 200-foot gilded spires, not completed until after Suryavarman's death, revealed his power to all of his Cambodian subjects.

Suryavarman II died around 1150, after waging an ineffectual attack on the Vietnamese kingdom.

Legacy

Suryavarman II ensured great prosperity and prestige to the Cambodian elites, but in doing so he bankrupted the country's economy. He ushered in an age of strife that exceeded the one he had ended, and encouraged a profound social and cultural shift in Cambodia that endures to the present.

In the twelfth century, Cambodia's population consisted of a small, competitive, and often corrupt elite and a mass of downtrodden slaves and peasants. Elite individuals and groups competed with and demonstrated personal holiness to each other by showing material achievement through the construction of beautiful and costly temples. Because Suryavarman initially brought so much wealth to Cambodia and initiated a vast temple construction campaign to prove his spiritual worth, he sparked early, intense competition among elites to show their own worthiness. When the production of wealth through conquest and large harvests declined during the second half of his reign, in order to keep up with the progress on Angkor Wat, elites brutally exploited their slaves and peasants to speed their own projects along. Although he unified the country, expanded its borders, and made its internal administration more efficient, Suryavarman's zealousness left Cambodia bankrupt and on the verge of civil war.

Suryavarman left the world one of its most impressive monuments. The construction of Angkor Wat, however, overextended Cambodia's economic means and brought to an end its position as an expansive regional power. After Suryavarman's death, the bloody suppression of a massive slave revolt, and a humiliating counterattack by the Champa, Cambodia's elites turned toward orthodox Buddhism, which forbade excessive displays of wealth and, more important, discouraged violence. Suryavarman and the elites had also consumed so much of Cambodia's national wealth that no money was left to maintain the irrigation networks, causing a fateful decline in agricultural production and a loss of control over much of the country. In the face of expanding Vietnamese and Thai kingdoms, Cambodia was impoverished and unable to resist incursions; by the eighteenth and nineteenth centuries, Cambodia had become overrun and occupied by Vietnam. Suryavarman II's empire, however, remained an inspiration to many Cambodians for its wealth and to some, such as the Khmer Rouge, for its crusading spirit and purifying violence.

Del Testa

For Further Reading
Audric, John. *Angkor and the Khmer Empire.* London: Robert Hale, 1972.
Chandler, David P. *A History of Cambodia,* 2nd ed. Boulder, Colo.: Westview Press, 1992.

Thatcher, Margaret

British Prime Minister
1925–

Life and Work

Margaret Thatcher (née Roberts) became one of Britain's most influential and controversial prime ministers.

Thatcher was born on October 13, 1925, to a moderately successful grocer and local political leader in Grantham, England. She entered Oxford University as a chemistry major in 1943. At Oxford, she discovered politics and joined the Conservative Association, a branch of the Conservative Party, and has remained active in that party ever since.

After graduating in 1947, she worked briefly as a chemist for a plastics firm and, later, for an ice cream manufacturer, relatively rare positions for a woman at the time. She soon ran for the town of Dartford's seat in Parliament in 1950 as the youngest woman candidate in Britain. After losing the election, she became a barrister (lawyer) in 1953. Her ability to leave work and to study for a second profession was assisted by her marriage in 1951 to Dennis Thatcher, a wealthy business owner.

In 1959, Thatcher won a seat in parliament from Finchley, near London. Between 1959 and 1970, Thatcher held a series of junior posts in various Conservative governments. With the election of Edward Heath as prime minister in 1970, Thatcher became minister of education, a post she held until 1974. In 1975, Thatcher, representing a more conservative Conservatism that emerged during the 1970s, replaced Heath as leader of the Conservative Party, an astounding change given Thatcher's gender and youth.

In 1979, Thatcher was elected prime minister on a wave of middle-class disgust over labor troubles, economic sluggishness, and a controversial plan by the Labour Party to devolve Scotland and Wales into autonomous regions. Thatcher immediately began a long series of reforms that privatized several nationalized industries and utilities and tied health care and education to market forces rather than government support. She was highly unpopular at first with many Britons, but the 1982 Falklands War boosted her popularity, as did a firm stance against the Soviet Union. However, although her fiscal austerity helped to improve the British economy and her popularity, her stance against the monetary and political integration of members of the European Community cost her the support of her party, and she lost an election in 1990. Her support of Britain's retention of Northern Ireland almost threatened her life; in 1984, at a government meeting in Brighton, she narrowly escaped a bomb blast, planted by the Irish Republican Army. Thatcher retired from her parliamentary seat in Finchley and active politics in 1992.

Legacy

Margaret Thatcher, at a high social cost, made Britain competitive again in the world market. She also reconfirmed the ability of women to lead national governments.

When Thatcher left office in 1990, Britain was a rising star of economic development in which the government and management had broken the grip of unions. Over the course of 11 years, Thatcher and her conservative Conservatives (known as "drys") had formulated a profound restructuring of the relationship of Britain's government to its people, destroying both the concept and some of the substance of a welfare state. In return, Britons faced a choice between adaptation and abandonment, in which those who adopted new skills succeeded and those who did not were left behind in misery and poverty. The abrupt change jarred many accustomed to a culture of work and support, in which unions guaranteed political representation and the government provided for the public welfare. The shock affected even the more socially liberal Conservatives. Thatcher's economic reforms created great divides in British society that have only just begun to come together under the leadership of Labour Party Prime Minister Tony Blair, elected in 1997.

The ability to force British society to abandon the arrangements of a public welfare state took incredible determination on Thatcher's part, both because it had long benefitted so much of the British electorate and it had become so much a part of British society. Thatcher led by learning the facts behind particular issues and by working closely with those who wielded power in government and business. Her icy public demeanor and determination earned her the sobriquet "the Iron Lady." All the more impressive was that Thatcher led, successfully, through war and severe social dislocation, as a woman in a society not known to often appreciate "public women." Margaret Thatcher, Britain's first woman prime minister, served longer in that post than anyone in the twentieth century. She was made a baroness by the Queen in 1992.

Del Testa

For Further Reading

Lewis, Russell. *Margaret Thatcher: A Personal and Political Biography.* Boston: Routledge & Kegan Paul, 1984.

Thatcher, Margaret. *The Downing Street Years.* London: HarperCollins, 1993.

Young, Hugo. *Margaret Thatcher: A Political Biography.* London: Macmillan, 1989.

WORLD EVENTS		THATCHER'S LIFE
Russian Revolution	1917	
	1925	Margaret Thatcher (née Roberts) is born
Great Depression	1929–39	
World War II	1939–45	
	1943	Thatcher enters Oxford University
	1947	Thatcher graduates from Oxford
Communist China is established	1949	
	1959	Thatcher wins seat in Parliament
Israel defeats Arab nations in Six-Day War	1967	
	1970–74	Thatcher serves as minister of education
Vietnam War ends	1975	Thatcher becomes head of Conservative Party
	1979–91	Thatcher repeatedly elected as prime minister
Dissolution of Soviet Union	1991	

Timur

Central Asian Conqueror
c. 1336–1405

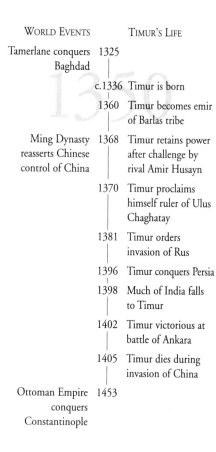

World Events		Timur's Life
Tamerlane conquers Baghdad	1325	
	c.1336	Timur is born
	1360	Timur becomes emir of Barlas tribe
Ming Dynasty reasserts Chinese control of China	1368	Timur retains power after challenge by rival Amir Husayn
	1370	Timur proclaims himself ruler of Ulus Chaghatay
	1381	Timur orders invasion of Rus
	1396	Timur conquers Persia
	1398	Much of India falls to Timur
	1402	Timur victorious at battle of Ankara
	1405	Timur dies during invasion of China
Ottoman Empire conquers Constantinople	1453	

Life and Work

The ruthless architect of a sprawling empire centered in Central Asia, Timur (Tamerlane) was the last nomadic conqueror to threaten the civilizations of China, India, and the Near East.

Timur was born about 1336, into a Turkic-speaking and Islamic tribe called the Barlas, then a part of a confederation called the Ulus Chaghatay. Although endowed with a powerful and imposing stature, he suffered an injury in battle early in life and thereby gained the nickname in English of Timur the Lame, or Tamerlane.

Timur had an inauspicious beginning. Born near the city of Samarkand, in Transoxiana, he spent part of his youth stealing sheep from neighboring herders. After creating a personal following through this brigandage, he gained the title of emir among the Barlas in 1360. This introduced him to the broader struggles that dominated the confederation of the Ulus Chaghatay. In 1368, a rival named Amir Husayn tried to usurp Timur's authority. His power held, however, and after he had the male line of Husayn's family executed, he took four of his former rival's wives as his own.

Timur proclaimed himself ruler of the Ulus Chaghatay in 1370. Eager to emulate his Mongol predecessors, he established a royal court at Samarkand. He also took a deep interest in learning, and although illiterate himself he became famous for his ability to debate with scholars about religion, science, and history. He came also to earn the reputation of a brutal warrior. His behavior in the field was notoriously cruel, and he had the habit of decorating the walls of fallen cities with the heads of his victims. Significantly, after establishing his rule, he began to claim lineage to GENGHIS KHAN (d. 1227).

Like his Mongol predecessor, Timur was not content with ruling only Central Asia. Soon after his triumph in the Ulus Chaghatay, he began a long series of brutal campaigns that took him through virtually all the regions of the world known to him. In 1381 he sent his armies north to the lands of Rus, reaching as far as the Volga River and threatening Moscow. In 1396

Persia fell, and in 1398 he crippled India when he sacked the city of Delhi. After returning briefly to Samarkand, he set out to the distant west. In 1402 he met the Turks at the Battle of Ankara, and even captured the sultan. His next target was China, for which he launched an invasion in 1405. However, he died en route at the city of Utrar in Central Asia.

Legacy

The empire that Timur imposed upon Central Asia and the Near East exacted a heavy cost from the subject population. The weakness of his civil administration and the brutality of his conquests left a state that was unable to maintain its integrity in subsequent decades.

Timur spent very little time at his capital in Samarkand because he believed his presence at the head of his wandering armies was more important. As a result, he failed to establish a strong administrative structure for his sprawling domains. At the same time, he did improve on the system used by his Mongol predecessors by investing in lands with settled agriculture. This was especially true in Persia, where he used a fairly efficient native bureaucracy. In Central Asia, however, he employed a system of personal appointments that tended to divide his rule rather than integrate it. He was forever wary of rebellion among his princes, especially his own sons. Thus when Timur died the empire lacked a strong government that could survive the loss of his charismatic leadership. As his sons battled each other, often employing the same brutal methods as their late father, the empire dissolved almost as rapidly as it had been formed.

Nevertheless, the memory of Timur's conquests lived on in Central Asia. Although conquered by the Russian Empire in the nineteenth century, its peoples maintained the Turkic customs and Islamic faith that Timur had embraced during his rule. In the twentieth century, Uzbeks and other Central Asian nationalities would draw upon this historical legacy in an effort to legitimate their own claims to sovereignty.

Strickland

For Further Reading

González de Clavijo, Ruy. *Embassy to Tamerlane, 1403–1406.* Translated by Guy Le Strange. London: Routledge, 1928.
Lamb, Harold. *Tamerlane: The Earth Shaker.* New York: Robert M. McBride, 1928.
Manz, Beatrice Forbes. *The Rise and Rule of Tamerlane.* Cambridge: Cambridge University Press, 1989.

Tito

Leader of Yugoslavia
1892–1980

Life and Work

Tito led an independent Yugoslavia that defied the Soviet Union and created a relatively stable and prosperous communist state. However, his policies ultimately unleashed ethnic nationalism that destroyed his country 10 years after his death.

Tito was born Josip Broz on May 7, 1892, in Croatia, a Balkan state controlled by the Austro-Hungarian Empire. The son of peasant farmers, Tito (a name he adopted later in his life) was apprenticed to a locksmith and moved to Zagreb, the capital of Croatia, in 1910. In 1913 Tito began his obligatory military service for the Austro-Hungarian Empire. After World War I broke out in 1914, Tito served honorably until March 1915, when he was captured by Russian forces.

The confusion created by the March 1917 revolution in Russia enabled Tito to escape. He joined the Bolshevik Red Guards (Russian communists, who overturned the provisional government in November 1917) until he returned to Croatia in 1920. By that time the Balkan states of Serbia, Croatia, and Slovenia had combined to form the new, independent state of Yugoslavia ruled by a Serbian royal family.

In 1923 Tito joined the Communist Party of Yugoslavia (CPY), engaging in organizational activities that got him imprisoned from 1928 to

1934, after which he joined other CPY exiles in Vienna. Rising in the CPY's hierarchy, Tito was appointed general secretary of the party in 1937. When Germany invaded Yugoslavia and the Soviet Union in 1941, Tito organized the National Liberation Partisan Detachments (the Partisans), who drove the Germans from Yugoslavia, despite having to fight a civil war against the royalist Chetniks and fascist Croatian Ustasi. The better-organized Partisans gained popular support and, by 1943, the support of the Allies. The CPY organized a government, and on November 29, 1945, Tito abolished the monarchy and declared the Federal Republic of Yugoslavia, a communist regime.

When Tito asserted a measure of independence from Soviet dominance, JOSEPH STALIN expelled Yugoslavia from the Cominform (an international association of communist parties) in 1948 and sent agents to assassinate Tito. With economic and military assistance from the West, Tito was ably to defy Stalin. His prestige high, Tito was elected president in 1953, a position he held to the end of his life. During the 1960s he accorded a measure of local autonomy to the individual states that made up Yugoslavia.

Although he never completely repudiated Soviet-style communism, Tito also sought a leadership role among nonaligned nations, such as Egypt and India, that refused to ally with either superpower during the Cold War. Tito died on May 4, 1980, still holding the reins of power in Yugoslavia.

Legacy

Tito reunified a Yugoslavia torn by bitter civil war during World War II. However, the ethnic nationalism at the root of the civil war reemerged after his death in large part because of the nature of his leadership.

Yugoslavia under Tito was a curious combination of relative economic and cultural freedom and total political repression and control. The lack of political freedom made debate on the role of ethnic identity in Yugoslavia impossible. Tito's regime had created temporary stability in a historically unstable region.

Treated almost as a mythic hero in his lifetime, Tito's image began to decay in the years following his death, undermining the legitimacy of the regime so connected to his cult of personality. At the end of the Cold War a widespread and increasingly open debate arose about the nature of the Yugoslav state and viability of com-

munist single-party rule. Sensing that communism was on the way out in Eastern Europe, Slobodan Milosevic, a rising member of the Communist Party in Serbia, transformed himself into a nationalist in 1989, a tactic that won him the first free elections in the post–Cold War era. Tito's state system was beginning to unravel.

Fearful of Serbian domination, one republic after another seceded from the Yugoslav federation, starting in 1990 with Croatia and Slovenia, followed by Bosnia-Herzegovina in 1992 and Macedonia in 1993. The Serbs in Croatia and Bosnia rebelled, hoping to carve out territory to create a Greater Serbia. Their brutal "ethnic cleansing" tactics against Croatians and Bosnian Muslims, and in 1999 against the Albanians of Kosovo, brought United Nations and NATO (North Atlantic Treaty Organization) military intervention in the region in March 1999 and ongoing efforts to resolve these conflicts. Many southern Slavs, rightly or wrongly, blamed Tito for the breakup of Yugoslavia into ethnic states.

Lemoine

WORLD EVENTS	TITO'S LIFE
Germany is united 1871	
	1892 Josep Broz, later Tito, is born
Russo-Japanese War 1905	
World War I 1914–18	
	1915 Tito is captured in World War I
Russian Revolution 1917	
	1920 Tito returns to new nation of Yugoslavia
	1928 Tito imprisoned
Great Depression 1929–39	
	1937 Tito becomes general secretary of Communist Party of Yugoslavia
World War II 1939–45	
	1945 Tito declares creation of Federal Republic of Yugoslavia
Communist China 1949 is established	
	1953 Tito is elected president of Yugoslavia
Israel defeats 1967 Arab nations in Six-Day War	
Vietnam War ends 1975	
	1980 Tito dies
Dissolution of 1991 Soviet Union	

For Further Reading

Pavlowitch, Stevan K. *Tito, Yugoslavia's Great Dictator: A Reassessment.* London: C. Hurst, 1992.

West, Richard. *Tito and the Rise and Fall of Yugoslavia.* London: Sinclair-Stevenson, 1994.

Tojo Hideki

Japanese Military and Political
Leader
1884–1948

Life and Work

Tojo Hideki is often portrayed as a cruel dictator who, during World War II, single-handedly orchestrated brutal conquests of European and American colonies in Asia. In fact, he was but one of many narrow-minded leaders in the beleaguered, paranoid, and ultra-patriotic Japan of the 1930s and 1940s.

Tojo Hideki was born in 1884 to a Japanese military officer. In 1904 he graduated from a military academy and immediately joined Japanese troops occupying Manchuria, in northeast China. Between 1907 and 1911, after returning from Manchuria, Tojo attended Staff College, a school for promising young officers. Tojo's superiors sent him to serve as Japan's military attache to Germany from 1919 to 1922. After 1931, because of his discretion, Tojo served in sensitive staff positions in occupied Manchuria, culminating with his 1935 appointment as a lieutenant general in charge of the Japanese military's secret police, the Kenpeitei.

World Events		Tojo's Life
Germany is united	1871	
	1884	Tojo Hideki is born
Russo-Japanese War	1905	
	1907–11	Tojo attends Staff College
World War I	1914–18	
Russian Revolution	1917	
Great Depression	1929–39	
	1931	Tojo begins serving in a series of staff positions in Manchuria
	1935	Tojo is appointed head of Kenpeitei, Japanese secret police
World War II	1939–45	
	1940	Tojo is made minister of war
	1941	Tojo is named prime minister
	1944	United States attacks Tokyo; Tojo resigns
	1948	Tojo is executed
Communist China is established	1949	

Tojo moved into increasingly political positions, such as the Manchurian army's chief of staff in 1937, vice–minister of war in 1938, and finally, minister of war in 1940. In the context of an increasingly militarized government at home, military adventurism abroad, and diplomatic isolation, Tojo became a supporter of the "strike South" faction. This faction argued for conquering Europe's Southeast Asian colonies and dealing the United States Navy a stunning blow so that Japan would have access to vital resources and could assume a dominant political position in Asia. In 1941, Tojo became prime minister. The United States' stubborn attitude toward Japan concerned Tojo, and he ordered a "strike South" for December 1941.

On December 7, 1941, the Japanese navy destroyed much of the United States' Pacific Fleet at Pearl Harbor, Hawaii, and by mid–1942, the Japanese army had captured all of Southeast Asia to the border of India. Thereafter, the Japanese military retreated, and the losses, especially after the firebombing of Tokyo in 1944, were blamed on Tojo, who in fact had taken on too much responsibility in both civilian and military affairs to lead effectively. On July 18, 1944, Tojo was forced to resign as prime minister. Thereafter, he retired to his home in Tokyo's suburbs. When the United States Occupation Forces police came to to arrest him, Tojo tried to commit suicide. He then endured three years of imprisonment and trial as a war criminal. On September 22, 1948, the Allied forces executed Tojo.

Legacy

The wartime characterization of Tojo Hideki as a brutal megalomaniac resembling Hitler or Stalin belies his true legacy, for Tojo never sought personal aggrandizement and always conducted himself as a normal, rational individual. This rationality, however, points the way to Tojo's legacy, for he revealed the dangers of excessive duty and of militarism.

Full of social tension encouraged by the worldwide Great Depression, the Japan of the late 1920s and 1930s wavered between democracy and military dictatorship, with extremists regularly assassinating moderate military and political leaders. The extremists wanted to end the distinction between military and civilian life in a way that supposedly recalled the pre–1868 Japan of the shogun. The uncommitted Tojo's unwavering obedience to the general staff of the

imperial army marked him as a useful, moderate loyalist. In 1941, when the general staff decided that capturing Southeast Asia was necessary and war with the United States inevitable, Tojo served its needs for a prime minister who shared its patriotic zeal and who had the organizational capability to carry out such plans. But Tojo was narrow–minded and had little nonmilitary experience. He conducted war, both a civilian and military affair, poorly. In addition, although he was personally compassionate and tried to moderate the excesses of his field commanders, he proved incapable of preventing horrible cruelties against Allied prisoners of war and subjugated civilians.

After 1945, Japan, strictly tutored by the Allied occupying powers, completely abandoned militarism and aggressive war, focusing successfully instead on economic expansion and material prosperity. In 1945, much as Germany did, Japan ended military culture and veneration of warriors. Tojo, in a sense, made this possible, because he had so clearly demonstrated the perils of permitting the military to have roles in civilian government and of placing unwaveringly obedient military men in leadership positions. Although not exactly a pawn of Japan's ruling military–industrial oligarchy during World War II, Tojo certainly was entirely beholden to their paranoia about Euro–American encroachment and their dreams of a Japanese Asia. Only recently, under threat from an aggressive North Korea and belligerent People's Republic of China, has Japan reluctantly agreed to any kind of enlargement of its military capability beyond a small but professional self–defense force.

Del Testa

For Further Reading

Browne, Courtney. *Tojo: The Last Banzai*. London: Angus and Robertson, 1967.
Hoyt, Edwin P. *Warlord—Tojo Against the World*. Lanham, Md.: Scarborough House, 1993.

Tokugawa Ieyasu

Shogun of Japan
1543–1616

Life and Work

Although beset with challenges to his rule and social unrest, Tokugawa Ieyasu completed and solidified the work of unifying and pacifying Japan that TOYOTOMI HIDEYOSHI had begun in 1580s. In so doing, he established a hereditary central leadership for Japan that endured from 1600 to 1867 and a culture of stability that has endured to the present.

Born on January 31, 1543, into the Tokugawa family in Mikawa province, south of modern Tokyo, Ieyasu, the son of a minor lord, spent much of his early life in the castle town of Sumpu as the privileged hostage of a strong *daimyo*, or local lord, Imagawa Yoshimoto. Ieyasu was born in the middle of Japan's century-long civil war during which local lords abandoned their loyalty to the Japanese emperor and his appointed dictator, the shogun, and battled each other for supremacy. Ieyasu received military and athletic training at Sumpu and studied the classics and Japanese literature at a local Buddhist temple.

In 1558, like many young men of his class, Ieyasu became a commander in Imagawa's army, proving himself an excellent leader. In 1560, with the death of *daimyo* Imagawa, Ieyasu was permitted to reclaim his lands at Mikawa and his rights as a minor *daimyo*. Thereafter, Ieyasu worked very hard and very shrewdly to expand his domains, making and breaking pacts with neighboring leaders and waging wars against the weak. For example, in 1569–70, Ieyasu conquered Totomi, an old and large domain immediately to the east of his possessions in Mikawa. But in 1570 and again in 1571, because he was too bold, Ieyasu lost many men and was barely able to save his own life.

After 1571, Ieyasu became more cautious for a time, relying more on alliances than direct confrontations to achieve his conquests. In 1584, Ieyasu skirmished with, and then became an ally of, Toyotomi Hideyoshi, who had just begun to try to concentrate his control of Japan's shogun. Ieyasu and Hideyoshi became closer allies, intermarrying their families and culminating in Ieyasu's loyalty oath to Hideyoshi

in 1588. During the 1590s, Hideyoshi defeated or gained the loyalty of all of Japan's *daimyo*. Although appointed as one of the five guardians of Hideyoshi's heir, Ieyasu backed away from Hideyoshi, setting up his headquarters in Edo, now Tokyo, and carefully avoiding Hideyoshi's campaign in Korea. When Hideyoshi died in 1598, Ieyasu continued to work with his fellow *daimyo* until, in 1600, he defeated a great army raised against him at the battle of Sekigghara. Thereafter, Ieyasu enjoyed essentially unchallenged authority in Japan, confirmed in 1603 with his appointment as hereditary shogun in the new Tokugawa line.

Ieyasu retired as shogun in 1605 in favor of his heir, Hidetada, but continued to run Japan's political life. Ieyasu continued to build on the social and economic reforms begun by Hideyoshi in the 1580s. He patronized the arts, improved transportation and communication, encouraged domestic and international commercial contacts, and ran very productive mines. After 1610, Ieyasu began to notice some discontent, because the peace left many people restless. Between 1610 and 1615, Ieyasu issued edicts on religion that reinforced Buddhism and destroyed Christianity in Japan. He also promulgated laws regulating court activity so that it did not interfere with the shogun's rule. At Osaka, in 1615, Ieyasu had to put down one final uprising, that of another heir, Hideyori, whom he compelled to commit suicide. Ieyasu died shortly thereafter, on April 17, 1616.

Legacy

Enforcing the centralization and pacification of Japan begun by Hideyoshi, Tokugawa Ieyasu ensured a hereditary stability in Japanese political life by making the shogun its political center again.

By 1591, Hideyoshi had subjugated Japan's warring *daimyo*, pacified them through rigid social codes and obligations, and created social stability and even prosperity in Japan. Ieyasu was able to institutionalize Hideyoshi's reforms through the office of the shogun.

Ieyasu's dealings with the outside world were perhaps less successful than those of Hideyoshi, but they may have been more significant. Ieyasu, even more so than Hideyoshi, badly wanted reciprocal trade with the countries of the world. Foreign trade, however, brought foreign ideas, especially Christianity, and wealth to

those *daimyo* involved in overseas trade. Christianity disrupted the traditional social order of Buddhism, Confucianism, and a divine emperor. Wealth meant imported firearms to challenge the shogun's authority. At first, Ieyasu tried to balance trade and Christianity by ejecting missionaries and making traders agree that they would not mix religion and commerce. His successors, Hidetada and Iemitsu, in the face of a revolt by angry *daimyo* in 1635 and a Christian-inspired revolt in 1637–38, slaughtered any Christian not willing to convert, and made Japan a *sakuko*, or closed country. Thereafter, only a trickle of trade flowed in through the Dutch and Chinese at Nagasaki. Social laws were tightened even further, so that after 1635, the shogun compelled *daimyo* to stay at the Edo headquarters one out of two years and to leave hostages there permanently.

The social system worked, and worked well, as long as no alternatives presented themselves. Although Japan's nineteenth-century leaders were aware of the changes going on in the world around them, only the shock of foreign powers beginning to impose their will on Japan forced them to open the country and adapt society to modern ways.

Del Testa

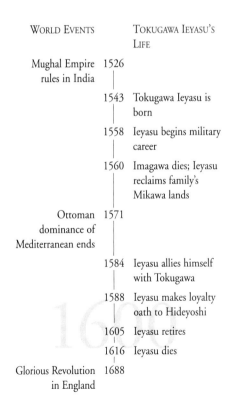

WORLD EVENTS		TOKUGAWA IEYASU'S LIFE
Mughal Empire rules in India	1526	
	1543	Tokugawa Ieyasu is born
	1558	Ieyasu begins military career
	1560	Imagawa dies; Ieyasu reclaims family's Mikawa lands
Ottoman dominance of Mediterranean ends	1571	
	1584	Ieyasu allies himself with Tokugawa
	1588	Ieyasu makes loyalty oath to Hideyoshi
	1605	Ieyasu retires
	1616	Ieyasu dies
Glorious Revolution in England	1688	

For Further Reading

Chie Nakane and Shinzabur Aishi, eds. *Tokugawa Japan: The Social and Economic Antecedents of Modern Japan*. Tokyo: University of Tokyo Press, 1990.

Totman, Conrad. *Tokugawa Ieyasu: Shogun, a Biography*. San Francisco: Heian International, 1983.

Topa Inca Yupanqui

Incan Emperor
c. 1440–1493

Life and Work

Building on the work of his eminent father, PACHACUTI INCA YUPANQUI, Topa Inca Yupanqui strengthened the frontiers and the internal administration of the Incan Empire and reigned during its period of greatest prosperity.

Topa was born about 1440 into the imperial house of the Inca. His father, Pachacuti, had created the Inca Empire and the administrative structure to perpetuate it after his death. However, an aging Pachacuti felt the need to expand the empire before he died so that it would not face external threats and that the administrative structure would have sufficient resources to draw upon for general prosperity. Therefore, in 1463 Pachacuti made Topa, despite his youth, commander-in-chief of the Incan armies so that his favored son and heir could gain experience and achieve Pachacuti's goals for an enlarged empire. He sent young Topa into the field on a long series conquests. Topa had probably had the education of most young Inca nobles of the time, including the study of the Quechua language, Incan religion, the military arts, and the *quipu*, a kind of abacus made up of knotted strings.

As military commander, Topa first struck northward, toward Ecuador, the homeland of three great peoples—the Chimú, the Cananri, and, most formidable, the Quitu. Using forced marches through difficult terrain, Topa surprised his enemies by being "everywhere and nowhere" at the same time. Topa conquered the lesser coastal states of Peru and made the Inca Empire a coastal and mountain domain that stretched from Ecuador to northern Chile.

In 1471, Pachacuti, well into his fifties or sixties, abdicated to his son so that the succession to the throne was clear. After participating in the ceremonies of office, Topa immediately left on campaign toward the east, where he vainly battled marauding lowland tribes from the Amazon and set up a string of large fortresses. While at the edge of the Amazon, Topa heard that the Colla, Lupaca, Pacasa, and Omasuyu tribes, the first groups conquered by his father, had revolted. He returned to Cuzco, the Incan capital, and struck against the rebels, defeating them in a series of bloody victories. With the rebels quelled, Topa had the northern and southern boundaries of the empire permanently established, and returned to Cuzco, where he lived and ruled in peace until his death in 1493.

Legacy

Topa Inca Yupanqui transformed the Incan Empire from the powerful regional entity of Pachacuti into a universal state, called the Tahuantinsuyu, or "land of four quarters." This unity enabled a flowering of culture and a period of prosperity previously unknown in South America.

Throughout his political life, Topa actively practiced and promoted the characteristic synthesis and absorption of culture and people that made the Inca so formidable and irresistible. During his youth, Topa, like his father, always tried to leave conquered people to their own business, requiring only that they conform to Incan administrative norms such as labor service and a hierarchical administration. However, Topa also knew that he had to integrate Incan and conquered societies more thoroughly than would happen through simple administrative measures. For example, the Inca readily accepted the art of other people; Topa's conquest of the Chimú had brought about a productive and beautiful synthesis of artistic styles that came to define Incan pottery and painting. In addition, Topa ensured that officials of conquered peoples learned to appreciate Incan ways by sending them to Cuzco for administrative training. In this way, more and more conquered peoples became Incan in culture, and yet subjugated tribes could see their culture blended with, not overtaken by, that of the Inca.

Just as important, Topa, using the forms initiated by his father, made the Inca into a mighty empire that endures as a point of South American pride to this day. By spreading Incan architecture, art, and administration across western South America forcefully and adroitly, Topa would have ensured, except for the unanticpated and devastating arrival of the Spaniards in the 1520s, the endurance of the Inca for many decades after his death.

Del Testa

For Further Reading

Hyams, Edward, and George Ordish. *The Last of the Incas: The Rise and Fall of an American Empire.* New York: Simon and Schuster, 1963.

Rostworowski de Diez Canseco, Maria. *History of the Inca Realm.* Translated by Harry B. Iceland. New York: Cambridge University Press, 1999.

Toussaint-Louverture

Revolutionary Leader of Haiti
c. 1743–1803

Life and Work

Toussaint-Louverture led an army of Haitians against the French colonial government during the French Revolution. Although he was ultimately captured, his military victories sparked the movement that brought independence to the island nation.

Toussaint-Louverture, born François Dominique Toussaint, was born a slave on a Haitian plantation around 1743. His father, the son of an African chieftain, had been brought to the island after being enslaved in a war in Africa. Toussaint grew up enjoying privileges such as lighter work and access to learning through a godfather who taught him to read. On the plantation he was made a steward, and this gave him experience in administration. He also had the opportunity to read European works on the themes of politics and military history, including such authors as JULIUS CAESAR and the Enlightenment philosopher Abbé Raynal. His reading almost surely developed in him a strong consciousness of alternatives to the condition of the black slaves on Haiti. He was eventually freed from slavery and joined Haiti's French forces.

When the French Revolution of 1789 inspired many of Haiti's black slaves and mulattoes (people of mixed race) to revolt, Toussaint was in an excellent position to offer leadership. Promising an end to slavery, in 1791 he gathered together a large army and for the remainder of the decade fought with great effectiveness against the French forces that were dispatched to the island to suppress the revolt. Toussaint benefitted from French preoccupation with battles in Europe and other parts of the New World. Assuming dictatorial powers over those parts of the island that he controlled, Toussaint decreed an end to slavery. He never formally declared independence from France, however. His rule was harsh, and in time some of Haiti's blacks and mulattoes began to offer resistance.

Toussaint continued to win battles and, in 1801, finally captured Santo Domingo, now capital of the Dominican Republic and the island's main city. He marked his victory the same year by convening a constitutional convention to decide the political future of the island. In the meantime, his rule continued to alienate large numbers of former slaves. When a fresh army arrived from France under General Leclerc in 1802, Toussaint was unable to organize a defense. He was captured the same year and taken to France, dying there in a prison on April 7, 1803.

Legacy

Toussaint-Louverture's twelve-year career as revolutionary leader ended in personal failure. The insurrection he inspired, however, continued, resulting in independence for Haiti in less than a year.

After his capture and deportation in 1802, two of Toussaint's comrades, General Jean-Jacques Dessalines, a former slave, and General Henri Christophe, prepared for a decisive revolution against French colonial authority. The resumption of the Napoleonic Wars between France and England provided them (as it had Toussaint) with the opportunity to build military strength. They mopped up small detachments of French soldiers on the island and even constructed light ships for use in attacking coastal patrols. At last they turned on the remaining French stronghold of La Cap. With an English naval blockade preventing reinforcements, the French commander Rochambeau was forced to abandon the island with only a handful of the 60,000 soldiers he had started with. On December 31, 1803, just eight months after the death of Toussaint in France, Dessalines and Christophe issued a formal declaration of independence.

The immediate aftermath of independence was bloody, however. The victorious generals had no intention of ruling democratically, and in 1804 Dessalines proclaimed himself emperor. Possibly encouraged by the promise of English trading relations, he issued an order early in 1805 to massacre all of the French remaining on the island. After the first round of killing ended, many French managed to escape into hiding. Dessalines then issued a call for them to give themselves up, promising a pardon. As soon as they showed themselves, however, he had them annihilated. Nearly three centuries of brutal colonial domination had thus been returned in kind and without mercy.

Strickland

WORLD EVENTS		TOUSSAINT-LOUVERTURE'S LIFE
English seize Calcutta	1690	
	c. 1743	Toussaint-Louverture is born
United States declares independence	1776	
French Revolution begins	1789	
	1791	Toussaint organizes army of blacks and mulattoes
	1801	Toussaint captures Santo Domingo
	1802	Toussaint is captured by General Leclerc
	1803	Toussaint dies; eight months later, Haiti's independence is declared
Latin American independence movement begins	1811	

For Further Reading

Alexis, Stephen. *Black Liberator: The Life of Toussaint Louverture.* Translated by William Stirling. New York: Macmillan, 1949.
James, C. L. R. *The Black Jacobins: Toussaint L'Ouverture and the San Domingo Revolution.* 2nd ed. New York: Vintage, 1989.
Ott, Thomas O. *The Haitian Revolution, 1789–1804.* Knoxville: University of Tennessee Press, 1973.

Toyotomi Hideyoshi

Unifier of Modern Japan
1536–1598

Life and Work

Toyotomi Hideyoshi ended a century-long civil war in Japan by negotiating with or conquering rebellious local lords and by imposing on the Japanese a social code that restricted the possibility of civil strife.

In 1536, Hideyoshi was born to a farming family in Nakamura, a village near Kyoto. Before Hideyoshi's time, shogun, or dictators, customarily managed the affairs of Japan's emperor, who mainly concerned himself with religion. The shogun managed *daimyo*, or local lords, who controlled various amounts of land and resources. By the mid-1400s, many *daimyo* began to control their possessions directly, rather than answering to the shogun. Thereafter, for over a century, groups of *daimyo* started wars of conquest against one another, fracturing Japan

World Events		Toyotomi Hideyoshi's Life
Mughal Empire rules in India	1526	
	1536	Hideyoshi born near Kyoto
	1568	Hideyoshi participates in Norabunga's attack on Kyoto
Ottoman dominance of Mediterranean ends	1571	
	1582	Norabunga is assassinated; Hideyoshi replaces him
	1590	Hideyoshi's conquest of Japan is complete
	1592–98	Hideyoshi invades Korea
	1598	Hideyoshi dies
Glorious Revolution in England	1688	

into warring territories. Hideyoshi left home in 1551 and joined these struggles. He became a messenger in the army of a local *daimyo*, Imagawa Yoshimoto, and, in 1558, joined the army of a more powerful *daimyo*, Oda Norabunga, who was trying to bring all of Japan's *daimyo* under his control. Through sheer martial ability, Hideyoshi rose in the ranks of Norabunga's army, participating in his 1568 attack on Kyoto and in the infamous 1571 destruction of Enryakuji, the center of the influential Tendai Buddhist sect. Known for his innovative tactics, Hideyoshi became one of Japan's ablest military leaders. As a reward for good service, Norabunga gave lands to Hideyoshi, and Hideyoshi became a *daimyo* himself. In 1582, an embittered rival killed Norabunga. Hideyoshi took Norabunga's place, waging war until, in 1590, he controlled all of Japan.

As Japan's de facto political leader, and in the aftermath of a century of disunity and destruction, Hideyoshi made peace with his enemies. To show that he did not seek to reign over the *daimyo*, Hideyoshi shunned the title of shogun, posing instead as an advisor to the emperor. In addition, Hideyoshi showed his generosity by allowing his enemies to keep their possessions as long as they swore loyalty to him. Beginning in 1587, to limit conflict and protect his regime, Hideyoshi disarmed all Japanese except samurai, the hereditary warriors. In 1591, Hideyoshi issued decrees that made most professions hereditary and bound the samurai and *daimyo* to him through service requirements. To limit future scheming, Hideyoshi burdened his *daimyo* with heavy military and construction expenditures, ensuring that they would have neither the men nor the money available for rebellion. Furthermore, between 1592 and 1598, Hideyoshi invaded Korea, with the intention of taking China. Although he may have seen this invasion as a way to reward those who had shown loyalty to him with new lands and glory, Hideyoshi may have also wanted the generation of soldiers who had grown up with violence and political intrigue to grind themselves down against an inevitable counterattack from China. Hideyoshi died in late 1598.

Legacy

Toyotomi Hideyoshi laid the foundation for 250 years of stability, prosperity, and creativity in Japan by unifying the *daimyo*

through conquest and by limiting civil strife through a rigid social code.

Hideyoshi realized that centralization of power alone did not guarantee an end to civil strife; Norabunga had temporarily unified much of central Japan in the 1580s, but the *daimyo* hated his violent and exploitative rule. Hideyoshi's system, building on Norabunga's conquests, was popular and therefore endured. It gave the *daimyo* a sense of managing their own affairs. The *daimyo*, with certain restrictions, collected taxes and administered justice in their holdings. However, in exchange for peace, the *daimyo* permanently mortgaged their lives and resources to the central government. The *daimyo* and his samurai had to support second homes in Tokyo, where they lived halftime and parts of their families lived permanently as hostages. They also had to buy expensive clothes and swords for court functions. Indeed, many of the lower samurai quickly sank into poverty and back into the peasantry.

It appeared, however, that the Japanese felt the benefits of Hideyoshi's system were worth its costs. The peace conferred by Hideyoshi's management of Japan's politics allowed commerce, industry, and the arts to flourish. The Japanese had to look around them to find or develop a culture suited to their needs, and it was no longer the precious Chinese styles that had been popular before the mid-1400s. Korean artisans brought to Japan during Hideoyoshi's invasion introduced a warmer, more textured quality to many of Japan's crafts. During Hideyoshi's rule, the Japanese mixed local folk culture with the Korean influences and produced a culture that many see as central to Japan's sense of self.

Hideyoshi made Japanese society and politics predictable and, within limits, immense creative energies flowed. And yet, Hideyoshi's system tolerated very little outside influence. Although Hideyoshi and the subsequent shogun craved new ideas, they mercilessly stamped out foreign cultural influences, such as Christianity, and kept tight control of the few Dutch and Chinese permitted to trade in Japan. This rigidity made Japan unprepared for the threat of Western imperialism in the 1800s; only the creativity and discipline facilitated by Hideyoshi's peace helped Japan respond to foreigners who forced themselves on the Japanese after 1853.

Del Testa

For Further Reading

Berry, Mary Elizabeth. *Hideyoshi*. Cambridge, Mass: Harvard University Press, 1982.
Dening, Walter. *The Life of Toyotomi Hideyoshi*. 5th ed. New York: AMS Press, 1971.

Trotsky, Leon

Communist Revolutionary and
Opponent of Stalinism
1879–1940

Life and Work

A tireless revolutionary and a rousing orator, Leon Trotsky helped organize the Bolshevik Revolution in Russia. Although driven from his homeland by political intrigue, he managed to form an independent communist movement until he was finally murdered.

Trotsky was born on October 26, 1879, in Yanovka in the Ukraine, which was then a part of the Russian Empire. His family name was Bronstein and his parents were prosperous Jewish peasants. In 1897 he was introduced to Marxism by Alexandra Sokolovskaia, a young woman with whom he was in love. Together the two organized a revolutionary group in southern Russia, but it was soon uncovered by the police. Sentenced to prison in 1898, he married Sokolovskaia in jail and was accompanied by her to exile in Siberia. Adopting the name Trotsky in ironic commemoration of one of his guards, he broke out of prison camp in 1902 and fled to England.

The years that followed were occupied mainly with disputes about how to bring about a revolution in Russia. He maintained an independent course, though he was sympathetic to the Bolshevik Party that VLADIMIR LENIN formed in 1903. During the revolution of 1905,

he returned to Russia to head the Petersburg Soviet (council), but was forced to flee again soon after. Following the March Revolution of 1917, he returned to join Lenin and played a key role in the Bolshevik seizure of power on November 7 (an event known as the October Revolution, according to the Julian calendar then in use). Trotsky was thereafter given important responsibilities in the Soviet government, including commissar of foreign relations (1918) and commissar of war (1918–21).

Trotsky's reputation was very strong at the time of Lenin's death in 1924. With the rise of JOSEPH STALIN in the years that followed, however, Trotsky was increasingly excluded from political life. In 1927 he was ejected from the Communist Party and in 1929 deported from the Soviet Union altogether. He spent the remainder of his years as a bitter opponent of Stalin and his regime, living in various countries and trying to organize an opposition from abroad. In his book, *The Revolution Betrayed* (1937), he claimed that the Soviet Union had deviated from the course set by Lenin, and this inspired his creation in 1938 of an alternative organization of communists called the Fourth International. His activities proved futile, however, and on August 21, 1940, on the secret orders of Stalin, a Spanish communist murdered Trotsky with an ice pick in Mexico City.

Legacy

L eon Trotsky played a central role in establishing the Soviet Union, yet his failure to oppose Stalin prevented his vision of communism from being realized there. Only in the West did he have a lasting impact on revolutionaries.

At the time of Lenin's death in 1924, Trotsky was regarded as the most influential and powerful member of the Soviet government. He was celebrated for his sharp oratory and writings, and he had proven his devotion to communism during the civil war as leader of the Red Army. Nevertheless, he kept aloof from other party leaders and preferred to leave the responsibilities of party management to people like Stalin. Stalin was able to exploit this by forming a rival bloc of party leaders that prevented Trotsky from exercising the authority that might have accompanied his status. Trotsky's highly theoretical approach to the nature of revolution also proved politically inexpedient. He espoused a theory called "per-

manent revolution," which claimed that Russia's communist regime could survive only if it fostered other revolutions throughout the world. When this failed to happen in the 1920s, and as Stalin emerged with an alternative theory of "socialism in one country," Trotsky found himself increasingly isolated and powerless.

Once he was banished from the Soviet Union, Trotsky developed a critique of Stalinism that inspired revolutionaries throughout the world after his death. His attacks on Stalin's use of terror against loyal party members within the Soviet Union were joined by Marxists in the West. More importantly, he developed a form of communism, often dubbed Trotskyism, that emphasized the importance of improving the conditions of the working class, which had been burdened by an ever-growing state bureaucracy under Stalin. For many Marxist revolutionaries and scholars, Trotskyism seemed to offer a corrective to the increasingly unpleasant spectacle of Soviet communism under Stalin, and was influential during the protests led by DANIEL COHN-BENDIT and other students throughout the world in 1968.

Strickland

WORLD EVENTS		TROTSKY'S LIFE
Germany is united	1871	
	1879	Leon Trotsky is born
	1897	Trotsky discovers Marxism
Russo-Japanese War	1905	Trotsky serves as chairman of Petersburg Soviet
World War I	1914–18	
Russian Revolution	1917	Trotsky plays key role in Bolshevik Revolution
	1918	Trotsky serves as Soviet commissar of foreign relations
	1918–21	Trotsky serves as commissar of war
	1924	Lenin's death
Great Depression	1929–39	
	1929	Trotsky is deported from Soviet Union
	1937	Trotsky publishes *The Revolution Betrayed*
World War II	1939–45	
	1940	Trotsky is murdered in Mexico City
Communist China is established	1949	

For Further Reading
Deutscher, Isaac. *The Prophet Armed: Trotsky, 1879–1921*. Oxford: Oxford University Press, 1954.
———. *The Prophet Outcast: Trotsky, 1929–1940*. Oxford: Oxford University Press, 1963.
———. *The Prophet Unarmed: Trotsky, 1921–1929*. Oxford: Oxford University Press, 1959.
Volkogonov, Dmitri. *Trotsky: The Eternal Revolutionary*. Translated by Harold Shukman. New York: Free Press, 1996.

Truman, Harry S.

Thirty-Third President of the United States

1884–1972

Life and Work

Harry S. Truman oversaw the transformation of the United States into a global superpower and the country's presidency into the most important public office in the world.

Born on May 8, 1884, in Lamar, Missouri, Truman grew up on a farm near Independence, Missouri. After graduating from high school, he took a number of office jobs and joined the National Guard. When the United States entered World War I in 1917, Truman joined the army. He was promoted to captain and ably led his troops into a number of battles. Returning to civilian life, Truman started a business, which soon failed, leading to many years of debt.

Truman began to participate in Democratic Party politics in Missouri, where he was elected county judge. In 1934, Truman was elected to the U.S. Senate, and served as chairman of the committee to investigate the national defense program after the United States entered World War II. In 1944, while still a senator, he was nominated as FRANKLIN DELANO ROOSEVELT's vice-president; Roosevelt and Truman were successful—Roosevelt won his fourth term in office.

Truman served only 83 days as vice-president. Roosevelt's died on April 12, 1945, and Truman was sworn in as president. His first major decision was to order the dropping of atomic bombs on Hiroshima and Nagasaki, Japan, to end the war in the Pacific theater. With the end of the war, Truman faced domestic demands for quick demobilization and a return to a peacetime economy. He also confronted a deterioration in relations with the Soviet Union, a breakdown of cooperation that was clear as early as the Potsdam Conference, which Truman attended in the summer of 1945.

In 1947 Truman formulated his so-called Truman Doctrine, in which the United States took on the responsibility for helping non-communist regimes defeat both foreign and domestic communist opponents, and began sending aid to Greece and Turkey to combat communist threats there. He also adopted GEORGE F. KENNAN's policy of containment of the Soviet Union. In 1948 Truman implemented the Marshall Plan, which provided funds to Western European countries to rebuild their economies. Truman also continued Roosevelt's New Deal programs.

Truman's policies were not always popular, yet he was re-elected in 1948, despite many predictions that he would lose. After the Communist Party gained power in China (1949), Truman expanded the policy of containment to Asia, sending troops to combat the invasion of South Korea by the communist North Koreans (1950). Truman's popularity at home sunk to new lows after he removed General Douglas MacArthur from the Korean command in 1951 for insubordination. Deciding not to run for re-election in 1952, Truman retired from public life. He gave lectures and wrote opinion pieces, continuing to influence American politics. He died on December 26, 1972, in Kansas City, Missouri.

WORLD EVENTS		TRUMAN'S LIFE
Germany is united	1871	
	1884	Harry S. Truman is born
Russo-Japanese War	1905	
World War I	1914–18	
	1917	Truman joins army in World War I
Russian Revolution	1917	
Great Depression	1929–39	
	1934	Truman is elected to U.S. Senate
World War II	1939–45	
	1944	Truman is elected vice-president
	1945	Truman becomes president after Roosevelt's death
		Truman OKs use of atomic bombs on Japan
	1948	Truman is re-elected to presidency
Communist China is established	1949	
	1950	Truman sends troops to Korea
	1952	Truman retires
Israel defeats Arab nations in Six-Day War	1967	
	1972	Truman dies
Vietnam War ends	1975	

Legacy

Harry S. Truman guided the United States into its new role as postwar global superpower and maintained the expanded role of the federal government in American life initiated by his predecessor, Franklin D. Roosevelt.

Recognizing the increased importance of the presidency in the new Cold War and welfare-state era, Truman transformed the executive branch of the government. He expanded the staff, and created or expanded advisory agencies such as the Council of Economic Advisors and the National Security Council, increasing the federal government's efficiency and organization.

Truman's decision to use the atomic bomb against Japan confirmed the United States as a superpower. Recognizing this new role, Truman abandoned isolationism, crafting instead enduring alliances with nations in both Europe and Asia against communist regimes. However, some accuse Truman of misunderstanding Soviet leader JOSEPH STALIN's motivations, causing a downward spiral of mistrust that led to the Cold War and the need for these alliances.

Truman's decision to continue the development of nuclear weapons, combined with the Cold War rivalry between the United States and the Soviet Union, led to a frightening arms race. The Cold War standoff lasted more than 40 years, until the fall of the Berlin Wall in 1989, although the proliferation of arms that the Cold War engendered continues to threaten the world's population today.

Lemoine

For Further Reading

Ferrell, Robert H. *Harry S. Truman and the Modern American Presidency.* Boston: Little, Brown, 1983.

McCoy, Donald R. *The Presidency of Harry S. Truman.* Lawrence: University Press of Kansas, 1984.

McCullough, David. *Truman.* New York: Simon and Schuster, 1992.

Tupac Amarú

Peruvian Rebel

c. 1742–1781

Life and Work

Tupac Amarú led a mass revolt against the colonial government of eighteenth-century Peru. Although ultimately defeated, his rebellion revived consciousness of the Incan past and further weakened the declining Spanish Empire.

Tupac Amarú was born in the southern region of modern Peru in the middle of the eighteenth century. His family descended both from the royalty of the old Incan Empire and from European settlers. This identity as a *mestizo*, or person of mixed blood, enhanced Tupac Amarú's status even more. Due to his lineage he became a *curaca*, or district headman, and was able to build close relations with the peasants who lived in his region of the Andes. Many of these peasants resented the Spanish provincial magistrates, such as Antonio de Arriaga, who occasionally tyrannized the district in which Tupac Amarú served.

During the Epiphany celebration in January 1780, the Indian peasants of Tupac Amarú's district petitioned their priest for the transfer of a nativity scene to their church. When the priest rejected the petition, his black servant began to circulate a story that Arriaga was behind the action, and that he was, in fact, preparing an attack on the district. Although untrue, the story greatly alarmed the peasants. In subsequent months many began to speak out against Arriaga's authority, and Tupac Amarú, eager both to claim the glory of his family heritage and bring improvements to his community, took this opportunity to revolt.

On November 10, 1780, Tupac Amarú had Arriaga seized and subjected to a hastily assembled popular tribunal. The death sentence was passed, and Arriaga was hanged on the spot. Tupac Amarú now called for a general insurrection against the colonial administration. Significantly, he did not challenge the authority of the king of Spain and even claimed to be acting in his name. Referring to his family background, he claimed to have been sent by divine powers to rescue the Incan people from bondage.

After seven months of rebellion, however, Tupac Amarú's forces were exhausted. Spanish authorities finally captured him, and, on May 18, 1781, he and several of his family were publicly executed. Their bodies were displayed afterward as a grisly warning to the peasants.

Legacy

Tupac Amarú's failed rebellion fostered the emergence of Incan nationalism and served to weaken the colonial authority of Spain. Furthermore, in modern times his memory came to inspire revolutionaries opposed to the political system of contemporary Peru.

Tupac Amarú's family background was crucial to his influence on the Indian peasants who participated in the revolt. His ability to instill the proud belief that they belonged to a historical people with a glorious past was a significant step toward the creation of modern Peruvian national self-consciousness. In addition to his blood ties, he also brought attention to the religious traditions of the Incan past. Without renouncing Christianity, to which many of the peasants adhered, he celebrated pagan customs that offered an alternative to the religious faith brought to the Andes from Europe. While this resulted in gross outrages during the rebellion (in some cases his followers devoured the hearts of the Christians they killed), the pagan themes of Tupac Amarú's image were combined with Incan memory to produce a nationalist ideology in later years.

While the Spanish crown showed itself capable of suppressing the insurrection, the example of Tupac Amarú was remembered among other colonial rebels in the decades after 1781. As resentments among the native peoples continued to simmer, colonial elites increasingly entertained thoughts of creating an independent state. Tupac Amarú had shown that massive support for a revolt against the established order was possible. Thus in 1811 SIMÓN BOLÍVAR received support when leading the Latin American wars of independence that finally brought colonial rule to an end in much of the region.

The memory of Tupac Amarú continued to inspire revolutionaries in independent Peru during the twentieth century. The Shining Path guerrilla movement saw him as a primitive example of peasant resistance to capitalist economic exploitation, and a revolutionary party called the Tupac Amarú Revolutionary Movement (MRTA) even looked to him for its name.

Strickland

WORLD EVENTS		TUPAC AMARÚ'S LIFE
English seize Calcutta	1690	
	c. 1742	Tupac Amarú is born
United States declares independence	1776	
	1780	Tupac Amarú executes Antonio de Arriaga and launches insurrection
	1781	Tupac Amarú is captured and executed
French Revolution begins	1789	

For Further Reading

Anna, Timothy. *The Fall of the Royal Government in Peru*. Lincoln: University of Nebraska Press, 1979.

Stavig, Ward. *The World of Tupac Amaru: Conflict, Community, and Identity in Colonial Peru*. Lincoln: University of Nebraska Press, 1999.

Stern, Steve J., ed. *Resistance, Rebellion, and Consciousness in the Andean Peasant World, Eighteenth to Twentieth Centuries*. Madison: University of Wisconsin Press, 1987.

Tutu, Desmond

Anglican Archbishop of South
Africa; Opponent of Apartheid
1931–

Life and Work

At a time of growing tension between
blacks and whites in South Africa,
Desmond Tutu called for the abolition of
apartheid. He used his status as a Christian
bishop to organize international opposition to
the government and to prevent racial violence.

Desmond Mpilo Tutu was born on October
7, 1931, in the Transvaal town of Klerksdorp.
As a boy, his interest was piqued by a missionary priest whose sermons challenged the system
of apartheid that deprived South Africa's blacks
of civil rights. Tutu became a high school
teacher in 1955, but resigned in 1957 to
protest new, racially discriminatory laws.
Feeling increasingly called to a religious life, he
was ordained an Anglican priest in 1961. He
then traveled to England for graduate study
and in 1966 received a master's degree in theology from the University of London. From
1972 to 1975 he served as associate director of

the World Council of Churches, an ecumenical
body designed to promote Christian unity and
social justice throughout the world. In 1978 he
became secretary-general of the South African
Council of Churches, an affiliate of the World
Council concerned specifically with the elimination of apartheid.

As leader of the South African Council, Tutu
entered political life more forcefully, earning the
reputation of a prophet for his use of Christian
teaching when attacking the apartheid system.
He organized negotiations with the government
to express the council's demands, but his calls
while abroad for economic sanctions against the
regime led to police harassment and the confiscation of his passport. His demand for a peaceful end to the regime was expressed in 1984
when he denounced violent uprisings that had
broken out in South Africa's townships. In the
same year he received the Nobel Prize for Peace.
In 1986 his moral authority reached its height
when he became archbishop of Cape Town, the
Anglican primate of South Africa.

Tutu witnessed the final dismantling of
apartheid after 1991, when NELSON MANDELA
was released from prison and his African
National Congress (ANC) was legalized. After
Mandela was elected president in 1994, he
appointed Tutu chairman of a Truth and
Reconciliation Commission in 1995 to study
the human rights abuses of the old regime.

Having contributed to the peaceful abolition of apartheid in South Africa, Tutu spent
the remainder of the decade traveling to areas
of the world divided by racial, ethnic, and religious violence, including Rwanda (1995),
Northern Ireland (1998), and Jerusalem,
where in 1999 he made a highly publicized
visit to the Holocaust Memorial of Yad
Vashem. In each of these places he delivered
addresses calling for peace, which, he claimed,
was possible only through forgiveness.

Legacy

Desmond Tutu's leadership of the Anglican
church and his calls for an end to
apartheid played an important role in the
peaceful abolition of white rule in South Africa.

Before Tutu entered South Africa's political
life, opposition to apartheid had long threatened
to bring civil war. Approximately three-quarters
of the population was black, and militant groups

such as the African National Congress were able
to draw support from a large number of people.
In the Sharpeville Uprising of 1960 and the
Soweto Uprising of 1976, for instance, violence
provoked by police attacks spread throughout the
country and claimed the lives of hundreds. From
prison, Nelson Mandela refused to renounce the
option of using violence, even when he was
offered freedom in exchange for doing so in
1985. Nevertheless, by maintaining a demand
for the peaceful overthrow of apartheid, Tutu
served to discredit proponents of violence among
blacks and fostered reconciliation between the
government and the opposition.

When President Pieter Botha resigned from
office in 1990, his successor, FREDERIK WILLEM
DE KLERK, was able to utilize the climate of
goodwill nurtured by Tutu. De Klerk offered to
release Mandela unconditionally. Mandela
agreed to meet with de Klerk and pledged to
pursue a nonviolent policy. De Klerk legalized
the African National Congress, which then won
the majority of seats to the Parliament in 1994.
Mandela was thereafter elected president, and a
new constitution in 1996 formalized the abolition of apartheid. While these dizzying events
were accompanied by some disturbances and
bloodshed, on the whole abolition of white rule
occurred peacefully. Thus it seemed particularly
appropriate when, in 1996, President Mandela
appointed Archbishop Tutu head of the commission designed to promote reconciliation
among South Africa's blacks and whites as the
century closed.

Strickland

World Events	Tutu's Life
Great Depression 1929–39	
	1931 Desmond Tutu is born
World War II 1939–45	
Communist China 1949 is established	
	1961 Tutu is ordained Anglican priest
Israel defeats 1967 Arab nations in Six-Day War	
Vietnam War ends 1975	
	1978 Tutu appointed secretary-general of South African Council of Churches
	1984 Tutu receives Nobel Prize for Peace
	1986 Tutu is named arch- bishop of Cape Town
Dissolution of 1991 Soviet Union	
	1995 Tutu is appointed chairman of a Truth and Reconciliation Commission

For Further Reading

Bock, Paul. *In Search of a Responsible World Society: The Social Teachings of the World Council of Churches.* Philadelphia:
    Westminster, 1974.

Du Boulay, Shirley. *Tutu: Voice of the Voiceless.* London: Hodder and Stoughton, 1988.

Kuperus, Tracy. *State, Civil Society, and Apartheid in South Africa.* New York: St. Martin's Press, 1999.

'Ubayd Allāh

Founder of the Fatimid Empire
in Africa
d. 936

Life and Work

By manipulating a strong religious identity and the dissatisfaction of many Muslims, 'Ubayd Allāh broke the authority of the Abbasids in North Africa and began the Fatimid dynasty.

Little is known about the early life of 'Ubayd Allāh, who was born Sa'id ibn Ahmed. He was an Ismaili, a member of a secret, radical, ultra-orthodox sect of Islam that, since the 800s, had perpetrated terror throughout the Muslim world in order to destroy the oppressive and, in their eyes, heretical Abbasid Caliphate (which had ruled parts of North Africa, the Near East, and the Middle East since 750). From early in his life, 'Ubayd Allāh claimed descent from Fatima, daughter of the prophet Muhammad.

In 902 and 904, 'Ubayd Allāh became known to the wider world when he led attacks against Abbasid authorities in Syria in order to become the province's imam, or leader. He must have had significant religious authority to rally the kind of support he did, because Syria was at the heart of the Abbasid Empire. These revolts were the latest round of terrorism sponsored by the Ismaili. After the failure of the revolts, 'Ubayd Allāh traveled to North Africa to meet with Abdullah, another Ismaili, to spread revolt among the Berbers, a people living in the mountains of present-day Algeria and Morocco in North Africa. North Africa had slipped from the control of the Muslim caliphs during the civil wars that brought the Abbasid Caliphate to power in the 700s and was ruled over by three small Muslim states. Although 'Ubayd Allāh was captured and imprisoned in northern Algeria, Abdullah managed to inspire a revolt among the Berbers. This revolt led to the collapse of the Aghlabids, the dynasty ruling over much of western North Africa.

When Abdullah and the agitated Berbers finished destroying the Aghlabids, he rescued 'Ubayd Allāh from prison and proclaimed him both caliph ("successor") and *mahdi* ("the chosen one"). Why Abdullah supported 'Ubayd Allāh over himself is unclear, but a rift grew between the two, and, in 912, 'Ubayd Allāh had Abdullah put to death.

'Ubayd Allāh launched two campaigns, in 914 and 921, against the Abbasids in Egypt—both of which failed. He then began taking the weak states of North Africa and the Mediterranean, claiming Morocco in 921 and Sicily in 933, and throughout his reign harassing the shores of the western Mediterranean with looting raids and hostage taking. He set up a capital at Mahdiyah, on the east coast of present-day Tunisia. In 925, 'Ubayd Allāh also threatened the Umayyad Caliphate in Spain; although he was unsuccessful, the effect was to push the Umayyads definitively away from the Abbasids. Thereafter, the Islamic world had three centers of power (Spain, North Africa, and the Middle East) and would never again be unified in the way it had been before 'Ubayd Allāh.

'Ubayd Allāh died in 936; the dynasty he established endured until 1171, when Adid, the last of the Fatimid rulers, died.

Legacy

'Ubayd Allāh successfully challenged the centralizing tendency of Islam and forced it into independent polities and rival sects that never reunited under one state again.

The emergence of the Fatimid dynasty under 'Ubayd Allāh represented a major transformation of Islam. 'Ubayd Allāh and subsequent Fatimids were, above all, the leaders of a sect of Islam; they challenged accepted orthodoxy and the leadership of the Abbasids in Baghdad and paved the way for increasing division in the Muslim world, weakening the unifying identity created by a shared religion that had made Muslims such powerful conquerors between 650 and 750. In addition, 'Ubayd Allāh combined the office of imam and caliph, uniting military and religious authority in one semidivine person. 'Ubayd Allāh was the first of a very small number of Islamic leaders who governed through violence and terror rather than the peaceful coexistence and accommodation encouraged by the Koran and Islamic custom.

'Ubayd Allāh's extremism, born from that of the Ismailis, gave great inspiration to his fanatical followers, who nearly succeeded in destroying the Abbasids. That extremism, however, gradually alienated those who had first brought him to power, the Berbers and peasantry of North Africa, because 'Ubayd Allāh did not allow them to share power with him in his expanded state. The consequences of this alienation were felt under subsequent Fatimid leaders, who had to quell vicious uprisings against their authority by the Berbers and others who felt excluded from Fatimid power and prosperity. After 'Ubayd Allāh, Islam never again had a central leadership for the vast population of Muslims, even when subsequent Fatimid leaders pushed as far east as Mecca. With separate Fatimid, Abbasid, and Umayyad Caliphates, the Islamic world lost the kind of unity it had enjoyed before 'Ubayd Allāh; the separate religious, political, and social developments in each of these divisions after they were founded made a return to an earlier unity increasingly difficult.

Del Testa

WORLD EVENTS		'UBAYD ALLĀH'S LIFE
Battle of Talas halts Islam's north Asian expansion	751	
	902 and 904	'Ubayd Allāh leads revolts in Syria
	905	'Ubayd Allāh is rescued from prison by Abdullah
	912	'Ubayd Allāh has Abdullah executed; 'Ubayd Allāh becomes caliph
	914	'Ubayd Allāh makes first of two failed attacks on Abbasid Egypt
	921	'Ubayd Allāh takes Morocco
	933	'Ubayd Allāh conquers Sicily
	936	'Ubayd Allāh dies
Ethnic Chinese rule is reasserted in northern China	980	

For Further Reading
Abun–Nasr, Jamal M. *A History of the Maghrib in the Islamic Period.* New York: Cambridge University Press, 1987.

'Umar I

Early Proponent of Islam and
Second Caliph
c. 586–644

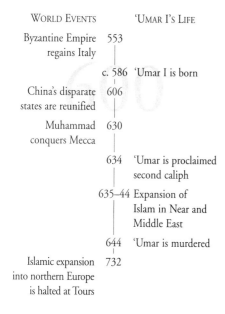

WORLD EVENTS		'UMAR I'S LIFE
Byzantine Empire regains Italy	553	
	c. 586	'Umar I is born
China's disparate states are reunified	606	
Muhammad conquers Mecca	630	
	634	'Umar is proclaimed second caliph
	635–44	Expansion of Islam in Near and Middle East
	644	'Umar is murdered
Islamic expansion into northern Europe is halted at Tours	732	

Life and Work

Through his faith and ability, 'Umar I ('Umar ibn al-Khattab) took a divided state of Muslim Arabs and created a powerful Islamic Empire.

'Umar was born around 586 into the unimportant Abi ibn Kab clan of Medina, a city in the south-central part of the Arabian Peninsula that had initially opposed Islam. 'Umar converted to Islam in 616 and became linked to Muhammad through the marriage of his daughter Hafsa. 'Umar became an advisor to Muhammad.

In 634, upon the death of the first caliph ("successor"), Abu Bakr, Muhammad's son-in-law and closest friend, a council of religious and clan authorities elected 'Umar as Islam's second caliph. 'Umar received valuable support from Aisha, Abu Bakr's daughter. Despite an almost complete lack of political experience, 'Umar immediately set about consolidating the gains of the rapidly expanding Islamic Empire by setting up an efficient and just administration and strengthening the army in preparations for future conquests.

The consolidation ordered by 'Umar permitted, between 635 and 644, the rapid conquest and Islamicization of Syria, Palestine, Iraq, Iran, and Egypt. It also caused the fall of the mighty Persian Empire and made destructive inroads into the Byzantine Empire. Only an outbreak of a plague in Syria in 639 slowed the progress of Islam across the Middle East. The advance of Muslim armies owed as much to internal divisions within the conquered countries as it did to 'Umar's organizational skill. In Syria, the Byzantine Empire attempted to defend itself against the Muslims with an enormous army drawn from all of its different possessions; lacking the cohesion that a common identity such as Islam inspired, the Byzantines were badly beaten. In Iraq, the people despised the rule of the Persians, whose language and culture were foreign to them and eagerly welcomed their Arab cousins. In addition, throughout the region, the violent religious conflicts within the Byzantine Empire and the military exhaustion of both the Byzantines and the Persians, who had struggled vainly against one another between 608 and 640, sapped the will of people to resist the spread of Islam.

On November 3, 644, a Persian slave, Abu Lulua, murdered 'Umar over a personal disagreement.

Legacy

The unification ordered by 'Umar I, his dedication to justice, and his personal humility engendered a massive conversion to Islam throughout North Africa, the Middle East, and western Asia, and created a powerful pan-Arab identity that has endured to the present.

'Umar permitted Islam to make great strides against strong opposition because of his keen judgment of men and their intentions. Through piety, duty, and a gift for administration, 'Umar managed to impose order and effective governance on the disparate peoples and regions of Islam. 'Umar imposed and administrative structure on the Islamic state wherever possible, dividing it up into small, fixed provinces ruled over by a governor appointed by him. Officials and soldiers received fixed stipends, the state generated revenue through land and personal taxes, and the communities of Muslims and non-Muslims were separated, with the religious leaders of the latter responsible for collecting taxes from the community. The Muslim tolerance of Jewish and Christian communities and the lightening of the tax load on them instilled great confidence in the entire Islamic world. 'Umar frequently recalled that Christian Africans had sheltered and cared for Muhammad when pagan Arabs would not.

More than just an able administrator, 'Umar instilled an enduring Muslim identity in Arabia and all the lands in which Islam subsequently became influential. In 639, 'Umar introduced the Muslim calendar, which dated the beginning of a new era for all Muslims from the time when Muhammad traveled from Mecca to Medina in 622. Building on the work of his predecessor, Abu Bakr, to end the believers' idolatry of Muhammad and to focus worship on Allah alone, 'Umar promoted the growth of centers of Muslim culture and worship throughout the Near and Middle East. Binding together all of his progress was a deep personal humility and piety that assured his subjects of his good intentions; 'Umar was reputed to have worn only tattered clothing, prayed often, and ridden camels, a lowly but common form of transportation, with his slaves. The pan-Arab state reemerged in political organizations such as the 1945 Arab League, which continues to operate, and the 1958–61 United Arab Republic, which in theory united Egypt and Syria.

Del Testa

For Further Reading

Madelung, Wilfred. *The Succession to Muhammad: A Study of the Early Caliphate.* New York: Cambridge University Press, 1997.

Walesa, Lech

Founder of Solidarity and
President of Poland
1943–

Life and Work

Lech Walesa helped organize opposition to the Polish communist regime and was elected president of Poland after that regime's collapse.

Walesa was born on September 29, 1943, in Popowo. The son of a carpenter, he moved to the shipping port of Gdansk while still a youth. As an electrician in the large Lenin Shipping Yards in 1970, he witnessed a strike among workers against the communist regime; in 1976 he participated in another strike and was fired. Disillusioned by the government's treatment of workers, between 1976 and 1980 he edited an underground newspaper that sought to organize political opposition. A devout Roman Catholic, he looked especially to members of the church for support.

When another strike broke out in Gdansk in 1980, Walesa was made its leader. To express the strikers' demands, a new independent trade union called Solidarity was formed in September. Walesa assumed leadership of it as well, and by the end of the year he had attracted nearly 10 million workers to the union. Although the government at first indicated willingness to accede to Walesa's demands for recognition of Solidarity and the right to free speech, in December 1981 Wojciech Jaruzelski, the Communist Party leader, declared martial law. The activities of Solidarity were suspended and Walesa was placed under house arrest.

After Walesa's release in 1982, he worked tirelessly to restore Solidarity's influence. In 1983 his efforts were recognized internationally when he received the Nobel Prize for Peace, the proceeds of which he donated to charity. His hopes grew after 1985 as MIKHAIL GORBACHEV sought to reform Soviet communism through his program of *perestroika* ("restructuring"). Jaruzelski was unable to hold his increasingly isolated government together, and Solidarity was legalized in January 1989. Walesa immediately entered into negotiations with the regime, and the Roman Catholic church was also invited to participate. After Tadeusz Mazowiecki, who was not a communist and had long collaborated with Walesa, was elected prime minister in September, the communist regime ceased to exist.

In 1990 Walesa decided to enter the race for a newly created presidency. Although increasingly estranged from Mazowiecki, he nevertheless won in December. During his tenure, he supported policies to expand the powers of his office at the expense of the Parliament. He also used the state's power to protect the Roman Catholic church and to restore some of the privileges it had lost under communism. Abandoned by many of his former supporters in Solidarity, he failed to win reelection in 1995.

Legacy

Lech Walesa's contributions to the Solidarity movement and the collapse of communism had a great impact on contemporaries in Poland and Eastern Europe.

Poland had been ruled by a communist regime since 1944, when the Soviet army liberated it from Nazi Germany. Although Polish communism never reached the same level of repression as in the Soviet Union under JOSEPH STALIN, the regime was forced to rely upon the police and censorship to retain its power. Walesa, by helping organize Solidarity, created communist Poland's first independent political movement. After 1981 millions of workers joined the movement he headed and actively supported the political ideals of free speech and economic justice he articulated. This explosion of civil society was the force that finally brought the communist regime to its knees in 1989.

Walesa's leadership of Solidarity did not rely upon organized labor alone, however, but utilized the immense strength of the Roman Catholic church. A practicing believer, Walesa was convinced that the church's participation was needed to reach a settlement with the communist regime. By working with the church and inviting it to participate in the negotiations of 1989, Walesa succeeded in harnessing an extremely powerful institution to help bring down communism.

While Walesa achieved brilliant results in leading efforts to destroy communism, he has been widely criticized by historians for failing to establish a stable government in its place. His policies as president between 1990 and 1995 proved in the short term to be only partly successful. To his credit he was able to maintain stability in a time of extreme political and economic transformation. In particular, his policies helped the economy adapt to a free market. But while the early 1990s saw improvements in productivity and the value of currency, many sectors of the economy remained subject to mismanagement and inefficiency. The fact that Walesa lost his reelection bid to the former communist Aleksander Kwasniewcki revealed the uncertainty of many Poles during the decade after the collapse of communism and the difficulties in charting a new course.

Strickland

For Further Reading
Boyes, Roger. *The Naked President: A Political Life of Lech Walesa.* London: Secker and Warburg, 1994.
Goodwyn, Lawrence. *Breaking the Barrier: The Rise of Solidarity in Poland.* Oxford: Oxford University Press, 1991.
Walesa, Lech. *The Struggle and the Triumph: An Autobiography.* Translated by Franklin Philip. New York: Arcade, 1992.

WORLD EVENTS		WALESA'S LIFE
World War II	1939–45	
	1943	Lech Walesa is born
Communist China is established	1949	
Israel defeats Arab nations in Six-Day War	1967	
	1970	Walesa witnesses Gdansk strike
Vietnam War ends	1975	
	1980	Walesa helps form solidarity
	1983	Walesa receives Nobel Prize for Peace
	1989	Walsea helps organize negotiations with government
	1990	Walesa is elected president
Dissolution of Soviet Union	1991	
	1995	Walesa loses reelection bid

Washington, Booker Taliaferro

African-American Leader and Educator
1856–1915

Life and Work

Booker Taliaferro Washington, recognized by many as the principal leader of African Americans at the end of the nineteenth century, founded the Tuskegee Institute, promoted economic advancement for African-Americans, and advocated accommodation with whites at the expense of political enfranchisement.

Washington was born a slave on a farm in Franklin County, Virginia. His mother was a mulatto slave and his father a white man. After the Civil War ended in 1865, Washington's stepfather moved the family to Malden, West Virginia. As a boy, Washington worked in the salt furnaces and coal mines, but also sought an education by attending evening classes. In 1872, he enrolled at the Hampton Institute, a school in Virginia dedicated to the education of former slaves, working as a janitor to earn room and board.

Washington graduated from the institute in 1875, convinced that black Americans should work toward economic advancement through self-help rather than fight for political rights and civil liberties. He taught at Hampton and at a school for black children in Malden, then studied at the Wayland Seminary in Washington, D.C. In 1881 he was appointed by General Samuel Armstrong, founder of the Hampton Institute, to be the principal of the new Tuskegee Normal and Industrial Institute in Tuskegee, Alabama.

For the next several years Washington supervised the creation of the campus and expanded enrollment to 400 students. The Tuskegee Institute's goal was to train African Americans in practical manual trades and professions such as farming, carpentry, shoemaking, and cooking. By successfully soliciting the financial assistance of white philanthropists, Washington transformed Tuskegee into the nation's foremost African-American educational institution.

Washington sought to expand his educational philosophy nationwide. In 1895 he gave a short but influential speech to a mostly white audience at the Atlanta Cotton States Exposition, where he appealed to white Americans, northern and southern, to permit the economic and educational self-improvement of black Americans. In exchange, African Americans would not agitate for political rights, social equality, or an end to segregation. Later known as the "Atlanta Compromise," the speech propelled Washington into national prominence, and some controversy; black leader W. E. B. Du Bois, for one, denounced the speech. In 1900, Washington founded the National Negro Business League.

Washington's autobiography, *Up From Slavery,* published in 1901, also enhanced his reputation. That year he was invited to dine with President THEODORE ROOSEVELT, and became the president's informal advisor in racial matters thereafter. Although conciliatory toward whites in his public appearances, he quietly worked to reduce segregation, lynching, and disenfranchisement during the era when Jim Crow laws severely discriminated against African Americans in the South.

Falling ill during a lecture tour in 1915, Washington returned to Tuskegee, where he died on November 14.

Legacy

Booker Taliaferro Washington sought educational and economic advancement for African Americans and cordial relations with the white population in an effort to gain acceptance for black Americans in the post–Civil War South. While many African Americans have embraced Washington's call for a greater degree of economic independence, they have generally disregarded his "accommodationist" strategy as being not only ineffectual but self-defeating.

The immediate impact of Washington's leadership stems from his overly manipulative control of African-American leadership, earning him the nickname "Wizard." He wielded his influence through the so-called Tuskegee Machine by having his supporters appointed to government offices, controlling many black American newspapers and journals, and using spies and intimidation against those who opposed him or criticized his approach.

Washington's leadership style and attitude of humility in front of whites created opposition groups, defining the cleavages in the African-American community that would last for decades. In 1905 Du Bois founded the Niagara Movement, a forerunner of the NAACP (founded in 1909) and posed a serious challenge to Washington's influence and accommodationist stance. Future civil rights leaders such as MARTIN LUTHER KING, JR. also rejected Washington's "gradual" approach to full civil and political rights for African Americans, opting instead for a more confrontational, though nonviolent, strategy.

Despite Washington's controversial stance toward white American society and strong-arm tactics toward his opponents, his efforts instilled a sense of pride among working-class African Americans and encouraged the growth of black-owned businesses through the auspices of the National Negro Business League. Washington himself was a symbol of personal progress, an "American success-hero," rising "up from slavery" to a position of power and influence.

However, his efforts to advance African-American economic independence through the practical manual trades largely failed, in part because rapid industrialization in the United States made many of those trades obsolete and also made city life attractive to an increasing number of African Americans.

Lemoine

WORLD EVENTS		WASHINGTON'S LIFE
Congress of Vienna reorganizes Europe	1815	
	1856	Booker Taliaferro Washington is born
Germany is united	1871	
	1872–75	Washington attends Hampton Institute
	1881	Washington becomes principal of Tuskegee Institute
	1895	Washington speaks at the Atlanta Cotton States Exposition
	1901	Washington publishes *Up From Slavery*
Russo-Japanese War	1905	
World War I	1914–18	
	1915	Washington dies
Russian Revolution	1917	

For Further Reading

Franklin, Robert Michael. *Liberating Visions: Human Fulfillment and Social Justice in African American Thought.* Minneapolis, Minn.: Fortress Press, 1990.

Harlan, Louis R. *Booker T. Washington: The Making of a Black Leader, 1856–1901.* Oxford: Oxford University Press, 1972.

Washington, George

First President of the United States
1732–1799

Life and Work

George Washington's military leadership in the American Revolution ensured victory over British forces and the secure establishment of the American republic. His moderate civilian leadership as first president of the United States ensured the nation's survival.

Born on February 22, 1732, to a moderately prosperous farmer in Virginia, Washington did not receive much formal education. He gained military and leadership skills—and rose rapidly through the ranks—in the conflicts between the British and the French, imperial rivals in North America during the 1750s. Commissioned as a major in the Virginia militia, Washington began to resent the disdainful treatment by English-born colonial administrators and military officers. In 1758 Washington was elected to the Virginia House of Burgesses, a colonial assembly, where he gained political skills that would serve him in the future.

The policies of the British government toward the colonies, especially regarding taxation, began to trouble Washington in the late 1760s and early 1770s. In 1774 he was appointed as a Virginia delegate to the Continental Congress convened in Philadelphia to discuss the colonists' response to the British. The result was open conflict.

When the conflict turned into war in 1775, Washington was named by the Continental Congress to lead the colonial forces and was granted extensive power to direct the war effort. Washington transformed a motley collection of patriots into a national army and created the United States Navy. He carefully balanced his duties between winning the war and maintaining civilian leadership.

Despite defeats in New York in 1776, Washington was able to rally the remnants of his army to win battles at Trenton and Princeton, New Jersey, but subsequently lost two battles in 1777, which cost the Americans Philadelphia. He then retreated, stationed his troops in Valley Forge, Pennsylvania, and struggled to keep the army intact during a bitter winter. In 1781, accompanied by crucial French forces, he defeated the British at the Battle of Yorktown, effectively ending the American Revolution. Washington returned his powers to the Congress in 1783 and retired to his estate at Mount Vernon, Virginia.

In 1787 Washington presided over the Constitutional Convention, convened to draft a new constitution to replace the ineffective Articles of Confederation. He was unanimously elected president in 1789. He served two terms, and, refusing to run a third time, retired once again to his estate in 1797. He died on December 14, 1799 at Mount Vernon.

Legacy

George Washington bolstered the legitimacy of the fledgling American republic, setting many precedents as both military leader and civilian president that have endured to the present.

Although Washington was granted wide-ranging powers during the American Revolution, he refused to allow the army to have an overtly political role, thereby eliminating the risk of a military dictatorship. The U.S. military still follows this policy.

As a war hero, Washington's participation in the Constitutional Convention helped to legitimize the republic and its new Constitution. Because the drafters of the Constitution trusted Washington, whom they all considered would be president following the convention, the executive branch was given a wider range of powers than it would have had if the first president had been someone else.

Washington proved an effective leader, organizing the administration and establishing the practical structure of the federal government—including cabinet positions, titles, ceremony, official etiquette, and other protocol, much of which has endured. Washington also maintained neutrality during the European wars sparked by the French Revolution, keeping the new republic safe from dangerous military conflict so soon after establishing its independence.

During Washington's administration, financial and commercial structures beneficial to merchants and creditors were set up by Treasury Secretary Alexander Hamilton. Supporters of Washington and Hamilton became known as the Federalists. Their position, which favored the social and economic elite of Northern merchants, fostered divisions within the American polity that contributed to the creation of parties representing competing political, social, and economic interests. THOMAS JEFFERSON formed the Democratic-Republican Party to oppose the Federalists and promote the interests of farmers in both the North and the South, setting the stage for future conflicts between these groups.

Soon after his death, Washington became a symbol of the republic, treated with almost religious fervor at times, standing for patriotic courage. He continues to embody the political ideals of the past and the present. Because of Washington's leadership, the United States has maintained a strong national government that is nonetheless relatively successful in restraining demagogic tendencies in the presidency.

Lemoine

For Further Reading
Elkins, Stanley, and Eric McKitrik. *The Age of Federalism.* Oxford: Oxford University Press, 1993.
Ferling, John E. *The First of Men: A Life of George Washington.* Knoxville: University of Tennessee Press, 1988.

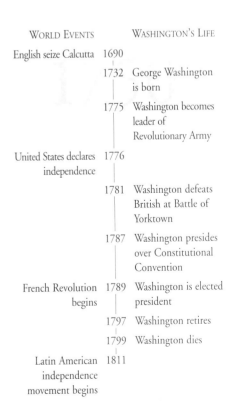

WORLD EVENTS		WASHINGTON'S LIFE
English seize Calcutta	1690	
	1732	George Washington is born
	1775	Washington becomes leader of Revolutionary Army
United States declares independence	1776	
	1781	Washington defeats British at Battle of Yorktown
	1787	Washington presides over Constitutional Convention
French Revolution begins	1789	Washington is elected president
	1797	Washington retires
	1799	Washington dies
Latin American independence movement begins	1811	

Wen-ti

Chinese Emperor
541–604

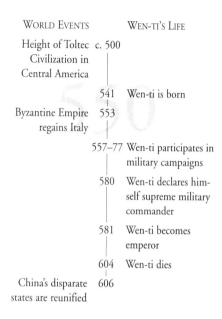

WORLD EVENTS		WEN-TI'S LIFE
Height of Toltec Civilization in Central America	c. 500	
	541	Wen-ti is born
Byzantine Empire regains Italy	553	
	557–77	Wen-ti participates in military campaigns
	580	Wen-ti declares himself supreme military commander
	581	Wen-ti becomes emperor
	604	Wen-ti dies
China's disparate states are reunified	606	

Life and Work

Wen-ti (Wendi), born Yang Chien, came of age during a time of great instability and disunity in China but overcame the divisions to reunite China for the first time in 800 years.

A few years after SHIH HUANG-TI had briefly unified the various states of what is known today as China in 217 B.C.E., much of northern and central China had fractured into smaller states and come under the domination of tribes of Turkic and Mongol peoples. These tribes vied for control of the steppes and fertile river valleys and occasionally advanced toward the richer lands of southern China, which were still under the control of ethnic Chinese dynasties. Wen-ti, the son of a duke, came from a family that dominated some of the highest offices of the Mongol dynasties of northern China and was of mixed Chinese and Hsien-pei blood (the Hsien-pei were a Mongolian people).

A Buddhist nun raised Wen-ti until he was 14, and he remained deeply religious throughout his life. At 14, he briefly attended a school for the sons of nobles and officials, where he probably studied writing, history, the basic theory of government, and some of the Confucian morality that was supposed to guide young leaders in their decision making. Wen-ti also spent much time learning the military arts, including archery, horseback riding, falconry, and tactics.

Because of his natural abilities, Wen-ti rose rapidly in the ranks of the Northern Chou dynasty. In 577, he was made a field commander in the armies of Emperor Wu, the leader of the Northern Chou who, between 557 and 577, gained control of all of northern China. Wen-ti soon came to hold administrative posts in the leadership of newly conquered territories to the west and south. For his exemplary services, Emperor Wu permitted Wen-ti to marry off one of his daughters to the Chou crown prince, a marriage that linked Wen-ti firmly to the Northern Chou dynasty.

In 579, Emperor Wu died, and his son Yü-weh came to the throne. Yü-weh, a corrupt and decadent individual, disliked Wen-ti and threatened Wen-ti's family directly. However, Yü-weh died suddenly in 580, and Wen-ti forged an imperial proclamation naming him commander of all of the Northern Chou's army. This deception, when discovered, almost provoked civil war, but Wen-ti's potential opponents never managed to unite against him. Wen-ti became emperor on March 4, 581.

During his reign, Wen-ti tried to undo the divisions of the previous 800 years. He clarified astrological charts, issued a new law code, and employed censors to ensure that it was obeyed. He embarked on numerous military expeditions that eventually brought the whole of southern China under his control. In short, Wen-ti recreated an empire for China, even if his own dynasty, the Sui, didn't last 20 years after his death in 604. In 618, Li Yuan, an official in the Sui governemnt who, like many of his peers, hated the depotism of the Sui, toppled the third and last Sui emperor and began the T'ang dynasty.

Legacy

Wen-ti made maintaining a unified China the basis for subsequent dynasties and Chinese international politics.

Much like the Emperor Shih Huang-ti, to whom historians sometimes compare him, Wen-ti welded the fractured pieces of China into a single state. However, China was a far different place in 600 C.E. than it had been in 250 B.C.E., when Shih Huang-ti ruled. Wen-ti realized that his rule could not have the arbitrary nature of Shih Huang-ti's. He realized that, after a conquest, he had to capture and hold the loyalty of the local leaders and assure them an active role in the administration, rather than simply occupying them militarily. The recognition of the need to satisfy local leaders' endured long after Wen-ti and became the basis for political accommodation throughout the rest of Chinese history until the Chinese Revolution of 1911. But because Wen-ti did not have enough time to cement these loyalties, his son, Yang-ti, was not able to hold the empire or the Sui dynasty together for very long.

In a sense, Wen-ti was the very embodiment of accommodation. He began a tradition of barbarian people of the North invading and conquering China and then mixing their own culture with that of the Chinese. However, the trend of accommodation and cultural mixture begun by Wen-ti also inspired a reaction among ethnic Chinese, who would oppose barbarian invasions by appealing to a sense of cultural purity that the barbarians might destroy if allowed to prevail.

Del Testa

For Further Reading

Bingham, Woodbridge. *The Founding of the T'ang Dynasty: The Fall of Sui and Rise of T'ang: A Preliminary Survey.* New York: Octogon Books, 1970.

Wright, Arthur F. *The Sui Dynasty.* New York: Knopf, 1978.

William I

First Norman King of England

c. 1027–1087

Life and Work

William I (William the Conqueror) invaded England and brought an end to its Anglo-Saxon dynasty. He reformed the economic and political order, making England one of the most powerful states in medieval Europe.

William was born around 1027, the bastard son of Robert, duke of Normandy (a province in the north of France). In 1035 his father died while on a pilgrimage to the Holy Land and the duchy was left to William. Many Norman nobles rose up against the succession, however, both because of William's youth and his bastard status. Happily for William, King Henry I of France favored him, and, with a French army at his side, William was able to recover his inheritance in 1047. Not content with just Normandy, the duke began organizing a plan to obtain the throne of England. In 1051 he met with his cousin, England's childless King Edward the Confessor and may have received his support in the matter of succession. After Edward's death in 1066, however, an Anglo-Saxon claimant named Harold seized the throne. William immediately raised an army and crossed the English Channel. At the Battle of Hastings on October 14 Harold was killed and the Anglo-Saxons were defeated. England now had a Norman king.

For Further Reading

Bates, David. *William the Conqueror.* London: G. Philip, 1989.

Sawyer, Peter, ed. *The Domesday Book: A Reassessment.* London: E. Arnold, 1985.

Walker, David. *The Normans in Britain.* Oxford: Blackwell, 1995.

Having secured his throne, William set about to consolidate his government. The most important measure to this end was the compilation of the Domesday Book, ordered by the king at Christmas in 1085. The Domesday Book, considered to be the most ambitious census taken in Europe since Roman rule, recorded the landholdings of the entire population of England and made the results available to the crown for the purpose of granting lands to loyal barons and increasing taxes.

Despite his great achievements in England, William never forgot his possessions in northern France. Much of his time after 1066 was spent there on military campaigns. In 1073 he was compelled to mount an invasion of Maine (a region south of Normandy) to defend a title he had acquired years earlier. In 1087, on news that his possessions were again under threat, he returned to Normandy. As he was passing through the town of Mantes, his horse bolted and he was injured. Removed to Rouen, he died in November.

Legacy

William I established a powerful and centralized foreign government that would influence English history for centuries.

After the conquest of 1066, the English monarchy gained greater power in the face of local officials and lords. While England under the Anglo-Saxon kings had already begun to establish a centralized administration, local officials called sheriffs retained considerable authority in raising taxes and armies. William's reforms, made possible by the Domesday Book, served to reduce the power of these sheriffs. Henceforth, the crown would assume a greater role in administration and economic affairs. Later kings such as HENRY II used this power to introduce legal reforms and to impose greater uniformity of rule throughout the land. This was facilitated by the use of itinerant royal officials who visited the various shires of England to inspect landholdings and ensure that the law was administered in conformity with the king's will. The crown also gained greater control over taxation. Under William's successor, Henry I, a special institution called the exchequer was created to oversee collection of revenue. Thus, within a century of William's death, England possessed the most highly centralized monarchy in Europe.

William's conquest of England also represented a turning point in the relationship of England to the rest of Europe. Prior to 1066 the Anglo-Saxon monarchy often maintained a native political orientation that tended to isolate England from continental affairs. After the Norman conquest, England decisively entered a period of close interaction with European powers, especially France. William's Norman origins facilitated this, of course, and much of the relationship between England and France in subsequent centuries grew out of the English crown's claims to French territories. Both Henry II and RICHARD I would devote themselves to retaining and even expanding their French possessions, and in the late Middle Ages the two great monarchies would become tragically locked in the conflict known as the Hundred Years War (1337–1453).

The legacy established by the Battle of Hastings was not solely military, however. William was accompanied by thousands of Normans, many of whom were soon enfeoffed (established as owners and rulers of a fiefdom) with lands acquired by the crown by way of the Domesday Book. Culturally, England was greatly enriched by the arrival of the French and their language. The flowering of the high Middle Ages, much of which took place in France, would be borne across the channel by individuals such as ELEANOR OF AQUITAINE. England, while integrated into Europe through Christianity centuries earlier, now became an even more inseparable part of its civilization.

Strickland

WORLD EVENTS		WILLIAM I'S LIFE
Ethnic Chinese rule is reasserted in northern China	980	
	c. 1027	William I is born
	1035	William inherits duchy of Normandy
	1047	William allies with France and recovers Normandy
Roman Catholic and Orthodox Christian churches separate in the Great Schism	1054	
Normans conquer England	1066	William invades England and wins Battle of Hastings
	1085	William orders compilation of Domesday Book
	1087	William dies
First Crusade begins	1095	

William II

Emperor of Germany
1859–1941

Life and Work

William II ruled Germany in a time of growing international tension. His reckless leadership wrecked havoc with Europe's diplomatic order and helped precipitate World War I.

Frederick Wilhelm Viktor Albert was born to the ruling Hohenzollern dynasty of Prussia in 1859. Born with a withered left arm, he developed an irritable and aggressive temperament. His petulance outlived childhood, and soon after becoming kaiser in 1888, he came to resent the dominant position in the government that Chancellor OTTO VON BISMARCK had established for himself. In 1890 William rashly dismissed Bismarck.

William revealed his incompetence almost immediately when he decided to cancel one of Bismarck's most important diplomatic achievements, the Reinsurance Treaty with Russia. By this treaty Germany had pledged never to join its ally Austria in a war of conquest against Russia. The effect had been to prevent Russia from seeking an alliance with Germany's chief potential adversary, France. The predictable consequence of William's cancellation was the alienation of Russia and the formation of a Franco–Russian alliance in 1894. William soon followed this blunder with the 1897 announcement that Germany must become a "world power" with overseas colonial interests equal to those of Britain. The resulting naval arms race compelled the frightened British to establish the Entente Cordiale, a co-operation treaty, with France in 1904. In case of war, Germany was now left alone with a declining Austria, but William remained certain that divine providence, to which he often made pious reference, was on his side. His recklessness was evidenced in 1904 when he landed unexpectedly at the Moroccan port of Tangiers to issue a challenge to French colonial interests there. The diplomatic crisis that ensued culminated in the Algeciras Conference in 1906. As a result, Germany found itself isolated and its potential adversaries in the West more united than ever.

In 1914 William committed the most costly miscalculation of his reign. In response to Austria's appeal for support in launching a war against Serbia, which was certain to escalate into a war also with Russia, he issued what was later called a "blank check" to Vienna in support of war. The resulting catastrophe, World War I, killed approximately 10 million men and threatened to destroy European civilization. By 1918 Germany, blockaded by the still superior British navy, was forced to surrender and William was driven from his throne. As the imperial system fell to pieces he fled to the Netherlands, where he died on June 4, 1941, never having set foot on German soil again.

Legacy

The impact of William II's reign was felt in Germany and throughout Europe during the troubled period following his downfall.

Within Germany there was initially a general repudiation of William's rule. In November 1918, just as William was fleeing, a revolution established the Weimar Republic. Considered the most progressive political system in Europe at the time, the new regime featured a liberal constitution, parliamentary government, full voting rights for adults (including women), and welfare support for workers. A dynamic and avant-garde culture also arose in which Bertolt Brecht, Walter Gropius, and Kurt Weill used drama, architecture, and music, respectively, to challenge capitalism and the elitism they claimed had been at the heart of Wilhelmine society. For many among the Weimar generation, the spike-helmeted image of William II became an emblem for a corrupt civilization with no future.

Outside Germany William also provided a negative example. In 1919 the Treaty of Versailles included a war guilt clause that burdened Germany with responsibility for the carnage of World War I and thus implicated the militaristic policies of its former kaiser. Although this was unfair (all major European powers had played a role in bringing about the war), it highlighted a growing conviction in Europe that confrontational methods of diplomacy would only bring similar cataclysms in the future. In this way William's example served as a foil for an emerging internationalist approach to diplomacy, embodied in the ill-fated League of Nations. Although this body failed to prevent renewed military aggression in Europe, its successor, the United Nations, would prove more successful after 1947.

The repudiation of William II was neither universal nor permanent, however. Within Germany itself a political movement arose during the course of the Weimar period that sought to reestablish an authoritarian and militaristic order. The 1920s were years of great uncertainty, and representatives of the old regime such as Field Marshal von Hindenburg, elected Germany's president in 1925, entertained the idea of diminishing the freedoms of the new order. Some of these archconservatives even supported radical right-wing parties such as the aspiring National Socialists of ADOLF HITLER. General Ludendorff, for example, who had served William during the war, participated in Hitler's abortive Beer Hall Putsch in 1923. And when Hitler's party won the greatest percentage of seats to the Reichstag in 1932, Hindenburg was the one who appointed him chancellor early in the following year. The Nazi dictatorship that followed would destroy these Wilhelmine remnants along with everything else.

Strickland

WORLD EVENTS		WILLIAM II'S LIFE
Congress of Vienna reorganizes Europe	1815	
	1859	William II is born
Germany is united	1871	
	1888	William accedes to throne
	1890	William dismisses Otto von Bismarck
	1904	William visits Tangiers
Russo-Japanese War	1905	
World War I	1914–18	
	1914	William issues "blank check" to Austria in support of war
Russian Revolution	1917	
	1918	William abdicates following end of World War I and flees Germany
Great Depression	1929–39	
World War II	1939–45	
	1941	William dies
Communist China is established	1949	

For Further Reading

Cecil, Lamar. *Wilhelm II*. 2 vols. Chapel Hill: University of North Carolina Press, 1989, 1996.

Cowles, Virginia. *The Kaiser*. New York: Harper and Row, 1963.

Joll, James. *The Origins of the First World War*. 2nd ed. London: Longman, 1992.

Retallack, James N. *Germany in the Age of Kaiser Wilhelm II*. New York: St. Martin's Press, 1996.

Wilson, Woodrow

Twenty-Eighth President of the
United States
1856–1924

Life and Work

One of the most idealistic of American presidents, Woodrow Wilson enacted progressive legislation for domestic reform that increased government regulation of business. He also defined an agenda for world peace following World War I that led to U.S. predominance in world affairs after World War II.

Thomas Woodrow Wilson was born on December 28, 1856, in Staunton, Virginia. The son of a Presbyterian pastor, he grew up believing in the moral superiority of Anglo-American political and cultural institutions. Despite his dyslexia, Wilson obtained a bachelor's degree at Princeton University in 1879 and a Ph.D. at Johns Hopkins in 1886. His election as president of Princeton in 1902 gained him prominence in New Jersey, where he was elected governor in 1911.

An able coalition-builder, Wilson was persuaded to run for president of the United States. Elected in 1912, he served two terms. Wilson pursued a liberal and progressive domestic policy, which included antitrust and banking reforms, lower tariffs, a child labor law, and other social reform legislation.

World War I and its aftermath took up most of Wilson's energies, however. At first Wilson

tried to maintain U.S. neutrality, but when Germany adopted a policy of unrestricted submarine warfare in 1917, sinking U.S. merchant ships, Wilson persuaded Congress to declare war on Germany and join the Allies (Britain, France, and Russia) to, as he put it, make the world "safe for democracy."

In a January 1918 speech to Congress, Wilson proposed a plan, called the Fourteen Points, to shape a "just peace" after the war, to accord national self-determination and independence to subject peoples, encourage open diplomacy and free trade, and establish the League of Nations, an organization of nation-states dedicated to maintaining world peace. United States participation proved crucial to the Allied victory over Germany, and the armistice signed on November 11, 1918 was based on the Fourteen Points.

Wilson attended the Paris Peace Conference (1919), where he oversaw the establishment of the League of Nations and participated in the drafting of the Treaty of Versailles, which dictated the terms of peace with Germany. Wilson fell ill during the unsuccessful effort to persuade Congress to ratify the Treaty of Versailles and was incapacitated for the remainder of his term. In declining health, he retired from politics and died on February 3, 1924.

Legacy

Woodrow Wilson's leadership increased government involvement in the social and economic life of the United States. His vision shaped the conduct of the United States as a world power during World War II and the Cold War.

Wilson's domestic agenda marked the high point of the Progressive Era (begun at the turn of the century). The federal government gained powerful tools to control the economy. Wilson's legislation set the stage for the New Deal, when President FRANKLIN DELANO ROOSEVELT's administration made use of these tools to combat the effects of the Great Depression.

Wilson's vision for world peace was initially foiled by French and British demands for excessive reparations from Germany, leading to bitter resentment among many Germans. A weak and ineffective League of Nations, which, despite Wilson's strenuous efforts, the isolationist U.S. Congress declined to join, proved incapable of opposing expansionist countries such

as Italy, Japan, and Germany, and failed to prevent the outbreak of World War II.

Following World War I, Wilson's principle of national self-determination was applied only to Europe—Poland, Czechoslovakia, and Yugoslavia—not to colonial territories in Asia, Africa, and the Middle East. Instead, the League of Nations expanded imperialism by granting Great Britain, France, and Belgium mandates, a form of trusteeship, to administer the former colonies and territories of Germany and the Turkish Ottoman Empire (an ally of Germany in the war). Full independence for these regions came only after World War II.

Wilson's legacy actually expanded in the decades following World War II. Both his progressive legislation and his leadership during World War I increased the power of the presidency and of the federal government to manage the economy. After World War II, U.S. administrations rejected a return to isolationism, setting the stage for United States dominance in postwar international affairs. American leadership also ensured that the United Nations, formed in 1945 to replace the discredited League of Nations, would survive as an institution of international arbitration.

Lemoine

WORLD EVENTS		WILSON'S LIFE
Congress of Vienna reorganizes Europe	1815	
	1856	Thomas Woodrow Wilson is born
Germany is united	1871	
	1902–10	Wilson serves as president of Princeton University
Russo-Japanese War	1905	
	1912	Wilson is elected president of the United States
World War I	1914–18	
Russian Revolution	1917	Congress declares war on Germany
	1918	Wilson announces his "Fourteen Points"
	1919	Wilson attends Paris Peace Conference and becomes seriously ill
	1924	Wilson dies
Great Depression	1929–39	

For Further Reading

Blum, John Morton. *Woodrow Wilson and the Politics of Morality.* Boston: Little, Brown, 1956.

Clements, Kendrick A. *The Presidency of Woodrow Wilson.* Lawrence: University Press of Kansas, 1992.

Heckscher, August. *Woodrow Wilson: A Biography.* New York: Scribner's, 1991.

Wollstonecraft, Mary

British Author and Feminist
1759–1797

Life and Work

Mary Wollstonecraft, who argued in favor of a new role for women in late-eighteenth-century European society, is considered one of the earliest modern feminists.

Wollstonecraft was born the second of seven children on April 27, 1759. Her father, abusive and alcoholic, did not prosper as a farmer. Limited family resources denied her formal schooling, and she was largely self-educated. Her first job was as a companion (a kind of servant) to a middle-class woman. In 1784 Wollstonecraft opened a girls' school with a close friend, which she closed after her friend died. In 1786 she accepted a job as a governess for an aristocratic family in Ireland. However, she soon decided to pursue a literary career, unusual for women at that time.

Returning to England after one year, Wollstonecraft worked for her supportive publisher, Joseph Johnson, translating foreign works and reviewing books. Johnson, a Dissenter (Britons who worshiped in Protestant sects outside the Anglican church and suffered discrimination as a result), introduced her to the intellectual world of the Dissenters, influencing her future work.

The French Revolution of 1789 launched Wollstonecraft's career. In 1789 she wrote *A Vindication of the Rights of Man,* a hurried response to EDMUND BURKE's reactionary *Reflections on the Revolution in France,* winning her instant renown. In 1792, *A Vindication of the Rights of Women* was published. Critical of the societal conventions that limited opportunities for women, it made a plea for women's equality in all spheres and became her most famous work. That same year she went to Paris, where she spent two years observing the revolution in its most radical phase, and wrote *A Historical and Moral View of the French Revolution* (1792).

In Paris she met an American army captain, Gilbert Imlay, with whom she had a daughter. She returned to Great Britain in 1794, hoping to continue her relationship with Imlay. However, she discovered his numerous infidelities, which drove her to attempt suicide. She survived and later met radical philosopher and writer William Godwin. They were married in 1797 after she became pregnant. She died later that year, on September 10, of blood poisoning after giving birth to her second child, the future Mary Shelley, author of the novel *Frankenstein.*

Legacy:

Mary Wollstonecraft is chiefly known as the founder and forerunner of modern feminism.

Inspired by the ideals of liberty, equality, and fraternity proposed by the French Revolution,

Wollstonecraft argued that the role of women needed to change from that of social ornament and mere object of male sexual desire to one based on virtue and the value of motherhood to society. Women, she argued, must establish their identity apart from men if they are to reason independently. This made them better companions to men and better mothers to raise responsible citizens. Future feminists adopted much of her argument.

The personal struggles and tragedies of Wollstonecraft's life have added poignancy to her impassioned intellectual arguments in favor of emancipation for women. Having been denied a formal education, she argued strongly that women needed to be well educated to better fulfill their roles in society. Education remained a vital issue for feminists in the nineteenth and twentieth centuries, as they increasingly demanded admission to universities. Wollstonecraft's struggles to find meaningful work as an unmarried woman underscored her critique of society's lack of opportunity for most women. Equal access to career opportunities has remained a major concern for feminists.

Wollstonecraft linked feminism with political and social radicalism, and many later feminists also combined feminist thought with liberalism, democratic socialism, or communism. Although feminism has since gone in many directions, feminists still challenge conventional society, not only in terms of gender relations, but also on political, economic, and legal terms.

Lemoine

World Events		Wollstonecraft's Life
English seize Calcutta	1690	
	1759	Mary Wollstonecraft is born
United States declares independence	1776	
	1784	Wollstonecraft opens girls' school
French Revolution begins	1789	Wollstonecraft publishes *A Vindication of the Rights of Man*
	1792	Wollstonecraft publishes *A Vindication of the Rights of Woman*
		Wollstonecraft goes to France and writes *A Historical and Moral View of the French Revolution*
	1797	Wollstonecraft dies after giving birth to daughter
Latin American independence movement begins	1811	

For Further Reading

Kelly, Gary. *Revolutionary Feminism: The Mind and Career of Mary Wollstonecraft.* London: Macmillan, 1992.
Lorch, Jennifer. *Mary Wollstonecraft: The Making of a Radical Feminist.* New York: Berg, 1990.
Moore, Jane. *Mary Wollstonecraft.* Plymouth, England: Northcote House, 1999.

Yeltsin, Boris

President of Russia
1931–

Life and Work

Assuming the presidency of the Russian Federation when it was still part of the Soviet Union, Boris Nikolaevich Yeltsin led the democratic forces that overthrew communism in 1991.

Yeltsin was born on February 1, 1931, near the Urals town of Sverdlovsk (Ekaterinburg). Receiving an engineering degree from the Urals Polytechnic Institute in 1955, he joined the Communist Party in 1961 and within 15 years became the head of the party organization in Sverdlovsk. In 1985 party General Secretary MIKHAIL GORBACHEV brought him to Moscow to help promote the policy of *perestroika* ("restructuring"); within a year Yeltsin had become a candidate member of the Politburo. His radical approach to reform, which included a public resignation from the Communist Party in 1990, soon put him and his patron at odds. Yeltsin's populist manner created enormous public support in Moscow, however, and this electoral base sent him to the new Congress of People's Deputies in 1989. On June 12, 1991, he was elected president of the Russian Federation. During the August putsch of 1991, he emerged as the principal defender of democracy, going so far as to climb atop a tank to rebuke conservative commu-

nists. In the wake of the putsch's failure, he effectively disbanded the Soviet Union by banning the Communist Party and forming a new Commonwealth of Independent States (CIS) with Belarus and the Ukraine.

His efforts to establish a free market by means of radical economic "shock therapy," however, soon provoked a revolt by the democratically elected Congress of People's Deputies. On November 4, 1993, he ordered tanks to shell the Congress building (known as the White House) and in the aftermath was able to have a new constitution accepted assigning even greater powers to the presidency. In the meantime, a new parliamentary body was formed called the Duma, which became the center of opposition to Yeltsin. When he ordered an unsuccessful assault on the breakaway Russian Republic of Chechnya in 1994, a chorus of Duma deputies including radical nationalists and communists (Yeltsin's ban of the party had since been judged unconstitutional) rang out in denunciation. In the 1996 presidential elections he narrowly escaped defeat. Despite severe drinking sprees and recurring heart attacks, Yeltsin remained in power through a series of minor political crises, until New Year's Eve 1999, when he resigned from office after having assured the succession of his protege Vladimir Putin.

Legacy

Boris Yeltsin's leadership of the former Soviet Union in the 1990s helped establish a constitutional system of government in Russia. Nevertheless, deep economic and political problems were left to his successor.

Yeltsin's greatest achievement was the consolidation of a constitutional system of government in a country that had few democratic traditions. While many political leaders had sought democracy in 1917, the communist regime created by VLADIMIR LENIN after the Bolshevik Revolution that year ruled dictatorially for the next 74 years. The establishment of a democratic constitution in December 1993 was an important step toward building democracy. Yeltsin's achievement is reflected in the fact that after Communist Party leader Gennady Ziuganov lost the presidential elections of 1996, he called upon his supporters to honor the results and obey the constitution.

Yeltsin's economic policies were much less successful. Hoping to propel Russia from command economy to free market overnight, his programs resulted in inflation, mass unemployment, and a flood of foreign goods. As Russian factories closed and elderly pensioners watched their savings evaporate, cynicism and despair began to spread among the population. Even when opposition forced Yeltsin to abandon extreme measures, widespread tax evasion made it difficult for the government to pay wages and subsidize programs such as space exploration and classical music, areas of major accopmlishment during the Soviet period. Yeltsin's toleration of political corruption was linked by historians to the rise of a plutocracy in which a small number of wealthy magnates oversaw an economy weakened by organized crime.

Finally, even the democratic political order that Yeltsin helped establish failed to create general satisfaction. Yeltsin himself was partly responsible for this disappointment, as his capricious and heavy-handed methods of rule came to alienate many earlier supporters. A celebrated populist in 1991, by 2000 his departure was celebrated by many of Russia's most committed democrats.

Strickland

For Further Reading

Morrison, John. *Boris Yeltsin: From Bolshevik to Democrat.* New York: Dutton, 1991.

Solovyov, Vladimir, and Elena Klepikova. *Boris Yeltsin: A Political Biography.* Translated by David Gurevich. New York: Putnam, 1992.

WORLD EVENTS		YELTSIN'S LIFE
Great Depression	1929–39	
	1931	Boris Yeltsin is born
World War II	1939–45	
Communist China is established	1949	
	1961	Yeltsin joins Communist Party
Israel defeats Arab nations in Six-Day War	1967	
Vietnam War ends	1975	
	1989	Yeltsin is elected to Congress of People's Deputies
	1990	Yeltsin resigns from Communist Party
Dissolution of Soviet Union	1991	Yeltsin is elected president of Russian Federation; dissolves Soviet Union
	1993	Yeltsin orders assault on Russian Congress building
	1999	Yeltsin resigns

Zapata, Emiliano

Mexican Revolutionary
1879–1919

Life and Work

Emiliano Zapata transformed his experience of injustice and oppression into a popular political movement that provoked a revolution and gave voice to Mexico's peasants.

Born on August 8, 1879, in Anenecuilco, Mexico, into a poor *mestizo* ("mixed-blood") family that trained and sold horses for a living, Zapata grew up knowing hardship and receiving little formal education. When he was 17, his parents died, leaving him in charge of his family farm and his brothers and sisters. In

World Events		Zapata's Life
Germany is united	1871	
	1879	Emiliano Zapata is born
	1897	Zapata organizes resistance to land confiscation
Russo-Japanese War	1905	
	1909	Zapata is elected to board of defense by villagers
World War I	1914–18	
	1914	Zapata enters Mexico City
Russian Revolution	1917	
	1919	Zapata is assassinated
Great Depression	1929–39	

1897, during a period of intensifying abuse of the peasantry by landowners, a *hacienda* ("estate") owner appropriated the lands of Zapata and his fellow villagers, and Zapata participated in a noisy protest of this action. Arrested as a consequence, Zapata avoided a long sentence only after receiving an official pardon. Upon release, he immediately began organizing new protests against the continuing expropriation of peasant lands. (Between 1870 and 1910, 90% of Mexico's peasants lost land to larger landowners.) In response, the government drafted Zapata into the army.

Zapata spent six months in the army but was discharged to a landowner near his home village to act as his horse trainer. In 1909, villagers elected Zapata to a board of defense for their village, and he began to negotiate for the return of confiscated lands. The negotiations proved fruitless and the peasants occupied the confiscated lands by force, redistributing them among themselves. The Mexican government sent in the army, but the peasant group resisted successfully. Calling for social and economic reforms that benefitted the peasantry and receiving a positive response throughout the state of Morelos, the group became known as the Zapatistas.

In 1910 and 1911, during the violent transition of power from Mexico's longtime dictator Porfirio Díaz to a new leader, Zapata's tiny peasant organization supported for president Francisco Madero, a populist landowner of the north.

For all of his populist rhetoric, Madero proved not to be the friend of the people that Zapata expected. In April 1911, Zapata asked Madero to return Mexico to the *ejido* system of communal land ownership; Madero refused. Even worse, Madero offered Zapata money with which to buy land if he would disarm his troops and stop pressing peasant claims. After the presidential elections of October 1911, in which Madero won 98% of the vote, Zapata had begun to disarm as part of a larger treaty that had facilitated Díaz's resignation, but stopped when Madero sent the army against him for not disarming quickly enough. In reaction, Zapata and his followers struck back against Madero's army, eventually capturing several states. Zapata's victories and the backlash against the limited land and labor reforms Madero had begun caused a coup within the Mexican government, and in February 1913

Madero was deposed and killed—to be replaced by an even worse despot, General Victoriano Huerta, a friend of the landed classes.

To combat Huerta, Zapata joined with other dissatisfied local leaders and revolutionaries. Together they resisted government forces loyal to Heurta and entered Mexico City on December 6, 1914. For the next three years, Mexico descended into near anarchy; Zapata was reluctant to take the role of national leadership. Zapata continued to push for land reform and peasants' rights, but after a Constitutional Convention in 1917 and the adoption of some reforms by the governement, Zapata had fewer and fewer supporters. He was assassinated in Morelos on April 10, 1919.

Legacy

Emiliano Zapata gave Mexico, a populist, land-based revolutionary movement that sought to shift the locus of the Mexican economy from city elites and rural landowners to the rural peasantry.

Zapata's main contribution to modern Mexico was a deep concern for equality and justice, most especially for the rural poor. Zapata believed that land redistribution and local decision making would produce economic growth and social peace among Mexico's rural poor. Although frequently turning to violence to achieve his goals, he refrained from violence as often as possible to give those who resisted his ideas the time to reconsider or to retreat. The combination of land reform and social justice became known as Zapatismo, or Zapatism, and continues to inspire many Mexicans today. However, Zapatismo did not have a place in it for any group other than the landless poor, and therefore alienated potential allies such as Mexico's new working classes.

Most recently, Zapatismo inspired the indigenous people of south-central Mexico to revolt against the central government and demand local autonomy and land reform. Despite a growing middle class and an improved economy, much of Mexico's rural poor remain outside the economic growth of the cities. Zapatismo and the echoes of its calls for land reform appear to remain a powerful message for a remedy to a continuing lack of economic and social opportunity.

Del Testa

For Further Reading

Brunk, Samuel. *Emiliano Zapata: Revolution & Betrayal in Mexico.* Albuquerque: University of New Mexico Press, 1995.
Newell, Peter E. *Zapata of Mexico.* New York: Black Rose Books, 1997.

Appendices,
Bibliography, and Index

Highlights of Government, Military, and Political Events

2925 After being crowned king of a province in Upper Egypt, Menes unites Upper and Lower Egypt into one country.

1787–60 Hammurabi conquers and unites the independent city-states of Mesopotamia, forming the political foundations of one of humankind's first great civilizations.

1472 Hatshepsut promotes herself as sole ruler of Egypt.

1279 Ramses II comes to power and begins expanding the borders of Egypt to what will become their greatest extent while concurrently maintaining internal peace.

c. 1000–962 David, ruler of Israel, unites the Jews and helps to establish the system of religious worship that will shape Jewish life for more than a millennium.

539 Cyrus II attacks and conquers Babylonia for the Persian Empire, incorporating the last of the ancient Near Eastern kingdoms into its expanse.

522 Darius I claims the throne of the Persian Empire; his rule, though marked by vast military expansion, will lead to disaster when he tries to conquer Greece.

461 Pericles defeats rivals in an election to become ruler of Athens and establishes a popular dictatorship.

336 Alexander III succeeds his father as king of Macedonia and launches a 10-year military campaign that will transform Macedonia into a vast empire and foster the spread of Greek culture into Asia and Egypt.

322 Candragupta makes himself head of the Maurya dynasty and emperor of India and attempts to unite and expand the Indian Empire by reclaiming Hellenized India, by pushing India's boundaries westward toward Persia, and by establishing friendly relations with both the Romans and the Persians.

c. 269 Aśoka takes the throne of the Indian Empire and converts the empire to Buddhism, elevating it from a small sect to the status of a major world religion.

246 Shih Huang-ti becomes head of the Ch'in dynasty and accedes to the throne of China; during his reign he will unify China through bribery, espionage, and keen military strategy.

73–71 Spartacus and his army of fellow slaves battle Roman legions in one of the greatest slave rebellions in ancient Rome.

55–44 Building on a series of military victories, Julius Caesar becomes dictator of the Roman Empire; during his rule his military expansion, dictatorial rule, and claims to divinity will undermine the republic and lay the groundwork for an imperial system of government that will last for centuries.

51–31 Cleopatra VII, of the Greek Ptolemaic dynasty and the last pharaoh of Egypt, rules with ambition and charm, delaying Egypt's fall to the Roman Empire.

31 Emperor Octavian defeats the forces of Antony and Cleopatra at the Battle of Actium, securing his succession to Julius Caesar; he has the title Augustus (Venerable) bestowed upon him by the Senate.

117 Hadrian becomes emperor of Rome, leading the empire during one of its longest periods of peace and prosperity.

135 Bar Kokhba, Jewish rebel leader and martyr, is killed by Hadrian's troops during one of many revolts against Roman efforts to destroy Jewish culture in the Middle East; his martyrdom will reinforce the cultural identity that will maintain Jewish civilization in the face of systematic persecution.

161 Marcus Aurelius becomes emperor of Rome; he devotes himself to defending the empire and preserving the Roman Golden Age.

285 Diocletian, after defeating a rival army at the Battle of Margus River, claims the title of Roman emperor, or Augustus, the most important symbol of imperial rule.

324 Constantine I becomes sole ruler of the Roman Empire; by converting to Christianity and building a new capital in the East, he will lay the foundation for Rome's successor, the Byzantine Empire.

443–53 Attila, a Hunnish king, expands his kingdom in both eastern and western Europe, threatening both ends of the Roman Empire.

527 Justinian I becomes emperor of Rome; he will renew the legal, territorial, and religious foundations of the Byzantine Empire and establish a close relationship between church and state, paving the way for future rulers such as Charlemagne.

581 Wen-ti becomes emperor of China; during his reign, he will issue a new law code, employ censors to ensure that it is obeyed, and embark on numerous military expeditions that will bring all of southern China under his control.

635–44 'Umar I, second caliph of Islam, orders the consolidation and Islamicization of Syria, Palestine, Iraq, Iran, and Egypt; the spread of Islam will cause the fall of the Persian Empire and make destructive inroads into the Byzantine Empire.

660   Mu'āwiyah I declares himself caliph of Islam; by 661 he will rule an Islamic empire that stretches from Morocco to the edge of India.

786   Hārūn ar-Rashid becomes caliph of the Abbasid Empire; during his reign he will maintain peace throughout his empire and bring material and intellectual prosperity to millions.

800   Charlemagne is crowned emperor of the Carolingian Empire by Pope Leo III, founding the first Christian empire in the West.

912   After spreading revolt throughout the Islamic empire, 'Ubayd Allāh becomes caliph and founder of the Fatimid Empire, representing a major transformation of Islam and breaking the authority of the Abbasids in North Africa.

962   Otto I creates the Holy Roman Empire (and is crowned emperor) after restoring unity to the eastern half of the Carolingian Empire after more than a century of disunity.

1066   William I wins the throne of England for Normandy at the Battle of Hastings and, in an attempt to consolidate his territories, begins compiling a census of the population called the Domesday Book.

1113   Suryavarman II comes to the Cambodian throne; during his reign he will expand Cambodian territory, construct Angkor Wat, and usher in an age of strife that will exceed the one he ended when he came to power.

1137–54 Eleanor of Aquitaine uses marital alliances to become one of the most important women in medieval Europe; at 15 she marries King Louis VII, making her the queen of France; 17 years later she marries King Henry II of England.

1154   Henry II ascends to the English throne and will control lands stretching from the Scots highlands to the Pyrenees; during his reign he will enact many legal reforms and wage a daring struggle against the privileges of the clergy.

1155   Frederick I is elected Holy Roman Emperor; during his rule he will successfully acquire territories in parts of Burgundy, Poland, Denmark, Sicily, and southern Italy.

1187   Saladin captures Jerusalem for the Muslims in a campaign for expansion of Islam against the Frankish Christian crusaders in the Middle East.

1189   Richard I is crowned king of England; his rule will be marked by the ideals of the age of chivalry, his predilection for combat, and indifference to the responsibilities of government.

1206   Temujin, the undisputed ruler of all the Mongol tribes, earns the name Genghis Khan ("Universal Ruler") and embarks on a campaign of imperial expansion that will eventually make the Mongol Empire one of the most powerful in the world.

1274   Edward I is crowned king of England; during his reign he will rely on his clerks for financial, legal, and administrative advice to extricate the country from the financial and diplomatic mess left by his father.

1307–37 Mansa Mūsā unites, centralizes, and expands Mali, transforming it into a prosperous trading empire.

1370   Timur, a nomadic conqueror, proclaims himself ruler of the central Asian Islamic tribe Ulus Chaghatay and begins a series of brutal conquests of neighboring territories and the Near East.

1415   Portuguese explorer Henry the Navigator leads a naval campaign that captures the port of Ceuta on the coast of North Africa, a victory that will prompt the Portuguese to pursue exploration and conquest along the Atlantic Coast and west coast of Africa.

1429   Joan of Arc leads the French army to victory against the English during a turning point in the Hundred Years War, lifting an English siege at Orléans and assuring continued French resistance.

1438   Pachacuti Inca Yupanqui successfully defends Cuzco, the capital of the Incan Empire, from neighboring invaders and is crowned king; he will spend the next 25 years expanding the empire.

1451   Mehmed II becomes ruler of the Ottoman Empire; he will spend the rest of his reign consolidating and expanding the empire.

1462   Ivan III succeeds his father to the throne of the kingdom of Muscovy and begins establishing the political foundations of the Russian Empire by eliminating all rival Russian states in eastern Europe and forming an autocratic system of government.

1464–92 Sunni Ali, ruler of the Songhay Empire, expands his realm over northwestern Africa and significantly influences the development of global trade.

1469   Isabella I unites the Spanish kingdoms of Castile and Aragon by marrying Ferdinand II; they begin to make Spain one of the most powerful states of early modern Europe.

1471   Topa Inca Yupanqui succeeds his father as Incan emperor; he will rule the empire during its time of greatest property.

1492   Christopher Columbus embarks on the first of four voyages during which he will inadvertently discover the Americas and open them to European conquest.

1493   Huayna Capac becomes head of the Incan Empire; during his reign the empire will grow to its greatest extent.

1518–20 Montezuma II, supreme leader of the Aztec Empire, accommodates invading Spaniards; the scheming of Spanish leader Hernán Cortés and a smallpox epidemic will eventually devastate the people of Mexico.

1520   Nineteen-year-old Charles V is elected Holy Roman Emperor and is crowned by Pope Leo X; his failure to check the Reformation and to unify his vast territories will influence the development of modern Europe.

       Suleyman I succeeds his father to the throne of the Turkish Ottoman Empire and continues his father's path of conquest until the empire reaches its largest size.

1521   Hernán Cortés recaptures Tenochtitlán for the Spanish, thanks to a smallpox epidemic and a starving Aztec population; two years later he will be appointed governor of the new imperial lands by Holy Roman emperor Charles V.

1532 Francisco Pizarro and his Spanish army travel to Peru where they defeat the Incan emperor Atahualpa, and claim the empire's capital, Cuzco, for Spain.

1534 King Henry VIII of England breaks from the Roman Catholic church when Pope Leo X refuses to annul his marriage; he will persuade Parliament to issue the Act of Supremacy, by which the monarch declares himself the "supreme head of the church of England."

1540 Pope Paul III approves Ignatius of Loyola's rule for a religious order "for the propagation of the faith," called the Society of Jesus (the Jesuits).

1542 Bartolomé de las Casas persuades Emperor Charles V of Spain to issue the New Laws, banning Indian slavery in the New World.

1547 Ivan IV crowns himself the first tsar of Russia and thus creates the Russian Empire; he will pursue major legal and administrative reforms, but face civil unrest and political instability, ultimately weakening the empire.

1556 Islamic Mughal emperor Akbar inherits the throne, and over the next 50 years he creates a stable and powerful empire characterized by religious tolerance.

1557–88 King Philip II of Spain increases Spanish power and advances the interests of the Roman Catholic church through wars, establishing Spain as the dominant military power in Europe.

1558 Elizabeth I succeeds her sister Mary as queen of England; the religious policies instituted and naval expansion undertaken during her reign will help make England one of the most prosperous states in Europe during subsequent centuries.

1561 Catherine de Médicis is named regent of France upon the coronation of her son, Charles IX; she will try to reconcile the opposing Roman Catholic and Protestant groups that spark the Wars of Religion in 1562.

1582 Toyotomi Hideyoshi rises to the rank of *daimyo*, or local lord, and begins waging war until he controls all of Japan by 1590.

1589 Henry of Navarre is crowned Henry IV of France and converts to Roman Catholicism in an attempt to decrease the country's religious turmoil; he will issue the Edict of Nantes, according the Huguenots some political, military, and religious autonomy and putting an end to the religious wars in France.

1603 Tokugawa Ieyasu, after battling various shoguns for provincial supremacy in Japan, is appointed hereditary shogun in the new Tokugawa line; he will establish a central leadership for Japan that will endure until 1867.

1611–32 Gustavus Adolphus wages tireless wars in the Baltic region to defend and expand the power of the Swedish Empire, transforming what had formerly been a kingdom limited to Scandinavia into the major imperial power of eastern Europe.

1624 Armand-Jean du Plessis Richelieu is appointed chief minister of France, a position that enables him to enact various economic and foreign policy reforms that will maintain Louis XIII's power and elevate France's international status.

1649 Oliver Cromwell orders the death of King Charles I, destroying the English absolute monarchy and establishing a commonwealth that he will rule as a military dictator, or lord protector.

1654–1715 During Louis XIV's reign as king of France, he expands French territory and power until the country is the most powerful in Europe.

1658 After defeating and killing his three brothers, Aurangzeb takes the throne of the Mughal Empire in 1658; his extensive campaigns expand the empire's territory to its greatest extent.

1689 Peter I assumes absolute authority in the Russian Empire; he will change the character of Russian life and link the continent to Europe through military conquest and political reform.

1740 Maria Theresa accedes to the throne of the Habsburg Austrian Empire; her leadership and the resilience of the army will enable the state to defend its territories during the War of Austrian Succession (1740–48) and during the Seven Years War (1756–63).

Frederick II succeeds his father as king of Prussia; he will make Prussia the dominant power of northern Germany by guiding his domestic policy with the ideals of the Enlightenment and his foreign policy with sheer cunning.

1762 After Catherine II orders the abdication of King Peter III of Russia, she is installed as ruler; during her reign she will develop Russia culturally and expand its territories.

1776 Thomas Jefferson and fellow writers present the Declaration of Independence to the U.S. Congress; his leadership and intellectual acuity will make him the third president of the United States and a founder of the Democratic-Republican Party.

1780 Tupac Amarú leads a general insurrection against the colonial administration of eighteenth-century Peru, reviving consciousness of the Incan past and further weakening the declining Spanish Empire.

1781 George Washington, defeating the British at the Battle of Yorktown, effectively ends the American Revolution; his military leadership assures him a position as first president of the United States.

1781–83 U.S. inventor, intellectual, and military leader Benjamin Franklin negotiates independence for America's 13 colonies, signing an official peace in Britain in 1783.

1783–88 James Madison actively participates in the drafting and ratification of the new U.S. Constitution, which forms the government that has endured to the present; he will serve as the fourth president of the United States.

1790 Edmund Burke writes *Reflections on the Revolution in France*, an attack on the revolutionary overthrow of King Louis XVI.

1791 Olympe de Gouges writes *Esprit Français, ou Problème à resoudre sur le labyrinthe de divers complots* (*The French Spirit, or a Problem to Resolve in Regards to the Maze of Many Plots*) and *Declaration of the Rights of Women*; through these works she will make women's rights synonymous with revolutionary rights.

1792 Mary Wollstonecraft publishes *A Vindication of the Rights of Woman*, one of the earliest treatises on feminism.

1793–94 Maximilien Robespierre leads the most radical phase of the French Revolution, the Reign of Terror, establishing a precedent for the totalitarian governments of the twentieth century.

1801 Toussaint-Louverture and his army capture Santo Domingo from the French, paving the way for Haitian independence a year later.

1804 After overthrowing the revolutionary government in France, Napoléon I proclaims himself emperor of a new ruling dynasty; he will go on to conquer most of Europe in the first decade of the nineteenth century and will introduce political, legal, and administrative reforms, centralize government administration, and help to develop liberal traditions in Europe.

1812–21 José de San Martín participates in the liberation movement against the Spaniards in Argentina, Chile, and Peru.

1813 Robert Owen writes *A New View of Society*, a plan for an industrial society united by cooperation rather than exploitation, and applies this vision, based on the traditions of Enlightenment rationalism and Christian charity, to his factories in Scotland.

1814 John Quincy Adams, who will become sixth president of the United States, while serving as ambassador to Great Britain, negotiates and signs the Treaty of Ghent, ending the destructive War of 1812 with Britain.

1815–48 Klemens von Metternich's diplomatic skills and philosophy of government give order to the international relations between European states from the time of Napoléon I's defeat in 1815 to the time of great national and liberal insurrections in the Austrian Empire in 1848.

1816–28 The Zulu nation, led by Shaka, engages in a series of wars of expansion, forcing a migration of neighboring peoples; he will foster a long-lasting sense of national pride among South African Zulus but severely disrupt the populations of central and southern Africa.

1822–25 Simón Bolívar, during his war against Spanish imperialism, liberates five South American nations from Spain.

1824 Osei Bonsu, leader of the West African Asante Empire, defeats the British at the Battle of Nsamankow, preventing Great Britain from extending its African imperial territory in the Gold Coast region for another 75 years.

1840–43 Louis Blanc publishes *The Organization of Labor* and *The History of Ten Years, 1830–1840*; both works will have a major impact on nineteenth-century socialist thought and twentieth-century democratic socialism.

1842 Russian anarchist Mikhail Bakunin writes an inflammatory article ending with a famous claim that "the passion for destruction is also a creative passion"; this statement will become the leitmotif of his revolutionary anarchist movement.

1848 Karl Marx and Friedrich Engels publish the *Communist Manifesto*; this statement will help establish a revolutionary movement that will transform the world in the twentieth century.

Susan B. Anthony and Elizabeth Cady Stanton assemble a convention for women's rights in Seneca Falls, N.Y., bringing the abuse and second-class status of women to the world's attention.

Giuseppe Mazzini, Italian nationalist and proponent of Italian unification, takes part in a revolt against Austrian control of Lombard and becomes ruler of the new Roman Republic as part of a governing triumvirate.

1850 Hung Hsui-ch'üan, disturbed leader of the the Taiping Rebellion, scores military success in China and founds the authoritarian and utopian "Heavenly Kingdom"; Hung's movement will inspire anti-Manchu nationalists such as Sun Yat-sen and Chinese communists such as Mao Tse-tung.

1851 Rama IV becomes king of Siam (Thailand); during his reign he will build a base on which a modern Siam can prosper from European commerce yet remain independent.

1854 Florence Nightingale and a unit of women nurses travel to military hospitals in Turkey during the Crimean War to introduce new standards of hygiene and improved medical equipment, lowering the mortality rate at the Scutari hospital from 42% to 2% between 1854 and 1855.

1855 Alexander II accedes to Russia's throne and initiates a series of legislative and social changes known as the Great Reforms in a bold effort to improve and strengthen the Russian Empire.

1857 David Livingstone, Scots missionary and explorer, publishes *Missionary Travels and Researches in South Africa*, an account of his expeditions to the African interior.

1860–61 Giuseppe Garibaldi deposes the king of Naples, handing over the kingdom to Piedmont-Sardinia; the Kingdom of Italy is finally proclaimed.

1861–65 Abraham Lincoln serves as sixteenth president of the United States and guides the Union (North) to a hard-won victory over the Confederacy (South), preserving the unity of the nation and putting an end to slavery in the United States.

1861 Camillo Benso di Cavour, who negotiated the unification process of the Kingdom of Italy, is appointed Italy's first prime minister.

1865 Leopold II accedes to the throne of Belgium and sets the kingdom on a course of overseas expansion, particularly in Africa; during his reign over the Congo region, he will subject the residents to immense brutality.

1867	William Ewart Gladstone assumes leadership of Britain's Liberal Party and, both before and after he serves two terms as prime minister, becomes a voice for Victorian leftist issues such as voting rights, self-rule, and anti-imperialism.
1871	Prussian chancellor Otto von Bismark successfully unites the German Empire under Kaiser William I.
1875	British Prime Minister Benjamin Disraeli successfully reconciles conservatism and modern democratic politics, transforming the Conservative Party into a mass party acceptable to the newly enfranchised working class when he passes bills in support of striking laborers.
1877	Chief Joseph and his followers attempt to flee the oppressive Indian reservation system of the United States by embarking on a three-month, 1,000-mile trek toward Canada.
1881	Booker Taliaferro Washington is appointed principal of the Tuskegee Normal and Industrial Institute in Tuskegee, Alabama, and converts it into the nation's foremost African-American educational institution, expanding educational opportunities for African Americans nationwide.
1889	Menelik II becomes emperor of Ethiopia and sets about modernizing his country to protect it from external invasions.
	Cecil Rhodes obtains a Royal Charter from the British government, giving the British South Africa Company (BSAC) the authority to negotiate with African rulers; these negotiations will facilitate the expansion of British control over great amounts of African territory.
1897	Founder of Zionism Theodor Herzl leads the First Zionist Congress in Switzerland, marking the foundation of the World Zionist Organization.
	Labor union organizer Eugene Debs joins the Socialist Party in an attempt to unite labor reform with political action; Debs will run for president of the United States on the Socialist Party's ticket five times between 1900 and 1920.
1901–08	Theodore Roosevelt serves as twenty-sixth president of the United States; during his term he will introduce new responsibilities to the presidency such as environmental advocacy, progressive social reforms in government, and expansion of foreign policy.
1902	Jean Jaurès founds the French Socialist Party, establishing himself as one of the first and most successful socialists to work within the parliamentary system in France.
1903	Emmeline Pankhurst founds the Women's Social and Political Union (WSPU) as a part of her campaign for women's suffrage in Britain.
1908	Two-year-old P'u-i is made emperor of China with his father as regent; as the last emperor of China, he will become a political pawn and a symbolic leader during the increasingly nationalistic struggles of the twentieth century.
1909	Mexican revolutionary and champion of peasant rights, Emiliano Zapata is elected to a board of defense for a small village and negotiates with the government for the return of confiscated lands to peasants; he will organize his supporters into a group known as the Zapatistas.

1911–12	Sun Yat-sen inspires the revolt that will lead to the abduction of the Chi'ing emperor and the establishment of China as a republic; he is named provisional president of the Republic of China, and he founds the Kuomintang, or "Revolutionary Party."
1914	Rosa Luxemburg, along with Karl Liebknecht, forms the revolutionary Spartacus League, a radical faction within the German Social Democratic Party.
	William II, emperor of Germany, gives Austria permission to go to war with Serbia, resulting in a war with Germany and culminating in World War I.
1914–18	Thomas Edward Lawrence, British soldier, plays a leading role in the Arab Revolt against Turkish rule during World War I, ultimately paving the way for Arab independence.
1917	Former British prime minister Arthur Balfour drafts the Balfour Declaration, encouraging Zionists to found the state of Palestine in 1948.
	British diplomat and Arab expert Gertrude Bell helps the British establish the state of Iraq.
	Alexander Kerensky is appointed prime minister of Russia and of the provisional government during the Russian Revolution; his failure to prevent the Bolshevik Party from seizing power by the end of the year will lead to the transformation of Russia into a socialist society.
	Vladimir Ilich Lenin, founder of the Russian Communist Party, comes to power in Russia; the uncompromising political tradition established by Lenin will lead to gross abuses of power.
	Leon Trotsky plays a key role in the Bolshevik seizure of power in Russia and he is thereafter given important responsibilities in the Soviet government, including commissar of foreign relations (1918) and commissar of war (1918–21).
1917–18	Georges Clemenceau is appointed premier during France's weakest point in World War I; he will establish a virtual civilian dictatorship and pull France to victory in 1918.
1918	Russian socialist Aleksandra Kollontai helps draft a law granting women the right to abortion and divorce, and publishes *The New Morality and the Working Class*, an essay that will inspire the women's movement in the Soviet Union.
	Nicholas II is murdered along with his family by Vladimir Ilich Lenin's Bolshevik government; the failure of Nicholas II to preserve the Russian monarchy will have an enormous impact on subsequent generations of Russians.
	U.S. president Woodrow Wilson proposes the Fourteen Points after World War I in an effort to encourage open diplomacy and free trade and to establish the League of Nations; the armistice signed ending the war will be based on Wilson's diplomatic effort.
1920	Mohandas Gandhi launches his first nationwide *satyagraha*, or nonviolent campaign of civil disobedience, in response to the Amritsar Massacre of Indians by British colonial troops; he will set a precedent for other

independence movements in European colonies and social reform movements in the United States and elsewhere

1922   Benito Mussolini stages the fascist "March on Rome" to seize power and is named prime minister by King Victor Emmanuel III; his tactics—advocating violence, discipline, aggressive imperialism, and war—will be imitated by Adolf Hitler and others.

1923   Kemal Atatürk, elected the first president of the Turkish Republic, begins the transformation of the Ottoman Empire into the modern state of Turkey.

1924–28   Chiang Kai-shek recaptures China from warlords who had ruled the country since 1911; he will preserve China as a single political entity in the face of enemies who want to divide and conquer it.

1926   Hirohito become Japan's 124th emperor; during his reign he will stabilize Japanese politics and society.

1928   Joseph Stalin begins his brutal dictatorship with the "revolution from above," a transformation of the Soviet Union from an agricultural to an industrial economy.

1932   Arabian leader Abd al-Aziz ibn Sa'ūd declares the Arabian peninsula to be the kingdom of Saudi Arabia.

1932–45   Franklin Delano Roosevelt serves as thirty-second president of the United States; during his term he will propose new government programs and legislation, the New Deal, to address the social and economic impact of the Depression; he will also engage in personal diplomacy with Winston Churchill and Joseph Stalin.

1933   Adolf Hitler is appointed chancellor of Germany and given dictatorial powers, later subjecting Germany to a cruel dictatorship and directly causing World War II; he will sweep away much of traditional Germany, overthrow numerous governments, and cause the deaths of approximately 40 million people.

1939   Winning the Spanish Civil War for the unified Nationalists, Francisco Franco declares himself supreme leader of Spain; he will go on to rule the country for 36 years with ruthless authoritarianism.

1940   Winston Churchill assumes the office of prime minister of Great Britain; he will serve the British government for more than half a century and help an isolated Britain survive the Battle of Britain and ultimately triumph over Nazi Germany during World War II.

1941   Tojo Hideki is appointed prime minister of Japan because of his extensive military experience and his plan to improve Japan's political position in Asia in World War II.

1944   Dwight David Eisenhower, Allied supreme commander during World War II, successfully leads the huge Normandy invasion force that will liberate Nazi-occupied Western Europe; his popularity as a war hero will help him serve as U.S. president for two terms (1953–61).

1945   Tito, leader of the Communist Party of Yugoslavia, abolishes the country's monarchy and declares the Federal Republic of Yugoslavia a communist regime.

1945–52   Harry S. Truman serves as thirty-third president of the United States; he will guide the United States through the end of World War II, seal an American victory with nuclear weapons, and establish the country's new role as a postwar global superpower.

1945–54   Vietnamese revolutionary and post-colonial leader Ho Chi Minh ejects the French from Vietnam and is eventually left in charge of Communist North Vietnam.

1946   U.S. diplomat George Kennan formulates the policy of containment employed against the Soviet Union during the Cold War, eventually leading to expansion of the U.S. political and military global presence.

1946–52   Eva Duarte de Perón, during her husband's term as president of Argentina, campaigns tirelessly to improve the lives of the poor, to give women the right to vote, and to establish a foundation that will grow into a massive welfare organization.

1947   George Marshall is named secretary of state by U.S. President Harry S. Truman; he designs the European Recovery Act, better known as the Marshall Plan, to help Europe recover from World War II and to keep the communists in Western Europe from gaining power.

Britain grants India full independence and Jawaharlal Nehru becomes the country's first prime minister, leading India during its transformation from a British colony into the world's largest democracy.

1948   David Ben-Gurion declares Israel's independence and becomes Israel's first prime minister in 1949.

Eleanor Roosevelt, political activist, former First Lady, and a delegate to the United Nations, helps author an international declaration on human rights that the organization will eventually adopt.

1949   Konrad Adenauer becomes the first chancellor of the Federal Republic of Germany; he will win back (West) German sovereignty by 1955, making West Germany an equal partner in the postwar world order.

Simone de Beauvoir publishes her masterpiece, *The Second Sex*, an analysis of the status of women that will revolutionize Western feminism and inspire a wide variety of theoretical and activist philosophies worldwide.

After declaring Indonesian independence four years earlier, Sukarno becomes president of Dutch-liberated Indonesia.

After the end of the war with Japan, Mao Tse-tung becomes chairman of the new People's Republic of China; during his rule he will forcibly redistribute wealth, and therefore power, from an isolated and entrenched elite to China's long-suffering common people.

1950   European economist and devout Roman Catholic Robert Schuman develops the Schuman Plan, calling for the creation of a Common Market in European coal and steel; Schuman's vision of a united Europe will be realized during the second half of the twentieth century.

1952   Malcolm Little becomes Malcolm X and joins the Nation of Islam, eventually rising in its ranks to become minister of the temple in New York City and one of the most important figures in the African-American struggle for social justice.

1952–56 Gamal Abdel Nasser and the Free Officers depose King Farouk of Egypt and dissolve parliament, replacing it with the Revolutionary Command Council under Nasser's leadership; they will declare a republic in 1953, and in 1956 Nasser will be elected president of a one-party state.

1953 Soviet physicist and political dissident Andrei Sakharov and colleague Igor Tamm contribute to the detonation of first Soviet hydrogen bomb, putting the Soviet military on a par with that of the United States.

Nikita Khrushchev succeeds Joseph Stalin as the leader of the Soviet Union; his attempts at economic reform will fail, provoking a conservative reaction that will last more than 20 years.

1957 Kwame Nkrumah leads the Gold Coast to independence, renaming it Ghana after an eleventh-century West African kingdom; in 1960 he is elected president.

1958 World War II hero Charles de Gaulle forms the Fifth Republic of France; he will force France to relinquish its colonial possessions while promoting French international presence.

1959 Fidel Castro and guerrilla leader Ernesto Guevara overthrow Cuban dictator Fulgencio Batista and seize Havana, establishing Castro as the head of a new communist regime.

1960 Léopold Sédar Senghor becomes the first elected president of the newly independent nation of Senegal and serves until 1981.

1961 Tanganyika African National Union achieves full independence from Great Britain and Julius Nyerere is appointed the nation's first prime minister; a year later he will become president, and in 1964 he will lead the unification of Tanganyika and Zanzibar to form the new state of Tanzania.

1962 Peter Benenson forms Amnesty International, an influential, concerted, nonpartisan organization dedicated to liberating people unjustly oppressed for their beliefs.

1963 Betty Friedan writes *The Feminine Mystique*, a best-selling book that launches a worldwide women's rights movement.

Martin Luther King, Jr., advocate of nonviolent civil disobedience to combat racial injustice, leads a mass march on Washington, D.C., where he will make his now-famous "I Have a Dream" speech; he will inspire many Americans and bolster the ideals of democracy.

1964 Jomo Kenyatta, leader of Kenya's independence movement, is elected that country's first president.

Leonid Brezhnev helps unseat Nikita Khrushchev as Soviet leader and is elevated to the post of party general secretary; during his 18-year rule he will contribute to the rise of the Soviet Union as a global military power and to the decline of communism.

1965 Suharto initiates a coup d'état, deposing and arresting Indonesia's president, Sukarno; he will install himself as president for life in 1968.

1967–72 Gloria Steinem, feminist activist, joins and promotes a wide array of feminist coalitions and causes, including the women's strike for peace, the National Organization for Women (NOW), the Equal Rights Amendment, and *Ms.* magazine.

1968 Daniel Cohn-Bendit leads a student demonstration at Nanterre, France, in protest of the Vietnam War, sparking a political group called "Mouvement du 22 mars" (March 22 Movement) that, in turn, will spark a sympathetic national workers' strike and will shut down the French economy for a number of weeks.

1969 Stephen Biko, South African civil rights activist, co-founds the all-black South African Students' Organization (SASO) as part of his campaign to abolish apartheid.

1970 Anwar as-Sadat succeeds Gamal Abdel Nasser as president of Egypt; Sadat will take Egypt in new directions and promote peace with Israel when he signs the Camp David accords (1978) with Israeli Prime Minister Menachem Begin, eventually earning him (and Begin) the Nobel Prize for Peace.

1975 Phnom Penh falls to the Khmer Rouge and Cambodian leader Pol Pot begins instituting a complete transformation of Cambodian society based on an extreme form of Maoism; during his rule he will empty the cities, collectivize all aspects of life, and be responsible for the deaths of over one million people.

1977 Oscar Romero is made archbishop of San Salvador during a time of increasing poverty and governmental repression; until his murder in 1980, he will serve as an advocate for the poor and a critic of the right-wing political regime.

Deng Xiaoping is reinstated as leader of the Communist Party in China, after the death of Mao Tse-tung in 1976.

1978 Israeli prime minister Menachem Begin negotiates a peace treaty with Egyptian president Anwar as-Sadat, signing the Camp David accords in 1978 and the Egyptian–Israeli treaty in 1979, eventually earning him (and Sadat) the Nobel Prize for Peace.

1979 Margaret Thatcher, leader of the Conservative Party in England, is elected prime minister of Great Britain; she is the first woman to lead the British national government.

Saddam Hussein is proclaimed president of Iraq; his aggressive military tactics and authoritarianism will destabilize the Middle East in the early 1990s and culminate in the Gulf War.

Ruhollah Khomeini, leader of an Iranian fundamentalist religious and political movement, becomes leader of Iran.

1980 Lech Walesa helps organize the independent trade union called Solidarity, beginning communist Poland's first independent political movement, and generating a force of civil society that will bring the communist regime to its knees in 1989.

Robert Mugabe becomes the first black president of Zimbabwe.

1985–91   Mikhail Gorbachev, general secretary of the Communist Party, carries out a series of reforms called *perestroika* ("restructuring") in an attempt to strengthen the Soviet Union's economy and institues *glasnost* ("openness"), a policy designed to encourage public discussion of the Soviet Union's problems; both policies will serve to undermine the communist system.

1986   Desmond Tutu is named archbishop of Cape Town, the Anglican primate of South Africa, two years after winning the Nobel Prize for Peace for his efforts in preventing racial violence and in combating the apartheid system.

Oscar Arias Sánchez becomes president of Costa Rica; during his presidency he will prevent his country from becoming embroiled in the destructive conflicts that rocked Central America throughout the 1980s, eventually earning the Nobel Prize for Peace in 1987.

1989   President of South Africa Frederik Willem de Klerk initiates a series of monumental reforms that will end apartheid and help transform South Africa into a functioning multiracial

country; for his efforts, he will receive the Nobel Prize for Peace with Nelson Mandela in 1993.

Vaclav Havel plays a leading role in the "Velvet Revolution," or the nonviolent transfer of power from the communists in Czechoslovakia; shortly thereafter Havel is elected interim president and reelected in July 1990.

1991   Aung San Suu Kyi is awarded the Nobel Prize for Peace for challenging the corrupt military regime, the SLORC (State Law and Order Restoration Council), that rules Burma, and for leading a continuing nonviolent campaign for human rights.

Boris Yeltsin is elected president of the Russian Federation, and, as a symbol of democracy, he effectively disbands the Soviet Union by banning the Communist Party and forming a new Commonwealth of Independent States (CIS) with Belarus and the Ukraine.

1993   Yasir Arafat signs the Oslo accords, establishing the state of Palestine in the occupied territories of the West Bank.

1994   Nelson Mandela is elected president of South Africa, representing the African National Congress in South Africa's first all-race national elections.

Chronological Listing of Biographies

Menes	Egyptian Pharaoh	c. 2925 B.C.E.
Hammurabi	Sumerian King	1820/1810–c. 1750 B.C.E.
Hatshepsut	Female Pharoh	c. 1522–1458 B.C.E.
Ramses II	Egyptian Pharaoh	d. 1213 B.C.E.
David	King of Ancient Israel	Tenth Century B.C.E.
Cyrus II	Founder of the Persian Empire	c. 600–530 B.C.E.
Darius I	Ruler of Ancient Persia	550–486 B.C.E.
Pericles	Ruler of Ancient Athens	c. 495–429 B.C.E.
Alexander III	Greco–Macedonian Conqueror	356–323 B.C.E.
Candragupta	Emperor and Unifier of India	c. 348–c. 298 B.C.E.
Aśoka	Indian Emperor	c. 292–c. 233 B.C.E.
Shih Huang-ti	Unifier of Ancient China	c. 259–210/209 B.C.E.
Caesar, Julius	Roman Dictator	100–44 B.C.E.
Spartacus	Leader of Roman Slave Rebellion	d. 71 B.C.E.
Cleopatra VII	Queen of Egypt	69–30 B.C.E.
Augustus	First Roman Emperor	63 B.C.E.–14 C.E.
Hadrian	Emperor of Rome	76–138
Marcus Aurelius	Roman Emperor and Philosopher	121–180
Kokhba, Bar	Jewish Rebel Leader	d. 135
Diocletian	Roman Emperor	c. 243–312
Constantine I	First Christian Emperor	c. 274–337
Attila	Hunnish King	c. 400–453
Justinian I	Byzantine Emperor	482–565
Wen-ti	Chinese Emperor	541–604
ʿUmar I	Early Proponent of Islam and Second Caliph	c. 586–644
Muʿāwiyah I	Founder of the Umayyad Dynasty	c. 605–680
Charlemagne	Founder of the First Christian Empire in the West	c. 742–814
Rashid, Hārūn ar-	Caliph of Abbasid Empire	766–809
Otto I	Founder of the Holy Roman Empire	912–973
ʿUbayd Allāh	Founder of the Fatimid Empire in Africa	d. 936
William I	First Norman King of England	c. 1027–1087
Suryavyarman II	Cambodian King and Builder of Angkor Wat	1098–c. 1150
Eleanor of Aquitaine	Medieval Queen and Patron of Culture	1122–1204
Frederick I	Holy Roman Emperor	c. 1123–1190
Henry II	King of England	1133–1189
Saladin	Muslim Military and Political Leader	1137–1195
Richard I	King of England and Leader of the Third Crusade	1157–1199
Genghis Khan	Founder of the Mongol Empire	1162–1227

Edward I	King of England	1239–1307
Timur	Central Asian Conqueror	c. 1336–1405
Mansa Mūsā	Emperor of Mali	d. 1337
Pachacuti Inca Yupanqui	Founder of the Incan Empire	c. 1408–c. 1474
Henry the Navigator	Portuguese Prince and Patron of Exploration	1394–1460
Joan of Arc	Defender of France and Roman Catholic Saint	1412–1431
Mehmed II	Ottoman Sultan	c. 1432–1481
Sunni Ali	Ruler of Songhay Empire	c. 1440–1492
Topa Inca Yupanqui	Incan Emperor	c. 1440–1493
Ivan III	Medieval Russian Tsar	1440–1505
Isabella I	Queen of Spain	1451–1504
Columbus, Christopher	First European Explorer of the Americas	1451–1506
Montezuma II	Aztec Leader	c. 1466–1520
Pizarro, Francisco	Spanish Conqueror of Peru	c. 1470–1541
Las Casas, Bartolomé de	Roman Catholic Missionary and Opponent of Slavery	1474–1566
Huayna Capac	Incan Emperor	c. 1480–1527
Cortés, Hernán	Spanish Conqueror of Mexico	1485–1547
Henry VIII	King of England	1491–1547
Ignatius of Loyola	Founder of the Society of Jesus	1491–1556
Suleyman I	Ottoman Sultan	c. 1494–1566
Charles V	Holy Roman Emperor	1500–1558
Catherine de Médicis	Queen, Regent, and Queen Mother in France	1519–1589
Philip II	King of Spain	1527–1598
Ivan IV	Ruler of Russia	1530–1584
Elizabeth I	Queen of England	1533–1603
Toyotomi Hideyoshi	Unifier of Modern Japan	1536–1598
Akbar	Indian Mughal Emperor	1542–1605
Tokugawa Ieyasu	Shogun of Japan	1543–1616
Henry IV	King of France	1553–1610
Richelieu, Armand-Jean du Plessis	Royal Advisor to King Louis XIII	1585–1642
Gustavus Adolphus	King of Sweden	1594–1632
Cromwell, Oliver	Leader of the English Civil War	1599–1658
Aurangzeb	Indian Mughal Emperor	1618–1707
Louis XIV	King of France	1638–1715
Peter I	Reformer of the Russian Empire	1672–1725
Franklin, Benjamin	American Philosopher and Revolutionary Patriot	1706–1790
Frederick II	King of Prussia	1712–1786
Maria Theresa	Empress of Austria	1717–1780
Catherine II	Empress of Russia	1729–1796
Burke, Edmund	British Statesman	1729–1797
Washington, George	First President of the United States	1732–1799
Tupac Amarú	Peruvian Rebel	c. 1742–1781
Toussaint-Louverture	Revolutionary Leader of Haiti	c. 1743–1803
Jefferson, Thomas	Third President of the United States	1743–1826
de Gouges, Olympe	French Political Thinker	1748–1793

Madison, James	Fourth President of the United States	1751–1836
Robespierre, Maximilien	French Revolutionary and Leader of the Radical Jacobin Club	1758–1794
Wollstonecraft, Mary	British Author and Feminist	1759–1797
Adams, John Quincy	Sixth President of the United States	1767–1848
Napoléon I	Emperor of France	1769–1821
Owen, Robert	Utopian Visionary	1771–1858
Metternich, Klemens von	Austrian Diplomat	1773–1859
San Martin, José de	South American Revolutionary	1778–1850
Osei Bonsu	Ruler of African Asante Kingdom	1779–1824
Bolívar, Simón	South American Independence Leader	1783–1830
Shaka	Zulu Ruler	c. 1787–1828
Rama IV	King of Siam (Thailand) and Modernizer	1804–1868
Disraeli, Benjamin	British Politician and Leader of the Conservative Party	1804–1881
Mazzini, Giuseppe	Nineteenth-Century Italian Nationalist	1805–1872
Garibaldi, Giuseppe	Nineteenth-Century Leader of Italian Unification	1807–1882
Lincoln, Abraham	Sixteenth President of the United States	1809–1865
Gladstone, William Ewart	British Politician and Leader of the Liberal Party	1809–1898
Cavour, Camillo Benso di	Leader of Italian Unification	1810–1861
Blanc, Louis	French Socialist and Historian	1811–1882
Livingstone, David	Scots Missionary and Explorer	1813–1873
Hung Hsiu-ch'üan	Leader of the Chinese Taiping Rebellion	1814–1864
Bakunin, Mikhail	Russian Anarchist	1814–1876
Bismarck, Otto von	German Statesman and Diplomat	1815–1898
Alexander II	Russian Tsar and Reformer	1818–1881
Marx, Karl	Revolutionary Socialist	1818–1883
Anthony, Susan Brownell	American Women's Rights Advocate	1820–1906
Nightingale, Florence	Pioneer of Modern Nursing	1820–1910
Leopold II	King of Belgium and Colonial Ruler	1835–1909
Joseph, Chief	Native American Chief of the Nez Percé	c. 1840–1904
Clemanceau, Georges	French Politician and Journalist	1841–1929
Menelik II	Ethiopian Emperor	1844–1913
Balfour, Arthur	British Politician, Author of the Balfour Declaration	1848–1930
Rhodes, Cecil	British Administrator in South Africa	1853–1902
Debs, Eugene Victor	American Politician and Labor Activist	1855–1926
Washington, Booker Taliaferro	African-American Leader and Educator	1856–1915
Wilson, Woodrow	Twenty-Eighth President of the United States	1856–1924
Roosevelt, Theodore	Twenty-Sixth President of the United States	1858–1919
Pankhurst, Emmeline	Leader of Women's Suffrage Movement in Great Britain	1858–1928
Jaurès, Jean	French Socialist and Politician	1859–1914
William II	Emperor of Germany	1859–1941
Herzl, Theodor	Founder of Zionism	1860–1904
Sun Yat-sen	Founder of Chinese Republic	1866–1925
Nicholas II	Last Tsar of Russia	1868–1918
Bell, Gertrude	British Diplomat	1868–1926
Gandhi, Mohandas	Indian Nationalist; Spiritual Leader	1869–1948

Lenin, Vladimir Ilich	Founder of Soviet Communism	1870–1924
Luxemburg, Rosa	German Radical Socialist	1871–1919
Kollontai, Aleksandra	Russian Socialist Feminist	1872–1952
Churchill, Winston	British Statesman	1874–1965
Sa'ūd, Abd al-Aziz ibn	Creator of Modern Saudi Arabia	c. 1876–1953
Adenauer, Konrad	German Chancellor	1876–1967
Zapata, Emiliano	Mexican Revolutionary	1879–1919
Trotsky, Leon	Communist Revolutionary and Opponent of Stalinism	1879–1940
Stalin, Joseph	Soviet Dictator	1879–1953
Marshall, George	U.S. Soldier and Diplomat, Drafter of the Marshall Plan	1880–1959
Atatürk, Kemal	Founder of Modern Turkey	1881–1938
Kerensky, Alexander	Prime Minister of Russia	1881–1970
Roosevelt, Franklin Delano	Thirty-Second President of the United States	1882–1945
Mussolini, Benito	Italian Dictator and Founder of the Fascist Movement	1883–1945
Tojo Hideki	Japanese Military and Political Leader	1884–1948
Roosevelt, Eleanor	American Political Activist and First Lady	1884–1962
Truman, Harry S.	Thirty-Third U.S. President, World War II and Cold War Leader	1884–1972
Schuman, Robert	Architect of European Unity	1886–1963
Ben-Gurion, David	First Prime Minister of Israel	1886–1973
Chiang Kai-shek	Leader of Nationalist China	1887–1975
Lawrence, Thomas Edward	British Soldier and Writer	1888–1935
Hitler, Adolf	Ruler of Nazi Germany	1889–1945
Nehru, Jawaharlal	First Prime Minister of India	1889–1964
Eisenhower, Dwight David	Thirty-Fourth President of the United States	1890–1969
Ho Chi Minh	Vietnamese Revolutionary and Leader	c. 1890–1969
de Gaulle, Charles	French Politician and Military Leader	1890–1970
Kenyatta, Jomo	First President of Kenya	c. 1891–1978
Franco, Francisco	Spanish General and Dictator	1892–1975
Tito	Leader of Yugoslavia	1892–1980
Mao Tse-tung	Chinese Communist Leader	1893–1976
Khrushchev, Nikita	Soviet Leader and Reformer	1894–1971
Sukarno	Indonesian Political Leader	1901–1970
Hirohito	Emperor of Japan	1901–1989
Khomeini, Ruhollah	Iranian Religious Leader	1902–1989
Kennan, George F.	U.S. Diplomat and Scholar	1904–
Deng Xiaoping	Leader of China, 1978–1997	1904–1997
P'u-i	Last Emperor of China	1906–1967
Brezhnev, Leonid	Soviet Leader	1906–1982
Senghor, Léopold Sédar	Writer and Leader of Senegal	1906–
de Beauvoir, Simone	French Philosopher and Feminist	1908–1986
Nkrumah, Kwame	Leader of Ghana	1909–1972
Begin, Menachem	Prime Minister of Israel	1913–1992
Romero, Oscar	Roman Catholic Archbishop of El Salvador	1917–1980
Nasser, Gamal Abdel	President of Egypt	1918–1970
Sadat, Anwar as-	President of Egypt	1918–1981

Mandela, Nelson	President of South Africa, Human Rights Leader	1918–
Péron, Eva Duarte de	Argentinean Populist	1919–1952
Sakharov, Andrei	Soviet Nuclear Weapons Researcher and Political Dissident	1921–1989
Benenson, Peter	Founder, Amnesty International	1921–
Friedan, Betty	Feminist Leader	1921–
Suharto	Indonesian Political Leader	1921–
Nyerere, Julius	First Leader of Independent Tanzania	1922–1999
Mugabe, Robert	President of Zimbabwe	1924–
Malcolm X	African-American Political and Religious Leader	1925–1965
Pol Pot	Cambodian Political Leader	c. 1925–1998
Thatcher, Margaret	British Prime Minister	1925–
Castro, Fidel	Cuban Revolutionary and Leader	1926–
Guevara, Ernesto	Marxist Revolutionary and Guerrilla Leader	1928–1967
King, Martin Luther, Jr.	U.S. Civil Rights Leader	1929–1968
Arafat, Yasir	Leader of the Palestinian Liberation Organization	1929–
Gorbachev, Mikhail	Last Soviet Leader	1931–
Tutu, Desmond	Anglican Archbishop and Opponent of Apartheid	1931–
Yeltsin, Boris	President of Russia	1931–
Steinem, Gloria	Feminist Activist and Writer	1934–
de Klerk, Frederik Willem	South African Political Leader	1936–
Havel, Vaclav	Writer and President of the Czech Republic	1936–
Hussein, Saddam	Iraqi Political Leader	1938–
Arias Sánchez, Oscar	President of Costa Rica	1941–
Walesa, Lech	Founder of Solidarity and President of Poland	1943–
Aung San Suu Kyi	Burmese Political Activist	1945–
Cohn-Bendit, Daniel	Leader of French Student Protests	1945–
Biko, Stephen	South African Civil Rights Activist	1946–1977

Alphabetical Listing of Biographies

Adams, John Quincy	Sixth President of the United States	1767–1848
Adenauer, Konrad	German Chancellor	1876–1967
Akbar	Indian Mughal Emperor	1542–1605
Alexander II	Russian Tsar and Reformer	1818–1881
Alexander III	Greco–Macedonian Conqueror	356–323 B.C.E.
Anthony, Susan Brownell	American Women's Rights Advocate	1820–1906
Arafat, Yasir	Leader of the Palestinian Liberation Organization	1929–
Arias Sánchez, Oscar	President of Costa Rica	1941–
Aśoka	Indian Emperor	c. 292–c. 233 B.C.E.
Atatürk, Kemal	Founder of Modern Turkey	1881–1938
Attila	Hunnish King	c. 400–453
Augustus	First Roman Emperor	63 B.C.E.–14 C.E.
Aung San Suu Kyi	Burmese Political Activist	1945–
Aurangzeb	Indian Mughal Emperor	1618–1707
Bakunin, Mikhail	Russian Anarchist	1814–1876
Balfour, Arthur	British Politician, Author of the Balfour Declaration	1848–1930
Begin, Menachem	Prime Minister of Israel	1913–1992
Bell, Gertrude	British Diplomat	1868–1926
Ben-Gurion, David	First Prime Minister of Israel	1886–1973
Benenson, Peter	Founder, Amnesty International	1921–
Biko, Stephen	South African Civil Rights Activist	1946–1977
Bismarck, Otto von	German Statesman and Diplomat	1815–1898
Blanc, Louis	French Socialist and Historian	1811–1882
Bolívar, Simón	South American Independence Leader	1783–1830
Brezhnev, Leonid	Soviet Leader	1906–1982
Burke, Edmund	British Statesman	1729–1797
Caesar, Julius	Roman Dictator	100–44 B.C.E.
Candragupta	Emperor and Unifier of India	c. 348–c. 298 B.C.E.
Castro, Fidel	Cuban Revolutionary and Leader	1926–
Catherine de Médicis	Queen, Regent, and Queen Mother in France	1519–1589
Catherine II	Empress of Russia	1729–1796
Cavour, Camillo Benso di	Nineteenth-Century Leader of the Unification of Italy	1810–1861
Charlemagne	Founder of the First Christian Empire in the West	c. 742–814
Charles V	Holy Roman Emperor	1500–1558
Chiang Kai-shek	Leader of Nationalist China	1887–1975
Churchill, Winston	British Statesman	1874–1965
Clemenceau, Georges	French Politician and Journalist	1841–1929
Cleopatra VII	Queen of Egypt	69–30 B.C.E.

Cohn-Bendit, Daniel	Leader of French Student Protest	1945–
Columbus, Christopher	First European Explorer of the Americas	1451–1506
Constantine I	First Christian Emperor	c. 274–337
Cortés, Hernán	Spanish Conqueror of Mexico	1485–1547
Cromwell, Oliver	Leader of the English Civil War	1599–1658
Cyrus II	Founder of the Persian Empire	c. 600–530 B.C.E.
Darius I	Ruler of Ancient Persia	550–486 B.C.E.
David	King of Ancient Israel	c. Tenth Century B.C.E.
de Beauvoir, Simone	French Philosopher and Feminist	1908–1986
Debs, Eugene Victor	American Politician and Labor Activist	1855–1926
de Gaulle, Charles	French Politician and Military Leader	1890–1970
de Gouges, Olympe	French Political Thinker	1748–1793
de Klerk, Frederik Willem	South African Political Leader	1936–
Deng Xiaoping	Leader of China, 1978–1997	1904–1997
Diocletian	Roman Emperor	c. 243–312
Disraeli, Benjamin	British Politician and Leader of the Conservative Party	1804–1881
Edward I	King of England	1239–1307
Eisenhower, Dwight David	Thirty-Fourth President of the United States	1890–1969
Eleanor of Aquitaine	Medieval Queen and Patron of Culture	1122–1204
Elizabeth I	Queen of England	1533–1603
Franco, Francisco	Spanish General and Dictator	1892–1975
Franklin, Benjamin	American Philosopher and Revolutionary Patriot	1706–1790
Frederick I	Holy Roman Emperor	c. 1123–1190
Frederick II	King of Prussia	1712–1786
Friedan, Betty	Feminist Leader	1921–
Gandhi, Mohandas	Indian Nationalist; Spiritual Leader	1869–1948
Garibaldi, Giuseppe	Nineteenth-Century Leader of Italian Unification	1807–1882
Genghis Khan	Founder of the Mongol Empire	1162–1227
Gladstone, William Ewart	British Politician and Leader of the Liberal Party	1809–1898
Gorbachev, Mikhail	Last Soviet Leader	1931–
Guevara, Ernesto	Marxist Revolutionary and Guerrilla Leader	1928–1967
Gustavus Adolphus	King of Sweden	1594–1632
Hadrian	Emperor of Rome	76–138
Hammurabi	Sumerian King	1820/1810–c. 1750 B.C.E.
Hatshepsut	Female Pharaoh	c. 1522–1458 B.C.E.
Havel, Vaclav	Writer and President of the Czech Republic	1936–
Henry II	King of England	1133–1189
Henry IV	King of France	1553–1610
Henry VIII	King of England	1491–1547
Henry the Navigator	Portuguese Prince and Patron of Exploration	1394–1460
Herzl, Theodor	Founder of Zionism	1860–1904
Hirohito	Emperor of Japan	1901–1989
Hitler, Adolf	Ruler of Nazi Germany	1889–1945
Ho Chi Minh	Vietnamese Revolutionary Leader	c. 1890–1969
Huayna Capac	Incan Emperor	c. 1480–1527

Hung Hsiu-ch'üan	Leader of the Chinese Taiping Rebellion	1814–1864
Hussein, Saddam	Iraqi Political Leader	1938–
Ignatius of Loyola	Founder of the Society of Jesus	1491–1556
Isabella I	Queen of Spain	1451–1504
Ivan III	Medieval Russian Tsar	1440–1505
Ivan IV	Ruler of Russia	1530–1584
Jaurès, Jean	French Socialist and Politician	1859–1914
Jefferson, Thomas	Third President of the United States	1743–1826
Joan of Arc	Defender of France and Roman Catholic Saint	1412–1431
Joseph, Chief	Native American Chief of the Nez Percé	c. 1840–1904
Justinian I	Byzantine Emperor	482–565
Kennan, George F.	U.S. Diplomat and Scholar	1904–
Kenyatta, Jomo	First President of Kenya	c. 1891–1978
Kerensky, Alexander	Prime Minister of Russia	1881–1970
Khomeini, Ruhollah	Iranian Religious Leader	1902–1989
Khrushchev, Nikita	Soviet Leader and Reformer	1894–1971
King, Martin Luther, Jr.	U.S. Civil Rights Leader	1929–1968
Kokhba, Bar	Jewish Rebel Leader	d. 135
Kollontai, Aleksandra	Russian Socialist Feminist	1872–1952
Las Casas, Bartolomé de	Roman Catholic Missionary and Opponent of Slavery	1474–1566
Lawrence, Thomas Edward	British Soldier and Writer	1888–1935
Lenin, Vladimir Ilich	Founder of Soviet Communism	1870–1924
Leopold II	King of Belgium and Colonial Ruler	1835–1909
Lincoln, Abraham	Sixteenth President of the United States	1809–1865
Livingstone, David	Scots Missionary and Explorer	1813–1873
Louis XIV	King of France	1638–1715
Luxemburg, Rosa	German Radical Socialist	1871–1919
Madison, James	Fourth President of the United States	1751–1836
Malcolm X	African-American Political and Religious Leader	1925–1965
Mandela, Nelson	President of South Africa, Human Rights Leader	1918–
Mansa Mūsā	Emperor of Mali	d. 1337
Mao Tse-Tung	Chinese Communist Leader	1893–1976
Marcus Aurelius	Roman Emperor and Philosopher	121–180
Maria Theresa	Empress of Austria	1717–1780
Marshall, George	U.S. Soldier and Diplomat, Drafter of the Marshall Plan	1880–1959
Marx, Karl	Revolutionary Socialist	1818–1883
Mazzini, Giuseppe	Nineteenth-Century Italian Nationalist	1805–1872
Mehmed II	Ottoman Sultan	c. 1432–1481
Menelik II	Ethiopian Emperor	1844–1913
Menes	Egyptian Pharaoh	c. 2925 B.C.E.
Metternich, Klemens von	Austrian Diplomat	1773–1859
Montezuma II	Aztec Leader	c. 1466–1520
Mu'āwiyah I	Founder of the Umayyad Dynasty	c. 605–680
Mugabe, Robert	President of Zimbabwe	1924–
Mussolini, Benito	Italian Dictator and Founder of the Fascist Movement	1883–1945

Napoléon I	Emperor of France	1769–1821
Nasser, Gamal Abdel	President of Egypt	1918–1970
Nehru, Jawaharlal	First Prime Minister of India	1889–1964
Nicholas II	Last Tsar of Russia	1868–1918
Nightingale, Florence	Pioneer of Modern Nursing	1820–1910
Nkrumah, Kwame	Leader of Ghana	1909–1972
Nyerere, Julius	First Leader of Independent Tanzania	1922–1999
Osei Bonsu	Ruler of African Asante Kingdom	1779–1824
Otto I	Founder of the Holy Roman Empire	912–973
Owen, Robert	Utopian Visionary	1771–1858
Pachacuti Inca Yupanqui	Founder of the Incan Empire	c. 1408–c. 1474
Pankhurst, Emmeline	Leader of Women's Suffrage Movement in Great Britain	1858–1928
Pericles	Ruler of Ancient Athens	c. 495–429 B.C.E.
Péron, Eva Duarte de	Argentinean Populist	1919–1952
Peter I	Reformer of the Russian Empire	1672–1725
Philip II	King of Spain	1527–1598
Pizarro, Francisco	Spanish Conqueror of Peru	c. 1470–1541
Pol Pot	Cambodian Political Leader	c. 1925–1998
P'u-i	Last Emperor of China	1906–1967
Rama IV	King of Siam (Thailand) and Modernizer	1804–1868
Ramses II	Egyptian Pharaoh	d. 1213 B.C.E.
Rashid, Hārūn ar-	Caliph of Abbasid Empire	766–809
Rhodes, Cecil	British Administrator in South Africa	1853–1902
Richard I	King of England and Leader of the Third Crusade	1157–1199
Richelieu, Armand-Jean du Plessis	Royal Advisor to King Louis XIII	1585–1642
Robespierre, Maximilien	French Revolutionary and Leader of the Radical Jacobin Club	1758–1794
Romero, Oscar	Roman Catholic Archbishop of El Salvador	1917–1980
Roosevelt, Eleanor	American Political Activist and First Lady	1884–1962
Roosevelt, Franklin Delano	Thirty-Second President of the United States	1882–1945
Roosevelt, Theodore	Twenty-Sixth President of the United States	1858–1919
Sadat, Anwar as-	President of Egypt	1918–1981
Sakharov, Andrei	Soviet Nuclear Weapons Researcher and Political Dissident	1921–1989
Saladin	Muslim Military and Political Leader	1137–1195
San Martin, José de	South American Revolutionary	1778–1850
Sa'ūd, Abd al-Aziz ibn	Creator of Modern Saudi Arabia	c. 1876–1953
Schuman, Robert	Architect of European Unity	1886–1963
Senghor, Léopold Sédar	Writer and Leader of Senegal	1906–
Shaka	Zulu Ruler	c. 1787–1828
Shih Huang-ti	Unifier of Ancient China	c. 259–210/209 B.C.E.
Spartacus	Leader of Roman Slave Rebellion	d. 71 B.C.E.
Stalin, Joseph	Soviet Dictator	1879–1953
Steinem, Gloria	Feminist Activist and Writer	1934–
Suharto	Indonesian Political Leader	1921–
Sukarno	Indonesian Political Leader	1901–1970
Suleyman I	Ottoman Sultan	c. 1494–1566

Bibliography

GENERAL BIOGRAPHICAL AND HISTORICAL REFERENCES

Included in this section are various sources that will provide readers with further biographical and historical information on many of the individuals included in this volume as well as information on others not included. The sources here range from basic biographical and historical encyclopedias and dictionaries to sources that specialize in particular eras, regions, or countries.

Adamson, Lynda G. *Notable Women in American History.* Westport, Conn.: Greenwood Press, 1999.

Berson, Robin Kadison. *Young Heroes in World History.* Westport, Conn.: Greenwood Press, 1999.

Bowman, John S., ed. *The Cambridge Dictionary of American Biography.* Cambridge and New York: Cambridge University Press, 1995.

Brown, Archie, ed. *The Soviet Union: A Biographical Dictionary.* New York: Macmillan, 1991.

Bunson, Matthew. *Encyclopedia of the Middle Ages.* New York: Facts On File, 1995.

Concise Dictionary of American Biography. 5th ed. New York: Scribner's, 1997.

Diller, Daniel C., and Stephen L. Robertson. *The Presidents, First Ladies and Vice-Presidents.* New York: CQ Press, 2001.

Fraser, Antonia, ed. *The Lives of the Kings and Queens of England.* Berkeley: University of California Press, 1995.

Griffiths, Martin. *Fifty Key Thinkers in International Relations.* New York: Routledge, 1999.

Hughes, Sarah S., and Brady Hughes. *Women in World History.* 2 vols. Armonk, N.Y.: M.E. Sharpe, 1995–97.

Jackson, Kenneth T., ed. *The Scribner Encyclopedia of American Lives.* 5 vols. New York: Scribner's, 1998.

Keegan, John, and Andrew Wheatcroft. *Who's Who in Military History: From 1433 to the Present Day.* 2nd ed. New York: Routledge, 1996.

Latin American Lives: Selected Biographies from the Five-Volume Encyclopedia of Latin American History and Culture. New York: Macmillan Library Reference USA, 1998

Lucas, Eileen. *Contemporary Human Rights Activists.* New York: Facts On File, 1997.

Palmer, Alan. *Who's Who in World Politics: From 1860 to the Present Day.* New York: Routledge, 1996.

Price-Groff, Claire. *Twentieth-Century Women Political Leaders.* New York: Facts On File, 1998.

Rasmussen, R. Kent. *Modern African Political Leaders.* New York: Facts On File, 1998.

Rice, Michael. *Who's Who in Ancient Egypt.* New York: Routledge, 1996.

Thackeray, Frank W., and John E. Findling, eds. *Events that Changed the World.* 3 vols. Westport, Conn.: Greenwood Press, 1995–99.

Van Creveld, Martin, ed. *The Encyclopedia of Revolutions and Revolutionaries.* New York: Facts On File, 1996.

Wakin, Eric. *Asian Independence Leaders.* New York: Facts On File, 1997.

———. *Contemporary Political Leaders of the Middle East.* New York: Facts On File, 1996.

Weston, Mark, and Walter F. Mondale. *Giants of Japan: The Lives of Japan's Greatest Men and Women.* New York: Kodansha International, 1999.

REGION BY REGION

Each section below presents a list of sources for a particular region of the world. They include general histories, analyses of major historical developments, and individual biographies. Some sources cited here may also be included in other sections of the bibliography.

Anglo America

Blum, John Morton. *Woodrow Wilson and the Politics of Morality.* Boston: Little, Brown, 1956.

Elkins, Stanley, and Eric McKitrik. *The Age of Federalism.* Oxford: Oxford University Press, 1993.

Ferrell, Robert H. *Harry S. Truman and the Modern American Presidency.* Boston: Little, Brown, 1983.

Franklin, Robert Michael. *Liberating Visions: Human Fulfillment and Social Justice in African-American Thought.* Minneapolis, Minn.: Fortress Press, 1990.

Harlan, Louis R. *Booker T. Washington: The Making of a Black Leader, 1856–1901.* Oxford: Oxford University Press, 1972.

Harrison, J. F. C. *Quest for the New Moral World: Robert Owen and the Owenites in Britain and America.* New York: Scribner's, 1969.

Howard, Helen Addison. *The Saga of Chief Joseph*. Lincoln: University of Nebraska Press, 1978.

McPherson, James M. *Abraham Lincoln and the Second American Revolution*. Oxford: Oxford University Press, 1990.

Miscamble, Wilson. *George Kennan and the Making of American Foreign Policy, 1947–1950*. Princeton, N.J.: Princeton University Press, 1992.

Perry, Bruce. *Malcolm: The Life of a Man Who Changed Black America*. Barrytown, N.Y.: Station Hill Press, 1991.

Rakove, Jack N. *James Madison and the Creation of the American Republic*. Glenview, Ill.: Scott, Foresman/Little, Brown Higher Education, 1990.

Weatherford, Doris. *A History of the American Suffragist Movement*. Denver, Colo.: ABC-CLIO, 1998.

East Asia and the Pacific

Bix, Herbert P. *Hirohito and the Making of Modern Japan*. New York: HarperCollins, 2000.

Chie Nakane, and Shinzabur Aishi, eds. *Tokugawa Japan: The Social and Economic Antecedents of Modern Japan*. Tokyo: University of Tokyo Press, 1990.

Dening, Walter. *The Life of Toyotomi Hideyoshi*. 5th ed. New York, AMS Press, 1971.

Hoyt, Edwin P. *Warlord—Tojo Against the World*. Lanham, Md.: Scarborough House, 1993.

Europe

Ashley, Maurice. *The English Civil War*. Rev. ed. Gloucester, England: A. Sutton, 1990.

Babinger, Franz. *Mehmed the Conquerer and His Time*. Translated by Ralph Manheim. Princeton, N.J.: Princeton University Press, 1978.

Barlow, Frank. *Thomas Becket*. London: Weidenfeld and Nicolson, 1986.

Barnes, Timothy. *The New Empire of Diocletian and Constantine*. Cambridge, Mass.: Harvard University Press, 1982.

Baum, Franz H. *Medieval Civilization in Germany, 800–1273*. New York: Praeger, 1969.

Berenger, Jean. *A History of the Habsburg Empire*. Translated by C. A. Simpson. London: Longman, 1994.

Billinger, Robert D., Jr. *Metternich and the German Question: States' Rights and Federal Duties, 1820–1834*. Newark: University of Delaware Press, 1991.

Borza, Eugene N., ed. *The Impact of Alexander the Great*. Hinsdale, Ill.: Dryden Press, 1974.

Bosworth, A. B. *Conquest and Empire: The Reign of Alexander the Great*. Cambridge: Cambridge University Press, 1988.

Bradley, Keith R. *Slavery and Rebellion in the Roman World, 140 B.C.–70 B.C.* Bloomington: Indiana University Press, 1989.

Brunt, P. A. *Italian Manpower, 225 B.C.–A.D. 14*. Oxford: Oxford University Press, 1971.

Buckley, Terry. *Aspects of Greek History, 750–323*. London: Routledge, 1996.

Bullock, Allen. *Hitler: A Study in Tyranny*. New York: Harper & Row, 1952.

Carter, John M. *The Battle of Actium: The Rise and Triumph of Augustus Caesar*. New York: Weybright and Talley, 1970.

Caute, David. *The Year of the Barricades: A Journey Through 1968*. New York: Harper & Row, 1988.

Chamberlin, Muriel Evelyn. *The Scramble for Africa*. London: Longman, 1974.

Chamberlin, Russell. *Charlemagne: Emperor of the Western World*. London: Grafton, 1986.

Chancellor, John. *The Life and Times of Edward I*. London: Weidenfeld and Nicolson, 1981.

Chandler, Daniel. *The Campaigns of Napoleon: The Mind and Method of History's Greatest Soldier*. New York: Macmillan, 1966.

Clot, André. *Suleiman the Magnificent: The Man, His Life, His Epoch*. Translated by Matthew J. Reisz. London: Saqi Books, 1989.

Daniels, Robert V. *Year of the Heroic Guerrilla: World Revolution and Counterrevolution in 1968*. New York: Basic Books, 1989.

Diebold, William. *The Schuman Plan: A Study in Economic Cooperation, 1950–1959*. New York: Praeger, 1959.

Evans, J. A. S. *The Age of Justinian: The Circumstances of Imperial Power*. London: Routledge, 1996.

Fuhrmann, Horst. *Germany in the High Middle Ages, c. 1050–1200*. Translated by Timothy Reuter. Cambridge: Cambridge University Press, 1986.

Gillingham, John. *Richard Coeur de Lion: Kingship, Chivalry, and War in the Twelfth Century*. London: Hambledon, 1994.

Godineau, Dominique. *The Women of Paris and Their French Revolution*. Translated by Katherine Streip. Berkeley: University of California Press, 1998.

Goodwyn, Lawrence. *Breaking the Barrier: The Rise of Solidarity in Poland*. Oxford: Oxford University Press, 1991.

Harris, William V. *War and Imperialism in Republican Rome, 327–70 B.C.* Oxford: Oxford University Press, 1979.

Heater, Derek. *The Idea of European Unity*. London: Leicester University Press, 1992.

Joll, James. *The Origins of the First World War*. 2nd ed. London: Longman, 1992.

Jones, A. H. M. *Constantine and the Conversion of Europe*. New York: Collier, 1962.

Kagan, Donald. *Pericles of Athens and the Birth of Athenian Democracy*. New York: Macmillan, 1991.

Kamen, Henry Arthur Francis. *The Spanish Inquisition: An Historical Revision*. London: Weidenfeld and Nicholson, 1997.

Kelly, Aileen. *Mikhail Bakunin: A Study in the Psychology and Politics of Utopianism*. Oxford: Oxford University Press, 1982.

Kelly, Amy Ruth. *Eleanor of Aquitaine and the Four Kings*. Cambridge, Mass.: Harvard University Press, 1950.

Kelly, Linda. *Women of the French Revolution*. London: Hamish Hamilton, 1987.

Knecht, R. J. *French Renaissance Monarchy: Francis I and Henry II*. London: Longman, 1996.

Leyser, Karl. *Rule and Conflict in Early Medieval Society: Ottonian Saxony*. London: E. Arnold, 1979.

McKitterick, Rosamund, ed. *Carolingian Culture: Emulation and Innovation*. Cambridge: Cambridge University Press, 1994.

May, Arthur James. *The Age of Metternich: 1814–1848*. Rev. ed. New York: Holt, Rinehart and Winston, 1963.

Milford, Nancy. *The Sun King*. New York: Viking Penguin, 1995.

Munz, Peter. *Frederick Barbarossa: A Study in Medieval Politics*. Ithaca, N.Y.: Cornell University Press, 1969.

Norwich, John Julius. *Byzantium*. 3 vols. New York: Knopf, 1988–95.

Retallack, James N. *Germany in the Age of Kaiser Wilhelm II*. New York: St. Martin's Press, 1996.

Reuter, Timothy. *Germany in the Early Middle Ages, c. 800–1056*. London: Longman, 1991.

Ricciotti, Giuseppe. *The Age of the Martyrs: Christianity from Diocletian to Constantine*. Translated by Anthony Bull. Milwaukee, Wis.: Bruce, 1959.

Roberts, Michael. *The Swedish Imperial Experience, 1560–1718*. Cambridge: Cambridge University Press, 1979.

Rowell, Henry Thompson. *Rome in the Augustan Age*. Norman: University of Oklahoma Press, 1962.

Royal, Edward. *Robert Owen and the Commencement of the Millennium: A Study of the Harmony Community*. Manchester, England: Manchester University Press, 1998.

Rubin, Nancy. *Isabella of Castile: The First Renaissance Queen*. New York: St. Martin's Press, 1991.

Runciman, Steven. *A History of the Crusades*. 3 vols. Cambridge: Cambridge University Press, 1951–54.

Sawyer, Peter, ed. *The Domesday Book: A Reassessment*. London: E. Arnold, 1985.

Schoeps, Julius H. *Theodor Herzl and the Zionist Dream*. Translated by Annemarie and Francis Clark-Lowes. London: Thames and Hudson, 1997.

Schwarz, Hans-Peter. *Konrad Adenauer: A German Politician and Statesman in a Period of War, Revolution and Reconstruction*. 2 vols. Oxford: Berghahn, 1995.

Sewell, William H., Jr. *Work and Revolution in France: The Language of Labor from the Old Regime to 1848*. Cambridge: Cambridge University Press, 1980.

Showalter, Dennis. *The Wars of Frederick the Great*. London: Longman, 1996.

Smith, Denis Mack. *Cavour and Garibaldi, 1860*. Cambridge: Cambridge Univsersity Press, 1954.

Solt, Leo F. *Church and State in Early Modern England, 1509–1640*. Oxford: Oxford University Press, 1990.

Sumption, Jonathan. *The Hundred Years War*. London: Faber and Faber, 1990.

Tachau, Frank. *Turkey: The Politics of Authority, Democracy, and Development*. New York: Greenwood Publishing, 1984.

Trachtenberg, Mark. *A Constructed Peace: The Making of the European Settlement, 1945–1963*. Princeton, N.J.: Princeton University Press, 1999.

Walker, David. *The Normans in Britain*. Oxford: Blackwell, 1995.

Wehler, Hans-Ulrich. *The German Empire, 1871–1918*. Translated by Kim Traynor. New York: Allen and Unwin, 1985.

Weiker, Walter F. *The Modernization of Turkey: From Atatürk to the Present Day*. New York: Holmes and Meier, 1981.

Weinstein, Harold Richard. *Jean Jaurès: A Study of Patriotism in the French Socialist Movement*. New York: Octagon Books, 1973.

West, Richard. *Tito and the Rise and Fall of Yugoslavia*. London: Sinclair-Stevenson, 1994.

Williams, Stephen. *Diocletian and the Roman Recovery*. London: B. T. Batsford, 1985.

Wingerden, Sophia A. *The Women's Suffrage Movement in Britain, 1866–1928*. New York: St. Martin's Press, 1999.

Latin America

Anna, Timothy. *The Fall of the Royal Government in Peru*. Lincoln: University of Nebraska Press, 1979.

Arias Sánchez, Oscar. *Horizons of Peace: The Costa Rican Contribution to the Peace Process in Central America*. Translated by Bernice G. Romero and Joaquín Tacsan. San José, Costa Rica: Arias Foundation for Peace and Human Progress, 1994.

Booth, John A., and Thomas W. Walker. *Understanding Central America*. 3rd ed. Boulder, Colo.: Westview, 1999.

Brading, D. A. *Classical Republicanism and Creole Patriotism: Simon Bolívar (1783–1830) and the Spanish American Revolution*. Cambridge: Center of Latin American Studies, University of Cambridge, 1983.

Brunk, Samuel. *Emiliano Zapata: Revolution & Betrayal in Mexico.* Albuquerque: University of New Mexico Press, 1995.

Hyams, Edward, and George Ordish. *The Last of the Incas: The Rise and Fall of an American Empire.* New York: Simon & Schuster, 1963.

James, C. L. R. *The Black Jacobins: Toussaint L'Ouverture and the San Domingo Revolution.* 2nd ed. New York: Vintage, 1989.

Johnson, John J. *Simon Bolívar and Spanish American Independence: 1783–1830.* Princeton, N.J.: D. Van Nostrand, 1968.

Lockhart, James. *The Men of Cajamarca: A Social and Biographical Study of the First Conquerors of Peru.* Austin: University of Texas Press, 1972.

Lynch, Edward A. *Religion and Politics in Latin America: Liberation Theology and Christian Democracy.* New York: Praeger, 1991.

Nicholson, Irene. *The Liberators: A Study of Independence Movements in Spanish America.* New York: Praeger, 1968.

Ott, Thomas O. *The Haitian Revolution, 1789–1804.* Knoxville: University of Tennessee Press, 1973.

Prescott, W. H. *History of the Conquest of Mexico.* New York: Cooper Square Press, 1999.

———. *History of the Conquest of Peru.* New York: Cooper Square Press, 1999.

Roche, David. *Argentina, 1516–1982: From Spanish Colonization to the Falklands War.* New York: Oxford, 1988.

Rostworowski de Diez Canseco, Maria. *History of the Inca Realm.* Translated by Harry B. Iceland. New York: Cambridge University Press, 1999.

Simpson, Lesley Byrd. *The Encomienda in New Spain: Forced Labor in the Spanish Colonies, 1492–1550.* Berkeley: University of California Press, 1929.

Stavig, Ward. *The World of Tupac Amaru: Conflict, Community, and Identity in Colonial Peru.* Lincoln: University of Nebraska Press, 1999.

Stern, Steve J., ed. *Resistence, Rebellion, and Consciousness in the Andean Peasant World, Eighteenth to Twentieth Centuries.* Madison: University of Wisconsin Press, 1987.

Thomas, Hugh. *Conquest: Montezuma, Cortés, and the Fall of Old Mexico.* New York: Simon & Schuster, 1993.

Wagner, Henry. *The Life and Writings of Bartolomé de las Casas.* Albuquerque: University of New Mexico Press, 1967.

North Africa and the Middle East

Abun-Nasr, Jamal M. *A History of the Maghrib in the Islamic Period.* New York: Cambridge University Press, 1987.

Amjad, Mohammed. *Iran: From Royal Dictatorship to Theocracy.* New York: Greenwood Publishing, 1989.

Arkell, A. J. *A History of the Sudan.* 2nd ed. London: Athlone, 1961.

Babinger, Franz. *Mehmed the Conqueror and His Time.* Translated by Ralph Manheim. Princeton, N.J.: Princeton University Press, 1978.

Borza, Eugene N., ed. *The Impact of Alexander the Great.* Hinsdale, Ill.: Dryden Press, 1974.

Bosworth, A. B. *Conquest and Empire: The Reign of Alexander the Great.* Cambridge: Cambridge University Press, 1988.

Brueggemann, Walter. *David's Truth in Israel's Imagination and Memory.* Philadelphia: Fortress, 1985.

Burn, A. R. *Persia and the Greeks.* New York: St. Martin's Press, 1962.

Clot, André. *Harun al-Rashid and the World of the Thousand and One Nights.* Translated by John Howe. London: Saqi Books, 1986.

———. *Suleiman the Magnificent: The Man, His Life, His Epoch.* Translated by Matthew J. Reisz. London: Saqi Books, 1989.

Cook, J. M. *The Persian Empire.* London: J. M. Dent and Sons, 1983.

Dandamaev, Muhammad A., and Vladimir G. Lukonin. *The Culture and Social Institutions of Ancient Iran.* Translated by Philip C. Kohl. Cambridge: Cambridge University Press, 1989.

Davidson, Basil. *Modern Africa: A Social and Political History.* 3rd ed. New York: Longman, 1994.

de Vaux, Roland. *Ancient Israel: Its Life and Institutions.* Translated by John McHugh. New York: McGraw Hill, 1961.

Foreman, Laura. *Cleopatra's Palace: In Search of a Legend.* New York: Random House, 1999.

Glubb, John Bagot. *Haroon al Rasheed and the Great Abbasids.* London: Hodder and Stoughton, 1976.

Hawting, G. R. *The First Dynasty of Islam: The Umayyad Caliphate, A.D. 661–750.* London: Croom Helm, 1986.

James, T. G. H. *A Short History of Ancient Egypt: From Predynastic to Roman.* London: Cassell, 1995.

McLoughlin, Leslie. *Ibn Saud: Founder of a Kingdom.* New York: St. Martin's Press, 1993.

Madelung, Wilfred. *The Succession to Muhammad: A Study of the Early Caliphate.* New York: Cambridge University Press, 1997.

Olmstead, A. T. *History of the Persian Empire: Achaeminid Period.* Chicago: University of Chicago Press, 1948.

Oppenheim, A. Leo. *Ancient Mesopotamia: Portrait of a Dead Civilization.* Chicago: University of Chicago Press, 1964.

Reade, Julian. *Mesopotamia.* Cambridge, Mass.: Harvard University Press, 1991.

Regan, Geoffrey. *Saladin and the Fall of Jerusalem.* New York: Croom Helm, 1987.

Rosenthal, Monroe. *Wars of the Jews: A Military History from Biblical to Modern Times.* New York: Hippocrene, 1990.

Runciman, Steven. *A History of the Crusades.* 3 vols. Cambridge: Cambridge University Press, 1951–54.

Saad, Elias N. *Social History of Timbuktu: The Role of Muslim Scholars and Notables, 1400–1900.* Cambridge: Cambridge University Press, 1983.

Schweitzer, Avraham. *Israel: The Changing National Agenda.* Dover, N.H.: Croom Helm, 1986.

Smith, Charles D. *Palestine and the Arab-Israeli Conflict.* 3rd ed. New York: St. Martin's Press, 1996.

Thobhani, Akbarali. *Mansa Musa: The Golden King of Ancient Mali.* Dubuque, Iowa: Kendall/Hill Publishing, 1998.

Wilkinson, Toby A. H. *Early Dynastic Egypt.* New York: Routledge, 1999.

Zweig, Ronald W., ed. *David Ben-Gurion: Politics and Leadership in Israel.* London: Frank Cass, 1991.

Russia and Central Asia

Anisimov, Evgenii V. *The Reforms of Peter the Great: Progress through Coercion in Russia.* Translated by John T. Alexander. Armonk, N.Y.: M. E. Sharpe, 1993.

Bingham, Woodbridge. *The Founding of the T'ang Dynasty: The Fall of Sui and Rise of T'ang: A Preliminary Survey.* New York: Octogon Books, 1970.

Bosworth, A. B. *Conquest and Empire: The Reign of Alexander the Great.* Cambridge: Cambridge University Press, 1988.

Breslauer, George W. *Khrushchev and Brezhnev as Leaders: Building Authority in Soviet Politics.* London: Allen and Unwin, 1981.

Chambers, James. *The Devil's Horsemen: The Mongol Invasion of Europe.* New York: Atheneum, 1979.

Cotterell, Arthur. *The First Emperor of China.* London: Macmillan, 1981.

Crummey, Robert O. *The Formation of Muscovy, 1304–1613.* London: Longman, 1987.

de Madariaga, Isabel. *Russia in the Age of Catherine the Great.* London: Weidenfeld and Nicolson, 1981.

Edmonds, Robin. *Soviet Foreign Policy: The Brezhnev Years.* Oxford: Oxford University Press, 1983.

Evans, Richard. *Deng Xiaoping and the Making of Modern China.* New York: Viking Penguin, 1997.

González de Clavijo, Ruy. *Embassy to Tamerlane, 1403–1406.* Translated by Guy Le Strange. London: Routledge, 1928.

Hosking, Geoffrey. *The Awakening of the Soviet Union.* 2nd ed. Cambridge, Mass.: Harvard University Press, 1991.

Hughes, Lindsey. *Russia in the Age of Peter the Great.* New Haven, Conn.: Yale University Press, 1998.

Jen Yu-wen. *The Taiping Revolutionary Movement.* New Haven, Conn.: Yale University Press, 1973.

Kaiser, Robert G. *Why Gorbachev Happened.* New York: Simon & Schuster, 1992.

Keep, John L. H. *Last of the Empires: A History of the Soviet Union, 1945–1991.* Oxford: Oxford University Press, 1995.

Lewin, Moshe. *The Gorbachev Phenomenon: A Historical Interpretation.* Berkeley: University of California Press, 1991.

Lincoln, W. Bruce. *The Great Reforms: Autocracy, Bureaucracy, and the Politics of Change in Imperial Russia.* DeKalb: Northern Illinois University Press, 1990.

————. *In War's Dark Shadow: The Russians before the Great War.* New York: Simon & Schuster, 1983.

Maenchen-Helfen, Otto J. *The World of the Huns: Studies in Their History and Culture.* Berkeley: University of California Press, 1973.

Malia, Martin. *The Soviet Tragedy: A History of Socialism in Russia, 1917–1991.* New York: Free Press, 1994.

Manz, Beatrice Forbes. *The Rise and Rule of Tamerlane.* Cambridge: Cambridge University Press, 1989.

Medvedev, Roy A., and Zhores A. Medvedev. *Khrushchev: The Years in Power.* New York: Columbia University Press, 1976.

Meyer, Alfred G. *Leninism.* Cambridge, Mass.: Harvard University Press, 1957.

Morgan, David. *The Mongols.* Oxford: Blackwell, 1986.

Neville, John Iröns. *The Last Emperor: The Life of the Hsüan-t'ung Emperor Aisin-Gioro P'u-yi, 1906–1967.* London: House of Fans, 1983.

Ostrowski, Donald. *Muscovy and the Mongols: Cross-Cultural Influences on the Steppe Frontier, 1304–1589.* Cambridge: Cambridge University Press, 1998.

Pipes, Richard. *The Russian Revolution.* New York: Alfred A. Knopf, 1990.

Seton-Watson, Hugh. *The Russian Empire, 1801–1917.* Oxford: Oxford University Press, 1967.

Stites, Richard. *The Women's Liberation Movement in Russia: Feminism, Nihilism, and Bolshevism, 1860–1930.* Princeton, N.J.: Princeton University Press, 1978.

Thompson, E. A. *A History of Attila and the Huns.* Oxford: Blackwell Publishers, 1996.

Tucker, Robert C. *Stalin as Revolutionary, 1879–1929: A Study in History and Personality.* New York: Norton, 1973.

————. *Stalin in Power: The Revolution from Above, 1928–1941.* New York: Norton, 1990.

Ulam, Adam. *The Bolsheviks: The Intellectual, Personal, and Political History of the Triumph of Communism in Russia.* New York: Macmillan, 1965.

Warth, Robert D. *Nicholas II: The Life and Reign of Russia's Last Monarch.* Westport, Conn.: Praeger, 1997.

Weller, Robert P. *Resistance, Chaos and Control in China: Taiping Rebels, Taiwanese Ghosts and Tiananmen.* Seattle: University of Washington Press, 1994.

Wright, Arthur F. *The Sui Dynasty.* New York: Knopf, 1978.

Yanov, Alexander. *The Origins of Autocracy: Ivan the Terrible in Russian History.* Translated by Stephen Dunn. Berkeley: University of California Press, 1981.

South and Southeast Asia

Audric, John. *Angkor and the Khmer Empire.* London: Robert Hale, 1972.

Burke, S. M. *Akbar: The Greatest Mogul.* New Delhi: Munshiram Manoharlal, 1989.

Chandler, David P. *A History of Cambodia.* 2nd ed. Boulder, Colo.: Westview Press, 1992.

Faruki, Zahiruddin. *Aurangzeb and His Times.* Delhi: Idarah-I Adabiyat-I Delli, 1972.

Habib, Irfan. *Akbar & His India II.* New York: Oxford University Press, 1997.

Kiernan, Ben. *The Pol Pot Regime: Race, Power, and Genocide in Cambodia under the Khmer Rouge, 1975-1979.* New York: Yale University Press, 1996.

Ling, Bettina. *Aung San Suu Kyi: Standing Up for Democracy in Burma.* New York: Feminist Press at the City University of New York, 1999.

Misra, Kashi Prasad. *Nonalignment Movement: India's Chairmanship.* New Delhi: Lancers Books, 1987.

Mookerji, Radhakumud. *Candragupta Maurya and His Times.* Delhi: Motilal Banarsidass, 1966.

Nikan, N. A., and Richard McKeon. *The Edicts of Asoka.* Chicago: University of Chicago Press, 1978.

Vatikiotis, Michael R. J. *Indonesian Politics under Suharto: The Rise and Fall of the New Order.* New York: Routledge, 1998.

Wyatt, David K. *Thailand: A Short History.* New Haven, Conn.: Yale University Press, 1982, 1984.

Sub-Saharan Africa

Arkell, A. J. *A History of the Sudan.* 2nd ed. London: Athlone, 1961.

Assensoh, A. B. *African Political Leadership: Jomo Kenyatta, Kwame Nkrumah, and Julius K. Nyerere.* Melbourne, Fla.: Krieger, 1998.

Birmingham, David. *Kwame Nkrumah: The Father of African Nationalism.* Rev. ed. Athens: Ohio University Press, 1990.

Chamberlin, Muriel Evelyn. *The Scramble for Africa.* London: Longman, 1974.

Davidson, Basil. *Modern Africa: A Social and Political History.* 3rd ed. New York: Longman, 1994.

Edgerton, Robert B. *The Fall of the Asante Empire: The Hundred-Year War for Africa's Gold Coast.* New York: Free Press, 1995.

Hale, Thomas A. *Scribe, Griot, and Novelist: Narrative Interpretations of the Songhay Empire.* Gainesville: University of Florida Press, 1990.

Hochschild, Adam. *King Leopold's Ghost: A Story of Greed, Terror, and Heroism in Colonial Africa.* Boston: Houghton Mifflin, 1998.

Juckes, Tim J. *The Opposition in South Africa: The Leadership of Z. K. Matthews, Nelson Mandela, and Stephen Biko.* Westport, Conn.: Praeger, 1995.

Kuperus, Tracy. *State, Civil Society, and Apartheid in South Africa.* New York: St. Martin's Press, 1999.

Levitzion, Nehemia. *Ancient Ghana and Mali.* London: Methuen, 1973.

Marcus, Harold G. *The Life and Times of Menelik II: Ethiopia 1844–1913.* Oxford: Clarendon Press, 1975.

Markovitz, Irving Leonard. *Léopold Sédar Senghor and the Politics of Negritude.* New York: Atheneum, 1969.

Miller, Norman, and Rodger Yeager. *Kenya: The Quest for Prosperity.* 2nd ed. Boulder, Colo.: Westview, 1994.

Omer-Cooper, J. D. *The Zulu Aftermath: A Nineteenth-Century Revolution in Bantu Africa.* Evanston, Ill.: Northwestern University Press, 1966.

Parsons, Neil. *A New History of Southern Africa.* 2nd ed. London: Macmillan, 1993.

Rotberg, Robert I. *The Founder: Cecil Rhodes and the Pursuit of Power.* Oxford: Oxford University Press, 1988.

Saad, Elias N. *Social History of Timbuktu: The Role of Muslim Scholars and Notables, 1400–1900.* Cambridge: Cambridge University Press, 1983.

Thobhani, Akbarali. *Mansa Musa: The Golden King of Ancient Mali.* Dubuque, Iowa: Kendall/Hill Publishing, 1998.

Welsh, Frank. *A History of South Africa.* London: HarperCollins, 1998.

Worth, Richard. *Robert Mugabe of Zimbabwe.* Englewood Cliffs, N.J.: J. Messner, 1990.

Index

Note: Page numbers in **boldface** indicate subjects of articles.

Committee of Union and Progress (Turkey), 12
common law, 77
Common Market. *See* European Economic Community
Commonwealth of Independent States, 70, 201
communism
    Cambodia, 148
    China. *See* Communist China
    Cuba, 31, 121, 160
    Fourth International, 187
    Indonesia, 173, 174
    "iron curtain" speech, 38
    left-wing opposition, 41
    Polish opposition, 193
    Soviet. *See* Soviet Union
    Soviet bloc, 27, 76, 120, 188
    Trotskyism vs. Stalinism, 187
    Vietnam, 84
    Yugoslavia, 121, 181
    See also anticommunism; Cold War; Marxism
Communist China
    Cambodian alliance, 148
    economic transformation, 54
    "Four Modernizations," 54
    historical influences, 86
    leaders, 37, 54, 117, 121, 149, 188
    Maoism, 117
    Nationalist conflict, 37, 54, 120
    pro-democracy protests, 54, 70
    treatment of figurehead emperor, 149
    U.S. containment policy, 97, 188
    U.S. relations, 54, 117
Communist Manifesto (Marx and Engels), 121, 140
Communist Party, Cambodian. *See* Khmer Rouge
Communist Party, Chinese. *See* Chinese Communist Party
Communist Party, Czech, 76
Communist Party, French, 41
Communist Party, German, 112
Communist Party, Soviet, 27, 70, 101, 201
    ejection of Trotsky, 187
    founding of, 107
    militancy of, 121
Communist Party, Yugoslavia, 181
Communist Youth League, 54
concentration camps, 153
Confederate States of America, 109
Confederation of the Rhine, 131
Confucianism, 86, 88, 183, 196
Congo Free State, 108
Congo River basin, 80
Congress, U.S., 3, 65, 113, 140, 199
Congress of People's Deputies (Soviet), 162, 201
Congress of Vienna (1815), 24, 119, 126
    prescription principle, 28
Congress Party (India), 133
Congro River basin, 108
Coningsby (Disraeli), 56
conquistadors, 44, 127, 147
conscription, Sweden, 72
conservatism
    Austria, 28, 126
    Britain, 28, 38, 56, 179
    European nationalism, 34
    fascist, 130
    feminist backlash, 172
    Germany, 24, 198
    Japan, 82
    as moral pessimism, 28
    Prussia, 64
    Reflections on the Revolution in France exposition of, 28, 200
    Russia, 6
    Saudi Arabia, 165
    Soviet Union, 27, 70
    Spain, 61

working class, 56
Conservative Party (South Africa), 53
Conservative Party (Tories; Britain), 18, 28, 38, 56, 69, 142, 179
Constantine I (the Great), Emperor of Rome, 35, **43**, 55, 96, 123
Constantinople, 13, 81
    as capital of eastern Roman empire, 43, 55, 96
    Egypt under, 40
    excommunication of eastern bishops, 35
    fall to Islam, 90, 96, 123
    Nika Riots of 532, 96
    as Ottoman capital, 123, 152, 175
Constantius, Emperor of Rome, 43
Constitution, U.S., 8, 113, 142, 195
Constitutional Charter (Sweden), 74
Constitutional Convention (Mexico; 1917), 202
Constitutional Convention (U.S.; 1787), 113, 195
constitutional monarchy
    Belgium, 108
    Britain, 45, 154
    Italy, 34, 122
    Spain, 61
constitutions
    France, 51, 167
    Italy, 34
    Russian Federation, 201
    South Africa, 190
    Turkey, 12
Constitutions of Clarendon (1164), 77
containment policy, 97, 188
Continental Congress (U.S.), 62, 93, 113, 195
Continental System, 131
Contras (Nicaragua), 10
Convention People's Party (Gold Coast), 136
conversos, 89
Corn Laws (Britain), 56, 69
Corpus juris civilis (Roman Law), 96
Corsica, 130
Cortés, Hernán, 36, **44**, 127, 147
Costa Rica, 10, 157
cotton mills, 140
Council of Economic Advisors (U.S.), 188
Council of Nicea (325), 43
Council of the Indies, 44, 147
Counter-Reformation, 88
Crassus, 29, 170
Creoles, 26, 164
Crimean War (1854–56), 6, 33, 34
    modern nursing, 135
Croatia, 130
Croesus, King of Lydia, 46
Cromwell, Oliver, **45**, 60
Cromwell, Richard, 45
Cromwell, Thomas, 79
crops, 44, 147
crucifixion, 170
Crusades, 59, 63, 123, 154, 163
Cuba
    socialist revolution, 31, 71, 121
    Soviet missiles in, 31, 101, 162
    Spanish-American War, 160
    Spanish exploration, 42
Cuban Missile Crisis (1962), 31, 101, 162
Cuban Revolution (1959), 31, 71
Cuhanca (people), 141
cult of personality, 115, 136, 181
cultural conflicts
    India, 11
    Native American-white settlers, 95
cultural influences
    by Greco-Macedonian empire, 7
    by Spanish conquistadors, 44, 147
    by Spanish missionaries, 105
    in Turkey, 12
Cultural Revolution (China; 1965–76), 54, 71, 117

culture
    Arab, 20, 106, 152
    Athenian, 143
    Egyptian, 125
    Greek, 7, 30, 40, 46, 123
    Inca, 184
    Japanese, 186
    Jewish retention of, 103
    Nazi, 83
    Russian, 33
    Weimar Republic, 198
    See also arts
Cuzco, 85, 141, 147, 184
Cyprus, 56
Cyrus II (the Great), King of Persia, 46, 47, 48
Czechoslovakia, 27, 70, 76, 199
Czech Republic, 76, 120

D

Dacia, 73
daimyo, 183, 186
Damascus (Syria), 106, 163
Danube River, 47, 118
Darius I (the Great), King of Persia, 46, 47
Darius III, King of Persia, 7
Daughters of the American Revolution, 158
David, King of Israel, 46, **48**, 96
Davidic dynasty, 48
Dawn, The (newspaper), 39
Day of Dupes (France; 1630), 155
death squads, 88, 157
de Beauvoir, Simone, **49**, 52, 104
De Beers Mining Company, 153
Debs, Eugene, **50**
Decembrist Revolt (1825), 6
Declaration of Independence (U.S.), 62, 93
Declaration of the Rights of Man and Citizen (France), 52
Declaration of the Rights of Women (de Gouges), 52
Defense Army of Indonesia, 173
Defense Department, U.S., 120
de Gaulle, Charles, 41, **51**, 166
de Gouges, Olympe, **52**
de Klerk, Frederik Willem, **53**, 115, 190
Delhi (India), 16, 180
Delian League, 143
democracy
    ancient Athens, 143
    Costa Rica, 10
    Czech Republic, 76
    direct vs. representative, 113
    as French Revolution ideal, 156
    India, 133
    Israel, 21
    South Africa, 115
    Soviet bloc, 70
    Soviet transition, 70, 201
    Thailand, 150
    United States, 93, 113
Democratic Party (Turkey), 12
Democratic Party (U.S.), 93, 158, 159, 160, 188, 199
Democratic-Republican Party (U.S.), 93, 113, 195
democratic socialism, 25
Demons (Dostoevsky), 17
demonstrations and protests
    African American, 102
    by American students, 65
    Chinese pro-democracy, 54, 70
    by French students, 41, 49, 51, 187
    Palestinian, 19
    woman suffrage, 142
Deng Xiaoping, **54**, 70
Denmark, 24, 63, 72, 166
depression (economic). *See* Great Depression
desegregation, 58, 102
Dessalines, Jean-Jacques, 185
détente policy, 27

developing nations. *See* Third World
Devil's Island, 39
Dexter Avenue Baptist Church (Montgomery, Ala.), 102
Dia, Mamadou, 167
dialectical materialism, 121
diamonds, 110, 153
Dias, Bartolomeu, 80
Díaz, Porfirio, 202
dictatorship
    Africa, 136
    ancient Athens, 143
    British Cromwellian, 45
    Burma, 15
    fascist Italy, 67, 130
    human rights abuses, 22
    Latin America, 164
    Nazi Germany, 83, 198
    revolutionary, 156
    Rome, 29
    Soviet Union, 99, 107, 171, 201
    Spain, 61
    See also authoritarianism; totalitarianism
Dien Bien Phu, battle of (1954), 84
Diet of Worms (1521), 36
Dingane, 168
Dingiswayo, 168
Diocletian, Emperor of Rome, 29, 43, 55
Diouf, Abdou, 167
diplomacy
    appeasement of Hitler, 38
    Austria, 119, 126
    Britain, 3, 18, 20, 198
    Egyptian-Israeli accord, 19, 161
    France, 93
    Germany, 24, 198
    internationalism, 198
    Russia, 3, 33
    Siam, 150
    Soviet Union, 27, 101, 104
    United States, 3, 93, 97, 120, 159, 160
    See also foreign policy
discrimination
    against women, 8, 65
    racial, 23, 53, 58, 102, 115, 158
Disraeli, Benjamin, **56**, 69
Dissenters (British Protestants), 200
dissidents
    Czechoslovakia, 76
    Soviet intolerance of, 27, 107, 162
divine lineage, 29, 40, 75, 150, 178
divine right, 111, 131, 155
divorce, 104
Domesday Book, 197
Dominican Republic, 147, 185
Domrémy (France), 94
Doric columns, 143
Dostoevsky, Fyodor, 17, 28, 33, 89, 145
Douglas, Stephen, 109
Drake, Sir Francis, 60, 146
drama
    ancient Athens, 143
    Czechoslovakia, 76
    Elizabethan, 60
    France, 52
    Weimar Republic, 198
Dresden (Germany), 17
Dreyfus, Alfred (Dreyfus affair), 39, 81, 92
Drogheda, battle of (1649), 45
Du Bois, W.E.B., 136, 194
Dual Alliance (1879), 24
Duma (Russia), 6, 99, 134, 201
Dumish clan, 165

E

East Africa, 98, 137, 153
East African Association, 98
Eastern Church. *See* Orthodox Christianity
Eastern Europe

Jews (*continued*)
 Balfour Declaration, 18, 21, 81
 Davidic line, 48
 expulsion from Western Europe, 42, 57, 89
 German persecution of, 24
 Holocaust, 19, 81, 83, 89
 importance of homeland to, 18, 19, 21, 48, 81, 103
 Persian rule, 46, 48
 rebellion against Romans, 103
 refugees from Nazism, 158
 in Roman Empire, 29, 48, 73, 103
 Zionism, 18, 19, 21, 81
 See also anti-Semitism; Israel
Jiangxi Soviet, 117
jihad (holy war), 175
Jim Crow laws, 102, 194
Joan of Arc, **94**
Jogisches, Leo, 112
John XII, Pope, 139
John, King of England, 57, 59, 77, 154
John, King of Portugal, 80
John Paul II, Pope, 157, 166
Johnson, Joseph, 200
Johnson, Reginald, 149
Joint Chiefs of Staff (U.S.), 120
Jordan, 9, 106, 132, 161
Joseph II, Emperor of Austria, 119
Joseph, Chief, **95**
journalism, 25, 39, 61, 92
Juan II, King of Castile, 89
Juan Carlos, King of Spain, 61
Judaism. *See* Jews
Judea, 14, 73, 103
Judicial Reform Edict (Russia; 1864), 6
Julian the Apostate, Emperor of Rome, 6
Junkers, 64
jury system, 77
Justice, La (newspaper), 39
Justin I, Byzantine Emperor, 96
Justinian I (the Great), Byzantine Emperor, 35, **96**

K

Kabul, 5
Kalahari Desert, 168
Kalinga (India), 11
Kansas-Nebraska Act (U.S.; 1854), 109
Kapital, Das (Marx), 121
Karaman (Anatolia), 123
Karl IX, King of Sweden, 74
Karlsbad Decree (1819), 126
Kashmir (India), 5
Kassites, 74
Kautalya, 30
Kazan, 91
Kennan, George F., **97**, 188
Kennedy, John F., 158, 160
Kenpeitei (Japan), 182
Kentucky and Virginia Resolutions, 93, 103
Kenya, 98
Kenya African National Union, 98
Kenyatta, Jomo, **98**
Kerensky, Alexander, **99**, 107, 134
KGB (Soviet Union), 101, 162
Khin Kyi, 15
Khmer Rouge, 148, 178
Khomeini, Ruhollah (Ayatollah), **100**
Khrushchev, Nikita, 27, **101**, 162, 171
kibbutz, 21
Kiev, Mongol sacking of (1240), 68
Kikuyu (people), 98
Kikuyu Central Association, 98
Kimberley (Orange Free State), 153
King, Martin Luther, Jr., 66, **102**, 114, 194
King David Hotel bombing (Jerusalem), 19
Kingdom of Poland Social Democratic Party, 112
Kipling, Rudyard, 108
Kirsi, 74

Klaus, Vaclav, 76
KMT. *See* Kuomintang Party
Knäred, Treaty of (1613), 72
knighthood, 59
Koines, 7
Kokhba, Bar, **103**
Kollontai, Aleksandra, **104**, 112
Koni River, 176
Koran, 152, 163
Korea, 186
Korean War (1950–53), 97, 120, 188
Kosovo, 181
Kuang Hsu, Emperor of China, 149
Kublai Khan, 68
Kuchuk-Kainarji, Treaty of (1774), 33
Ku Klux Klan, 114
Kulturkampf, 24
Kuomintang Party (China), 37, 54, 86, 117, 120, 177
Kurdistan, 12, 175
Kurds (people), 12
Kuwait, 87, 165
Kwasniewski, Aleksandr, 193
Kyoto (Japan), 186

L

labor movement
 first English union, 140
 Poland, 193
 U.S. activism, 50, 158, 159
Labor Party (Israel), 19, 21
Labour Party (Britain), 69, 179
Lake Ngami, 110
Lake Titicaca, 85
Lake Victoria, 168
land reform
 China, 86, 117
 Cuba, 31, 71
 Iran, 100
 Ireland, 69
 Kenya, 98
 Mexico, 202
land rights
 Britain, 79
 Mexican confiscation, 202
 Native American dispossession, 95
 Russia, 33, 91
 Zimbabwe, 129
language
 German, 119
 Greco–Macedonian Empire, 7
 Inca, 141
 Latin alphabet, 12
 Latin influence, 29
 Latin literature, 14
 Portuguese, 80
 Quechua, 85, 141, 184
Laos, 150
La Rochelle (France), 155
Larsa, 74
Las Casas, Bartolomé de, **105**, 146
Latin America
 Aztec Empire, 36, 44, 127, 147, 189
 Inca Empire, 85, 141, 184
 independence struggle, 26, 71, 164, 189
 Jesuits in, 88
 liberation theology, 157
 Marxist guerrilla movement, 71, 189
 Monroe Doctrine, 3, 160
 native Roman Catholicism, 105
 Portuguese claims, 80
 Roosevelt Corollary, 160
 Spanish cultural influence, 89, 146, 147
 U.S. Cold War policy, 120
 U.S. interventions in, 160
 See also Central America; *specific countries*
Latin language, 12, 14, 29
law
 Britain, 77, 154, 197
 Hammurabi's Code, 74
 human rights activism, 22
 Islamic, 100

Napoleonic Code, 131
 Ottoman codification, 123
 Roman codification, 96
 Russia, 91
 United States, 3
 U.S. civil rights, 65, 102, 109
Lawrence, Thomas Edward (Lawrence of Arabia), 20, **106**
lay investiture, 139
League of Nations, 198, 199
 mandates, 18, 19, 81, 106, 132, 199
Lebanon, 9, 19, 132
Le Cap (Haiti), 185
Lechfeld, battle of (955), 139
Leclerc, Charles-Victor-Emmanuel, 185
Lee, Robert E., 109
Left Hegelians, 17, 121
left-wing politics
 France, 39, 41, 92
 Italy, 122
 liberation theology, 157
 Spain, 61
 student revolts, 41
 See also socialism
legalism, 169
legal tradition. *See* law
Legations (Papal Estates), 34
Legislative Commission (Russia), 33
Legnano, battle of (1176), 63
Lenin, Vladimir Ilich, 6, 17, 41, 55, 99, 104, **107**, 121, 171
 Bolshevik Party founding, 187
 as elite revolutionary, 156
 fate of Russian royal family, 134
 Soviet dictatorship, 201
Leninist Marxism, 117
Lenin's Tomb, 101
Leo I, Pope, 13
Leo III, Byzantine Emperor, 96
Leo III, Pope, 35
Leo X, Pope, 36, 79
Leopold I, King of Belgium, 108
Leopold II, King of Belgium, **108**
Lepanto, battle of (1571), 146
Lepidus, 14
lesbian rights, 172
"Letter from a Birmingham Jail" (King), 102
liberal feminism, 104, 200
liberalism
 Britain, 69
 German suppression, 24
 Italian *Risorgimento,* 34
 Soviet *perestroika,* 70, 193, 201
Liberal Party (Whigs; Britain), 28, 56, 69, 142
liberation theology, 157
Libya, 151
Liebknecht, Karl, 112
Likud Party (Israel), 19, 21
Lima (Peru), 147, 164
Lincoln, Abraham, 93, **109**, 150
literature
 ancient Athens, 143
 Britain, 56, 60, 77, 154, 200
 Carolingian, 35
 epics, 7, 14
 French, 49
 Joan of Arc legend, 94
 Latin, 14
 manuscript copying, 35
 medieval, 59
 Russian, 33, 145
 Soviet, 101
 utopian, 140
Lithuania, 70
Liudolf, 139
livestock, 147
Livingstone, David, **110**
Livingstonia Central Africa Company, 110
Livonia, 72
Livy, 14
Li Yuan, Emperor of China, 196
Lloyd George, David, 38

Lobengula, King of the Ndebele, 153
Lombard League, 63
Lombardy, 34, 35, 63, 67, 122
London Missionary Society, 110
Long March (Chinese Communists; 1934–35), 54, 117
Long Parliament (Britain), 45
Louis VII, King of France, 59
Louis XIII, King of France, 32, 78, 111, 155
Louis XIV, King of France, 32, 72, 78, 111, 145, 155
Louis XV, King of France, 111
Louis XVI, King of France, 111, 131, 156
Louisiana Purchase (1803), 93
Louis-Philippe (French king), 25
Lower (Baja) California, 44
Loyalists (Spain), 61
Lübeck, Gustav, 112
Ludendorff, Erich, 198
Lupaca (people), 184
Lü Pu-wei, 169
Luther, Martin, 36, 79, 88
Lutheranism, 36
Lützen, battle of (1632), 72
Luxembourg, 166
Luxembourg Commission, 25
Luxemburg, Rosa, **112**, 170
Lydia, kingdom of, 46, 47

M

Maastricht Treaty (1991), 166
maat (divine rule mandate), 75
MacArthur, Douglas, 58, 188
Macedonia (ancient), 7, 14, 40
Macedonia (modern), 181
machine gun, 72, 138
Madeira, 80
Madero, Francisco, 202
Madison, James, 3, 93, **113**
Madras (India), 16
Magdeburg massacre (1631), 72
Magna Carta (1215), 57, 77, 154
mahdi, 191
Mahdiyah (Tunisia), 191
Maita, 141
Malatesta, Enrico, 17
Malaysia, 150, 173, 174
Malcolm X, **114**, 129
Malenkov, Georgii, 101
Mali, 116, 167, 176
Manchester (England), 140, 142
Manchukuo. *See* Manchuria
Manchuria, 37, 82, 149, 182
Manchus, 37, 86, 149
Manco Capac, 147
Mandarins, Les (de Beauvoir), 49
Mandela, Nelson, 23, 53, 102, **115**, 136, 137, 190
mansabdari system, 5
Mansa Mūsā, Emperor of Mali, **116**
manuscript copying, 35
Maoism, 147
Mao Tse-tung, 37, 54, 71, 86, **117**, 120, 121, 149
Marathas, 16
Marathon, battle of (490 B.C.E.), 47
March 22 Movement, 41
March on Rome (1922), 130
March on Washington (1963), 102
Marcus Aurelius, Emperor of Rome, 55, **118**
Marguerite, Princess of France, 32, 78
Margus River, battle of (285), 55
Maria Theresa, Empress of Austria, 64, **119**
Marie, Countess of Champagne, 59
Marie Antoinette, Queen of France, 119
Marie de Médicis, Queen Regent of France, 78, 155
Marie-Louise, Princess of Austria, 126, 131
Marius (Roman consul), 29
Marlowe, Christopher, 60

Marne River, 13
Married Women's Property Bill (Britain; 1882), 142
Marshall, George, 97, **120**
Marshall Plan, 4, 97, 120, 188
Marston Moor, battle of (1644), 45
martyrdom, 55, 66, 103, 157
Marx, Karl, 17, 71, 92, 104, 107, **121**, 171
    as liberation theology influence, 157
    scientific socialism, 140
Marxism
    China, 117
    Latin American guerrillas, 71, 189
    orthodox radical, 112
    philosophical development of, 121
    in Russia 6, 107, 171, 187. *See also* Soviet Union
    Spartacus symbolism, 170
    Tanzanian version, 137
    Trotskyite, 187
Mary I, Queen of England, 60, 79
Mary II, Queen of England, 45
Mary Stuart, Queen of Scots, 60
Masada, 103
Massachusetts, 3
massacres
    of Aztecs, 127
    by Crusaders, 154
    of French in Haiti, 185
    of French Protestants, 32, 78
    in Germany, 72
    by Huns, 13
    of Incas, 147
    in India, 66
    of Indonesian communists, 173
    in Ireland, 45
    in Nanking, 82, 86
    of Palestinian refugees, 19
    in St. Petersburg (Russia), 99
    in South Africa, 115
Matilda, Princess of England, 77
Matteotti, Giacomo, 130
Matthew, Gospel of, 48
Mau Mau, 98
Mauritania, 116
Mauryan Empire, 11, 30
Maximian, Emperor of Rome, 43, 55
Maximilian I, Holy Roman Emperor, 36
Mazarin, Cardinal Jules, 111
Mazowiecki, Tadeusz, 193
Mazzini, Giuseppe, 66, **122**
McCarthy, Joseph, 58, 120
McKinley, William, 17, 160
Mecca, 112, 116, 165, 192
Media, kingdom of, 46
Médici family, 32, 78
medieval culture
    Arab exchanges, 152
    in Britain, 197
    British jurisprudence, 77
    chivalry, 59, 154
    Christian statecraft, 48
    Church supremacy, 77
    foundations, 35
Medina, 128, 192
Meditations (Marcus Aurelius), 118
Mediterranean Sea
    British influence, 56
    Fatimid raids, 191
    Ottoman Empire, 123, 175
    Roman Empire, 14, 40
    strategic importance of, 20
    Turkish naval power decline, 146
Mehmed II (the Conqueror), Ottoman Sultan, **123**
Mehmed IV, Ottoman Sultan, 12
Meiji dynasty, 82
Mei-ling Soong (Mme. Chiang Kai-Shek), 37
Mein Kampf (Hitler), 83
Memphis (Egypt), 125
Menelik II, Emperor of Ethiopia, **124**
Menem, Carlos, 144
Menes, King of Egypt, **125**

Mesopotamia, 46, 48, 73, 125
    unification, 74
    See also Iraq
Messiah, 48
mestizos, 147, 164, 189, 202
Metternich, Klemens von, 17, 24, 28, 119, **126**
Mexican-American War (1846–48), 3
Mexico
    Aztec Empire, 127, 36, 44
    Indian conversions, 105
    revolution, 202
    Spanish conquest, 44
    U.S. intervention, 160
Mexico City, 44, 127, 202
Mfecane (forced migration), 168
Michael, Archangel, 94
Middle Ages. *See* medieval culture
Middle East
    Arabists, 20, 106
    Arab revolts, 81, 106
    Balfour Declaration, 18, 21, 81
    Cold War policies, 21, 100, 132, 161
    Islamicization, 128, 163, 192
    mandates, 18, 19, 81, 106, 132
    Nile Valley cultures, 125
    Ottoman control, 106
    See also Arab-Israeli conflict; Arabs; *specific countries and regions*
Mikawa (Japan), 183
Milan, sack of (1162), 63
Miles, Nelson A., 95
military
    Austria, 119
    Britain, 135
    China, 86
    France, 51, 131
    Iraq, 87
    Japan, 82, 182
    Mughal Empire, 5
    nursing, 135
    professional armies, 72
    Prussia, 64
    Roman Empire, 73, 118
    Russia, 6, 33
    Spain, 146
    Swedish honor code, 72
    United States, 195
    See also naval power
military governments
    Argentina, 144
    Britain, 45
    Burma, 15
    Spain, 61
military-industrial complex, 58, 182
military leaders
    ancient Athens, 143
    ancient Israel, 48
    ancient Rome, 29, 55, 73
    Arab nationalist, 106
    Asante, 138
    Aztec, 127
    Babylonia, 74
    Britain, 45, 154
    China, 37, 169, 196
    Egypt, 132, 151
    France, 51, 94, 131
    Greco–Macedonian Empire, 7
    Huns, 13
    Inca, 141, 184
    India, 30
    Islam, 163
    Israel, 21
    Japan, 182, 183, 186
    Latin American independence, 26, 164
    Mongol, 68
    Mughal, 5, 16
    Persia, 47
    Russia, 91, 134, 145
    Songhay, 176
    Spain, 61, 146
    Sweden, 72
    Timur, 180

United States, 62, 120, 195
    Zulu, 168
Military Reform Edict (Russia; 1874), 6
military strength
    ancient Rome, 29
    Egypt, 75
    France, 111
    Russian Empire, 33, 91, 145
    Soviet Union, 27, 162
    Sweden, 72
    See also weapons
military tactics
    air supremacy, 38
    amphibious assault, 58
    cannon siege, 123
    cavalry, 13, 72, 163
    commando, 106
    of conquistadors, 127
    flanking maneuvers, 168
    guerrilla, 71
    infantry lines, 72
    of Islamic forces, 163
    mobile strategy, 51
    Mongol terror, 68
    submarine warfare, 199
    volley, 72
    See also weapons
Miliukov, Paul, 134
millets (Ottoman structure), 123
Milosevic, Slobodan, 181
Milvian Bridge, battle of (312), 43
Mindszenty, Cardinal Josef, 22
mining, 153
missiles. *See* nuclear weapons
Missionary Travels and Researches in South Africa (Livingstone), 110
missionizing
    in Africa, 108, 110
    Byzantine Orthodox, 43, 96
    Jesuit, 88
    Roman Catholic, 42, 43, 44, 105, 146
Missouri Compromise (U.S.; 1820), 109
Modena (Italy), 34
modernization
    Ethiopia, 124
    Japan, 82
    Kenya, 98
    Russia, 33, 145
    Siam, 150
    Turkey, 12, 106
    See also Westernization
Mogul Empire, 5, 180
Mohammed. *See* Muhammad, prophet
Moi, Daniel arap, 98
monarchy
    absolute, 24, 32, 45, 111, 145, 155
    antimonarchism, 3
    conservative prescription principle, 28, 126
    constitutional, 34, 45, 61, 108, 122, 154
    divine right to, 29, 40, 111, 131, 155
    enlightened absolutism, 33, 64
    European nationalism and, 34
    humanization of, 150
    opulent courts, 152
    parliamentary, 45, 57
    succession, 32
    See also specific countries and rulers
monasteries
    British dissolution of, 79
    Buddhist, 11
    Russian land restrictions, 91
    scholarship and copying, 35
Monge, Luis Alberto, 10
Mongkut. *See* Rama IV
Mongol Empire, 68, 90, 116, 196
Monnet, Jean, 166
Monroe, James, 3
Monroe Doctrine, 3
    Roosevelt Corollary, 160

Montesquieu, Baron de, 33, 88
Montezuma II, Aztec Emperor, 44, **127**
Montfort, Simon de, 57
Montgomery (Ala.) bus boycott, 102
Monticello (Virginia), 93
monuments, 46, 151, 178
Moors, 35, 42, 80, 89, 146
morality, 3, 100
moral pessimism, 28
More, Sir Thomas, 79, 140
Moriscos, 146
Morley, Thomas, 60
Morocco, 61, 116, 152, 161, 191, 198
Mosaic Law, 48
Moscow, 90, 101, 180
Moses, 48
Mossi, 176
Mount Gilboa, battle of, 48
Mount Vernon (Virginia), 195
Mount Zion, 48
Mouvement du 22 mars, 41
Mozambique, 110
Mozart, Wolfgang Amadeus, 119
Ms. (magazine), 172
Mu'āwiyah I, Umayyad Caliph, **128**
Mubarak, Husni, 161
Mugabe, Robert, **129**
Mughal Empire, 5, 16
Muhammad, prophet, 128, 152, 191, 192
Muhammad, Elijah, 114
multiparty system, 12, 115, 133, 137
Munich Conference (1938), 38
Munich putsch of 1923, 130
Murad II, Ottoman Sultan, 123
Muscovy, kingdom of, 68, 90, 91, 96, 145
music, 60, 64, 119, 198
Muslim Mosque, Inc., 112
Muslims. *See* Islam
Mussolini, Benito, 34, 61, 67, 122, **130**
Myanmar. *See* Burma

N

NAACP, 194
Nabunaid, King of Babylon, 46
Nagasaki (Japan), 88, 183, 188
Namibia, 53
Nanda family, 30
Nandi (Shaka's mother), 168
Nanking (China), 37, 82, 86
Nanterre (France), 41
Naples, kingdom of, 36, 67, 126
Napoléon I, Emperor of France, 7, 25, 33, **131**, 176
    dissolution of Holy Roman Empire, 131, 139
    invasion of Spain, 26, 164
    marriage to Austrian princess, 126, 131
    ultimate defeat, 111, 126, 131
Napoléon III, Emperor of France, 34, 39, 67
Napoleonic Code, 131
Napoleonic Wars
    Austria, 119, 126, 131
    Congress of Vienna, 24, 28, 119, 126
    conservative aftermath, 28
    French ultimate defeat, 111
    Haitian independence, 185
    Hundred Days, 131
    Latin American independence, 26
    peace terms, 126
    Russia, 33, 126, 131
    successes and defeats, 131
    U.S. policies, 3, 93
Narodnaya Volya (People's Will), 6
narodniki (populists), 6
NASAKOM (Indonesia), 174
Naseby, battle of (1645), 45
Nasser, Gamal Abdel, 21, 40, **132**, 161
Natal, 153, 168
Nathan, prophet, 48

DAVID W. DEL TESTA has a Ph.D. in History from the University of California at Davis. He is a member of the American Historical Association and the Association of Asian Studies. Del Testa has been a history teaching instructor and teaching assistant for the past eight years.